1990

THE PHILOSOPHY OF
ALFRED NORTH WHITEHEAD

THE LIBRARY OF LIVING PHILOSOPHERS

PAUL ARTHUR, *Editor*

Already Published:

THE PHILOSOPHY OF JOHN DEWEY (1939)
THE PHILOSOPHY OF GEORGE SANTAYANA (1940)
THE PHILOSOPHY OF ALFRED NORTH WHITEHEAD (1941)
THE PHILOSOPHY OF G. E. MOORE (1942)
THE PHILOSOPHY OF BERTRAND RUSSELL (1944)
THE PHILOSOPHY OF ERNST CASSIRER (1949)
ALBERT EINSTEIN: PHILOSOPHER-SCIENTIST (1949)
THE PHILOSOPHY OF SARVEPALLI RADHAKRISHNAN (1952)
THE PHILOSOPHY OF KARL JASPERS (1957)
THE PHILOSOPHY OF C. D. BROAD (1959)
THE PHILOSOPHY OF RUDOLF CARNAP (1963)
THE PHILOSOPHY OF MARTIN BUBER (1967)
THE PHILOSOPHY OF C. I. LEWIS (1968)

In Preparation:

THE PHILOSOPHY OF KARL R. POPPER
THE PHILOSOPHY OF GABRIEL MARCEL

THE PHILOSOPHY OF BRAND BLANSHARD

Other volumes to be announced later

ACKNOWLEDGMENTS

GRATEFUL ACKNOWLEDGMENT is hereby made to the publishers of all of Professor Whitehead's books as well as to the editors and publishers of philosophical and literary journals and magazines for their kind permission to quote from the works of Professor Whitehead as well as for their courtesy in not insisting upon a detailed enumeration of the books and articles quoted. In this connection special gratitude is due to The Macmillan Company, New York, who are the American publishers of by far the most of Professor Whitehead's works. Exact title, name of publisher, and place and dates of publication of each of Professor Whitehead's works are given in the bibliography, which will be found on pp. 751 to 778 of this volume.

Grateful acknowledgment is further made to the publishers of other works quoted in the following pages, who have also been kind enough not to require the specific enumeration of the works thus quoted. In a few instances special permission to quote is given in the footnotes.

Alfred North Whitehead

THE LIBRARY OF LIVING PHILOSOPHERS

VOLUME III

THE

PHILOSOPHY

OF

ALFRED NORTH WHITEHEAD

EDITED BY

PAUL ARTHUR SCHILPP

NORTHWESTERN UNIVERSITY &
SOUTHERN ILLINOIS UNIVERSITY

LA SALLE, ILLINOIS • OPEN COURT • ESTABLISHED 1887

THE PHILOSOPHY OF ALFRED NORTH WHITEHEAD

Copyright 1941 and 1951
by the Library of Living Philosophers, Inc.

SECOND EDITION

1951

SECOND PRINTING, 1971

Library of Congress Catalog Card Number: 72-149316

All rights in this book are reserved.

Printed in the United States of America

GENERAL INTRODUCTION*

TO

"THE LIBRARY OF LIVING PHILOSOPHERS"

ACCORDING to the late F. C. S. Schiller, the greatest obstacle to fruitful discussion in philosophy is "the curious etiquette which apparently taboos the asking of questions about a philosopher's meaning while he is alive." The "interminable controversies which fill the histories of philosophy," he goes on to say, "could have been ended at once by asking the living philosophers a few searching questions."

The confident optimism of this last remark undoubtedly goes too far. Living thinkers have often been asked "a few searching questions," but their answers have not stopped "interminable controversies" about their real meaning. It is none the less true that there would be far greater clarity of understanding than is now often the case, if more such searching questions had been directed to great thinkers while they were still alive.

This, at any rate, is the basic thought behind the present undertaking. The volumes of *The Library of Living Philosophers* can in no sense take the place of the major writings of great and original thinkers. Students who would know the philosophies of such men as John Dewey, George Santayana, Alfred North Whitehead, Benedetto Croce, G. E. Moore, Bertrand Russell, Ernst Cassirer, Léon Brunschvicg, Martin Heidegger, *et al.*, will still need to read the writings of these men. There is no substitute for first-hand contact with the original thought of the philosopher himself. Least of all does this *Library* pretend to be such a substitute. The *Library* in fact, will spare neither effort nor expense in offering to the student the best possible guide to the published writings of a given thinker. We shall attempt to

* This *General Introduction*, setting forth the underlying conception of this *Library*, is purposely reprinted in each volume (with only very minor changes).

meet this aim by providing at the end of each volume in our series a complete bibliography of the published work of the philosopher in question. Nor should one overlook the fact that the essays in each volume cannot but finally lead to this same goal. The interpretative and critical discussions of the various phases of a great thinker's work and, most of all, the reply of the thinker himself, are bound to lead the reader to the works of the philosopher himself.

At the same time, there is no blinking the fact that different experts find different ideas in the writings of the same philosopher. This is as true of the appreciative interpreter and grateful disciple as it is of the critical opponent. Nor can it be denied that such differences of reading and of interpretation on the part of other experts often leave the neophyte aghast before the whole maze of widely varying and even opposing interpretations. Who is right and whose interpretation shall he accept? When the doctors disagree among themselves, what is the poor student to do? If, finally, in desperation, he decides that all of the interpreters are probably wrong and that the only thing for him to do is to go back to the original writings of the philosopher himself and then make his own decision—uninfluenced (as if this were possible!) by the interpretation of any one else—the result is not that he has actually come to the meaning of the original philosopher himself, but rather that he has set up one more interpretation, which may differ to a greater or lesser degree from the interpretations already existing. It is clear that in this direction lies chaos, just the kind of chaos which Schiller has so graphically and inimitably described.[1]

It is strange that until now no way of escaping this difficulty has been seriously considered. It has not occurred to students of philosophy that one effective way of partially meeting the problem is to put these varying interpretations and critiques before the philosopher while he is still alive and to ask him to act at one and the same time as both defendant and judge. If the world's great living philosophers can be induced to coöperate in an enterprise whereby their own work can at least partially be saved from

[1] In his essay on "Must Philosophers Disagree?" in the volume by the same title (Macmillan, London, 1934), from which the above quotations were taken.

becoming merely "desiccated lecture-fodder," which on the one hand "provides innocuous sustenance for ruminant professors," and, on the other hand, gives an opportunity to such ruminants and their understudies to "speculate safely, endlessly, and fruitlessly, about what a philosopher must have meant," (Schiller) they will have taken a long step toward making their intentions clearly comprehensible.

With this in mind *The Library of Living Philosophers* expects to publish at more or less regular intervals a volume on each of the greater among the world's living philosophers. In each case it will be the purpose of the editors of *The Library* to bring together in the volume the interpretations and criticisms of a wide range of that particular thinker's scholarly contemporaries, each of whom will be given a free hand to discuss the particular phase of the thinker's work which has been assigned to him. All contributed essays will finally be submitted to the philosopher with whose work and thought they are concerned, for his careful perusal and reply. And, although it would be expecting too much to imagine that the philosopher's reply will be able to stop all differences of interpretation and of critique, this should at least serve the purpose of stopping certain of the grosser and more general kinds of misinterpretations. If no further gain than this were to come from the present and projected volumes of this *Library*, it would seem to be fully justified.

In carrying out this principal purpose of the *Library*, the editor announces that (in so far as humanly possible) each volume will conform to the following pattern:

First, a series of expository and critical articles written by the leading exponents and opponents of the philosopher's thought;

Second, the reply to the critics and commentators by the philosopher himself;[2]

---

[2] In the present volume there are substituted for this feature two new essays from the pen of Professor Whitehead. The reasons for this substitution the reader will find both in a personal statement from Professor Whitehead, a statement which introduces "The Philosopher's Summary" (cf. pp. 664 and 665 below), and also in the editor's Preface to this volume.

Third, an intellectual autobiography of the thinker whenever this can be secured; in any case an authoritative and authorized biography; and

Fourth, a bibliography of the writings of the philosopher to provide a ready instrument to give access to his writings and thought.

Future volumes in this series will appear in as rapid succession as is feasible in view of the scholarly nature of this *Library.* The editor hopes to publish at least one new volume each year.

It is a real pleasure, finally, to make grateful acknowledgment for the financial assistance which this project has already received. Without such help the work on this *Library* could never have been undertaken. The first three volumes have been (and are being) made possible in part by funds granted by the Carnegie Corporation of New York. Additional financial assistance, for the first volume, came from the Alumni Foundation Fund of the College of Liberal Arts of Northwestern University, and for the third (present) volume from Mr. Lessing Rosenthal of Chicago. To these donors the editor desires to express his sincere gratitude and deep appreciation. Neither the Carnegie Corporation nor the other donors are, however, in any sense the authors, owners, publishers, or proprietors of this *Library* and they are therefore not to be understood as approving by virtue of their grants any of the statements made in this or in any succeeding volume.

PAUL ARTHUR SCHILPP
Editor

302 HARRIS HALL
NORTHWESTERN UNIVERSITY
EVANSTON, ILLINOIS

TABLE OF CONTENTS

TABLE OF CONTENTS

PREFACE*

WHEN, in December 1940, the second volume in this series (that on *The Philosophy of George Santayana*) came off the press, and the editor was at the same time privileged to announce that volumes on the philosophies of Benedetto Croce, G. E. Moore, Bertrand Russell, Ernst Cassirer, and Léon Brunschvicg had already been agreed to, there were only two major regrets marring the immediate prospects of our *Library*. One of these consisted in the fact that, on March 10, 1939, Professor Henri Bergson had found it necessary to decline his coöperation on a volume which was to have dealt with his philosophy.

As the here reproduced facsimile of a letter from Professor Bergson indicates, the editor, on February 27, 1939, had invited M. Bergson to become the subject of one of the early volumes in this *Library*. As can also be seen from Professor Bergson's letter, it was with real disappointment and for good personal reasons that he found it necessary to decline our invitation. It is, of course, a source of very great regret to everyone interested in this series that the present *Library* got under way too late to be able to include in its titles volumes on the philosophies of such recently deceased great philosophers as M. Bergson, Samuel Alexander, and Edmund Husserl. But we are proud to reproduce herewith at least the evidence of our attempts in that direction and also of the very keen interest in our undertaking which is evinced by Professor Bergson's letter. Since we cannot give our readers a volume on Bergson, we are glad to present to them at least what in all likelihood is one of the last handwritten letters received in the United States from the pen of M. Bergson before his death on January 4, 1941. The publication of this Bergson letter would have been appropriate in any philosophical volume in the year 1941, but certainly in no

*Written for the first edition, December, 1941.

47, BOULEVARD BEAUSEJOUR XVIᵉ

Paris, 10 Mars 1939

à Mr. Paul Arthur Schilpp
Evanston Illinois

Cher Monsieur,

En réponse à votre lettre du 27 février,
je viens à vous dire que votre projet d'une
« Library of living Philosophers » me paraît
appelé à rendre de réels services, et que je suis
très touché de la pensée que vous avez eue de
me consacrer un des premiers volumes. Mais
il ne me sera malheureusement pas possible
d'accepter votre aimable proposition. Depuis
quinze ans je souffre d'une grave affection
rhumatismale qui m'oblige à de grands soins
et me laisse bien peu de temps dans ma
journée pour le travail. Je n'aurai pas trop
de tout ce temps pour certaines recherches que
j'ai entreprises et par lesquelles je terminerai
probablement ma carrière (je vais avoir
80 ans). Accepter, dans ces conditions, de répondre
à des questions et à des critiques concernant
l'ensemble de mes écrits me serait tout-à-fait
impossible. Croyez à tout mon regret, et
agréez, je vous prie, l'assurance de mes sentiments
très distingués

H. Bergson

FACSIMILE REPRODUCTION OF A LETTER FROM HENRI BERGSON, DATED IN PARIS, MARCH 10, 1939 volume more so than in one dealing with Professor Whitehead's philosophy, since Whitehead has always acknowledged his indebtedness to this great French philosophical contemporary.

The other source of regret lay in the fact that—despite repeated efforts in that direction—the editor had been unable to secure the consent and coöperation of Professor Alfred North Whitehead for a volume on Whitehead's philosophy. If, then, despite that fact, we are now able to present to the philosophical public *The Philosophy of Alfred North Whitehead* as Volume III of our *Library of Living Philosophers*, it can readily be seen that this fills a niche in the present series, the permanent emptiness of which would have been inexcusable. Professor Whitehead's personal coöperation, which finally was secured early in 1941, has made possible a volume the importance of which will be immediately apparent to every philosopher and student of philosophy. The editor desires to take this opportunity of expressing both to Professor and to Mrs. Whitehead his deep appreciation and profound gratitude for their gracious helpfulness and never failing courtesy throughout the preparation of this volume.

It is, of course, quite unfortunate that, at one point at least, the present volume not merely differs widely from its predecessors, but fails to carry out one of the major promises of our *Library*. This volume contains no actual "Reply" from the pen of Professor Whitehead to the descriptive and critical articles of his commentators and critics. However, no living person can be blamed for this omission. It was due to a series of unfortunate circumstances and events over which no one could have any control. It lay in no one's power to keep Professor Whitehead, at the age of eighty, from a serious illness which for weeks endangered his very life and his convalescence from which is even now not yet complete.

In lieu of his "Reply" Professor Whitehead has given us, for first publication, his two most recent philosophical papers and utterances: papers concerning which he himself writes that they "summarize" his "final point of view" and constitute, to his own mind, a sufficient answer to his questioners and critics. These essays, respectively entitled, "Mathematics and The Good" and

"Immortality," will be found under the general head of "The Philosopher's Summary." Professor Whitehead himself has been so kind as to explain to readers of this volume the reasons for the absence of a more formal "Reply," a statement which we are happy to print in facsimile reproduction as the very first item of "The Philosopher's Summary."

At all other points, however, the present volume fully carries out the intentions and promises of this *Library*. We are particularly pleased to be able to present herewith the first and only existing Whitehead autobiography under the unassuming title, "Autobiographical Notes." Anyone who knows Professor Whitehead himself will not merely be grateful for these "Notes," but will see the sterling character and extreme modesty of the man in every paragraph.

The editor's thanks are again due to everyone of the contributors to this volume. As was true in the case of the Dewey volume, many of the contributors to the present tome were willing, temporarily at least, to lay aside other important philosophical work in order to participate in significant fashion in the present undertaking. I can only express the hope that the finished volume will justify their interests and their effort to their own minds, and that despite the fact that most of them will, of course, feel greatly disappointed at the absence of a more formal reply to their specific questions and criticisms.

A special word of explanation is perhaps in order in connection with the essay from the pen of Dr. Victor Lowe. The length of the essay—it runs to 110 pages—is certainly extraordinary, especially by comparison with the size of any of the other essays. In all fairness to Dr. Lowe it must be said that he offered to cut the length of the essay as much as the size of the volume might require. After having read the manuscript in its original form, however, the editor decided that this explicit, thoroughgoing, and detailed description of the historical unfolding and "Development of Whitehead's Philosophy" was entirely too important a contribution to the present volume to justify any cutting at any point. In fact, the editor is convinced that the very detailed character and thoroughness of Dr. Lowe's tracing of Whitehead's philosophical development will do more than perhaps any other single contribution to help students of philosophy to understand and appreciate Whitehead's thought. Despite the unusual length of the essay, it would have been an inexcusable mistake, therefore, to have tried to shorten Dr. Lowe's contribution.

There are two further counts on which the editor is obligated to Dr. Lowe. Due to the fact of his residence in Cambridge, and of his high regard for and close contact with Professor Whitehead, Dr. Lowe was so kind as to act, during the larger part of the year, as the most helpful and conscientious intermediary between Professor Whitehead and the editor. Although this may have been a real labor of love, it added greatly to Dr. Lowe's burdens. Even that, however, was not yet enough. In collaboration with Dr. Robert C. Baldwin, of the University of Connecticut, Dr. Lowe undertook and brought to successful conclusion the admirable "Bibliography of the Writings of Alfred North Whitehead" which the reader will find at the end of the present volume, a bibliography which—in spite of certain obvious and to some extent insurmountable difficulties occasioned by the present international situation—continues the high standard set in this regard by the previous volumes in our *Library*. The inclusion of some carefully "Selected Reviews" in this bibliography should make it even more serviceable and useful than it would have been in any event. This new feature we also owe to the industry and care of the bibliographers. In a Prefatory Note to the Bibliography Drs. Lowe and Baldwin have voiced their own gratitude for help and services rendered them. The editor gladly joins them in this expression.

The editor also gratefully acknowledges again his indebtedness to Dr. Arturo Fallico, of the Chicago State Teachers College, who has not only provided the pen-drawing of Mr. Whitehead for the jacket of the present volume, but who, during last spring vacation, with the editor journeyed all the way to Cambridge for the sole purpose of making the pen-drawing directly from life.

In conclusion the editor may be permitted a personal word. No one could possibly be more aware of the obvious shortcomings of any and all of the volumes in this series than is the editor himself. Even with the very best of intentions the ultimate limitations of space simply make it physically impossible to present every possible aspect of any specific philosopher from every conceivable point of view. There has to be selection, both of subject-matter and of contributors, *somewhere*. And it stands, of course, to reason that no such selection could ever be expected to satisfy *every* type of mind or *every* philosophical temperament. There are bound to be differences of opinion on any such selection actually made. The editor's final appeal to the reader, on this account, is to have each volume judged by *what it contains* rather than by what it omits. Thus judged the first three volumes in this *Library* speak for themselves.

P. A. S.

DEPARTMENT OF PHILOSOPHY
NORTHWESTERN UNIVERSITY
EVANSTON, ILLINOIS
December 1, 1941

PREFATORY NOTE ADDED IN 1971

The editor wishes to express his appreciation to the new publishers of the Library—The Open Court Publishing Company —for undertaking to keep all of the volumes of the Library permanently in print; to the Advisory Board of the Library, for their help in planning future volumes (the present membership of the Board is listed below); and to the National Endowment for the Humanities, Washington, D. C., for generous grants for the years 1967-1969.

Paul A. Schilpp

Department of Philosophy
Southern Illinois University
Carbondale, Illinois

ADVISORY BOARD

Herbert Feigl
  University of Minnesota

Eugene Freeman
  San Jose State College

Cornelius Krusé
  Wesleyan University

Victor Lowe
  Johns Hopkins University

Richard P. McKeon
  University of Chicago

Sterling M. McMurrin
  University of Utah

Herbert W. Schneider
  Claremont Graduate School

Alfred North Whitehead

AUTOBIOGRAPHICAL NOTES

AUTOBIOGRAPHICAL NOTES

I WAS born in 1861, February 15, at Ramsgate in the Isle of Thanet, Kent. The family, grandfather, father, uncles, brothers engaged in activities concerned with education, religion and Local Administration: my grandfather born of yeoman stock in Isle of Sheppey, was probably a descendant of the Quaker George Whitehead, whom George Fox in his *Journal* mentions as living there in the year 1670. In the year 1815, my grandfather, Thomas Whitehead, at the age of twenty-one, became head of a private school in Ramsgate, Isle of Thanet, to which my father Alfred Whitehead succeeded at the correspondingly early age of twenty-five, in the year 1852. They were, both of them, most successful schoolmasters, though my grandfather was by far the more remarkable man.

About 1860 my father was ordained as a clergyman of the Anglican Church; and about 1866 or 1867 he gave up his school for clerical duty, first in Ramsgate, and later in 1871 he was appointed Vicar of St. Peters Parish, a large district mostly rural, with its church about two or three miles from Ramsgate. The North Foreland belongs to the parish. He remained there till his death in 1898.

He became influential among the clergy of East Kent, occupying the offices of Rural Dean, Honorary Canon of Canterbury, and Proctor in Convocation for the Diocese. But the central fact of his influence was based on his popularity with the general mass of the population in the Island. He never lost his interest in education, and daily visited his three parochial schools, for infants, for girls, and for boys. As a small boy, before I left home for school in 1875, I often accompanied him. He was a man with local interests and influence; apart from an understanding of such provincial figures, the social and political history of England in the nineteenth century cannot be

3

comprehended. England was governed by the influence of personality: this does not mean 'intellect'.

My father was not intellectual, but he possessed personality. Archbishop Tait had his summer residence in the parish, and he and his family were close friends of my parents. He and my father illustrated the survival of the better (and recessive) side of the eighteenth century throughout its successor. Thus, at the time unconsciously, I watched the history of England by my vision of grandfather, father, Archbishop Tait, Sir Moses Montefiore, the Pugin family, and others. When the Baptist minister in the parish was dying, it was my father who read the Bible to him. Such was England in those days, guided by local men with strong mutual antagonisms and intimate community of feeling. This vision was one source of my interest in history, and in education.

Another influence in the same direction was the mass of archaeological remains with their interest and beauty. Canterbury Cathedral with its splendor and its memories was sixteen miles distant. As I now write I can visualize the very spot where Becket fell A.D. 1170, and can recall my reconstruction of the incident in my young imagination. Also there is the tomb of Edward, The Black Prince (died A.D. 1376).

But closer to my home, within the Island or just beyond its borders, English history had left every type of relic. There stood the great walls of Richborough Castle built by the Romans, and the shores of Ebbes Fleet where the Saxons and Augustine landed. A mile or so inland was the village of Minster with its wonderful Abbey Church, retaining some touches of Roman stone-work, but dominated by its glorious Norman architecture. On this spot Augustine preached his first sermon. Indeed the Island was furnished with Norman, and other medieval churches, built by the Minster monks, and second only to their Abbey. My father's church was one of them, with a Norman nave.

Just beyond Richborough is the town of Sandwich. At that time it retained the sixteenth and seventeenth centuries, with its Flemish houses lining the streets. Its town-records state that in order to check the silting up of the harbour, the citizens invited skilful men from the Low Countries—'cunning in waterworks'. Unfortunately they failed, so that the town remained static from that period. In the last half century, it has been revived by a golf-course, one of the best in England. I feel a sense of profanation amidst the relics of the Romans, of the Saxons, of Augustine, the medieval monks, and the ships of the Tudors and the Stuarts. Golf seems rather a cheap ending to the story.

At the age of fifteen, in the year 1875, I was sent to school at Sherborne in Dorsetshire, at the opposite end of southern England. Here the relics of the past were even more obvious. In this year (1941) the school is to celebrate its twelve-hundredth anniversary. It dates from St. Aldhelm, and claims Alfred the Great as a pupil. The school acquired the monastery buildings, and its grounds are bounded by one of the most magnificent Abbeys in existence, with tombs of Saxon princes. In my last two years there the Abbots' room (as we believed) was my private study; and we worked under the sound of the Abbey bells, brought from the Field of The Cloth of Gold by Henry VIII.

I have written thus far in order to show by example how the imaginative life of the southern English professional class during the last half of the nineteenth century was molded. My own experience was not in the least bit exceptional. Of course details differ, but the type was fairly uniform for provincial people.

This tale has another reference to the purpose of this slight autobiography. It shows how historical tradition is handed down by the direct experience of physical surroundings.

On the intellectual side, my education also conformed to the normal standard of the time. Latin began at the age of ten years, and Greek at twelve. Holidays excepted, my recollection is that daily, up to the age of nineteen and a half years, some pages of Latin and Greek authors were construed, and their grammar examined. Before going to school pages of rules of Latin grammar could be repeated, all in Latin, and exemplified by quotations. The classical studies were interspersed with mathematics. Of course, such studies included history—namely, Herodotus, Xenophon, Thucydides, Sallust, Livy, and Tacitus. I can still feel the dullness of Xenophon, Sallust, and Livy. Of course we all know that they are great authors; but this is a candid autobiography.

The others were enjoyable. Indeed my recollection is that the classics were well taught, with an unconscious comparison of the older civilization with modern life. I was excused in the composition of Latin Verse and the reading of some Latin poetry, in order to give more time for mathematics. We read the Bible in Greek, namely, with the Septuagint for the Old Testament. Such Scripture lessons, on each Sunday afternoon and Monday morning, were popular, because the authors did not seem to know much more Greek than we did, and so kept their grammar simple.

We were not overworked; and in my final year my time was mostly occupied with duties as Head of the School with its responsibility for discipline outside the class-rooms, on the Rugby model derived from Thomas Arnold, and as Captain of the Games, chiefly cricket and football, very enjoyable but taking time. There was however spare time for private reading. Poetry, more especially Wordsworth and Shelley, became a major interest, and also history.

My university life at Trinity College, Cambridge, commenced in the autumn of 1880; and, so far as residence is concerned, continued without interruption until the summer of 1910. But my membership of the College, first as 'scholar' and then as 'fellow' continues unbroken. I cannot exaggerate my obligation to the University of Cambridge, and in particular to Trinity College, for social and intellectual training.

The education of a human being is a most complex topic, which we have hardly begun to understand. The only point on which I feel certain is that there is no widespread, simple solution. We have to consider the particular problem set to each institution by its type of students, and their future opportunities. Of course, for the moment and for a particular social system, some forms of the problem are more widespread than others—for instance, the problem now set to the majority of State Universities in the U.S.A. Throughout the nineteenth century, the University of Cambridge did a brilliant job. But its habits were adapted to very special circumstances.

The formal teaching at Cambridge was competently done, by interesting men of first-rate ability. But courses assigned to each undergraduate might cover a narrow range. For example, during my whole undergraduate period at Trinity, all my lectures were on mathematics, pure and applied. I never went inside another lecture room. But the lectures were only one side of the education. The missing portions were supplied by incessant conversation, with our friends, undergraduates, or members of the staff. This started with dinner at about six or seven, and went on till about ten o'clock in the evening, stopping sometimes earlier and sometimes later. In my own case, there would then follow two or three hours' work at mathematics.

Groups of friends were not created by identity of subjects for study. We all came from the same sort of school, with the same sort of previous training. We discussed everything—politics, religion, philosophy, literature—with a bias toward literature. This experience led to a large amount of miscellaneous reading. For example, by the time that I gained my fellowship in 1885 I nearly knew by heart parts of Kant's *Critique of Pure Reason*. Now I have forgotten it, because I was early disenchanted. I have never been able to read Hegel: I initiated my attempt by studying some remarks of his on mathematics which struck me as complete nonsense. It was foolish of me, but I am not writing to explain my good sense.

Looking backwards across more than half a century, the conversations have the appearance of a daily Platonic dialogue. Henry Head, D'Arcy Thompson, Jim Stephen, the Llewellen Davies brothers, Lowes Dickinson, Nat Wedd, Sorley, and many others—some of them subsequently famous, and others, equally able, attracting no subsequent public attention. That was the way by which Cambridge educated her sons. It was a replica of the Platonic method. The 'Apostles' who met on Saturdays in each others' rooms, from 10 P.M. to any time next morning, were the concentration of this experience. The active members were eight or ten undergraduates or young B.A.'s, but older members who had 'taken wings' often attended. There we discussed with Maitland, the historian, Verrall, Henry Jackson, Sidgwick, and casual judges, or scientists, or members of

Parliament who had come up to Cambridge for the weekend. It was a wonderful influence. The club was started in the late 1820's by Tennyson and his friends. It is still flourishing.

My Cambridge education with its emphasis on mathematics and on free discussion among friends would have gained Plato's approval. As times changed, Cambridge University has reformed its methods. Its success in the nineteenth century was a happy accident dependent on social circumstances which have passed away—fortunately. The Platonic education was very limited in its application to life.

In the autumn of 1885, the fellowship at Trinity was acquired, and with additional luck a teaching job was added. The final position as a Senior Lecturer was resigned in the year 1910, when we removed to London.

In December 1890 my marriage with Evelyn Willoughby Wade took place. The effect of my wife upon my outlook on the world has been so fundamental, that it must be mentioned as an essential factor in my philosophic output. So far I have been describing the narrow English education for English professional life. The prevalence of this social grade, influencing the aristocrats above them, and leading the masses below them, is one of the reasons why the England of the nineteenth century exhibited its failures and successes. It is one of the recessive factors of national life which hardly ever enters into historical narrative.

My wife's background is completely different, namely military and diplomatic. Her vivid life has taught me that beauty, moral and aesthetic, is the aim of existence; and that kindness, and love, and artistic satisfaction are among its modes of attainment. Logic and Science are the disclosure of relevant patterns, and also procure the avoidance of irrelevancies.

This outlook somewhat shifts the ordinary philosophic emphasis upon the past. It directs attention to the periods of great art and literature, as best expressing the essential values of life. The summit of human attainment does not wait for the emergence of systematized doctrine, though system has its essential functions in the rise of civilization. It provides the gradual up-growth of a stabilized social system.

Our three children were born between 1891 and 1898. They all served in the first war: our eldest son throughout its whole extent, in France, in East Africa, and in England; our daughter in the Foreign Office in England and Paris; our youngest boy served in the Air Force: his plane was shot down in France with fatal results, in March 1918.

For about eight years (1898-1906) we lived in the Old Mill House at Grantchester, about three miles from Cambridge. Our windows overlooked a mill pool, and at that time the mill was still working. It has all gone now. There are two mill pools there; the older one, about a couple of hundred yards higher up the river, was the one mentioned by Chaucer. Some parts of our house were very old, probably from the sixteenth century. The whole spot was intrinsically beautiful and was filled with reminiscences, from Chaucer to Byron and Wordsworth. Later on another poet, Rupert Brooke, lived in the neighbouring house, the Old Vicarage. But that was after our time and did not enter into our life. I must mention the Shuckburghs (translator of Cicero's letters) and the William Batesons (the geneticist) who also lived in the village and were dear friends of ours. We owed our happy life at Grantchester to the Shuckburghs, who found the house for us. It had a lovely garden, with flowering creepers over the house, and with a yew tree which Chaucer might have planted. In the spring nightingales kept us awake, and king-fishers haunted the river.

My first book, *A Treatise on Universal Algebra*, was published in February, 1898. It was commenced in January, 1891. The ideas in it were largely founded on Hermann Grassmann's two books, the *Ausdehnungslehre* of 1844, and the *Ausdehnungslehre* of 1862. The earlier of the two books is by far the most fundamental. Unfortunately when it was published no one understood it; he was a century ahead of his time. Also Sir William Rowan Hamilton's *Quaternions* of 1853, and a preliminary paper in 1844, and Boole's *Symbolic Logic* of 1859, were almost equally influential on my thoughts. My whole subsequent work on Mathematical Logic is derived from these sources. Grassmann was an original genius, never sufficiently recognized. Leibniz, Saccheri, and Grassmann wrote on these topics before people could understand them, or grasp their importance. Indeed poor Saccheri himself failed to grasp what he had achieved, and Leibniz did not publish his work on this subject.

My knowledge of Leibniz's investigations was entirely based on L. Couturat's book, *La Logique de Leibniz,* published in 1901.

This mention of Couturat suggests the insertion of two other experiences connected with France. Elie Halévy, the historian of England in the early nineteenth century, frequently visited Cambridge, and we greatly enjoyed our friendship with him and his wife.

The other experience is that of a Congress on Mathematical Logic held in Paris in March, 1914. Couturat was there, and Xavier Leon, and (I think) Halévy. It was crammed with Italians, Germans, and a few English including Bertrand Russell and ourselves. The Congress was lavishly entertained by various notables, including a reception by the President of the Republic. At the end of the last session, the President of the Congress congratulated us warmly on its success and concluded with the hope that we should return to our homes carrying happy memories of 'La Douce France'. In less than five months the first World War broke out. It was the end of an epoch, but we did not know it.

The *Treatise on Universal Algebra* led to my election to the Royal Society in 1903. Nearly thirty years later (in 1931) came the fellowship of the British Academy as the result of work on philosophy, commencing about 1918. Meanwhile between 1898 and 1903, my second volume of Universal Algebra was in preparation. It was never published.

In 1903 Bertrand Russell published *The Principles of Mathematics.* This was also a 'first volume'. We then discovered that our projected second volumes were practically on identical topics, so we coalesced to produce a joint work. We hoped that a short period of one year or so would complete the job. Then our horizon extended and, in the course of eight or nine years, *Principia Mathematica* was produced. It lies outside the scope of this sketch to discuss this work. Russell had entered the Uni-

versity at the beginning of the eighteen nineties. Like the rest
of the world, we enjoyed his brilliance, first as my pupil and
then as a colleague and friend. He was a great factor in our
lives, during our Cambridge period. But our fundamental points
of view—philosophic and sociological—diverged, and so with
different interests our collaboration came to a natural end.

At the close of the University session, in the summer of 1910,
we left Cambridge. During our residence in London, we lived
in Chelsea, for most of the time in Carlyle Square. Wherever
we went, my wife's aesthetic taste gave a wonderful charm to
the houses, sometimes almost miraculously. The remark applies
especially to some of our London residences, which seemed im-
pervious to beauty. I remember the policeman who saw a beautiful girl let herself into our house in the early hours after mid-
night. She had been presented at Court and had then gone to a
party. The policeman later enquired of our maid whether he
had seen a real person or the Virgin Mary. He could hardly
believe that a real person in a lovely dress would be living there.
But inside there was beauty.

During my first academic session (1910-1911) in London
I held no academic position. My *Introduction to Mathematics*
dates from that period. During the sessions from 1911 to the
summer of 1914, I held various positions at University College
London, and from 1914 to the summer of 1924 a professorship
at the Imperial College of Science and Technology in Kensing-
ton. During the later years of this period I was Dean of the
Faculty of Science in the University, Chairman of the Academic
Council which manages the internal affairs concerned with London education, and a member of the Senate. I was also Chairman
of the Council which managed The Goldsmith's College, and
a member of the Council of the Borough Polytechnic. There
were endless other committees involved in these positions. In
fact, participation in the supervision of London education, University and Technological, joined to the teaching duties of my
professorship at the Imperial College constituted a busy life.
It was made possible by the marvelous efficiency of the secre-
tarial staff of the University.

This experience of the problems of London, extending for

fourteen years, transformed my views as to the problem of higher education in a modern industrial civilization. It was then the fashion—not yet extinct—to take a narrow view of the function of Universities. There were the Oxford and Cambridge type, and the German type. Any other type was viewed with ignorant contempt. The seething mass of artisans seeking intellectual enlightenment, of young people from every social grade craving for adequate knowledge, the variety of problems thus introduced—all this was a new factor in civilization. But the learned world is immersed in the past.

The University of London is a confederation of various institutions of different types for the purpose of meeting this novel problem of modern life. It had recently been remodelled under the influence of Lord Haldane, and was a marvelous success. The group of men and women—business men, lawyers, doctors, scientists, literary scholars, administrative heads of departments—who gave their time, wholly or in part, to this new problem of education were achieving a much needed transformation. They were not unique in this enterprise: in the U.S.A. under different circumstances analogous groups were solving analogous problems. It is not too much to say that this novel adaptation of education is one of the factors which may save civilization. The nearest analogy is that of the monasteries a thousand years earlier.

The point of these personal reminiscences is the way in which latent capabilities have been elicited by favorable circumstances of my life. It is impossible for me to judge of any permanent value in the output. But I am aware of the love, and kindness, and encouragement by which it was developed.

To turn now to another side of life, during my later years at Cambridge, there was considerable political and academic controversy in which I participated. The great question of the emancipation of women suddenly flared up, after simmering for half a century. I was a member of the University Syndicate which reported in favour of equality of status in the University. We were defeated, after stormy discussions and riotous behaviour on the part of students. If my memory is correct, the date was about 1898. But later on, until the war in 1914, there were stormy episodes in London and elsewhere. The division of opinion cut across party lines; for example, the conservative Balfour was pro-woman, and the liberal Asquith was against. The success of the movement came at the end of the war in 1918.

My political opinions were, and are, on the liberal side, as against the conservatives. I am now writing in terms of English party divisions. The Liberal party has now (1941) practically vanished; and in England my vote would be given for the moderate side of the Labour party. However at present there are no 'parties' in England.

During our residence at Grantchester, I did a considerable amount of political speaking in Grantchester and in the country villages of the district. The meetings were in the parish school-rooms, during the evening. It was exciting work, as the whole village attended and expressed itself vigorously. English villages have no use for regular party agents. They require local residents to address them. I always found that a party agent was a nuisance. Rotten eggs and oranges were effective party weapons, and I have often been covered by them. But they were indications of vigour, rather than of bad feeling. Our worst experience was at a meeting in the Guildhall at Cambridge, addressed by Keir Hardie who was then the leading member of the new Labour Party. My wife and I were on the platform, sitting behind him, and there was a riotous undergraduate audience. The result was that any rotten oranges that missed Keir Hardie had a good chance of hitting one of us. When we lived in London my activities were wholly educational.

My philosophic writings started in London, at the latter end of the war. The London Aristotelian Society was a pleasant centre of discussion, and close friendships were formed.

During the year 1924 at the age of sixty-three, I received the honour of an invitation to join the Faculty of Harvard University in the Philosophy Department. I became Professor Emeritus at the close of the session 1936-1937. It is impossible to express too strongly the encouragement and help that has been rendered to me by the University authorities, my colleagues on the Faculty, students, and friends. My wife and I have been overwhelmed with kindness. The shortcomings of my published work, which of course are many, are due to myself alone. I venture upon one remark which applies to all philosophic work:—Philosophy is an attempt to express the infinity of the universe in terms of the limitations of language.

It is out of the question to deal with Harvard and its many influences at the end of a chapter. Nor is such a topic quite relevant to the purpose of this book. Today in America, there is a zeal for knowledge which is reminiscent of the great periods of Greece and the Renaissance. But above all, there is in all sections of the population a warm-hearted kindness which is unsurpassed in any large social system.

Alfred North Whitehead

CAMBRIDGE, MASSACHUSETTS
1941

I

Victor Lowe

THE DEVELOPMENT OF
WHITEHEAD'S PHILOSOPHY

SYNOPSIS

THE DEVELOPMENT OF
WHITEHEAD'S PHILOSOPHY

THE problem of this essay is the unity of Whitehead's thought. A somewhat analogous problem occurs in a simpler form in the case of William James, who was first a physiologist, and then a psychologist, before he became publicly a philosopher. Ralph Barton Perry concluded that "If he [James] was ever a philosopher he was always a philosopher."[1] Now Whitehead during far the greater part of his life was regarded, and regarded himself, as a mathematician. In what sense his mind was always a philosopher's mind, can be discovered only the long way—by considering his writings *seriatim*, and noting the ways in which each, in its purpose, its treatment, and its conclusions agrees and differs from its predecessors. Since I cannot assume that the reader is acquainted with Whitehead's early writings, a good deal of exposition will have to be given them. That will also ensure the performance of some useful service, regardless of whether my general conclusions be accepted or rejected.

It is usual to distinguish three periods of Whitehead's activity: a first devoted primarily to mathematical and logical investigations, a second to the philosophy of physical science, and a third to metaphysics and the historical rôle of metaphysical ideas in civilization. (These are the topics, respectively, of divisions I to III, IV and V, VI and VII in the present essay.) The progress of Whitehead's logic within the first period is discussed in this volume—along with its successes and defects— by Professor Quine. But such opinions and modes of thinking, occurring in the first period, as either show the nature of Whitehead's interest, or recur later, are of concern here. In fact, at-

---

[1] *The Thought and Character of William James* (N.Y., 1935), I, 449.

tending to them will considerably modify the prevailing conception of Whitehead's pre-metaphysical background. The question we are most interested to answer in the end is: What do
Whitehead's writings of the first and second periods provide
for those of the second and third? Premises? Presuppositions?
Or, as Metz would have it,[1a] "Presuppositions in principle"
(whatever that means)? Or, what? Too many critics have
assumed that the relationships are simple enough to allow them
to distill the essence of Whitehead from the texts of some one
period, one book, or even one chapter.

I. The *UNIVERSAL ALGEBRA* (1898)

A substantial part of the history of Whitehead's development must be given over to *UA*.[2] Whitehead devoted seven
years to this book. It is entirely mathematical, yes; but in an
unusual way that is of the greatest relevance to Whitehead's
semi-mathematical, rationalistic metaphysics. To set forth the
significance of this book without technicalities—for I wish this
essay to be useful to all who are interested in Whitehead's philosophy—is the object of the next dozen pages.

1. The title phrase calls to mind Leibniz and his vision of
a universal calculus of reasoning. C. I. Lewis, in his examination of Leibniz's contribution to symbolic logic, concludes that
this calculus, as conceived in Leibniz's later studies,

was intended to be the science of mathematical and deductive form in
general (it is doubtful whether induction was included), and such as
to make possible the application of the analytic method of mathematics
to all subjects of which scientific knowledge is possible.[3]

Compare this with the statement in Whitehead's Preface:

The ideal of mathematics should be to erect a calculus to facilitate
reasoning in connection with every province of thought, or of external
experience, in which the succession of thoughts, or of events can be

---

[1a] *A Hundred Years of British Philosophy* (Eng. tr., 1938), 592.

[2] For convenience as well as for brevity I shall, in the body of the text, usually
refer to Whitehead's books, after their first mention, by their initials: to the
Universal Alegebra as *UA*, to the *Principles of Natural Knowledge* as *PNK*, etc.

[3] C. I. Lewis, *A Survey of Symbolic Logic* (University of California Press,
1918), 9.

definitely ascertained and precisely stated. So that all serious thought which is not philosophy, or inductive reasoning, or imaginative literature, shall be mathematics developed by means of a calculus.[4]

The exception made of *philosophy* is to be noted. "Logic as the essence of philosophy" is a Leibnizian conception which took complete possession of Russell's imagination, but never of Whitehead's.

This view of the ideal of mathematics Whitehead maintains (roughly speaking) throughout the years. I find in its first working out three points of particular interest with respect to his later thought.

2. In the first place, there is an emphasis on the provision of means (a "calculus") for the *facilitation* of reasoning. Of course this strain is extremely Leibnizian; though with a difference. The universal calculus which Leibniz conceived was intended, in Professor Lewis' words, "to afford some systematic abridgment of the labor of rational investigation in all fields, much as mathematical formulae abridge the labor of dealing with quantity and number."[5] It should be possible to devise labor-saving symbolic schemes for other fields, Leibniz asserts, because, "All our reasoning is nothing but the relating and substituting of characters, whether these characters be words or marks or images."[6]

This last statement has a positivistic sound; as a positivist friend of mine said when it was read to him—it "has quite a modern ring." But Whitehead does not subscribe to it. His recognition of the tremendous importance of a comprehensive symbolism rests on a conception of the fundamental difference between reasoning and the manipulation of characters. The importance of the latter is that it conserves the precious supply of the former, and places it at new vantage-points. "The use of a calculus," Whitehead writes, "is after all nothing but a way of avoiding reasoning." "The signs of a Mathematical Calculus are substitutive signs:" they are not, like words, instruments

[4] Whitehead, *A Treatise on Universal Algebra*, viii.
[5] Lewis, *op. cit.*, 6.
[6] Gerhardt, *Phil. Schriften von Leibniz* (Berlin, 1890), VII, 31; quoted by Lewis, *op. cit.*, 9.

for thinking about the meanings expressed, but rather, as Stout had roughly put it, "means of not thinking" about the meanings symbolized.[7] In the chapter on "Symbolism" in his *Introduction to Mathematics* (1911), Whitehead brings the point home with one of his most beautiful similes:

It is a profoundly erroneous truism . . . that we should cultivate the habit of thinking of what we are doing. . . . Civilization advances by extending the number of important operations which we can perform without thinking about them. Operations of thought are like cavalry charges in a battle—they are strictly limited in number, they require fresh horses, and must only be made at decisive moments.[8]

In *UA*, he equates the difference between the factors that Leibniz (sometimes, at least) tended to identify, explicitly with Bradley's distinction between "inference" and "external demonstration." Inference Whitehead describes as "an ideal combination or construction within the mind of the reasoner which results in the intuitive evidence of a new fact or relation between the data."[9] In external demonstration, the combination is performed with marks on paper in accordance with fixed rules, and this art of manipulation throws up the result for sense-perception and subsequent interpretation.[10]

[7] Whitehead, *op. cit.*, §§47, 1. Stout, G. F., "Thought and Language," *Mind*, April 1891.

[8] P. 61.

[9] Whitehead, *op. cit.*, §6. F. H. Bradley, *Principles of Logic*, Bk. II, Pt. I, Ch. III.

[10] Since Leibniz's mind is more akin to Whitehead's than is that of any other philosopher, except possibly Plato, it is worth pointing out that the divergence just noticed is symptomatic of an important general difference between the two men. Whitehead lacks a certain mechanical, metallic quality that Leibniz possessed. I do not mean that Leibniz's thinking in any sense lacked elasticity. He had a very superior, active mind. He could have written *UA*, or the categoreal framework of *Process and Reality*, and probably he would have made them shorter and more elegant. He could not have written *Modes of Thought* or *The Aims of Education*. He had a concern and an unparalleled ability for a meticulous efficiency in thinking out the formal inter-relations between the things that make up the world. Whitehead has a much deeper feeling for the inner natures of these things, and a more delicate perception of the inquiring mind's relation to their totality. This difference is in part the difference between the late seventeenth century and the wisdom that was possible two hundred years later. But there is also an ultimate difference of the individual minds, which can be brought out in this way. If we imagine Leibniz now alive, and universities at the low level

This early appreciation and contrasting of two elements essential to the advance of thought, is to be compared on the one hand with the doctrine of self-evidence as the goal of thought, which is set forth in Whitehead's latest book, *Modes of Thought* (1938; see Chap. III); and, on the other hand, with the high place which, in various books of all periods, he gives to the invention and organization of mechanical aids to thinking. John Dewey has recently quoted with emphatic approval the declaration in *Science and the Modern World,* that "the reason why we are on a higher imaginative level is not because we have finer imagination, but because we have better instruments."[11] The instruments referred to are physical instruments, but their relation to discovery in physical science is analogous to the function of symbols in pure mathematics. Instruments and calculi are like railroads, which make walks in distant mountains possible.

All the expressions on this topic that are scattered through Whitehead's writings should, furthermore, be set in the context of his observations on education, observations which penetrate to the general nature of advance in human knowledge. From the autobiographical sketch in the present volume, we can see how great a part of Whitehead's activities, all through his life, has been expended on education. He wrote essays on it before he began to write as a philosopher, even a philosopher of physics. (Most of the important ones are collected in *The Organisation of Thought* or *The Aims of Education.*) But just as education is not an isolable subject, irrelevant if one does not happen to possess children or an interest in schools, so Whitehead's reflections on education are not confined within these essays. *Principia Mathematica* (hereafter *PM*) is probably the only book bearing his name in which an interest in the activities of the mind does not often show itself. To quote one

---

to which they had sunk in his time, we can easily conceive his service of a prince replaced by the service of a large corporation in the capacity of chief accountant. We see him devising some beautiful systems, with much of the work done by machines of his own invention. But Whitehead as an accountant is not conceivable.

[11] *Science and the Modern World* (N.Y., 1925), 161; Dewey, *Logic* (N.Y., 1938), 391n.

example from the *UA* (Sec. 7): "No sooner has a substitutive scheme [of manipulable symbols] been devised to assist in the investigation of any originals, than the imagination begins to use the originals to assist in the investigation of the substitutive scheme."[12] A simple remark this, doubtless not original with Whitehead. A logician might describe it as "of merely psychological interest." What is it doing in a mathematical treatise? But it happens to be true; and it indicates that *this* mathematician has an interest in analyzing the way things happen. A mind that will remark the psychological interplay that occurs in the consideration of symbols and things symbolized is, perhaps, not so likely to take the pains always to distinguish the two in the sharp manner required by the modern school of semanticists. Such a mind will instinctively go ahead and develop its subject, allowing the analyses that add precision and fix the theory of the subject to constitute a second stage. By then that type of mind will probably have passed on to other subjects, leaving the original field to specialists.

3. The second point about Whitehead's conception of mathematics that we have to consider is its relation to the logic of propositions. The Preface states, "Mathematics in its widest signification is the development of all types of formal, necessary, deductive reasoning. . . . The sole concern of mathematics is the inference of proposition from proposition."[13] Perhaps the most important part of this definition is the implied suggestion that there are a great many unexplored deductive sciences.

The second sentence quoted expresses what Whitehead has since come to consider an unwarranted limitation. The positive statement made by the first sentence expresses what was then a great advance in the conception of mathematics. At the time *UA* was written, the development of a wide variety of geometries from alternative hypotheses (axioms), along with the extrusion of appeals to spatial intuition from geometrical proofs, had led many mathematicians to identify geometrical propositions with logical implications. The eventual extension of this view to all mathematics was, I take it, a plausible supposition

---

[12] §7.
[13] *Universal Algebra*, Preface, vi.

to those who, like Whitehead, had observed the success of Boole and Schrocder in organizing deductive logic itself as an algebra. But this must be distinguished from the thesis demonstrated in *PM*. In 1898 neither Whitehead nor anyone else (except Frege, whose work was unknown) had advanced toward the exhibition of mathematics as the science concerned with the logical deduction of consequences from the general premises of all reasoning. According to Whitehead,[14] the full expression of this definition and its development into a philosophy of mathematics is due to Russell in his *Principles of Mathematics,* published in 1903. In 1898 Russell's ideas were still in confusion.[15]

As for the calculus of propositions itself: the symbolic relations worked out in *UA* hold between "terms," and the interpretation of the primitive terms as propositions is but one, and not the first, interpretation of the algebra of logic as Whitehead expounds it; furthermore, that algebra takes up but a small fraction of Whitehead's book.

The point of view of *UA* toward the rules of inference is that

The justification of the rules of inference in any branch of mathematics is not properly part of mathematics: it is the business of experience or of philosophy. The business of mathematics is simply to follow the rule.[16]

This is an early point of view; Whitehead's later transcendence of it is probably due in the main to Russell. Quantities of the ingredient hereby excluded are mixed into the composition of the *Principia*.[17] Some writers may contend that the exclusion amounts to the denial of the possibility of mathematical logic. The question is controversial, and we need not enter upon it. It suffices to say that no one should turn to the *UA* to study the whys and wherefores of inference itself, or—speaking generally—the ultimate problems since raised for logicians by the unification of mathematics and logic.

[14] Article, "Mathematics, Nature of," *Encyclopædia Britannica,* ed. 14, Vol. 15, 87n.

[15] According to a letter from Lord Russell to the present author, June 18, 1941 (referred to by permission).

[16] P. vi.

[17] See H. M. Sheffer, review of ed. 2, Vol. I of *Principia Mathematica, Isis,* Vol. 8 (1926), 228.

4. The third feature of the philosophy of mathematics held by Whitehead in 1898 is of the greatest importance for an understanding of the method, and of many of the special theses, of his later philosophy. This feature is an attack on the classical conception of mathematics as the science of number and quantity only (or, as it was sometimes expressed, "of discrete and continuous magnitude"): a conception then accepted by a great many mathematicians, and still assumed by some of them today and by the great majority of laymen. The mathematical constructions of the *UA* constitute an exhibition of the inadequacy of the traditional conception; which is furthermore, as in Whitehead's writings of all periods, subjected to direct criticism. It is in the highest degree doubtful if the Whiteheadian type of rationalistic method in the field of metaphysics would have been developed at all, had not the traditional conception of the scope of mathematics first been broken down.

The fact is that in Whitehead's work as a whole there are three great assaults on traditional notions, which pave the way for his own contributions. (Of course the phrase, "pave the way," is most inadequate as a description of the intimate connection between his criticism of a narrow concept and his envisagement of a wider one.) The first assault is this, on the quantitative conception of mathematics. One reason for its importance is that the other two do not merely succeed it, but are superimposed while it is maintained, as it were, a pedal point. The second assault is directed against "scientific materialism" as a cosmology of the physical world. The third attacks the sense-percepta conception of experience, which Hume had expressed to perfection. These three assaults determine the problems of Whitehead's three periods of activity.

Let us set forth the origins of Whitehead's first attack. We have already come upon one. The identification of mathematical meanings with logical implications, while in one sense a restriction, at the same time liberates mathematics from confinement within certain frontiers of fact, and gives it, in theory, free rein in the realm of possibility. The full effect of this line of thought waited upon the composition of *Principia*. Whitehead's attack on the traditional limits of mathematics was stimulated in the first place by certain achievements that may be singled out from the tremendous progress made by that science in the half-century preceding the composition of *UA*. Besides the invention of the algebra of logic by George Boole, four other advances, having nothing directly to do with mathematical logic, had a great effect. They are: (1) the discovery of means to eliminate "infinitesimals" and to replace statements involving them by statements about classes of finites; (2) the enlargement of algebra effected by the introduction of the "complex quantity" and similar conceptions; (3) the invention of non-Euclidean geometries; (4) the expansion of that type of geometry, called "projective," which involves no reference to size, distance or measurement, and the subsequent demonstration that the various metrical geometries, Euclidean and non-Euclidean, can be regarded as so many alternative specializations of this geometry.

One or another of these four advances, selected from nineteenth century mathematics, affects Whitehead's thinking in every one of his books. Taken together, the four are capable of inspiring, in a mathematician inclined toward philosophy, a vision of a new cosmology to be developed by a mathematics no longer held within the bounds of the quantitative. In comparison with what might be developed, mathematics that labors under this restriction appears to Whitehead much as "school-mathematics" appeared to Descartes. Of course the analogy must be qualified: Whitehead's vision did not come in a youthful dream, but opened up gradually; the advance in mathematics that formed its basis was not provided by the philosopher himself, but by the specialists of the preceding generation; the reason Whitehead prizes the *mathematical* investigation of the world is not the absolute certainty which Descartes fancied was thereby gained; and non-mathematical factors are equally important in the genesis of Whitehead's philosophy, whereas the mathematical vision is the central factor in Descartes'. But for all that, with respect to the significance of recent mathematical discovery for cosmology, Whitehead is the modern Descartes.

The first of the four developments named above is not particularly relevant to any of Whitehead's work before his inven-

tion of the "method of extensive abstraction." But, inasmuch
as a sense of the importance of the other three dominates *UA*,
I shall at this point introduce a partial, non-technical account
of their meaning.

To an unprejudiced observer, it is plain that the world in
which we live is by no means exhausted by those properties
which can be measured, added, subtracted, multiplied. Such
properties are, in the strict sense, "quantitative." But suppose
we deal with that which cannot be added or multiplied, by
specifying that the definitions of addition and multiplication
shall be enlarged so as to be adequate to this instance and still
include their ordinary meanings as particular cases. If we then
continue to speak of terms so operated upon as "quantities," we
have enlarged the field of "the quantitative." A very important
step of this kind was taken in algebra when expressions involving
the square root of minus one were so handled, and christened
"complex quantities." Bigger steps beyond numerical quantity
were taken in the 1840's, when Hamilton invented quaternions
and Grassmann invented his calculus of extension. Now how, or
indeed why, should any stop be put to this process, so long as
conventional definitions set up in this way prove useful in
exhibiting widespread patterns of connection among the elements of some subject-matter? The process has in fact gone so
far that dictionaries now give as the first meaning of "quantity"
in mathematics, "whatever may be operated upon according to
fixed mutually consistent laws." In short, the elements of any
pattern the conditions of which can be precisely stated may now
be called "quantities,"—so far have mathematicians gone beyond quantity.

While other mathematicians were engaged in this process,
Whitehead observed it; the idea of "universal algebra" is an
expression of its possibilities, then not nearly so well recognized
as now.

In almost all his books, Whitehead somewhere points the
moral for philosophy of the discoveries of geometries alternative
to what had been supposed to be the one system of geometrical
knowledge. The *UA* weaves Euclidean and non-Euclidean
geometries together. Almost all the algebraical developments

in Whitehead's book are worked out in terms of a geometrical interpretation, so that the book might be said to be mainly about geometry. At the time it was written, the subject of non-Euclidean geometry had passed through the stage in which it merely presented one alternative to Euclid (that developed by Lobachevski, Bolyai and Gauss); and through a second stage in which another alternative (the Riemannian geometry) was developed, and the investigation of the possible types of geometry was provided with a wide field through generalization of the ordinary conception of three-dimensional space into that of an *n*-dimensional structured set, or manifold, of points. In the latter decades of the nineteenth century, a third stage was in full progress: it was being shown that transformations from any one of these geometries to another were possible through alteration of the definitions of "distance" in the manifold; more, it was demonstrated that the very idea of distance, with all its possible specifications, could be introduced as a late addition to the axioms and definitions of non-metrical geometry. Thus the line of mathematical development which began with the invention of one alternative to the geometry of Euclid was opening up the vista of a vast and extremely general science of order in which the metrical systems appear as so many sub-sciences.[18]

There were hints that an existing but neglected algebra contained powerful symbolic machinery for handling this rich new field as one unit. In 1844, prior to all but the first stage of non-Euclidean geometry, Hermann Grassmann had published his Calculus of Extension (*Ausdehnungslehre*). Its leading idea, for which its author gave the original credit to Leibniz, was to set up, by means of a calculus, a general science of *form*, to which the sciences of geometrical magnitude should appear as subordinate and posterior. Consequently, it was ignored on the ground that it was "too philosophical." Grassmann himself expressed the belief that his work was most likely to be recognized

[18] There are many accounts to which the reader may turn for a fuller description of the historical development. A good full account, written by Whitehead and Russell, is Part VI, "Non-Euclidean Geometry," of the article, "Geometry," in the eleventh edition of the *Encyclopædia Britannica*.

by those inclined to philosophy.[19] Thirty to fifty years later, *some* mathematicians were noticing Grassmann's work; now mathematicians honor him, but do not read him overmuch.

These, then, are the mathematical developments that gave Whitehead his initial push. Algebra and geometry were both advancing to new fronts. The *UA* is an attempt to integrate many of the new sectors.

5. The explicit aim of the book is "to present a thorough investigation of the various systems of Symbolic Reasoning allied to ordinary Algebra" (which is assumed).[20] There are two coeval lines of unification. (1) All algebras, regardless of subject-matter, deal in some sense with the composition of terms, and employ two general types of composition: addition and multiplication. Accordingly, Whitehead defines "Universal Algebra" as "that calculus which symbolizes general operations, . . . which are called Addition and Multiplication."[21] He gives a general description of these processes which will hold for all algebras (his definitions are stated by Prof. Quine, pp. 127f below) and specifies the particular laws and definitions concerning them, in which the various algebras differ. (2) The terms which are thus operated on seem, in all algebras, to be susceptible to interpretation as spatial elements (not necessarily points). To give a few examples: ordinary algebra was developed with the numerical interpretation of its terms in mind; none other was thought of,—but with Descartes an associated geometrical interpretation was discovered. Boole's algebra of logic is capable of a spatial as well as a propositional interpretation. Grassmann's algebra is a "geometrical calculus."

Thus Whitehead's book is a study in comparative algebras, knit together both formally (through specification of abstract laws) and concretely, through uniformity of interpretation. Its ultimate object is nothing else than to elaborate the widest, most differentiable "modes of togetherness" that can be handled by exact abstract thought, and to display the patterns, thus pre-

---

[19] Preface to *Ausdehnungslehre* of 1862. See A. E. Heath's three articles on Grassmann in the *Monist*, Vol. 27, no. 1 (1917); E. Nagel, *Osiris*, Vol. 7, 168.

[20] P. v.

[21] §12.

cipitated, by interpreting the variables as positions in space generally conceived (i.e., so that the particular number of dimensions, the Euclidean parallelism, and the metrical characteristics appear as specializations); the entire project, by its performance, *to provide evidence* for those interested in the general theory of symbolic reasoning.

Whitehead did not complete his program, because he set aside the second volume of *UA* in order to combine forces with Russell in the writing of *PM*. The published first volume is devoted to two unusual algebras which attracted Whitehead's attention precisely because of their "bold extension beyond the traditional domain of pure quantity:"[22] these are Boole's algebra of logic, and the algebra of Grassmann referred to above. Four-fifths of the bulk of the volume are taken up by the statement of Grassmann's principles in an appropriate form and their extended application in turn to a non-metrical theory of forces (which may be called line geometry or a contribution to pure dynamics, depending upon one's interest), to non-Euclidean geometry, and to the ordinary Euclidean space of three dimensions. Whitehead shows how this calculus can get behind even projective geometry, the theorems of which can be set out as consequences of the definitions of the calculus. He aims not so much at discovering new propositions, as at proving whole groups of known propositions more simply, from new and more general standpoints, thus showing the power and the use of a branch of mathematics which members of the profession had looked upon as queer and excessively philosophical.[23]

[22] P. viii.

[23] As to the achievement of the book, only a mathematician would be competent to judge. For estimates of the section on the algebra of logic, Sec. 1 of Professor Quine's essay in this volume, or C. I. Lewis' *Survey of Symbolic Logic*, may be consulted. There are very few reviews of the *UA as a whole*. The mathematician G. B. Mathews, writing in *Nature*, thought it brilliant: the wealth of applications removed the last excuse for ignoring Grassmann; while it was too early to say whether a great instrument of discovery had been presented, the power of the calculus as a means of expression and organization was amply demonstrated; and the author included substantial contributions of his own to mathematical research. In England, Whitehead's election to the Royal Society resulted from the book. But mathematicians elsewhere generally did not read it. *Possibly* they might have, had not the "contributions" which Whitehead considered

6. Certainly, the *UA* is philosophical. No set, well-known subject is treated for its own sake, in methodological separation from other fields susceptible to algebraic treatment. Scientific research usually proceeds by deducing new possibilities of detail from the deposition of recent work in a specific field, and but seldom turns round deliberately to reorganize general ideas; whereas Whitehead's work here, as later, seems to run in the opposite direction. By preference, he usually does what the scientist only sometimes does: he seeks a higher level of generality than what is currently employed. To this end, Whitehead does two things: he brings together the characteristic ideas of diverse fields and in an imaginative construction organizes them into a unity on a different level with its own concepts; and then deduces "applications," namely, a considerable body of known propositions, and some new propositions, so as to show that this unity is not a trivial correlation, but a promising unification. That is his procedure with respect to algebra and geometry here, and it was to be his procedure with respect to the physics of space and time in his investigations of twenty years later. It is the procedure recommended for speculative philosophy in the great opening chapter of *Process and Reality*.

The whole object of the *UA*, Whitehead says, is not completeness in details, but "unity of idea."[24] In pursuit of that, he breaks out of boundaries and surprises the professions, not entirely to their pleasure. Had he written instead of this book a mathematical memoir presenting polished additions to knowledge, mathematicians would have read it. Had he written an essay on symbolic reasoning, in which certain grand generalities were suggested, philosophers would have read it; but the

---

most novel been anticipated in a book published by Burali-Forte one year earlier, but which had not been seen by Whitehead until the *UA* was through the press.

What mathematicians usually say about the *UA* is that "there are some good things in it," but that it "had no influence." Symbolic logicians read the short section on the algebra of logic only; algebraists, interested mainly in the theory of equations and the theory of numbers, continued to develop their own discipline; geometers gathered, at second hand, that some of the discoveries of Cayley and Klein on the relations among the non-Euclidean geometries had been restated and discussed from a slightly different point of view. The fact is that Whitehead's work suffered (in a lesser degree) the fate of Grassmann's, and for a like reason.

[24] P. viii.

essay would have been worthless all the same. Whitehead has always been eager to show the *usefulness* of speculation. A philosophic idea, he holds, is trivial unless it can be shown to illuminate something and to organize ideas of lesser generality. Again, had Whitehead confined himself to the general principles of uninterpreted algebras, his appeal for symbolic logicians as a class would have been increased; but he has never been much interested in the uninterpreted. He makes it a point, early in the development of a logical scheme, to introduce a particular, though broad, interpretation, in connection with which the scheme is worked out and rendered fruitful.[25] The subtitle "With Applications" is of the essence of the *UA*. (And the *UA* is not the only book of Whitehead's bearing that subtitle.) Even that phrase misleads, through suggesting that the interpretations of the algebraic scheme are tacked on to it, whereas they are worked out concurrently with it.

Thus the dominating characteristic of the *UA* is its combination of an inductive and comparative procedure with a speculative rationalism directed toward breaking down boundaries. The rarity of that combination in our time is the reason why Whitehead is generally acknowledged to be unique and to be rather too much for us.

The *UA* is Whiteheadian in its secondary characteristics also. It displays the Whiteheadian ingenuity of thought and the Whiteheadian complexity of presentation so often complained of. There is the Whiteheadian carelessness, too: for example, in Section 22 the significance of the fact that all algebras seem to be capable of spatial interpretation is remarked, and an appendix promised "on a mode of arrangement of the axioms of geometry," but the appendix is not in the book. The author had moved on to a fresh topic, and was probably too busy pioneering on the theory of cardinal numbers to see to it that Volume I of the *UA* was perfected. The book, in its treatment of Grassmann, also shows the well-known Whiteheadian desire to bring out the truth and power of general ideas earlier stated,

[25] See *Universal Algebra*, Bk. I, Ch. I; also §§ 22, 25. Cf. *Science and the Modern World* (N.Y., 1925), 44: "It is the large generalisation, limited by a happy particularity, which is the fruitful conception."

but short-circuited by history and left out of account in prevalent modes of thought.

7. Since this first book of Whitehead's deals with abstract ideas in hierarchical patterns, it is natural for a philosopher to raise in connection with it the question as to the source of the Platonic strain in Whitehead's metaphysics, manifest in his doctrine of "eternal objects." If one reads his works in chronological order, one comes upon no evidence whatever that this doctrine ever appeared doubtful to Whitehead, or that he adopted his Platonic attitude at a certain juncture for specific reasons. If one may ever judge of such matters from the general character of the texts and acquaintance with their author, it seems to me allowable to suppose that the attitude, in Whitehead's case, was almost second nature; possibly intensified gradually through the years.

It is otherwise with the question whether Whitehead ever had the *pure* Platonic temper of mind. The *UA* does not enter upon metaphysics, but there are indications that its author might be expected, were he a metaphysician, to adopt a modified Platonism. "Philosophical" remarks are frequent in the book; none of them hints that concepts have a status superior to things. The position taken is that the importance of a logical scheme derives from its interpretation as "representing" properties of "the world of existing things."[26] This position is adhered to through all Whitehead's works. I believe it to be connected with his great, and rather heterodox, interest in geometry, among all the branches of mathematics. Although every mathematician "interprets" his logical schemes in order to prove their consistency, the interpretation of geometry most frequently employed by mathematicians, in which the elements are interpreted as sets of real numbers, is markedly rare in Whitehead's geometrical investigations. Before long he comes to ask, "What is the meaning of a 'point', in Nature?" Such questions are not raised in the *UA*; but its author does take care to state that his logically primitive conception, that of a "manifold of elements," is abstracted from the concrete situation, a "scheme of things,"

_____

[26] P. vii; also §§ 5, 8.

which is first explained.[27] The ideal of a universal algebra he justifies through its relation to "almost every event, phenomenal or intellectual, which can occur."[28]

Anyone who contrasts this, Whitehead's first handling of the realm of possibility, with Russell's early Platonic articles and books, and with G. E. Moore's early articles, will perceive in Whitehead's case a certain maturity and absence of single-minded faith; which, though it does not settle any metaphysical issues, leads naturally to a modified rather than a rigorous Platonism. And if we suppose—what would surely be false—that Whitehead was born dogmatic, we should still be able to infer from his writings that the doctrine of evolution and the discovery of alternative geometries—either one would have been sufficient—had entirely unbent him. The moral of the geometrical development is that not *one* pattern of ideas, but many patterns of ideas, are illustrated in Nature. It is because of our particular purposes and our limited insight that we discover some and not others. Again, consider an abstract idea such as "equivalence:" the propositions of a calculus, Whitehead says, assert equivalences. But, he observes, we employ no idea of equivalence *simpliciter*. Distinct things can only be asserted to be equivalent relatively to "a certain defined purpose in view, a certain limitation of thought or of action."[29] This mathematician, in short, has already the reflective self-consciousness of a discerning philosopher.

II. "MATHEMATICAL CONCEPTS OF THE MATERIAL WORLD" (1905)

1. The year in which the *UA* appeared saw also the publication of a paper by Whitehead on non-Euclidean geometry. In 1899 he submitted to the Royal Society a paper, read but not published (so far as can be discovered),[30] in which an additional type of algebra, that of groups of finite order, was investigated. He seems then, and for some years thereafter, to have been at

[27] §§ 8, 5.
[28] P. viii.
[29] §3.
[30] See Bibliography, p. 706 below.

work on the second—never published—volume of the *Universal Algebra*. The important novel element that came to him at this time was his first intimate acquaintance with the work of Peano and Frege. With this, and probably as a result of it, came a concentration of his interest on what is now called mathematical logic, and in particular on the analysis of the foundations of arithmetic (finite and infinite) by its methods. Whitehead's papers of 1901 to 1904 on this subject are discussed by Professor Quine in the present volume. This is also the period in which the collaboration with Bertrand Russell began. The writing, with him, of *Principia Mathematica* occupied most of Whitehead's energies during the decade 1900 to 1910.

But the middle of this decade is marked by the appearance of a memoir (published in the *Philosophical Transactions of the Royal Society*), which Whitehead considers one of the best pieces of work he has done. The title is, "On Mathematical Concepts of the Material World." Its object is, using the symbolism developed for the writing of the *Principia*, "to initiate the mathematical investigation of various possible ways of conceiving the nature of the material world. In so far as its results are worked out in precise mathematical detail, the memoir is concerned with the possible relations to space of the ultimate entities which (in ordinary language) constitute the 'stuff' in space."[31]

This paper was submitted to the Royal Society in the same year, 1905, in which Einstein's first paper on relativity appeared. Einstein's paper presented only the Special Theory of Relativity, and did not touch the unification of the theory of space and the theory of matter. But "Mathematical Concepts of the Material World" presents several proposals for their unification into a single theory of the material world.[32] Such a diving behind the apparent independence of sciences is just what we should expect from the author of the *Universal Alge-*

---

[31] *Philosophical Transactions of the Royal Society of London*, Series A., Vol. 205 (1905-06), 465. This memoir will hereafter be referred to, in the body of the text, as the memoir of 1905.

[32] I am not suggesting that any of Whitehead's proposals are at all similar to the General Theory of Relativity presented by Einstein in 1916.

bra. Yet, so far as I know, only Morris Cohen has so much as referred to this paper in print.[33] Did writers on Whitehead's philosophy but know of it, it would be impossible for them to make such errors in their conception of the genesis of his philosophy as are made, for example, by even the generally reliable Dr. Metz.

In the history of Whitehead's philosophical development, the memoir of 1905 is noteworthy because it presents his first criticism of "scientific materialism." The criticism is logical, not physical or philosophical. Also, what is criticized is not called "scientific materialism" (a term introduced in *Science and the Modern World*[34]), but "the classical concept of the material world." Evidently it is of the first importance to know clearly what this classical concept, as conceived by Whitehead, is.

2. The memoir was written during a period of great activity in the investigation of various sets of axioms for geometry. Oswald Veblen, for example,[35] had just constructed the whole of Euclidean geometry from axioms referring to but one class of undefined entities, "points," and one undefined triadic relation among points, "between." (The properties of points and of betweenness are said to be "defined" solely by the axioms.) Whitehead, in his memoir, makes use of Veblen's set of postulates as the most convenient organization of geometry; his own great originality lies in applying this axiomatic method to the expression and, beyond that, the improvement, of the theoretical basis of physics:—truly a grand achievement! The explicit goal is to try out different ways of embracing in a single deductive scheme both the relations of points *inter se* and the relations of points to matter. A "concept of the material world" is the name he gives to such a complete set of axioms, definitions, and resulting propositions. The "classical concept" embodies the prevailing habits of thought. It employs three mutually exclusive classes of entities: points of space, instants of time, and particles of matter. The theory of the motion of matter is superposed

[33] *Symposium in Honor of the Seventieth Birthday of Alfred North Whitehead* (Harvard University Press, 1932), 12.

[34] New York (1925), 24.

[35] *Trans. Amer. Math. Soc.*, Vol. 5 (1904).

on a presupposed independent theory of space and a presupposed independent theory of time. (In fact, the classical concept arose in an age when geometry was the only developed science.) The superposition (according to an analysis first suggested by Russell in *The Principles of Mathematics*[36]) requires a class of relations of "occupation of a point at an instant," a new relation being required for each permanent particle. The general laws of dynamics, and all independent physical laws, are then added to the deductive scheme as axioms about the properties of this class of relations.

The criticism which Whitehead, as logician and mathematician, makes of the classical concept, is as follows. Occam's razor gives a sufficient reason for trying to reduce the number of relations involved, and to make a construction which does not require three independent classes of entities, if fewer will suffice. And Whitehead, being Whitehead, looks upon the segregation of geometry from the other physical sciences as a challenge to theoretical thought. His aim in this memoir is to propose alternative concepts of the material world.

After formulating the classical concept ("Concept I") in terms of the precise symbolic logic of relations developed for the *Principia*—something in itself well worth doing—Whitehead states two variants in which geometry is brought into closer contact with physics. "Concept II," based on a suggestion of Russell's,[37] replaces "material particles" by dyadic relations between points and instants; "Concept III," which may in part be traced back to Leibniz, replaces the two classes, points and particles, by what may be called either moving points or particles of ether. Then in Concepts IV and V ultimate physical entities that are *linear* rather than punctual in nature are introduced, resulting in a tremendous difference from the classical concept. These linear or directional ultimates are analogous to lines of force, though endless. The points of space are defined in terms of their properties, and the lines and figures of ordinary geometry are defined as complexes of these *defined* points.

[36] Chap. LIII. See Whitehead, "On Mathematical Concepts of the Material World," 479.

[37] *The Principles of Mathematics* (Camb. Univ. Press, 1903), Ch. LIII.

In Concept V, the development of which climaxes the memoir, particles of matter are also derivative. The memoir concludes with a sketch of a way in which Concept V might be used to make possible a simple formulation of electromagnetic physics. Classical dynamics and, Whitehead hopes, eventually all of physics, is in this concept expressible in terms of a single polyadic relation, holding between the members of a single class of ultimate physical entities and the instants of time, and one auxiliary relation (required to determine kinetic axes of reference). The single undefined relation, R, is the intersection in order of three linear ultimates by a fourth at an instant of time.

3. Certain specific features of this work now claim our attention. First, Whitehead's treatment of time. There is here no trace of the novel idea which forms the basis of his later physical constructions and is carried over into his metaphysics: the idea that the instant of time, or, in physics, the "configuration at an instant," should not be assumed as primitive and undefined, but, like the point of space, be derived from physical elements which are epistemologically more primitive, though their logical properties are more complex. Whitehead here asserts, on the contrary: "Time must be composed of *Instants. . . . Instants of time* will be found to be included among the ultimate existents of every concept." Again, "In every concept a dyadic serial relation, having for its field the instants of time and these only, is necessary."[38]

Those of us who were educated in the post-Relativity era may mistakenly suppose it to be obvious that instants of time should have been treated as points of space were treated in the memoir. Besides committing an anachronism, we should be forgetting that the purposes of the memoir were mathematical, not at all epistemological. And we ought not to expect a man who is very busy working a new field with a new instrument (symbolic logic) to think up a new theory of time as well as new theories of space and matter. It is not humanly possible to make progress if one tries to revise all prevailing concepts at one stroke. Whitehead had been a geometer for years, and the idea of the

[38] "On Mathematical Concepts of the Material World," 467 and 468 (italics in text).

point as complex was easily suggested to him by the "projective point" of geometry, which is a bundle of straight lines. The chances are that he did not in 1905 give any appreciable thought to the analysis of time; he assumed the obvious, accepted analysis, into instants.

4. Whitehead's treatment of points next requires comment. He writes that "Geometers are already used to the idea of the point as complex," but adds that they nevertheless assume points as ultimate entities, since the definition of the projective point is introduced subsequently to a geometry of points; in fact, the straight lines referred to in the definition are those concurrent at a point. His investigation, he says, grew out of an endeavor to remove this circularity.[39] Two independent geometrical theories, the "Theory of Interpoints" and the "Theory of Dimensions," are offered to that end. Their mathematical merit and novelty—the Theory of Dimensions, Whitehead says, "is based on a new definition of the dimensions of a space"[40]—must be left to the judgment of mathematicians. The general significance of these theories to us lies in the fact that they make possible in the memoir the precise mathematical development of the two "concepts of the material world" that differ widely from the classical concept. The theories themselves are unintelligible if one is not acquainted both with advanced geometry and with the symbolism of *Principia Mathematica*. The facts about them which can here be set down for students of Whitehead are as follows.

First, logicians and mathematicians interested in the full project of *Principia* will find in these theories (along with a paper written in 1914, to be discussed below) the closest existing indication of the manner in which the polyadic relations, essential to Geometry, would have been worked out in the fourth volume of the *Principia*. The Theory of Dimensions, furthermore, is first presented in its most general form, in which it is a contribution to the theory of classes, before the application to geometry is made. Secondly, in the Theory of Interpoints Whitehead for the first time employs the procedure

[39] *Ibid.*, 482, 483, 466.
[40] *Ibid.*, 466.

which he pushed to the limit in his books on the philosophy of physics, namely, the inclusion of temporal entities (the instant in this case, the "duration" later) in the statement of the point-defining relation. Thirdly, one notices in these theories White-head's first employment of certain concepts, notably "cogredi-ence" in the Theory of Interpoints and "primeness" in the Theory of Dimensions,[41] which have a basic rôle in the technical development of the theories of space and time in all his later works. The meanings of these concepts are generalized later on, to be sure. Thus, in the later books, cogredience is the com-mon characteristic of those events which are comprised within a temporally thick slab of three-dimensional nature, which is taken to be what is given to sense-perception; whereas cogredi-ence here has no perceptual significance; it is merely an abstract characteristic (suggested by the theory of "points at infinity") possessed, under certain conditions, by the linear ultimates at an instant of time. Nevertheless there is a recognizable similarity, which deserves to be investigated by anyone interested in White-head's physical theory. Fourthly, these two theories must be looked upon by students of Whitehead's "method of extensive abstraction" as the first beginnings of that method, though the name is only introduced later. This is particularly true of the Theory of Interpoints, which explicitly defines points of space in terms of proposed ultimate material entities. The method of extensive abstraction, as later developed, grows out of two purposes: to define meanings for "point," "line," "instant," etc., thus giving the relational theory of space and time the exact mathematical formulation which its adherents had pre-viously neglected to provide; and to answer the epistemological question (of central importance for an empirical science): "how is the space of physics based upon experience?" Whitehead's dis-cussions of extensive abstraction join the two questions in the way they are customarily joined, or rather fused, by relationists —through the fact that our experience of space is an experience of the order of physical things, not of points. But only the first question is raised in the 1905 memoir,—all epistemological

[41] *Ibid.*, 508-509, 493.

questions being excluded from an investigation that is purely logical.

On the relative merits of the relational and absolute theories of space and time, "Mathematical Concepts of the Material World" makes no decisive pronouncement; quite properly, since the memoir is not concerned with philosophical questions, nor with winning acceptance for any theory of the material world. It is quite plain, however, from the memoir and from subsequent papers, that Whitehead was in fact interested in this controversy, but had not made up his mind about it; and there is no indication that he had yet really tried to do so. The topic is not discussed in its application to time, but the treatment of time is entirely in accord with the absolutist point of view; and when Whitehead asserts that "Time must be composed of Instants,"[42] he refers the reader to Russell's article, "Is Position in Time and Space Absolute or Relative?"[43]—an article devoted to demolishing the relational theories, and to showing that points and instants *must* be assumed as ultimate simple entities, independent and prior to matter. Yet in his discussion of theories of space Whitehead indicates a preference for the relational type (which he calls "Leibniz's theory of the Relativity of Space"), on the ground that since "entities are not to be multiplied beyond necessity," space-elements and material elements should not be accepted as two ultimately independent classes, if a monistic alternative be possible. Thus the absolute theory of space is part of the classical concept of the material world, as here conceived,[44] and is a source of weakness in it. The concept which Whitehead emphasizes, "Concept V," is a "Leibnizian monistic concept."[45]

5. Theoretical thought, when philosophic or nearly philosophic in its breadth, is mere star-gazing unless it springs, in part at least, from specific advances in knowledge.[46] The reader

[42] *Ibid.*, 467.

[43] *Mind*, n.s., Vol. 10, No. 39 (July, 1901), 293-317.

[44] And as repeated elsewhere, e.g., *Aims of Education* (written 10 years later), 235.

[45] *Op. cit.* (cf. footnote 31 above), 467-468, 505.

[46] The advances that seem to have nourished Whitehead's work in this memoir,

will have already perceived how very much this memoir has to do with the progress of geometry. Two points concerning geometry remain to be noticed. (i) Whitehead, as we might expect of the author of the *Universal Algebra,* chooses for his Concepts of the material world sets of axioms which contain no reference to metrical ideas. Such ideas, which must of course appear in any geometry that is to meet the demands of physics, are subsequently introduced by definition.[47] (ii) Non-Euclidean geometries are not discussed. Whitehead adopts the natural course of taking the geometry as Euclidean throughout, and remarks that non-Euclidean structures can be obtained, if desired, by appropriate alterations in the properties of the fundamental polyadic relation from which the propositions of geometry spring in each Concept.[48] In fact, however, a novel analysis of Euclidean parallelism is an essential part of "Concept V" as elaborated with the aid of the Theory of Interpoints and the Theory of Dimensions. One wonders whether this fact has anything to do with Whitehead's choice of a Euclidean structure for the geometry of space-time in his later work on the Theory of Relativity as developed by extensive abstraction.

In this memoir we meet, for the first time, the plain and decisive contribution made by physical conceptions to Whitehead's speculative thought. When all Whitehead's work is surveyed, six influences from physics are found. This group and the group of mathematical discoveries discussed earlier were equally indispensable stimuli—though the physical influences have been more favored by the notice of commentators. At this point I shall touch only on the three that antedate the memoir of 1905. They are: the development of *vector* physics, the development of the theories of molecular and sub-molecular energetic vibration, and thirdly the rise of *field* as a basic concept. Later come the statistical conception of physical laws, the theory of relativity, and the quantum theory.

The first of these six is probably the weightiest of all scientific

other than the great advance in the symbolic logic of classes and relations provided by Russell and Whitehead himself, are physical and geometrical.

[47] *Op. cit.* (cf. footnote 31), 477.

[48] *Ibid.,* 476.

influences on Whitehead's philosophy. A favorite comparison in *Process and Reality* is that of "prehension" with its physical model, the "vector," or directed magnitude describing transmission. In all his later books Whitehead makes it clear that he thinks the great advance of modern over ancient and medieval cosmology has been the gradual replacement of a "procession of forms" by the various "forms of process,"—and this achievement is mainly the gift of physics.[49] The achievement was gradual, and effectively began with the establishment of the transmission theories of light and sound in the seventeenth century: an event of the greatest importance to philosophy,[50] though one usually misunderstood as merely providing the historical occasion for an epistemological distinction among qualities. The molecular theories developed in the nineteenth century, such as the kinetic theory of gases, extended the process, and applied the concept of energy, to all bodies. Finally, in the late nineteenth century, the mathematical theory of vectors and the physical concept of a field provided the means for tracing and integrating the propagation of vibratory energy through all space.

In the latter chapters of the *Universal Algebra* Whitehead made contributions to vector theory. In "Mathematical Concepts of the Material World" the term, vector, is not used, for a vector requires an origin and a length. But it is highly significant that, in order to embrace all geometrical concepts and so many physical concepts as possible in a single-based set of axioms, Whitehead chose for his base-class physical lines considered as simple entities. He notes, too, that on this basis the controversy as to how physical forces can possibly act at a distance (which bears some analogy to the epistemological controversy as to how a subject can possibly have knowledge of a world external to him) is resolved by the fact that two distant particles possess linear ultimates in common.

In the memoir of 1905, the essential thing that is done with each concept of the material world is the demonstration that

---

[49] *Nature and Life* (Univ. of Chicago Press, 1934), 15; reprinted in *Modes of Thought* (Macmillan, N.Y., 1938), 192.

[50] See *The Concept of Nature* (Camb. Univ. Press, 1920), 26.

the theorems of Euclidean geometry follow from its axioms and definitions, and that the motion of matter is expressible. But the existence of relatively permanent "corpuscles," that is, units of matter such as electrons, is also considered. The general line followed consists in defining a corpuscle as a volume, whose permanence is the persistence of some peculiarity of motion of the linear ultimates "passing through" it. This is an example of the now familiar idea of "knots in the ether." It also suggests, to one familiar with Whitehead's metaphysics, his interpretation there of a relatively permanent body, such as an electron, as a succession of occasions, or space-time regions, in each of which a characteristic togetherness of prehensions is repeated. There, as here, Whitehead is carrying out the scientific effort to conceive of that which seems to be an ultimate, enduring fact as in reality a particular result of the aggregate operation of vector forces.

It is a curious fact that this magnificent paper had even less influence on the development of physics than did the *Universal Algebra* on the development of mathematics. Though Whitehead offered only a few general suggestions as to how physicists might fit existing theories into the structure of Concept V, the advantages to be hoped for from success in this enterprise were so great that the attempt might well have been worth while.

What is wanted at this stage is some simple hypothesis concerning the motion of [the linear ultimates] . . . and correlating it with the motion of electric points and electrons. From such a hypothesis the whole electromagnetic and gravitational laws might follow with the utmost simplicity. The complete concept involves the assumption of only one class of entities as forming the universe. Properties of "space" and of the physical phenomena "in space" become simply the properties of this single class of entities.[51]

Whitehead's knowledge of the psychology of research warned him that this ideal would not be carried out in the near future.

In physical research so much depends upon a trained imaginative intuition, that it seems most unlikely that existing physicists would, in general, gain any advantage from deserting familiar habits of thought.[52]

---

[51] *Philos. Trans.*, etc., 525.
[52] *Ibid.*, 466.

But the chief reason why the attempt was not made seems to me to have been the non-existence of a sufficient number of theoretical physicists who were both interested in the axiomatic method and willing to work through the highly complex *Principia* symbolism of Whitehead's memoir.[53]

6. There remains to be considered the relation of "Mathematical Concepts of the Material World" to logic and to philosophy.

What Whitehead calls "philosophic questions" are excluded. To give a striking example: on remarking that possibly the material world, as described in Concept II, "labours under the defect that it can never be perceived," he adds, "But this is a philosophic question with which we have no concern."[54] The general problem, of formulating mathematical concepts of the material world, is, then, "discussed purely for the sake of its logical (i.e., mathematical) interest. It has an indirect bearing on philosophy by disentangling the essentials of the idea of a material world from the accidents of one particular concept."[55]

The most obvious characteristic of the memoir is that it was written by one of the authors of *Principia Mathematica*, who was fired with a vision of the possibilities of mathematical logic, and was applying it to new regions, geometry and physics. (Most of the theorems, Whitehead says, were first worked out in symbolic form.) Logic, as a body of principles of inference, is assumed and employed in the memoir just as in any other mathematical investigation; there are no pre-geometrical propositions (except in the Theory of Dimensions). But all the relations between the variables are expressed in terms of "logical constants," such as negation, disjunction, class membership, etc. The primitive symbols and first definitions are thus a selection from the first symbols and definitions of the *Principia;* and from propositional functions the memoir passes to the symbolic defini-

---

[53] This statement is not to be construed as *blaming* anyone. Only, one cannot but regret the distance between the physicists and this memoir; and wonder how much different the development of physics in the twentieth century might have been had Whitehead been a physicist interested in the axiomatic method, instead of a mathematical logician interested in physical applications.

[54] *Philos. Trans.*, etc., 480.

[55] *Ibid.*, 465.

tions of non-propositional functions and of relations. The first propositions that are asserted are hypotheses as to the formal conditions satisfied by the entities forming the field of the "geometrical" relation, R; these hypotheses are the "axioms" of a concept of the material world. Thus the fundamental relation in terms of which all geometry and, in the advanced concepts, dynamics as well, is expressible, is itself specified by logical ideas only, though it is immediately given a physical interpretation. Consequently, the paper may be said to broach the idea that physics is "one application of a logical system;"[56] or, alternatively, to exhibit the logical component of physics.

A pure logician is likely to misconceive "Mathematical Concepts of the Material World." The phrases used at the close of the preceding paragraph are accurate only when applied to the logician's endeavor to state the conceptual structure of physics *as physics stands,* the existing science being called upon to supply the entities and relationships among entities which, substituted for the logical variables, give the conceptual structure its important interpretation. But it is of the essence of Whitehead's work to propose for physics new entities and new relationships among entities. Symbolic logic is only the great instrument, which by its generalizing symbolism makes these novel possibilities visible. Thus the work is more than a logician's analysis of the structure of physics. It is also an excursion in mathematical cosmology.

We have to make an effort if we are to recover the true early Whitehead. The prevailing impression is that, before he began to write philosophy, this man was entirely a professional mathematician and a mathematical logician, interested primarily in the same things that interested Russell: the foundations of symbolic logic and arithmetic, the logic of classes and relations, the definition of implication, the theory of descriptions, the theory of logical types. Of course—though the last three named are Russell's brain-children—Whitehead was deeply interested in these topics and did an enormous amount of work on them (in-

[56] Morris R. Cohen, describing the paper in *Symposium in Honor of the Seventieth Birthday of Alfred North Whitehead* (Harvard Univ. Press, 1932), 12.

cluding half of the work in *Principia*[57]). But the prevailing opinion is a mistake, and has resulted from the fact that the *Universal Algebra* is not read (except for its short section on the algebra
of logic), nor is this memoir of 1905, nor any volume of *Principia* beyond the first, which is primarily logical; and that the
fourth volume of *Principia*, which was to deal with Geometry
and was to be written by Whitehead alone, never appeared. If
we look into these writings and into the books Whitehead wrote
later as a kind of preliminary to the completion of *Principia*,
we see that the early Whitehead was as much interested in
mathematical cosmology as in symbolic logic. The logical inelegance of the classical concept of the material world is nothing
more than that unnecessary disconnection of first principles which
has goaded on all of Whitehead's intellectual efforts, and which
is named "incoherence" in the opening chapter of *Process and
Reality*. Whitehead's career as a whole shows the kinship
between the mathematician's interest in creating a single theory
where formerly two were required, and the philosopher's
interest in gaining synoptic vision. *Principia Mathematica* itself
is a colossal endeavor to replace two sciences, logic and mathematics, by one.

It is important to observe that logic does not provide the
reason for the logical inelegance of the classical concept. The
situation, as Whitehead describes it after setting forth a modified
form of Veblen's axioms for geometry, is this:

Nothing could be more beautiful than the above issue of the classical
concept, if only we limit ourselves to the consideration of an unchanging
world of space. Unfortunately, it is a changing world to which the complete concept must apply, and the intrusion at this stage into the classical
concept of the necessity of providing for change can only spoil a harmonious and complete whole.[58]

The integral inclusion of geometry—the perfect static science
—within the world of change: that was to be Whitehead's
favorite problem for years.

[57] According to a letter from Lord Russell to the present author, July 3, 1941
(referred to by permission).

[58] Whitehead, *op. cit.*, 479.

III. 1906-1914

1. Whitehead's next publications are two short companion books, *The Axioms of Projective Geometry* (1906) and *The Axioms of Descriptive Geometry* (1907)—numbers 4 and 5, respectively, in the series of "Cambridge Tracts in Mathematics and Mathematical Physics." They should perhaps be looked upon as finally providing the Appendix on the axioms of geometry which was promised in the *Universal Algebra*. The interest of these tracts is almost entirely mathematical. They present no original set of axioms. Yet they show their authorship. The axioms of projective geometry are presented only after a chapter is devoted to the nature of the axiomatic method and an original definition of geometry in general. On the former subject, this chapter deserves recognition as a marvelously compressed account, still worth reading for its lucidity and reasonableness. The definition of geometry makes it "the science of *cross*-classification,"[59] in contrast with the mutually exclusive classification of things into species and genera according to the Aristotelian system. This definition—it is repeated in *Adventures of Ideas* (1933)[60]—accords with the view that geometry has no determinate subject-matter in the usual sense of the term, but deals merely with types of relation, and applies to any entities whose interrelations satisfy the formal axioms.[61]

[59] *Axioms of Projective Geometry*, §3. To this statement Whitehead later adds the following comment, of capital importance: "Projective Geometry is only one example of a science of cross-classification. Other such sciences have not been developed, partly because no obvious applications have obtruded themselves, and partly because the abstract interest of such sciences have not engaged the interest of any large group of mathematicians. For example, in *Principia Mathematica*, Section 93, 'On the Inductive Analysis of the Field of a Relation', is a suggestion for another science of that type. Indeed, the whole of Vol. I is devoted to the initiation of non-numerical quasi-geometrical sciences, together with a technique for their elaboration. The subsequent parts of the book specialize on those more special mathematical sciences which involve number and quantity." *Adventures of Ideas*, Ch. VIII, §IX (p. 176).

[60] *Adventures of Ideas*, 176.

[61] The definition of geometry given by Russell in *The Principles of Mathematics* also emphasizes the formalistic view: "Geometry is the study of series of two or more dimensions." (§352) On the actual usage of mathematicians, O. Veblen and J. H. C. Whitehead have written that there is probably no definite answer to the question why the name "geometry" is given to some mathematical sciences

Whitehead's division of geometries into "projective" and
"descriptive" is rather unusual, though Russell also employed
it in his *Principles of Mathematics*.[62] A geometry is called "projective" if two coplanar lines necessarily intersect, "descriptive"
if they do not. Doubtless Whitehead believed that this classification led to a more unified conception of geometry than did the
prevailing nomenclature, but he has not explained its advantages sufficiently to win the acceptance of mathematicians.[63]
Another Whiteheadian touch is the endeavor to fit the expositions in these tracts to the preparation of students, already introduced to the subject, for reading the detached treatises on it.
Thus the effort is not to exhaust the possibilities of a set of
axioms, but to lead the reader to see whether and when a
fresh axiom is required if a particular proposition is to be proved.
However, the tracts alone, without a teacher, fail to accomplish
their educational aim, because of their extreme compression
and the absence of external aids. In an ideal society every man
of genius would be provided with a well-educated slave whose
duty it would be to take charge of a manuscript as soon as the
author's creative interest moves on, and proceed to eliminate
slips and add the explanations and the bold-faced type that the
ordinary reader requires.

and not to others: "A branch of mathematics is called a geometry because the
name seems good, on emotional and traditional grounds, to a sufficient number
of competent people." (*Foundations of Differential Geometry*, Cambridge, 1932,
17.)

[62] §§362, 374.

[63] The subject-matter of the first tract is easily seen to coincide with "geometry
of position," or "projective geometry" in the usual meaning of the phrase. The
set of axioms used is mainly due to Pieri. Axioms of order are introduced subsequently to axioms of classification. The latter part of this tract stresses the
fact that numerical coördinates can be introduced without having recourse to
"distance" as a primitive idea. The tract on "Descriptive Geometry" deals first
with what others might call "affine geometry;" Veblen's axioms, for which the
undefined ideas are "point" and "between," are mainly used, though others are
discussed. The latter half of this tract is written round the theory of transformation groups, and stresses Sophus Lie's work on the analysis and definition
of Congruence, as superior to using Congruence as an undefined idea. This
mathematical definability of Congruence later becomes an essential point in
Whitehead's battle against the operational approach of orthodox Relativity
Theory (thus, Lie's work is again appealed to on p. 49 of *The Principle of Relativity* (1922)).

2. In 1910 the first volume of *Principia Mathematica* was published. From Whitehead's pen there have since come two short expositions of it that are not sufficiently known. The account given in the latter half of his 1916 essay on "The Organisation of Thought"[64] is a masterpiece of exposition. Attention should be called to Whitehead's way of expressing the significance of the achievement:

... the whole apparatus of special indefinable mathematical concepts, and special *a priori* mathematical premises, respecting number, quantity, and space, has vanished.[65]

The other account of *Principia* is incidental to Whitehead's article, "Mathematics," written for the eleventh edition of the *Encyclopædia Britannica*.[66] The article is entirely an attack on the traditional definition of mathematics as the science of magnitude. The main attack is the novel one developed by Whitehead and Russell themselves. The central point is that the theory of cardinal numbers is shown in *Principia* to be but a subdivision of the general theory of classes and relations; and the proof of Peano's "axioms of cardinal number" takes us to the premises of logic only. After placing ordinal numbers, infinite numbers, the real number system, and geometry also within the general science of classes and relations, Whitehead in this article presents Russell's theory about the use of classes (the "theory of types"), which is intended to make possible the deduction of the general properties of classes and relations from the ultimate logical properties of propositions. The conclusion is that mathematics in general is the "science concerned with the logical deduction of consequences from the general premises of all reasoning."[67] This is the definition due to Russell, as previously mentioned (p. 23, above).

3. A condensed account of his two tracts on Geometry,

[64] *The Organisation of Thought* (1917), 116-128; reprinted in *The Aims of Education* (1929), 163-175.

[65] *Ibid.*, 126 (in reprint, 172); cf. in this connection the passage quoted from *Adventures of Ideas*, footnote 59 above.

[66] Vol. 17, 878-883 (Cambridge, 1911). Reprinted under the title, "Mathematics, Nature of," in the 14th ed., Vol. 15, 85-89 (New York, 1929).

[67] *Enc. Brit.*, 14th ed., Vol. 15, 87.

together with some interesting philosophical discussions, may be found in Whitehead's article on "The Axioms of Geometry," which appears in this same edition (eleventh) of the *Britannica*. It is Division VII (Vol. 11, pp. 730-736) of the many-authored article, "Geometry."[68] This was published in 1910. Here Whitehead associates the respected name of Kant with the quantitative conception of the subject. We should not say that "space is a quantity," but rather that "systems of quantities can be found [as properties of congruence-groups] in a space."[69] Another interesting point occurs in Whitehead's discussion of the controversy between adherents of the relational and the absolute theories of space. The latter is defined as asserting, "it is not intrinsically unmeaning to say that any definite body occupies *this* part of space, and not *that* part of space, without reference to other bodies occupying space." Whitehead offers the opinion that "No decisive argument for either view has at present been elaborated."[70] This remark makes it possible to date his own arrival at a conclusion, in favor of the relational theory, at some time between 1910 and 1914. The latter year is that of the delivery of Russell's lectures on *Our Knowledge of the External World*, in which there was published for the first time a construction of the points and instants of absolute space and time out of entities of a perceptible type, according to the method of "extensive abstraction;" and Russell referred to Whitehead as having originated the method and the definition of points.[71]

The importance of this decision of Whitehead's, as will appear from the sequel, extends far beyond the mere philosophy of space. What caused Whitehead to adopt the relational theory can at the present date only be conjectured; but the conjecture is highly plausible. Whitehead was getting the fourth volume of *Principia*, on Geometry, under way. In view of his habit of concentrating on the particular task in hand, it would be most

[68] Not reprinted in the 14th ed.
[69] P. 734.
[70] P. 730.
[71] *Our Knowledge of the External World* (1914), Preface. Cf. also Russell's *Analysis of Matter* (1927), 290.

improbable if his rejection of the absolute theory were not a result of the procedure planned for that volume. It would have been hardly worth while to treat geometry as arithmetic, by associating "points" with triples (or, more generally, with *n*-ads) of numbers. It would be more interesting to develop points as classes of entities of some general type not peculiarly "geometrical" in nature—just as in the earlier volumes cardinal numbers were developed as particular classes of entities not essentially numerical in nature—the classes to be so constructed that the relations between them would have the precise mathematical properties of points. This would also be in line with his bias against the absolute theory with its purely spatial entities, which was manifested in "Mathematical Concepts of the Material World." A second influence, equally important, is the continued effect of Whitehead's philosophic or reflective way of thinking of intellectual processes; this factor, which gives the method of extensive abstraction its epistemological aspect, I shall describe in the next division of the present essay.

4. No account of Whitehead's writings in this period would be complete if it omitted mention of his masterly "shilling shocker," *An Introduction to Mathematics,* written for the Home University Library, and published in 1911. It shows his great ability in sheer exposition, when there is no problem of working out new ideas. With reference to the four advances in nineteenth century mathematics that I singled out as particularly influencing Whitehead, it is to be noted that while the *Introduction to Mathematics* quite properly stops short of projective and non-Euclidean geometry, it does include a superb account of the enlargement of algebra effected by the introduction of complex quantities, and of the elimination of the infinitesimal.[72] Students of Whitehead's philosophy could also profit by looking between the covers of this book, since the explanations of the nature and importance of exact science contain short statements of philosophical doctrines, not intended to be such, but therefore all the more revealing of the selective emphases and the natural bent of Whitehead's thoughts in his—so-called

[72] Chaps. VI-VIII; XI, XV.

—pre-philosophical period. Thus, there is the discussion of the value of symbolism, referred to earlier;[73] a discussion of the *periodicity* exhibited in nature;[74] an assertion that the idea of a vector "is the root-idea of physical science;"[75] a characteristic insistence that "The really profound changes in human life all have their ultimate origin in knowledge pursued for its own sake;"[76] a simple exposition of the abstract character of mathematics;[77] and an account (using coördinate geometry as an example)[78] of the importance for the growth of science of that integrating generalization which has been characteristic of Whitehead's own writings.

IV. Pre-Speculative Epistemology (1914-1917)

1. Whitehead is set apart from the typical philosophers of our time by having produced a metaphysics instead of confining himself to epistemology or attacks on epistemology. But he is a typical modern in this, that reflections on the nature of knowledge prepared the path for his metaphysical speculation. The fact is not generally appreciated, and his critics have a habit of supposing that the connection consists in minimizing the importance of clear knowledge and assigning a high value to the vague merely in order to have an excuse for "going off the deep end." Actually, Whitehead's epistemological preparation was a study of how the evident model of clear and precise knowledge of the world—mathematical physics—is arrived at. This is an epistemological study, to which logical construction, and physical and psychological knowledge, are relevant.

The phase now to be described begins somewhere between 1911 and 1914, its initial motive being merely to provide a logical analysis of space for the fourth volume of the *Principia*. Reflections on what is meant by space inaugurate an epistemological development, which culminates in an *epistemological* criticism of the Classical Concept of the material world, and

---

[73] P. 20 above; see *Introduction to Mathematics*, Ch. V, *passim*.
[74] *Ibid.*, chap. XII.
[75] *Ibid.*, 126.
[76] *Ibid.*, 32. Compare chaps. I and II of *Science and the Modern World* (1925).
[77] *Ibid.*, chaps. I, II, XVI; cf. *Science and the Modern World*, chap. II.
[78] *Ibid.*, chap. IX.

the elaboration of a new Concept from a different empirical base. The books published in 1919 and 1920 present the culmination of this development. The years preceding it show more tentative groping, more shifts in position, than do any others, in the development of Whitehead's philosophy. Compared with this progress, the expansion of the new Concept of the material world into a metaphysics, that is, a Concept of the world in all its aspects, is fairly straightforward. But in that development, which takes place in the 1920's, an epistemological inquiry— into our experience of causality—is again an essential step, though not one marked out as a temporally separate phase.

The published evidence of the original phase of epistemological preparation consists of four papers, completed, respectively, in 1914, 1915, 1916 and 1917. (And the educational essays of this period have a general relevance.) Every one of these papers is important, but it would be tedious to analyze each in turn. The last three are written from one and the same point of view, and I shall accordingly treat them as a unit after briefly noticing the first, in which the discussion is on a different level.

2. The paper of 1914 is called "La Théorie Relationniste de l'Espace." It was read before a Congress of mathematical logicians which met in Paris, early in April.[79] The paper seems poorly written and unnecessarily long. But to the student of Whitehead's development it is an interesting document of transition—of the typical Whiteheadian transition, which is not a change of opinion so much as an enlargement of interest.

The relational theory of space is now adopted, and its standpoint expressed in a manner that will evidently take its adherent far afield: it forbids us to consider physical bodies as first in space and then acting on each other—rather, they are in space because they *interact,* and space is only the expression of certain properties of their interaction.[80] (The doctrine of *Process and*

---

[79] Publication, in the *Revue de Métaphysique et de Morale,* was delayed two years. A report of the meeting, given in *L'Enseignement Mathématique,* Vol. 16 (1914), records (pp. 375-376) a delegate's remark that Whitehead's opinions did not agree with Russell's conclusions in *The Principles of Mathematics;* and Whitehead's reply,—that his collaboration with Russell did not preclude divergences, and that, besides, Russell's ideas on space had since developed.

[80] *Revue de Métaphysique et de Morale,* Vol. 23 (1916), 429-30.

Reality is that "geometry is . . . the morphology of nexūs."[81])
The exact point of application of the relational theory, i.e., what
the original relata should be, Whitehead has not settled upon.
It will be another year before he has his epistemological biases
organized and ready for publication. He is now in the process
of making the necessary distinctions, e.g., between the space of
mathematical physics, "immediate apparent space," which is a
fragment of the world as actually perceived by a particular individual, and "complete apparent space," or the public space of
common sense, which is constructed from immediate apparent
space. Whitehead is also trying to clear the way of *a priori*
dogmatisms, such as the dictum that space must be infinitely
divisible. The *must* is better replaced by an expression of infinite
divisibility in precise logical symbolism, and a study of the way
the assumption affects the mathematical statement of the relational theory of space.

Thus the epistemological discussions are accompanied by contributions in mathematical logic, along the lines of "extensive
abstraction;" for the fact that one is not ready to speak one's
mind about the data of perception and the meanings of "space"
does not prevent one from working out some of the formal
conditions that must obtain if geometry, as used in physics, is
to be the issue of the investigation. The chief contribution is a
definition of "point" in the manner familiar to readers of *The
Concept of Nature:* the assumption of a point is the assumption
that relations of inclusion-of-a-part-within-a-whole exist among
extended objects, such that we can define the class of all those
convergent series of objects which would, in ordinary language,
be said to include the point. The symbolism of *Principia Mathematica* is employed to state the axioms required. Whitehead's
position is that there undoubtedly exist many possible ways of
defining geometrical entities; he urges that a variety of ways
be tried, and an effort made to find those that best accord with
the facts of perception (for apparent space) or with scientific
hypotheses (for physical space).[82] Evidently, his conviction that

---

[81] Pt. IV, chap. III, §I. I am not implying that in 1914 Whitehead had worked
out a doctrine of interaction; most certainly he had not.

[82] *Revue de Métaphysique et de Morale*, Vol. 23, 441-442.

geometry is part of physics has pushed Whitehead's problem of working out the foundations of geometry for the *Principia*, into an epistemological arena.

3. The papers of 1915, 1916 and 1917 are entitled, respectively, "Space, Time, and Relativity," "The Organisation of Thought," and "The Anatomy of Some Scientific Ideas." They were first published in book form in 1917[83] as the concluding chapters of *The Organisation of Thought* (a book otherwise devoted to essays on education), and reprinted in 1929 (the former book being out of print)[84] as Chapters X, VIII and IX, respectively, of *The Aims of Education and Other Essays*.

These papers are the first pieces of writing that would ordinarily be called "philosophical." Whitehead has come to questions that are immediately—as opposed to ultimately—of interest to scientists as a group and to philosophers, not only to mathematicians and logicians. He is beginning to take an active part in the discussions of the Aristotelian Society in London, and in the British Association for the Advancement of Science. His essays consist of suggestions proposed for the consideration of such audiences. The symbolism of *Principia* does not appear in print again for twenty years.

The nerve of the epistemological thought developed in these essays is given in the following quotation.

I insist on the radically untidy, ill-adjusted character of the fields of actual experience from which science starts. To grasp this fundamental truth is the first step in wisdom, when constructing a philosophy of science. This fact is concealed by the influence of language, moulded by science, which foists on us exact concepts as though they represented the immediate deliverances of experience. The result is, that we imagine that we have immediate experience of a world of perfectly defined objects implicated in perfectly defined events which, as known to us by the direct deliverance of our senses, happen at exact instants of time, in a space formed by exact points, without parts and without magnitude: the neat, trim, tidy, exact world which is the goal of scientific thought.

My contention is, that this world is a world of ideas, and that its internal relations are relations between abstract concepts, and that the

[83] For other publications see the Bibliography in this volume.
[84] I shall therefore make my page references to this latter reprint.

elucidation of the precise connection between this world and the feelings of actual experience is the fundamental question of scientific philosophy.[85]

This passage is of the utmost importance. It beautifully states the eternal problem of all those who concern themselves with the relation of experience to scientific concepts; it shows how Whitehead's position in these essays has its origin in his great natural gift of psychological awareness; and it shows how his position is connected, on the one hand, with his examination of geometry as a physical science, and on the other hand with the criticism of abstractions—what his critics call his anti-intellectualism—which dominates *Science and the Modern World.* It is not too much to say that the general condition that is necessary, and sufficient, for understanding the development of Whitehead's philosophy is to bear jointly in mind his aim at mathematical cosmology and his doctrine of "the rough world and the smooth world" (as I shall call the doctrine that is expounded in this quotation). Notice that in the passage there is nothing that the author of *Process and Reality* need reject.

4. Whitehead's method of solving the "fundamental question of scientific philosophy," however, is built round four ideas which are all severely modified later on. The great difference between Whitehead and Russell consists in Russell's refusal to modify these ideas. In fact, the difference begins now, since Russell's expressions of the problem (in *Our Knowledge of the External World* and in his essays which followed it) are, in contrast to Whitehead's, such as to exclude the possibility of the Whiteheadian modifications.

To state the four ideas. *First,* an acceptance of the characteristic starting point of British empiricism:

Fragmentary individual experiences are all that we know, and . . . all speculation must start from these *disjecta membra* as its sole datum.

Consider in your mind some definite chair. The concept of that chair is simply the concept of all the interrelated experiences connected with that chair—namely, of the experience of the folk who made it, of the folk who sold it, of the folk who . . .

---

[85] *Aims of Education,* 157-158. The date of the passage is 1916.

The material pyramids of Egypt are a conception, what is actual are the fragmentary experiences of the races who have gazed on them.

. . . an extended body is nothing else than the class of perception[s] of it by all its percipients, actual or ideal.[86]

There is no evidence in the Whiteheadian corpus that Whitehead considered any alternative to this empiricism. It is the natural beginning for an Englishman's investigation into the data of science. This Englishman, Whitehead, is a philosopher of experience in all his later writings. His panpsychism will change everything; but he is now deliberately excluding all metaphysical questions, and asking only about the observational basis of science. The only special comment that need be made is that Whitehead's natural bias in favor of immediate experience was probably strengthened at this time by the contrast between life in London and his former life in Cambridge, by his reflections on education, and by the rise of relativity in physics.

Whitehead, become conscious of his empiricism, is no longer interested in the absolute theory of space.

All space measurement is from stuff in space to stuff in space. The geometrical entities of empty space never appear. The only geometrical properties of which we have any direct knowledge are properties of those shifting, changeable appearances which we call things in space. It is the sun which is distant, and the ball which is round, and the lamp-posts which are in linear order.[87]

And obviously the same reasoning applies to time.

It needs very little reflection to convince us that a point in time is no direct deliverance of experience. We live in durations, and not in points.[88]

Whitehead's empiricism in this stage approaches the narrow "scientific empiricism" of the positivists, but that is mainly because of a *second* idea, that of the independence of science from metaphysics.

One of the points which I am urging in this address is, that the basis

[86] *Ibid.*, 245-246, 159, 243, 176.
[87] *Ibid.*, 233.
[88] *Ibid.*, 237.

of science does not depend on the assumption of any of the conclusions of metaphysics; but that both science and metaphysics start from the same given groundwork of immediate experience, and in the main proceed in opposite directions on their diverse tasks.

For example, metaphysics inquires how our perceptions of the chair relate us to some true reality. Science gathers up these perceptions into a determinate class, adds to them ideal perceptions of analogous sort, which under assignable circumstances would be obtained, and this single concept of that set of perceptions is all that science needs; unless indeed you prefer that thought find its origin in some legend of those great twin brethren, the Cock and Bull.[89]

Its task is the discovery of the relations which exist within that flux of perceptions, sensations, and emotions which forms our experience of life. The panorama yielded by sight, sound, taste, smell, touch, and by more inchoate sensible feelings, is the sole field of activity. It is in this way that science is the thought organisation of experience.[90]

How different from the metaphysical Whitehead that we know! The reference to "the more inchoate sensible feelings" (which are of no value to science) was probably much less noticed by Whitehead's public than the reference to a cock and bull story. The latter is probably a thrust at the current idealistic metaphysics; it was graciously deleted in the 1929 reprint, but originally it was printed not only in *The Organisation of Thought,* but in the *Proceedings of the Aristotelian Society* and in the *Report of the British Association for the Advancement of Science* as well. The wide circulation of the essays of this period among English philosophers and men of science is doubtless one cause of the resentment later entertained in many quarters toward the doctrines of *Science and the Modern World.* In America, where these essays are too little known, the process is sometimes reversed: a positivist of my acquaintance, who saw no merit in Whitehead as a philosopher, after reading the essays changed his opinion; and recommended them to his class, which was studying modern developments from Hume's position.

For Whitehead's work in this period is indeed—we are com-

---

[89] *The Organisation of Thought,* 114. Also in *Aims of Education,* 161, except for the clause following the last semicolon.
[90] *Aims of Education,* 157.

ing to his *third* idea, which may be called the idea of inferential constructions[91]—in many respects a fresh development of Hume's principle that the connected world we take for granted is in reality a product of the habits of the imagination. "In my view," writes Whitehead, "the creation of the world is the first unconscious act of speculative thought; and the first task of a self-conscious philosophy is to explain how it has been done."[92] In the long essay on "The Anatomy of Some Scientific Ideas" (1917) he digs out several "fundamental principles of mental construction according to which our conception of the external physical world is constructed."[93] These principles are not *a priori*, as in Kant, but matters of fact observed through empirical reflection. Their origination and their present automatic operation are viewed as due to long ages of historical evolution.[94]

Our idea of a thing, such as an orange, is built up out of percepts ("sense-objects," in Whitehead's terminology) by the unconscious application of various principles. For example,

The essential ground of the association of sense-objects of various types, perceived within one short duration, into a first crude thought-object of perception is the coincidence of their space-relations, that is, in general an approximate coincidence of such relations perhaps only vaguely apprehended.[95]

There are also various principles of association according to type, quality and intensity of sense. This is the kind of analysis that is continued by C. D. Broad in the second Part of *Scientific Thought*.

Such concepts as a "force *at a point*," and a "configuration *at an instant*" are indispensable to the physical scientist in his effort to attain accuracy and system. What is the origin of these concepts?

The master-key by which we confine our attention to such parts as

[91] The phrase occurs in *ibid.*, 191.
[92] *Ibid.*, 246.
[93] *Ibid.*, 191.
[94] *Ibid.*, 158-159.
[95] *Ibid.*, 193-194.

possess mutual relations sufficiently simple for our intellects to consider is the principle of convergence to simplicity with diminution of extent.

The origin of points is the effort to take full advantage of the principle of convergence to simplicity.

What are the precise properties [of classes of thought-objects of perception] meant when a point is described as an ideal limit?[96]

The answer to the question is the method of extensive abstraction, which Whitehead now applies to time as well as to space. It is the advance of mathematics that makes it impossible for us any longer to shirk the problem:

It may be observed that, before the ordinary mathematical meanings of limit had received a precise explanation, the idea of a point as a limit might be considered as one among other examples of an idea only to be apprehended by direct intuition. This view is not now open to us.[97]

Many critics of Whitehead's method of extensive abstraction —especially those who follow Broad's account of it instead of Whitehead's—have erroneous impressions which may be dispelled by reading the beautiful expositions included in these essays.[98]

The *fourth* idea is, that with mathematical logic, which can precisely specify the conditions required for membership in a class, if the class is to have certain formal properties, we can hope to exhibit *all* the concepts of science as concepts of classes of percepts. The process begins with concepts that are directly exhibited, as, e.g., the whole-part relation is exhibited in space-perception, and proceeds to concepts of classification and order which apply to these primary concepts, and so on, until conceptions are reached

whose logical relations have a peculiar smoothness. For example, conceptions of mathematical time, of mathematical space, are such smooth

---

[96] *Ibid.*, 191, 206, 207.

[97] *Ibid.*, 207.

[98] A sample error is the charge that extensive abstraction forgets that the relevance of "points" and "instants" lies in their application (to state this relevance is the whole point of the method!), and aims instead to define these entities in such a way as to guarantee their existence (this is an auxiliary interpretation).

conceptions. No one lives in "an infinite given whole," but in a set of fragmentary experiences. The problem is to exhibit the concepts of mathematical space and time as the necessary outcome of these fragments by a process of logical building up.[99]

Whitehead at this time held high hopes for the class theory. It would have been most unnatural to confine the exploration of its possibilities to the concepts of space and time alone.

5. One reason, besides intrinsic importance, for quoting at such length from Whitehead's essays of 1915 to 1917 is that public familiarity with the program they broach is due almost entirely to Russell's more widely read expositions; and Whitehead and Russell do not talk the same language.

What are the un-russellian, un-Humian, un-positivistic traits discernible in Whitehead's own exposition? Five such traits can be picked out.

(i) Consider Whitehead's attitude toward metaphysics. Here is a man who has been developing the logic of classes and relations and applying it to space, and who has an eye on what I have called mathematical cosmology. He wants to work his instruments of discovery to the uttermost. But his metaphysical friends tell him that the meaning of scientific concepts requires reference to the nature of ultimate reality, not forgetting mind. Naturally, he retorts,

But, for the purpose of science, what is the actual world? Has science to wait for the termination of the metaphysical debate till it can determine its own subject-matter? (*AE*, 157.)

The initial independence from metaphysics that is here claimed for science is, like Whitehead's later (and better known) insistence that the philosophy of natural science should proceed without discussing the mind's synthesis with nature,[100] essentially the natural demand of the creative intellect for freedom from interference in its chosen task. *Today* Whitehead would say that the manner in which a scientist approaches his subject-matter reflects his implicit metaphysics. But there is no excuse for a positivist's supposing that the pre-metaphysical Whitehead was

[99] *Op. cit.* (*AE*), 243.
[100] *Concept of Nature* (1920), chaps. I, II.

anti-metaphysical. On the contrary, "Science does not diminish the need of a metaphysics." The relationship of possibility to actuality, in particular, calls for metaphysical analysis. And, stronger yet, "Science only renders the metaphysical need more urgent."[101] The conclusion of "The Anatomy of Some Scientific Ideas" runs,

We commenced by excluding judgments of worth and ontological judgments. We conclude by recalling them. Judgments of worth are no part of the texture of physical science, but they are part of the motive of its production.

Again, ontological judgments were not excluded by reason of any lack of interest. They are in fact presupposed in every act of life: in our affections, in our self-restraints, and in our constructive efforts.[102]

There is here, in short, no closed positivism, but a development of thought within a certain region, namely the analysis of the perceptual basis (as opposed to the ontological significance) of scientific concepts.

(ii) Secondly, let us consider the total absence in these essays of the sceptical motive which is so characteristic of Russell, of Hume, and of most positivists. Radical scepticism does not interest Whitehead:

The question which I am inviting you to consider is this: How does exact thought apply to the fragmentary, vague *continua* of experience? I am not saying that it does not apply: quite the contrary. But I want to know how it applies . . . in detail how the correspondence is effected.

Whitehead goes further and asserts that

science is rooted in . . . the whole apparatus of commonsense thought [which has been developed in the evolution of man and by which he arranges his experience]. That is the *datum* from which it starts, and to which it must recur. . . . You may polish up commonsense, you may contradict in detail, you may surprise it. But ultimately your whole task is to satisfy it.[103]

The refusal of the philosophy of organism to accept Hume's

[101] *Aims of Education*, 229, 231.
[102] *Ibid.*, 228, 229.
[103] *Ibid.*, 158, 159-160.

epistemology is based on the doctrine that practice is the ultimate touchstone of theory.

(iii) By the school of Hume, Russell, and the Carnap of *Der Logische Aufbau der Welt*, the construction of the concepts of common sense and of science is looked upon as the building up of a *public* world from *private* experiences. But Whitehead's emphasis is in another direction, namely, the attainment of accuracy, logical smoothness, and completeness of detail. In a few more years he will denounce the problem of building up publicity from privacy as a false one; now he seems to agree that there is a problem; and he enumerates "universal logical truths, moral and aesthetic truths, and truths embodied in hypothetical propositions," as being "the immediate objects of perception which are other than the mere affections of the perceiving subject."[104] This is Russell's position in *Our Knowledge of the External World*. Furthermore, when Whitehead read "Space, Time, and Relativity" before the Aristotelian Society in 1915, he commented that there may be a good deal in the time-lag argument against "an immediate presentation to us of an aspect of the world as it in fact is."[105] Plainly he is not at this time a neo-realist, so far as perception of external nature is concerned. But, unlike Russell, he initiates no attack on natural realism. Since his epistemological inquiry does not revolve around the antithesis between the private and the public, his subsequent move into realism will require no revolution in his ideas.

(iv) Were we to search the doctrines of metaphysics to find that one which is most uncongenial to positivism, we might well choose the doctrine of the immanence of the past in the present, which is emphasized by Bergson's and Whitehead's metaphysics. But Whitehead now, although suggesting that our conception of past events is built up from the before-after relation observed in the present event by means of repeated applications of a "Principle of Aggregation," also anticipates the doctrine of immanence:

[104] *Ibid.*, 230.
[105] *Organisation of Thought*, 225. The passage is omitted in *The Aims of Education* reprint.

If it be admitted, as stated above, that we live in durations and not in instants, . . . the distinction between memory and immediate presentation cannot be quite fundamental; for always we have with us the fading present as it becomes the immediate past.[106]

The passage reminds us of William James; indeed, Whitehead's account of the field of perception is James', not Hume's.

(v) We come finally to what will turn out to be the most important deviation from "scientific" empiricism. After describing the manner in which he proposes to arrive at "that connected infinite world in which in our thoughts we live," Whitehead comments,

The fact that immediate experience is capable of this deductive superstructure must mean that it itself has a certain uniformity of texture. So this great fact still remains.[107]

Whitehead's system of natural knowledge in *The Principles of Natural Knowledge* (1919) rests on this doctrine—here so briefly alluded to—of the *texture* of immediate experience. The doctrine is the progenitor of the metaphysical doctrine of prehensions.

In fact, Whitehead's fundamental object of explicit criticism in these essays is no particular doctrine (save that of absolute space and time, and, in passing, the subject-predicate logic), but the false neatness of abstract intellectualism, the attitude of mind which supposes that there is a stock of concepts, at once general and precise, on hand for use by scientists and philosophers. The physicist "assumes geometry," and is satisfied. He has another job to do. The intellectualist philosopher, without the physicist's justification, thoughtlessly assumes a similarly precise set of concepts. Evidently, while Whitehead's intentions at this time are limited, he is attacking the great "fallacy of misplaced concreteness."

V. The Philosophy of Natural Science
(1918 to 1924)

1. The three books—the *Enquiry Concerning the Principles*

---

[106] *Aims of Education*, 189-190.
[107] *Ibid.*, 246.

of Natural Knowledge (1919), *The Concept of Nature* (1920), and *The Principle of Relativity* (1922)—may be considered as forming a unit. I shall call them, for short, the 1920 books. They have, all of them, but one subject—a new philosophy of natural science, with special applications to physics. Inconsistencies between the three are minor. The first is the indispensable volume, *CN* being mainly a beautifully smooth and less technical explanation of its predecessor, whereas the novel element in the last of the triad is the deduction of a General Theory of Relativity. Fortunately, we have come at last to the part of Whitehead's output that is sufficiently well known to enable us to embark on discussion with little prior exposition.

The main specific changes that have occurred in the history of Whitehead's thought are the considerable modification of his empiricism and the almost entire rejection of the three other ideas which were presented above[108] as involved in his first epistemology. The changes were well under way by the time *CN* appeared; in fact, practically all that their completion then required was the expansion of certain doctrines of that book beyond the field of the philosophy of science. The chief reason why this change was hardly noticed, until *SMW* startled the public, is that *CN*, by reason of its realism and certain logical distinctions, drew to its author a fresh set of sympathies, strongly held by most of the philosophers who inclined toward Hume and positivism. Whitehead was conquering new worlds, and had so far given little encouragement to metaphysicians. One outcome of the discussion of the 1920 books will be to show how very much the anti-metaphysicians should have been on their guard. For Whitehead's empiricism, in appearance retained, is now in fact greatly altered through the replacement of the base-class, viz., sense-objects (percepts), by two types of primitive entities, "objects" and "events." The class theory is gradually seen to involve a false simplification when extended beyond purely spatio-temporal concepts like points and instants. Principles of inferential construction play a correspondingly

---

[108] In Section 4 of the preceding division of this essay.

lesser rôle than formerly. Only Whitehead's working attitude toward metaphysics remains what it was.

He is, as before, discussing the rationale of natural science. But his discussion is now inspired by the conviction that the classical scientific materialism, taken as a whole, does not stand up under empirical examination any better than did the absolute theory of space; and furthermore in certain respects (which had escaped attention in the memoir of 1905, on "Mathematical Concepts of the Material World"), it lacks coherence. Scientific materialism was already under attack from all sides, but the usual mode of its correction consisted in restricting meanings to laboratory operations together with conventions. The problem of the philosophy of natural science, for Whitehead, is to offer the scientist, in place of the ancient trinity of time, space and matter, a coherent set of meanings based on relations exhibited in all sensory observation. Such a set of general meanings will constitute a philosophy for the reorganization of theoretical physics.

2. The relation of Whitehead's thought to physical science is easily misconceived. A reviewer of *PNK* expressed the belief that Whitehead had felt very strongly the force of Bergson's criticism of physical science, and had written the book in response to it—to acknowledge that science *was* guilty of spatialization, and to show that science could be reformed so as to be free of that trait. The reviewer must have had inside information, since the only reference to Bergson in the book is a statement that Whitehead believes his doctrine of the "passage of nature" is "in full accord with Bergson." On putting the reviewer's opinion before Whitehead, several years ago, I received the reply that he had read Bergson, but was not much worried by him; what did worry him at that time was "the muddle geometry had got into" (in relation to the physical world).

Another natural misconception about this period—in relation to the logical period that preceded and the metaphysical period that followed it—is that Einstein's theory of relativity acted on Whitehead as an impulse from the outside that was needed to release his latent philosophical powers. Dr. Rudolf Metz, by asserting this opinion as fact, in his excellent and reasonably lengthy account of Whitehead,[109] has recently given it a strong push towards entrenchment in the public mind. Metz's authority is: Whitehead himself.

His awakening from dogmatic slumber resulted, as he himself confessed, from the great changes in the field of mathematical physics that came especially from Einstein's theory of relativity and its criticism of the traditional doctrine of space and time.[110]

The confession referred to appears in the opening paragraph of the preface to *The Principle of Relativity*, as follows:

The present work is an exposition of an alternative rendering of the theory of relativity. It takes its rise from that "awakening from dogmatic slumber"—to use Kant's phrase—which we owe to Einstein and Minkowski.

Now as to the inferences drawn from the above. In the first place, Dr. Metz has converted the plural "we" into the singular "I." Whitehead's allusion to Kant's "dogmatic slumber" is impersonal, and refers to a general awakening to possibilities, formerly undreamt of, concerning the relativity of space, time, and matter. Dr. Metz's reading may be a simple slip, or it may be the result of unconsciously assuming that the subject whose philosophy he is reviewing was at that time thinking of himself as the author of a philosophy. In the second place, even if Whitehead had said "I" instead of "we," such a statement, coming from a notoriously modest man, would have proved nothing about what the man might have done in the absence of Einstein's work. Thirdly, although it is doubtless quite improbable that the theory of relativity contained in the book would have been written had Einstein's theory not preceded it, that still leaves us a long way from *philosophy*. Fourthly, Dr. Metz implies that Whitehead had been quietly acquiescing in "the traditional doctrine of space and time." As a matter of fact, Whitehead had for years been criticizing the traditional doctrine, both from a logical and from an epistemological point of

---

[109] *A Hundred Years of British Philosophy*, English trans. (London and New York, 1938), 589-622.

[110] Metz, R., *op. cit.*, 591.

view—as we have seen. He was now spurred on by the great advance toward unification initiated by physicists.

Dr. Metz's assumption of a slumber and a need to awaken is dictated by acceptance of the usual misinterpretation of Whitehead's thought of the first period, as having been entirely that of a member of the mathematical profession, whose work has nothing to do with anything else. Thus the passage I have criticized is immediately preceded by this opinion of Whitehead's work on *PM*:

Although this also, being concerned with a special science, has little to do with philosophy in the full sense of the word, it led Whitehead nearer to a philosophical attitude. But this was not independently reached by a process of inner development, but was imposed upon him by his collaborator and merely taken over by him. There was needed a further impulse from without to bring him finally into the paths of philosophy and to release him from the fetters of Russell's way of thinking.[111]

Dismiss the non-existent fetters from your mind, remember that Whitehead has a very independent mind and that he had already developed an epistemology of space and time (which Russell had taken over in 1914!), and the supposed need of an impulse from the world of science to release Whitehead and turn him into a philosopher vanishes.

Exactly what rôle is to be ascribed to the theory of relativity in Whitehead's development, it is impossible to say. The case is typical. His own intellectual history has never interested Whitehead, and nothing would appall him more than the idea of putting out in speech or writing a "General Confession" in the manner of Santayana.[112] The observer can construct no *neat* picture of the whole. He *can*, by studying the so-called non-philosophical writings, avoid the deeper pitfalls; and he can, on the basis of the published evidence, draw probable conclusions. In the case of the theory of relativity, it is practically certain that Minkowski's work influenced Whitehead considerably, and that Einstein's spurred him on. The whole physical development agitated him very much, as it did every live mind that

[111] *Ibid.*

[112] Cf. *The Philosophy of George Santayana* (Evanston and Chicago, 1940), 3-30.

had an interest in the philosophy of science. It incited Whitehead to devise a theory of space-time, from which both the
Lorentz Transformation and the observable consequences of
Einstein's general theory could be deduced, but which should
have an altogether different foundation.

In the fourth volume of *PM*, he would have to take cognizance of the interrelations of space, time, and matter—both
because the author of "Mathematical Concepts of the Material
World" was inclined to do so, and because experimental physics
demanded it. Meantime, physicists would be getting fixed in
their minds a conception of these interrelations which was, according to Whitehead, far too narrow. In these matters, time
is of the essence. So, I take it, nothing was more natural than
to postpone the completion of the *Principia* in order to "lay the
basis of a natural philosophy which is the necessary presupposition of a reorganised speculative [i.e., theoretical] physics,"[113]
and to deduce the accepted experimental results from that basis.

In fact, Whitehead failed to deflect the path of physics.
Around 1933 Eddington, who had done much to get Einstein's
interpretations accepted, remarked in a physical journal that
he could now see that the philosopher's insight had been superior, but that it had come out of season for the physicist.[114]
There is a bare possibility that Whitehead's theory of relativity
may yet affect the history of science, for he deduced several
consequences which differ from those of Einstein's theory by
minute quantities still beyond our powers of observation.

The main effect of relativity theory on Whitehead was probably to accelerate the application of his logical and epistemological studies on a grand scale; it catalyzed their synthesis into a
theory of physics. A comparison of *PNK* with Whitehead's
earlier writings suggests that, among specific ideas, thinking
about the idea of *time* was what the physical theory most sharply
stimulated in him. His work on time had lagged behind his
work on space; naturally, since he was a geometer. But he had
long been peculiarly interested in relating geometry to motion,

[113] *The Concept of Nature*, vii.
[114] However, this refers to only one important aspect of the general divergence
between the two.

and, but for the time consumed by the *Principia* and by the educational activities he plunged into after that was done, he might much earlier have worked out a theory of space-time. Einstein's special theory, and Minkowski's work, had been before the public for years. Whitehead had already pointed out the desirability of conducting discussions of relativity on a broad basis, in which the points of view of psychology and of the axiomatic foundations of mathematics should be joined to the physical point of view. Now the general theory of relativity had brought matters to a head. A new theory of natural science was required of him.

3. The pith of Whitehead's theory is to be found by consulting the opening chapter of *PNK* and then the fine summary of that book written by him for a meeting of the Aristotelian Society.[115] The opening chapter of *PNK* is magnificent and infinitely more important than Whitehead's celebrated polemic against the bifurcation of nature. When reading this man it is an indispensable rule to read every preface and first chapter at least six times: there he usually states very clearly what he is about.

The argument starts from a fresh criticism of that traditional "Concept of the material world" that Whitehead had examined in his memoir of 1905. His present efforts are aimed at supplying a rational connection between geometry and physics, with the tremendously important additional specification that the connection must be in principle observable. He carries much of the outcome directly into his metaphysics.

The aspect of the traditional scheme now singled out is its employment of "nature at an instant" (an instantaneous configuration of material) as a fundamental conception.[116] It will

---

[115] "Symposium: Time, Space, and Material," *Aristotelian Society Supplementary Vol. 2, Problems of Science and Philosophy*, 1919, 44-57. C. D. Broad's well-known summary (*Mind*, n.s., Vol. 29, 216-231) fails to reflect the essential character of the book, as presenting a unitary *theory of nature*, and converts it from an essay in Speculative natural philosophy into a series of chapters of Critical philosophy, contributing to the technical problem of defining the existential status of "ideal" entities like points and instants.

[116] Cf. *Principles of Natural Knowledge*, arts. 1.2, 2.5. "Symposium: Time, Space, and Material," 44-46.

be recalled[117] that Whitehead had assumed this to be ultimate in all Concepts of the material world, and had found no fault with it. But in fact the idea of "nature at an instant" embodies the classical prejudice that "the essential relationship between bits of matter is purely spatial."[118]

The [classical] theory demands that there should be an instantaneous space corresponding to each instant, and provides for no correlation between these spaces; while nature has provided us with no apparatus for observing them.[119]

Thus "no physical relation between nature at one instant and nature at another instant"[120] is provided for. Conceptions like velocity and kinetic energy, which express such relations and are essential to physics, are tacked on, instead of being integrally included in the foundations.[121] The remedy is to include among the undefined elements of science the notion of a state of change.[122] Furthermore, if a relational theory of space be adopted (and the absolute theory is of no use to an observational science), it will be seen that the persistence of matter (e.g., of a measuring rod or other instrument during the time required to make an observation) is not expressible in the traditional scheme, since we cannot then appeal to "occupation of the same *spatial* entities at two different instants" as the basis of the observed persistence. We must set instants aside, and admit that "the ultimate fact for observational knowledge is perception through a duration."[123]

An analogous difficulty prevents the classical materialism from expressing a physical relation between two *places* even (e.g., a stress). For the physical entities of the scheme are point-particles, and no two points are in contact, nor are there any "infinitely small volumes"—the notion of such being in fact a muddled notion that was plausible only so long as it seemed

---

[117] Part II, sec. 3, above.

[118] This phrasing, so reminiscent of Whitehead's 1905 memoir, is from *Nature and Life* (1934), 5 (as reprinted in *Modes of Thought*, 179).

[119] *Principles of Natural Knowledge*, art. 2.2.

[120] "Symposium: Time, Space, and Material," 45.

[121] *Ibid.*, 45.

[122] *Principles of Natural Knowledge*, art. 1.2.

[123] *Ibid.*, art. 2.4.

necessary to the infinitesimal calculus: but Weierstrass and his
school had knocked the bottom out of that necessity.[124] Of
course, this difficulty of defining physical relationships that
extend across space had been discussed for generations, but
without much effect on either physics or metaphysics. Whitehead himself had discussed it on previous occasions without arriving at a conclusion;[125] and in 1905 he had pointed to its
avoidance as a merit in his proposed linear Concepts of the
material world.[126] But he had missed the full application of the
difficulty to physical action through time.[127]

That the ultimates of natural science are states of change,
conceived as single unities and extended in both space and time
—this is a fundamental result which Whitehead carries over
bodily into his metaphysics. That the specious present is an
example of such a unity, is for him at once the ground of the
harmony of his theory of nature with observation, and the
ground of the possibility of applying his result to a metaphysics
of experience. Thus Whitehead's unification of experiences and
nature in one Concept has its first origin here.

In *PNK* these unities are called "events:" Whitehead proceeds to state the facts about them that are exhibited in every
observation of external nature. He calls these facts the "constants of externality;" they are the assumptions common to all
the sciences of nature. I do not recall ever having seen a discussion of these "constants:" but they are what the book is
about! They concern chiefly the relation of "cogredience"
(definition of a presented expanse by a percipient event)
and "extension" (the mutual overlapping and inclusion of
events).[128] The development of Whitehead's scheme is dominated by the embracing of spatial and temporal extendedness

[124] *Ibid.*, art. 1.3. The effect of this mathematical advance was to immensely
clarify and sharpen the problem of relating geometrical to natural entities.

[125] In §II, "Physical Objects and Physical Space," of the 1914 paper which I
earlier discussed (Part IV, sec. 2); and in "The Anatomy of Some Scientific Ideas"
(1917; see *Aims of Education*, 222-225).

[126] See sec. 5 of Part II above.

[127] The reader will notice the kinship of this argument to Whitehead's famous
criticism of Zeno in *Process and Reality*; but the later argument can stand on its
own feet.

[128] Cf. "Symposium: Time, Space, and Material," 47-50.

as two species of a general relation of extension. That is the sort of thing we should expect from the Whitehead we became acquainted with in the earlier portions of this paper. Besides, Minkowski's work had given Whitehead a great stimulus in that direction.

Of course Whitehead does not ask physics to confine the span of an event to that of the specious present; his point is that the idea of spatio-temporal spans, of whatever magnitude, must replace instants and points, if what is observed (not in its specificity, to be sure) is to fall within the Concept of the material world. The unusual character of Whitehead's theory of nature, which distinguishes it both from contemporary theories and from his mathematical theory of 1905, is precisely this statement of the general character of observation and the inclusion of the general character as the basis of a unified speculative construction.[129] The whole thing is the product of a most unusual English philosopher-scientist, who *fuses* (and does not merely happen to hold simultaneously in his mind) the Berkeleian criticism of scientific concepts and an unlimited interest in mathematical cosmology.

The relation which holds between the basis adopted in the *Principles of Natural Knowledge* and the bricks and mortar of Whitehead's metaphysical system can be expressed in another way, the full import of which will appear in our next section. The physicists had discovered the relativity of space and time to the circumstances of the observer, but they had not been bold enough to build entirely on the general character of a-perception-from-a-standpoint-here-and-now. It is because Whitehead's physical inquiry does build on this basis, that the conclusion of the inquiry leads naturally to the further question:—what is the full character of the relation which holds between a percipient event and other events?—in other words, what base-relations for a pluralistic and temporalistic cosmology are discernible in the percipient event?[130]

---

[129] Current physical views employ no Concept of Nature (at least not explicitly), and advance through an indefinite succession of laboratory operations, assumptions about them, and formal theories, fitted together as circumstances require.

[130] When he presented his metaphysics of Time to the Sixth International Con-

4. One of the most striking features of Whitehead's philosophy of nature is its sharp distinction between two fundamentally different sorts of entities in nature: "events" and "objects," or "recognita,"[131] which are recurring characters of events. This distinction is the clear beginning of the great duality in his metaphysics between "actual occasions or entities," and "eternal objects." And, of course, the analysis of the celebrated relation of "ingression" begins here, so far as the relationships evident in sense-perception are concerned. The original duality, however, was not intended to be an assertion about the ultimate character of reality, but only to correspond to a difference evident in perception and indispensable for a clear philosophy of natural science. My own belief is that nothing better than a pragmatic reason can be given for making "recognita" as ultimate as "events" in the theory of nature. Only a writer so Platonically minded as Whitehead would assert, without attempting to justify himself, that "Objects are of course essential for process, as appears clearly enough in the course of any analysis of process."[132] To Professor L. S. Stebbing the fundamental distinction between recognita and events was the source of the greatest merit in Whitehead's work: he had produced a philosophy of nature in which universals and particulars could not be confused.[133]

The purpose of the dual apparatus is, with the help of the method of extensive abstraction, "to express the essential scientific concepts of time, space and material as issuing from fundamental relations between events [extension and cogredience]

gress of Philosophy in 1926 (one year after *Science and the Modern World*), Whitehead said that his "whole paper" was directed toward explaining "the relativistic conclusion that individual perceptivity is the ultimate physical fact." (Sec. V of paper on "Time," in *Proc. Sixth Int. Congress of Philos.*).

[131] "Symposium: Time, Space, and Material," 51.

[132] *Principles of Natural Knowledge* (ed. 2), 202.

[133] Stebbing, "Concerning Substance," *Proc. Aristotelian Soc.*, n.s., Vol. 30 (1929-30), p. 300; see also other articles and reviews by this critic in *Mind* and in *Proc. Aristotelian Soc.* during the decade following the publication of *PNK*.

Because clearing away confusion was a necessity, much of *PNK* is given over to drawing distinctions of one kind or another; and this was a source of delight to many intellectualist philosophers with whom Whitehead had little in common (see the close of Division IV, above).

and from recognitions of the characters of events."[134] The choice of the object and the event for this purpose is natural enough; and the new basis is what makes possible Whitehead's advance from the mere suggestions of his epistemological period to the grand construction of a theory of nature. But, in the process, Whitehead's previous sense-empiricism is left far behind. Alongside of sense-objects he introduces several other types of objects ("percipient," "perceptual," and later "physical" objects), which are equally said to be "yielded for our knowledge by our perceptions of nature."[135] His manner of describing our perception of events is even more significant, and deserves close attention.

The fundamental datum is a "duration;" other events and various objects are discriminated only as given in a duration. This givenness is of two kinds. There is full awareness, and there is awareness of "significance." Thus we look at the closed door of a cupboard, and are aware that an event (bounded by the edges of the cupboard and by the beginning and end of our act of seeing) has a certain character (color and form). But we are also aware that inside the cupboard there are events whose space-relations complete the space-relations of the things that are fully seen (the exterior of the cupboard, other objects seen in the room) to myself as a point of origin. Similarly for contemporary events so distant that we can learn of their characters only indirectly, say by reading newspapers. And this awareness of the relations of which undiscriminated events are known to be relata is for Whitehead as immediate, as given, as plainly posited in an act of observation, as awareness of sense-data, strictly so called.

The difference between these two types of perception is described in *CN* as the difference between "the discerned" and "the discernible," in *The Principle of Relativity* as the difference between "cognizance by adjective" and "cognizance by relatedness only." The doctrine is called the doctrine of "significance," namely, events whose characters are not discerned

[134] *Principles of Natural Knowledge*, art. 2.5.
[135] *Ibid.*, art. 13.2, and p. 203 in the second edition.

are known through being signified, in a uniform manner, by other events.[136] You may discern in the doctrine a touch of Kant's transcendental aesthetic; or you may see in it other historical affiliations. Whitehead observes that to start with an experience of percepts, and then add a theory of significance, is to subject yourself to Hume's criticism of Berkeley; Kant's method, "the essential point" of which was "the assumption that 'significance' is an essential element in concrete experience,"[137] was superior. Whitehead argues also that the modern method [practiced by Russell] of constructing a visual space out of colored patches, then an auditory space out of sounds, and so on for the other senses, and then fitting all these spaces together, sets an impossible task for "inferential construction."[138]

Two facts are certain. *First,* that *the doctrine of significance underlies Whitehead's whole theory of nature.* Every application of the method of extensive abstraction is based on it. This doctrine also (together with his appeal to a uniform non-metrical geometry as presupposed in every application of metrics) makes possible the distinction he draws between geometry and the rest of physics; and this distinction constitutes the essential difference between his theory of relativity and Einstein's. *Second,* that *the doctrine of significance is not a doctrine of ordinary empiricism.* Every regular empiricist (and also every Critical Realist and positivist) will insist that the network of relationships affirmed by Whitehead is not a direct datum of knowledge, but *either* (as for Russell prior to *The Analysis of Matter*) a shorthand way of referring to classes of hypothetical percepts *or* (and this is more usual) a result of inference. Thus, in *The Revolt Against Dualism,* part of Professor Lovejoy's argument that Whitehead merely re-enunciates epistemological dualism in novel terminology, is a warning to the reader to bear in mind "a rather constant peculiarity of Professor Whitehead's way of putting things—his custom of speaking of that which is cognized indirectly or inferentially in terms which

[136] *Ibid.,* arts. 3.3-3.8, 16.1, 16.2, 19.4, 20, 21; *Concept of Nature,* 49-53, 186-188, 184, 197f.; *Principle of Relativity,* chaps. II, IV.

[137] *Principles of Natural Knowledge,* art. 3.4.

[138] *Ibid.,* arts. 62-63.

would ordinarily be regarded as appropriate only to the 'objects of immediate appearance'."[139] On the contrary, Whitehead means what he says when he includes in immediate experience what is excluded from it by orthodox epistemology.

As for the antecedents of "significance" in his own writings, one has already been mentioned: the ascription of a "uniform texture" to "immediate experience" in the essay of 1915. At that time Whitehead spoke of this uniformity as "a most curious and arresting fact," and remarked that he was "quite ready to believe that it is a mere illusion."[140] Perhaps he was; and perhaps he was not so ready as he thought. The expansion of this ascription of "texture" into a central doctrine was probably due to his search—evident in the essays of 1915 to 1917[141]—for the best way to formulate the ideal or hypothetical perceptions which seemed to be necessary additions to sense-data if a geometry, smooth and complete enough to be a scientific concept, was to be constructed. Probably he had something like "significance" vaguely in mind.

In a note which Whitehead appended to CN while reading proof (this is in 1920), he removes the limitation of significance to space-relations within a duration, and asserts that there is a significance of a percipient event "involving its extension through a whole time-system [of durations] backwards and forwards.[142] In other words the essential 'beyond' in nature is a definite beyond in time as well as in space."[143] The expansion pleases him, because it furthers the assimilation of time and space in one theory of extension.

Any reader of SMW will see how readily this doctrine suggests the description given in that book, of the perceiver as cognizant of "aspects" of an entire universe of other events.

But Whitehead, while still engaged on the philosophy of

[139] *The Revolt Against Dualism* (1930), 180.

[140] *Aims of Education*, 245.

[141] *Ibid.*, 160, 177, 218-220.

[142] As he later puts it, "my life in the morning" and "my life in the afternoon of the same day" fit on to each other in a continuum apprehended as dominating my experience. ("Uniformity and Contingency," *Proc. Aristotelian Soc.*, n.s., Vol. 23 (1922-23), 7.

[143] *Concept of Nature*, 198.

natural science, carries the doctrine of significance well beyond the scope assigned to it in *The Concept of Nature*. In a lecture delivered in June, 1922,[144] he expounds it as central to the general question of the relation of finite to infinite: each finite fact is embedded in the whole of factuality, but a uniform significance, pervading experience in certain respects, makes it possible to know something without knowing everything. Whitehead's presidential address to the Aristotelian Society in November, 1922, is entirely concerned with the doctrine of significance. It is there described as the doctrine of spatio-temporal relations covertly assumed by Hume, and the first conception that we have to make explicit if we are to solve the problem of induction bequeathed by him.[145] (Compare *Science and the Modern World*, p. 63.) And the passage of the mind from sense-data to an ordinary perceptual object (e.g., of a dog's mind from "smell and a pat" to "master") is in that address said to be no inference from a class of sense-data, but a further instance of significance: this is Whitehead's first adumbration of his conception of "symbolic reference," which gets fully developed in the little book on *Symbolism*, published in 1927. We must finally notice in this address an identification[146] of the converse of significance with the transmission of causal force from a focus throughout a field: apparently Whitehead, thinking often both of induction and of field physics, is slowly transmuting his idea of significance from a mere description of the spatial relatedness disclosed in a single perception, into a description of the causal bonds—prehensions—through which one occasion affects the rise of another

---

[144] Before the Royal Society of Edinburgh. The lecture is printed as ch. II in *The Principle of Relativity* (1922).

[145] Whitehead agrees with Hume's principle, that "there is nothing in a number of instances, different from every single instance, which is supposed to be exactly similar;" he infers that "the key to the mystery must be found in the intrinsic character of each instance." ("Uniformity and Contingency," *Proc. Aristotelian Soc.*, n.s., Vol. 23, 1922-23, 14; the quotation from Hume is from Essay VII, "The Idea of Necessary Connection," in the *Philosophical Essays Concerning the Human Understanding*.) Every student of Whitehead's reply to Hume should consult this lecture. Whitehead there incidentally distinguishes his conception from those by which idealism has aimed to secure the conformation of experience not yet examined to present experience.

[146] "Uniformity and Contingency," 17.

in the creative advance of nature. In a few years that train of thought will be completed, and (in *Symbolism*) the concept of a secondary significance that is again purely spatial will be introduced as a product of the temporal action of prehensions.

Whitehead's investigation of significance cannot safely be assimilated to any other development in modern philosophy. With a non-Newtonian physics of vector fields in his mind, Whitehead seems to be giving us a progressive elaboration of the premise that "perception is a natural event."

5. There has thus far in this essay been no occasion to allude to the school of modern realism. No influence from it is discernible in any of Whitehead's writings prior to *PNK;* and the main object of that book was easily describable without reference to realistic doctrine. Whitehead does not write his books out of a desire to decide the battles of epistemologists. However, his familiarity with realistic doctrine is attested by his reference, in the Preface, to discussions with Dawes Hicks and T. P. Nunn, and, of course, Russell; and also by references in later books. That his sympathies were with the realists as against the idealists, there can be no doubt. But there is no evidence that he was ever a member of the Moore-Russell school, as is commonly supposed. In fact, anyone who accepts the doctrine of the rough world and the smooth world, which is the central doctrine of his epistemological period (1914 to 1917), will have Moore's and Russell's original epistemological essays thoroughly spoiled for him. My belief is that Whitehead was a spectator of the battles fought by these realists, and that he privately agreed—for reasons of his own, which he was too busy to develop—with some of their theses, and with very few of the theses of their opponents.

It is an important characteristic of Whitehead's *metaphysics* that it is realistic, in a fundamental sense; this depends on his pluralism, and his final doctrine of prehensions as causal links. The natural philosophy of his 1920 books adumbrates this metaphysical realism through its doctrine of the mutual significance of events. But in these books the obvious realism, which was noticed and either hailed or refuted, is of a more special kind. Its thesis is that immediate appearance is a datum which, for the philosophy of natural science, can and must be considered without reference to the mind to which it appears. Whitehead makes the essential and simple claim that in scientific observation something, not thought or mind, is perceived. G. E. Moore's celebrated article, "The Refutation of Idealism," had been one of the principal agents—perhaps *the* agent—in getting this claim before the philosophic public. *The Aims and Achievements of Scientific Method,* published in 1907 by Whitehead's friend Nunn, propounds a doctrine of "the Objective" that was probably closer to his own mode of thought. "The Objective" is a closed system, separate from and "prior" to perception and thought; the chief basis of this assertion is "the direct and simple perception of the presence of Objectivity as such;"[147] also the assumption of this objectivity is tacitly made in every scientific investigation. Both these arguments are congenial to Whitehead. But the reasons for the realistic character of his philosophy of nature may be found by considering in order his assertions: (1) "Nature is the terminus of sense-perception;" (2) "Nature is closed to mind."[148]

(1) The first statement itself includes two propositions, both of which are emphasized by Whitehead in this period, and which are too seldom distinguished by him. As defining the status of sensa for natural science, the statement is indispensable, and is never repudiated in Whitehead's writings. As a sweeping definition of nature, that is, of the subject-matter of the natural sciences, the statement is thought indispensable, but is dropped in a few years. The point of the narrower proposition is that what is perceived is a part of nature and not merely content of mind; in fact, for natural science the datum is not mental at all. Whitehead subjects the opposite opinion to a variety of devastating criticisms, but it will be sufficient to state his reason for including this polemic in his exposition of the concept of nature—a reason noticed, he said, by hardly any of those who had commented on it. If what is perceived be considered a fact of individual psychology only, no assertions about

---

[147] Nunn, 6.
[148] *Concept of Nature,* 4.

nature can be verified. This is the indispensable core of White-head's protest against bifurcation.

Just what the definition of nature as solely "the terminus of sense-perception" comes to, is very hard to say, in view of the broad manner in which—owing to his doctrine of significance—Whitehead understands sense-perception. Clearly his theory is no simple phenomenalism. But his often repeated references to "sense-awareness" have naturally led people to think of these books as phenomenalistic. An example is his declaration, in *The Principle of Relativity*, that "the keynote of everything" is adherence to Poynting's aphorism, "I have no doubt what-ever that our ultimate aim must be to describe the sensible in terms of the sensible."[149] Now "the sensible," in the philosophy of science, is a pinning-down word. I do not think Whitehead realized how very far he was from pinning himself down to its usual meaning. Of course, these contexts are complicated by Whitehead's desire to pin Einstein down, and make individual perceptivity the basis of relativity.

There were in fact several possible causes for Whitehead's adoption of this definition of nature, though we are completely in the dark as to their relative weights. Possibly the influence of neo-realism was decisive; perhaps the definition is to be understood as the remaining effect of the narrow empiricism and the class-theory he was gradually shedding; perhaps he was influenced most by the advantage of defining nature as one homogenous subject; or by realization that his defense of simul-taneity would get no hearing on any other than an empiricist basis. Probably his choice of the definition was "instinctive" rather than the result of specific deliberation.

(2) If we follow the course of the argument in the opening chapter of *CN*, the reason for adopting the closure of nature to mind is the adoption of the definition of nature described above, as "that which we observe in perception through the senses," followed by adoption of the realistic premise that the object of sense-observation is not thought but something which is "self-contained for thought."[150] In his next chapter Whitehead gives

[149] *The Principle of Relativity*, 5.
[150] *Concept of Nature*, 3, 4.

other reasons—weightier, it seems to me—for closing nature to mind. These reasons would be sufficient even if nature were not defined in neo-realistic fashion. The point is that the aim of the whole inquiry is not to state everything that is true about nature, but to express the unity of the initial subject-matter of the natural sciences in a single Concept, with interrelated factors. It is a fact, acknowledged by everyone, that the natural sciences form a group with a certain unity; and essential factors in this unity are the assumption (made in every observation of nature) of the externality of nature to mind, and the concentration on that which is external. The study of mind forms another department of science, and the synthesis of nature and the observant mind is a task for metaphysics. Trying to embrace either of these other studies in the chosen inquiry is a fatal distraction: "It blows up the whole arena."[151] What minds do in the natural sciences is not left out of the account, but on the contrary investigated; thus the mind—Whitehead usually writes "we"—achieves accuracy by confining its attention to places and times of small extent. But in all this the assumption of the externality of the object of the mind's attention is maintained. What has to be made explicit is the unity which nature has *for the natural scientist.*

It would be a great mistake to identify this point of view with that of positivism. Surely we must distinguish between a limited inquiry and the philosophic doctrine of positivism. Here are no declarations that metaphysics is merely emotive. Instead, Whitehead writes of the "need of a metaphysics whose scope transcends the limitation to nature."[152] He postpones the attempt to satisfy that need, because there is another job which he must first do cleanly. Yet philosophers have been known to quote, "Nature is closed to mind," and disregard the sentence that follows it: "This closure of nature does not carry with it any metaphysical doctrine of the disjunction of nature and mind."[153]

Whitehead's whole procedure here is really an example of

---

[151] *Ibid.*, 29.
[152] *Ibid.*, 32.
[153] *Ibid.*, 4.

one of his primary metaphysical tenets—that all achievement requires exclusion.

6. The condemnation of the bifurcation of nature has probably been more debated than anything else in Whitehead's work. The essential core of his criticism has already been pointed out. We may add the observation that nothing was more natural for Whitehead than to criticize this bifurcation. For years he had been fastening on incoherence, or absence of rational connection, between two theories, each accepted; and particularly on incoherence in the theory of the relation of geometry to physics—"the muddle geometry had got into." Prevailing notions about space and about the things spread out in space exhibit a striking incoherence. Generally accepted is the bifurcation of nature into data which appear to a mind, and are really subjective, mental and private; and physical objects that cause perceptions to occur, but do not themselves appear at all. Yet the relational theory of space is also accepted, and rightly. Take this relational theory seriously, and we must say that

the space in which apparent nature is set is the expression of certain relations between the apparent objects. It is a set of apparent relations between apparent relata. . . . Similarly the space in which causal nature is set is the expression of certain relations between the causal objects. . . . of certain facts about the causal activity which is going on behind the scenes. Accordingly causal space belongs to a different order of reality to apparent space. Hence there is no pointwise connection between the two. . . . The case is even worse if we admit the relativity of time.[154]

It is through some such line of thought as this, I believe, that Whitehead first became an enemy of bifurcation. In his logical-epistemological essay on the relational theory of space, written in 1914, he had, we remember, joined the analysis of the relational theory with the drawing of distinctions between the diverse meanings of "space," apparent or physical.

It should be noticed that the argument given above would not occur to anyone who had not passed beyond a purely logical point of view. The natural comment of a logician on the argument would be that it is the relations, not the relata, that are

[154] *Ibid.*, 41f.

essential to geometry, which deals with any relata whatever, so long as they satisfy the specified relations. Whitehead would recommend the logician's point of view so far as research into geometry is concerned; but he is now asking how geometry applies to nature. The import of the relational theory is that the relata do make a difference; if they don't, we had better keep on with the clean and simple points of the absolute theory of space.

An important fact, which may be inferred from the preceding portions of this essay but deserves to be stated explicitly, is that much of Whitehead's work in his second, or physical, period was instigated through the success of mathematicians in their investigations into the axioms of geometry. Whitehead observes that if the absolute theory of space be true, the mathematicians have said all that needs to be said about space.[155] But if points are not natural entities, a whole new region for inquiry appears: what *are* the entities of the spatial world we live in?

To recur to Whitehead's argument against bifurcation. Some philosophers think that it is essentially an attack on the causal relation as the instrument of physical explanation. They then infer that his metaphysics repudiates his philosophy of nature. In fact, the polemic contains no objection to causal explanation—*within nature*. (Whitehead draws the distinction.[155a]) What he does require of the causal relation is exactly what he requires of every other relation employed in natural science: that it should operate in a single field, and not mysteriously leap a chasm between two alien types of entity, namely, material molecules and affections of the mind. Also, it is a mistake to suppose that causality enters into Whitehead's philosophy only with the lectures on *Symbolism*, delivered in 1927. What is true is that the rôle of causality is then greatly expanded. But his position now is (to quote from an explanation of the point of his chapter on bifurcation):

It is the problem of science to conjecture the characters in the three-way spreads [durations] of the past which shall express the dependence of

---

[155] *Principles of Natural Knowledge*, v and art. 2.1.
[155a] *The Concept of Nature*, 31.

the three-way spread of my present experience upon the past history of Nature. These characters are collections of molecules, . . . and light waves [in the case of vision] . . . , and finally disturbances in my body.[156]

Again, no objectionable bifurcation is introduced by recognizing that perceived change in what is regarded as the same object is a function of a number of variables. The causes of change may be as many and as complex as you please—provided only that they are not wholly alien in nature from the perceived datum that changes.

What must be acknowledged about Whitehead's protest against bifurcation is that in his zeal he overstates his case. Harping so much on "apparent nature," he must describe causes as "characters of apparent characters," which does violence to what the scientist means by a cause. When he says, "Our experiences of the apparent world are nature itself,"[157] the conception that these experiences, which display an apparent world, are processes of reception and appropriation of not-alien antecedent causal events, is needed to distinguish his resolution of bifurcation from that of ordinary scientific phenomenalism. For you cannot get away from a division into past world and present experience: you must unite the two through the idea of an immediate experience of process. This is what is supplied in 1927. A beginning for it was already made by the application of the doctrine of our awareness of significance to temporal extension, and by the doctrine of the "passage" of events. In Note II (written in 1924) to the second edition of *PNK*, Whitehead said of the first edition (1919) that ". . . the true doctrine, that 'process' is the fundamental idea, was not in my mind with sufficient emphasis. Extension is derivative from process, and is required by it."[158]

7. The final comment to be made on the 1920 books is that there is both much more and much less in them than is commonly supposed. For example: Whitehead did not simply decide on pluralism when he came to write a metaphysics. The

---

[156] "Symposium: The Problem of Simultaneity," *Aristotelian Soc., Supplementary Vol. 3: Relativity, Logic, and Mysticism*, 1923, 41.

[157] *Principles of Natural Knowledge*, art. 61.9; *Principle of Relativity*, 62.

[158] P. 202.

1920 books, which showed the preoccupation with the continuity of change that is natural for a man reforming the theory of space and time, also search for unities of rhythm which require blocks of time for their realization. In the magnificent attack on the classical conceptions of time, space, and matter with which *PNK* opens, not the least of Whitehead's criticisms is that the classical scheme makes such unities illusory or at the most derivative facts. The book closes with a chapter on Rhythms, which adumbrates his later conception of "living occasions." In fact, the kinship of that final chapter with the whole theory of grades of organic and inorganic occasions that appears in *Process and Reality* will be evident to anyone who reads it.

There is also less in the 1920 books than is commonly found there. In order to "prevent the reader from bolting up side tracks in pursuit of misunderstandings," Whitehead included in *CN* two chapters of a philosophic character, which inevitably trod on the toes of some philosophers and elated others. As a result there has arisen a bad habit of discussing these philosophical chapters in separation from the inquiry to which they are but auxiliaries; and this habit (which in itself would not have such evil effects, if the chapters were but carefully read) has engendered the worse habit of forgetting the specific and philosophically limited context of all of Whitehead's assertions in each of these three books. This in spite of very plain warnings in the texts. These books are admittedly philosophical, but in a limited sense only:

> . . . "philosophy" in this connection . . . is solely engaged in determining the most general conceptions which apply to things observed by the senses. Accordingly it is not even metaphysics: it should be called pan-physics.[159]

There are, moreover, specific warnings to philosophers not to look to "pan-physics" for solutions of metaphysical problems. The entire project is relative to the reorganization of physics.

Concerning "the values of nature," the introduction of which, in *Science and the Modern World,* surprised so many of the "tough-minded," Whitehead wrote, "The values of nature are perhaps the key to the metaphysical synthesis of existence. But

---

[159] *Principle of Relativity,* 4.

such a synthesis is exactly what I am not attempting."[160] Of course,

It is difficult for a philosopher to realise that anyone really is confining his discussion within the limits that I have set before you. The boundary is set up just where he is beginning to get excited.[161]

Some philosophers are excited about teleology, perhaps rightly; but certainly they go wrong if they assert that "According to these . . . works the external world had little if any teleology within it," and argue that the subsequent expansion of the "events" of this Whiteheadian period into the "prehending subjects" of the philosophy of organism shows that Whitehead was driven to acknowledge his philosophy of natural science to be "weak," "inadequate," or "wrong."[162] The cause of the expansion is not so simple as this. Teleology in nature, or the efficacy of mental functionings in nature, are perfectly compatible with the answers the books of this period give to their own questions. They make no attempt to assess the degree or state the kind of teleology that exists; for their purpose no attempt is necessary, unless one believes that a man in love, for example, "necessarily measures space and time differently from a man given over to avarice."[163]

Whitehead's philosophy of nature, then, "speaks to the condition" of physics only. It cares not a whit for the intrinsic significance of any event. The understanding of the physical level from the perspective of a metaphysical level is postponed. It is promised in the Preface to the second edition of *PNK*, written in August, 1924. Since "nature" is then used with a wider meaning, "Whitehead's philosophy of natural science" is a better name for what we have been examining than "Whitehead's philosophy of nature."

We must not be so naïve as to suppose that any expanding

[160] *The Concept of Nature*, 5.

[161] *Ibid.*, 48.

[162] David L. Miller, "Purpose, Design and Physical Relativity," *Philos. of Science*, July, 1936 (esp. p. 268).

[163] Whitehead, replying to H. Wildon Carr in a Symposium on the idealistic interpretation of the theory of relativity: *Proc. Aristotelian Soc.*, n.s., Vol. 22 (1921-22), 133f.

and philosophic mind succeeds in confining itself absolutely to a specified level of thought. Whitehead's way of talking about the "creative advance" of nature, for example, is sometimes a metaphysical note in these books. There is in the production of ideas a ferment which interferes with their bottling. This remark applies in some degree to every part of Whitehead's work.

But the only course open to a philosophic critic who has doubts about Whitehead's philosophy of natural science is to show that in some respect—for example, in stating what we mean by measurement or by extension—Whitehead falsifies the *essential* character of all scientific investigation that is directed toward nature. Conversely, if a philosopher disbelieves, let us say, Whitehead's Platonism, he must criticize the doctrines of *Process and Reality;* he must not rest content with demolishing the special form in which that Platonism appears earlier—the theory of the "recognition of natural objects"—and then referring to *PR* merely in passing.[164] Nothing is proved by showing that a theory, offered as adequate for physics, is inadequate for metaphysics. And if it be shown that "recognition of objects" is not an irreducible *in physics,* that is a blow to the general (metaphysical) theory of objects, but no disproof of it; since the theories, and the physical-metaphysical relationship, and the possibilities of demonstration, are never so precisely drawn that this situation is an instance of the situation in formal logic where a universal proposition may be disproved by a single negative instance.

VI. METAPHYSICS (1925—)

1. Whitehead's turning toward an all-inclusive speculative

---

[164] The late Professor A. A. Bowman's extensive criticism of Whitehead, in the third chapter of his *A Sacramental Universe* (1939), rests on this mistake. His reference to *Process and Reality* as "a speculative completion of the train of thought which began on a different plane with the *Principles of Natural Knowledge,*" is useless to him unless it means—what is not true—that *Process and Reality* is describable with sufficient accuracy, as the completion of *that* train of thought only. The phrase, "on a different plane," is quite accurate. The planes being different, the assumption underlying Professor Bowman's criticism, namely, that "Yet the conclusions of the later work are dependent upon premises supplied by the earlier, and must stand or fall with these" (p. 85), becomes a mere assertion, supported by the single word, "Yet."

construction after his books on the philosophy of natural science would not have been in the least surprising, even if he had not been encouraged by outside causes. He had written several times of the need for a metaphysics which should synthesize mind with nature, and value with fact. In his Tarner Lectures of 1919 he had described the aim of philosophy as "attainment of some unifying concept which will set in assigned relationships within itself all that there is for knowledge, for feeling, and for emotion,"[165]—which is both an accurate prescription for the philosophy of organism, and the sort of conception of philosophy we should expect from the unusual mathematician who wrote the *Universal Algebra* and "Mathematical Concepts of the Material World."

But he was also led toward metaphysics by external events. (I do not mean that we can safely assign great weight to these external events.) His appointment to a philosophical professorship and his migration to America probably stimulated him enormously. Also, tragedy has a liberating effect on minds that are capable of expansion. Probably the national tragedy and the personal tragedy of the war of 1914 to 1918 played a part in extending the horizon of his thoughts. There is, however, no evidence that his metaphysics might, under other circumstances, have taken on a different character.

It is possible that the production of a grand metaphysical scheme by Samuel Alexander encouraged him to try his hand. But there is no *need* whatever to assume that. Although Whitehead thinks highly of Alexander's work, and has been sensitive to the lively originality of James and Bergson also, I can find in his metaphysical writings no clear demonstration of their influence either in his choice of problems or in the essentials of his solutions. The references to contemporary philosophers in his prefaces are partly mere appreciations, partly the overstatements of a modest man.

It should be noted, as regards Bergson, that Whitehead's advance from physics to metaphysics is of an entirely different type from the French philosopher's. In an Aristotelian Society

[165] *Concept of Nature*, 2.

Symposium on the question, "Time, Space and Material: are they, and if so in what sense, the ultimate data of science?", Mrs. Adrian Stephen (Karin Costelloe), who is a skillful interpreter of Bergson, said that, "If our question were put to him, Bergson would, I think, reply: Material is the ultimate datum of science, space is the form which science imposes upon its objects, science cannot deal with time."[166] Whitehead's answer, however, is not, like this, *restrictive*. His advance is toward a single unifying concept, not toward a contrasting pair of concepts, the inferior member of which is to be supplied by physical science. When Whitehead first (in print) looks toward metaphysics, he writes that he hopes to *embody* his philosophy of nature "in a more complete metaphysical study."[167]

In all of Whitehead's later writings one can see that a strong motive for metaphysical exposition is his belief that the educated man's implicit conception of the universe has not responded to the advance from the seventeenth century physics of inert matter to the late nineteenth century physics of energetic vibrations described in terms of vectors. He sees that, whereas a number of philosophic systems have been produced in the modern period, it is not systems of philosophy, but the success of the materialistic ideas of science, which has shaped the philosophy unconsciously held by our society. No epistemology and no philosophy of religion, but only a new and equally scientific set of ideas about nature and nature's relation to human experience, can hope to get this philosophy displaced.

There is no evidence that any twentieth century developments in the field of science lured Whitehead into metaphysics at this time. The four mathematical developments and the three physical developments earlier enumerated, had been active in his mind for many years. It is natural to include the quantum theory among influences on him; I think, however, that in fact this was to him a supporting illustration rather than a formative influence in the creation of his atomic pluralism. As for the

---

[166] *Aristotelian Soc., Supplementary Vol. 2: Problems of Science and Philosophy* (1919), 87. I have already quoted (pp. 70-74, above) from Whitehead's contribution to this Symposium.

[167] *Principles of Natural Knowledge*, Preface to second ed. (1925).

theory of relativity, Whitehead had already made his response to it.[168]

Probably the scientific influences whose force on Whitehead increased at this time are those which naturally accompany the turning of his gaze upon the vastness of the universe. Such are the statistical theory of physical laws, and the general theory of evolution. The latter, it must always be remembered, is for Whitehead—who was born in 1861, and once visited Darwin's house—a real and living force, not an item in the intellectual history of the nineteenth century; and that is a great advantage which his metaphysical thinking enjoys over that of the present generation.

My general conclusion on this subject is that we should accept at face value Whitehead's statement, in the preface to PR (*Process and Reality*), that he is endeavoring to "compress the material derived from years of meditation."[169] Indeed, no other supposition is compatible with the fact that in but a few years,

[168] Elsewhere I have discussed the claim that, ". . . the problems around which his philosophy of organism is focused have arisen for the most part out of an attempt to reconcile his realistic position in philosophy with the theory of physical relativity." (Miller, David L., *op. cit.*, 272. My reply is in *Philos. of Science*, April, 1938.)

In absurdity, this claim is equalled only by the assertion of a certain reviewer of *Process and Reality*, that Whitehead's elaboration of a "philosophy of *organism*" was due to his having, at a time when his thinking was fluid and ready to respond to influences, migrated to Harvard and come under the influence of L. J. Henderson. Prof. Henderson is a positivist, fundamentally at odds with Whitehead. What *is* possible is that Henderson's book on *The Fitness of the Environment*, written around 1912 (partly under the influence of Josiah Royce), either led Whitehead in the direction of, or strengthened his belief in, the doctrine of order that is at the heart of his panpsychism: the doctrine that all order is relative to adaptation for the attainment of an end.

One may look for an influence from the organismically minded biologist-philosopher J. S. Haldane; such search also will prove futile. In fact, there is no need at all to assume that a special influence from a biological quarter was required for Whitehead to set about constructing a philosophy of organism. It is sufficient to remember that a great deal of his life has been spent in conversation with friends who were engaged in every branch of scientific activity; for example, there were Bateson and Sir Henry Head, on the biological side. Furthermore, the concept of organism in Whitehead's metaphysics is by no means cut altogether, or even for the most part, out of biological cloth. (See p. 95, below.)

[169] P. x in Macmillan ed. (1929). (All references to *Process and Reality* in this essay will be to the American [Macmillan] ed. of 1929.)

devoted mainly to teaching, he constructed so intricate and so vast a system of philosophy, and expounded it in several books.

2. Many problems were raised by the 1920 books—as Whitehead well realized when he wrote them. For one thing, his definitions of spatial concepts needed reconsidering. Their defect was brought out by Theodore de Laguna: if the definitions were correct, men *could not* have known what they meant by "points" before the days of the Michelson-Morley experiment—which is contrary to common sense meanings, and also to Whitehead's own appeal to common sense meanings in his arguments defending simultaneity against Einstein's criticism. *PR* contains a new construction, in which extensive abstraction is applied, not first to durations and then to space alone, but first to regions of space-time, so that the definitions of spatial entities are not dependent on the prior defining of temporal entities, but can be introduced side by side with them.[170] The more powerful apparatus employed makes possible the definition of a "straight line." Since this is all done in terms of pure extension, without any reference to processes of measurement, it is quite important. It is the final issue of one of the lines of emphasis we picked up in expounding the *Universal Algebra*.[171] And of course it seems to Whitehead entirely natural to include the definition of so general a property of the world in a book on metaphysics.

The other problems that were leading him to the speculative theories of *SMW* (1925) appear in the Notes he appended to the second edition of *PNK* in 1924. Since these notes are not intelligible to a person who has not freshly studied the book, some of the problems will bear enumeration here.

In the first place, full abandonment of the class-theory necessitates a full reconsideration of the question: What, in empirical terms, is a physical object? It is, however, impossible to answer that question without introducing the concept of possibility in addition to that of actuality. Also, Whitehead had noted that his general distinction between an "object"—i.e., what *can*

[170] This advantage is connected with a change in Whitehead's epistemology of space (p. 102, below).

[171] Pp. 25ff., above.

recur—and an "event" followed roughly the lines of the general division between possibility and actuality; he would like to work out that division. Another contrast, which he had already suggested to be associated with the event-object distinction, is that between continuity and atomism. If only objects have parts, what is the sense in which an event is one thing? We must particularly ask about the events we directly live through, which are perceptions of durations.

What is most striking in these Notes is that Whitehead uses for the first time the phrases, "social entity," and "realisation." "The main point [concerning "fuller and more systematic treatment" of his fundamental concepts of events and objects] hinges onto the ingression of objects into social entities, and onto the analysis of the process of the realisation of social entities."[172] He also writes of a "duration" as "the realisation of a social entity." The difference between the words "relatedness" and "realisation" is precisely the difference between the standpoints of the 1920 books and of *SMW*, respectively. The former books had set forth the extensive relatedness displayed in every duration and in the passage of durations. Whitehead's mind is now probably following the simple and important thought that relatedness does not just happen, but is the skeleton of an active process of becoming, which is, in ways that he wishes to analyze, both a complex of objects and an outcome of other becomings.[173]

The passage from "relatedness" to "realisation" can also be looked upon as indicating that Whitehead, having begun with *the percipient event as one entity*, is now asking what is its internal process of constitution.

These Notes suggest pretty clearly that Whitehead thinks of the metaphysical study toward which he is heading, as a working out of the "implications" of the ideas which, in the 1920 books, "had not shaped themselves with sufficient emphasis in my mind."[174]

---

[172] *Principles of Natural Knowledge*, 201, 202.

[173] This transition in thought seems also to be at the bottom of the more complex transition from "nature lifeless" to "nature alive," which is described in *Nature and Life* (1934), 20ff. (as reprinted in *Modes of Thought* (1938), 200ff).

[174] *Principles of Natural Knowledge* (ed. 2), 201.

It seems to me that the idea of significance, above all others, was in need of further elaboration. This is an indispensable idea, but so far it has hardly been more than asserted and assigned a variety of tasks. What does "significance" come to, as a factor in the universe? If the converse of the doctrine is that "Relations are perceived in the making and because of the making,"[175] what is the story of their making?

3. Two series of Lowell Lectures gave Whitehead the opportunity to complete the kind of work that, on his own view, should precede a full-scale attempt at metaphysical construction. Such construction is really the boldest of imaginative generalizations. Consequently it "must have its origin in the generalization of particular factors discerned in particular topics of human interest; for example, in physics, or in physiology, or .... In this way the prime requisite, that anyhow there shall be some important application, is secured."[176] To start from an eclectic point of view is to assure a result befitting a dilettante. Whitehead already had hold of an origin. In *SMW* one of the two threads in his main line of generalization—that coming from physics— is traced.

The critical portions of the early chapters of this book are essentially restatements of the previous examination of perceptual knowledge that was made for the sake of the foundations of physics. Thus, it was through the contrast between what in *SMW* are called the "separative character" and the "prehensive character" of space[177] that he had, in the first article of *PNK*, sharply distinguished his assumptions from those of scientific materialism. Again, that no element in our perceptual knowledge has the characteristic of being "simply located" in space and time (this "simple location" being the defining characteristic of matter, and being "the very foundation of the seventeenth century scheme of nature"[178]), had been very clearly set forth—without the use of that phrase, but with

---

[175] *Ibid.*, art. 3.7.

[176] *Process and Reality*, Pt. I, chap. I, §II. See p. 31, above.

[177] *Science and the Modern World* (N.Y., 1925), 90. (All references to *Science and the Modern World* in this essay will be to the 1925 [Macmillan] ed.)

[178] *Ibid.*, 81.

the help of the same quotation from Berkeley that starts the discussion in SMW^{179}—in a very fundamental passage in PNK.[180] In fact, the assertion of "significance" and the denial of "simple location" are one and the same thing in Whitehead.[181]

As I see the argument of SMW, the "organic theory of nature" is then reached from the position of the 1920 books by thinking of their "percipient event" as a temporal process with an internal constitution, and making the following steps.

(1) The "unity of the perceptual field," which had been set down as an ultimate character of observations, is interpreted as "what it claims to be: the self-knowledge of our bodily event."[182]

(2) The previously discriminated awareness, in the percipient event, of "significance" of all other events with respect to it as a focus, is converted into a process of awareness of aspects of all other events as "grasped into a unity," or "prehended," in the bodily event.[183] The unity is called an "organism," its constituents being concurrent (more accurately, as in PR, concrescent) prehensions. By "organism," Whitehead generally means a temporally bounded process which *organizes* a variety of given elements into a new fact.[184]

(3) The occurrence of an organism is described as "some-

[179] P. 95. The quotation is from §10 of the Fourth Dialogue of Berkeley's *Alciphron*.

[180] Arts. 3.5, 3.6.

[181] In *The Revolt Against Dualism* (1930, chap. V), Professor A. O. Lovejoy finds that seven meanings of "simple location" are contained in Whitehead's texts. I doubt that this would have been possible, had the critic remembered that Whitehead was concentrating on the contrast between the classical conception of matter and our actual observations of place. Also, it seems to me that Whitehead's remarks on the connection between the idea of simple location and the relational view of space might not have puzzled Professor Lovejoy (*Revolt*, 160) if he had stuck to *Whitehead's* conception of the relational view, instead of going afield to find in a definition by C. D. Broad the usual—and, he seems to assume, most proper—statement of the relational view. Broad's definition is quite foreign to all Whitehead's discussions of that subject.

[182] *Science and the Modern World*, 103.

[183] *Ibid.*, 98.

[184] Paper on "Time," Sec. II. (*Proc. Sixth International Congress of Philosophy*, Harvard Univ., 1926.)

thing which is for its own sake," or the emergence of a particular *value* in the world.[185]

(4) On the principle that the bodily event is a natural event
in nature, it is inferred that every event in nature arises as a
unity of concurrent prehensions,[186] and is an emergence of value.

(5) This conception of natural events is applied to the
problem of mechanism and freedom: since every event arises
as a prehension of its environment, the characters of the events
in the human body are not entirely determined by any absolute
properties of the components of bodies in general (molecules),
but are modified by the fact that the molecules are in a particular human body (the theory of "organic mechanism").[187]

(6) The persistence or endurance characteristic of matter
is explained[188] as reiteration of the same pattern in a succession
(the "nexus" of *PR*) of events that prehend each other.

(7) It is explained how biological evolution, or the rise of
complex organisms, is describable in terms of the maintenance
and alteration of such nexūs. "Enduring things are . . . the outcome of a temporal process; . . . Only if you take *material* to be
fundamental, this property of endurance is an arbitrary fact
at the base of the order of nature; but if you take *organism*
to be fundamental, this property is the result of evolution."[189]
The concept later called "creativity" is introduced, as a "substantial activity" "underlying" the evolution of the organisms
in which it is embodied; this is said to be required by the doctrine of evolution.

(8) On the basis of the earlier expressed premise that "Time
is known to me as an abstraction from the passage of events,"[190]

---

[185] *Science and the Modern World,* 131. Whitehead argues, "These unities,
which I call events, are the emergence into actuality of something. How are we to
characterise the something which thus emerges? . . . no one word can be adequate.
But conversely, nothing must be left out. . . . 'Value' is the word I use for the
intrinsic reality of an event."

[186] *Ibid.,* 103.

[187] *Ibid.,* 108-112.

[188] *Ibid.,* 152ff.

[189] *Ibid.,* 152, 154. Cf. 152: "On the materialistic theory, there is material—
such as matter or electricity—which endures. On the organic theory, the only en-
durances are structures of activity, and the structures are evolved."

[190] *Concept of Nature,* 34.

it is held that Time is in its fundamental character a discrete succession of epochs, or arrests, each being the duration required for the emergence of a prehensive unity as a single fact. (This is the "epochal theory of time," which might better have been called the epochal or atomic theory of process.)

(9) There is a general description of the quantum character of physical action as a fact to be expected if nature is conceived as a complex of organisms.

(10) In each of the above steps, objects are implicated along with events, in accordance with their dual association as described in Whitehead's preceding books. In addition, the realm of objects is widened by being explicitly identified with the realm of possibility. The emergence of new properties in events, which is required for (7), is due to the prehension of objects other than those that characterize the events prehended.

This enumeration is not, of course, intended as a substitute for a logical analysis. The appeals to evidence are also omitted. Their general character will appear below (pp. 108f.).

It may be useful to remark that Whitehead has not yet, at this point, got his labels fixed; so that he often uses "event," "prehension" and "organism" synonymously, and even says, "A 'prehension' is a 'prehensive occasion'."[191] In *PR* a determinate terminology is introduced: "prehensions" are the threads of process, the vectors, between "actual occasions," which are concrescent unities analyzable into such threads.

In addition to the argument just summarized, Whitehead's writings contain another line that leads from physics to metaphysics. This second line is occasionally discussed in *SMW* in connection with the main argument. It may be found clearly presented in its own unity in *Nature and Life* (1934). It does not begin with Whitehead's own analysis of physical observation, but with the general character of physical theory in which mass is subordinated to energy, and "simple location" has evaporated, being replaced by vector relations and fields; Whitehead's generalization proceeds toward a panpsychistic metaphysics.

[191] *Science and the Modern World,* 101.

4. We now come to the generalization from religious experience. Religious experience and theology in general—if not the specific faith of his fathers—has been a continued and vital interest for Whitehead. Because his concept of God is indispensable to the coherence of the realm of possibility with the realm of actuality, and because he endeavors to assimilate the formal characteristics of God to those of every other actual entity, it is sometimes supposed that Whitehead's God is a mere binder for the theoretical structure of the philosophy of organism, and lacks all religious character. The criticism is based either on a misunderstanding of what "system" is for Whitehead and why he seeks it, or on a limited range of religious feeling. *Religion in the Making,* and the closing Part of *PR,* are intensely religious. A valid and significant, though in itself minor, objection is that Whitehead's summing up in Section V of the last chapter of *PR*—"It is as true to say that God is permanent and the World is fluent, as that the World is permanent and God is fluent,"[192] etc.—is either mystical, or reflects too much the author's long familiarity with the "principle of duality" in projective geometry;—and the passage is not mystical.

Though Whitehead's basic metaphysical concepts—creativity, prehension, eternal objects, actual occasions—had made their bow in the latter chapters of *SMW,* the best introduction to their metaphysical relationships occurs in Section III of Chap. III of *RM* (*Religion in the Making*). Another point, relevant to the general subject of the present essay, is that the conception of God in *SMW* seems to be somewhat stronger than in *PR.* Applied to the earlier exposition, but not to the later, I see some cogency in A. E. Taylor's criticism[193] that Whitehead, denying omnipotence to God in order to absolve him of responsibility for evil, had made him just as responsible in this matter as if he were omnipotent. The "consequent nature of God"—God as the end—is, the reader will remember, not fully expounded before *PR.*

[192] *Process and Reality,* 528.
[193] The criticism is contained in "Dr. Whitehead's Philosophy of Religion," *Dublin Rev.,* Vol. 181, July, 1927, 17-41.

5. The most casual reader of *SMW* will observe that no account of sense-perception alone can possibly provide an epistemology corresponding to the "organic theory of nature." That theory implies that our *general* response to nature, or prehension of our environment, includes a reception of causality: the "intrinsic reality" of one event is affected by the "extrinsic reality" of another. But this was not elaborated. The main outline of Whitehead's mature epistemology is laid down in another book (*Symbolism, Its Meaning and Effect*, 1927) which precedes the publication of his metaphysics. He writes no more of the Newtonian deposition thereafter, but of "the Hume-Newton situation." Two thoughts guide his criticism: that Hume was entirely right in what he said about sense-perception, and that sense-perception is the superficial part of our experience, the overlay. In every succeeding book the strength and centrality of his conviction about the superficiality of sense-perception grows greater.

There is no need to hunt for a cause for the omission of the perception of causal efficacy from Whitehead's writings on the philosophy of natural science. Scientific observations are perceptions of sense-data. Whitehead comes to another kind of experience when he comes to consider other aspects of human activity. Even in the scientific field he had limited himself to the perceptual basis; he might, I imagine, have now proceeded by examination of the character of scientific laws.[194] His main course, perhaps more natural for an empiricist who is also trying to englobe physical science in a wider sphere, is an examination of experience generally.

An auxiliary course is more closely connected with Whitehead's earlier work: in a valuable paper of 1926[195] he arrives at the causal character of physical prehension through an analysis of time. That paper includes Whitehead's first exposition of his new theory that the perception of sense-data is an act of

---

[194] There were starting points for such an examination in his 1920 books, and in his paper of 1922 on "Uniformity and Contingency." Whitehead's final position on scientific laws appears in chaps. VII and VIII of *Adventures of Ideas* (1933).

[195] "Time," *Proc. Sixth International Congress of Philos.* (Longmans, Green & Co., N.Y., 1927), 59-64.

"physical imagination, in a generalized sense of the word,"[196]—
an act that is useful because of a symbolic reference to causal
actualities.

In *Symbolism*, Whitehead's theory of perception suffers from
a confusion which seems to be due to his tendency always to
think of the two elements of a dualism as on a par with each
other.[197] Thus he balances "the two pure modes of perception"
("causal efficacy" and "presentational immediacy"), and discusses their "intersection." At the same time, he obviously believes that perception of causal efficacy is by far the more fundamental. Again, in *PR*, I do not know what to make of his assigning an experience of "sensa" to even the lowest grades of actual
existents,—except on the assumption that he could not entirely
cease from thinking in dualities. Of course, having in the meantime worked out his panpsychism, he is using "sensa" in a
highly generalized meaning; but the difficulty remains: if
sense-perception is not a metaphysical characteristic, it should
not be assigned to *every* existent.

In this connection we must remember that the stage of Whitehead's thought under discussion was preceded by one in which
causality was little analyzed. A contemporary world of things
was assumed as a datum, and the characteristics of the sense-data
were related together by a primarily atemporal theory of their
multiple inherence in events. Their transmission and generation
could but lightly be touched on, in the absence of a theory of the
full functioning of events. There was a systematic relatedness
evident in nature which had to be got hold of somehow,—from
some limited standpoint. One does not, at first trial, find the
adequate conception for all purposes. Whitehead got hold of
"significance in a presented duration," and expanded the notion
and shifted its emphasis as he expanded his field of inquiry. On
passing from examination of perception to examination of experience, he adopted the view that it is the *antecedent* environment that is the datum for an occasion of experience.[198] Then
there is no awareness of absolutely contemporary occasions:

---

[196] *Ibid.*, sec. V.

[197] See p. 107, below.

[198] Why he adopted this will be discussed in sec. 7, below.

they constitute no datum for the present. But after that we find, as we must expect, that some of Whitehead's discussions of the contemporary world retain language which, as ordinarily used, is appropriate only if that world is considered as a datum.

It is of the essence of the philosophy of organism that its epistemological realism is based squarely on the rehabilitation of causality. If Hume is right about sense-data, then a realist must appeal to some other given, unless he is to abandon all idea of providing his "common world" with empirical credentials. In fact, this is no predicament, but an opportunity for the realist to build a much deeper realism than is possible on a phenomenalistic basis. For "experience," instead of being a "selection" of sense-data—a notion that is logically possible, but which has no evidence in its favor and requires a devious recasting (at best) of the physiological evidence—instead of this, experience becomes a reaction to things which exist for their own sakes and are felt as imposing their own weight and value on the experient.[199]

One of the many important functions of the theory of symbolic reference in Whitehead's philosophy is to replace the principle of inferential constructions which we discussed in Division IV. It was faulty psychology to try to explain our knowledge of common sense objects entirely in terms of that principle.[200] But on looking at this change from a broad point of view, we can see the similarity of approach as between Whitehead's pre-speculative epistemology and the epistemology which he now develops to be the empirical anchorage of his metaphysics. Both were written out of an awareness of a fundamental contrast in experience—between elements of inescapable actuality, and the response of thought, creating elements that provide "accurate definition." The contrast is pushed to a deeper level in the second inquiry—that is all. The sense-perceptions which constituted the primordial pole in the first

---

[199] A "real" causality is indispensable to a system of realistic pluralism. With causality accepted, one can work out a scheme in which, "though each event is necessary for the community of events, the weight of its contribution is determined by something intrinsic in itself" (*Science and the Modern World*, 147).

[200] See *Symbolism*, 3.

inquiry—rightly, in view of the limitation to the observational basis of natural science—have become the derivative pole now.[201]

The theory of symbolic reference effects a considerable change, or rather expansion, of Whitehead's theory of space-time. The earlier theory becomes more plausible (and also more complicated, so that it is difficult to understand its details from the imperfect exposition given in Part IV of *PR*). When nature is no longer conceived as the terminus of sense-perception, but as a great expanding nexus of occurrences, it is hard to suppose that the spatio-temporal relatedness throughout this universe is uniform; in fact, it is impossible to do so while holding— as Whitehead does—that the spatio-temporal relations are the outcome of the natures of the occurrences, and with these natures shift from cosmic epoch to cosmic epoch. Thus the uniform geometry of the 1920 books does not characterize the universe itself. But that geometry was always assumed to be defined by a percipient standpoint, and such definition is still held to occur; it becomes a natural event with its cause, context, and purpose. The act of "spatialization" (as it can accurately be called) is part of the process of responding to the qualitative and geometrical complexity of the world of things by transmuting it into a definitely colored and uniformly structured "projected" field. This is an act which animals have learned to perform through long ages of the evolution of their sense-organs and nervous systems.

The theory of symbolic reference has, if I am not mistaken, a very great importance, entirely apart from the rôle it plays in Whitehead's speculative construction. But this is not the place to urge philosophers to work with it. My final comment on the theory must concern the belief of some philosophers, that it is its author's way of returning to the bifurcation of nature which

---

[201] The intermediate period, in which common sense objects have an independent but not clearly elucidated status with respect to sense-data, begins with the adoption of "significance" and the event-object duality in 1919. See the statement on p. 204 of ed. 2 of *The Principles of Natural Knowledge*, to the effect that Whitehead in the first edition "wavered between the 'class-theory' of perceptual objects and the 'control-theory' of physical objects," and was endeavoring to get away from the class-theory. "Uniformity and Contingency" (*Proc. Aristotelian Soc.*, 1922-23) should also be consulted.

he had previously condemned. To those who bifurcate nature, the connection between private sense-data and physical causes may be summed up in the word, "somehow" (sometimes dressed up as "animal faith" or "peculiar but well-known transcendent reference"); and only the sense-data are experienced. Whitehead admits, nay insists upon, the numerical and qualitative distinction between sense-data and things. But (1) he has offered a theory of the "somehow;" (2) this theory is based on an independently established doctrine that we experience causes. The true defect of Whitehead's earlier description of nature has been mentioned above.[202] The supposition that he reaffirms the bifurcation he had previously condemned is often aided by passing in discussion from the 1920 books to *Symbolism*, in defiance of the difference between them in subject-matter and in the aim of the analysis.

6. After Whitehead's generalizations from science and from religion, and his development of an epistemology, comes the full metaphysical scheme itself. That it will be semi-mathematical in form is a foregone conclusion. An exposition closer than Whitehead's to the axiomatic method of mathematics may perhaps be made of this cosmology by someone in the future. The expression of metaphysical schemes in symbolic logic has not yet progressed very far. But it is important now to realize that the semi-mathematical method employed in *Process and Reality* is not a result of the *bare fact* that the author happened to have been a mathematician before he became a philosopher. The method is mathematical because the author is aiming at a single Concept of the universe, in which the various ideas form a natural circle from which none can be excised without leaving a gap between principles involving the others—for each fundamental idea is metaphysical, i.e., expresses an ultimate factor relevant to everything that happens. Now the various ideas in a branch of mathematics form such a natural circle. In fact, mathematics, divested of its limitation to quantity and number, is nothing but the instrument for expressing such connectedness. (Also, as in speculative philosophy, there are alternative circles, some wider than others.)

[202] P. 85.

I am not forgetting that one of the famous sentences in *PR* is, "Philosophy has been misled by the example of mathematics" (p. 12). What is referred to in that dictum is the fact that the great historical branches of mathematics have been able to start from premises which were reasonably regarded as clear, distinct, and certain (and the secondary fact that mathematicians have been able to use *ex absurdo* arguments with a justified freedom, because in practice there was little doubt as to what premise was at fault). Philosophical discussion, Whitehead holds, is not mathematical deduction, but an examination of experience. Neither the philosopher, nor the scientist, should look *first* to mathematics,—that is medievalism. But when the universal factors—what Dewey calls the generic traits—of experience have been so far as possible discerned, the effort to understand their operation should proceed by conjecturing a scheme, in form analogous to a set of interrelated assumptions, primitive ideas, and definitions. The reason for this ideal is at bottom the same as the reason why every science frames mathematical schemes whenever possible.

Dewey tells us that natural events display beginnings, integrations, consummations. Whitehead employs a fundamental concept of Concrescence. The two men, in this respect, see the world similarly. But Whitehead proposes assumptions and definitions which organize the "generic traits" of processes of concrescence. The organization may be faulty, the terms may not be the best; but it is the first step toward the deduction of consequences, by which philosophies submit themselves to the judgment of experience.[203]

Whitehead's ideal of coherence is seldom understood. It is in fact very difficult to explain it precisely. But the ideal is certainly *not* either a revival of the ancient tyranny of philosophic rationalism, or an attempt to "derive the matter of experience"

---

[203] The wider (or more metaphysical) thought is, the farther we must travel to verify it. It is true that insofar as categories are genuinely metaphysical they will be exemplified in every experience. But what a given experience, or the total experience of a man, or the total experience of an age, *tells* about such categories is a slight fragment of the truth. To verify a comprehensive scheme like Whitehead's, we need centuries.

(whatever that may mean) from "the necessities of logic." Neither of these cliches has *anything* to do with the subject. Sometimes it is supposed that Whitehead, in those magnificent passages on coherence in the opening chapters of *PR*, is merely saying something to which no one objects: that the parts of a philosophy should hang together. This is nearer the truth. The error is the implicit supposition that we all know what is involved in the ideal of "hanging together," and that, even if it be an ideal hard to attain, it involves nothing more than proceeding "as logically as possible."[204]

In his philosophy of nature Whitehead had pursued the same ideal of coherence, in a limited region:

. . . in the place of emphasising space and time in their capacity of disconnecting, we shall build up an account of their complex essences as derivative from the ultimate ways in which those things, ultimate in science, are interconnected.[205]

In *PR*, "the ideal of speculative philosophy that its fundamental notions shall not seem capable of abstraction from each other," is intended to be met by the cosmological principle that "the

[204] Dewey, criticizing Whitehead, suggests that possibly this is all he means by "coherence:" *Philos. Rev.*, Vol. 46, 1937, 171.

[205] *Principles of Natural Knowledge*, Art. 1.5. Anyone who thinks that on turning to metaphysics Whitehead for the sake of an ontology of internal relations abandoned a supposed contrary manner of thought, has forgotten all the passages whose burden is akin to this from *The Concept of Nature* (pp. 141-142): "The false idea which we have to get rid of is that of nature as a mere aggregate of independent entities, each capable of isolation. According to this conception these entities, whose characters are capable of isolated definition, come together and by their accidental relations form the system of nature. . . . With this theory space might be without time, and time might be without space. [Compare Whitehead's reference to Descartes' philosophy as an example of "incoherence," in Sec. II of the first chapter in *Process and Reality*.] . . . The explanation of nature which I urge as an alternative ideal to this accidental view of nature, is that nothing in nature could be what it is except as an ingredient in nature as it is. . . . An isolated event is not an event. . . . The isolation of an entity in thought, when we think of it as a bare 'it', has no counterpart in any corresponding isolation in nature. Such isolation is merely part of the procedure of intellectual knowledge." In *The Principle of Relativity* we have this (p. 17): "The point of this doctrine [of "significance"] on which I want to insist is that any factor, by virtue of its status as a limitation within totality, necessarily refers to factors of totality other than itself."

process, or concrescence, of any one actual entity involves the
other actual entities among its components."[206]

Here a result of Whitehead's early logical investigations
comes to play a rôle in the constructive task of the metaphysical
period. I refer to the inadequacy of the subject-predicate logic.
Whitehead thinks—I believe rightly—that the orthodox conception of "having an experience" is shaped according to the
subject-predicate mould: the experient is the subject, and is
qualified by his sensations. In *The Principle of Relativity* Whitehead had said,

If you once conceive fundamental fact as a multiplicity of subjects qualified by predicates, you must fail to give a coherent account of experience. The disjunction of subjects is the presupposition from which you
start, and you can only account for conjunctive relations by some fallacious sleight of hand, such as Leibniz's metaphor of his monads engaged in mirroring. The alternative philosophic position must commence with denouncing the whole idea of 'subject qualified by predicate'
as a trap set for philosophers by the syntax of language.[207]

Thus Whitehead's philosophic endeavor is to state literally that
coherence of factors which Leibniz could express only meta-
phorically.

In philosophy as it has come down to us, *dualisms* form, with
multiple solipsisms, the two main types of incoherence. The
source of multiple solipsisms is the dualism of subject and object, the private and the public. The *duality* of private subject
and public object is a fundamental fact stamped on the face of
experience. To achieve coherence, Whitehead begins with the
principle that, "The sole concrete facts, in terms of which actualities can be analysed, are prehensions [of objects by subjects];
and every prehension has its public side and its private side."[208]
But, further, his basic conceptions are intended to be so inclusive
in scope, and so interlocked, as to overcome all the classical
dualisms of metaphysics: mind and matter, God and the world,
permanence and transience, causality and teleology, atomism

---

[206] *Process and Reality,* 5, 10.
[207] *Principle of Relativity,* 13f.
[208] *Process and Reality,* IV, I, §V, p. 444.

and continuity, sensation and emotion, internal and external relations, etc., as well as subject and object. Thus, e.g., "physical" inheritance from the environment, and novel "mental" reaction to it, are both, in principle, ascribed to *every* occasion, as respectively its "public" basis and its "private" culmination. It makes no difference that the "mentality" involved in inorganic occasions is slight in proportion as spontaneity is negligible. The objections to this are not as good as the objections to calling "zero" a number.

The standing danger in pursuing the ideal of coherence after Whitehead's manner is, I think, the acceptance of both poles of historical and practically important antitheses as equally fundamental. There is, for example, a historical antithesis between change and permanence (better, timelessness). Whitehead assumes that the satisfactory theory "must embody an understanding of the interweaving of change and permanence, each required by the other."[209] He does not consider that the continual recurrence of the idea of the timeless may be due to the human habit of wishful thinking.

7. There is a human temptation for idealists to believe that in erecting his metaphysics Whitehead in fact turned his back on "his previous realism." But, as may be seen from the discussion in Division V,[210] that realism was relative to a limited purpose. The closure of nature to the observing mind, interpreted as it was intended to be interpreted, is not repudiated at any later point. In Whitehead's metaphysics, it is true, sense-data are creations of mentality; but this is *on Whitehead's definition* of "mentality," which is so far from the idealistic epistemologist's notion of the conscious mentality of the observing human mind, that it might be called, *per contra*, biological. The creation is really a transmutation (so evolved in man's history as to be now automatic) of given elements which are physical. There is compensation for idealists in the fact that Whitehead's final account of the occurrence of sense-perception is equally distant from the account given in G. E. Moore's "Refutation of Idealism."

[209] *Modes of Thought*, 73.
[210] Especially pp. 79-82 and 86f.

Idealists are right in seeing *a certain* kinship between White-head's pursuit of a coherent scheme and their pursuit of a coherent system of experience; there is every difference in the *manner* of the pursuit.

The world, as Whitehead finally describes it, is in some fundamental respects similar to the world idealism has tradi-tionally pictured. His working hypothesis is that the structure of every organism is analogous to that of an occasion of experi-ence. (I do not see what other hypothesis would be compatible with the aim at the coherence of all human experience and all nature.) The employment of the hypothesis consists in rounding out our immediate knowledge of our experiences by interpret-ing them in the light of what we know of other events in nature,[211] and conversely interpreting the other events in the light of the generic traits of the experiences we live through.[212] Thus Whitehead tries to make full utilization of natural science and of immediate experience.

A result is that he ascribes value, feeling, purpose to every existent. This accords with the results of idealistic philosophies. But the setting of the metaphysical problem is realistic. What is "experience?" It is "the self-enjoyment of being one among many, and of being one arising out of the composition of many."[213] Whitehead starts as the American realists did, with the notion of a "common world" in which we find ourselves, a world full of minds and of other things which also exist in their own right.

The really important moral for idealism concerns the way in which teleology and value take their place in this philosophy. Whitehead's difference from many others who arrive at idealism from the study of physics, lies in the fact that he does *not* look at the structure of the spatio-temporal continuum, or some other aspect of the physical scheme, and ask, "What rôle did mind play here?" or "How is all this understandable without tele-

---

[211] For example, we know—and Whitehead takes it very seriously—that man is one of the animals.

[212] An example is the fourth step in the account I gave of the argument of *Science and the Modern World* (p. 96, above).

[213] *Process and Reality*, II, VI, §I, 220.

ology?" He first examines the logical and empirical defects in the orthodox scientific conception of nature ("scientific materialism"); then he proposes an amazingly detailed, comprehensive theory of nature—nature taken, as the scientist must take her, in and for herself; he next examines our immediate, naïve experience of nature and our practice of life (and appeals to the romantic poets to remind us "how strained and paradoxical is the view of nature which modern science imposes on our thoughts"[214]); *then,* and then only, guided by the ratio: alist ideal of one set of concepts in which human experience and physical nature are understood together, he frames such an account of the teleologic and non-teleologic factors involved in our experience as will allow of their universal conjoint application in the understanding of existence. (Anybody can raise a cry about "the omissions of science.")

The advance *pronto* from physical theory or refined experimental results to the teleology of actual things achieves nothing. Like Whitehead, we must advance by way of a theory of the nature of the actual things.

8. There seems to me to be a natural reason why so many philosophers think, as noted before, that there must be a lack of harmony between the Whitehead of 1920 and the Whitehead of 1930. There are many differences separating philosophies; but I think that the real continental divide in modern philosophy runs between those which do, and those which do not, inquire how experiences are constituted. Whitehead's crossing of a divide which is a natural barrier to most philosophers is at the bottom of the difficulties about Whitehead and the bifurcation of nature. Let us look into the matter from a rather general point of view.

On one side lie the philosophies which start with given presentations and aim to arrive at a world which is objective, at least in the sense of exhibiting enough regularity to live by. They consider themselves successful if they show "how two minds can know one thing" and "justify" the concepts of the sciences. Members of this school have sometimes tried to construct

[214] *Science and the Modern World,* 118.

"proofs" by taking the "given" as a basis and analyzing meanings. On the farther slope of the divide lie the philosophies that start with an organism in an environment:—in more general terms, they start with a given world, the fundamental relations in which are set forth in working hypotheses; and they aim to explain the subjective experiences, which we actually enjoy, as showing the general patterns which occasions of experience would show in arising from such a world. Here are included the philosophies for which knowledge, and perhaps consciousness itself, is only one of the emergent characteristics to be explained; and which address no proofs to philosophical skepticism, but may make a bold effort to englobe and precede, or at least accompany, science, as well as to follow, analyze, and justify it.

"Experience" is for the former group of philosophies primarily a collective name for given qualia—though the word may also be applied to these as interpreted and organized by thought and language. The latter group of philosophies speaks more often of experiences; it understands by an experience a complete event in the history of a sentient organism. The term refers primarily to a process in which contents, or qualia, are displayed,—though also, by inclusion, to the display itself. For these philosophies, theory enters to complete the notion of an experience, rather than to complete the construction of the objective world, though that may be done also. The attempt is to lay bare the constitution of an experience; whereas for philosophies of the former type, to say that an experience has a constitution would be to ascribe to the given a characteristic of knowledge, and thus fail to push skepticism to its farthest limits before embarking on construction.

William James affords a good example of these two points of view. (Let the philosophies be labeled "Type I" and "Type II.") As a psychologist, James held that to ascribe a constitution to an experience was to commit "the psychologist's fallacy," that is, to speak from the standpoint of the laboratory observer instead of the laboratory subject; and as a philosopher, he never passed beyond the standpoint of Type I. At the same time, he entertained a behavioristic strain in his psychology. Recent work of Type II has usually taken the form of the "biological approach." The standpoint of Type I has been refined and broadened by Professor C. I. Lewis' conceptualistic pragmatism. I note that in introducing his system Professor Lewis expressly rejected the biological approach to philosophy.[215]

As a usual thing, these two types of philosophers speak different languages, and can only abuse each other. To the first group, the second are pseudo-scientists; to the second, the first are mere epistemologists. That a man should both analyze experience and expand scientific theory, is felt to be excessive,—almost incredible; and—though the thought is not consciously entertained—*unprofessional*. He will be said to contradict himself.

Whitehead's pre-speculative epistemology and his philosophy of natural science evidently fall under Type I. "The physical world is, in some general sense of the term, a deduced concept. Our problem is, in fact, to fit the world to our perceptions, and not our perceptions to the world."[216] This is, certainly, an analysis of meanings. Professor Lewis praised *PNK* and *CN*. But Whitehead was not analyzing meanings for their own sakes; he was criticizing the accepted Concept of the physical world. His intellectual radicalism, and his very great interest in theory, drove him to build a different physical world, and so to produce a speculative cosmology. The empirical anchorage of the cosmology is his doctrine that the environment-organism relation is directly felt in experience. That was no great departure from a point, previously noted, in his analysis of perceptual knowledge: "relations are perceived in the making and because of the making."[217] The converse, or organism-environment relation, had a ground prepared for it in his doctrine of "significance." He concludes by ascribing to experience, as an outcome of the world, a constitution which in fact fits into the accurate introspective account of the stream of consciousness given by William James.[218]

[215] *Mind and the World-Order* (N.Y., 1929), 35, 426.
[216] *Aims of Education*, 247. The date of the passage is 1915.
[217] *Principles of Natural Knowledge*, art. 3.7.
[218] Compare chap. IX of James's *Psychology* with §§12-14 of chap. XI of *Ad-*

9. One very important originative factor in the development of Whitehead's philosophy has not yet been taken up in this essay. I shall introduce it by considering again the doctrine of the little book on *Symbolism*, which lies at the very heart of Whitehead's philosophy. When a student finishes the first two chapters of this book and turns to the third, where the meaning and effect of symbolism in human society are discussed, he is likely to stop because the epistemological analysis is over. If he does, he misses the true Whitehead altogether. Although the arguments of the first two chapters are not as a rule dependent on any other considerations for their validity, they are dependent on the third chapter for their full setting and import. The evidence from which the epistemology grows has a much wider base than inspection of given experience (about which disagreement is notorious). Whitehead's central doctrine of causal inheritance seems to me to have sprung chiefly from his reflections on the characteristics of human society. The reflections are of the sort made, on a smaller scale, by Burke in his conception of "prejudice." Whitehead sees the actual, specific character of human individuals, and the specific character of a part of human society (such as New England), and the specific character of a home, or of a tree, as the outcome of an inescapable inheritance transmitted from the past, and of sporadic or purposed deviations from that inheritance. Such a conclusion is obvious to an Englishman considering the institutions, the edifices, the customs about him. In an article on "The Education of an Englishman,"[219] Whitehead describes this beautifully; but even an American can see its truth. He has only to observe the comparatively insignificant effect which the actually presented sense-data of the moment have in determining the diverse judgments, mental processes, and reactions of different men. What is important is not the presented sense-datum, but the cumulative effect of the past history of the organism.

One should never think of Whitehead as writing primarily out of a scientific background. By science I mean here the sys-

---

ventures of Ideas. See my article, "William James and Whitehead's Doctrine of Prehensions," *Jour. of Philos.*, Vol. 38 (Feb. 27, 1941), 113-126.

[219] *Atlantic Monthly*, Vol. 138 (Aug., 1926), 192-198.

tematic study of the causes of various types of natural events. Whitehead is *aware* of practically everything; but the two primary sources of his thought are sociological reflection, of the kind just described (and, more generally, what might crudely be called "humanistic reflection"), and the study of Theory, of mathematics in the widest sense, in which it is far more than the study of quantities.

Some critics, observing the humanistic setting of Whitehead's argument in *Symbolism*, condemn him for giving us vague reflections instead of the accurate logical analyses of his earlier books. They forget that the subject-matter is not the same. Eventually, Whitehead hopes, we may be able to use symbolic logic in the description of our experience generally, not merely of its spatio-temporal aspects. For the present, we must look for generic traits and formulate them as well as we can.

A cardinal point about Whitehead's humanistic reflections is that the concept of evolution (not necessarily progress), biological, sociological, intellectual, has constantly colored and reinforced them. Whitehead believes that when a philosopher talks, say about language and reality, he should not forget the obvious fact that the precise entities he is holding up "by the scruff of the neck" for examination did not long have their present character, and are not going to keep it for long; they are occurrences thrown up from a long, long past. The eternally fixed term ought to have gone out of philosophical discussion when the eternally fixed species went out of biology. The retention of the former gives a show of exactness which is a "fake," to use the language of Whitehead's recent Ingersoll Lecture.[220]

Exactness should be pursued, but never assumed. It is of the highest importance to uphold the banner of accuracy, but we have to be knowing about it. We must be aware of the roughness of our knowledge, consider what assumptions we are making, and advance by defining a path of increasing approximations. In expounding extensive abstraction to his classes at

---

[220] Concluding paragraph (p. 700 in this volume).

Harvard, Whitehead used to say that the same considerations about exactness and routes of approximation apply to morals, politics, and so on, as apply to the ideal entities of space and time (which have the advantage of permitting dispassionate discussion). Here is a consistent strain which runs through all of Whitehead's thought, bursts into print with the doctrine of the rough world and the smooth world in the essays of 1915 to 1917, and continues to increase in force. An incidental fact, amusing if not significant, is that Whitehead's first serious publication, a paper in mathematical physics dated 1888, bears the subtitle, "A method of approximation."[221]

To recur to the doctrine of evolution. The bifurcation of nature that Whitehead condemned in *CN* originated as an effect of the transmission theories of seventeenth century physics on the common sense conception that matter is the passive support of qualities. But the culminating bifurcation is the one discussed in Sec. 8, above,—that between "given experience" and "reaction to the environment." This bifurcation became acute for cosmology with the emergence of evolution in the nineteenth century. It is the foil of Whitehead's final delineation of experience. It is in order to bridge it, that he designs his account of experience so that it will apply to the unborn child, the infant in the cradle, our hours of sleep, as well as "normal" perception.

To understand Whitehead's central doctrine of causal inheritance, we have to remember Darwin and Burke and—we must not forget it—mathematics. The logic of relations and series is an instrument with which the dependence on each other of derivation-series of various complexity can be defined.[222] The definitions in *PR* of "society" in general, and of several types of societies, are examples.[223] The vector character of physics, and the absolute generality of the mathematical notion of a series, and the way in which the functioning of the human body is centered mainly toward the experience enjoyed by the

[221] "On the Motion of Viscous Incompressible Fluids," *Quart. Jour. of pure and applied Math.*, Vol. 23, 1888, 78-93.

[222] Russell aptly said, "The old logic put thought in fetters, while the new logic gives it wings." (*Our Knowledge of the External World*, 68.)

[223] *Process and Reality*, Pt. I, chap. III, §II; Pt. II, chaps. III, IV.

brain: these are the reasons why the doctrine of inheritance, whose truth is discerned in human society, can be applied to all events in the universe. Physics and mathematics and physiology together make possible a generalization from sociology.

Of course there is no one line of generalization in Whitehead's philosophy. Several lines, which have been meditated upon for years, mingle. In the succession of Whitehead's pre-metaphysical books we can see the line which comes from physics, and that which comes from religion. But the fundamental rôle of the sociological line is apparent to any student of *PR* and *Adventures of Ideas*. The grand vision of the possibilities of abstract theory, or mathematics (which was discussed in the first division of this essay), makes this whole development possible.

I suggest that thinking about the patterns discernible equally in—to take one example—the conditions of the growth of human individuals or societies, and the conditions of the growth of forests, is at the bottom of Whitehead's whole constructive effort. Ordinarily one does not join thoughts about such different things. Only a philosopher or a mathematician might be expected to do so. One would say that the philosopher was aiming at a synthesis, the mathematician making an abstraction. It comes to the same thing. It is "seeking the forms in the facts."

It must finally be noted that for some characteristics of a philosophy no derivation, however general, can be offered. *That* is the way *that* philosopher sees the world. That the general aspect of nature is one of evolutionary expansiveness, which can only be expressed by adopting some such concept as "Creativity" as a metaphysical ultimate, is a case in point. So also, in part, is Whitehead's pluralism.

10. Whitehead's humanistic background requires a little more comment. His doctrine of inheritance is surely only one among the doctrines that were primarily nurtured here. We should include (in part) his pluralism—look at his essays on education; his doctrine of the necessity of finitude and exclusion for achievement—here look again at his essays on education; his doctrine of purpose; his doctrine of alternative potentialities; and several others. The discussions in which he exhibits and

justifies these doctrines appeal primarily to their universality in human living. And no aspect of human living has been excluded from what I so crudely call his humanistic background: he has noticed the conditions of achievement in art, and in science, and in education; and equally the conditions involved in the mere survival and destruction of societies.

In drawing on a very deep general understanding of human history—human custom and human originality—to contribute, equally with his own professional studies, toward the building of a philosophy, Whitehead is very English. He is also very Whiteheadian: he could not have done otherwise. What might, by critics at least, be called the contribution to his philosophy that comes from his *amateur* side, had been a subject of meditation for decades; this appears plainly in every account he has ever given of his life's activities.

Whitehead has made no attempt to be a scholar in the humanistic field. That would have been impossible. Relying considerably on secondary sources, he has repeated old errors of historical fact. But that does not affect his *philosophy*. Anyone who supposes that in criticizing such errors he criticizes Whitehead's thought, has a curious sense of importance. Among real criticisms that may be passed on Whitehead's humanistic side, I suggest this: when we remember that the system set forth in *PR* is an essay in cosmology, and reflect that its future may very well depend more on the scientists than on the philosophers, and also recall that on Whitehead's own grounds the system is a failure if science is not affected by it, then one wonders if his humanistic background has not been acquired at too great a price. *This* man had the ability to produce a new synthesis of the sciences, a new concept of the world, and to work it out enough to ensure some actual shaping effect on the progress of the sciences and the creation of new sciences. Whether or not the philosophic system he produced comes to have such an effect in some degree, is the responsibility of others. But one wishes Whitehead had encouraged the effect. The discussion in *PR* of some of the general theories of some of the sciences, and of the divisions between sciences, is far too short. If half the time Whitehead has spent reading and discussing theology

and political history had gone into the study of—let us say—
Freud and biology, he might have given scientists badly needed
theoretical unification in these and other fields. Perhaps I am
naïve; they might have used his system no more than did the
physicists. And doubtless this hypothetical Whitehead would
have been not so complete and civilized a man as is the actual
Whitehead. Parts of *AI*, too, would never have been written.
Whitehead, of course, is not worried about his philosophy.
Its real application may lie in a very remote future.

Another effect of his historical bent is his piety toward the
great philosophers. There is ample reason for expounding a
new philosophy in connection with their depositions. But I sympathize with those critics who call Whitehead's piety toward
them excessive. It cannot be salutary to tell the philosophers
of the future[224] that Plato divined "seven notions" and that "All
philosophical systems are endeavours to express . . . [their]
interweaving."[225] Then there is the raising of John Locke to
divinity. Of course Locke is a very useful man to study,—very:
and that for the reason Whitehead gives, his "admirable adequacy." Also, this adequacy can be of use to a man engaged in
Whitehead's great investigation, cosmology. But the type of
question raised by Locke is so infinitely narrower! When, in
the first paragraph of the preface to *PR*, Whitehead says,

The writer who most fully anticipated the main positions of the philosophy of organism is John Locke in his *Essay*, especially in its later books
(Cf. Bk. IV, Ch. VI, Sec. 11),[226]

one can be thankful that Whitehead's own work follows to set
the reader right.

Whitehead has read philosophy all his life. But possibly we
can see in the excessive space devoted to Descartes and Locke in
his essay on cosmology a bad effect of his philosophical professorship. Whitehead's comparisons of his doctrines with theirs are
helpful to students of philosophy.[227] But, since the future rests

---

[224] I doubt that Whitehead intends his statement to be purely historical.

[225] *Adventures of Ideas*, chap. IX, §VIII (p. 203).

[226] *Process and Reality*, v.

[227] But Whitehead's statement that "the philosophy of organism . . . does start
with a generalization of Locke's account of mental operations," and that "pre-

with the scientists, was it not far more important to emphasize the utilization of scientific and theoretical conceptions in the philosophy of organism, and to emphasize the importance of the philosophy for such conceptions, than to gain the authority of Descartes and Locke?

It is neither of these two, but Berkeley, who seems to me—judging from our examination of the foundations of Whitehead's philosophy of natural science—to have been the philosopher most relevant to Whitehead's own conceptions in their formative stage. We can, however, ascribe to no philosopher a relevance comparable to that of mathematical and physical conceptions, or to that of the doctrine of evolution. Even Plato must be put down as providing primarily—though on a grand scale—an illustration after the fact. Some of those who know Whitehead wonder if William Wordsworth did not influence him more than any other man.

VII. Conclusion

1. I think that after *PR* no novel departures occur in Whitehead's system of philosophy. And *PR* must always remain *the* indispensable book. The relationship of *AI* to *PR* is analogous to that of *CN* to *PNK*. The expositions of the first book, in each case, suffer from the pressure of the new ideas, burgeoning forth. But only the first book states the ideas in their theoretical completeness.

Incidental reference has already been made to some parts of *AI*. I assume that the reader is familiar with the plan of this book, and sees how Whitehead, in devoting himself to the historical rôle of metaphysical ideas in civilization, followed his system of metaphysics with the—to him—natural commentary on it. Only a few additional developments need to be pointed out. Whitehead now, by defining *beauty* in terms of his metaphysics, repays the debt which his systematic thought owed to that part of its "humanistic" background. The book's discussion

---

hensions" in particular "are a generalization from Descartes' mental 'cogitations', and from Locke's 'ideas' " (*Process and Reality*, Pt. I, chap. II, §I) gives a misleading idea of the sources from which the philosophy, and the concept of prehension, sprang in Whitehead's intellectual development.

of "Laws of Nature" rounds out his position on causality, so that one sees how the "passing events" of the 1920 books had to get expanded into the "actual occasions" of the philosophy of organism, with their "objective immortality."[228] His technical theory of the relation of sense-perception to reality is further explained, and connected with the ancient contrast between appearance and reality; and his last word on the topic—the rôle of God—emerges. A very valuable gloss on the first part of *PR* is provided by an account of the sources of its terminology and a discussion of the relation of theory to evidence. The chapter on "Objects and Subjects," which was Whitehead's presidential address to the eastern division of the American Philosophical Association in 1931, must be noticed, for three reasons. (1) It will, I imagine, come to be considered the *locus classicus* for Whitehead's conception of experience. (2) The many admirers of his philosophy who balk at his doctrine of eternal objects will find the chapter useful because of the accidental fact that it manages to summarize Whitehead's metaphysical position quite well, without once mentioning either these entities or God. (3) Those who object to Whitehead mainly because of his Jamesian theory of personal unity will be pleased to find that in this chapter he says that a problem remains; his further discussion of it, however, proceeds along his usual lines.

2. With the completion of *AI* the greatest productive period of Whitehead's life came to a close. In seven years, filled with teaching and departmental work, he had constructed the most comprehensive cosmology in history, and thoroughly expounded it from a variety of points of view. In the years immediately succeeding he suffered ill health, and published only a few papers. One of these[229] sketches a new theory of classes and relations, and a new definition of number, to make good certain serious defects of the treatment in the *Principia*.

Then in 1938 appeared what must always be one of the best-

---

[228] Critics who think this expansion involves a great repudiation should observe that Whitehead had long before described the "passage of events" as one thing with their "significance" (*Principle of Relativity*, 1922, 68).

[229] "Indication, Classes, Numbers, Validation," *Mind*, n.s., Vol. 43 (July, 1934), 281-297.

loved books, as *SMW* will always be one of the most exciting books, that philosophy possesses. In *Modes of Thought* system is kept entirely in the background. The metaphysician sets aside his conceptual definitions, and writes "the first chapter in philosophic approach"—"a free examination of some ultimate notions, as they occur naturally in daily life."[230] The whole has an extraordinary valedictory beauty.

Whitehead used to tell his students, in the thirties, that he could contemplate with pleasure a conflation of his philosophy with that of Samuel Alexander. That philosopher, he felt, had leaned a bit too much toward monism, whereas he himself had in *PR* leaned too much toward pluralism. In *MT* he seems to me to conceive of the universe somewhat more monistically. How, if at all, he would revise the categoreal scheme of *PR* could not be discussed in this type of book. One sees a tendency, sometimes checked, to refer "importance" to the ultimate unity (the God of *PR*), and the contrasting notion, "matter-of-fact," to finite individuals. But Whitehead is very far from going over to monism. "There is also equally fundamental in the Universe, a factor of multiplicity."[231]

The one topic which recurs again and again is the contrast that was so emphatically set forth even on its first appearance, in *Symbolism*. "The doctrine dominating these lectures," Whitehead now writes in his preface,

is that factors in our experience are 'clear and distinct' in proportion to their variability, provided that they sustain themselves for that moderate period required for importance. The necessities are invariable, and for that reason remain in the background of thought, dimly and vaguely. Thus philosophic truth is to be sought in the presuppositions of language rather than in its express statements.[232]

"Clear, conscious discrimination . . . is of the essence of our humanity," but "an accident of our existence."[233]

With the development of his metaphysics, Whitehead had passed gradually away from his first conception of mathematics, as concerned solely with "the inference of proposition from

[230] *Modes of Thought*, 1.
[231] *Ibid.*, 70.
[232] *Ibid.*, vii.
[233] *Ibid.*, 158.

proposition," and had come to conceive of it as dealing with the connectedness between passing things insofar as the facts of connection are general, that is, form "patterns." He now brings out the radical character of his final position. Every mathematical statement is a statement about a process and its issue. He thinks this is obvious in the case of the mathematical conception of an infinite series; but it holds equally of the multiplication table.[234]

There is however not a hair's breadth of deviation from his constant position that mathematics abstracts utterly from particular things and processes. It is just because mathematics aims to state forms universally exemplified that it is kin to metaphysics. In *PR* when "a metaphysical proposition" is defined, the example chosen for discussion is "one and one make two." In the late logical paper, referred to in the preceding Section, the definition of number in *PM* is condemned because it entails "the dependence of number upon shifting accidents of factual existence (unless 'change' be conceived as illusory)."[235]

From the doctrine of the essential connection of mathematical forms with the world there issues, in *Modes of Thought*, an arresting comparison of logical consistency with aesthetic consistency. Another consequence is Whitehead's belief that the logic of propositions, if based on inconsistency (H. M. Sheffer showed how the system of *PM* could be based on inconsistency as the sole undefined relation[236]), reflects the fundamental fact of a pluralistic metaphysics of process; the existence of alternatives that are not conjointly realizable sets the problem for the becoming of every actual occasion.

The doctrine of the autonomy of form, and the worse doctrine of the autonomy of propositional forms, are pieces of bad metaphysics. They have—for one thing—the same defect as the absolute theory of space (which Whitehead had so long criticized) and the conception of natural laws as absolute: they forget that the relata always make a difference. Yet every science, as a science, progresses by making an abstraction, and considering the relata only in certain respects: thus "spaciness" is

[234] *Ibid.*, 112, 123-126.
[235] *Mind*, n.s., Vol. 43, 288.
[236] *Trans. Amer. Math. Soc.*, Vol. 14, 481-488. Sheffer does not speak of the relation of inconsistency, but of an operation called "rejection" or "nonconjunction." See his review of ed. 2 of *PM: Isis*, vol. 8 (1926), p. 229.

absent from geometry, process from arithmetic.[237] Speculative philosophy is important because it is important to aim at "a right adjustment of abstractions." This is what is missed by the critics who think that Whitehead denies the principles of scientific method when he turns philosopher.[238] Far from making general war on acts of abstraction, he insists that such acts are indispensable to the advance of thought. What he objects to is a bigoted

[237] *Modes of Thought,* 64. In his pre-speculative period Whitehead overemphasized this fact. He would probably no longer say that, "The fact which is essential for science is our conception; its meaning in regard to the metaphysics of reality is of no scientific importance, so far as physical science is concerned." ("The Anatomy of Some Scientific Ideas" (1917), *Aims of Education,* 196.)

[238] Ernest Nagel, reviewing *Process and Reality,* made this objection: "When Whitehead declares that by the 'coherence' of ideas he understands that no entity be conceivable in 'complete abstraction' from the system of the universe, one may retort that no relational way of thought can declare itself otherwise. But one must also add, that while there can be no 'complete abstraction' in this sense, there undoubtedly is a 'relative abstraction' so that one must not make the impossible demand that the nature of the whole universe be presupposed in whatever we may say. Whitehead's pursuit of [the totality of truth] . . . is fortunately not his only occupation, otherwise the *Universal Algebra* and the *Principia* would never have been written." (*Symposium,* v. 1, 1930, p. 396.)

The comments to be made on this are: (1) Nagel begins by declaring that he agrees with Whitehead's ideal of coherence. How, on Nagel's view, are we to offer the ideal more than lip-service? (2) One must admit that though the necessity of "also" making "relative abstractions" is repeatedly insisted upon in *Adventures of Ideas* and *Modes of Thought,* it is not prominent in *Process and Reality.* And in *The Function of Reason,* Whitehead, in the heat of argument, makes statements which are either ambiguous or excessive (e.g., the statement on p. 49 that "Insofar as philosophers have failed, scientists do not know what they are talking about when they pursue their own methods"). (3) What is meant by the key phrase of the quotation: "one must not make the impossible *demand*"? Whitehead is not proposing to stop speech. The only *demand* he makes is that no limit be imposed on the philosopher's "gradual definition of habitual ideas" (*Adventures of Ideas,* p. 185) in terms of the nature of the universe from which they rise.

Whitehead holds that science and philosophy are engaged in a joint enterprise (*Ibid.,* chap. IX). Our knowledge is reached by stages; abstractions fall into clusters, of greater or less circumference. The most ambitious philosophers "cannot produce that final adjustment of well-defined generalities which constitute a complete metaphysics. But . . . [they] can produce a variety of partial systems of limited generality." (*Ibid.,* pp. 185-186.) Whitehead's pursuit of both scientific and philosophic theory is simply the pursuit of the double necessity: "We have to analyse and to abstract, *and* to understand the natural status of our abstractions." (*Nature and Life,* p. 1; as reprinted in *Modes of Thought,* p. 173; my italics.)

insistence that only fools investigate the totality from which the abstraction has been made. If philosophers keep to the same abstractions that sciences make, they are scientists in disguise, or possibly pseudo-scientists, who happen to earn their living by teaching philosophy. If a man of Whitehead's ability delves behind the abstractions made by particular sciences, it becomes possible for philosophy to "point out fields for research."[239] Whitehead thinks that the *development* of those fields must be assigned to specialists.

I have been sketching Whitehead's final conception of philosophy in its relation to exact thought. The relation of philosophy to life—from the point of view of this essay, the union of Whitehead's humanistic side with his aim at mathematical coherence—is beautifully stated in the final paragraph of *MT*.

Philosophy is akin to poetry, and both of them seek to express that ultimate good sense which we term civilization. In each case there is reference to form beyond the direct meanings of words. Poetry allies itself to metre, philosophy to mathematic pattern.[240]

3. The reader who has had the courage to come thus far will see from the evidence presented that the only possible answer to the question, "Mathematician or Philosopher?" is: "At all times, both." (This is a *rough* answer: any other kind would involve "fake" exactness.) By way of illustration, consider Whitehead's battle against the idea of an independently existing entity, which his philosophy has fought more than anything else. He began as a mathematician; now a mathematical scheme is the complete denial of entities which might exist independently and merely happen to fall into relationships. As a mathematician, Whitehead was a bit unusual in that he worked so much at bringing different schemes together, out of *their* independence. Independent existence was exemplified in physical thought primarily by the concepts of Space and material particle. Whitehead attacked each in turn. Then he came to attack

---

The theory of "Coördinate Division" in Part IV of *Process and Reality* is to be understood as the culmination of Whitehead's long effort to provide a right place of relative independence for the abstractions of physical science.

[239] *Modes of Thought*, 30.
[240] *Modes of Thought*, 237f.

the Humian epistemology of perceptions which have no intrinsic reference to other perceptions.

Many other threads run through his life-work. A very important one is his concern over the integral inclusion of geometry in the world of change. We traced that back to 1905.

But that his conclusions at one time provide premises for later conclusions, cannot be assumed without severe qualifications, which destroy the simple notion of a "premise." There is a difference in the level of his discussions. We need say no more about this, since the sore spots have been examined in the body of this essay. The mistaken assumption rests on a very naïve notion of the logic and the psychology involved in expanding investigations.

4. Finally, let us glance at a few general conditions that made Whitehead's development possible. The nineteenth century was a peaceful century, and sheltered the pursuit of thought; Whitehead was fifty-three years old at the beginning of the World War. As a youth, he went to Cambridge during one of her great ages. Fortunate occasions arose, at various times, for the exercise of his powers. But the division of his activity into distinct periods, each of high accomplishment, is equally the result of his extraordinary concentration. His first object was a great intellectual synthesis, universal algebra. He went on to another, and another, always one at a time—but in his conversations and reflections he was constantly touching on all the conditions involved in human existence. If it be also true that mathematics and metaphysics are naturally akin, then it is impossible to imagine a set of conditions more favorable to the creation of a philosophy.

The man fitted the conditions perfectly. The philosophy of organism is the ultimate intellectual achievement of the nineteenth century. The centuries to come will profit far more than we.

VICTOR LOWE

DEPARTMENT OF PHILOSOPHY
SYRACUSE UNIVERSITY

2

Willard V. Quine

WHITEHEAD AND THE RISE OF
MODERN LOGIC

WHITEHEAD AND THE RISE OF
MODERN LOGIC

I

"ALGEBRA," for centuries, meant numerical algebra: arithmetic formulated with help of variables. Complex numbers came as an extension, but an extension still of number, arithmetically motivated; not as a departure from number. During the short period from 1843 to 1847, then, three utterly non-numerical theories came to be created in the partial image of numerical algebra: Sir William Rowan Hamilton's theory of quaternions, Hermann Grassmann's theory of extension (*Ausdehnungslehre*), and George Boole's algebra of logic. Mathematicians began to recognize that there was no necessary connection between the algebraic type of approach and the numerical type of subject matter, and indeed that the algorithmic laws of an algebra might fruitfully be studied in abstraction from all subject matter. Benjamin Peirce's *Linear Associative Algebras* (1870), a generalization of Hamilton's quaternion theory, was explicitly a comparative study of certain uninterpreted algebras. Thus it was that a wide new field came to be cleared which is today undergoing intensive cultivation under the name of abstract algebra.

It was as a pioneer in this field that Whitehead wrote his first book, *A Treatise on Universal Algebra* (1898). In Book I of this work he undertook to characterize such algebraic notions as equivalence, addition, and multiplication along lines general enough to suit any algebra, irrespective of the more special laws of the algebra and irrespective of the interpretation. The laws:

$$x+y = y+x, \quad (x+y) +z = x+(y+z), \quad x(y+z) = xy+xz,$$

e.g., he regarded as common to algebras generally; whereas algebras might differ in point of various other laws, including:

$$xy = yx, \qquad (xy)z = x(yz), \qquad x + x = x.$$

Algebras violating the law '$x + x = x$' he called *numerical*, and classified in turn into *species* substantially as follows: a numerical algebra is of nth species if from its elements we can form a class α such that (i) any two members of α can meaningfully be added and multiplied, (ii) every element of the whole algebra is a product of two or more members of α, and (iii) anything is a product of n members of α if and only if it likewise belongs to α.

The projected second volume of *Universal Algebra*, which never appeared, was to deal with linear algebras, or algebras of first *species*. The existing Volume I is concerned, in the last five of its seven Books, with algebras of higher species. This portion of the work constitutes a detailed investigation of the calculus of extension founded by Grassmann. Book II of the volume deals with a non-numerical algebra, namely the Boolean algebra of logic. This Book will concern us to the exclusion of the five succeeding Books. But meanwhile there is an aspect of Book I that calls for discussion: the general doctrine of equivalence.

Whitehead regarded '$=$' as expressing a relation of equivalence, short of identity. His defense was that laws such as '$x + y = y + x$' would otherwise, like '$z = z$', make no assertion at all. This reasoning, which hints strongly of Wittgenstein's more recent polemic against identity,[1] loses its force if we attend closely to the distinction between notation and subject matter. Let us tentatively suppose, contrary to Whitehead as of 1898, that '$x + y = y + x$' does hold as a genuine identity; i.e., that the order of summands is wholly immaterial. A notation of addition more suggestive than '$x + y$', then, would consist in simply superimposing 'x' and 'y' in the manner of a monogram. This notation quite properly refrains from suggesting any order of summands; and there ceases to be any analogue of '$x + y = y + x$', the nearest approach being of the vacuous type '$z = z$'. Now the one objection to this procedure is the expense of casting monograms; and thus it is that we revert to

---

[1] Ludwig Wittgenstein, *Tractatus Logico-Philosophicus* (London, 1922), esp. 5·5303.

a linear notation which imposes an arbitrary notational order on summands. The printer foists upon us a redundant notation, issuing in synonyms. One and the same sum can now be expressed in two ways, '$x + y$' and '$y + x$'. The law '$x + y = y + x$' comes to be needed as a means of neutralizing this excess of notation over subject matter. The law thus preserves a consequential role, even with ' $=$ ' construed in the strict sense of identity.

It is not easy to imagine a notation capable of absorbing various other laws, e.g., '$x(y + z) = xy + xz$', in the manner in which the monogram notation absorbed '$x + y = y + x$'; nor is it easy to imagine a notation capable even of absorbing '$x + y = y + x$' and yet leaving '$x + x = x$' unprejudiced. For most purposes, notations teeming with synonyms are forced upon us by circumstances yet more compelling than the cost of monograms. Hence the utility of the identity concept.

Continuing his discussion of equivalence ('$=$'), Whitehead pointed out that an equivalence formula or equation implies replaceability of the one side by the other in all algebraic contexts, whereas this does not hold for certain non-algebraic contexts. In the differential calculus, e.g., we cannot assert that if $x^3 = 8$ then $dx^3/dx = d8/dx$; for dx^3/dx is $3x^2$ (hence 12 where $x^3 = 8$) whereas $d8/dx$ is 0. This was no doubt further ground for his construing ' $=$ ' as meaning something short of identity; for if x^3 *is* simply 8, so that dx^3/dx and $d8/dx$ are d/dx of one and the same thing, then surely $dx^3/dx = d8/dx$.

As is now known, however, this apparent anomaly calls for no departure from the strict identity relation. It is functions or relations, not numbers, that have derivatives. The expression 'dx^3/dx', which may for logical purposes be rendered more clearly in the fashion '$D \lambda_x(x^3)$', designates the derivative not of the number x^3 but of a relation $\lambda_x(x^3)$—the relation "cube of."[2] Likewise '$d8/dx$' or '$D \lambda_x 8$' designates the derivative not of the number 8 but of the relation $\lambda_x 8$—the relation that 8 bears to everything.[3] The 'x' of '$\lambda_x(x^3)$' and similar contexts is

---

[2] Cf. §VIII, below. For the logical definition of the derivative see my *Mathematical Logic* (New York, 1940), 279.

[3] Incidentally dx^3/dx or $D \lambda_x(x^3)$ is itself not a number, $3x^2$, but a relation in turn, viz. $\lambda_x(3x^2)$—"triple of square of;" and $d8/dx$ or $D \lambda_x 8$ is not 0 but $\lambda_x 0$.

a so-called bound (or apparent) variable, a relative pronoun in effect, having no relevance beyond the immediate 'λ' context. Both '$\lambda_x(x^3)$' and '$\lambda_x 8$' are constants referring to fixed relations, and they are quite unaffected by special numerical hypotheses such as '$x^3 = 8$'.

Whitehead's version of '$=$' as equivalence-in-diversity does not reappear in his later work. Hinted in the contrast which he drew on this early occasion between algebra and the differential calculus, still, there is this sound characterization of an algebra: its terms are constructed from one another without any binding of variables.

II

The elements of the Boolean algebra are classes. The product xy is construed as the class whose members are the common members of the classes x and y, and the sum $x + y$ is construed as the class obtained by pooling the members of x and y.[4] A further notion is that of the *complement* $\bar{x}$, whose members comprise everything except the members of x. Finally there is the empty class o, and the exhaustive class 1. Equations constructed of these materials admit of an algorithm which is rather like that of the familiar numerical algebra, but simpler.

The algebra is subject, as Schröder showed in 1877,[5] to a neat principle of *duality:* every law remains true when 'plus' is switched with 'times' and 'o' with '1'. Another important principle is that of *development*, which goes back to Boole: any function $f(x)$ of the algebra is expressible as a sum $ax + b\bar{x}$, wherein the coefficients a and b are respectively $f(1)$ and $f(0)$; likewise any function $f(x, y)$ is expressible as a sum:

$$(1) \qquad axy + b\bar{x}y + cx\bar{y} + d\bar{x}\bar{y},$$

wherein the coefficients are respectively $f(1, 1), f(0, 1), f(1, 0),$

---

[4] This version of the sum goes back to Leibniz (*Opera*, Erdmann edition of 1840, Vol. 1, 94 f.). In Boole's own books, *The Mathematical Analysis of Logic* (London and Cambridge, 1847) and *An Investigation of the Laws of Thought* (London, 1854), the sum was construed in a slightly different and less convenient way; but Leibniz's version was revived by W. S. Jevons (*Pure Logic*, London, 1864), and became usual.

[5] Ernst Schröder, *Der Operationskreis des Logikkalkuls* (Leipzig, 1877). Whitehead gives the credit rather to C. S. Peirce. For a clarification of the point see Alonzo Church's review of E. T. Bell in *Journal of Symbolic Logic*, Vol. 5 (1940), 152.

and $f(0, 0)$; and correspondingly for higher functions $f(x, y, z)$, $f(x, y, z, w)$, etc.

Any equation of the logical algebra can be converted into another whose right member is '0'; for '$z = w$' is equivalent to '$z\bar{w} + \bar{z}w = 0$'. Having thus converted any equation, we may proceed to develop its left member after the manner exemplified in (I). Any logical equation thus admits of a standard form wherein a sort of polynomial is equated to 0. Since there are such striking analogies between equations of logic and those of ordinary algebra, the problem of solving logical equations for unknowns was among the first to command interest in connection with Boole's algebra.

The general equation in one unknown, '$ax + b\bar{x} = 0$', can be satisfied just in case $ab = 0$; and, where this condition is fulfilled, the equation proves to be satisfied by $\bar{a}c + b\bar{c}$ for every choice of c, and by nothing else. The nearest thing to a solution of '$ax + b\bar{x} = 0$', in short, is '$x = \bar{a}c + b\bar{c}$'. This was known to Boole. The "solution"—in the same sense—of the general equation in two unknowns was given by Schröder in 1890.

Whitehead sets all these matters forth systematically in Chapters I and II of his Book II, and derives new results of his own. Among these is the solution of the general equation in three or more unknowns; also the general solution of n simultaneous equations in one unknown. An interesting principle which he establishes in the course of these developments is that a function $f(x, y, z, \cdots)$, in any number of unknowns, is capable of assuming all and only those values which can be assumed by this function in one unknown:

$$abc \cdots k + u(a + b + c + \cdots + k),$$

where $a, b, c, \cdots, k$ are the successive coefficients of f according to the law of development. These findings are accompanied by numerous others in the same vein.

In his "Memoir on the algebra of symbolic logic" of three years later, Whitehead delves yet further into the theory of equations and theory of functions of Boolean algebra. He investigates the problem of factoring any function into a product of so-called *linear primes*. By a linear prime he means any function $f(x, y, z, \cdots)$ that is expressible in the fashion:

$$\bar{a}x + a\bar{x} + \bar{b}y + b\bar{y} + \bar{c}z + c\bar{z} + \cdots.$$

The importance of this notion is reflected in these principles: (i) a function capable of the value o is a linear prime if and only if no factor of it (other than itself) is capable of the value o; (ii) no sum of distinct linear primes, with the same variables, is capable of the value o. In arriving at various laws of factoring, Whitehead makes extensive use of *invariants*—in striking analogy to the procedure of ordinary theory of equations. His invariants are symmetric functions of the coefficients a, b, etc. obtained under the principle of development. He shows on the basis of the principle of duality that another theory, closely parallel to all this, subsists for what he calls *separable primes*— complements of linear primes. This parallel theory is concerned not with factoring but with resolving into summands.

The second part of the article deals with transformations of functions. Any transformation of x and y into u and v is represented by a pair of equations:

(2) $$x = f_1(u, v), \qquad y = f_2(u, v).$$

In case the equations (2) happen to be equivalent to another pair of the form:

$$u = F_1(x, y), \qquad v = F_2(x, y),$$

he calls the transformation a *substitution*. He shows that the substitutions, unlike the transformations generally, constitute a group; and that, given any function f, the substitutions that leave f unchanged constitute a group by themselves—the *identical group* of f, as he calls it. Among the many results that he establishes with regard to substitution groups, perhaps the most surprising is this: if the identical groups of two functions f_1 and f_2 have nothing in common (except the *vacuous* substitution), then (2) above is itself a substitution.

It was while this paper was at press that Whitehead came upon Giuseppe Peano's powerful mathematical logic; and forthwith he embarked with Bertrand Russell on *Principia Mathematica*. But he did not turn his back on Boolean algebra without according it one more paper, by way of extending his old theory of equations with the help of the new Peano devices. In this paper, "The logic of relations, logical substitution groups, and cardinal numbers," Whitehead formulated the general notion of a Boolean equation rigorously within Peano's formal notation. The following verbal sketch, though diverging somewhat from Whitehead's meaning, depicts the general type of approach. Given an expression of equational form, in n variables, we may think of each of its *solutions* as an n-place sequence of classes which, as values of the respective variables, make the expression true. Such a sequence may be explained in turn as a class of n pairs, wherein the first of the classes is paired with the number 1, the second with 2, etc. Finally an *equation* (as distinct from the equational expression) may be conceived as the class of the solutions. Equations become identified thus with certain classes of classes of class-number pairs; and the exact definition can be couched in Peano's symbols.

An interesting effect of defining equation along such lines was that the idea of an equation in infinitely many variables came to have meaning. Whitehead then extended various of his earlier results to apply to equations in this widened sense. He formulated a solution of the general equation, and he determined the number of possible solutions. As an instrument in these investigations he used Georg Cantor's theory of infinite numbers—a theory that had itself been the object meanwhile of investigations on Whitehead's part (cf. §IX).

III

Such, in outline, were Whitehead's mathematically oriented studies of Boolean algebra. But he also directed his attention, even in *Universal Algebra*, to the more strictly logical type of problem: that which concerns analysis and systematization of the basic forms of discourse. The equations of Boolean algebra provide directly for universal statements, to the effect that *everything* or that *nothing* belongs to a class x (viz., '$x = 1$' and '$x = 0$'); but they do not provide thus directly for existential statements, to the effect that *something* does or does not belong to x. Accordingly Whitehead[6] introduced a curious quasi-term 'j', which he thought of as a modification of '1' to the following effect: xj, like $x1$, is x; but the use of the notation 'xj' is under-

---

[6] *Universal Algebra*, Bk. II, Chap. III.

stood as implying incidentally the further information that something belongs to x. Analogously he introduced another quasi-term 'ω', thought of as a modification of 'o' to the following effect: $x + \omega$, like $x + \text{o}$, is x, but the use of the notation '$x + \omega$' implies incidentally that something does *not* belong to x. When used in isolation, rather than written in an equation, 'xj' drops its status of term altogether and comes to function simply as a statement to the effect that something belongs to x; and correspondingly for '$x + \omega$'. The expression 'xj' or '$x + \omega$' may also function simply as a statement when it stands as a member of an equation, provided the adjacent equality sign is modified in the fashion '$\equiv$' and read 'if and only if'.

Certain of the laws of Boolean algebra remain valid when 'j' and 'ω' occur among the terms, but the analogy is not thoroughgoing. Additional rules are formulated to guide the manipulation of 'j' and 'ω', and even some additional auxiliary notations are adopted. Seeing how this engine grates and creaks, we may wonder with Vacca[7] why Whitehead did not favor the simple expedient of expressing existence statements by means of inequalities: '$x \neq \text{o}$' for 'Something belongs to x', and '$x \neq 1$' for 'Something does not belong to x'. Perhaps the answer is that Whitehead was viewing algebras strictly as systems of equations, as opposed to inequalities.

The traditional formal logic falls neatly into two parts, which may for brevity be called the *categorical* and the *hypothetical*. The categorical logic embraces the theory of immediate inference and the categorical syllogism. The hypothetical logic received only fragmentary treatment in the Aristotelian tradition, under the head of hypothetical and disjunctive syllogisms; its fuller development took place rather at the hands of the Stoic logicians and their followers—notably Chrysippus in ancient times and Petrus Hispanus in the Middle Ages.[8] Now the algebra of classes deals, in a simple and systematic way, with the matters that were dealt with more haltingly and inelegantly in the old categorical logic. Whitehead accordingly devotes a chap-

---

[7] Giovanni Vacca, review of *Universal Algebra* (Italian), *Revue. de math.* (*Riv. di mat.*), Vol. 6 (1896–9), 101–104.

[8] See Jan Łukasiewicz, "Zur Geschichte der Aussagenlogik," *Erkenntnis*, Vol. 5 (1935–6), 111–131.

ter[9] to deriving the various moods of categorical syllogisms. But, as Boole was aware, the algebra can be made also to provide for hypothetical logic, simply by dropping the *classial* interpretation of the algebra in favor of a *propositional* interpretation. To this course Whitehead devotes a chapter in turn.[10]

Under the propositional interpretation of the algebra, $\bar{x}$ is construed as the *denial* of the proposition x; and xy is construed as the *conjunction* and $x + y$ as the *alternation* of the propositions x and y. Thus $\bar{x}$ is true just in case x is false, xy is true just in case x and y are both true, and $x + y$ is true just in case one or both of x and y are true. In construing ' $=$ ' propositionally, there was some divergence among Boole and his followers. The simplest choice is to construe ' $x = y$ ' as true whenever x and y are both true or both false. So construed, ' $x = y$ ' reduces to ' $xy + \bar{x}\bar{y}$ '. The sign ' $=$ ' becomes dispensable, and so do ' 1 ' and ' 0 '; in fact ' $x = 1$ ' and ' $x = 0$ ' reduce to ' x ' and ' $\bar{x}$ '. But Whitehead chose rather to construe ' $x = y$ ' as true only in case "any motives · · · to assent, which on presentation to the mind induce assent to x, also necessarily induce assent to y and conversely."[11] For him, ' $x = 1$ ' does not reduce to ' x '; it affirms rather that x is not merely true, but self-evident. Correspondingly ' $x = 0$ ' affirms that x is "self-condemned." Again ' $x\bar{j}$ ' and ' $x + \omega$ ' (which might have been ' $x \neq 0$ ' and ' $x \neq 1$ ') deny respectively that x is self-condemned and that x is self-evident. Substantially a logic of modalities—necessity, impossibility, possibility, contingency, equivalence—is thus forthcoming.

Let us take stock again of the subject matter of the algebra. Originally, under the classial interpretation, the elements x, y, etc. of the algebra were said to be classes; i.e., the *letters* ' x ', ' y ', etc. were thought of as replaceable by any actual names of specific classes. Now, under the propositional interpretation, the elements x, y, etc. are said to be propositions; and this means, correspondingly, that ' x ', ' y ', etc. are to be replaceable by *names of* propositions. Actually, in getting specific instances of the algebraic laws under the so-called propositional interpretation,

[9] *Universal Algebra*, Bk. II, Chap. IV.
[10] *Ibid.*, Chap. V.
[11] *Ibid.*, 108.

the letters are ordinarily replaced by *statements*; so we seem called upon to understand "propositions" no longer as statements, as was traditionally done, but rather as certain other entities—abstract and non-linguistic, presumably—whereof statements as wholes are names. A compound of the form '$x = y$', then, is to be true when the statements joined by ' $=$ ' are names of the same proposition; and perhaps Whitehead's vague criterion in terms of "motives to assent" is as reasonable a criterion as any for deciding whether two statements are names of the same proposition. It does seem more natural than the simpler alternative previously considered, whereby '$x = y$' holds whenever both components are true or both false.

By rephrasing the so-called propositional interpretation of the algebra, though, we can easily dispense with obscure entities and reinstate the common-sense view, according to which statements are not names at all. We may stipulate simply that the constant expressions substitutable for 'x', 'y', etc. are to be statements; we need not countenance any *entities* x, y, etc., whereof the substituted statements are names. Whereas ' $=$ ' in its ordinary sense of 'is' or 'is equivalent to' is a verb, a connective of names, we must now reconstrue it in a fashion appropriate for connecting statements; and the obvious reading is 'if and only if'. Just as 'xy' and '$x + y$' are read 'x and y' and 'x or y', so '$x = y$' is read 'x if and only if y'; verbs appear only inside the component statements that are thought of as supplanting 'x' and 'y'. And now it *is* quite natural to explain a compound of the form '$x = y$' as true whenever both its components are true or both false.

Modalities, e.g. logical necessity, logical impossibility, logical equivalence, are most clearly construed as properties and relations of statements, and treated in a theory that discourses *about* statements. In such a theory, known nowadays as *metalogic*, variables 'x', 'y', etc. occur which refer to statements and thus admit not statements but *names of* statements as substituends. Thus the modalities are lifted out of logic proper, and reserved to a discipline that *treats of* the expressions *used in* that logic. Whitehead's own subsequent work conformed to this trend; the modalities do not recur in his definitive formalization of logic.[12]

In *Universal Algebra*, however, Whitehead had a special use for his modal version of the algebra of logic; viz., in dealing with categorical statements by MacColl's method.[13] The method consists in rendering 'Every *A* is a *B*', 'No *A* is a *B*', etc., in the respective forms '$x\bar{y} = 0$', '$xy = 0$', etc., where '*x*' and '*y*' stand for 'It is an *A*' and 'It is a *B*'. The apparent advantage of this method is that it renders the propositional interpretation of the algebra adequate not only to the hypothetical logic but to the categorical logic as well; the shift to the classial interpretation for purposes of categorical logic becomes unnecessary. Thus it was that Whitehead conceived of the propositional interpretation as having "perhaps the best right to be called a system of Symbolic Logic."[14]

But the method has shortcomings. First, it requires us to extend the notion of statement or proposition to include such expressions as 'It is mortal', where 'it' is thought of as having no grammatical antecedent, expressed or implied. This extension is drastic, for clearly such expressions admit neither of truth nor of falsehood. Second, the method is not very clearly suited to Whitehead's versions of '$= 0$' and '$= 1$'. There is an excess of rationalism in the view that 'Every vertebrate has a heart' expresses impossibility or "self-condemnedness" of 'It is a vertebrate and it has no heart'. Third, the method cannot be extended to more complex cases. If e.g. we construe:

(3)   Whatever interests every man interests Socrates

as:

(4) (it interests every man and it does not interest Socrates) $= 0$,

and then we construe the fragment 'it interests every man' in (4) correspondingly as:

[12] For further discussion of these matters see §IV, below; also §§4–5 of my *Mathematical Logic*.

[13] Hugh MacColl, "The calculus of equivalent statements," *Proc. London Math. Soc.*, Vol. 9 (1877–8), 9–20, 177–186; Vol. 10 (1878–9), 16–28; Vol. 11 (1879–80), 113–121; Vol. 28 (1896–7), 156–183, 555–579; Vol. 29 (1897–8), 98–109.

[14] *Universal Algebra*, 111.

(5)   (it is a man and it does not interest it) = o,

we find ourselves involved in ambiguity; for the final result is
indistinguishable from the result obtained by starting not with
(3) but with:

(6)   Whatever every man interests interests Socrates.

Inadequacy to the analysis of complex cases like (3) is a limitation that is shared by the classial interpretation of the Boolean
algebra, and by the traditional formal logic as well; and that it
obtrudes itself particularly as a shortcoming of MacColl's device
is perhaps a virtue of the latter. Actually Frege had overcome
this limitation during the very period of MacColl's papers, and
nineteen years before the appearance of *Universal Algebra;* for
it was in 1879 that Frege created quantification theory and
thereby founded modern mathematical logic.[15] But Frege's
books remained long unnoticed. Only during the five years
preceding *Universal Algebra* had Peano come to make extensive use of techniques similar to Frege's; and not until two years
after *Universal Algebra* did Whitehead come to know Peano's
work. Frege remained unknown to Whitehead for yet another
two years.

IV

Peano's logic, together with certain emendations by Russell,
came to Whitehead's enthusiastic attention in 1900. "I believe,"
Whitehead wrote, "that the invention of the Peano and Russell
symbolism . . . forms an epoch in mathematical reasoning."[16] In
particular, he deemed it virtually indispensable as a tool for
exploring Cantor's new theory of infinite cardinal numbers.

The abstract nature of the [latter] subject makes ordinary language
totally ineffective, only gaining precision by verbosity, and imagination is very misleading, since it presents to us special aggregates which
are denumerable or of the power of the continuum. Thus we are
thrown back onto a strict logical deduction by the symbolic method.[17]

Russell, in 1900, was working on the first volume of his *Prin-*

[15] Gottlob Frege, *Begriffsschrift* (Halle, 1879). Quantification theory will be taken
up in §V.
[16] "On cardinal numbers," 367.
[17] *Ibid.,* 367.

ciples of Mathematics. Here he undertook to analyze the logical foundations of arithmetic and other parts of mathematics within the medium of ordinary language, without explicit recourse to Peano's symbolism. This volume, "which may be regarded either as a commentary upon, or as an introduction to, the second volume, is addressed in equal measure to the philosopher and to the mathematician."[18] The projected second volume, on the other hand, was to spare no rigor and no detail. Here the reader was to be exposed to the full blast of Peano's symbols. To quote Russell:

The second volume, in which I have had the great good fortune to secure the collaboration of Mr. A. N. Whitehead, will be addressed to mathematicians; it will contain chains of deductions, from the premisses of symbolic logic through Arithmetic, finite and infinite, to Geometry, in an order similar to that adopted in the present volume; it will also contain various original developments, in which the method of Professor Peano, as supplemented by the Logic of Relations, has shown itself a powerful instrument of mathematical investigation.[19]

Such was the collaboration on which Whitehead and Russell embarked in 1900, with little thought that they were to be engaged in it for eleven years. But, they recounted afterwards,

as we advanced it became increasingly evident that the subject is a very much larger one than we had supposed; moreover, on many fundamental questions which had been left obscure and doubtful in the former work, we have now arrived at what we believe to be satisfactory solutions. It therefore became necessary to make our book independent of *The Principles of Mathematics.*[20]

So Volume I of the *Principles* remained, like that of *Universal Algebra*, without a mate. Instead of Volume II there appeared, in 1910–13, one of the great intellectual monuments of all time: the three volumes of *Principia Mathematica.* Even this vast work stops short of the geometry that had been slated as part of Volume II of *Principles;* this material was deferred still to a projected fourth volume of *Principia.*[21]

---

[18] Bertrand Russell, *Principles of Mathematics* (Cambridge, Eng., 1903), Preface.
[19] *Ibid.*
[20] *Principia Mathematica,* Vol. 1, v.
[21] *Op. cit.,* Vol. 3, v–vi.

Part I of *Principia*, occupying the first half of the first volume, is entitled "Mathematical Logic."[22] It begins with what is substantially Boolean algebra in its simplest propositional interpretation; but without ' $=$ ', 'o', and '1', for we have seen (§III) that these are superfluous under this interpretation. The letters 'p', 'q', and others are used as propositional variables; and the Boolean operations of negation, addition, and multiplication— i.e., in the present interpretation, denial, alternation, and conjunction—are expressed in the fashion ' $\sim p$ ', '$p \lor q$', '$p \cdot q$'. Only the first two of these are taken as *primitive*, or undefined; the third is defined in terms of the other two as ' $\sim(\sim p \lor \sim q)$ '. Further defined compounds are '$p \supset q$' and '$p \equiv q$'; these are defined respectively as ' $\sim p \lor q$ ' and '$(p \supset q) \cdot (q \supset p)$', and are read '$p$ implies q' and 'p is equivalent to q'.

The laws:

$$(p \lor p) \supset p, \qquad q \supset (p \lor q), \qquad (p \lor q) \supset (q \lor p),$$
$$(q \supset r) \supset [(p \lor q) \supset (p \lor r)]$$

are adopted as formal axioms, together with a fifth that has since been proved redundant;[23] and a couple of hundred further laws, hitherto recorded for the most part by Boole's early followers C. S. Peirce and Ernst Schröder, are deduced from these axioms as theorems. The deductive procedures used are two: *substitution* of appropriate expressions for variables, and *modus ponens* (i.e., cancellation of the first part of a theorem or axiom of the form '$p \supset q$' when that first part is itself a theorem or axiom). Such rules of deductive procedure call for metalogical formulation (cf. §III), as rules *about* expressions of the sort that occur as axioms and theorems; however, the rule of *modus ponens* shows its metalogical status less clearly in *Principia* than it had in Frege's work, and the rule of substitution is left tacit altogether.[24]

---

[22] My discussion of *Principia* will relate solely to the first edition; for Whitehead had no hand in the Introduction and Appendices that were added to Vol. 1 in the second edition. Cf. *Mind*, n.s. Vol. 35 (1926), 130.

[23] Cf. Paul Bernays, "Axiomatische Untersuchungen des Aussagen-Kalkuls der 'Principia Mathematica'," *Math. Zeitschrift*, Vol. 25 (1926), 305-320.

[24] See Frege, *Grundgesetze der Arithmetik*, Vol. 1 (Jena, 1893), 25; Russell, *Introduction to Mathematical Philosophy* (London, 1919), 151.

Whitehead and Russell view definitions as conventions of abbreviation; thus '$p . q$', '$p \supset q$', and '$p \equiv q$' are mere shorthand for the more official renderings '$\sim(\sim p \vee \sim q)$', '$\sim p \vee q$', and '$(\sim p \vee q) . (\sim q \vee p)$'. Now over the legitimacy of such conventions there can be no dispute; but dispute may still arise over the attempt to paraphrase such a defined sign in words—e.g., '$.$' as 'and', '$\supset$' as 'implies', '$\equiv$' as 'is equivalent to'. Against reading '$\supset$' as 'implies', objections have indeed been raised.[25] It is objected that every false proposition then comes to imply every proposition, and that every true proposition comes to be implied by every proposition, in glaring violation of any ordinary idea of implication. Exception has been taken similarly to the proposed reading of '$\equiv$'.

This controversy would not have arisen if the notion of statements as naming had been carefully avoided, and the variables 'p', 'q', etc. had been treated explicitly as standing in positions appropriate to statements rather than names (cf. §III). The contested readings of '$\equiv$' and '$\supset$' would then never have suggested themselves. The natural readings are 'if and only if' and 'only if', which, like 'and' and 'or', are the sort of expressions that appropriately join statements to form statements. '$\equiv$' is the *biconditional* sign, and '$\supset$' the *conditional* sign. Implication and equivalence, on the other hand, are relations between statements, and hence are properly attributed by putting a verb 'implies' or 'is equivalent to' between *names of* the statements related. Such discourse belongs to metalogic.

In *Principia*, as in Frege's logic, one statement is capable of containing other statements *truth-functionally* only; i.e., in such a way that the truth value (truth or falsehood) of the whole remains unchanged when a true part is replaced by any other truth, or a false part by any other falsehood. Preservation of this principle of truth-functionality is essential to the simplicity and convenience of logical theory. In all departures from this norm that have to my knowledge ever been propounded, moreover, a sacrifice is made not only with regard to simplicity and convenience, but with regard even to the admissibility of a certain common-sense mode of inference: inference by inter-

---

[25] Notably by C. I. Lewis (*Survey of Symbolic Logic*, Berkeley, 1918, Chaps. IV–V).

changing terms that designate the same object.[26] On grounds
of technical expediency and on common-sense grounds as well,
thus, there is a strong case for the principle of truth-functionality. But it is a mistake to suppose that in order to preserve this
principle we must construe the relations of implication and
equivalence truth-functionally. It would be as reasonable to
suppose that we must so construe the relation of rhyming as to
make it depend on the truth values of the rhyming statements.
The principle of truth-functionality concerns only the constructing of statements from statements; whereas relationships such
as implication or equivalence or rhyming are properly ascribed
rather by attaching verbs to *names of* statements. It is regrettable that Frege's own scrupulous observance of this distinction
between an expression and its name, between use and mention,
was so little heeded by Whitehead, Russell, and their critics.

V

The theory of *quantification* occupies the next portion of Part
I of *Principia*. *Universal* quantification consists in attaching the
so-called *universal quantifier* '(x)' [or '(y)', etc.], which may be
read 'whatever object x [or y, etc.] may be', to an expression
that has the form of a statement but exhibits recurrences of the
variable 'x' [or 'y', etc.]. Thus (3), above, can be rendered as:

(7) $(x)(x$ interests every man $\supset x$ interests Socrates).

The part 'x interests every man' here can be rendered in turn as:

$(y)(y$ is a man $\supset x$ interests y),

so the whole becomes:

(8) $(x)((y)(y$ is a man $\supset x$ interests $y) \supset x$ interests Socrates),

whereas (6) becomes rather:

[26] C. I. Lewis and C. H. Langford (*Symbolic Logic*, New York, 1932), e.g., use a non-
truth-functional operator '$\Diamond$' to express logical possibility. Thus the statements:

$\Diamond$ (number of planets in solar system < 7),

$\Diamond$ $(9 < 7)$

would be judged as true and false respectively, despite the fact that they are intercon-
vertible by interchanging the terms '9' and 'number of planets in solar system', both of
which designate the same object. Similar examples are readily devised for the early
Whitehead system discussed in §III.

(9) $(x)((y)(y$ is a man $\supset y$ interests $x) \supset x$ interests Socrates).

Thus it is that quantification theory solves the problem of distinguishing between (3) and (6).

Existential quantification consists in applying rather the prefix '$(\exists x)$' [or '$(\exists y)$', etc.], which may be read 'there is an object x [or y, etc.] such that'. Thus 'Some primes are even' would be rendered:

(10) $(\exists x)(x$ is a prime . x is even).

Whitehead and Russell define this sort of quantification in terms of the other, by explaining '$(\exists x)$' as short for ' $\sim (x) \sim$ '.[27]

Just as in the simpler part of logic Whitehead and Russell used 'p', 'q', etc. to stand in place of statements, so in quantification theory they use 'ϕx', 'ψy', '$\chi(x, y)$', etc. to stand in place of expressions of the kind that I call *matrices*[28]—such expressions as 'x interests Socrates', 'y is a man', 'x interests y'. To the axioms hitherto noted, two more are now added:

$$(x)\phi x \supset \phi y, \qquad (x)(p \vee \phi x) \supset (p \vee (x)\phi x).$$

A hundred theorems are derived, by use of the two deductive procedures hitherto noted and three more: substitution for complexes such as 'ϕx', relettering of variables used in connection with quantifiers, and introduction of new initial quantifiers. The new rule of substitution, like the old one, is left tacit; and so is the rule of relettering. Correct formulation of these rules, particularly that of substitution, is not easy.[29]

In its main lines this theory of quantification follows Frege's. Peano's methods, though adequate to the same purposes, differed in essential respects and were not as elegant. Whitehead and Russell's notation, set forth above, is more expedient typographically than Frege's, but Frege's exposition was more precise.

---

[27] I am passing over the alternative development proposed in *9 of *Principia*. The main point of this alternative is in relation to the ramified theory of types, discussed in §VII below.

[28] *Mathematical Logic*, 71 ff.

[29] For a formulation of the rule of substitution see David Hilbert and Wilhelm Ackermann, *Grundzüge der theoretischen Logik*, 2d ed. (Berlin, 1938), 56 f. The attempted formulation in the 1st ed., p. 53, was wrong. For the rule of relettering, see my *Mathematical Logic*, §21.

Embedded within the midst of quantification theory, as rendered by Whitehead and Russell, there is an inconspicuous detail that embodies the germ of a Platonic ontology of universals. This detail is properly inessential to quantification theory itself, but in some form it is essential to any foundation of classical mathematics. It is just this: 'ϕ', 'ψ', etc. are allowed to occur in quantifiers. The significance of this inconspicuous detail will be clarified.

Let us consider again the letters 'p', 'q', etc. These belong to a schematism for diagrammatically depicting the patterns of compound statements. The letters enter the diagrams '$p \supset q$', '$\sim(p \,.\, \sim p)$', etc. as dummies for statements; they occupy positions that would be occupied by actual statements within any actual compound statement of the depicted pattern. Analogously, the complex variables 'ϕx', 'ϕy', 'ψx', '$\chi(x,y)$', etc. enter the diagrams as dummies for matrices; they are written in complex form only to remind us, e.g., that 'ϕx' and 'ϕy' supplant matrices that are alike except for their component variables 'x' and 'y'. Expressions involving dummies 'p', 'q', 'ϕx', etc. are from this point of view not statements, nor matrices, but diagrams or schemata; such in particular are the six axioms noted above. Moreover the variables 'p', 'q', etc., used thus in schemata, need not refer to objects of any sort as their *values;* nor do 'ϕx', 'ψy', etc. The statements and matrices that these variables supplant need not be viewed as *names of* anything at all (cf. §III).

The letters 'x', 'y', etc. themselves, fundamentally different in status from 'p', 'q', 'ϕx', etc., turn up not merely in schemata but also in the matrices themselves and even in actual statements—e.g. (7)–(10). These letters, adjuncts to the quantification notation, must be recognized as ordinary variables referring to objects. The context (10), e.g., is read 'There is *something x* such that *it* is prime and even'; and (7) is read '*Whatever entity x* may be, if *it* interests every man then *it* interests Socrates.' The letter 'x' does *refer*, in its pronominal fashion, to each of the entities of our universe—whatever those may be.[30]

[30] Cf. my "Designation and existence," *Journal of Philosophy*, Vol. 36 (1939), 701–709.

The effect of letting 'ϕ', 'ψ', etc. occur in quantifiers, now, is that these letters cease to be fragments merely of dummy matrices[31] 'ϕx', 'ψy', etc., and come to share the genuinely referential power of 'x', 'y', etc. They must now be regarded as variables in their own right, referring to some sort of abstract entities, perhaps *attributes*, as their values; and they are eligible now to occur in genuine matrices and statements.[32] One such statement is '$(\exists\phi)(x)\phi x$', which may be read 'There is an attribute ϕ such that, no matter what x may be, x has the attribute ϕ.' The juxtapositive notation 'ϕx', no longer an indissoluble dummy matrix, comes to express the *attribution* of an attribute ϕ on the one hand to an object x on the other. '$\phi(x, y)$', similarly, comes to express attribution of a *dyadic* or *relative* attribute ϕ to the respective objects x and y.

In putting 'ϕ', 'ψ', etc. in quantifiers Whitehead and Russell leap from quantification theory to a theory of attributes—a theory involving over and above quantification the notion of attribution. But this new notion is never explicitly recognized. The relevant distinctions are blurred by use of the phrase 'propositional function' to refer indiscriminately both to expressions of the kind that I have called matrices and to objects of the kind that I have called attributes.

It is properly on the theory of attributes, rather than that of quantification, that Whitehead and Russell's definition of *identity* is rested; for '$x = y$' is defined with help of quantified 'ϕ' as '$(\phi)(\phi x \supset \phi y)$',[33] i.e., 'Every attribute of x is an attribute of y'. The theory of identity is one of the many branches of logic and mathematics that are successively developed from the foregoing logical basis, in the course of *Principia*, by adop-

---

[31] My technical term for these is 'atomic matrix frames'. In general, diagrams or schemata for statements and matrices are in my terminology *frames*. The 'ϕ' occurring as a fragment of 'ϕx', 'ϕy', etc., I call a *predicate variable*; and 'p', 'q', etc., I call *statement variables*. Variables such as 'x', 'y', etc., that can occur in quantifiers and hence in actual matrices and statements, I call *pronominal variables*. See my *Elementary Logic* (Boston, 1941), §§14, 33, 42.

[32] I.e., the letters 'ϕ', 'ψ', etc. cease to be predicate variables and become pronominal variables whose values are attributes; cf. preceding footnote.

[33] I omit a complication involving the notion, discussed in §VII below, of "predicative function."

tion of appropriate definitions. The logical basis itself remains as above; further primitive equipment is never added.

The next branch of logical theory developed in *Principia* is that of *descriptions*. The notation of description consists in applying the prefix '$(\imath x)$' [or '$(\imath y)$', etc.] to a matrix in order to designate the one and only object x [or y, etc.] that satisfies the matrix; e.g., $(\imath x)(x^3 = 8)$ is the one and only number whose cube is 8, viz. 2. Notations to this effect were used by both Frege and Peano, but Russell was the first to define the device in terms of more basic notions.[34] His definition, used in *Principia*, is contextual: a description is explained not in isolation but as part of a broader context, which is defined as a whole. A whole context '$\psi(\imath x)\phi x$'—to use the schematic notation—is explained as an abbreviation for:

$$(\exists y)(x)((x = y \equiv \phi x) \cdot \psi y).$$

If there is one and only one object x such that ϕx—symbolically, if $(\exists y)(x)(x = y \equiv \phi x)$, or briefly $E!(\imath x)\phi x$—then the description '$(\imath x)\phi x$' as contextually defined comes to behave as if it designated that one object; and in other cases the context of the description simply becomes false. To speak of "the context" here is really ambiguous, since a single occurrence of a description commonly has many contexts of varying lengths; conventions are added, however, to resolve the ambiguity.

VI

In *Principia* the prefix '$\hat{x}$' (or '$\hat{y}$', etc.) is applied to a matrix to designate the class of all objects x (or y, etc.) satisfying that matrix. The class of all sons of lawyers, e.g., is

$$\hat{x}(\exists y)(y \text{ is a lawyer} \cdot x \text{ is son of } y).$$

This device of *abstraction of classes* had been used, under different notations, by Frege and Peano. A companion notation, due to Peano, is that of *membership:* '$x \, \epsilon \, \alpha$', meaning that x is a member of the class α. Thus the combination:

$$z \, \epsilon \, \hat{x}(\exists y)(y \text{ is a lawyer} \cdot x \text{ is son of } y)$$

[34] Russell, "On denoting," *Mind*, n.s. Vol. 14 (1905), 479–493; "Mathematical logic as based on the theory of types," *Amer. Journal of Math.*, Vol. 30 (1908), 222–262.

amounts merely to:

$$(\exists y)(y \text{ is a lawyer} . z \text{ is son of } y).$$

Any instance of the schema:

(11) $$(z \epsilon \hat{x}\phi x) \equiv \phi z$$

evidently holds in similar fashion.

But what sort of things are these classes? Not mere collections, or aggregates, in any concrete sense. A class α of concrete things is by no means identifiable with the concrete total object t made up of those things. On the contrary, α is not even determined by t; for α might have as members either many small parts of t or a few large ones. A class is an abstract entity, a universal, even if it happens to be a class of concrete things.

To the nominalist temper, accordingly, the elimination of classes in favor of expressions is a congenial objective; and this is what Russell is sometimes believed[35] to have done when he showed[36] how contexts ostensibly treating of classes could be construed as abbreviations of other expressions wherein reference is made only to "propositional functions." These constructions reappear in *Principia;* membership, abstraction, even quantification with respect to class variables 'α', 'β', etc., are introduced by contextual definition as notational abbreviations. The principle (11) is deduced, in view of these definitions, from the antecedent logical basis.

So long as 'propositional function' is thought of in the sense of 'matrix', such a construction would seem to serve its nominalistic objective; but actually Russell's construction involves use of 'ϕ', 'ψ', etc. in quantifiers, and hence calls for propositional functions in the sense rather of attributes. To have reduced classes to attributes is of little philosophical consequence, for attributes are no less universal, abstract, intangible, than classes themselves.

Indeed, there is no call even to distinguish attributes from classes, unless on this one technical score: classes are identified when they coincide in point of members, whereas it may be held that attributes sometimes differ though they are attributes

---

[35] See e.g. Hans Hahn, *Ueberflüssige Wesenheiten* (Vienna, 1930), 22.

[36] Russell, *op. cit.* (1908).

of just the same things. It is precisely this difference, in fact, and nothing more, that Russell's contextual definition of classes accommodates; his is a technical construction enabling us to speak ostensibly of identical classes by way of shorthand for discourse about coincident but perhaps non-identical attributes.

Such definition rests the clearer on the obscurer, and the more economical on the less. Classes are more economical than attributes because they are scarcer: they coalesce when their members are the same. Classes are clearer than attributes because they have a relatively definite principle of individuation: they differ from one another just in case their members differ, whereas attributes (if they diverge from classes at all) differ from one another also under additional circumstances whose nature is left, in *Principia*, quite unspecified. Furthermore any attempt to specify those additional circumstances may be expected eventually to run afoul of the rule of "putting equals for equals," analogously to what was observed earlier (§IV) in the case of non-truth-functional statement composition.

In any case there are no specific attributes that can be proved in *Principia* to be true of just the same things and yet to differ from one another. The theory of attributes receives no application, therefore, for which the theory of classes would not have served. Once classes have been introduced, attributes are scarcely mentioned again in the course of the three volumes.

The clear course would have been to introduce the membership notation '$x \in \alpha$' at an earlier point, as a primitive notation taking the place of the juxtapositive notation 'ϕx' insofar as the latter is used in its ill-recognized *attributional* sense. Thus, e.g., '$(\exists \alpha)(x)(x \in \alpha)$' would supplant '$(\exists \phi)(x)\phi x$'. The notation of class abstraction would still admit of definition, viz. by explaining '$\hat{x}\phi x$' as short for '$(\imath\alpha)(x)(x \in \alpha \equiv \phi x)$'.[37] Just one axiom schema would have to be added, viz. '$F\,!\hat{x}\phi x$';[38] whereupon (11) and all other principles of the *Principia* theory of classes would be forthcoming. The notation 'ϕx' might survive in the status of dummy matrix for expository convenience (as

[37] Substantially this definition was used by Whitehead on a later occasion ("Indication, classes, numbers, validation."

[38] Cf. §V, above. This schema combines P1 and R3 of my "New foundations for mathematical logic," *Amer. Math. Monthly*, Vol. 44 (1937), 70–80.

here), but 'ϕ' would never be isolated in quantifiers nor used in actual statements and matrices. The notion of attribute, insofar as it diverges from that of class, would not occur.

The course proposed would have been a little closer to Peano and Frege, and its adoption would have obviated some of the vaguest stretches of *Principia*. Perhaps it would have been adopted if the use of the phrase "propositional function" indiscriminately for matrices and for attributes had not obscured essential cleavages.

The contextual definition of classes is repeated in *Principia* for the dyadic case. Here, instead of classes properly so called, we have "relations in extension"—classes, substantially, of ordered pairs. Parallel to the notation '$x \epsilon \alpha$' of class membership, there is in the case of relations the notation 'xRy' to the effect that x bears the relation R to y. Abstraction, in the case of relations, is expressed by double prefixes such as '$\hat{x}\hat{y}$'.

The reform proposed above for the theory of classes carries over to the theory of relations in strict analogy. '$\hat{x}\hat{y}\phi(x, y)$' comes to be explained as short for:

$$(\imath R)(x)(y)[xRy \equiv \phi(x, y)],$$

while 'xRy' comes to figure as a primitive notation supplanting the attributional version of '$\phi(x, y)$'. An axiom schema analogous to '$E!\hat{x}\phi x$' has to be added, viz. '$E!\hat{x}\hat{y}\phi(x, y)$'.

This reform of the foundations does not affect the ensuing constructions. In the course of these constructions Boolean algebra is reconstructed in its classial interpretation, by defining the complement $-\alpha$ of a class α as $\hat{x}\sim(x \epsilon \alpha)$, the product of classes α and β as $\hat{x}(x \epsilon \alpha . x \epsilon \beta)$, and the sum as $\hat{x}(x \epsilon \alpha \lor x \epsilon \beta)$. The universal class, designated by 'V', is defined as $\hat{x}(x = x)$; and the null class Λ is defined in turn as $-V$. An exactly parallel algebra of relations is also developed, wherein the complement $\dot{-}R$ of a relation R is defined as $\hat{x}\hat{y}\sim(xRy)$, the product of relations $\mathcal{Q}$ and R as $\hat{x}\hat{y}(x\mathcal{Q}y . xRy)$, and so on. Theorems are deduced at considerable length in the class algebra, and then parallels are listed for relations.

This wasteful duality would have been avoided if, like Peano, the authors had treated relations quite literally as classes of ordered pairs. The notion of an ordered pair $x;y$ could be adopted as primitive, as in Peano, whereupon 'xRy' could be explained as short for '$x;y \in R$'. Relational abstraction, correspondingly, could be reduced to class abstraction by explaining $\hat{x}\hat{y}\phi(x, y)$ as

$$\hat{z}(\exists x)(\exists y)(z = x;y \cdot \phi(x, y)).$$

Such of relation theory as parallels general class theory then comes, in large part, simply to be absorbed into the latter. Incidentally the axiom schema '$E!\hat{x}\hat{y}\phi(x, y)$', noted above, now becomes dispensable in favor of:

$$(x;y = z;w) \supset (x = z \cdot y = w).$$

And one of the advances in logic since *Principia* is the discovery by Wiener[39] that this latter axiom and the primitive notion of ordered pair that it governs can be eliminated in turn. The ordered pair is satisfactorily definable on the basis of class theory alone.

VII

Russell was the first to discover that the principle (11), if admitted without special restrictions of one sort or another, leads to contradiction. If in particular we put 'α' for 'x', '$\sim(\alpha \in \alpha)$' for 'ϕx', and '$\hat{\alpha}\sim(\alpha \in \alpha)$' for '$z$', we get as an instance of (11) the self-contradictory statement:

(12) $[\hat{\alpha}\sim(\alpha \in \alpha) \in \hat{\alpha}\sim(\hat{\alpha} \in \alpha)] \equiv \sim[\hat{\alpha}\sim(\alpha \in \alpha) \in \hat{\alpha}\sim(\alpha \in \alpha)].$

Both Frege's logic and Peano's turn out, in this way, to be involved in contradiction.

Russell's remedy is his *theory of types*. Every class is conceived as belonging to one and only one of a hierarchy of so-called types; and any formula that represents membership as holding otherwise than between members of consecutive ascending types is rejected as meaningless, along with all its contexts. In particular, thus, '$\alpha \in \alpha$' and all its contexts are meaningless. Such is the status of (12), which thus ceases to count as an instance of (11). (12) is only one of infinitely many contradictions derivable from (11); but all these, so far as is known, are banished like (12) by the theory of types.

---

[39] Norbert Wiener, "A simplification of the logic of relations," *Proc. Camb. Phil. Soc.*, Vol. 17 (1912–14), 387–390.

Relation theory, though, involves analogous contradictions, so Russell has to extend the theory of types to cover relations as well as classes. The theory here is more complicated; the two degrees of freedom implicit in the ordered pair call for more than a simple hierarchy of types. The theory of "propositional functions," insofar as it makes use of 'ϕ', 'ψ', etc. in quantifiers, is of course no less liable to the contradictions than are class theory and relation theory; and from the point of view of *Principia* it is actually not to classes and relations but to "propositional functions" that the basic version of type theory applies. From this equivocal realm the theory is transmitted to classes and relations through the contextual definitions of these latter.

As applied to propositional functions the theory undergoes a special complication: a hierarchy of *orders* is superimposed, such that propositional functions may differ as to order even though they be of the same type. This ramification of type theory proves to subject logic and mathematics to certain intolerable restrictions, for the removal of which an *axiom of reducibility* is adopted. According to this axiom, every propositional function is satisfied by exactly the same arguments as some propositional function which is *predicative*, i.e., which has the lowest order compatible with its type.

This ramification of type theory is designed for the avoidance of certain contradictions of a quite different sort from (12). But the treatment is vague, on account of failure to distinguish between expressions and their names. On restoring this distinction one finds that the contradictions against which this part of type theory was directed are no business of logic anyway; they can arise only in discourse that goes beyond pure logic and imports semantic terms such as 'true' or 'designates'. The whole ramification, with the axiom of reducibility, calls simply for amputation.[40]

It is readily seen also on other grounds that this part of type theory was bound to be wholly idle. The axiom of reducibility assures us that from the beginning we could have construed the notations of *Principia* as referring exclusively to so-called pre-

[40] Cf. F. P. Ramsey, *Foundations of Mathematics* (London and New York, 1931), 20–29.

dicative "propositional functions" (predicative *attributes*); but when this is done, the resulting logic is the same as if neither "orders" nor "predicativity" nor "reducibility" had been thought of in the first place.[41] That this simple situation escaped the attention of the authors is attributable, again, to the ambiguity of "propositional function" and the underlying difficulty over use and mention.

The residual unramified type theory, as applied to classes and relations, is actually the only form of type theory that figures even in *Principia* after the first couple of hundred pages; for, as remarked, "propositional functions" are soon submerged. But even this simpler version of type theory is a source of much complexity of technical detail.

Because the theory allows a class to have members only of uniform type, the universal class V gives way to an infinite series of quasi-universal classes, one for each type. The negation $-\alpha$ ceases to comprise all non-members of α, and comes to comprise only those non-members of α which are next lower in type than α. Even the null class Λ gives way to an infinite series of null classes. The Boolean class algebra no longer applies to classes in general, but is reproduced rather within each type. The same is true of the calculus of relations. Even arithmetic, when introduced by definitions on the basis of logic, proves to be subject to the same reduplications. Thus the numbers cease to be unique; a new o appears for each type, likewise a new 1, and so on, just as in the case of V and Λ. Not only are all these cleavages and reduplications intuitively repugnant, but they call continually for more or less elaborate technical manoeuvres by way of restoring severed connections.[42]

In particular, an awkward effect is obstruction of the proof that $n \neq n + 1$ for all finite n; this principle comes rather to be cited as hypothesis where needed (cf. §IX), and Whitehead and Russell avoid it whenever they can at the cost of more circuitous proofs. In one way and another the theory of types accounts for perhaps a fifth of the page-count of the three volumes.

A few years ago Whitehead presented an alternative founda-

[41] Cf. my paper "On the axiom of reducibility," *Mind*, n.s. Vol. 45 (1936), 498–500.
[42] From my "New foundations for mathematical logic," *Amer. Math. Mo.*, Vol. 44, 78 f.

tion for arithmetic, designed both to obviate the reduplication of numbers and to render '$n \neq n + 1$' demonstrable in straightforward logical fashion.[43] His method, though, is costly; for it turns essentially on the use of statements in non-truth-functional contexts (cf. §IV). For all its cost, moreover, the method continues to presuppose the theory of attributes (using 'ϕ', 'ψ', etc. in quantifiers); and in that domain the theory of types remains intact.

Whatever the inconveniences of type theory, contradictions such as (12) show clearly enough that the previous naïve logic needed reforming. The theory of types (as applied to classes and relations, hence without the *ramus amputandus*) remains one of the important proposals for a reformed logic. There have been other proposals to the same end—one of them even coeval with the theory of types.[44] None of these other proposals involves that reduplicative situation whose irksomeness, for Whitehead among others, has been noted; and not all of these proposals obstruct the proof that $n \neq n + 1$.[45]

But a striking circumstance is that none of these proposals, type theory included, has any intuitive foundation. None has the backing of common sense. Common sense is bankrupt, for it wound up in contradiction. Deprived of his tradition, the logician has had to resort to myth-making. That myth will be best that engenders a form of logic most convenient for mathematics and the sciences; and perhaps it will become the common sense of another generation.

VIII

In the remainder of Part I numerous special notions having to do with relations are defined and hundreds of theorems are derived. One important notion is $R``\alpha$, the class of all objects bearing R to any members of α. The definition is obvious: $\hat{x}(\exists y)(y \in \alpha . xRy)$. Another is the *relative product* $R \mid S$, defined as $\hat{x}\hat{z}(\exists y)(xRy . ySz)$. Another is $\breve{R}$, the *converse* of R,

---

[43] "Indication, classes, numbers, validation."

[44] Ernst Zermelo, "Untersuchungen über die Grundlagen der Mengenlehre I," *Math. Annalen*, Vol. 65 (1908), 261–281.

[45] In my *Mathematical Logic*, e.g., this is readily deducible from †677 (p. 252) with help of mathematical induction.

defined as $\hat{y}\hat{x}(xRy)$. These notions had figured prominently in the early work on relation theory by Augustus De Morgan and C. S. Peirce. But these pioneers did not distinguish explicitly between the first two of the notions; Frege was the first to do so.

Another important notion is $R^{\iota}x$, defined as $(\imath y)(yRx)$. So long as one and only one thing bears R to x, that thing is $R^{\iota}x$. If in keeping with modern trends we explain a *function* in general as a one-many relation, i.e., a relation that no two things bear to the same thing,[46] then the notation '$R^{\iota}x$' may be spoken of as that of functional *application;* where R is a function, $R^{\iota}x$ is the value of R for the argument x.

Special functions D, ɑ, $\overrightarrow{R}$, and $\overleftarrow{R}$ are then defined, in such a way that D$^{\iota}R$, ɑ$^{\iota}R$, $\overrightarrow{R}^{\iota}x$, and $\overleftarrow{R}^{\iota}x$ turn out to be respectively $\hat{x}(\exists y)(xRy)$, $\hat{y}(\exists x)(xRy)$, $\hat{y}(yRx)$, and $\hat{y}(xRy)$. But this and other portions of *Principia* would have been shorter and better if every new notation had been required to pay its way or suffer deletion. D$^{\iota}R$ and ɑ$^{\iota}R$, called the *domain* and *converse domain* of R, could have been expressed quite as briefly in terms of previous notions, without further definition; viz., as $R^{\iota\iota}$V and $\breve{R}^{\iota\iota}$V. Also, given Peano's notation 'ιx' for the class $\hat{y}(y = x)$ whose sole member is x, the notations '$\overrightarrow{R}^{\iota}x$' and '$\overleftarrow{R}^{\iota}x$' could have been dropped in favor of $R^{\iota\iota}\iota x$ and $\breve{R}^{\iota\iota}\iota x$. Use of '$R^{\iota\iota}$V', '$\breve{R}^{\iota\iota}$V', '$R^{\iota\iota}\iota x$', and '$\breve{R}^{\iota\iota}\iota x$' would have called for very few special theorems, over and above the general ones governing '$R^{\iota\iota}\alpha$'. On the other hand the adoption of 'D$^{\iota}R$' and the rest calls for chapters of additional theorems by way of relating these new notations to old ones and to one another; and thereupon we find ourselves manipulating 'D$^{\iota}R$', 'ɑ$^{\iota}R$', etc. according to the new special laws, neglecting general laws about '$R^{\iota\iota}\alpha$' that would have served as well. It is important to remember that algorithmic power turns not on assorted occurrences of many signs, but on repeated occurrences of a few.

Functional application, under a different notation, played a

---

[46] Cf. Peano, "Sulla definizione di funzione," *Atti della Reale Accad. dei Lincei*, Rendiconti, classe di sci. fis., mat., e nat., Vol. 20 (1911), 3–5.

prominent role in Frege's logic; and so did a companion notion of functional *abstraction*. This latter consists in applying the prefix 'λ_x' (or 'λ_y', etc.)[47] to a term containing 'x' (or 'y', etc.), in order to designate the function whose value, for any argument x, is the object referred to by the original term; thus $\lambda_x(x^3)$ is the function "cube of," i.e., the function whose value for any argument x is x^3. Functional abstraction is related to functional application precisely as class abstraction is related to membership. Just as membership cancels class abstraction (cf. (11)), so application cancels functional abstraction; $\lambda_x(x^3)$ ' y, e.g., is y^3. Functional abstraction is readily introduced on the basis of relational abstraction; $\lambda_x(x^3)$, e.g., is simply $\hat{y}\hat{x}(y = x^3)$.

The fact that functional abstraction was not carried over into *Principia* accounts for a good deal of inelegance. A special definition is adopted, e.g., explaining 'R_ϵ' as short for '$\hat{\beta}\hat{\alpha}(\beta = R``\alpha)$'; whereas '$\lambda_\alpha(R``\alpha)$', if available, would have served instead of that special sign. The devious course of defining 'D' in isolation as '$\hat{\alpha}\hat{R}[\alpha = \hat{x}(\exists y)(xRy)]$', instead of defining 'DR' outright as '$\hat{x}(\exists y)(xRy)$' (or using '$R``V$' instead), is another consequence of the lack of functional abstraction. The course was prompted by the need of D, on rare occasions, as a function in its own right; but if functional abstraction had been at hand, the infrequent need of 'D' in isolation would have been served by '$\lambda_R DR$' (or '$\lambda_R(R``V)$'). The situation is precisely similar with '$\complement$', '$\overrightarrow{R}$', and '$\overleftarrow{R}$'; and the situation is similar also with 'ι', for Whitehead and Russell introduce Peano's 'ιx' as '$\iota`x$' in parallel fashion to 'D$`R$' and the rest. Profitable use might have been made of functional abstraction at many other places in *Principia* as well.[48]

IX

Classes are said to have the same *cardinal number* just in case they are respectively the domain and the converse domain of a *one-one* relation; i.e., of a function (in the sense lately ex-

[47] I depart from Frege's notation in favor of Church's, which is more familiar nowadays.

[48] Notably Vol. 1, *38 *passim;* Vol. 2, *150·01·02.

plained) whose converse is a function. Where α and β are any mutually exclusive classes whose respective cardinal numbers are μ and ν, the arithmetical *sum* of μ and ν is defined as the cardinal number of the logical sum of α and β; the arithmetical *product* of μ and ν is the cardinal number of the class of all pairs $i;j$ such that $i \in \alpha$ and $j \in \beta$; and μ to the *power* ν is the cardinal number of the class of all functions having β as converse domain and part or all of α as domain. A number is *infinite* if it is at once the cardinal number of distinct classes α and β such that $\alpha \subset \beta$, i.e., such that $(x)(x \in \alpha \supset x \in \beta)$; otherwise *finite*. o is defined as the cardinal number of the null class; 1 is the cardinal number of classes of the form ιx; and each further finite cardinal is expressible in terms of 1 and arithmetical addition. The first infinite cardinal, $\aleph_0$, is defined as the cardinal number of the class of all finite cardinals. The *ordering* of cardinals is fixed by the stipulation that $\mu \leq \nu$ wherever μ and ν are the cardinal numbers respectively of classes α and β such that $\alpha \subset \beta$.

Such are the elementary constructions of Cantor's theory of cardinal numbers. This much was set forth explicitly by Peano in his logical notation.[49] But note that the cardinal number of α, symbolically Num α, has bèen defined only in the context 'Num α = Num β'; not in isolation. Actually Num α could very easily be defined in isolation, viz. as the class of all domains of one-one relations having α as converse domain; and such, years earlier, was Frege's course.[50] But Peano rejected this course, asserting groundlessly that Num α and the class in question "ont des propriétés différentes."[51]

In early sections of Whitehead's 1902 paper "On cardinal numbers," Peano's formulation of Cantor's constructions is reproduced with certain emendations attributed to Russell. Here Frege's definition of cardinal number that Peano had rejected is adopted. Here also we find a definition of the class of finite cardinals that goes back to Frege; it turns not on the Cantorian

[49] Peano, *Formulaire de mathématiques*, Vol. 3 (Paris, 1901), 70–72.
[50] Frege, *Grundlagen der Arithmetik* (Breslau, 1884), 79–85; *Grundgesetze der Arithmetik*, Vol. 1 (Jena, 1893), 56 f.
[51] *Loc. it.*, 70.

criterion indicated above, but rather on the idea of accessibility from o by successive additions of 1. It goes into the *Principia* notation thus:

$$\hat{\mu}(\kappa)\,[(\nu)(\nu \,\epsilon\, \kappa \,\supset\, \nu+1 \,\epsilon\, \kappa) \,\supset\, (\text{o} \,\epsilon\, \kappa \,\supset\, \mu \,\epsilon\, \kappa)\,].$$

Russell had learned it through Dedekind, being ignorant still of Frege when this paper went to press.

In this paper Whitehead redefines the power μ^ν as the number of ways of picking exactly one member from each of ν mutually exclusive classes having μ members apiece; and he derives the old definition as a theorem. Further, he defines the sum and the product of any class of cardinals—covering the case where the cardinals belonging to the class are not merely infinite but infinitely numerous. He proves various familiar arithmetical theorems, in extension to infinite cardinals; the most striking case, perhaps, is the binomial theorem, whose explicit formulation alone is no small undertaking.

The proofs of various of the theorems in this paper and its sequel[52] depend on two hypotheses: (1) every infinite class is exhaustively resoluble into parts having $\aleph_0$ members apiece, and (2) of any two cardinal numbers one exceeds the other. Both are reducible to a far more basic hypothesis, Zermelo's famous *axiom of choice;* but this was for the future, for the axiom itself dates only from 1904.[53]

The definitions in the two Whitehead papers tend to be less rigorous than in Peano. Many of them omit essential quantifiers.[54] In the definition of the number 1 there is also a further defect, whereby the null class comes inadvertently to be admitted as a member of 1.[55] There is a notation of multiplication that receives no definition, though it appears in two theorems.[56] In general the proofs of theorems are sketchy; and in particular I have been unable to decipher the alleged proof that $n \neq n + 1$ for finite n.[57]

[52] Whitehead, "Theorems on cardinal numbers."

[53] Zermelo, "Beweis, dass jede Menge wohlgeordnet werden kann," *Math. Annalen*, Vol. 59 (1904), 514–516.

[54] I.e., essential subscripts; for Peano's notation is used.

[55] "On cardinal numbers," 378, also 373.

[56] *Ibid.*, 381 (4·21·22).

[57] *Ibid.*, 379 (2·1).

Still the two papers were highly significant, affording as they did the first considerable development of infinite arithmetic within mathematical logic. Cantor and others had used no logical formalism; Peano had deduced none but a few trivial theorems in infinite arithmetic; and Frege, though deducing the laws of finite arithmetic in rigorous detail, did little with infinite numbers.

Principia was in progress, and these two papers were early progress reports. Subsequent progress was both qualitative and quantitative. In the finished *Principia*, Parts II–III, the concepts of cardinal arithmetic are constructed more elegantly than before and a good level of rigor is maintained. The axiom of choice is now used explicitly as a hypothesis where needed; and so is another principle, the so-called *axiom of infinity*, which for *Principia* is equivalent to the troublesome law that $n \neq n + 1$ for finite n (cf. § VII). With and without the help of these hypotheses, hundreds of theorems on finite and infinite cardinals and ancillary topics are deduced. In Part V, Cantor's theory of finite and infinite *ordinal* numbers is developed, followed by remnants of cardinal arithmetic that depend on the theory of ordinals. In point both of rigor and of comprehensiveness, these portions of *Principia* remain the authoritative work on cardinals and ordinals.

The theory of ordinals is part of that of *ordered sets;* for, just as a cardinal is a class of classes all having the same number of members, so an ordinal is a class of so-called *well ordered* sets all having the same number of members arranged in similar orders. To an ordered set, two things matter—the members and their order; so we might think of an ordered set as a complex, somehow, of a class α and a "before-after" relation R among members of α. However, specification of α is superfluous; α is already determined by R, being simply the field of R, i.e., the logical sum $C'R$ of $D'R$ and $Q'R$. Hence the ordered set can be adequately treated simply by identifying it with R; and such is the course adopted by Whitehead and Russell. Ordered sets are not identified with relations in general, but with those relations R that have the "before-after" kind of structure. This condition on R breaks up into three:

Asymmetry: $(x)(y) \sim (xRy . yRx)$,

Transitivity: $(x)(y)(z) [(xRy . yRz) \supset xRz]$,

Connexity: $(x)(y) [(x \in C'R . y \in C'R) \supset (xRy \lor yRx \lor x = y)]$.

In *Principia* such a relation R is called *serial*. For *well*-ordering, yet a fourth condition is needed:

$$(\beta) [(\beta \subset \check{R}''\beta) \supset (\beta = \Lambda)].$$

Given all four conditions on R, there is still latitude as regards further details of structure; and the class of all well ordered serial relations that agree with R in all such further details is taken as the *ordinal number* of R.

It should be noted that Whitehead and Russell's identification of an ordered set with the relation of "before-after" therein is somewhat arbitrary; we could identify it rather with the relation "no later than" in the set (thus choosing the analogue of "$\leqq$" rather than that of "$<$"). This alternative approach, which is gaining in favor, has certain advantages; e.g., it restores the ordinal number 1,[58] anomalously missing under the Whitehead-Russell method.

The theory of ordered sets, or series, is broader than that of well ordered sets and ordinals. In general, ordered sets or serial relations that coincide in all further details of structure are said to belong to the same *order type*. Ordinal numbers are thus special sorts of order types, viz. those of well ordered series. In *Principia* order types are spoken of rather as *serial numbers;* but their analogy to numbers is slight, for, unlike the ordinals, they do not all fall into a serial order of "magnitude." In the theory of ordered sets generally, what has interested mathematicians is not a quasi-arithmetic of order types, but rather the notion of the *limit* of a set and derivative notions. This branch of theory, known as analytic set theory, is rigorously developed from logic in the course of Part V of *Principia*.

Order type or serial number is, we saw, the generalization of ordinal number that is reached by waiving the requirement of well-ordering. But a still broader generalization—called *relation number* in *Principia*—is reached by waiving the requirement of

[58] This was called to my attention by Dr. Alfred Tarski.

seriality in turn and considering relations generally. The theory of relation numbers is the general theory of isomorphism, i.e., of structural identity among relations. It embraces the theory of ordering and of well-ordering, inasmuch as serial numbers and ordinal numbers are simply the relation numbers of ordered and well ordered sets; but it also embraces wider theories, e.g., that of partial order. The theory of relation numbers occupies Part IV of *Principia;* serial and ordinal numbers appear only afterward, as specializations. Emphasis is put on the analogies, insofar as there are such, between relation numbers and cardinals; but these relationships would have come out somewhat more clearly and simply if relations had been treated literally as classes of ordered pairs (cf. §VI).

X

Part VI, "Quantity," occupies the last half of the last volume of *Principia.* Attention is here turned to the arithmetic of signed integers, ratios, and real numbers. Following Peano, the authors construe the signed integers $+\mu$ and $-\mu$ in effect as the function $\lambda_\nu(\nu + \mu)$ and its converse, where μ is any finite cardinal. Arithmetical notions such as sum, product, and power, defined hitherto for cardinals, are now defined again appropriately for signed integers; and a train of theorems is deduced.

Peano's way of construing ratios, viz. by identifying μ/ν with $\hat{\mu}'\hat{\nu}'(\mu \times \nu' = \mu' \times \nu)$ for all finite cardinals μ and ν, is abandoned by Whitehead and Russell in favor of a version whereby μ/ν becomes a relation not between cardinal numbers but between relations. Roughly, μ/ν is construed as the relation which $\mathcal{Q}$ bears to R just in case there are things x and y such that x bears $\mathcal{Q}|\mathcal{Q}| \cdots$ (ν times) and likewise $R|R| \cdots$ (μ times) to y. Think of $\mathcal{Q}$ and R as vectors or transformations, applicable over and over; then $\mathcal{Q}$ bears μ/ν to R if ν applications of $\mathcal{Q}$ do the work of μ applications of R. (In the definition actually adopted a complication is added whose purpose is to minimize the dependence of rational arithmetic on the axiom of infinity; but it is a complication engendered merely by the theory of types.)

This version of ratios is interesting in that it makes ratios immediately applicable to relations generally, arithmetical and otherwise. The grandparent relation, e.g., stands in the ratio 2/5 to the great-great-great-grandparent relation. Such applicability proves useful in a subsequently expounded theory of measurement. A further virtue of this version is the naturalness with which the series of ratios so construed admits of extension to include negatives. The negative of a ratio P is defined in effect as $P \mid \lambda_R \breve{R}$. The negative of the ratio 2/5 obtains, e.g., between the grandparent relation and the great-great-great-grandchild relation.

A real number is explained, substantially, as any class of ratios that (1) does not contain all the ratios, but (2) contains any given ratio if and only if it contains also a higher. (Actually an exception is made, inelegantly and gratuitously, in connection with 0.[59]) That those classes form a model of the traditional real number series was first pointed out by Dedekind.[60] In this version of real numbers, the ratios alluded to are to be understood of course as just positive and zero; and the real numbers thus accounted for are likewise just positive and zero. But one can build the negative reals on the negative ratios in quite analogous fashion; and Whitehead and Russell do so.

They also develop an attractive alternative construction of real numbers, the effect of which is to increase the kinship between real numbers and ratios. Here a real number is identified not with a class α of ratios, as above, but rather with the relation whose ordered pairs are got by pooling all the ratios belonging to such a class α. Real numbers so construed are, like ratios, relations between relations.

For real numbers in both senses, as well as for ratios, Whitehead and Russell set up the full complement of associated arithmetical notions and prove many theorems. Then they turn to the concluding topic of *Principia*, which is *measurement*. In dim outline, the development of this topic proceeds as follows.

Any one-one relation R that is *repeatable* (i.e., such that everything to which R is borne bears R to something in turn) is called a *vector*. A class κ ($\neq \Lambda$) of vectors all having the same field α, and such further that the order of applying any two of

[59] *Principia*, Vol. 3, 316 f.
[60] Richard Dedekind, *Stetigkeit und irrationale Zahlen* (Brunswick, 1872).

the vectors is immaterial $(P|\mathcal{Q} = \mathcal{Q}|P)$, is called a *vector-family of α*. Now a *magnitude* is thought of as a vector; the gram, e.g., is thought of as the vector "a gram more than." *Kinds* of magnitude, e.g., mass, length, etc., are certain vector-families. *Measurement*, finally, consists in determining ratios between members of some vector-family κ; and here we see the special utility of the adopted version of ratios as relations of relations. In cases where irrational measures are called for, use is made not of ratios but of real numbers—which still are relations of relations, under the second version. A general theory of so-called *nets* is begun, with a view to the introduction of geometrical coördinates in the projected fourth volume.

Measurement is ordinarily thought of as a concern of natural science; and we should scarcely venture to derive the concepts of natural science from pure logic. But we may still venture to formulate the conceptual *structure* of natural science in purely logical terms. Insofar as certain terms, say of physics, are constructible from other more basic ones by logical devices, we may reproduce the constructions using variables in place of those basic physical terms. Along these lines we arrive at purely logical functions that make up—more and more exhaustively as we proceed—the logical component of natural science. "Application" of these logical constructs to the world consists merely in assigning values, of the appropriate extra-logical sort, to the variables.

Such is the intended status of the theory of measurement developed in *Principia*. When we take κ as a certain physically specified class of vectors, we have a rudimentary theory of mass; when we take κ as another class, we have a rudimentary theory of length; and so on. Physical laws, insofar as they imply relevant differences between these various choices of κ, will supply differences in detail between the theory of mass, the theory of length, etc.

Application of the general theory in this wise encounters some difficulty on the score of the repeatability clause in the definition of vector. If we construe the gram, e.g., as the relation "heavier by a gram than" as between physical objects, then after a certain point the finitude of mass of the universe will obstruct repeatability. If we are to take the gram as a vector, it seems we must take it not as the described relation between bodies but rather as the relation "a gram more than" as between entities that are in turn abstract quantities in some sense or other. Such, indeed, is the intention of Whitehead and Russell;[61] but then we are left farther frum the physical application than might have been desired.

Analysis of the logical structure of natural science had been occupying Whitehead as early as 1906, when he published a paper "to initiate the mathematical investigation of various possible ways of conceiving the nature of the material world."[62] The constructions in that paper are couched in the regular *Principia* notation, and foreshadow to some degree the projected volume on geometry; and a continuation is outlined in Whitehead's later writings[63] under the head of "extensive abstraction." Other constructions in the 1906 paper go far outside geometry; this was the beginning of a quest for the broadest, most basic concepts and principles of nature, and in the decades since *Principia* the quest has issued in a metaphysics.

WILLARD V. QUINE

DEPARTMENT OF PHILOSOPHY
HARVARD UNIVERSITY

[61] Cf. *Principia*, Vol. 3, 339.
[62] "On mathematical concepts of the material world," 465.
[63] "La théorie rélationniste de l'espace;" *The Principles of Natural Knowledge; The Concept of Nature; Process and Reality.*

3

Filmer S. C. Northrop

WHITEHEAD'S PHILOSOPHY OF SCIENCE

3
WHITEHEAD'S PHILOSOPHY OF SCIENCE

THE number of philosophers of the first order who were scientists before they became philosophers is notable. Democritus, Leucippus, Plato, Aristotle, Albertus Magnus, Descartes, Leibniz, and Kant are but a few. Professor Whitehead continues this great tradition.

Forty years of his life, following his election as a Fellow in Trinity College in Cambridge University, were given to mathematical science. During these years his treatise on *Universal Algebra* was published and *Principia Mathematica* was written in collaboration with Bertrand Russell. The normally ripe age of sixty-one found him still teaching mathematical physics at the Imperial College of Science and Technology in London. Not until most thinkers consider their creative work to be over did our subject leave science for professional philosophy.

This move he regarded as a pursuit of rather than a retreat from science. Four books written during the later years of his professional scientific career had prepared the way for this development. They were *The Organization of Thought* (1917), *The Principles of Natural Knowledge* (1919), *The Concept of Nature* (1920), and *The Principle of Relativity* (1922). Dealing with the reconstruction in our scientific concepts necessitated by contemporary scientific discoveries, and especially by Einstein's theory of relativity, these treatises initiated a new philosophy in order adequately to meet the problems and express the findings of a new science.

It has been necessary to remind ourselves of these historical facts because since then *Process and Reality* has been published. The novelty, imaginative scope, and metaphysical subtlety of this work have tended to cover up the earlier treatises, to the detriment not merely of a study and appreciation of Whitehead's philosophy of science but also of *Process and Reality* itself. For it must be noted that the last third of this work is given exclusively to the philosophy of science. Not merely in its chronological origin but also in its final conclusion Whitehead's most systematic and definitive metaphysical book is part and parcel of his philosophy of science.

The time has come, therefore, to turn back from *Process and Reality* to Whitehead's earlier scientific and philosophical treatises. In them we find his doctrine taking its inception, we discover the factors which have made it what it is, and we have it in close relation to technical scientific evidence as well as to general philosophical intuition, where we can judge of its truth or falsity.

A complete study of his philosophy of science should include the last third of *Process and Reality* as well as the four earlier treatises. The spatial limitations of this chapter force us to select and concentrate. We restrict ourselves to the earlier works and in particular to *The Concept of Nature* and *The Principle of Relativity*. In this there is gain as well as loss, as it gives us the philosophy of science which he held before his metaphysics became systematically articulate. A later study may indicate the extent, if any, to which the formulation of his metaphysics modified his philosophy of science. Here we pursue the philosophy of science which prepared the way for *Process and Reality*.

Three major factors determined its character. The first was the reconstruction in the basic concepts of science made necessary by Einstein's theory of relativity. The story here is a technical and complicated one, since Whitehead both follows and departs from Einstein. The second factor was the epistemological difficulties into which the traditional modern scientific theories had forced modern philosophy. This led to Whitehead's rejection of "the bifurcation of nature," where by "bifurcation" is meant the distinction between nature as sensed and nature as designated by scientific theory.[1] The third was a Bergsonian influence which came to Whitehead through his personal friend, the late H. Wildon Carr. During those impressionable war

---

[1] *The Concept of Nature*, 30, 40; *The Principle of Relativity*, 39.

years, when Whitehead's philosophy of science was taking shape, Carr was writing a book on Bergson and continuously conversing with Whitehead concerning the French philosopher. From this source came the doctrine of the primacy of process, which is as basic to Whitehead's philosophy of science as it is to his metaphysics. Alexander reinforced this tendency, as the Preface to *The Concept of Nature* indicates.

THE IMPORTANCE OF THE BERGSONIAN INFLUENCE

This factor can hardly be exaggerated. It presented the basic concept and doctrine of Whitehead's entire scientific and philosophical outlook.

With only one major point in Bergson's doctrine did Whitehead disagree. This was Bergson's contention that spatialization in science is falsification. Whitehead found himself unable to understand how the use of spatial concepts in scientific procedure could enable the scientists to predict with the precision they achieve, were spatialization the falsification of fact which Bergson maintained.

Consequently, Whitehead conceived it to be one of his major tasks to follow Bergson in accepting duration and process as primary and at the same time to derive the concepts of space in a manner that will exhibit them as concrete factors in fact. In *The Concept of Nature* this is achieved. As we shall show later, the relatedness of space and its order for a given moment of time is defined in terms of temporal concepts.

The Bergsonian emphasis on immediate intuition led Whitehead to deny any scientific knowledge except that given by sense awareness. "Nature," Whitehead writes in *The Concept of Nature*, "is nothing else than the deliverance of sense-awareness."[2] All scientific concepts are consequently derivable from what is immediately sensed by mere abstraction, and any "bifurcation of nature" into the sensed and the postulated must be rejected.[3] There are other reasons for the rejection of bifurcation.

[2] P. 185.
[3] *The Concept of Nature*, chap. III and IV.

The Epistemological Difficulties of
Modern Philosophy

One of the most acute of contemporary epistemologists, Professor A. E. Murphy, after having examined the diverse attempts to solve the epistemological problems of modern philosophy and after developing a theory of his own known as objective relativism, only apparently to become disillusioned by it, has finally decided that any motion to consider any particular theory as having provided the solution had best be tabled.[4]

Two decades earlier Whitehead had reached the same conclusion and arrived at a theory concerning why it is necessary. The theory is that the problems of modern epistemology are insoluble within the assumptions which define them. These assumptions were imposed upon modern philosophy by "the bifurcation of nature" into the immediately sensed and the postulated-but-not-sensed which Galilei and Newton first introduced and which Einstein and the contemporary physicists, as Whitehead realizes[5] and as we shall show, are still continuing. In this connection it is relevant to note that all modern philosophers took Newton's physics for granted and that Locke and Kant were devout followers of Newton, Kant being a mathematician and physicist who discovered the nebular hypothesis by the aid of Newton's principles before he became a philosopher.

Impressed by the insolubility of the epistemological problems of modern philosophy within the scientific assumptions which give rise to them, Whitehead concludes that the only way out is a new theory of the fundamental concepts of science which, by avoiding bifurcation, prevents these insoluble epistemological problems from arising.

In his book *The Principle of Relativity*,[6] Whitehead writes:

The molecular theory, the wave theory of light, and finally the electromagnetic theory of things in general have, as it seems, set up for scientific

[4] *The Journal of Philosophy*, Vol. XXXIV, pp. 281-292.
[5] *The Concept of Nature*, chap. II.
[6] Pp. 61, 62.

investigation a society of entities, such as ether, molecules, and electrons, which are intrinsically incapable of direct observation. When Sir Ernest Rutherford at Cambridge knocks a molecule to pieces, he does not see a molecule or an electron. What he observes is a flash of light. . . . I suggest to you that, unless we are careful in our formulation of principles, the outcome of this train of thought is apt to be unsatisfactory and very misleading to scientific imagination. The apparent world becomes an individual psychological reaction to the stimulus of an entirely disparate interplay of electrons and ether. There is at most a parallelism between his observations and the conjectural molecular catastrophe. On this theory we must entirely separate psychological time, space, external perceptions, and bodily feelings from the scientific world of molecular interaction. . . . If we are to avoid this unfortunate bifurcation, we must construe our knowledge of the apparent world as being an individual experience of something which is more than personal. Nature is thus a totality including individual experiences, so that we must reject the distinction between nature as it really is and experiences of it which are purely psychological. Our experiences of the apparent world are nature itself.

We must examine the precise manner in which modern science introduced bifurcation.

Concerning heat, Galilei writes as follows:

But first I want to propose some examination of that which we call heat, whose generally accepted notion comes very far from the truth if my serious doubts be correct, inasmuch as it is supposed to be a true . . . quality really residing in the thing which we perceive to be heated. . . . I say that I am inclined sufficiently to believe . . . that the thing that produces heat in us and makes us perceive it, which we call by the general name fire, is a multitude of minute corpuscles thus and thus figured, moved with such and such a velocity; . . . and I judge that if the animate and sensitive body were removed, heat would remain nothing more than a simple word.[7]

At the beginning of his *Principia,* after designating the eight definitions of the basic concepts of modern science, Newton immediately adds:

Hitherto I have laid down the definitions of such words as are less known, and explained the sense in which I would have them to be

[7] Quoted by E. A. Burtt, *Metaphysical Foundations of Physics* (Harcourt, Brace and Company, Inc., New York, 1925), 75, 78.

understood in the following discourse. I do not define time, space, place, and motion, as being well known to all. Only I must observe, that the common people conceive those quantities under no other notions but from the relation they bear to sensible objects. And thence arise certain prejudices, for the removing of which it will be convenient to distinguish them into absolute and relative, true and apparent, mathematical and common.[8]

These quotations indicate that Galilei bifurcated nature by distinguishing "heat" as immediately sensed and "heat" considered as an unobserved motion of atoms too small for the senses to detect, after the manner of the modern kinetic theory of heat and gases. They show, too, that Newton enlarged this bifurcation by applying it not merely to sense qualities but also to space, time, and motion. For Newton the time and space we immediately sense are not the time and space of the science of physics.

Precisely the same distinction holds in Einstein's theory. The fact is that sensed time does not flow uniformly. Time, as it enters into physics, is postulated, to use Newton's language, as "flowing equably." Einstein's theory agrees with Newton upon this particular point. When we consider the simultaneity of spatially separated events this bifurcation not merely for Einstein's physics but also for common sense will become even more evident.

One other fact enforces the same conclusion. Time as immediately sensed would seem to be capable of relating states separated only by a relatively short specious present, since by its very nature sense awareness can only disclose what is given in the present; one cannot, it would seem, sense the past or the future. Yet time as it enters into physics relates the state of a physical system in the present to states of that system in the distant past and future so far away in time that by no stretching of the imagination can the scientific knowledge of these past and future states be said to be given by sense awareness. Kant, because of his use of Newton's physics in the discovery and development of the nebular hypothesis, was tremendously im-

[8] P. 6.

pressed by this fact. It made him see, as Newton maintained, that time as it enters into physics has a character and reference far beyond the present, which is quite different from time as immediately sensed.[9] To this point we shall return shortly.

The bifurcation between the sensed and the postulated which Newton introduced for time he applied also to space. At best we sense only a finite local part of space and, if Berkeley is correct, only two dimensions and these with a structure distorted according to the degree of one's astigmatism, not the infinitely extended three-dimensional space which Newton's physics postulated, or the Riemannian three-dimensional space with the finite curvature of Einstein's later theory.

Moreover, Newton defined a physical object as that which has position in absolute postulated public space. This follows from Newton's first law, according to which any object in motion without any forces acting on it will move on forever with a constant velocity in a straight line. It is quite clear that such motion would take a body completely out of sensed space. In the *Principia*, Newton adds: "All things are placed in time as to order of succession; and in space as to order of situation. It is from their essence or nature that they are places; . . ."[10] When it is noted that "essence" means that which is given by definition, the inclusion of position in absolute space in the definition of a physical object becomes clear. There are many reasons for this.

First, Newton held to a kinetic atomic theory. This theory conceives of nature as composed of atoms of matter every one of which is moving, as the word "kinetic" indicates. On a relational theory of space such a theory is meaningless, since it defines motion not as a relation of atoms to a common public referent but as a relation of physical atoms to some other physical atom taken as a referent. On this basis it would be possible to talk about all the atoms but the one taken as referent as being in motion, but meaningless to talk about all of them as having the property of moving, as the kinetic atomic

[9] See the writer's "Natural Science and the Critical Philosophy of Kant" in *The Heritage of Kant*, edited by Whitney and Bowers (Princeton University Press, 1939).
[10] P. 8.

theory maintains. This follows because to take an atom as a frame of reference automatically defines rest and thus renders it impossible to talk about the atom which is the referent as moving. It is this necessity of a referent other than any one of the moving atoms, if motion of all the atoms is to be meaningful, which Newton has in mind when he writes that the physicist's concept of a physical object carries with it as a part of its definition the notion of position with respect to some common publicly existing referent, which he and his predecessors identified with absolute postulated space.

A second reason for Newton's distinction between sensed and postulated space and his conception of postulated space as absolute is that on any other basis Newton's first law of motion would be meaningless. This was first proved by the famous mathematical physicist Euler and had a notable influence upon Kant.

Kant, following Leibniz, first held a relational theory of space and supposed that Newton's formulation of his physics in terms of absolute space was quite unnecessary. Euler's proof convinced him to the contrary. The proof is as follows: Newton's first law asserts that any object not acted on by an external force keeps its velocity constant. In short, it makes it meaningful to speak of an object not acted upon by any external force as moving. Such an object would be a solitary object in nature, since Newton's second law prescribes that were even one other physical object present an external force would be brought to bear upon the first object. But on a relational theory of space the motion of a solitary physical object is meaningless, since, according to this theory, motion is a relation between one physical object and another physical object, and hence cannot exist unless nature contains at least two physical objects. Thus Euler showed that Newton's first law of motion is incompatible with a relational theory of space.

This proof led Kant to reject the Leibnizian relational theory for Newton's absolute theory and to inquire whether there are not purely geometrical, as opposed to Newton's and Euler's kinematic, arguments for absolute space. Kant found such a proof in the fact of "incongruent counterparts," illustrated in two otherwise similar right and left hands. Providing only three dimensions of space are assumed, he had no difficulty in showing that on a relational theory of space only the similarity and not the difference between the right and left hands can be accounted for.[11] An expert contemporary mathematician informs me that this investigation by Kant inaugurated the science of analysis situs and that, providing only three dimensions of space are assumed, Kant's conclusion is valid.

Since Einstein's theory postulates only three dimensions for space, these considerations from Newton, Kant, and Euler indicate that Einstein's rejection of absolute space carries with it, as Whitehead has emphasized, a more far-reaching reorganization in the fundamental concepts of science than most contemporary physicists have supposed. To these factual considerations against a relational theory of space must be added Newton's famous rotating bucket experiment and its contemporary counterpart, Foucault's pendulum. As Whitehead has indicated, the contemporary physicist's explanation of this fact, which Newton brought forward against the relational theory of space, is exceedingly artificial.[12]

It is one of the merits of Whitehead's philosophy of science that it reconciles the relational theory of space necessitated by Einstein's theory of relativity with these logical and factual considerations brought forward by Newton, Euler, and Kant. It does this by rejecting Einstein's theory of space as a relation between physical objects and substituting for it a relational theory which conceives of space as a relation between immediately sensed phenomenal events.[13] By defining objects, both "perceptual" and "scientific," in terms of "adjectives" which enter into events in external relations,[14] while conceiving of the relation between events as internal and quite independent of the "ingression of objects," Whitehead has a meaning for space quite

[11] *Immanuel Kants Werke*, Herausgegeben von E. Cassirer (Berlin, 1912), Vol. II, 391-400.

[12] Cf. *The Principle of Relativity*, 87; *The Principles of Natural Knowledge*, 36; and *The Concept of Nature*, 138, 194.

[13] Cf. *The Principles of Natural Knowledge*, 8; *The Principle of Relativity*, 53, 58, 71.

[14] *The Principle of Relativity*, 58, 64.

independent of matter and hence can express the notion of the motion of any or all objects in terms of a relation of objects to space—in this respect following Newton, Euler, and Kant rather than Einstein[15]—while at the same time holding a relational theory of space and thus, at this point, going with Einstein against Newton and the latter's devotees.[16]

We now understand part of what Whitehead means when he writes, "We owe the whole conception notably to Einstein," and then adds, "I do not agree with his way of handling his discovery."[17]

Certainly Whitehead's position is a possible one and most original. It faces facts and proofs given by Newton, Euler, and Kant which Einstein and his followers leave either unintelligible or with rather artificial explanations. Kant's "incongruent counterparts" is the most telling one of these. Moreover, the identification of space with the relatedness of immediately sensed events enables Whitehead to avoid the bifurcation of nature introduced by Newton and carried on, as we shall show, by Einstein.

The consequences of this bifurcation for the development of modern philosophy must now be pursued.

Once Galilei and Newton have introduced the distinction between nature as sensed and nature as conceived according to the postulates of physics, the question immediately arises concerning what the relation is between the unobserved atoms in absolute space and uniformly flowing time and the colors and sounds in the non-uniformly flowing time and the distorted space which we immediately sense. That the colors and sounds and intuited space and time exist even theoretical physicists cannot deny, since it is only by appealing to these directly observable factors that the deductive consequences of their postulated theory can be put to an empirical test to determine their truth or falsity.

The reply of a traditional modern physicist to this question would run somewhat as follows: The extended colors and sounds

[15] *Ibid.*, 23, 25.
[16] *The Concept of Nature*, 105, 117.
[17] *The Principle of Relativity*, 59.

which we immediately sense are the way in which atoms with diameters too small for one's crude senses to detect appear to the observer. Put more precisely, this means that Galilei's and Newton's sensed "heat," "space," "time," and "motion" are related to the postulated colorless atoms with certain mean free paths, located in absolute space and equably flowing time, by a three-termed relation of appearance in which the unobserved moving atoms in absolute space are one term, the immediately sensed colors and sounds a second term, and the observer the third term.

The question then arose concerning the nature of this observer. Hobbes and others proposed that the observer be conceived as merely another collection of moving physical atoms similar to those in the object. A little reflection showed, however, that such an observer would not satisfy this three-termed relation of appearance. Such an observer could have no properties other than those which the postulates of physics prescribe for physical atoms and their molar aggregates. These properties are merely a capacity to move and undergo acceleration as prescribed by Newton's three laws of motion. Upon this basis all that could possibly happen as a consequence of the action of an object composed of atoms upon an observer would be the production of accelerations in the atoms of the observer. Such accelerations are not an immediately sensed awareness of colors and sounds and sensed space or time. In short, were the observer merely such an entity, colors, sounds, odors, and sensed space and time should not exist.

Locke, who was Newton's most trusted friend and correspondent, saw the point. A type of observer must be introduced which satisfies this three-termed relation of appearance. This necessitates that it cannot be a material substance, since such substances, as we have just noted, have only the property—when acted upon by other material substances—of undergoing accelerations, whereas what is required to satisfy the three-termed relation of appearance is a substance which, when acted upon by the material substances of physics, will have an immediate awareness of colors and sounds and sensed space and time. It is precisely the latter characteristic which is the defining property of Locke's mental substance. It is an immaterial atomic entity identified with the observer in scientific knowledge such that, when the postulated material substances in Newton's "real, true and mathematical" space and time act upon it, colors and sounds in Newton's sensed space and time are immediately apprehended. To complete the account Locke had to add to the material substances of physics one property not given them by Newton's physics. This additional property Locke called "the power" to act upon mental substances and thereby give rise in the latter to an awareness of colors and sounds, etc. This "power" of the material substance to produce an awareness of colors and sounds in the mental substance, and not the colors and sounds themselves, as so many careless readers of Locke suppose, is what Locke means by a "secondary quality."[18]

Note what has happened. To the bifurcation introduced by Newton between the object of knowledge as sensed and the object of knowledge as postulated is added a second bifurcation between the object of scientific knowledge, whether sensed or postulated, and the observer. The consequence of this second bifurcation is to throw the observer out of nature and to place him in such a relation to what he is supposed to know that, as Berkeley showed, he should have knowledge only of his impressions and hence could not possibly know the material objects which the theory assumes that he does know. In this manner "the bifurcation of nature" introduced by Galilei and Newton, when made articulate with respect to its psychological and epistemological consequences by Locke, gives rise to a contradiction. The theory asserts an observer's knowledge of material substance which, on its own account of the relation of the observer to these material substances, this observer could not possibly know. With Hume it became clear that such an observer could not know himself, conceived as the persistent atomic mental substance which the theory asserts the observer to be; there would be knowledge only of the sequence of impressions.

Such was the epistemological impasse bequeathed to modern philosophy by traditional modern physics. Several attempts were

[18] Locke's *Essay Concerning Human Understanding*, Fraser Edition (Oxford Press), Vol. I, 170.

made to escape from it. One was the positivistic thesis, usually identified with Hume—although it is doubtful whether Hume ever drew such conclusions from his analysis—to the effect that what physics "really means" by atoms, and postulated space and time are linguistic statements about sensed space and sensed time and sensed data. The difficulty with this thesis is that, if this is what physicists meant, they would have said so by taking immediately intuited colors and sounds and surfaces as the basic concepts in their physics, instead of the concepts they did take. The fact is that the objects, space, and time of physics are assigned different properties, as Newton explicitly indicates, from those which Hume's analysis of the deliverances of sense awareness shows sensed factors to possess. Furthermore, the deductions in Newton's physics, and as we shall show later also in Einstein's physics, simply do not follow unless we take as the basic assumptions of the science, physical objects, space, and time with the postulated properties differing from those given by sensed space, time, and objects.

A second attempt to escape the epistemological impasse was made by Leibniz. It merely served to make the untenability of the situation more evident.

Leibniz noted that the material substances, by definition, are located in space and hence their action upon anything else can occur only in space. The mental substances, on the other hand, are not in space; instead, for them, space is merely a relational item within the content of their consciousness. Thus, the notion of the action of a material substance which can act only in space upon a mental substance with respect to which space is but an item of consciousness becomes nonsensical and meaningless.

Either the material substances must be brought within the space in the field of awareness of the mental substance which, since it is not ordered in anything such as space or time, must be "windowless," or the mental substance must be defined in terms of the material substances, Leibniz reasoned. The unfortunate consequences, indicated above, of Hobbes' attempt to develop the latter thesis left Leibniz with the former alternative. Accordingly he concluded that space is a relational item within the consciousness of the observer conceived as a windowless monad. This explains how Leibniz, in thinking out the epistemological consequences of the new physics, was driven to his doctrine of windowless monads and to his relational theory of space, notwithstanding Newton's position to the contrary.

It explains also why Kant—who was the culmination of the rationalistic movement through Leibniz as well as of the empirical movement through Locke, Berkeley, and Hume—came naturally to regard the concepts of substance, causality, space, and time not as referring to an ontological order of existing physical objects in existent absolute space, but merely as forms contributed by the active ego in ordering and understanding the bare materials of sense awareness, which Hume convinced Kant to be quite incapable by themselves of giving the concepts of Newton's physics.

In this connection, it is relevant to note that, apart from epistemological philosophy, Berkeley was a bishop and Hume the clerk to a politician. Neither one knew much about science at first hand. This background left them quite competent to designate the meanings provided by immediate sense awareness. It left them equally *in*competent to determine whether these are the meanings required by physical science. For the latter inquiry Kant is much more to be trusted than Berkeley or Hume, since Kant was a mathematician and a physicist before he became a philosopher. So precise and expert was his mastery of the technical and scientific meanings of the basic concepts and principles of Newtonian mechanics that by means of them he solved for the first time certain scientific problems set by the Berlin Royal Academy of Science and discovered and developed the nebular hypothesis. In fact, it was because of the way in which Kant found the concepts of space, time, and causality to function in this theory of the nebular hypothesis as well as by his reading of Newton's bifurcation between the sensed and the mathematically postulated, that Kant became quite correctly and inescapably aware that what modern physics means by its basic concepts simply is not what the mere deliverances of sense awareness designated by Hume would provide.[19] No alternative remained, therefore, for Kant but to find

[19] See the writer's previously cited "Natural Science and the Critical Philosophy of Kant."

some other source for the concepts of modern science than sense awareness alone.

Upon all these points Einstein, as well as Newton, agrees with Kant. Einstein sees very clearly from his acquaintance with Berkeley's arguments that the existence of scientific objects, such as atoms, and even of common sense objects is not given by sense awareness but by postulation, confirmed only indirectly through its deductive consequences.[20] He sees also, from his knowledge of Hume that the concept of causality, as it enters into Newtonian and Einsteinian scientific theory, is not abstracted from the deliverances of sense awareness. At the last Princeton meeting of the Eastern Division of the American Philosophical Association, Einstein spoke roughly as follows: "The first thing which we have to realize about causality is that it is not given empirically. This was Hume's great insight. The second is that nevertheless causality occurs in modern physics." The point is that Hume's analysis showed that, were causality derived by abstraction from sense awareness, then one could mean by it nothing more than an habitual anticipation of repetition. Clearly, this could not give a relation of necessary connection joining the present state of a system in nature to its future state to make unequivocal temporal prediction possible. Yet it is precisely the latter type of relation of necessary connection which modern and contemporary physics means by causality as it actually uses the concept.

It is considerations such as these, arising out of the discrepancy between the deliverances of mere sense awareness as disclosed to him by Hume and the demands of physics as revealed in his own first-hand acquaintance with the precise manner in which the concepts of physical objects, space, time, and causality actually function in this science, which convinced Kant that these concepts simply do not have their basis in sense awareness, and led him to his own particular theory of their necessary, universal, and hence *a priori* source. The development of modern mathematics has revealed, however, that these concepts possess a merely hypothetical, postulated, and indirectly verified, and hence contingent, status rather than the necessary categorical

---

[20] A. Einstein *The World As I See It* (New York, 1934), 60.

status which Kant's positive thesis requires; so Kant's attempt to escape the epistemological impasse into which the bifurcation of nature, introduced by modern science, drove modern philosophy fails also. Need we wonder, therefore, that Whitehead's reflection upon modern philosophy leads him to reject any theory of the concepts of science or philosophy which bifurcates nature.

Nevertheless, the fact remains that space and time actually function in science in ways different from the way concepts derived by mere abstraction from sense awareness, according to Hume's account of the latter, would do. Moreover, Whitehead's knowledge of science, like Kant's, is sufficiently professional to make him aware that this is the case. Thus, even though Kant's positive theory of the source of the concepts of space and time in Newton's physics fails, the fact that the scientific concepts are not those which Hume's description of the deliverances of sense awareness would give persists. How is a theory which would deny any source for the concepts of science except sense awareness to meet this difficulty? It is the answer to this question which drives Whitehead to his particular doctrine of spatio-temporal relatedness.

His answer takes the following form: Hume's description of the deliverances of sense awareness is incomplete. It designates only "knowledge by adjective" and ignores "knowledge by relatedness."[21] Concentrating attention only on "knowledge by adjective," it reports only the awareness of sense data and their contingent relations and overlooks that what one actually senses are sense data which are in a unique here and now. This unique here-now insures that we sense "events" within which adjectives "ingress." The relation between adjectives is contingent and external.[22] Consequently, were sense awareness to disclose nothing but sense data and their contingent relations, the existence of a concept of time in science which relates the present to the distant past and future would be indeed a mystery, and recourse to a concept of nature known in some other way than

---

[21] *The Principle of Relativity*, 18-19. Cf. the distinction between the 'discerned' and the 'discernible' in *The Concept of Nature*, 49.

[22] *Ibid.*, 64.

by sense awareness would be necessary to account for it, as Kant maintained. But since we sense "adjectives" such as blue or green in this unique here and now, the situation with respect to the deliverance of sense awareness is not so limited.

The uniqueness of this event here-now carries the knowledge that it is other than any other event, no matter how far distant in space and time any other event may be. But this is impossible unless the sensed knowledge of the local, immediately present event carries with it at least sufficient knowledge of all other events, no matter how far distant, and of its relation to them, to enable sense awareness to convey a meaningful distinction of the local, present event from them, as sense awareness most certainly does when it exhibits the event here and now as unique. It follows, therefore, Whitehead concludes, that sense awareness of a local event gives "by relatedness" a knowledge of all other events in nature, no matter how far distant they may be spatially and temporally.[23]

Lest this account seem to assert more for sense awareness than it does, we must hasten to emphasize that knowledge in the present of events "by relatedness" in the distant past and future entails knowledge of the latter events only as bare terms or relata in the systematic spatio-temporal relatedness; it does not entail knowledge of the adjectives within these spatially and temporally distant events.[24] It is for this reason that Whitehead describes the relation of adjectives to each other and to events as external.

Note how this solves Kant's problem. It explains why space and time as they enter into physics are not limited to the adjectivally sensed local here and the adjectivally very brief specious present, but are instead systematic ordering relations joining nature in the present to nature in the distant past and future, while also being derivable from sense awareness by abstraction *a posteriori,* thereby avoiding the bifurcation which Kant's recourse to a categorical *a priori* source for the concepts of modern physics made necessary.[25]

[23] *The Principle of Relativity,* 26, 64; *The Concept of Nature,* chap. III.
[24] *The Concept of Nature,* 51.
[25] Cf. *The Principle of Relativity,* 25, 64.

It has equally impressive merits when considered from the standpoint of common sense. For it explains why, in sensing the present, we know there has been a past and will be a future, although we do not know necessarily by present sense awareness what the adjectival character of this past has been or what the adjectival character of the future will be. Such are the consequences of making the relation between events internal, so that the sense awareness of an event here-now carries with it the knowledge by relatedness of all other spatially and temporally distant events as bare relata, and of treating the relation of adjectives to events and to each other as external, so that knowledge by adjective of certain sense data now does not give either the knowledge by adjective or by relatedness of sensa in distant events.

It is precisely this complicated doctrine of internal and external relatedness, however, which gets Whitehead's philosophy of science into conflict with Einstein's physics.[26] In order to make the relation between events an internal relation Whitehead has to regard the metric of space as homogeneous and uniform,[27] and in order to make the relation between adjectives and events external he has to maintain, since he defines matter in terms of the "adjectives," that the metric of space is not affected by and has no essential connection with the distribution of the matter of the universe.[28] Both of these points Einstein and contemporary physicists unequivocally deny because of the general theory of relativity.

In one of his scientific papers, Einstein writes,

According to the general theory of relativity the metrical character (curvature) of the four-dimensional space-time continuum is defined at every point by the matter at that point and the state of that matter. Therefore, on account of the lack of uniformity in the distribution of matter, the metrical structure of this continuum must necessarily be extremely complicated. . . .[29]

[26] Ibid., 65.
[27] Ibid., 64, 73.
[28] Ibid., v-vi.
[29] A. Einstein and Others, The Principle of Relativity (Methuen & Co., London, 1923), 183.

That this is explicit in the mathematics of the theory is shown by the fundamental equation of the general theory:

$$G_{ik} - \tfrac{1}{2}\, g_{ik}G = T_{ik}.$$

The expression to the left of the equality sign defines the metric of space-time; that to the right, matter and energy. Consequently, the equating of the two makes the connection between matter and space essential to the theory and not a mere possible interpretation.

Before one allows this conflict with Einstein's theory to cause one hastily to dismiss Whitehead's philosophy of science, two points must be noted.

First, a theory may be quite satisfactory from the standpoint of a physicist, yet false from the standpoint of the philosopher of science. Our consideration of the epistemological consequences of the bifurcation of nature makes this clear. The physicist does not have to face these epistemological problems; hence this weakness in his theory does not come to his attention, at least not in his capacity as a physicist. But the philosopher of science must face the epistemological consequences of a given set of basic concepts for physics as well as their purely scientific and experimental consequences. There is nothing necessarily to prevent a scientific theory from being quite adequate from the scientific standpoint and equally inadequate from the epistemological standpoint. Whitehead believes this to be the case with respect to Einstein's physics, in the form in which Einstein has left it. Consequently, if, in order to make the primitive concepts of science adequate with respect to their epistemological consequences, it is necessary to deviate from present scientific doctrines, then, unfortunate as this additional reconstruction' in our scientific theory may be, it must be made. The failure of all attempts of modern philosophers to solve the epistemological problems bequeathed to modern philosophy by the modern scientists' bifurcation of nature gives weight to Whitehead's conclusion.

Even so, certain things remain to be said. Whitehead's argument that in sense awareness we have a homogeneous uniform systematic internal relatedness of all the events in all space and all time has been put as effectively as possible. I have tried to convince myself that it is true. When I consult the deliverances of my own sense awareness, however, I find myself oppressed with skepticism. At best, I find merely that his doctrine is plausible, not that it is as self-evidently certain as an immediate deliverance of sense awareness should be. When, in addition, I find that its acceptance, in order to avoid bifurcation, gets one into conflict with Einstein's general theory which, at every point where physicists have been able to check it against unequivocal sense awareness, has been confirmed, I must be doubly skeptical, even though the latter consideration by itself need not be absolutely decisive.

Let us suppose, however, that my skepticism is quite ill-founded and that what Whitehead asserts concerning spatio-temporal relatedness is given in sense awareness. Even so, has he avoided bifurcation?

One concept in scientific theory shows that he has not. It is causality.

Here again Whitehead is forced to maintain that Hume failed to describe everything which sense awareness discloses. Thus, Whitehead identifies causality with the "control" which nature exerts over "the ingression of sense objects into nature."[30] Precisely how sense awareness discloses such "control" is not clear. In support of the thesis that it does, he appeals to Locke's notion of "power." But, as we have previously noted, Locke's notion of power was not anything empirically sensed, but a postulated property ascribed to the material substances of physics in addition to those assigned by the physicist, in order to explain how material substances could act upon mental substances to give the latter an awareness of colors and sounds.

But even if we grant the presence in sense awareness of the "control" and the "power" which Whitehead identifies with causality, this has no more to do with causality as it actually enters into physical science than has Hume's notion of an habitual expectation of repetition. Causality in Newton's, Max-

[30] *The Concept of Nature*, 144-146; cf. also *The Principle of Relativity*, chap. II.

well's, and Einstein's physics is a relation of necessary connection between the states of physical systems at different times such that, given the determination of the state of the system at one time, its state at any future time can be logically deduced.[31] Clearly, this is something quite different from an intuition of "power" or "control over the ingression of sense objects" given immediately in sense awareness. We have no alternative therefore but to conclude with Newton, Kant, and Einstein that the concept of causality in the science of physics is not given empirically as a deliverance of sense awareness. This means that Whitehead has not succeeded in avoiding bifurcation. Further evidence of this will appear.

Nevertheless, the conflict between Whitehead's philosophy and contemporary physics has a second consideration to justify itself. Purely within the physics of the situation, quite apart from the epistemological problem resulting from bifurcation, there are difficulties raised by the advent of Einstein's theory which the latter's formulation does not seem to meet, and which Whitehead's philosophy of science does resolve. This brings us to the third major factor which, notwithstanding Whitehead's deviations from Einstein, has determined Whitehead's philosophy of science.

EINSTEIN'S THEORY OF RELATIVITY

The first consequence of this theory is to enforce the rejection of Newton's absolute space and the substitution for it of a relational theory of space. This happened in the Special Theory of Relativity. Later, in the General Theory of Relativity, as our previous reference to its fundamental mathematical equation has shown, this relatedness was shown to have physical objects or events defined in terms of collocations of physical objects as its relata. The special theory also had shown this when it indicated that there is no meaning to space apart from the particular physical object with which one identifies the zero point in one's coördinate system and which thereby one takes as one's reference system when one observes and measures. This

[31] See the writer's two articles in *Philosophy of Science*, Vol. 3: 215-232 and Vol. 5: 166-180.

demonstrated clearly that space is relative to physical objects. We can understand, therefore, why Einstein and the contemporary physicists hold a relational theory of space and regard the relata which relational space relates as physical objects or as events defined in terms of collisions or collocations of such objects. We shall call this relational theory of space the physical relational theory of space, to distinguish it from Whitehead's relational theory, which we shall term the phenomenal relational theory of space.

Whitehead asks us to pursue this physical relational theory of space to certain of its logical consequences.

Let us start with the relata, the physical objects, rather than the relations. Our quotations from Newton show that position in absolute space was part of the scientist's definition of what physics means by a physical object. It follows, therefore, that Einstein's rejection of absolute space for a relational theory of space entails a reconstruction not merely in our scientific theory of space and time but also in our scientific theory of a physical object. We can no longer mean by a physical object what we meant before Einstein's theory came along. Until this reconstruction is made, it does not mean very much to say that space is a relation between physical objects. The latter statement seems to be meaningful only because we take the relational theory of space and couple it with the old pre-relativistic concept of a physical object, forgetting that this is a contradiction in terms, since the pre-relativistic concept of a physical object prescribed position in absolute space as an essential part of what is meant by a physical object, and this is clearly incompatible with a relational theory of space.

This failure of Einstein and the contemporary physicists to reconstruct their theory of a physical object as well as their theory of space and time as a consequence of Einstein's rejection of absolute space, suggests to Whitehead that Einstein's physical relational theory of space is but a half-way point in the reconstruction of the concepts of modern science which the acceptance of Einstein's theory entails, and hence is not to be taken too seriously.

Whitehead moved beyond this half-way point, at which he

regards Einstein as stopping, in the following manner: Since physical objects can no longer be conceived as Newton defined them, as entities with position in postulated absolute space, how are we to conceive them? Postulated absolute space being untenable, Whitehead believes that postulated physical objects, either molar or atomic, cannot be maintained either. This makes it impossible to define away the events we immediately sense, as Newton's and Einstein's physics does, in terms of postulated physical objects and propagations. Thus, bifurcation disappears, and the only events with which physics is left are the immediately sensed ones, and the only possible relata for the relational theory of space and time to relate are these immediately sensed events. In this manner, when the reconstruction in our scientific concept of a physical object, which Einstein's rejection of absolute space entails, is carried out, the physical relational theory of space of Einstein is seen to give way to the phenomenal relational theory of space of Whitehead.

Furthermore, since this entails that the source of our scientific concept of physical objects cannot be located beyond the continuum of immediately sensed events in unobserved postulated collocations of atomic entities too small for the senses to detect, nothing remains but to define the different objects of science in terms of immediately sensed factors. These immediately sensed factors are either the "events" or the "adjectives." Since events are here-now and then pass, whereas objects persist through different events, as do adjectives, it is in terms of the latter that objects must be defined, Whitehead concludes.[32]

The objects of nature are of three kinds, which Whitehead terms "sense objects" such as colors and sounds, "perceptual objects" such as tables and chairs, and "scientific objects" such as atoms, molecules, and electrons.[33] Consider the relation between sense objects and scientific objects. He distinguished between them, not as does Newtonian and Einsteinian physics on the old bifurcation basis, according to which the colors and sounds are sensed data and the electrons and protons are unobserved postulated entities too small for the senses to detect,

[32] *The Principle of Relativity*, 58.
[33] *The Concept of Nature*, chap. VII.

but upon the basis that both atoms and sense data are immediately sensed adjectives of immediately sensed events, the difference between them being that the adjectives which are colors and sounds depend upon the relation between the event which is their sensed locus and the percipient event which is the sensed observer, whereas the adjectives which are scientific objects such as electrons are more persistent and are a function only of the events which are their sensed locus.[34]

In this manner Whitehead avoids bifurcation, while providing a meaning for the difference between sense objects and scientific objects. A reading of Chapter VII in *The Concept of Nature* will show that their distinction from perceptual objects is indicated also. Certainly this is a remarkable and most original achievement.

But whether it is original and remarkable enough to accomplish its purpose is doubtful. Even Whitehead realized in the case of the "perceptual objects" of common-sense knowledge, during the period between the writing of *The Principles of Natural Knowledge* and *The Concept of Nature*, that the mere persistence and collocation of "sense objects" is not sufficient to define a "perceptual object." To overcome this deficiency he appeals to the same questionable intuitively given notion of "the control of nature's passage over the ingression of sense objects into nature" which he introduced to account for causality, thereby escaping bifurcation only by putting a greater demand upon the deliverance of sense awareness than the latter seems capable of fulfilling.

If this is suggested in the case of perceptual objects, it is inescapable in the case of "scientific objects." An electron is, according to Whitehead's theory, a sensed adjective qualifying all the event particles in a "historical route," i.e., a Minkowskean world-line.[35] Such a world-line extends from the distant past through the briefly extended specious present to the unlimitedly distant future. Now, even on Whitehead's theory, one can only sense adjectives in the present; knowledge of them

[34] *The Principle of Relativity,* 33, 69; cf. *The Concept of Nature,* 155-158.
[35] *The Principles of Relativity,* 32.

in the present does not, as in the case of knowledge of events in the present in relation to events in the past and future, entail knowledge of adjectives in the past and the future.[36] Thus his definition of an electron as a "historical route," every event of which is qualified by the same adjective, clearly takes one beyond what sense awareness, even on his own exceedingly generous theory of its capacity, can provide.

But suppose that we overlook the difficulty with respect to the past and the future and concentrate attention on a very long present. Does any physicist or anyone else mean by an electron, that he senses or that it is possible for him to sense a persistent adjective through all the time that he is watching the Wilson cloud chamber experiment? Even in this experiment, which is the nearest one ever comes to an electron in sense awareness, there is merely a disconnected sequence of flashes, and this for only a few very brief "historical routes." Most of the trillions upon trillions of electrons which the physicist's verified theory leads him to believe make up the collection of scientific objects in the cloud chamber, exhibit during the present period when he watches the experiment no sensible adjectives whatever; only a few "tracks" appear on the photographic plate. Thus, immediately sensed adjectives permanently qualifying all the events in "historical routes" simply cannot be what a physicist means by a scientific object such as an electron.

At best, if the language of "events," "historical routes," and "adjectives" is to be used in defining an electron, it must be something postulated, not something sensed. But the moment this distinction between the sensed and the postulated is admitted, Whitehead's doctrine that "nature is only what is disclosed in sense awareness" is rejected and bifurcation cannot be escaped.

We conclude, therefore, that Whitehead's use of the reconstruction in our scientific theory of a physical object, necessitated by Einstein's rejection of absolute space which warranted substituting Whitehead's phenomenal relational theory of space for Einstein's physical relational theory of space, fails because,

[36] *Ibid.*, 26.

among other things, it leads to an inadequate theory of the "scientific object." It appears also that, whether epistemologists and philosophers like it or not, *science requires bifurcation.*

Whitehead has another argument against Einstein's physical relational theory of space which is more telling. Assume that the old concept of a physical object is still meaningful, even after the rejection of absolute space, and hence that it is meaningful to think of space as a relation between physical objects. According to the traditional and current theory these physical objects are made up of particles such as chemical atoms or physical electrons which are in motion. By space we must mean then a relation between these entities. But clearly, since these entities are in constant motion, the relatedness between them must be one thing at one instant of their motion and a quite different thing at another. It follows therefore that space should never have the same metrical properties at any two instants of time. Yet even Einstein's theory assumes that it does.[37] Thus, when one stops thinking about Einstein's physical relational theory in the abstract, and actually expresses it in terms of the real physical objects which physics tells us exist, the type of approximate metrical constancy in space which Einstein's theory requires is not the one which space, conceived as a relation between the existent objects of physics, would provide.

Whitehead concludes, therefore, that the relational theory of space, necessitated by Einstein's rejection of Newton's absolute space, must be conceived not as relating physical objects, or events, defined in terms of physical objects or propagations as Einstein maintains, but as relating immediately sensed non-physically defined phenomenal events. That Whitehead's doctrine of a homogeneous systematic internal relatedness of such events meets this real difficulty cannot be denied. Its only weakness is that it conflicts with Einstein's general theory, as we have previously shown. Elsewhere I have shown how the above-mentioned difficulty, together with the facts brought forward by Newton, Euler, and Kant against a physical relational theory of space, can be met within the latter theory and without any

---

[37] *The Principle of Relativity,* 58-59; *The Concept of Nature,* 97, 105.

conflict with either Einstein's special theory or his general theory.[38]

Whitehead's way of meeting these difficulties has one other unfortunate consequence. It leads him into even greater conflict with the generally accepted conclusions of contemporary physics by forcing the rejection of the basic definition of simultaneity for spatially separated events upon which the entire theory of relativity rests.

If the events of physics are immediately sensed events with spatio-temporal relations to each other, not defined in terms of physical objects, as Whitehead's doctrine of the contingent external relation between "adjectives" and "events" necessitates, then it follows that the temporal relation of simultaneity between even spatially separated events cannot be defined, as Einstein's physics defines it, in terms of the propagation of light waves. Also, since for Whitehead the entire space-time structure of events is given in sense awareness, the relation of simultaneity between spatially separated events must be intuitively given there also. Thus Whitehead affirms an intuitively given meaning for the simultaneity of spatially separated events, not merely for events a considerable distance apart, but for events even at the utmost spatial extremes of the whole of nature.[39]

This brings him into unequivocal conflict with the special theory of relativity. It is essential to the latter theory, as Einstein has emphasized[40] that there is an intuitively given (i.e., immediately sensed) meaning for simultaneity only for spatially coexistent events (i.e., events side by side) and that the simultaneity of spatially separated events is not given intuitively in sense awareness, but depends upon an appeal to space and to physical light propagation. This appears in Einstein's famous definition: Two spatially separated events are simultaneous if light rays leaving each upon their occurrence arrive at a mid-

[38] *Proceedings of the National Academy of Sciences*, Vol. 16; *Science and First Principles*, by F. S. C. Northrop (Macmillan Co., New York, 1931), chap. II.

[39] *The Principle of Relativity*, 66-67; *The Concept of Nature*, 53.

[40] A. Einstein, *The Theory of Relativity*, 4th Edition (London, 1921), chap. VIII.

point, equidistant from each, simultaneously. It is to be noted that the appearance of the word "simultaneously" in the definition does not make the definition circular. What it means is that Einstein has defined the simultaneity of spatially separated events, which is not given intuitively, in terms of equal distances in space, physical light propagation, and the simultaneity of spatially coexistent events which is given intuitively.

From this definition, in conjunction with the two other postulates of the special theory, the relativity of time and space for different frames of reference can be deduced, and the Lorentzian transformation equations, connecting values of time or space in one frame to their different values in another frame, can be derived. It is important to note that Einstein's definition is essential to these transformation equations, since it provides the invariant constant c, the numerical value of the velocity of light, which enters into them.

There are several reasons for Whitehead's rejection of Einstein's concept of simultaneity. The first is Whitehead's rejection of bifurcation.[41] Einstein's doctrine of simultaneity limits the simultaneity which is known by sense awareness purely to that of events which are immediately beside each other and the observer. Consequently, when science refers, as it does, to events far away in space as occurring simultaneously with events observed by the observer, this scientific knowledge of spatially separated simultaneity, according to Einstein's theory, simply is not given by sense awareness. It is known by postulated theory, which is confirmed indirectly through its deductive consequences and not by immediate apprehension. But to maintain such a conception of science is to distinguish very sharply between the very limited part or aspect of simultaneous nature which is disclosed in direct sense awareness and the concept of simultaneous nature as it is prescribed in one's deductively formulated scientific theory, and forthwith to admit bifurcation.

There is a second reason. It follows from the Bergsonian influence and its attendant doctrine of the primacy of process. If duration and process are primary, then the concept of time

[41] Cf. *The Principle of Relativity*, 96.

ought to be usable to define the secondary concepts of space. In a remarkable manner this is precisely what Whitehead accomplishes in *The Concept of Nature*. It is the assumption of an intuitively given simultaneity for spatially separated events that makes this achievement possible.

The initial fact disclosed in sense awareness, according to Whitehead, is the extension of all intuitively given nature in the process of passing. Clearly, what we immediately apprehend is everything which we apprehend. This, according to Whitehead's description, is an extended manifold which does not have an immediately sensed largest extension or an immediately sensed smallest extension.[42] Moreover, of this manifold, passage and duration are immediately perceived as constituting its very nature. We do not immediately sense nature at an instant, nor do we immediately sense geometrical points with a minimum of extension. Instead, we immediately intuit an extended manifold which is enduring through time and passing. Thus sense awareness supports the primacy of passage.

Within this all-embracing intuited passage factors or parts, which also endure and pass, are exhibited. These factors of total fact Whitehead, in *The Concept of Nature*, terms "events." These events, as we noted previously in our account of Whitehead's "knowledge by relatedness," are internally related to each other. Some of these events known by relatedness are in the past; some are in the present; and some are given, through knowledge by relatedness, as in the future. The initial fact, however, is the internal relatedness of these events by the relation of extension, where extension is not distinguished yet into spatial extension and temporal extension.

This distinction arises with the introduction of the intuitively given relation of simultaneity for all nature.[43] This relation throws together into one class all partial events throughout the whole of nature which occur now, and separates this class of events from events non-simultaneous with these in the past and in the future. By this means Whitehead succeeds in de-

[42] *The Concept of Nature,* 59.
[43] *The Principles of Natural Knowledge,* 68.

fining spatial relations in terms of temporal concepts. Space is that relation between events which occurs when the events are simultaneous. That this ensues is shown by the following consideration. Clearly, events that happen at the same time are not separated temporally; hence they can only be separated spatially. Thus Whitehead succeeds in using the concept of simultaneity applied to the whole of nature to define the spatial relatedness of events at a given moment of time.

It is to be emphasized that when the intuited concept of simultaneity for spatially separated events throws into one class all events happening in a given now, this now must be conceived, because of the fundamental property of duration characterizing all events, not as an instant but as a now with temporal extension. One of these extended nows joining events related by the intuitively given relation of simultaneity Whitehead, in *The Concept of Nature,* terms a "duration." A duration is the whole of spatially extended nature intuited for a given extended now. Events which are not simultaneous with those in a given duration fall into other durations of simultaneous events. Two such durations cannot intersect, since to intersect an event in one of the durations would have to be at the same time as an event in the other duration, and this the relation of non-simultaneity between the events of the two durations prevents. Thus, just as the relation of simultaneity within the exetension of space-time separates out the purely spatial relatedness of events, so the relation of non-simultaneity gives the purely temporal order between them and the durations of which they are a part. Such a family of non-intersecting durations Whitehead calls a time-system. The non-intersection of the durations of such a time-system constitutes what Whitehead terms a "parallelism" of durations.

Since any duration has temporal extension, its now-ness is not instantaneous and sharp. This absence of sharpness informs us that the events of the immediately apprehended spatio-temporal extension of nature can be thrown together into durations in more than one way by the intuitively given relation of simultaneity. Hence, there arise different families of parallel durations and different time systems.[44] Thus, without any appeal to physical objects or light propagations, the relativity of time, and, as can easily be shown, also of space, is provided.

By purely temporal concepts, Whitehead succeeds in defining the order of the parts of space in the space of a given duration. It is easy to show that durations belonging to different time-systems intersect, i.e., have events in common. The order of space in the moment of a duration of one time-system is defined by its intersection with the moments of the durations of another time-system.[45] In this detailed and precise way, Whitehead, by the use of nothing but the temporal concept of simultaneity and its negate, shows the capacity of the doctrine of the primacy of process to derive spatial concepts. The weakness in Bergson's treatment of space is corrected.

So far Whitehead has provided merely a concept of space for a given duration. Were this all, this phenomenal relational theory of space would be subject to the same objection which Whitehead made against Einstein's physical relational theory; there would be a meaning for space at an instant, but no meaning for the space required by physics which, at least to a first approximation, keeps its metrical properties constant through time. Note that all the distinctions up to this point have been defined not merely without any reference to physical objects, as they must be if Whitehead is to maintain his thesis that space-time relates phenomenal events rather than physical objects or events defined in terms of them, but also without any recourse even to immediately sensed adjectives. It is considerations such as this which give one a tremendous respect for Whitehead's philosophy of science. He has paid what it costs to reject Einstein's physically defined theory, working his own doctrine out in detail. By appeal to an immediately sensed adjective, at rest relative to the immediately sensed percipient event which is the observer, yet persisting through time, a "historical route" is defined which relates the instantaneous point in the space of one moment to instantaneous points in the instantaneous spaces

[44] *The Concept of Nature,* 72-73, 85.
[45] *Ibid.,* 90-91.

of other moments of the same time-system and thereby defines a space which persists through time.[46]

Unfortunately, there are also unsatisfactory results which must be noted. A philosophy of science, if it is to have anything to do with actual science, must provide transformation equations joining the measured numerical values for space and time in one time system to their measured values in any other time system.

These transformation equations are very unambiguous. They are mathematical expressions first discovered by Lorentz. In them an invariant constant c appears, referring to the velocity of light propagation and having the numerical value of 186,000 miles per second.

On Einstein's physical relational theory the presence of this constant in the transformation equations follows necessarily, since simultaneity for spatially separated events is defined in terms of light propagation, and the relativity of time and space for different physical frames of reference is deduced from this definition.

On Whitehead's theory all this is a mystery. As we have noted, for him the connection between space and time in a given time-system and between different time-systems has nothing to do with light propagation or physical frames of reference. This makes it difficult to understand why the constant c should have anything to do with the transformation equations. In fact, on Whitehead's theory it is difficult to see how there can be unambiguous transformation equations of any kind whatever. For we have noted that according to him the existence of different time-systems has its basis in an ambiguity in nature's passage which permits us to throw the same events together into durations in different ways by the use of the intuitively given relation of simultaneity. On this basis the relation between different time-systems is grounded in an ambiguity. How one can derive unambiguous transformation equations from an ambiguity is somewhat difficult to understand.

In his book *The Principle of Relativity*, Whitehead has faced

[46] *The Concept of Nature*, chap. V.

this problem. There a certain constant c appears, which by great good fortune turns out to have the empirical value of 186,000 miles per second.[47] I find it difficult to escape the conclusion that his philosophy of science is made to work at this point only by methods which are most artificial. Here his rejection of Einstein's definition of the simultaneity of spatially separated events in favor of an intuitively given meaning seems to have unfortunate consequences.

There is a third weighty reason, however, why Whitehead maintains the latter doctrine. The plain fact of the matter is that any observer does immediately sense such a simultaneity. I certainly do see a flash in the distant intuited sky while I hear an explosion beside me now. Clearly these two immediately sensed events are not side by side. Yet I immediately sense their occurence as simultaneous. No appeal to light propagation or to immediately intuited events side by side in a V-shaped mirror equidistant from the two spatially separated events is necessary to give me this knowledge. On this point there is no question but that Whitehead is correct. We do have an intuitively given knowledge of the simultaneity of spatially separated events.

Curiously enough, instead of confirming Whitehead's contention against Einstein, this fact turns out to be a boomerang against the Whiteheadian position.

The word "is" in the expression "There is an intuitively given simultaneity of spatially separated events" is ambiguous. It may mean "for the specific sense awareness of the individual observer only," or "publicly valid simultaneity the same for all observers on the same frame of reference." When Whitehead affirms an intuitively given simultaneity of spatially separated events, he is correct, but only in the first of the above two senses, as evidence shortly to be indicated will show. When Einstein denies an intuitively given simultaneity for such events, it is in the second of the above two senses, and in this he is correct. Thus there is no contradiction between the fact noted by Whitehead and Einstein's contention; on the contrary, the latter becomes clear because of the former.

[47] *The Principle of Relativity,* 76; *The Concept of Nature,* 131.

Unfortunately, Whitehead in his turn cannot account for the fact which Einstein has pointed out. This fact is that a publicly valid meaning for the simultaneity of spatially separated events is not given intuitively. Consider two immediately sensed explosions; one in West Haven and the other in East Haven, which are so loud that they can be heard at every point between the two places. Since West Haven and East Haven are on opposite sides of the city of New Haven, these two events are spatially separated. We all know it to be a phenomenological fact, and hence one which Whitehead cannot escape, that if a person midway between these two explosions immediately senses them as simultaneous, then all other observers who are nearer the one explosion than the other will not. This example shows both, that we do have an immediately sensed simultaneity for spatially separated events for the individual sense awareness of the individual observer, and that this intuitively given simultaneity does not provide a publicly valid simultaneity the same for all observers at rest relative to each other on the same frame of reference—in this instance on the earth's surface. In short, we discover that on Whitehead's theory there is no meaning for public time.

Whitehead's doctrine of intuitively given simultaneity seemed to work only because to the intuitively given simultaneity of spatially separated events—which he was quite correct in affirming, but only for the particular sense awareness of a single individual—he inadvertently attributed a public validity which it does not possess.

The reason for this error, quite apart from the ambiguity in the word "is," previously noted, can be easily appreciated. Otherwise, he cannot get a public time. The error follows also from his thesis that nature is nothing but what is disclosed in sense awareness. If this were true, there would be no concept of the simultaneity of spatially separated events, which is not intuitively given. It follows also from his rejection of bifurcation. For to admit a non-intuitively given relation of simultaneity between spatially separated events—as common sense and Einstein's physics does when it admits a public time the same for all observers on the same physical frame of reference—is to

bifurcate nature into the intuited relation of simultaneity varying from person to person (which is the only one immediately
sensed) and the postulated simultaneity of physical theory
which, since it is the same from person to person at rest relative
to each other on the same frame of reference, is quite different
from that which is immediately sensed.

Moreover, the events which these two bifurcated types of
simultaneity relate are also bifurcated. A simple childhood experience will illustrate this. As a young boy about five years of
age I remember once standing by the house on our farm in
southern Wisconsin on a very windy day and being puzzled by
the fact that the afternoon freight train, when it whistled as it
came across the farm boundary a quarter of a mile away, exhibited first the flash of the white puff of steam and then, several
seconds later, the noise of the whistle. At that age, clearly, I
knew nothing about the distinction in Newton's *Principia* between the many sensed events in sensed space and time which
vary from person to person and place to place and from one
sense to the other even for the same person, and hence do not
give an objective event or a public world, and the single, quite
different physically defined postulated event with its quite different temporal location earlier than any sensed event, and hence
by its very nature not given in sense awareness, which does provide a public world. Nor was I informed about the different
velocities of propagation of the unobserved postulated sound
and light waves. Yet in this childhood experience I had the
facts which have led both common sense and modern science,
including Einstein, to bifurcate nature into two types of events
and two types of time and space relating them.

What was my puzzle? I believed then, as all of us still believe, that there was but one event involved in the whistling of
this train. The engine did not first shoot forth steam and then
later emit a terrific noise. Yet clearly what I observed through
my senses were two events at two different times, not one event
at one time. If sense awareness alone is the criterion of what
happens in nature, there were two events here and not one, and
that is the end of the matter. It might be said that previously
I had stood immediately beside engines when they whistled and

thus knew that the emission of steam and sound were "really" one event and not two. But why accept the deliverance of sense awareness in the one case and reject it in the other? What I sensed I sensed in both cases, and there is equal justification so far as sense awareness is concerned for taking the later two-event experience as what "really" happened and rejecting the other. In fact, the only procedure justified by sense awareness is to accept both on the same footing as holding under the actual circumstances in which they are sensed as holding, namely, only for the individual sense awareness of the individual observer and thereby to give up sensed events as the criterion of the publicly objective in nature.

This is precisely what common sense and science does, and it is because of it that a bifurcation between two types of events of nature and their differing types of simultaneity is necessary. For if immediately sensed events and their simultaneity do not define the publicly objective in nature, then events of some other kind with their unobserved objectivity and simultaneity must be introduced.

But how, it may be asked, can science justify the postulation of such unobservable events and temporal relations? The answer is easy. When formal logic is applied to a present state of nature defined in terms of them, one can deduce future states of nature composed of such events which, when joined to immediately sensed phenomenal events by epistemic correlation, enable one to predict the latter events and their intuitively given simultaneity, varying in the spatially separated instances from person to person and place to place exactly as sense awareness discloses. In short, the objective world and the events defined in terms of the scientific objects which compose it are not known by observation but by trial and error postulation, confirmed only indirectly through its deductive consequences by recourse to the epistemic correlation of some of its events with the phenomenal events which are immediately sensed.

Since only part of the space of the unobserved postulated events correlates with the whole of the space of immediately sensed events, there is no difficulty in explaining how physical objects can exist after moving completely out of sensed space.

In this manner also the existence in science of causality in a sense other than that given by either Hume's or Whitehead's account of sense awareness is explained. Whereas present sensed events do not have properties enabling one to deduce sensed events in the future, postulated physically defined present events do logically entail future postulated physically defined events. This makes clear, also, why Aristotelian physics, which, like Whitehead's, refused to bifurcate nature, was descriptive of natural occurrences but lacked predictive power, whereas modern physics is less qualitatively descriptive of what we immediately sense but has tremendous predictive power.

Einstein's theory has not taken physics back from the postulated public time and physically defined events introduced by Newton to immediately sensed events with their relative time. The relativity of time in Einstein's physics is not the phenomenological relativity from person to person of immediately sensed events. The latter relativity of time was known long before Einstein or even Newton. The same bifurcation between immediately sensed time with its simultaneity varying from person to person on the same frame of reference and the postulated public time relating postulated physically defined objective events and holding for all observers on a given frame of reference is maintained in Einstein's theory as was maintained by Newton. The novelty of Einstein's discovery is that whereas Newton supposed that the publicly valid unobserved simultaneity between postulated spatially separated physical events relative to one frame of reference such as the earth held through transformation equations for all frames, Einstein has shown that this is not the case. Were the sun taken as one's frame of reference rather than the earth, there would be a public time the same for as many observers as one might conceive to be located on its surface, which would be quite different from the varying temporal relation between phenomenal events which each observer would immediately sense, but this public time for the sun would not be that for the earth. These considerations indicate that Einstein bifurcates nature for any frame of reference, between sensed events with their sensed space and time and postulated physically defined events with their quite different spatial and temporal relatedness exactly as did Newton. It is precisely for this reason that the definition of simultaneity of such spatially separated events depends upon light propagation, since the emission of light propagation is a necessary consequence of the defining properties of such events and hence is not arbitrary, as Whitehead has critically suggested.[48] It would be arbitrary only if the events of the verified deductive theory of physics were phenomenal immediately sensed events.

A few weeks ago I had a lengthy discussion with Professor Einstein with respect to the fundamental assumptions of his theory of relativity. Late in the discussion this question of Whitehead's difference from Einstein with respect to the simultaneity of spatially separated events arose. Einstein said, "I simply do not understand Whitehead." I replied, "There is no difficulty in understanding him. When Whitehead affirms an intuitively given meaning for the simultaneity of spatially separated events, he means immediately sensed phenomenological events, not postulated public physically defined events. On this point he is clearly right. We certainly do see a flash in the distant visual space of the sky now, while we hear an explosion beside us. His reason for maintaining that this is the only kind of simultaneity which is given arises from his desire, in order to meet epistemological philosophical difficulties, to have only one continuum of intuitively given events, and to avoid the bifurcation between these phenomenal events and the postulated physically defined public events." Einstein replied, "Oh! Is that what he means? That would be wonderful! So many problems would be solved were it true! Unfortunately, it is a fairy tale. Our world is not as simple as that." After a moment's silent reflection, he added, "On that theory there would be no meaning to two observers speaking about the same event." The explosions in East and West Haven show Einstein to be correct. Since the sensed event is not merely the heard noise but the sensed time at which it is heard, and this is different for each observer between East Haven and West Haven, there is no meaning, if sensed events are all that exist, in the statement that all the observers hear the same event in the case of either explosion. We have no

[48] *The Concept of Nature*, 195.

alternative but to conclude with Einstein that the attempt to avoid bifurcation fails because it entails a doctrine of simultaneity which leaves both technical science and ordinary daily human relations without any meaning for the public time not merely of two spatially separated events but also of any single event. It is not an accident that we have to go to the physically defined events of astronomical physics for our public time.

SUMMARY

Whitehead's philosophy of science has been produced by three factors: (1) Bergson's emphasis upon the all-sufficiency of immediate intuition and the primacy of process, (2) the epistemological difficulties into which the scientist's bifurcation of nature led modern philosophers, and (3) the reconstruction in the fundamental concepts of contemporary science necessitated by recent discoveries, especially Einstein's theory of relativity. It has both the strength and the weaknesses of these three influences. Both have appeared in our analysis.

The weaknesses are (1) a questionable theory of internal relatedness for sensed events, (2) an inadequate theory of scientific objects, and of transformation equations, (3) a failure to account for scientific causality or public time, (4) too radical a conflict with the accepted and verified results of contemporary science, and (5) a general tendency to find greater deliverances of knowledge in sense awareness than it exhibits. All these weaknesses go back to the first two influences. It is not that these influences are necessarily wrong; it is his doctrine of *nothing but* the intuited or the immediately sensed which accompanies them that does the damage. But, to drop the "nothing but" is to admit bifurcation.

The strength is that (1) Whitehead's theory, while being less compatible with the empirical evidence on many essential points than Einstein's, also accounts for certain facts for which Einstein's, to date, has given no explanation, notably Kant's "incongruent counterparts," and for others such as Newton's rotating bucket experiment, for which Einstein's explanation is somewhat artificial; and (2) Whitehead's philosophy of science faces the epistemological as well as the scientific difficulties, whereas

Einstein offers his theory only for the physics of the situation and thus leaves untouched the epistemological problem which the philosopher of science has to face.

The writer has shown[49] that the scientific difficulties which Whitehead's theory meets can be met within Einstein's assumptions in an alternative way. Whitehead admits that this alternative meets the scientific difficulties.[50]

Only the epistemological problem, therefore, remains for one who would follow Einstein rather than deviate from the latter in accepting Whitehead's philosophy of science.

We have noted that Einstein's physics follows Newton's in bifurcating nature and that the Newtonian bifurcation led to insoluble epistemological difficulties in modern philosophy. Our analysis showed that Newton's first bifurcation between the object as sensed and the object as postulated gave rise historically to Locke's second bifurcation between the object as postulated and the observer. Because of the insoluble difficulties of the second bifurcation, Whitehead concluded that the first also must be rejected.

But this does not follow. Common sense and science only require the first bifurcation. The fact that the second came after the first historically does not entail that the first gives rise to the second necessarily. Also, it is only the second bifurcation which is epistemologically vicious.

This suggests the way out. One must, for reasons derived from immediate intuition, common sense experience, and experimental physics indicated previously in our analysis, follow Newton and Einstein in accepting the first bifurcation and escape the epistemological impasse of traditional modern philosophy by rejecting the second bifurcation. Elsewhere[51] the writer has briefly sketched the direction which this must take. The working out of this alternative must await another occasion. Here we merely conclude that Whitehead was correct in rejecting the second

---

[49] *Proc. Nat'l Acad. of Sciences,* Vol. 16, 55-68; also *Science and First Principles* (New York and Cambridge, England, 1931), chap. II.

[50] *Process and Reality,* 508.

[51] *Research Publications of the Association for Nervous and Mental Diseases,* 1939, Vol. 19, 99-104.

bifurcation and incorrect in concluding therefrom that he must reject the first.

Nevertheless, Whitehead's philosophy of science is the most important achievement in this field in our time. Compared with Whitehead, others have not even seen the difficulties, to say nothing about providing solutions for them, worked out in detail. It is his great merit to have seen the entire problem in all its ramifications, intuitive, technical, scientific, and epistemological and to have developed a detailed systematic doctrine for its solution. If, for the reasons given in our analysis, this solution is destined not to be the one upon which the scientific and philosophical thought of the immediate future will settle, nevertheless, it is only by confronting current scientific theory with the difficulties Whitehead has indicated and with the specific philosophy of science he has developed that we are being guided to a more satisfactory answer.

FILMER S. C. NORTHROP

DEPARTMENT OF PHILOSOPHY
YALE UNIVERSITY

Evander Bradley McGilvary

SPACE-TIME, SIMPLE LOCATION, AND PREHENSION

4

SPACE-TIME, SIMPLE LOCATION, AND PREHENSION

IN retrospect we can now see that the publication of Mr. Whitehead's *Organisation of Thought* in 1917 was the herald of the coming of an important protagonist into the arena of philosophy. He was already well known in mathematical circles, but only a few philosophers, at least on this side of the water, had ever heard of him. Within three years we were all reading *The Principles of Natural Knowledge* and *The Concept of Nature*, greatly to our profit and enlightenment. And we needed the enlightenment. There had been a rumor for some time bruited about among us of a new theory in physics called the theory of relativity; but most of us had a vague idea that it was of concern only to physicists, that somehow it solved problems in that field by proving that space by itself and time by itself were only shadows cast by space-time which alone had independent reality. But the theory, so we were told, could be understood only by adepts in higher mathematics, mathematics so high as to be utterly out of reach of a pedestrian philosopher. We even heard that not more than a dozen mathematicians could master the elements of the theory. No wonder that we had all become defeatists, and drew into our own shells, where we might hope to withstand the assaults of the mystical giant Abracadabra, who could make the less appear the greater length.

Such was the general situation when along came Mr. Whitehead, speaking a language that for the most part we could understand and employing equations that after considerable brushing up we could follow. There might be some sense in relativity after all. At least it became evident that, for better or for worse, relativity had been plunked down right within our very shells by one who showed himself a philosopher. We could no longer ignore it. But it took some of us a long time to come to terms with it, and some of us apparently still regard it as an enemy of clear thought. But there it is, and there it bids fair to stay. And Mr. Whitehead is largely responsible for its being there in our own bailiwick.

For one I am very grateful to him for what he has done. But he not only has forced relativity upon our recognition, if not upon our acceptance. After he had rewritten relativity to his own liking in *The Principle of Relativity*, he proceeded to use it as a building stone in a new philosophical structure which he called "the philosophy of organism" or "organic mechanism," and beguiled us into reading it by writing some of the choicest prose ever used in a brief outline of the development of modern thought. This he did in the first two-thirds of *Science and the Modern World*. And when he had us thoroughly charmed, he thrust upon us his "prehensions" and his "fallacy of simple location," his God as "the ultimate limitation, and His existence" as "the ultimate irrationality." Mr. Whitehead is a master of propaedeutics: he would not have his disciples cross their bridges till they came to them, but when they did come, what staggeringly steep bridges! We had hardly caught our breaths before he displayed to us reality in process in *Process and Reality*. And most of us have not yet done with catching our breaths. There we have again, after years of dormancy, philosophy in the grand manner. It is truly a great work; few have ever been greater.

In my copy of it I put under my name the date of its purchase, "1929." I see that it is also the date of its publication. Ever since that date it has been the subject of recurrent study, both in privacy and in the fellowship of other students. The time thus spent has been repaid with usury, leaving me greatly in debt. There is much that I still do not understand, as will appear in the sequel. But even where I cannot understand the solutions Mr. Whitehead offers for the problems he discusses, I have come to realize more keenly the significance of the problems and the necessity of grappling with them afresh. And oddly enough, the failure to understand has often not had the result such failures usually have. I have in many cases the vague feeling that if I only could get the right hold on his solutions, I should see that they are tenable. Each item in his philosophy leaves on me the impression the famous "flower in the crannied wall" left on Tennyson. Or shall I make a more homely comparison? An attempt to get my teeth into Mr. Whitehead's philosophy reminds me of the struggle of a squirrel with a cocoanut. He knows that there is something inside that would satisfy could he but get at it; but all that he can do is to roll it around; his jaws are too small, or to put it the other way about, the nut is too big and too round.[1] But even a cocoanut has "eyes" through which teeth lucky enough to find them, may get at the meat inside. Sometimes I think that I have hit upon such eyes, but still there is meat beyond my reach.

Another difficulty in understanding Mr. Whitehead is what one should expect of any philosopher whose publications range through more than a score of years, during which his views have been developing. One has no right to expect him publicly to retract every sentence he has written that he now would not write again. Henry James tried to do this in part by rewriting some of his novels, but the result has not been such as to tempt a philosopher to follow his example. In studying Mr. Whitehead's earlier works, one is not seldom left wondering whether what one finds there will fit into the later scheme or whether it has been demoded by what follows. Hence it is the part of prudence to raise the question without flatly attributing contradiction to the philosopher. For this reason I will take up in this

---

[1] Some years ago a story was circulated here in Madison, and I got it from one of the participants in the events narrated. A distinguished dean and several other equally distinguished biologists, all of them enthusiastic investigators, decided on a novel experiment. A cocoanut was placed on the flat roof of a porch overhung by a branch of a tree frequented by squirrels; and the issue was eagerly awaited, with notebooks out and pencils poised, ready to record every item with split-second date. It was not long before things began to happen. A squirrel jumped down to the roof, squirrel enough to know a nut when he saw and smelt it. For minutes, long to the spectators and doubtless long also to the squirrel, the nut was pushed hither and yon, till it finally rolled off the roof and smashed the skull of a dog that happened to be strolling by.

The tale has a moral: had the nut been less round, the dog's head were now sound.

essay five of Mr. Whitehead's works in chronological order, confining my attention to five. Of these five *The Principles of Natural Knowledge, The Concept of Nature,* and *The Principle of Relativity,* all published within the course of three years, evidently constitute an integrated group. One important thought running through the three is that the universe consists in part of "contingent" facts and relations, and in part of "systematic relatedness," and that any definiteness of character "is gained through the relatedness and not the relatedness through the character."[2] This idea controls Whitehead's "exposition of an alternative rendering of the theory of relativity." "My whole course of thought," he tells us, "presupposes the magnificent stroke of genius by which Einstein and Minkowski assimilated time and space.[3] But he does not accept Einstein's philosophy of nature.

The metrical formulae finally arrived at are those of the earlier theory [of Einstein], but the meanings ascribed to the algebraic symbols are entirely different. As the result of a consideration of the character of our knowledge in general, and of our knowledge of nature in particular, undertaken in Part I of this book and in my two previous works on this subject, I deduce that our experience requires and exhibits a basis of uniformity, and that in the case of nature this basis exhibits itself as the uniformity of spatio-temporal relations. This conclusion entirely cuts away the casual heterogeneity of these relations which is the essential of Einstein's later theory. . . . It is inherent in my theory to maintain the old division between physics and geometry. Physics is the science of the contingent relations of nature and geometry expresses its uniform relatedness.[4]

Apparently results obtainable only by experiments exhibit "contingent relations of nature," whereas results obtained by purely logical processes are alone expressive of nature's "uniform relatedness." With this distinction in mind, let us review Mr. Whitehead's criticism of Einstein's special theory of relativity.

[2] *The Principle of Relativity,* 19.
[3] *Ibid.,* 88.
[4] *Ibid.,* v-vi.

The reason why the velocity of light has been adopted as the standard velocity in the definition of simultaneity is because the negative results of the experiments to determine the earth's motion require that this velocity, which is the '*c*' of Maxwell's equations, should have this property. Also light signals are after all our only way of detecting distant events. . . .

But there are certain objections to the acceptance of Einstein's definition of simultaneity, the 'signal-theory' as we will call it. In the first place, light signals are very important elements in our lives, but still we cannot but feel that the signal-theory somewhat exaggerates their position. The very meaning of simultaneity is made to depend on them. There are blind people and dark cloudy nights, and neither blind people nor people in the dark are deficient in a sense of simultaneity. They know quite well what it means to bark both their shins at the same instant. In fact the determination of simultaneity in this way is never made, and if it could be made would not be accurate; for we live in air and not *in vacuo*.[5]

This passage calls for several comments. In the first place Mr. Whitehead must have been aware of the fact that Einstein makes a fundamental distinction between simultaneity *at the same place* and simultaneity *at a distance*. Any man's two shins are (of course not precisely) in the same place, and so are my watch and a train I see arriving at a station. And yet of watch and train Einstein says:

If, for instance, I say, "That train arrives here at 7 o'clock," I mean something like this: "The pointing of the small hand of my watch to 7 and the arrival of the train are simultaneous events."

And he expressly says the simultaneity thus defined

is satisfactory when we are concerned with defining a time exclusively for the place where the watch is located; but it is no longer satisfactory when we have to connect in time series of events occurring at different places, or—what comes to the same thing—to evaluate the times of events occurring at places remote from the watch.[6]

[5] *The Principles of Natural Knowledge*, 53. Until further notice subsequent quotations are to the immediately following passages.

[6] "Zur Elektrodynamik bewegter Körper," reprinted in *Das Relativitätsprinzip: eine Sammlung von Abhandlungen*, 5te Aufl., (Leipzig, Berlin, 1923), 27; English translation by W. Perrett and G. B. Jeffery (London, 1923), 39. This translation

Of course such judgments of simultaneity are never ideally precise, not even, as we have seen, in the case of the barking of one's two shins. But without such direct experiences of simultaneity we probably should never have got any idea of simultaneity. Mr. Whitehead is thus obviously in error when he says of Einstein's definition of simultaneity: "The very meaning of simultaneity is made to depend on light signals." He is also in error when he says: "In fact the determination of simultaneity in this way [i.e., by electromagnetic signals] is never made." Any one who checks his clocks by radio is determining simultaneity at a distance in this way; and if it be objected that when this statement was made radio was not in very general use, the reply is that "Western Union clocks" have been in use in America for more than twenty-two years.

But is the telegraphic transmission of signals transmission *in vacuo?* Of course not. As Mr. Whitehead says, "we live in air and not *in vacuo,*" and telegraphy lives in metal wires. But it is of course not bringing news to him when it is pointed out that absolute precision is never attained in experimental physics. Einstein's problem was to "define" some method whereby we can determine with as great precision as possible what events at a distance from each other are simultaneous, since the extrapolation of the felt simultaneity of barked shins, without more ado, did not seem to him to be satisfactory. Such a fact as that "we live in air and not *in vacuo*" has never in modern physics been regarded as a valid objection against the assumption in physics that there are physical constants. Physics obtains its "constants" by devious methods of successive approximations, and the velocity of light *in vacuo* and in the absence of gravitational fields is one of these constants. These constants are indeed "contingent" facts, and therefore for the present we admit that Mr. White-

---

was made from the 4th German edition of the collection, and published under the title, *The Principle of Relativity*. Hereafter I shall, in the present paper, refer to the German edition with an "*R*" and to the English translation with "*Eng.*"

I shall put in parenthesis the name of the author of the paper referred to. In this way confusion is avoided between the collection of papers and Mr. Whitehead's volume which bears the same title, and will be referred to by this title without further specification.

head has scored a point—but we will return to this point later.

Also there are other physical messages from place to place; there is the transmission of material bodies, the transmission of sound, the transmission of waves and ripples on the surface of water, the transmission of nerve excitation through the body, and innumerable other forms which enter into habitual experience. The transmission of light is only one form among many.

But there has never been any evidence offered that these other innumerable forms of transmission have the character that the prevalent interpretation of innumerable experiments gives to the propagation of light *in vacuo*, namely, the character of having the same velocity in both of two systems in relative motion, a character that Mr. Whitehead grants to it "as an approximation."[1]

One of the most surprising objections that Mr. Whitehead makes to the 'signal theory' is given next:

Furthermore local time does not concern one material particle only. The same definition of simultaneity holds throughout the whole space of a consentient set in the Newtonian group. The message theory does not account for the consentience in time-reckoning which characterises a consentient set, nor does it account for the fundamental position of the Newtonian group.

The first of these sentences surely is not meant to imply that Einstein held to Lorentz's view with regard to "local time." It has been very generally recognized that Einstein did away with local time that concerned "one material particle only." He organized Lorentz's "local times" into time systems each extending throughout a whole system at rest. He did not call these time systems "consentient sets," but this at worst can only be regarded as failure to hit upon a felicitous terminology. He did not account for "the fundamental position of the Newtonian group" because he did not recognize that fundamental position. On the contrary he denied that the Newtonian group is fundamental. This group is for him a limiting group but not a fundamental group. To charge him with failure to account for "the fundamental position of the Newtonian group" is to beg the

[1] *The Concept of Nature*, 195.

question: *Is* the Newtonian group fundamental? It is difficult to see how this question can be answered dogmatically, in view of the fact that all pure geometries, Euclidean, Riemannian, and others, rest on postulates and not on self-evident axioms, whereas all physical geometries involve what Mr. Whitehead calls "contingent factors." *As a matter of fact and not of logic,* is physical space Euclidean, Riemannian, or other? It would seem as if the only way to answer this question is to go to the laboratory, and the results of laboratory experiments are "contingent." They are what they are, but they might conceivably have been otherwise.

This raises the whole question as to the relation between physics and mathematics in the construction of the philosophy of nature. Is the physicist required to dig into the foundations of mathematics and work out a satisfactory logical theory as to these foundations before he has a right to make use of whatever extant mathematics is available for his purpose? Is not the relation between physicist and mathematician one of co-operation, in which the physicist is entitled to depend on the mathematician for the mathematics he uses, just as the mathematician may follow the lead of the physicist in deciding what further developments in pure mathematics are in order to meet the demands of the physicist. "Once in the bluest of blue moons," a physicist may arise who is also a mathematical genius and who, in order to solve his physical problem, establishes a new branch of mathematics on a secure logical basis. Being an ignorant layman in the history of mathematics, I have to depend on hearsay evidence that Newton was such a genius. What Einstein did in working out his special theory was to accept from mathematics the Euclidean notions of straight lines, parallels and perpendiculars, without asking whether these notions could be defined by assuming families of parallel durations and by subjecting the durations to "the method of extensive abstraction." What Mr. Whitehead has done is to make this assumption and to develop this method, and then to go to the results of the laboratory to find that "within the limits of our inexactitude of observation the velocity of light is an approximation to the critical velocity 'c' which expresses the relation between our space and time units."[8] Mr. Whitehead and Einstein started from the opposite sides of the field of co-operative enterprise; and, when they met in the same equations, Mr. Whitehead seems in effect to have greeted his fellow worker with the charge that there is only one side from which to start in order to secure a philosophy of nature. In philosophy, uniform relatedness always must come first ('so he insistently asserts), and then find the contingent facts for it to relate—*never* the other way about! In other words, definiteness of character "is gained through the relatedness and not the relatedness through the character." Otherwise you have only "the casual heterogeneity of these relations!"

But before considering whether Einstein's "heterogeneity" of spatio-temporal relations was so hopelessly "casual," let us return to Einstein's definition of simultaneity at a distance. I am not sure whether I have touched upon the real nerve center controlling Mr. Whitehead's reaction to this definition. Other critics of this definition at any rate have argued that it is arbitrary; and the argument is so important that it is worth while here to discuss it, whether Mr. Whitehead would underwrite it or not. Let us quote the passage in which this definition is given.

If at the point A of space there is a clock, an observer at A can determine the time values of events in the immediate proximity of A by finding the positions of the hands which are simultaneous with these events. [The reader will observe here that Einstein repeats that something similar to the felt simultaneity of barked shins is the basis of his further discussion.] If there is at the point B of space another clock in all respects resembling the one at A, it is possible for an observer at B to determine the time values of events in the immediate neighborhood of B. But it is not possible without further assumption [Festsetzung] to compare, in respect of time, an event at A with an event at B. We have so far defined only an "A time" and a "B time." We have not defined a common "time" for A and B, for the latter cannot be defined at all unless we establish *by definition* [man *durch Definition* festsetzt] that the "time" required by light to travel from A to B equals the "time" it requires to travel from B to A. Let a ray of light start at the "A time" t_A from A toward B, let it at the "B time" t_B be reflected at B

[8] *The Concept of Nature*, 195.

in the direction of A, and arrive again at A at the "A time" t'_A. In accordance with definition the two clocks synchronize if

$$t_B - t_A = t'_A - t_B.^9$$

This passage requires especial attention. In the first place, it is to be noted that, beginning with the fourth sentence, the word "time" appears eight times, and every time it is enclosed in quotation marks. The reason should be obvious. The reason is that "time" is here used in three different senses. "A time" and "B time" are separate *dates* as given by the respective clocks on the occasions of the respective events mentioned; whereas in the clause "that the 'time' required by light to travel from A to B equals the 'time' it requires to travel from B to A," the word "time" means *time interval*. And there is a third "time," namely "a common 'time' for A and B."

In the second place, it is to be noted that what one "*durch Definition festsetzt*" is *not* the meaning of *simultaneity*, but the *equality of the two time intervals* here mentioned. And it should be obvious that the equality of two time intervals is not the same thing as the simultaneity of two events.

In the third place, we shall have to discover what is meant by the expression "*durch Definition festsetzt.*" Whatever be the meaning, it is natural that we should interpret the meaning of the verb "festsetzen" in the same way in which we interpret that of the noun "Festsetzung" used in the previous sentence.

In the fourth place, the paragraph we have quoted does not stand alone: there are six others following it in the same section which is entitled "Definition of Simultaneity;" and in the third paragraph of the next section there is a reference back to our paragraph. I suggest that we take the whole context into consideration; and since those who have worked forward have so sadly failed to see what Einstein was doing in the way of "defining" simultaneity of events at a distance, I suggest that we work backward. I therefore quote from the second section:

The following reflexions are based on the principle of relativity and on the principle of the constancy of the velocity of light. These two principles we define [please note this word "define"] as follows: . . .

⁹ *The Principle of Relativity* (Einstein), R, 28, *Eng.*, 39-40.

2. Any ray of light moves in the "stationary" system of co-ordinates with the determined [*bestimmten,* i.e., definite] velocity *c,* whether the ray be emitted by a stationary or by a moving body. Hence

velocity = (light path)/(time interval)

where time interval is to be taken in the sense of the definition in §1.[10]

I requested the reader to note the use of the word "define" in the second of these quoted sentences. Einstein's two "principles" are what we also call "postulates" or "assumptions," and what he does when he "defines" these postulates is *to lay them down in explicit terms.*

The closing reference to "definition in §1" given of "time interval," would seem to justify us in suggesting that perhaps "to define a principle or postulate" is another way of saying "to postulate by definition" (*durch Definition festzusetzen*), namely, to lay down a postulate *in explicit terms.* With this interpretation the last sentence of the earlier paragraph is a *sequitur:* "In accordance with what is thus laid down explicitly as a postulate (definitionsgemäss), the two clocks run synchronously if $t_B - t_A = t'_A - t_B$." I know of no other interpretation that would not involve a *non sequitur.* Nor do I recognize any arbitrariness in the whole procedure. Any one has a right in his theory of nature to lay down explicit postulates on which he operates—as much right as Mr. Whitehead has to lay down in his later theory his postulate of God in his two natures, "primordial" and "consequent." And it can be said of Einstein's postulate that it is at least subject to experimental test. This is of course to resort to "contingency," but most scientists prefer a theory that admits of such resort.

Now, whether my suggested interpretation of the puzzling "*durch Definition festsetzt*" be accepted or not, one thing is clear: what is "festgesetzt" is the *equality* of the two time *intervals,* and *not* a definition of simultaneity. And what has been obtained *as a logical consequence* is a clock at A and a clock at B, thus at a distance from each other, and known to be running synchronously. Now by universal acceptance, two clocks are synchronous when they run at the same rate and their equal

[10] *Ibid., R, 29, Eng., 41.*

readings are simultaneous. Hence, after two or three sentences which we need not here quote, Einstein could say:

we have settled [*festgelegt*] what is to be understood by synchronous stationary clocks located at different places, and have evidently obtained a definition of "simultaneous," or "synchronous," and of "time." The "time" of an event is that which is given simultaneously with the event by a stationary clock located at the place of the event, this clock being synchronous, and indeed synchronous for all time determinations, with a specified stationary clock . . . the time now defined being appropriate to the stationary system we call it "the time of the stationary system."

Thus, in spite of the conceded uncertainty as to the meaning of a single phrase, it must, I think, be also conceded that there is no uncertainty or ambiguity or arbitrariness in Einstein's method of defining "simultaneity at a distance." First he places two clocks "in all respects resembling" each other, one at A and the other at B, A and B being different points in a stationary system. At A and B he also stations observers. Since the clocks are *clocks*, they mark time, and since they resemble each other in all respects, their periods are equal, or, in other words, they run at the same rate. He signals by a light flash from A to B, which is reflected back to A. He assumes or postulates that the time intervals in the to and fro trips are equal. On this assumption he has his clocks set so that $t_B - t_A = t'_A - t_B$, where t_A is the reading of the clock at A at the time of sending the signal from A, t_B is the reading of the clock at B on the arrival of the signal at B, and t'_A is the reading of the clock at A on the return of the reflected signal. The clocks thus set are defined as "synchronous," and this definition is the definition of "simultaneity at a distance," since synchronous clocks are those which, having equal periods, have equal *simultaneous* readings. And, because simultaneity is a symmetrical and transitive relation, *other* events occurring at the places and times where and when synchronous clocks have equal readings, are simultaneous with each other. The symmetry and transitivity of synchronism is *expressly* postulated by Einstein in two sentences (not quoted) in this very connection.

It is to be noted that neither here nor anywhere else in the paper, *The Electrodynamics of Moving Bodies,* does Einstein so much as refer to any *actually measured value* of the velocity of light. Had he used such a value, as for instance 300,000 km/sec, basing his argument on such a value, it could be said that he had used a "contingent" fact as a basis of his argument. On the contrary, he based his argument on the "principle of the constancy of the velocity of light," explicitly defined as "light path divided by time interval." What more in the way of "the uniformity of spatio-temporal relations" would Mr. Whitehead exact of a philosophy of nature than such a constancy of the spatio-temporal relation of the velocity of light, when it is borne in mind that it is the *constancy of this relation* and *not* the experimentally measured value of this relation that plays the decisive part in Einstein's special theory?

It is true that in the general theory the velocity of light is not regarded as constant. But the general theory is based on the special theory, and it is by the employment of tensor analysis that the general theory is developed. And tensor analysis deals with nothing but spatio-temporal relations. It is quite true, also, that Einstein says with regard to the requirement of general covariance that it "takes away from space and time the last remnant of physical objectivity."[11] But this is because he had accepted from Minkowski the view that the special theory involved the reduction of space and time to mere shadows of space-time, which alone has independent reality. This view Mr. Whitehead himself in part accepts when he says:

My whole course of thought presupposes the magnificent stroke of genius by which Einstein and Minkowski assimilated time and space. It also presupposes the general method of seeking tensor or invariant relations as general expressions for the laws of the physical field, a method due to Einstein.[12]

The first sentence of this quotation accepts the assimilation of space and time, while the second accepts the method of tensor analysis adopted by Einstein, which Einstein regarded as depriving space and time of the last remnant of physical

[11] *Ibid.,* R, 86, Eng., 117.
[12] *The Principle of Relativity,* 88.

objectivity, but which Mr. Whitehead regarded as having no such implication. However, what Mr. Whitehead calls "the modern assimilation of time and space"[13] is, I think, exactly what deprived space and time of physical objectivity.

In a paper recently published,[14] I have attempted to show that "the modern assimilation of time and space" was not the work of Einstein but of Minkowski, and that it was accomplished by the use of the spurious equation $c = 1$, where c is the velocity of light, adopted as unit velocity. By substituting from this equation into the Einsteinian equation[15]

$$x^2 + y^2 + z^2 = c^2 t^2,$$

there is obtained the equation

$$x^2 + y^2 + z^2 = t^2.$$

This equation effects the "assimilation" of time and space, since the expression on the left is unquestionably a spatial expression, and that on the right a temporal expression. A mystical turn is given to this assimilation by introducing what Sir Arthur Eddington calls "the mysterious factor $\sqrt{-1}$, which seems to have the property of turning time into space."[16] As the result of this transformation, Minkowski finds Einstein's "relativity postulate" a very feeble word for what has become *"the postulate of the absolute world* (or briefly, the world-postulate)." And "the essence of this postulate," he tells us, "may be clothed mathematically in a very pregnant manner in the mystic formula

$$3.10^5 \text{ km} = \sqrt{-1} \text{ sec.}"[17]$$

The equation $c = 1$ is spurious because c is a *velocity* unit and *not* unity (i.e., the number 1). The correct equation is

$$c = \text{unit-length/unit-time} = 3.10^5 \text{ km/sec.} \quad . . . \quad [1]$$

In the paper referred to, I gave a new derivation of the Lorentz transformation in which the expression ct appears early in the process in the equation

[13] *Ibid.*, 58.

[14] "The Lorentz Transformation and 'Space-Time'," in *The Journal of Philosophy*, Vol. XXXVIII, No. 13, 337-349.

[15] *The Principle of Relativity* (Einstein), R, 33, *Eng.*, 46.

[16] *Space, Time and Gravitation* (Cambridge, 1929), 48.

[17] *The Principle of Relativity* (Minkowski), R, 60 and 64, *Eng.*, 83 and 88.

$$ct = \sqrt{(x^2 + y^2 + z^2)} \ . \ . \ . \ [2]$$

where the expressions on both sides are unquestionably measures of *spatial* length. By substituting from the spurious equation $c = 1$ we get

$$t = \sqrt{(x^2 + y^2 + z^2)} \ . \ . \ . \ [3]$$

and thus seem to have converted a *spatial* measure number, ct,
into a *temporal* measure number, t, or, to borrow from Sir
Arthur Eddington, we seem to have "turned time into space."
It is apparently this conversion that Mr. Whitehead calls the
"assimilation of time and space." I am not suggesting that anywhere in his mathematical reasoning he actually makes use of
the equation $c = 1$. He does, however, adopt "the modern
assimilation of time and space," which can be effected only by
that use.

But if we substitute in [2] from [1], the left side of
[2], where t is the number of time units, becomes

(unit-length/unit-time) $\times$ t units of time $= t$ length units, [4]

since in authentic kinematics the product of the number of units
of velocity by the number of units of time is the number of units
of *length*, and *not* the number of units of *time*. Substituting from
[4] into [2] we get

t units of length $= \sqrt{(x^2 + y^2 + z^2)}$ units of length,

a perfectly respectable equation, which asserts that the number
of units of a length, measured kinematically, is equal to the
number of units of the same length when measured analytically
by the use of co-ordinates. Here there is no turning of time into
space, no assimilation of space and time. Time measures *remain*
time measures, and space measures *remain* space measures, because unit velocity *remains* unit *velocity*, not having been il-
legitimately turned into a "pure" number. There is as much
difference between a unit of velocity and the number 1 as there
is between 1 cow and the number 1. It is the failure to recognize this logical fact that brought "Space-Time" into our world
and all the attendant mysticism. Minkowski was correct when he
said that his world-postulate "may be clothed mathematically in
a very pregnant manner in the mystic formula

$$3.10^5 \text{ km} = \sqrt{-1} \text{ sec."}$$

If a man's "genius" is to be measured by the influence he has exerted on the thought of his time, Minkowski deserves to be regarded as a genius. But whether his genius was "magnificent" is something else. At any rate, it is of a different sort from that of Einstein. Einstein unhappily was misled by Minkowski into accepting the assimilation of space and time, and therefore into depriving them of objectivity.

It is to Mr. Whitehead's credit that, in spite of his acceptance of the assimilation of time and space, he did not follow many other relativists into the realm of mysticism, but continued to insist on the "heterogeneity of time from space."[18] However, the assimilation of time and space has had one fortunate result, since

> There is some soul of goodness in things evil
> Would men observingly distil it out.

That assimilation has drawn men's observing attention to the sort of real union of time and space which has always prevailed, but the implications of which had been overlooked. For instance, the view that "the progressive advance of nature" consists of a succession of instantaneous presents seems to have been widely held until the present century, although there were notable exceptions, among which Bergson's philosophy occurs to every one. But there was nothing in the accepted equations of motion that implied that time is a succession of self-sufficient instants. Physicists spoke of "velocity at an instant," and apparently some of them regarded this concept as having a meaning even when the "instant" was taken as an isolated point in time. But this view was not universally held before the advent of relativity. I find even in an article on "Calculus" in a popular encyclopedia the following discussion:

> But as this idea of what a differential is is somewhat vague, owing to the difficulty of actually conceiving something that is 'infinitely small', the following considerations may be resorted to. Studying the motion of a ball thrown up in the air, we consider infinitely small intervals of time dt merely in order to be able to think of the motion as uniform; for within any finite interval the motion is variable. . . . We may, according-

[18] *The Principle of Relativity*, 68.

ly, define the differential of distance *dl* as the distance that *would be* traversed by the ball in an arbitrary finite interval of time, *dt*, beginning at a given instant, if at the instant the motion became uniform.[19]

It is unfair to attribute to any scientist or philosopher, who has not expressly said that "velocity at an instant" is a manner of speaking, the view that there is in actuality such a thing, as it would be unfair to attribute to a scientist who speaks of "acceleration from infinity" in connection with gravitation the view that actually any object ever starts at rest from an infinite distance and on reaching the earth has acquired the assigned "acceleration from infinity." I rather suspect that correct thinking on the union of space and time did not begin in 1908, just as the correct doctrine of "limits" was not initiated then.

Let us now turn to a consideration of what I cannot but regard as a strange denial of a patent fact of experience, when Mr. Whitehead says:

It is an error to ascribe parts to objects, where 'part' here means spatial or temporal part. The erroneousness of such ascription immediately follows from the premiss that primarily an object is not in space or in time. The absence of temporal parts of objects is a commonplace of thought. No one thinks that part of a stone is at one time and another part of the stone is at another time. The same stone is at both times, in the sense in which the stone is existing at those times (if it be existing). But spatial parts are in a different category, and it is natural to think of various parts of a stone, simultaneously existing. Such a conception confuses the stone as an object with the event which exhibits the actual relations of the stone within nature. . . . The fundamental rule is that events have parts and that—except in a derivative sense, from their relations to events—objects have no parts.[20]

As to temporal parts of a stone, how about the geological theory of the process of sedimentation by which rocks are

[19] *The New International Encyclopedia* (New York, 1902), Vol. III, 745, d. The author of this article could not have been influenced by either Einstein or Minkowski; and yet I wonder whether those under the influence of "the modern assimilation" could succeed much better in conveying to the lay reader the idea that velocity at an instant is not to be interpreted as something that has any meaning apart from "an *interval* of time *beginning* at an instant."

[20] *The Principles of Natural Knowledge*, 65f.

formed? If they have grown by sedimentary accretion, it would seem as if their parts are in time; or is Mr. Whitehead speaking only of such small stones as we find these days, and not of *rocks?* But even in this case, any one who has seen a stone crusher in operation naturally thinks of a part of a stone at one time and another part as at another time. A full discussion of the subject would take us over into the question of physical particles; but without entering into this subject, may one not ask whether the "fundamental rule" is not rather dogmatically stated? Mr. Whitehead's position is that of an uncompromising Platonist; and of course any one has a right to be a Platonist. It cannot be proved that Platonism is a false doctrine, but I wonder whether it can be proved that it is a true doctrine. I have discussed this question elsewhere and cannot here go into the matter again.[21] I only venture to remark that a fundamental cleavage within nature between eternal objects and events is as objectionable as a "bifurcation of nature" to which I object as much as does Mr. Whitehead. It seems to result in two mutually contradictory notions about events. The first is expressed in the passage just quoted: "events have parts and . . . —except in a derivative sense, from their relations to events—objects have no parts." This makes events distinct terms of a two-term relation of "ingression." The second is expressed when it is said:

I give the name 'event' to a spatio-temporal happening. An event does not in any way imply rapid change; the endurance of a block of marble is an event. Nature presents itself to us as essentially a becoming, and any limited portion of nature which preserves most completely such concreteness as attaches to nature itself is also a becoming and is what I call an event. By this I do not mean a bare portion of space-time. Such a concept is a further abstraction. I mean a part of the becomingness of nature, coloured with all the hues of its content.[22]

How the becomingness of nature can have "a part coloured with all the hues of its content," when all colors and hues have no parts, is beyond my understanding. I can understand when

[21] "Relations in General and Universals in Particular," in *The Journal of Philosophy*, Vol. XXXVI (1939), 5-15, 29-40.
[22] *The Principle of Relativity*, 21.

it is said that "there is no such entity as a bare event,"[23] but if this is the case, it seems that a relation of "ingression" is unnecessary for reconstituting an entity which abstraction has torn apart. All that is necessary is to let the event be the entirety it is before we have split it into an "event that has parts" and something else called an "object" which has no parts.

Let us pass to what Mr. Whitehead calls "the fallacy of simple location."

To say that a bit of matter has *simple location* means that, in expressing its spatio-temporal relations, it is adequate to state that it is where it is, in a definite finite region of space, and throughout a definite finite duration of time, apart from any essential reference of the relations of that bit of matter to other regions of space and to other durations of time. Again, this concept of simple location is independent of the controversy between the absolutist and the relativist views of space and time. So long as any theory of space, or of time, can give a meaning, either absolute or relative, to the idea of a definite region of space, and of a definite duration of time, the idea of simple location has a perfectly definite meaning. . . . I shall argue that among the primary elements of nature as apprehended in our immediate experience, there is no element whatever which possesses this character of simple location.[24]

Since the relativist theory of space and time maintains that no region of space (or duration of time) has any meaning apart from its spatial relations of distance and direction to other regions (or apart from its relation of before and after to other durations), I find it hard to distinguish the denial of "simple location" from the relativist doctrine, unless we emphasize the words "a bit of matter" at the beginning of the passage just quoted. That this is the intended emphasis is apparent when we consider the context in which the denial of "simple location" is made:

There will be some fundamental assumptions which adherents of all the variant systems within the epoch unconsciously presuppose. . . . One

[23] *Ibid.*, 26.

[24] *Science and the Modern World*, 81. A similar definition of "simple location" is given on pages 69-70. (Page references in this essay to *Science and the Modern World* are to the American edition, 1925.)

such assumption underlies the whole philosophy of nature during the modern period. It is embodied in the conception which is supposed to express the most concrete aspect of nature. The Ionian philosophers asked, What is nature made of? The answer is couched in terms of stuff, or matter, or material, . . . which has the property of simple location in space and time, or, if you adopt the more modern ideas, in space-time.[25]

Now Mr. Whitehead's answer substitutes "actual occasions" for stuff, or matter, or material, and it is by "prehensions" that any actual occasion effects its own concretion. What it prehends is, among other things, other actual occasions. These prehended occasions have their "locations" in space and time, and the pre-hending occasion also has its location. And the denial of "simple location" is the denial of the exclusiveness of these several locations. Each actual occasion is located not only where its own concrescence takes place, but is also in every other location where the prehension of it by other actual occasions occurs.

In a certain sense, everything is everywhere at all times. For every location involves an aspect of itself in every other location. Thus every spatio-temporal standpoint mirrors the world. If you try to imagine this doctrine in terms of our conventional views of space and time, which presuppose simple location, it is a great paradox. But if you think of it in terms of our naïve experience, it is a mere transcript of the obvious facts. You are in a certain place perceiving things. Your perception takes place where you are, and is entirely dependent on how your body is functioning. But this functioning of the body in one place, exhibits for your cognisance an aspect of the distant environment, fading away into the general knowledge that there are things beyond.[26]

Now this concept of "mirroring" reminds us of Leibniz, and Mr. Whitehead says: "It is evident that I can use Leibniz's language, and say that every volume mirrors in itself every other volume in space."[27] But Leibniz's mirroring monads had, as we all know, no windows through which they could *go out* and through which other monads could *enter*. Their mirroring took place by grace of "pre-established harmony." Not so with

[25] *Ibid.*, 69.
[26] *Ibid.*, 128-129.
[27] *Ibid.*, 92.

Mr. Whitehead's monads. "Each monadic creature [so he tells us] is a mode of the process of 'feeling' the world, of housing the world in one unit of complex feeling. . . . Such a unit is an 'actual occasion'."[28] It is like 'Omer, when he "smote 'is blooming lyre":

> An' what he thought 'e might require,
> 'E went an' took—the same as me.

This taking, which of course is the English for "prehension," is literal taking and bringing home; and, as with 'Omer's taking, what is thus taken is not *dislodged* from where it was; and the reason for this is that "everything is everywhere at all times." The qualification, "in a certain sense," thus is not left vague. The "sense" in which "everything is everywhere at all times" is that, except perhaps in "negative prehension," everything is actually and actively taken up into everything else. Not the *whole* of everything is thus taken up, but only what the prehending monad can use in effecting its concrescence.

The things which are grasped into a realised unity, here and now, are not the castle, the cloud, and the planet simply in themselves; but they are the castle, the cloud, and the planet from the standpoint, in space and time, of the prehensive unification. In other words, it is the perspective of the castle over there from the standpoint of the unification here. It is, therefore, aspects of the castle, the cloud, and the planet which are grasped into unity here. You will remember that the idea of perspectives is quite familiar in philosophy. It was introduced by Leibniz, in the notion of his monads mirroring perspectives of the universe. I am using the same notion, only I am toning down his monads into the unified events in space and time [i.e., into actual occasions].[29]

Thus we find that Mr. Whitehead's doctrine of denial of "simple location" is intimately connected with his view of "prehension," and that this is likewise intimately connected with his view of "perspectives." This implication of elements in a theory with other elements is, of course, what is to be expected in any truly systematic philosophy. We thus have to examine his doc-

---

[28] *Process and Reality*, 124. (Page references to *Process and Reality* in this essay are to the American edition, 1930.)
[29] *Science and the Modern World*, 98f.

trine of perspectives to see whether we can get additional light on the assertion that in a certain sense everything is everywhere at all times. Unfortunately, so far as concerns an attempt to discuss Mr. Whitehead's philosophy in any short paper, the doctrine of perspectives implies his doctrine of "objectification," and that implies other doctrines, and so on till we have come full circle.

But as we have seen, even a cocoanut has "eyes" through which teeth, lucky enough to find them, may possibly get at the meat inside. I suspect that the following "Categories of Explanation" may be such "eyes" in Mr. Whitehead's philosophy of organism, where everything is endowed with ubiquity and sempiternity.

(ii) That in the becoming of an actual entity, the *potential* unity of many entities—actual and non-actual—acquires the *real* unity of the one actual entity; so that the actual entity is the real concrescence of many potentials.

(iv) That the potentiality for being an element in a real concrescence of many entities into one actuality, is the one general metaphysical character attaching to all entities, actual and non-actual; and that every item in its universe is involved in each concrescence. In other words, it belongs to the nature of a 'being' that it is a potential for every 'becoming'. This is the 'principle of relativity'.

(v) That no two actual entities originate from an identical universe; though the difference between the two universes only consists in some actual entities, included in one and not in the other. . . .[30]

Thus each novel entity in its concrescence "includes" within itself other actual entities, which thus become "elements" within its constitution. In this way the novel entity is where and when its concrescence occurs. The other entities are where and when their concrescences occur; but in being included in the constitution of the novel entity, they are also where and when this entity occurs. It is in *this* sense that "everything is everywhere and all times."

To call this inclusion of other entities within the novel entity

[30] *Process and Reality,* 33f.

a "mirroring"[31] is an understatement by metaphor. A more adequate and more literal expression of what occurs in prehension is found when Mr. Whitehead says that an actual entity "objectifies" what it prehends. "The term 'objectification' refers to the particular mode in which the potentiality of one actual entity is realised in another actual entity."[32]

Some real component in the objectified entity assumes the rôle of being how that particular entity is a datum in the experience of the subject. In this case, the objectified contemporaries are only directly relevant to the subject in their character of arising from a datum which is an extensive continuum. . . . They thus exhibit the community of contemporary actualities as a common world with mathematical relations —where the term 'mathematical' is used in the sense in which it would have been understood by Plato, Euclid, and Descartes, before the modern discovery of the true definition of pure mathematics.[33]

Thus, an act of experience has an objective scheme of extensive order by reason of the double fact that its own *perspective* standpoint has extensive content, and that the other actual entities are objectified with the retention of their extensive relationships.[34]

But if we take the doctrine of objectification seriously, the extensive continuum at once becomes the primary factor in objectification. It provides the general scheme of extensive perspective which is exhibited in all the mutual objectifications by which actual entities prehend each other.[35]

This general scheme, as prehended by an actual entity from

[31] "The volumes [A and B] of space have no independent existence . . . the aspect of B from A is the *mode* in which B enters into the composition of A. This is the modal character of space, that the prehensive unity of A is the prehension into unity of the aspects of all other volumes from the standpoint of A. The shape of a volume is the formula from which the totality of its aspects can be derived. Thus the shape of a volume is more abstract than its aspects. It is evident that I can use Leibniz's language, and say that every volume mirrors in itself every other volume in space." (*Science and the Modern World,* 91-92.)

"It [the extensive continuum] is not a fact prior to the world; it is the first determination of order—that is, of real potentiality—arising out of the general character of the world. In its full generality beyond the present epoch, it does not involve shapes, dimensions, or measurability; these are additional determinations of real potentiality arising from our cosmic epoch." (*Process and Reality,* 103.)

[32] *Process and Reality,* 34.

[33] *Ibid.,* 97.

[34] *Ibid.,* 105 (my italics).

[35] *Ibid.,* 118.

its own perspective standpoint, is what Mr. Whitehead calls "geometrical perspective relatedness."[36]

I have now singled out a number of passages, taken each from its own context, and put them together in such a way that each forms a part of the context in which the others play a part. Whether in doing this I have done injustice to the author's thought, he alone can say; and, fortunately, he is here with us to say. All that I can claim is that, by doing this, I get into my perspective Mr. Whitehead's theory of perspectives—a perspective which for me at least "makes sense" out of his denial of simple location. I cannot agree with what Lord Russell said of Mr. Whitehead's "fallacy of simple location, when avoided": To his mind, "such a view, if taken seriously, is incompatible with science."[37]

On the contrary, I find a remarkable family resemblance between Mr. Whitehead's view of perspectives and Lord Russell's, with individual differences such as are found in all families except in case of identical twins. The resemblance, no doubt, appears to the two authors to be superficial, and yet it is there, superficial or not. Often it happens that members of the same family dislike and even resent attention called to family characteristics.

We have already seen what Mr. Whitehead's view is, if my interpretation of it proves to be correct. Let us look at Lord Russell's.

It will be observed that *two* places in perspective space are associated with every aspect of a thing: namely, the place where the thing is, and the place which is the perspective of which the aspect in question forms part.[38]

The "two places" will be indefinitely multiplied when it is

[36] *Ibid.,* 185.

[37] *The Analysis of Matter* (New York, London, 1927), 340f. He added, "and it involves a mystic pantheism." On this added stricture, I reserve my comments, for the reason that I am here considering only Mr. Whitehead's way of avoiding that "fallacy," and not the *other* features of his philosophy with which this avoidance may be implicated.

[38] *Our Knowledge of the External World as a Field for Scientific Method in Philosophy,* by Bertrand Russell (Chicago and London, Fourth Thousand, 1915), 92.

remembered that there is an indefinite number of places where the perspective is, of which the aspect in question forms part. But *this* resemblance is not what I have in mind, since something like this multiplicity of places associated with every aspect of a thing is found in any theory of perspectives. The resemblance I have in mind is deeper:

The two places associated with a single aspect correspond to the two ways of classifying it. We may distinguish the two places as that *at* which, and that *from* which, the aspect appears. The "place at which" is the place of the *thing* to which the aspect belongs; the "place from which" is the place of the *perspective* to which the aspect belongs.[39]

Note that the "aspect belongs" both to the thing and to the perspective. Just what this means requires explanation, which can be given by a few more quotations. Imagining that each mind looks out from the world, as in Leibniz's monadology, the author says:

Each mind sees at each moment an immensely complex three-dimensional world. . . . If two men are sitting in a room, two somewhat similar worlds are perceived by them; if a third man enters and sits between them, a third world, intermediate between the two previous worlds, begins to be perceived. . . . The system consisting of all views of the universe perceived and unperceived, I shall call the system of "perspectives;" I shall confine the expression "private worlds" to such views of the universe as are actually perceived . . . but there may be any number of unperceived perspectives.[40]

Perspective space is the system of "points of view" of private spaces (perspectives), or, since "points of view" have not been defined, we may say it is the system of the private spaces themselves. These private spaces will each count as one point, or at any rate as one element, in perspective space.[41]

---

[39] *Ibid.*, 92. (The last two italics are mine.)

[40] *Ibid.*, 87f. The same treatment of perspectives is given in Lecture VII of *The Analysis of Mind* (London, New York, 1921). I have purposely omitted important features of Lord Russell's theory, features that differentiate his theory from Mr. Whitehead's. An instance is the former's assertion that "there is absolutely nothing which is seen by two minds simultaneously." (*Ibid.*, 87.) I perpetrated this omission for the reason that I am now interested in pointing out the *resemblance* between the two authors.

[41] *Our Knowledge of the External World*, 89f.

Thus everything we ever see is at the point, or *is* the point, in perspective space where we are when we see it. This constitutes the point of resemblance between the two theories of perspective we are comparing, since for Mr. Whitehead the concrescent actual occasion in prehending "includes" the prehended datum in its own constitution. If I may use the vernacular, everything we see is, for both our philosophers, where we are when we see it.

But naturally both our philosophers were not content with leaving everything they see in their own physical heads—to speak Lord Russell's language—or in their own concrescent occasions, in Mr. Whitehead's language. The different ways in which they severally avoided such a predicament mark one of the distinctive differences between the two. Lord Russell went to work and constructed an entirely different space from the space in any perspective, called it "perspective space"—later he called it "physical space"—put the different perspectives at different places in this new space, and put the "thing" perceived in a different place in this space from that assigned to any perspective that contains an "aspect" of the "thing." In this way he successfully committed "the fallacy of simple location" as far as the "thing" is concerned. But partially to atone for this commission, he generously allowed the "aspect" to "belong" both to the "thing," now at one place, and to the "perspective," now at another place in the "perspective space." The atonement is only partial, since he did not say that the *same* "aspect" is *at* the two different places where its two owners are. And of course something can belong to two owners, without being where the owners are. Just what "belonging to" means in Lord Russell's theory we need not ask here, since the answer is part of another story. At any rate, everything has "aspects" scattered "all over the map," so to say. Its "aspects" are everywhere and, if not at all times, at any rate at many times: they are everywhere except, apparently, where the thing is to which they belong.

Mr. Whitehead, as we have seen, avoids the predicament by having declined at the start to commit the "fallacy of simple location." His "concrescent occasion" has therefore the good fortune of being able as it were both to eat its cake and have it. The actual occasion ingests all its cakes into its own "inner constitution" and also leaves them out where they were before.

It is not my purpose here to criticize in detail either of these doctrines of the nature of perspectives. Space will not permit. I can only say that neither seems necessitated by the facts or even plausible. When Mr. Whitehead argues that "among the primary elements of nature as apprehended in our immediate experience, there is no element whatever which possesses this character of simple location," I can only reply that this does not find confirmation in my experience. The very fact that he finds it necessary to relegate all apparently "immediate experience" that contravenes his assertion to the category of "perception in the mode of presentational immediacy," shows that "immediate experience" has to be categorized in order to be used as evidence on the question at issue. He himself has said:

> The verification of a rationalistic scheme is to be sought in its general success, and not in the peculiar certainty, or initial clarity, of its first principles. In this connection the misuse of the *ex absurdo* argument has to be noted; much philosophical reasoning is vitiated by it . . . in the absence of a well-defined categoreal scheme of entities, issuing in a satisfactory metaphysical system, every premise in a philosophical argument is under suspicion. . . . There may be rival schemes, inconsistent among themselves; each with its own merits and its own failures. . . . Metaphysical categories are not dogmatic statements of the obvious; they are tentative formulations of the ultimate generalities.[42]

To assert that the doctrine of simple location is a fallacy is a "misuse of the *ex absurdo* argument," since the very essence of a "fallacy" is that it is a logical absurdity, a self-contradiction. To condemn as fallacious rivals whose assumptions do not agree with one's own is not in keeping with the position that one's own categories are "*tentative* formulations of the ultimate generalities."

There is much else in Mr. Whitehead's philosophy of "space-time," on which I should like to have more light. I can mention here only one of the remaining perplexities. It concerns the

---

[42] *Process and Reality*, 12.

status of "the extensive continuum" among the "categories of
existence."

An extensive continuum is a complex of entities united by the various
allied relationships of whole to part, and of overlapping so as to possess
common parts, and of contact, and of other relationships derived from
these primary relationships. The notion of a 'continuum' involves both the
property of indefinite divisibility and the property of unbounded extension.
There are always entities beyond entities, because nonentity is no boundary. This extensive continuum expresses the solidarity of all possible standpoints throughout the whole process of the world. It is not a fact prior
to the world; it is the first determination of order—that is, of real potentiality—arising out of the general character of the world. . . . This
extensive continuum is 'real,' because it expresses a fact derived from the
actual world and concerning the contemporary actual world. All actual
entities are related according to the determinations of this continuum;
and all possible actual entities in the future must exemplify these determinations in their relations with the already actual world. The reality
of the future is bound up with the reality of this continuum. It is the
reality of what is potential, in its character of a real component of what
is actual. Such a real component must be interpreted in terms of the relatedness of prehensions.[43]

This passage, when compared with that quoted in footnote 31
above, suggests that any volume of space in this extensive continuum is to be interpreted as "the prehension into unity of the
aspects of all other volumes from the standpoint" of that
volume. Does that volume itself prehend into unity all other
volumes? If it does, then it is itself an *actual entity*, since Mr.
Whitehead has said: "I have adopted the term 'prehension', to
express the activity whereby an actual entity effects its own
concretion of other things."[44]

But in an earlier work Mr. Whitehead had said that "a bare
portion of space-time" is an "abstraction," and "any limited
portion of nature which preserves most completely such concreteness as attaches to nature itself," is "a part of the becomingness of nature, coloured with all the hues of its content."[45] Can

[43] *Ibid.*, 103f.
[44] *Ibid.*, 81.
[45] *The Principle of Relativity*, 21.

an "abstraction" be "an actual entity" which "effects its own concretion of other things" through the "activity" of "prehension"? I therefore repeat my former question, Where among the categories of existence does the extensive continuum find a place? Is it an "eternal object"?

All philosophers have much to look forward to, when a philosopher of Mr. Whitehead's eminence consents to elucidate his position in reply to critics. He himself has acknowledged that "the worst homage we can pay to genius is to accept uncritically formulations of truths which we owe to it." He should feel assured that our criticisms are our best expression of homage to his genius.

EVANDER BRADLEY McGILVARY

DEPARTMENT OF PHILOSOPHY
UNIVERSITY OF WISCONSIN

5

Joseph Needham

A BIOLOGIST'S VIEW OF WHITEHEAD'S PHILOSOPHY

A BIOLOGIST'S VIEW OF WHITEHEAD'S PHILOSOPHY

IT NEED hardly be said that the author of this modest contribution is very conscious, both of the honour which has been done him in an invitation to contribute to the present symposium, and of the pleasure which it is to be able to participate in a reasoned tribute to one of the greatest of living philosophers. The reader's indulgence is begged at the outset in case any of what follows should appear unduly trite, but in requesting the co-operation of a working biologist, the editor laid himself open to receiving a paper in which the finer points, to say the least, of Professor Whitehead's philosophy, should be but poorly appreciated.

The author's interest in "philosophical" or theoretical biology was probably awakened by the very fact of his being a biochemist. The zoological systematist may get along well enough by treating his data as an array of empty forms unconnected with a material substratum; the psychologist may do the same; and the organic chemist may reveal the structural formula of some compound once involved in a living cell, or analyse the constituents of blood or tissue fluids, without devoting much thought to the organisation of the living being which synthesised the one or secreted the other. But the true biochemist is deeply concerned about the structure and organisation of the living cell, with its "topography" permitting of innumerable simultaneously-proceeding chemical reactions, its faculty of getting things done just at the right time and place, and its remarkable properties of symmetry and polarity, exhibited in an aqueous colloidal medium of certain essential constituents, especially the proteins, carbohydrates, and fats. The ancient problem of body and mind, too, was always around the corner. How to reconcile the introspected "me" and the domain of mind and spirit with the world of flesh and blood, of macro-molecules and hydrogen ions, with which the former seemed to be so strangely connected? This interest in the organisation of the living cell, the borderline between biology and physics, was natural in Cambridge, where the tradition of W. B. Hardy and F. G. Hopkins was, and still is, in full vigor.

The author's first approach to the whole subject on the theoretical side was therefore a careful, if somewhat unrewarding, examination of the voluminous and polemical literature on "vitalism," "neo-vitalism," and "mechanism," which had appeared during the last decade of the past century and the first two of the present one. The writings of Hans Driesch, J. S. Haldane, and E. S. Russell on the one side, and of men such as H. S. Jennings and Judson Herrick on the other, were gone through. It would probably be well worth someone's while to take this literature and make a coherent historical summary of it, for it belongs to a distinct period which has been closed since about 1930. The vitalists systematically drew attention to the flaws in the over-simplified explanations of biological processes which workers such as Jacques Loeb, recognising them to be interim hypotheses only, were always putting forward. Their attitude was no doubt partly inspired by the human, all too human, but nevertheless obscurantist, desire to retain elements of mystery in the universe, and hence they fought decade after decade a stubborn withdrawing action against the ever-fresh shock-troops of the mechanists. The process had begun long before; it was familiar to the men of T. H. Huxley's time, as witness the interesting passage in the book of that curious character W. H. Mallock, *The New Republic* (1878):

Saunders (intended to be W. K. Clifford, the mathematician): One word more, one plain word, if you will allow me. All this talk about religion, poetry, morality, implies this—or it implies nothing—the recognition of some elements of inscrutable mystery in our lives and conduct; and to every mystery, to all mystery, science is the sworn, the deadly, foe. What she is daily branding into man's consciousness is that nothing is inscrutable that can practically concern him. Use, pleasure, self-preservation—on these everything depends; on these rocks of ages are all rules of conduct founded, and now that we have dug down to these foundations, what an entirely changed fabric of life shall we build upon them. Right and wrong, I say again, are entirely misleading terms, and the superstition that sees an unfathomable gulf yawning between them is the great bar to all health and progress.

Laurence (intended apparently to be Mallock himself): And I say, on the contrary, that it is on the recognition of this mysterious and unfathomable gulf that all the higher pleasures of life depend. . . .

The vitalists, in fact, were concerned, perhaps because of some misplaced sense of the numinous, to retain at all costs a measure of animistic mystery in the nature and behaviour of living organisms. The neo-vitalists, as they called themselves, centered this mystery in the very organisation of life itself, regarding organising relations as in principle inscrutable and axiomatic, rather than a subject for investigation.

The atmosphere surrounding these controversies was always somewhat polemical. As W. T. Marvin said in 1918: compare Driesch and Loeb—nobody could call them unimpassioned neutrals examining a body of evidence. He went on to suggest a psychological difference; the vitalist hoped that the scientific method as applied to life and mind would fail, the mechanist hoped it would succeed.

If science wins, the world will prove to be one in which man is thrown entirely upon his own resources and skill, upon his self-control, courage, and strength, and perhaps upon his ability to be happy by adjusting himself to pitiless fact. If science fails, there is room for the childlike hope that unseen powers may come to the relief of human weakness. If science wins, the world is the necessary consequences of logically related facts, and man's enterprise, . . . is the playing of a game of chess against an opponent who himself never errs and never overlooks errors. If science fails, the world resembles fairyland . . . ; and man's enterprise either is no longer a task for skill and knowledge or is conditioned by the 'goodness' of man's will or is in part a game of luck.[1]

Vitalists and neo-vitalists were found rather among the philosophers than among the biologists themselves. Certainly during the present century the vast majority of working biologists

[1] W. T. Marvin, *Philosophical Review* (1918), vol. 27, 616.

and biochemists have been "mechanists." Their conception of the task of biology was consistently that sketched out in T. H. Huxley's definition of physiology in 1867:

Zoological physiology is the doctrine of the functions or actions of animals. It regards animal bodies as machines impelled by certain forces and performing an amount of work which can be expressed in terms of the ordinary forces of nature. The final object of physiology is to deduce the facts of morphology on the one hand and those of ecology on the other, from the laws of the molecular forces of matter.[2]

This, however, though useful as a slogan, can never have satisfied even the working biologists. It must always have been obvious that the laws of chemistry do not appear until you are dealing with entities sufficiently large to show the phenomena of chemical combination, and similarly that the laws governing crystal structure do not appear until crystals have been formed, and *a fortiori* the laws of living organisms or social units cannot be studied except at their own level. This is the problem which the emergent evolutionists afterwards brought into prominence. If one were to know *all* there is to know about the properties of atoms, for instance, it may be said, one should be able to predict all the molecular combinations they would form, and all the living structures that could be built up from them; but in order to know all about the atoms one has to know a great deal about the molecules and the living cells first. In 1838 K. F. Burdach had said "Physiology will always be able to dispense with the aid of chemistry." This was not necessarily a vitalist statement. During the succeeding century it became quite clear that the regularities established in the biological sciences—physiology, experimental morphology and embryology, genetics, cytology, and the like—remained of durable validity, whatever discoveries might be made in biochemistry and the organic chemistry of substances of biological origin, to say nothing of biophysics. The question became critical; how are the levels related? How do biochemistry and biophysics contribute (as they obviously do) to a unified picture of life and nature? For certain studies the problem was a desperate one.

[2] T. H. Huxley, *Science Gossip* (1867), 74.

When Wilhelm Roux in the last two decades of the nineteenth century founded the science of experimental morphology (*Entwicklungsmechanik*) by the strict application of causal analysis of developmental processes instead of their mere description, he divided the biological factors into two, the "simple components" whose connection with physico-chemical factors could immediately be seen, and the "complex components" where the relation with physico-chemical factors was much less obvious, but might reasonably be expected to be revealed in due course.[3] The curling of a piece of ectoderm, for instance, if understood in relation to protein fibres, surface forces, lipoprotein monolayers, etc., would be a case of a simple component. The regularly reproducible self-differentiation of an isolated eye-cup under certain conditions, for instance, involving processes much too complicated at present for physico-chemical explanations, would be a case of a complex component. But the terminology of *components* (*einfache* & *complexe Komponenten*) never came into general use.

By 1928 the position of most working biologists could be summed up not unfairly as follows:

Mechanists do not say that nothing is true or intelligible unless expressed in physico-chemical terms, they do not say that nothing takes place differently in living matter from what takes place in the dead, they do not say that our present physics and chemistry are fully competent to explain the behaviour of living systems. What they do say is that the processes of living matter are subject to the same laws that govern the processes in dead matter, but that the laws operate in a more complicated medium; thus living things differ from dead things in degree and not in kind; they are, as it were, *extrapolations* from the inorganic.[4]

The nature of this relationship, however, still remained obscure. In the following year, however, the situation was greatly clarified by the appearance of J. H. Woodger's book *Biological Principles*. From his discussion it followed that the term "vitalism" ought henceforward to be restricted to all propositions of the type "the living being consists of an X in addition to carbon, hydrogen,

[3] See W. Roux, *Gesammelte Abhandlungen ü. Entwicklungsmechanik der Organismen* (Leipzig, 1895), 2 vols.

[4] J. Needham, *The Sceptical Biologist* (London, 1929), 247.

oxygen, nitrogen, etc., plus organising relations." This, for biologists, at any rate, was one of the first clear statements of the objectivity and importance of organising relations in the living system. They had always been recognised, but at the same time obscured, by the persistent opposition of progressive experimental science, implacable but correct, towards every form of lingering animism, the *spiritus rector*, the *nisus formativus*, the *archaeus*, the *entelechia*, etc., etc. And the situation had not been improved by the adoption of the organising relations by the neo-vitalists as the very citadel of the *anima* itself.

Organising relations, then, were to become the object of scientific study, not the home of an inscrutable vital principle, nor the axiom from which all biology must proceed. Since 1930 this point of view has penetrated widely through scientific circles, all the more so as it was really a description of what a large number of scientific workers had previously believed in a somewhat unconscious way. If space permitted, it would be interesting to consider the practical applications of these ideas, the question, for instance, of what methods may be adopted in the study of organised living structure. How far may wholes be made transparent, as by X-ray analysis of the crystalline and liquid crystalline arrangements which, as we now know, play such an important part in the structure of the living body? How far can living structure be so explored without interference with its delicate organisation (cf. the principle of indeterminacy)? What are the forces which hold morphological entities together, and how do they link up with forces at the molecular and sub-molecular level? We cannot go into these questions at this time. Biological organisation is not immune from scientific enquiry, it is not inscrutable, and it cannot be "reduced" to physico-chemical organisation, because nothing can ever be reduced to anything. As Samuel Butler once remarked "Nothing is ever *merely* anything." The laws of higher organisation only operate there.

Woodger's point of view, supported also by the Austrian theoretical biologist v. Bertalannfy,[5] was perhaps the most tech-

[5] L. v. Bertalannfy, *Theoretische Biologie* (Berlin, 1932).

nically well-informed manifestation of a great movement of modern thought which sought to base a philosophical world-view on ideas originating from biology rather than from the classical physics. It fused once again what Descartes had put asunder. It was Descartes, as Woodger acutely said, who introduced the practice of calling organisms machines, with the unfortunate consequence that transcendent mechanics had to be invented to drive them. Organicism, if not obscurantist, was bound to be the death of "vitalism" as well as of "mechanism." It was likely to be the death of animism too, since mental phenomena cannot but be considered in the light of the evolution of the central nervous system, as is discussed in the latest and most interesting work of this kind, the Gifford Lectures of Sir Charles Sherrington.[6]

From the scientist's standpoint, the organic conception of the world involves *succession* in time and *envelopes* in space. Taking the latter first, it is obvious that the different levels of organisation, for such we must call them, occur one within the other. Ultimate particles, the proton, electron, etc., build up atoms, atoms build molecules, molecules build large colloidal particles and cell-constituents and paracrystalline phases and the like, these in their turn are organised into the living cell. Above this level, cells form organs and tissues, the latter combine into the functioning living body, and the bodies of animals, especially men, form social communities. As the central nervous system becomes more complex so mental phenomena emerge, until the elaborate psychological life of man is attained. The remarkable thing about our world is, however, that these envelopes seem each to be analogous to past phases in the history of its development. There were "inorganic" molecules before there were living cells, the origin of which evidently depended upon the right environmental conditions for the flowering of the potentialities of the protein system; there were living cells before there were organs or tissues of metazoan organisms; there were primitive organisms before there were any higher ones, and higher organisms before there were any social associations.

[6] C. Sherrington, *Man on his Nature* (Cambridge, 1941).

The fundamental thread that seems to run through the history of our world is a continuous rise in level of organisation. Whether this organisation is the same as that to which physicists refer in their discussions of the shuffling process which underlies the second law of thermo-dynamics, and whether its rise in the domain of living organisms has entailed some corresponding loss of organisation somewhere else, are matters which we can not stop to deal with here.

The basically important fact that social evolution must be regarded as continuous with biological evolution was appreciated already by Herbert Spencer and Auguste Comte, who in this respect, though not of course in others, made an approach to the organic conception of the world. It has the extremely important corollary that any static or too conservative view of the present position of human institutions becomes impossible. If living organisation has such triumphs behind it as the first invention of the cell-membrane, the kidney-tubule, the notochord, the flint-knife and the plough, the art of language and the skill of ships, it is not likely that the agreements of Ottawa or Munich have any durable importance, or that human society will always remain separated into states with national sovereignties above the moral law, and social classes with different privileges and manners. This has generally been appreciated by upholders of the organic view of the world, but much more boldly by Marx and Engels, for instance, than by Smuts or Lloyd-Morgan.

It is probable, indeed, that the organic view of the world has considerable historical and social significance. The seventeenth century, the age of Gassendi and Newton, of Boyle and Descartes, was a time in which the capitalist system of economic individualism won its first decisive victories in taking over state power. The surrender of the last royalist troops in the English civil war was the final conclusion of centuries of feudalism, for though the monarchy was restored in England, feudalism was not. All later monarchs ruled by the grace of the City of London. Parallel with the breaking-up of the old guilds, and the absolute freeing of commercial enterprise in every kind of new exploitation, went the rediscovery of atomism by Gassendi and its application to chemistry as the "corpuscularian or mechanical hypothesis" by Boyle. The analogy between free merchants, projectors, and industrialists, and the fortuitous concourse of atoms, can even be found explicitly stated in seventeenth century books on economics. Is it not therefore of interest that in our time, when capitalist economics has worked itself through to a new state of society demanding everywhere more social control and organisation of human affairs, that there should be a rediscovery of the organic interpretation of the world, an interpretation in which the molecules "do not blindly run," in Whitehead's famous phrase,[7] but run in accordance with the whole of which they form a part. Function depends on position in the whole. Statistical regularity of fortuitous random motions is *not* the whole story; there is a plan of organising relations too. The world is not entirely like a perfect gas or an absolutely homogeneous solid, it also contains viscous phases, crystals rigid in one, two, or three dimensions, plasticity, and elastic deformability, living organisation. It may be that we are on the threshold of a long period, lasting perhaps for several centuries, in which the organic conception of the world will transform society, giving it a unity more comradely and equal than feudalism, but less chaotic and self-contradictory than the centuries of capitalist atomism. In Alfred North Whitehead we surely have to recognise the greatest living philosopher of the organic movement in philosophy and science.

About the historical origins of the organicistic viewpoint in biology a great deal could be said. Here there is space to refer only to one or two points. Samuel Taylor Coleridge is not generally regarded as having contributed much to theoretical biology, yet surely his essay "The Theory of Life," published in 1848, was more advanced than any other thought at the time, and than a great deal since. Coleridge wrote:

I define life as the principle of individuation, or the power which unites a given all into a whole that is presupposed by its parts. The link that combines the two, and acts throughout both, will, of course, be defined by this

_____

[7] *Science and the Modern World,* 110. (All quotations in this essay from *Science and the Modern World* are taken from the American edition, 1925.)

tendency to individuation. Thus, from its utmost latency, in which life is one with the elementary powers of mechanism . . . to its highest manifestation . . . there is an ascending series of intermediate classes, and of analogous gradations in each class. . . . In the lowest forms of the vegetable and animal world we perceive totality dawning into individuation, while in man, as the highest of the class, the individuality is not only perfected in its corporeal sense, but begins a new series beyond the appropriate limits of physiology.[8]

It is curious to think that Coleridge was as unconscious as Aristotle (who also recognised a "ladder of beings") of the evolutionary succession which has coloured all our thought on these subjects since the middle of the last century.

More important, some decades later, was the work of the London philosopher, Karl Marx,[9] and the Manchester business man Frederick Engels.[10] The views of the latter on scientific theory have in recent times become generally recognised as having been far in advance of his age. The author would disclaim any competence for presenting the contributions of these great thinkers as they deserve, but there are numerous handbooks which may be consulted, a process which is in this case especially necessary as the views of these men on political subjects, then unorthodox, caused them to be somewhat boycotted in academic circles.[11] Marx and Engels were of course profoundly influenced by Hegel, just as Coleridge had been. But whereas he tended to retain Hegel's metaphysical idealism, they "turned it right side up" and, while keeping Hegel's dialectical account of change and process, in which a synthesis arises out of the deadlock of the thesis and the antithesis, they adopted a realist metaphysics. Their materialism, however, was to be known as "dialectical materialism" as opposed to the old mechanical materialism, in order to show its naturalistic character,

---

[8] S. T. Coleridge, *Theory of Life* (1st ed. 1848, usual ed. London, 1885).

[9] See especially *The German Ideology* and *Theses on Feuerbach*.

[10] See especially *Anti-Dühring; Socialism, Utopian and Scientific*, and *Dialectics of Nature*.

[11] See e.g. T. A. Jackson, *Dialectics, the Logic of Marxism* (1936); D. Guest, *Textbook of Dialectical Materialism* (1939); R. Maublanc, *La Philosophie du marxisme et l'enseignement officiel* (1936); J. Lewis, *Introduction to Philosophy* (1937); M. Shirokov, *Textbook of Marxist Philosophy* (n.d.).

its determination to account for all the highest phenomena of mind and social organisation, without leaving the firm basis of the real objective existence of matter. Something of this kind was meant by Marx's saying that materialism must cease to be "ascetic." Of course, the only way in which such a naturalism could account for the highest phenomena of mind and social organisation, love and comradeship, justice and mercy, was by admitting a series of levels of organisation, arranged in the successions and envelopes of which we have already spoken. And so from this standpoint also there came a doctrine of levels of organisation. It had, however, the cardinal virtue, which not many other naturalisms have had, of emphasising the transitory character of human institutions. It showed that evolution of social systems continued from that of biological systems, and urged the optimistic but tolerably convincing view that human misery is essentially connected with a low and inferior stage of social organisation, that it had in the past been much worse than it is now, and that in the future it ought to be greatly decreased. This is not the place to discuss Marx's theory of history, but if history is the history of class-struggles (and to some extent it undeniably is), there is room for hope that when mankind has united in a world co-operative commonwealth unmarked by social classes, a good many of the more unpleasant features of life in a semi-barbarous state will have ceased to exist. And indeed this is not a hope at all, but a faith based on that guiding thread of rise in level of organisation, which we have seen running throughout the evolution of our world; and hence a scientific faith. It was for this reason that the kind of socialism advocated by Marx and Engels received the name which it bears to this day, "scientific" socialism, as opposed to the Utopian varieties, which based their hopes only on the goodness of human nature or similar more or less reliable factors.

Dialectical materialism has been called the theory of transformations, of the way in which the qualitatively new arises, of the nature of change in the natural world. Its outcome in biology—to return to our main theme—was certainly beneficial. In 1931 a Russian biologist, B. Zavadovsky, wrote for an English symposium as follows:

The true task of scientific research, is not the violent identification of the biological and the physical, but the discovery of the qualitatively specific controlling principles which characterise the main features of every phenomenon, and the finding of methods of research appropriate to the phenomena studied. . . . It is necessary to renounce both the simplified reduction of some sciences to others, and also the sharp demarcations between the physical, biological, and socio-historical sciences. . . . Biological phenomena, historically connected with physical phenomena in inorganic nature, are none the less not only not reducible to physico-chemical or mechanical laws, but within their own limits display different and qualitatively distinct laws. But biological laws do not in the least lose thereby their material quality and cognisability, requiring only in each case methods of investigation appropriate to the phenomena studied.[12]

A few years later there was an equally good statement from a French biologist, professor of zoology at the Sorbonne. Marcel Prenant wrote:

In biology dialectical materialism is opposed both to vitalism and to mechanical materialism, which are both really metaphysical theories. He refuses to make a sharp distinction between the physical and biological sciences, to reserve causal determinism to the former and to appeal to teleology in the latter. But neither does he suppose that biology must try to reduce itself to the physical sciences. He affirms the unity of the world, in which neither life nor human society constitute domains apart, but he also affirms that this unity expresses itself in qualitatively different forms of whose distinctive characters one should never lose sight.[13]

Dialectical materialism has been perhaps more successful in emphasising the existence of the levels of organisation than in elucidating the dialectical character of the transitions between them. There have, however, been some interesting suggestions. J. D. Bernal[14] has pointed out that natural processes are never 100% efficient. Besides the main process or reaction, there are always residual processes or side-reactions, which, if cyclic or if adjuvant to the main reaction, will not matter very much. But they may be opposing and cumulative, so that after some time a new situation will arise in which such opposing processes may

[12] B. Zavadovsky, essay in *Science at the Cross-roads* (London, 1931).

[13] M. Prenant, *Bull. Soc. Philomath.* (Paris, 1933), vol. 116, 84.

[14] J. D. Bernal, essay in *Aspects of Dialectical Materialism* (London, 1934).

make an antithesis to the main reaction's thesis. This situation may be unstable, and wherever instability occurs one of the possible resulting syntheses may be a level of higher organisation. Such a scheme can be worked out for the aggregation of particles in planets, the formation of hydrosphere and atmosphere, and the development of economic processes since the renaissance. J. B. S. Haldane,[15] too, has discussed evolution theory from this viewpoint, distinguishing three Hegelian triads:

Thesis	Antithesis	Synthesis
1) Heredity	Mutation	Variation
2) Variation	Selection	Evolution
3) Selection of the fittest individuals	Consequent loss of fitness in the species	Survival of species showing little intraspecific competition

The early conviction of Engels that Nature is through and through dialectical was rightly directed against the static conceptions of the scientists of his time, who were unprepared for the mass of contradictions that science was about to have to deal with, and who did not appreciate that Nature is full of apparently irreconcilable antagonisms and distinctions which are reconciled at higher organisational levels. The well-known rules of the passing of quantity into quality, the unity of opposites and the negation of negations, have all become commonplaces of scientific thought. What has not yet been done, however, is to elucidate the way in which each of the new great levels of organisation has arisen; and, although this must to some extent await the results of further experiments and observations, there is quite enough knowledge already available to permit of a good deal of theoretical thinking along these lines.

And so we come to consider Whitehead's own contributions from the biologist's point of view. Unlike so many philosophers, he has always appreciated the structure of our world in its *succession* and its *envelopes*. Perhaps one of his most famous and influential passages was that in which he said: "Science is taking

[15] J. B. S. Haldane, *Science and Society* (1937), vol. 1, 473.

on a new aspect which is neither purely physical, nor purely biological. It is becoming the study of organisms. Biology is the study of the larger organisms; whereas physics is the study of the smaller organisms."[16] And so, regarding envelopes: "In surveying nature, we must remember that there are not only basic organisms whose ingredients are merely aspects of eternal objects" (i.e., the ultimate particles of physics, each of which is related to everything else in the universe by its bare co-existence).

There are also organisms of organisms. Suppose for the moment and for the sake of simplicity, we assume, without any evidence, that electrons and hydrogen nuclei are such basic organisms. Then the atoms, and the molecules, are organisms of a higher type, which also represent a compact definite organic unity. But when we come to the larger aggregations of matter, the organic unity fades into the background. It appears to be but faint and elementary. It is there; but the pattern is vague and indecisive. It is a mere aggregation of effects. When we come to living beings, the definiteness of pattern is recovered, and the organic character again rises into prominence.[17]

Elsewhere, Whitehead elaborates all this at length.[18] "The Universe" he says

achieves its values by reason of its coördination into societies of societies, and into societies of societies of societies. Thus an army is a society of regiments, and regiments are societies of men, and men are societies of cells, of blood, and of bones, together with the dominant society of personal human experience, and cells are societies of smaller physical entities such as protons, and so on. Also all of these societies presuppose the circumambient space of social physical activity.

So also with the successions. According to Whitehead, Nature exhibits itself as exemplifying a philosophy of the evolution of organisms subject to determinate conditions. Surveying the levels of organisation, he writes:[19]

One conclusion is the diverse modes of functioning which are produced

[16] *Science and the Modern World*, 145.
[17] *Ibid.*, 156.
[18] *Adventures of Ideas*, 264; cf. also *Process and Reality* (American edition, 1929), 113ff.; *Modes of Thought*, 31ff.
[19] *Modes of Thought*, 215f.

by diverse modes of organisation. The second conclusion is the aspect of continuity between these different modes. There are border-line cases, which bridge the gaps. Often the border-line cases are unstable, and pass quickly. But span of existence is merely relative to our habits of human life. For inframolecular occurrences, a second is a vast period of time. A third conclusion is the difference in the aspects of nature according as we change the scale of observation. Each scale of observation presents us with average effects proper to that scale.

Here is how he speaks of the emergence of mind.[20]

In so far as conceptual mentality does not intervene, the grand patterns pervading the environment are passed on with the inherited modes of adjustment. Here we find the patterns of activity studied by the physicists and chemists. Mentality is merely latent in all these occasions as thus studied. In the case of inorganic nature any sporadic flashes are inoperative so far as our powers of discernment are concerned. The lowest stages of effective mentality, controlled by the inheritance of physical pattern, involves the faint direction of emphasis by unconscious ideal aim. The various examples of the higher forms of life exhibit the variety of grades of effectiveness of mentality. In the social habits of animals, there is evidence of flashes of mentality in the past which have degenerated into physical habits. Finally in the higher mammals and more particularly in mankind, we have clear evidence of mentality habitually effective. In our own experience, our knowledge consciously entertained and systematised can only mean such mentality, directly observed.

Turning to the border line of metaphysics, it is interesting to note that Whitehead goes so far as to say that

a thoroughgoing evolutionary philosophy is inconsistent with [mechanical] materialism. The aboriginal stuff, or material, from which a materialistic philosophy starts is incapable of evolution. This material is in itself the ultimate substance. Evolution, on the [mechanical] materialistic theory, is reduced to the rôle of being another word for the description of the changes of the external relations between portions of matter. There is nothing to evolve, because one set of external relations is as good as any other set of external relations. There can merely be change, purposeless and unprogressive. But the whole point of the modern doctrine is the evolution of the complex organisms from the antecedent states of less complex organisms. The doctrine thus cries aloud for a conception of

[20] *Ibid.*, 230f.

organism as fundamental for nature. It also requires an underlying activity—a substantial activity—expressing itself in individual embodiments, and evolving in achievements of organism. The organism is a unit of emergent value, a real fusion of the characters of eternal objects, emerging for its own sake.[21]

If in this passage Whitehead speaks like Lloyd-Morgan, we shall see others in which he speaks like Marx. Little though the philosophers of organic evolutionary naturalism may have borrowed from one another, they march in the same ranks.

Elsewhere Whitehead explains why he ignores for the most part nineteenth century idealism. It was, he says, too much divorced from the scientific outlook, yet at the same time it swallowed the scientific scheme in its entirety and then explained it away as being an idea in some ultimate mentality. He leaves open, however, a final decision on the metaphysical issue—

... however you take it, these idealistic schools have conspicuously failed to connect, in any organic fashion, the fact of nature with their idealistic philosophies. So far as concerns what will be said in these lectures [*Science and the Modern World*], your ultimate outlook may be realistic or idealistic. My point is that a further stage of provisional realism is required in which the scientific scheme is recast, and founded upon the ultimate concept of *organism*.[22]

While this failure to close the door definitely on idealism has endeared him to theologians such as Thornton,[23] many scientists have preferred the robuster materialism of the Marxists. No Marxist, however, could be more strongly opposed to mechanical materialism than Whitehead.

"My aim," he says[24]

... is briefly to point out how both Newton's contribution and Hume's contribution are, each in their way, gravely defective. They are right as far as they go. But they omit those aspects of the Universe as experienced, and of our modes of experiencing, which jointly lead to the more penetrating ways of understanding. In the recent situations at Washington, D.C., the Hume-Newton modes of thought can only discern a com-

[21] *Science and the Modern World*, 151f.
[22] *Ibid.*, 90.
[23] L. Thornton, *The Incarnate Lord* (London, 1930).
[24] *Modes of Thought*, 185.

plex transition of sensa, and an entangled locomotion of molecules, while the deepest intuition of the whole world discerns the President of the United States inaugurating a new chapter in the history of mankind. In such ways the Hume-Newton interpretation omits our intuitive modes of understanding.

In other words, what the President does is relevant to events at an extremely high level of organisation, and the concomitant atomic happenings are not directly concerned, though they underlie, and are entirely presupposed by, all that goes on at that high level.

Whitehead proceeds to his famous attack on the notion of "simple location."[25]

To say that a bit of matter has *simple location* means that, in expressing its spatio-temporal relations, it is adequate to state that it is where it is, in a definite finite region of space, and throughout a definite finite duration of time, *apart from any essential reference of the relations of that bit of matter to other regions of space and to other durations of time.* Again, this concept of simple location is independent of the controversy between the absolutist and the relativist views of space or of time. So long as any theory of space, or of time, can give a meaning, either absolute or relative, to the idea of a definite region of space, and of a definite duration of time, the idea of simple location has a perfectly definite meaning. This idea is the very foundation of the seventeenth century scheme of nature. Apart from it, the scheme is incapable of expression. I shall argue that among the primary elements of nature as apprehended in our immediate experience, there is no element whatever which possesses this character of simple location. It does not follow, however, that the science of the seventeenth century was simply wrong. I hold that by a process of constructive abstraction we can arrive at abstractions which are the simply-located bits of material, and at other abstractions which are the minds included in the scientific scheme. Accordingly, the real error is an example of what I have termed: The Fallacy of Misplaced Concreteness.

To the biologist all this was extremely welcome. If for three hundred years he had been a "mechanist" following in the footsteps of Descartes and la Mettrie, it was not because he felt satisfied with the seventeenth century statistical picture of the fortuitous concourse of particles, each with a momentarily

[25] *Science and the Modern World*, 81f. (Italics mine, except *simple location*.)

defined exact position in space, but because there was no other scheme by the aid of which he could proceed with the causal analysis of biological phenomena. The difficulties rose, of course, to a wild crescendo in the science of embryology at the turn of the century. When experimental embryology was put on a firm foundation by Wilhelm Roux, it was supposed that all eggs showed what is called "mosaic" development, that is to say, they would, if injured or divided, produce a finished organism lacking precisely all that would have developed from those parts which had been destroyed or removed. About 1895, however, the discovery was made (and this is what has secured Hans Driesch's name in history, not what he wrote long afterwards) that in many eggs, at any rate, all kinds of interferences could be made without affecting at all the embryo resulting. Large pieces could be removed from the egg, several blastomeres could be taken away, or the blastomeres could be shuffled at will, and yet a normal, though small-sized, embryo would result. Any one monad in the original egg-cell, then, was capable of forming any part of the finished embryo. Driesch was quite right in proclaiming that this was beyond the powers of any machine such as man has ever constructed, but he soon left the straight and narrow path by insinuating his non-material entelechy into the works as the inevitable transcendent mechanic or driver. C. D. Broad's comment deserves to be better known: "If you want a mind that will construct its own organism, you may as well postulate God at once. If he cannot perform such a feat, it is hardly likely that what has been hidden from the wise and prudent will be revealed to entelechies."[26] Looking at the matter to-day after the passage of forty years of research in experimental morphology, we realise that what these early workers were up against was a very general process in development which we now speak of as Determination. The individual cells of the very young organism are not strictly determined as to their fate in the finished product, and this determination comes about as development goes on, partly at least through the action of chemical substances, about which we already know a

[26] C. D. Broad, *Proc. Aristot. Soc.* (1919), vol. 19, 123.

good deal.[27] But the important point is that these chemical substances (the Evocators and Organisers) do not act at random, but faithfully in accordance with that plan of the body which is decreed by the characters of the species, whether embodied in the nuclear chromosomes or perhaps in the cytoplasm of the egg, a plan the field properties of which have given it the name of Individuation Field. Hence the fate of a given monad, protein molecule, atomic group, or what have you, in the original egg, is a function of its position in the whole. And thus we have a typical instance of the way in which the concept of simple location is hopelessly inadequate to cope with the facts arising in biological studies. The reader may be referred to Whitehead's own writings for an account of why it is inadequate in physics also; but others have made similar approaches, for example Wolfgang Köhler, starting from psychology, with his theory of physical "Gestalten."[28] According to Whitehead, all the things in the world are to be conceived as modifications of conditions within space-time, extending throughout its whole range, but having a central focal region, which is in common speech "where the thing is." In topographic analogy, such as thermodynamicians use, the influence of the thing grades off past successive contours, like the slopes of Fujiyama, in every direction. The connection of this idea with the sort of fact which we are always meeting in biology, namely phenomena of field character, is obvious, and to-day the concept of field is equally widespread and necessary in physics as in biology.

To this may be added the following. The abstraction of classical seventeenth century science from the life sciences had the effect, wrote Whitehead,[29] of bringing it about that dynamics, physics, and chemistry were the disciplines which guided the gradual transition from the full common-sense notions of the sixteenth century to the concept of Nature suggested by modern speculative physics. "This change of view, occupying four centuries, may be characterized as the transition from Space and Matter as the fundamental notions, to Process conceived of as

[27] Cf. J. Needham, *Order of Life* (Yale, 1936).
[28] Wolfgang Köhler, *Die Physischen Gestalten* (1920).
[29] Cf. *Science and the Modern World*, 58.

a complex of Activity with internal relations between its various factors."[30] The phrasing here is important in view of what has to be said below concerning the transition from the concepts of Form and Matter to those of Organisation and Energy. The older point of view abstracted from any long-continuing change and conceived of the full reality of Nature at a single instant. It abstracted from any temporal duration, and characterised the interrelations in Nature solely by the distribution of matter in space. For the modern view, process, activity, and change, are, as for the dialectical materialists, the matter of fact. "At an instant there is nothing. Each instant is only a way of grouping matters of fact . . . there is no Nature at an instant. Thus all the interrelations of matters of fact must involve transition in their essence. All realisation involves implication in the creative advance."[31]

It is extremely interesting that Whitehead in this century, and Engels in the last century, both selected an almost identical group of scientific advances which they felt to have been the deciding factors in necessitating the great transition from the Renaissance or Newtonian outlook in science to the modern, dialectical, or organic. Engels' three major discoveries were these:

The first was the proof of the transformation of energy. All the innumerable operative causes in nature, which until then had led a mysterious, inexplicable, existence as so-called 'forces'—mechanical force, heat, radiation, electricity, magnetism, chemical affinity, etc.—are now proved to be special forms, modes of existence of one and the same energy, i.e., motion. The unity of all motion in nature is no longer a philosophical assertion but a fact of natural science.

The second—chronologically earlier—discovery was that of the organic cell by Schleiden and Schwann, of the cell as a unit, out of the multiplication of which, and its differentiation, all organisms, except the very lowest, arise and develop.

But an essential gap still remained. If all multicellular organisms— plants as well as animals, including man—grow from a single cell according to the law of cell-division, whence, then, comes the infinite variety

[30] *Modes of Thought*, 198.
[31] *Ibid.*, 200.

of these organisms? This question was answered by the third great discovery, the theory of evolution, which was first presented in connected form and substantiated by Darwin.[32]

Whitehead speaks of four rather than three great advances, the first two being the idea of a field of physical activity pervading all space, and of atomism.[33] In the seventies of the last century some of the great departments of physics, such as light and electromagnetism, were established on the basis of waves in a continuous medium. But other sciences, such as chemistry, were established on the basis of ultimate particles or atoms and their interactions. Whitehead includes the cell-"theory" in biology as another example of the atomistic basis. It was, he says, in some respects, more revolutionary than the atomism of Dalton, for it introduced the notion of organism into the world of minute beings. There had been a tendency to treat the atom as an ultimate entity, capable only of external relations, but Pasteur showed the decisive importance of the idea of organism at the stage of infinitesimal magnitude. Whitehead's second group of two new ideas comprises the law of the conservation of energy, and the doctrine of evolution. In energy-transformations, permanence underlies change. In evolution, permanence abdicates and change takes its place. There is therefore in the world an aspect of permanence and an aspect of change. In modern physics, wrote Whitehead,[34]

mass . . . becomes the name for a quantity of energy considered in relation to some of its dynamical effects. This train of thought leads to the notion of energy being fundamental, thus displacing matter from that position. But energy is merely the name for the quantitative aspect of a structure of happenings; in short, it depends on the notion of the functioning of an organism.

And evolution is the evolution of organisms of ever increasing organisation. As for the dialectical contradiction between particles and waves, that has in our own time been, at any rate par-

---

[32] Appendix B to *Ludwig Feuerbach and the Outcome of Classical German Philosophy*.

[33] Cf. *Science and the Modern World*, 138ff.

[34] *Science and the Modern World*, 144.

tially, resolved, with the modern theories of wave-mechanics, quantum mechanics, etc., about which it is not fitting that a biologist should speak.

In parenthesis, having mentioned the agreement between Whitehead and Engels on the history of science, it is interesting to find at various places in Whitehead's writings remarkable echoes of Marxist thought. One conceives that these originate from the congruity that there is between the dialectical conception of Nature and the organic conception. For example, when discussing dualism, Whitehead says

The Universe is *many* because it is wholly and completely to be analysed into many final actualities. . . . The Universe is *one*, because of the universal immanence. There is thus a dualism in this contrast between the unity and multiplicity. Throughout the Universe there reigns the *union of opposites* which is the ground of dualism.[35]

And in another place: "In the past human life was lived in a bullock cart; in the future it will be lived in an aeroplane; and the change of speed amounts to a difference in *quality*."[36] More important, there are some fine passages where Whitehead expounds the changeableness of scientific formulations; the additions, distinctions, and modifications which have to be introduced perpetually into them; and the complete inadequacy of formal logic for science.[37] "We are told by logicians that a proposition must be either true or false, and that there is no middle term. But in practice, we may know that a proposition expresses an important truth, but that it is subject to limitations and qualifications which at present remain undiscovered." Clashes between theories are no sign of the failure of science, they are dialectical contradictions out of which much better approximations to truth will later arise. "A clash of doctrines is not a disaster—it is an opportunity."[38] A contradiction may be a sign of defeat in formal logic, but in science it marks the first step towards a victory. A reliance on scholastic and undialectical logic, which has marked so much writing in biological theory (e.g.,

[35] *Adventures of Ideas*, 245. (Last italics mine.)
[36] *Science and the Modern World*, 137. (Italics mine.)
[37] *Ibid.*, 255ff.
[38] *Ibid.*, 259.

the later works of H. Driesch) has been the reason why few biologists have troubled about it.

Reference was made above to Marx's phrase about making materialism not "ascetic." An admirable parallel passage is to be found in Whitehead.[39]

In the same way as Descartes introduced the tradition of thought which kept subsequent philosophy in some measure of contact with the scientific movement, so Leibnitz introduced the alternative tradition that the entities, which are the ultimate actual things, are in some sense procedures of organisation. . . . Kant reflected the two traditions, one upon the other. Kant was a scientist, but the schools derivative from Kant have had but slight effect on the mentality of the scientific world. It should be the task of the philosophical schools of this century to bring together the two streams into an expression of the world-picture derived from science, and thereby end the divorce of science from the affirmations of our aesthetic and ethical experiences.

This, then, can only be done by recognising them for what they are, manifestations of the highest organisational levels, sublime indeed, but connected as surely with all the lower levels as the physical hands of a man playing a violin in an orchestra are with the claws of a crab.

Such a connection involves what we have already had occasion to mention, the problem of the origin of mentality in evolution. There seems to be a bifurcation here. As we ascend the organisational levels, we seem to be led off in two separate directions, one the ascending series of social groups through animal associations to human community, the other the ascending series of stages of mental development. Perhaps it is not erroneous to regard the sociological and the psychological series as different aspects of one and the same set of high organisational levels. Only where the brain and central nervous system reaches its heights as in the primates does social organisation really develop, or conversely only where complexity is sufficient to allow of social life, intelligible communication and co-operative effort, does the mental life and its physical basis attain a high status.

The problem of "mind and matter" has always been the

[39] *Ibid.*, 217f.

skeleton in biology's cupboard. Though generally abandoned to the philosophers, biologists never felt any satisfaction at the way in which their colleagues were dealing with it. When some twenty years ago the present writer constructed a chart to show the historical development of biochemistry and physiology since the fifteenth century, he built it around the mind-body problem. Later for a long time he thought that this had been a mistake, but perhaps it was really a correct and useful plan, though now it would require considerable revision. Physiology has had a curious history in this respect. Though the word was first used in its present sense by John Fernel in the sixteenth century, the first textbook of physiology was the *De Homine* of Descartes, completed in 1637 but not published till 1662. Here mind and matter were absolutely separated. But as knowledge of the nervous system grew during the eighteenth and nineteenth centuries, it became more and more impossible to uphold this separation. As Whitehead acutely remarks,[40] "The effect of physiology was to put mind back into nature. The neurologist traces first the effect of stimuli along the bodily nerves, then integration at nerve centres, and finally the rise of a projective reference beyond the body with a resulting motor efficacy in renewed nervous excitement."

Elsewhere he sums up the situation thus:[41]

Descartes expresses this dualism with the utmost distinctness. For him, there are material substances with spatial relations, and mental substances. The mental substances are external to the material substances. Neither type requires the other type for the completion of its essence. Their unexplained interrelations are unnecessary for their respective existences. In truth, this formulation of the problem in terms of minds and matter is unfortunate. It omits the lower forms of life, such as vegetation and the lower animal types. These forms touch upon human mentality at their highest, and upon inorganic nature at their lowest.

The effect of this sharp division between nature and life has poisoned all subsequent philosophy. Even when the coördinate existence of the two types of actualities is abandoned, there is no proper fusion of the two in most modern schools of thought. For some, nature is mere appearance and mind is the sole reality. For others, physical nature is the sole reality

[40] *Ibid.*, 206.
[41] *Modes of Thought*, 204f.

and mind is an epiphenomenon. Here the phrases 'mere appearance' and 'epiphenomenon' obviously carry the implication of slight importance for the understanding of the final nature of things.

The doctrine that I am maintaining is that neither physical nature nor life can be understood unless we fuse them together as essential factors in the composition of 'really real' things whose inter-connections and individual characters constitute the universe.

This is a fine statement of the true scientific attitude to the problem of minds and bodies, and would be as acceptable to the dialectical materialists as to the emergent evolutionists. It means that when we speak of mind we mean "mind (in the sense of Pavlov and Sherrington)" and not "mind (loud and prolonged applause)."

Nearly all that has so far been said has been in praise of Whitehead's writings from the biological point of view, though with no attempt to pronounce upon the subtler points of his philosophy, a task impracticable for a working biologist. If any criticism were permitted, it would be that Whitehead has not been sufficiently outspoken in leading along the sociological and political directions in which his philosophy clearly points. It is true that he describes the creative aspect of evolution like any Marxist, as the creation of their own environment by organisms. He says that here the single organism is helpless and that adequate action needs societies of co-operating organisms. But what tendencies in the world to-day are showing a capacity for such adequate action? If it were possible for Marx and Engels in the days of a capitalism comparatively mild and progressive to state their views uncompromisingly, whether right or wrong, about the line humanity must take towards higher levels of organisation; how much more necessary would it be in our own time, when the state power of fascism has arisen in a tottering social system, a power purporting falsely to be a higher level of organisation, but really no more than a mechanical tyranny. One looks in vain in Whitehead's writings for some clear lead among the social tendencies of our times. This is not to say that he has not sketched out, sometimes with brilliant detail, the historical origin of many of the features of economic individualism. Just as we made a connection earlier in this paper between economic individualism and seventeenth century atomism, so Whitehead points out the connection between both these and the individualistic *"cogito, ergo sum"* of Descartes.[42] It led, he says, from private worlds of experience to private worlds of morals. Moreover he suggests, not unconvincingly, that the assumption of the bare valuelessness of mere matter led to a lack of reverence in the treatment of natural and artistic beauty. The supreme ugliness of industrial civilisation, as it first arose, would thus be connected with its utter failure to recognise the unity of mind and matter at all the levels of organisation. But this is not what we are looking for. Whitehead's apparent inability to give a lead in his own time comes out especially strikingly in *Adventures of Ideas*, where the adventure of civilisation is discussed.[43] It is too abstract. It does not interlock with the concrete realities of political life. The objection or the defence that philosophers are not to be expected to descend into the arena of political struggles has no force. Philosophers themselves have said that the world would not be well until philosophers became kings. To-day kingship lies open to whoever cares to take it. It is said that Stalin was once asked when and where did Lenin expound dialectical materialism? He answered: "When and where did he *not* expound it?"—a curiously Confucian reply.

But if the cobbler must stick to his last, the general upshot of this contribution is the great debt which biologists owe to A. N. Whitehead as the greatest living philosopher of organism. The epigram of old John Scott Haldane, neo-vitalist though he was, is coming true: "If physics and biology one day meet, and one of the two is swallowed up, that one will not be biology." In justice we should add that though it might perhaps be classical physics, it will not be physics itself, either; the two disciplines constituting indeed a Hegelian-Marxist contradiction, of which the philosophy of organism is the synthesis. In conclusion it may be of interest to give two examples, from the author's own field, of the way in which the newer attitude is changing previous conceptions.

[42] Cf. *Science and the Modern World*, 272ff.
[43] Cf. *Adventures of Ideas*, 352ff.

The question of the reducibility or irreducibility of biological facts to physico-chemical facts has already arisen several times above. Once the idea of a series of organic levels is reached, what we have to do is to seek to elucidate the regularities which occur at each of the levels without attempting either to force the higher or (anatomically) coarser processes into the framework of the lower or finer processes, or conversely to explain the lower by the higher. From this viewpoint the regularities discovered by experimental morphology will always have their validity; they cannot be affected by anything which either biochemistry or psychology may in the future discover. The behaviour, for instance, of an embryonic eye-cup isolated into saline solution—its capacity for self-differentiation, fusion with another eye-cup, lens-induction, regulation, etc.—will always remain the same however our knowledge of biochemistry or biophysics may advance. This is the reason why prediction is possible at levels which, strictly speaking, we do not "understand" at all, for example, genetics. But, though the biological regularities, once well and truly established, may remain for ever irrefragable, they will, considered alone, remain for ever meaningless. Meaning can only be introduced into our knowledge of the world by the simultaneous investigation of all the levels of complexity and organisation. Only in this way can we hope to understand how one is connected with the others. Only by understanding how one is connected with the others can we hope to see the meaningful integration of the evolving world in which organisation has been achieving its ever new triumphs.

The second question is one which has deeply concerned the present writer in his aim to unify biochemistry and morphology, namely the ancient problem of Form and Matter. Though not frequently discussed by Whitehead, it is fundamental for the biologist. The setting of μορφή and εἶδος against ὕλη by Aristotle has had an incalculably great influence on the historical development of biology. In the characteristic Greek art, sculpture, the form was certainly much more relevant to human interests than the marble or the bronze manifesting it. So for many centuries biologists devoted themselves to the study of animal form without much consideration of the matter with which it is indissolubly connected. It is not surprising that the numerous devils of vitalism found a congenial abode in the empty mansions of form thus suitably swept and garnished. The morphological tradition (originating perhaps from the idea of change as the privation of one form and the donation of another) was to think of matter far too simply, ignoring what we now know to be the vast complexity of chemical structures, and the unbroken line of sizes reaching from the sub-atomic levels to the particles of virus molecule size. Only in the light of the conception of organic levels can the saecular gulf between morphology and chemistry be bridged.

It is true that Aristotle held that there could be form without matter, though no matter without form. But according to him, the only entities which possessed form without matter, were the divine prime mover, the intelligent demiurges that moved the spheres, and perhaps the rational soul of man. Some of these are factors in which experimental science has never been very much interested. On the other hand, he maintained that there could be no matter without form, for however pure the matter was (even the chaotic primal menstrual matter which was the raw material of the embryo), it was always composed of the elements, i.e., always either hot or cold, wet or dry, and hence had a minimum of form. In its primitive way, this mirrors the position of modern science. Form is not the perquisite of the morphologist. It exists as the essential characteristic of the whole realm of organic chemistry, and cannot be excluded either from "inorganic" chemistry or from nuclear physics. But at that level it blends without distinction into order as such, and hence we should do well to give up all the old arguments about Form and Matter, replacing these factors with two others more in accordance with modern knowledge of the universe: Organisation and Energy. From this point of view there can no longer be any barrier between morphology and chemistry. We may hope that the future will show us, not only what laws the form of living organisms exhibits at its own level, but also how these laws are integrated with those which appear at lower levels of organisation. This formulation is surely in line with Whitehead's philosophy of organism, and no less so with that of the dialectical materialists and the emergent evolutionists.

Let us say once more then that in Whitehead's philosophy biologists find a view of the world which they are particularly well fitted to appreciate. Though dialectical materialism and emergent evolutionism have also much to teach them, they see in him the greatest and subtlest exponent of organic mechanism. These words are written in the College of Francis Glisson and William Harvey, of W. B. Hardy and Charles Sherrington. Isaac Newton's rooms, in that College of the Holy and Undivided Trinity to which A. N. Whitehead also belongs, lie only a stone's throw away. From the neighbouring biological stronghold a word of deep respect and salutation goes out to the repairer of the onesidedness of that Newtonian system which in its time was so profoundly progressive, the instaurator of the organic conception of the many-levelled world.

JOSEPH NEEDHAM

CONVILLE AND CAIUS COLLEGE
CAMBRIDGE UNIVERSITY, ENGLAND

6

Percy Hughes

IS WHITEHEAD'S PSYCHOLOGY ADEQUATE?

IS WHITEHEAD'S PSYCHOLOGY ADEQUATE?

I. The Question Defined

IN his last presentation of Psychology William James described it as still an abstract, truncated, would-be science of whose "underlying principles not one glimpse of clear insight exists." "Our perplexity is extreme," he concludes.[1] And this perplexity continues to this day, for J. R. Kantor's summary of *Current Trends in Psychological Theory*[2] seems to represent, fairly and comprehensively, the theoretical background of psychological laboratories and lecture rooms in this country. His bibliography cites 120 titles representing some 80 eminent psychologists of the day, expressing, I think, at least 13 mutually incompatible accounts of Psychology's first principles. These several doctrines, says Kantor, seem to be traditional rather than the fruit of intensive analysis. Frankly pessimistic, he advises psychologists either to work out a genuinely operational view or betake themselves to philosophies that have outgrown the "idealistic" or "dualistic" aberrations of the past. In either case psychologists, he warns, would have to modify profoundly their "hypotheses and procedures."[3]

Yet James also foretold with assurance a day when Psychology would be "taken up into the total body of philosophy," though not without profound modification of its formulas.[4] I am convinced that Whitehead has brought us much nearer to that "day;" though, like every other student of his works, I am in doubt how "adequate" my interpretation of his writings

[1] *Psychology* (1893), 238, 256, 464.
[2] *Psychological Bulletin*, Jan. 1941.
[3] *Ibid.*, 60.
[4] *Op. cit.*, 7.

is. But, as his psychologic doctrine seems to me the corridor of entrance to his "Cosmological Scheme," I take counsel of courage, and shall submit it to empirical test.

This psychologic doctrine also is essentially a logical scheme. Of such a structure we may properly demand, says Whitehead, that it be not merely logical or self-consistent, but also (1) coherent; that is, its fundamental ideas do not imply each other but do involve each other; (2) important; that is, it has methodological consequences; (3) widely applicable; and (4) adequate, in the sense that no item of experience defies interpretation in terms of that scheme.[5]

The coherence of Whitehead's doctrine is impressive, and, so far as I know, unassailable. Each piece of it seems to "ingress" with cries of delight to welcome new-found kin! Its importance has been acclaimed; it heralds a new day in philosophic method. The range of its applicability one hardly can compass within the limits of a chapter. But, to challenge its adequacy as regards a few items of experience that seem important is practicable, and should throw some new light on the doctrine. Such an inquiry should be predominatingly empirical. It is that kind of inquiry which I now attempt.

Whitehead does not define Psychology, and in fact seldom uses the term. This I explain partly by that current diversity of views among professed psychologists, which I noted above. Moreover, among philosophers Psychology has commonly signified "the study of mental functionings considered in themselves and in their mutual relations," in contrast with "epistemology, the theory of the knowledge of the external world." Preoccupation with this "uneasy division," says Whitehead, has given rise to a host of perplexities, and indeed has brought ruin to "modern philosophy."[6] He naturally would shrink from giving his doctrine a name that might suggest such parenthood. Other philosophers of note now disclaim the title psychologist. A book on Psychology now, from one or two of them, would greatly serve that science.

[5] *The Function of Reason* (1929), 53-55; *Process and Reality* (1930), 4.

[6] *Science and the Modern World*, 82, 210f. (Page references in this essay to *Science and the Modern World* are to the American edition, 1925, reprint 1926.)

Whitehead's rare use of the term, Psychology, occurs in two connections. He speaks of the unit private psychological field as "the event considered from its own standpoint."[7] This corresponds with the definition of Psychology proposed by some contemporary philosophers, that it is the study of modes of experiencing, in contrast with the study of data or objects experienced.[8] As his doctrine develops, this "private psychological field" becomes Whitehead's *subjective form*[9] which is *"how"* an act of experiencing goes on.

Whitehead also speaks of a "science still in the process of incubation," which he would call Psychological Physiology.[10]

This use of the term, Psychology, looks back to those days when psychology meant the study of the psyche or soul. For this embryonic science becomes with Whitehead the study of "a personal living society of high-grade occasions," which, he says, "is the soul of which Plato spoke."[11] Now, in Whitehead's terminology, such a society is a nexus, and a nexus is *"public* matter of fact;"* whereas, says he, a subjective form is *"private* matter of fact."[12] So my immediate task is to coördinate these two uses of the term, psychological, *and to show how private and public matters of fact are related in Whitehead's doctrine.*

II. The "Private Psychological Field"

Whitehead, we must recall, approached the problems of philosophy not from the notions of psychology but from the notions of modern physics.[13] From this modern viewpoint Nature is not merely an "entangled locomotion of molecules" but primarily "a complex of activities with internal relations between its various factors." Now, internally, or from its own standpoint, "an activity is a complex process of appropriating into a unity

---

[7] *Ibid.*, 216f.; *Process and Reality*, 444. (Page references to *Process and Reality* in this essay are to the American edition, 1930.)

[8] Cf. John Dewey, "Conduct and Experience," *Psychologies of 1930*, 417; *Philosophy and Civilization* (1931), 409-422.

[9] Cf. *Process and Reality*, 35.

[10] Cf. *Ibid.*, 157-167.

[11] *Adventures of Ideas* (1933), 267.

[12] *Process and Reality*, 32.

[13] Cf. *Science and the Modern World*, 219.

of existence the many data presented as relevant by the physical processes of nature."[14] Whitehead says this is true of the inorganic activities with which physics and chemistry deal; and I don't doubt it. He says it is also true of organic physiologic activities, such as the growth of a tree. And this seems obvious. In an act of growth many concrete processes are unified, and each of them is itself a unification and "appropriation" of "alien things," such as elements of soil, atmosphere, sunlight, etc. An act of growth not only is a concrescence of these processes (which Whitehead calls prehensions), but it originates them. Moreover each of these processes (or prehensions) is modified by the fact that it is a part of the act of growth as a whole. Indeed the "really real" thing is the act as a whole, which Whitehead therefore calls the "subject" and the actual "occasion of experience."

So the quality of the total concrescent act imposes itself on all its constituent processes. Having called the act the "subject," he calls this imposed quality the subjective form of the act. Also he occasionally calls it the *affective tone*. The term *active tone* seems to me transparent and of glovelike fit.

Not only is this concrescent structure of activity or act found in all physical acts and in all physiological acts; it is the structure essential in all conscious, cognitive acts, such as we ordinarily call acts of experiencing. As I perceive that gathering thunder-cloud sweep toward my study, there arise innumerable processes (prehensions) of bodily adaptation in which I appropriate or make my own the shape, color, coolness, and menace of the activities of nature that I am bent on perceiving. This activity of perceptual adaptation is a concrescence of prehensive processes, each of which has the quality of the act as a whole. It is Whitehead's "original and enduring contribution to philosophy, present and future," that he has shown that "acts in human experiencing are thus analogous with all acts, physical and physiological, which are involved in natural events."[15] Hence all acts or "occasions" in Nature involve the "private psychological field" of subjective form or "active tone."

[14] *Modes of Thought* (1938), 191, 198, 205.
[15] John Dewey, "Whitehead's Philosophy," *Phil. Rev.* (1937) Vol. XLVI, 173.

III. Questions of Terminology

In the history of Philosophy we find Plato bending words of common speech to his uses; whereas Aristotle invented many words or phrases more precisely to express his meaning. In time Plato's meaning came to be the standard interpretation of old words; while Aristotle's new tools of speech have been horribly misused. Mathematical physicists may follow Aristotle's practice with success; for they speak only to others who are learning their new language. But philosophy, Whitehead admirably says, seeks to correct in individuals their initial selective emphasis, so that generalizations derived from some specialty may find applications in fields beyond it.[16] It would seem that even according to this account of philosophic purpose, familiar words used in a new context would acquire new meanings just as rapidly as a new context would be recognized as genuine. And in so far as philosophy starts from the whole apparatus of common-sense thought and recurs to it[17]—an alternative view I much prefer—the Platonic procedure seems doubly justified. The great educational significance of Whitehead's doctrine will hardly be realized until his novel terminology is fairly construed in terms of common use.

Let us begin with a neutral term, events. When we discuss matters of fact it is events we talk about. But we know events don't bring themselves about; they are brought about by activities individualized in acts ("occasions of experience"), which therefore are the actualities, the really real things, of nature. But in an event acts take account of or deal with each other; what one act does is done to other acts, so that acts become matters of mutual and public concern. Dewey's familiar term, transaction, seems preferable to the term nexus, to indicate this involvement of doing and undergoing; it is more familiar and more expressive.

The tendency of any act is to initiate a procedure which may be analyzed into concrete processes *(prehensions)*; and upon this procedure—upon every process within it—the unity of the

---

[16] Cf. *Process and Reality*, 7f.
[17] Cf. *Aims of Education* (1917), 159.

act imposes its quality of seeking a certain fulfilment *(satisfaction)*. This qualifying affective tone we therefore well may call the active tone *(subjective form)* of the procedure. That fulfilment, from the standpoint of subsequent acts, is an achievement, a work, an effect. *(Superject.)* Some acts are members of a series, each responding to that which precedes and expressing itself in that which follows. We call this a course of action. In a personal life-career there are such one-dimensional series; but they are more common in other histories. Hence, to call all courses of action *personal orders* or *persons* is gratuitously confusing.

We need to speak of processes that contribute to the total concrescent procedure of an act by excluding certain data from consideration, as irrelevant. The forest tree responds to excessive shade by not beginning to grow branchlets below its crown of foliage. That reserve and irresponsiveness is why there is that crown. Shall we call them renunciations? No, for to renounce requires consideration. Let us speak of inhibitive responses *(negative prehensions)* as first aid to complacency; while facilitative responses *(positive prehensions)* enrich experience, even in negative judgments, and lend themselves to Adventure, and to that Peace, which is "the harmony of the soul's activities with ideal aims that lie beyond any personal satisfaction."[18]

IV. PHYSICS, PHYSIOLOGY AND PSYCHOLOGY

"The key notion from which such [cosmological] construction should start is that the energetic activity considered in physics is the emotional intensity entertained in life."[19] Clearly this statement has much significance for Whitehead's Psychology. I take it to mean that the flux of energy from act to act differs in the degree to which there occur transmutations—that is, qualitative and structural enrichments—rather than mere transmission of energy. Physics studies processes in which transmutation is at a minimum; psychology is concerned with acts

---

[18] *Adventures of Ideas*, 371.
[19] *Modes of Thought*, 231f.

and processes in which transmutation is at a maximum. Physiology occupies the middle position. Courses of physiological action are marked by attainment. In some the action is rhythmic, as in respiration; others are irreversible, as in maturation, and also in senescent decay.

Psychology is inseparable, says Whitehead, from physiology; and he shows also that it is inseparable from physics, or the study of the "inorganic apparatus." In any act of thought there is a highly complex procedure, embracing acts and processes that are the concern of all three sciences. All sciences study the flux of energetic activity. In psychological transaction novel attainment is emphatic; and this is what Whitehead means by "emotional intensity." A corollary of this doctrine is that acts of creative emphasis do affect, in some way, the merely quantitative flux of energy studied in physics, bringing about, in some measure, a "counter-tendency" to that "physical system" which "presents to us the spectacle of a finite system steadily running down—losing its activities and varieties."[20] How is this possible? Whitehead suggests that qualities may act like catalytic agents:[21] or they may involve strains that result in "deformation of the shape of an electron."[22]

V. Active Tone: Private and Public

Until we have grasped the internal constitution of an act our building of cosmologic schemes is in vain; and this inwardness is the originating of an active tone (subjective form) throughout the procedure of the act.[23] Until the act has moved toward its fulfilment in dealing with other acts and in being dealt with by them as their medium of activity, this active tone is private in nature, as it is to knowledge; but its tone consists in moving towards publicity in such transactions within events.

This publicity is twofold. On the one hand the tone of activity is *responsive*. Our acquaintance with a larch in early spring may begin in a private greeny tone of feeling, as it passes into a

[20] *The Function of Reason*, 72.
[21] Cf. *Process and Reality*, 163, 420; *Modes of Thought*, 231.
[22] Cf. *Process and Reality*, 152.
[23] Cf. *Ibid.*, 444.

public feeling of knowing that that larch is green.[24] On the other hand, this same tone is *expressive*. "Expression is the diffusion in the environment of something initially entertained"[25] as private active tone. Such expressiveness of all acts throughout nature is fundamental in nature. This general relationship of mutual immanence between all activities Whitehead learned from modern physics, not from "animal faith." Its applicability to human experience follows as a reasonable metaphysical assumption. It is not discredited by the fact that all animals believe it, even if they have learned from outworn physical doctrine to look on nature as "a realm of matter,"—a "self-sufficient meaningless complex of facts,"—"an unintelligible universe," that provokes in them some "mystic chant" of A Free Man's Worship, or some other intonation of dismay and despair.

Some speak of the privacy of "mind" accessible only to introspection. The term introspection is a befuddling metaphor, suggesting eyes and ears reversing their processes, to note what happens in a mind that presently admits it is not there or anywhere! But it was invented to identify acts of recalling previous acts. Trouble arises only when it is supposed that this act of recall is an act of resurrection. Acts do "not all die;" they persist commonly with diminishing efficacy to provoke and mould acts of recall. The act of recall will impose its active tone on what residual effect it encounters of the earlier act.

So when Whitehead says that introspection "lifts the clear-cut data of sensation into primacy, and cloaks the vague compulsions and derivations which form the main stuff of experience,"[26] he probably well describes one sort of introspection, still prevalent in some schools of thought. James, however, in his acts of recall, sought for those organic, cenesthetic sensations, which Whitehead evidently also sought and found, and called "nonsensory experiences" of causal efficacy. It is a case of one mode of introspective act, or recall, criticizing and supplementing another mode. Competent introspective technique psychologists develop in some laboratories; but this development depends on

[21] Cf. *Adventures of Ideas*, 315.
[25] *Modes of Thought* (1938), 29.
[26] *Adventures of Ideas*, 290.

knowledge that how a man is introspecting others often can judge better than he. So hard it is to be utterly private even in one's own mind!

By such deficiencies in introspection I would presently explain certain seeming inadequacies in Whitehead's psychological doctrine. But I now stress the fact that attentive acts and the active tone of their procedure may also be observed otherwise than by "introspective" recall. Attentive acts express themselves in differences they make in the world about them; "whatever merges into actuality, implants its aspects in every individual event."[27] And conscious, percipient acts are parts of the environing actuality of every act in Nature.

So we see that no concrete happening or act or process is without private, internal tone or without public imprint. Psychology's emphasis upon private fields, however, may serve to correct a crude species of naturalism which would blind us to aspects of nature that are generative of value. Though it warrants no belief in a region or realm of mind never perceived save by itself.

VI. PSYCHOLOGICAL PHYSIOLOGY

In section I I said that my immediate task is to coördinate two apparently distinct meanings that Whitehead has given to the word, psychological, the one indicating private, the other public, "matter-of-fact." In sections II to V I have said that this private fact or "Subjective form" is that tone of creativity, it is that genesis of value, which qualifies all processes in Nature, because they originate and are furthered in and by *acts*. So I give this genesis of value the more transparent name of "active tone;" and have described how this tone, privately born, becomes public to all other acts, in that all acts are both responsive and expressive to each other. Publicity consists in this interaction. So now the psychological problem becomes to find what type of transactions is in The Order of Nature best adapted to intensify active tone or creative emphasis.[28] For this emphasis clearly is

[27] *Science and the Modern World*, 216.
[28] Cf. *Process and Reality*, 127ff.

Nature's aim. Consciousness appears in Nature as its crowning achievement of this aim.

In the following passage[29] Whitehead provides the general frame within which this crowning achievement of nature is, so far as we know, best attained.

The brain is continuous with the body, and the body is continuous with the rest of the natural world. Human experience is an act of self-origination including the whole of nature, limited to the perspective of a focal region within the body, but not necessarily persisting in any fixed coördination with a definite part of the brain.

The details of this picture constitute the elements of a science "still in the process of incubation" which he appropriately calls Psychological Physiology. For his aim is not to reduce conscious experience to a physiological event, but to show how physiological structure lends itself to the realization of creative thought.[30]

Most of us have talked vaguely of conscious experience as the functioning of a living body, not without some uneasiness, I suppose, as to how a physiological mechanism could produce the flights of imaginative thought. So far as I know Whitehead is the first to suggest a "likely tale." His conception is startling, but grows in plausibility. We must distinguish between occupied space and empty space. Occupation means occupation by bodies. Emptiness means therefore a field of non-corporeal activities. For apart from activity there is indeed nothing.

Within a living body are interstices of such empty space, where activities both respond to the acts of the body and express themselves in those acts, yet themselves arise in an incorporeal though physical medium. For a body is an association of activities which condition each other in maintaining a pattern of conformity. This association is in the first place serial, so that, as acts arise and pass away, still the series remains as an "enduring object." And, in the second place, many such series maintain themselves in nature by constituting a "society" of contemporary acts, each playing a part in a pattern of activity, which we may call a mechanism.

[29] Cf. *Adventures of Ideas*, 290.
[30] Cf. *Process and Reality*, 157-167.

As the immediate environment of its "empty spaces" a body stabilizes and "canalizes" activities in them without binding them to conformity. The body performs the function of an "amplifier." This applies not only to the body as a whole, but to all its cells and organs; and in the human body the dominance of the brain over all other organs leads to the highest degree of intensification of acts in the enclosed "empty spaces."

The essential in life is originality and creativeness. Such empty spaces within bodies favor interaction between acts which retain their freedom. They form what Whitehead calls "entirely living nexūs," which in the human body, more than in any other known to us, are "regnant" over that body. Psychological Physiology is the study of these "entirely living nexūs," or spontaneous interactions, partly in abstraction from the physical, partly in response to the physical, and partly in response to each other. The first leads to the study of Feelings or "prehensions," the second to the study of the effect of food and of sense stimulation, and the third, as I understand it, raises the problem of the "living soul."

VII. The Living Soul

The two modern philosophers who most consistently reject the notion of a self-identical Soul-Substance are Hume and William James. But the problem remains for them, as it does for the philosophy of organism, to provide an adequate account of this undoubted personal unity, maintaining itself amidst the welter of circumstance.[31]

It is clear that Whitehead by "personal" means *here* what the rest of us do. He is dealing with a characteristic peculiarly human. "In some sense there is a unity in the life of each man, from birth to death."

Whitehead's answer to this problem is not wholly clear to me. I submit an interpretation that seems to me illuminating, and also quite in conformity with what Whitehead says upon the subject. But the interpretation is in part conjectural; some other interpretation may equally or better accord with what Whitehead says. His answer seems to me to involve, beside (1)

[31] *Adventures of Ideas*, 240.

the body, (2) the concept of a *Locus*, (3) the concept of personal order, or "series of high-grade occasions," "which is the *Soul* of which Plato spoke," and also (4) the concept of a "non-social nexus," or spontaneous interaction, which I wish to call *Spirit*. (In choosing this term I give expression to my conviction that there is the most remarkable correspondence between Whitehead's philosophy and that religious insight which inspires *The Testament of Beauty* of Robert Bridges. To interpret one of these great Englishmen in terms of the other might not please either, even when I interpret both in the light of the Anglican Prayer Book. But it has been and is an enjoyable exercise.)

The "Locus" is the region of empty space within the body which "provides an emplacement" for acts that are Personal and Spiritual. It contributes to the unity of personal life-career because it is within the enduring body, interacting with that body, in the way already explained. The Concept of Personal Order or Soul, is, for Whitehead, that of a one-dimensional, continuous, cumulative series of "high-grade occasions," culminating in "intellectual feelings." The concept is enriched and modified by the recognition that such a personal order would inherit not only from preceding members of the series but also from the environing body, with its innumerable strands of inheritance. None the less he speaks of this personal unity as a single strand in nature. In my judgment this one-dimensional strand persisting throughout life is a postulated unity such as all histories must assume. The facts exhibit at best only an approximation to this conception.[32]

But Whitehead has previously urged that, to the problem of life and freedom, the enduring Soul, with its inherited, persisting order, "is exactly the irrelevant answer." "The problem is, How can there be originality? And the answer explains how the Soul need be no more original than a stone." The true answer he finds in interactions between acts of which each is responsive to the physical conformal environment of the body, but in its own 'aim' is moved by "envisagement" of the possi-

[32] Cf. Percy Hughes, "The Technique of Philosophic Explanation," *Journal of Philosophy* (1939), Vol. XXXVI, 652f.

bilities inherent in Nature. The description of these possibilities as "eternal objects" maintained by the Primordial Nature of God, is to my view alone adequate to explain the facts. But that question takes us beyond the corridor of Psychological Physiology, I think, into a "court of learning" opening therefrom.

It is apparent that this spontaneous interaction of acts also contributes to such unity and continuity as exists in a personal life-career. For the advance of man in understanding Nature is dependent at least in some measure upon the Order of Nature, potential as well as actual. There is a "natural" relation expressed, for example, in the scientific progress of a man, or in any other form of intellectual or esthetic advance, in the life-career of a person. I believe we can not extract square roots without previous acquaintance with some way of adding, subtracting, and multiplying.

It is suggestive to reflect that such a strand of unity persists also in the life of a nation or a civilization. I have wondered that Whitehead has not extended the notion of bodies to include societies, rather than the notion of societies to include bodies! For it seems that social institutions do provide a nest of strands of enduring objects that facilitate, confirm, and strengthen, in the unoccupied region they enclose, spontaneous interactions of freedom, which in turn themselves have a scope of functioning within the living bodies of persons. It is not unprofitable to compare totalitarian and democratic societies in these terms. As with Psychological Physiology, so with Psychological Sociology, it seems to me, the underlying method of such a science must be after the pattern of history, not of mathematics. Though the latter is not excluded.

It is to the relation of these two patterns in psychological study, as they are exemplified in Whitehead's writings, that I now turn.

VIII. Method and Self-Education

In his *Emendation* Spinoza first describes his self-education, as it led him to the realization that to win "unceasing joy" he must attain the "knowledge of the union that the mind hath with the whole of Nature." He writes his Ethics, *de more geometrico*, to help him attain this knowledge; but many of his writings and the tradition of his life assure us that to many of the unlearned he attributed intuitive awareness, though not *scientia intuitiva*, of this union, in the form of true religion. Indeed we realize that the postulates of his "demonstration" rest upon such faith. That is to say, with Spinoza as with Whitehead, the employment of mathematical method appears only as a phase of that career or history of self-education which supplied the bases of that method.

This process of self-education Whitehead describes in essays written while he was turning from mathematical inquiry to cosmologic speculation.[33] Then he writes, "the essence of education is that it be religious," and inculcate Duty and Reverence. Duty requires that we attain knowledge of what is "relevant to decision and action;" and "morality of outlook" he later affirms, "is inseparably conjoined with generality of outlook."[34] So Speculative Philosophy, as a "necessary system of general ideas" is but the fulfilment of Duty—of "ultimate morality." In Whitehead, the man, such speculation is progress in his self-education, which is "essentially" a matter of religion. For "the foundation of reverence is this perception, that the present holds within itself the complete sum of existence, backwards and forwards, that whole amplitude of time, which is eternity."[35]

I contrast this account of self-education with his account of "the true method of discovery." "It starts from the ground of particular observation," we are told; but "must have its origin in *generalization* of particular factors" already discerned in existent theory. Then "it makes a flight in the thin air of imaginative generalization; and it again lands for renewed observation rendered acute by rational interpretation." In this method "generalization will, if derived from physics, find applications in fields of experience beyond physics."[36]

[33] *Aims of Education* (1929)—a volume that contains important essays written and published between 1916 and 1923. See especially pages 23, 29 and 57.

[34] *Process and Reality*, 23.

[35] *Aims of Education*, 23.

[36] *Process and Reality*, 7, 8 (italics mine).

This is one method of discovery, I have no doubt; but it takes place within a self-illuminating life-career which we recognize as self-education. What then is the place of this method within the personal life-career? Whitehead answers in terms of a Rhythm in Education. The first stage is one of "first realizations of the import of the unexplored relationships between bare facts." This is the stage of the ferment of romantic emotion. The second stage is that of analysis and of "exact formulation." Further disclosure is thus attained; but new facts acquired must now fit into the analysis. Only such facts are entertained, as accord with that analysis. The third stage, the stage of fruition, is a "reaction toward romance." We "relapse into the discursive adventures of the romantic stage," but with a mind now no longer a rabble but a disciplined regiment.

I do not question that the Method as above defined has some place in the personal life-career of self-education. But the Rhythm Whitehead thus noted in adolescent education he applies to the whole course of life and self-education. "Its whole aim is the production of active wisdom." "Without a previous stage of romance the stage of precision is barren," "its analyses are analyses of nothing." It appears to me that in his definition of the method of discovery Whitehead has finely identified the logico-mathematical method, but without bringing it into relation with this more comprehensive path of self-education.

Our philosophic tradition on the whole preserves a fairly close relation between life-careers of self-education and the speculative systems philosophers have, or have not set up. The aim of the system is to transcend, but not to ignore this relation. I think it must be clear that Psychology, and indeed Psychological Physiology is that part of the "Total Body of Philosophy" for which this relation is most relevant. Psychology proper is the corridor of entrance to and exit from any Cosmological scheme.

A Psychology "discovered" by "flights in the thin air of imaginative generalization" may be expected to show the fault of inadequacy or attenuation of observable reality. Whitehead has himself said that he has "attenuated human personality into a genetic relation between occasions of human experience."[37] I have shown, I think, that that attenuation he has not wholly corrected. There are in his psychology other attenuations also not wholly corrected. With this point of view I examine his doctrine of "Feelings." It is in most respects a "flight in the thin air of imaginative generalization."

IX. THE DOCTRINE OF FEELINGS

A "feeling" is a process of positively grasping (prehending) data, both responding to them and embracing them in the active urge toward the fulfilment of the act in which that feeling arose. Responsive feelings are termed physical, and feelings of aim are called mental. For my present purpose the important distinction is between conscious and unconscious feelings. Neither a mental nor a physical process need be conscious. An act in the growth of a tree, for example, unifies physical feelings as they are transmuted into mental feelings; the tree becomes a special case of a special variety of white oak.

Indeed, below the propositional level feelings have no active tones that are conscious.[38] Even many propositional feelings seem to be unconscious. Any feeling that contrasts in a transaction that which *is*, with that which *might be* is propositional; and such comparative feelings seem to be involved, for example, in the creative alchemy of germ plasm evolving new individuals and new species.

How then is this analysis of feelings, occupying about 100 pages of highly condensed matter, related to observation? Since, psychiatrists aside, we can only recall feelings that have been conscious, the method of introspection can not really be applied. Therefore such unconscious feelings, both primary and propositional, can only be known "derivatively, as they remain components" in conscious acts and processes.[39]

Such derivations may fairly then be called imaginative, though without branding them as false. But they do leave to

[37] *Adventures of Ideas*, 239.
[38] Cf. *Process and Reality*, 391.
[39] *Ibid.*, 246.

conscious procedure the selection of its data, and the selection also of possible modes of coördination. Yet, "Consciousness is only the last and greatest of elements by which the selective character of the individual obscures the external totality from which it originates and which it embodies."[40] Therefore "the task of philosophy is to recover the totality obscured by the selection," and "philosophy is consciousness correcting its own excess of subjectivity." Yet both by this method of imaginative analysis and also by the method of introspection, we see that the selective emphasis of consciousness may well be exaggerated, not corrected.

In my judgment Whitehead's bias of dominant interest is shown in his frequent identification of conscious quality with cognitive quality; it is shown also in his identification of causation with the mode of causal efficacy. How settle the issue? Only by reference to that other type of subject-matter in which consciousness may genuinely be self-corrective. This reference consists in returning to the concept of self-education as a phase, probably the essential phase, of the life-career of an individual person.

X. The Psychology of Life-Career

We have seen that the problem of Psychology, at least from the standpoint of philosophy, is to establish an authentic notion of the "experience" of ourselves, and of other things more or less like ourselves, as the corridor through which we may enter, and also leave, the tower of cosmological speculation. For clearly, our views of experience, or of action generally, must be based ultimately upon our own awareness of our own actions. Philosophy, we may agree, seeks to correct the subjective bias this involves; and the correction of the bias starts from recognizing its existence and origin.

In living we fulfill courses of action. In retrospective, retrovertive perception we first awake to this life's story, "placing ourselves back in it by a kind of sympathy." Consciousness "detaches itself from the already-made to attach itself to the being-

[40] *Ibid.*, 22.

made."[41] This perception we amplify as we acquire the arts of narrative, and develop the science of historical procedure. Histories construct narratives of courses of action throughout Nature, astronomic, biographic as well as national histories, histories of civilization and of thought. One's life-career sustains a course of self-education, in making itself, in enjoying itself, more or less, and also in understanding itself, orienting itself among courses of action throughout Nature.

Histories seek but hardly attain, a knowledge of action continuous in successive acts. We postulate a single life-stream with our body for its "bed," with power feebly to illuminate the acts that rise like waves upon its surface, deriving therefrom some insight into what goes on in its own depths. But to that insight all sciences "derivatively" contribute. Those waves are waves of attention, which in their radical discontinuity, present many types of act. Sometimes these acts are tidal waves of attending; but more often like ripples they endure for seconds only.

Whitehead's Physiological Psychology describes a pattern or mechanism in Nature apparently well-suited to relate the cumulative personal effect of acts, such as we indicate by the words comprehension, cognition, etc., with the act through and in which we attain that effect, indicated by such words as comprehend*ing*, cogniz*ing*, etc. Learning and understanding are words that obscure this distinction.

The general pattern of these acts Whitehead has well defined as a unification of processes (prehensions), all pervaded by the "tone" of the act, of the fulfilment which it seeks. But I think he has not sufficiently emphasized the diversity of process within a "pattern of dominance," so that an act which is dominantly practical subordinates within itself processes that are cognitive and algedonic. As with Spinoza, his interest is primarily cognitive; and in a sense he agrees with Spinoza that "the decision of the mind and the motion of the body are one and the same thing." But we must avoid the conclusion that when I dig potatoes my act is primarily one of finding out what digging

[41] H. Bergson, *Creative Evolution* (trans. 1911), 171, 232; Percy Hughes, "The Technique of Philosophic Explanation," *Journal of Philosophy* (1939) Vol. XXXVI, 650.

potatoes is like. Any cognitive gain here is quite subordinate to the practical.

Further, in an act of knowing, sometimes dominant emphasis is on contrasts of general possibilities. Here processes of perceptual adaptation to particular goings-on are present, if only to the words employed. But the act as a whole is one of *inhibiting* perceptual response, so that *general* contrasts may be amplified and rendered distinct. Often in such reflection we become almost deaf and blind. And again, conversely, even in our perceptual adaptation to circumstance, there are, present and effective, processes of conceptual contrast, but they occur as subordinate to the responsive adaptation of the whole body to what is being perceived.

This fact emphasizes the discontinuity and multidimensionality of human life-career. Somehow I gain in understanding, perhaps, and also in skills, and also in capacity to enjoy. These several channels of process may help or interfere with each other. Philosophy fixes its attention upon understanding. Gains in the pleasurable quality of life and in power to shape events to our purpose are secondary to it; but undue emphasis upon any one of these three types of act and process leads to condescension toward people whose dominating interest is other than our own; and it may lead to fanaticism in the pursuit of cognition, of pleasure, or of power. Such an outlook is totalitarian in its inward structure.

Similarly, again, even among acts of perceptual adaptation, one may distinguish three patterns of dominance. To *observe* is an exploration of the several factors mutually involved in a situation. To *explain*, in its primary perceptual meaning, is to unify some present event with the preceding course of action of which that present is the fulfilment. To *appreciate* is to respond to the present in terms of the promise it encloses, realizing its potential scope.

XI. The Inadequacies of Whitehead's Psychology of Perception

From my point of view some of Whitehead's inadequacies are readily explainable and therefore easily corrected. In 1917 he speaks of the sports of English schools as "nature returning with a cap and bells."[42] This seems to indicate a deficient appreciation of the place of enjoyment and of bodily skill in constituting the religious life not only of England, but of most vigorous peoples. For I suppose the essential religion of Englishmen is sportsmanship, and "in their sports is their prayer." Whitehead rather depreciates arms and legs, at least in theory, especially in comparison with ears. Miss Helen Keller does not! To abstract knowing and to center philosophy upon it is comparable to abstracting pleasure-pain, or power, or security, and centering philosophy on that. We know other acts than acts of knowing.

Also, I find that there are at least three distinct types of perceptual adaptation, acts of observing, acts of explaining, and acts of appreciating. Whitehead, on the other hand, recognizes only one type of "conscious perception." This is not a mere matter of omission. Whitehead stresses that our notion of cause rests on our perception of causes. But causation has a different aspect in these three types of perceptual adaptation. Laws are mere summaries of connections directly perceived.

The general tendency among philosophers today is to identify cause with that type of cause I call explanatory. All other types of causes are viewed as illegitimate or derivative. Whitehead says[43] causation is "the energizing of the past occasion as it claims its self-identical existence as a living issue in the present;" it is "the influx of the other into that self-identity which is the continued life of the immediate past within the immediacy of the present." Woodbridge says:[44] "Agents acting characteristically in historical processes we do identify, and also the consequences of their so acting. That is precisely what we mean by cause and effect." Says Dewey, causation is the "continuity of historical change," it is the "sequential order itself," "the growth process itself."[45] Montague identifies cause with "one experience generating another."[46]

[42] *The Aims of Education*, 78; Percy Hughes, "Sports in the Nation," *Journal of Social Philosophy* (1940), Vol. 5, 206-218.

[43] Cf. *Adventures of Ideas*, 233f.

[44] *An Essay on Nature* (1940), 201.

[45] *Experience and Nature* (1929), 99, 273, 275.

[46] *The Ways of Things* (1940), 183.

On the other hand, Aristotle's doctrine of "fourfold causation" is a magnificent summary of causation within a situation observed. There are at least four essential types of factors involved in such a situation. The root notion of cause is dependence; and in situations observed there is *mutual* dependence.[47] Indeed Whitehead's cosmologic doctrine is one of manifold mutual dependence of factors observed as involved in situations.[48]

This doctrine of fourfold causation Dewey rejects and ingeniously charges to the "social setting of Greek thought" and to an "anthropomorphic rendering of nature."[49] *All* our rendering of nature is anthropomorphic—should be, must be. There is much in our social setting that explains only too well this current philosophic emphasis on cause as "enforcement."

How does causation appear in acts of appreciation? The cause is the "not yet," it is the "promise," "the encloser of things to be," as Whitman says, "realizing an acme of things accomplished." Whitehead's God seems to me the only adequate concept of the cause of what we appreciate. We can not observe or explain Him; He is the "lure of feeling," He is what we *really* appreciate. I should call this a matter of adequate, well informed perceptual adaptation, of the type I call appreciation. The concept gives us "exact formulation" of what is thus felt.[50] In Santayana's mythic atlas I would place *appreciation* at the gateway of the Realm of Spirit, *observation* at that of the Realm of Truth, and explanation at the gateway of the Realm of Matter. Implication would admit us to *Essence!*

Similarly our concept of Individuality varies as it is derived from perceptual adaptation of one or other of these three types.

In fact, the psychological gateway and corridor into the Total Body of Philosophy needs widening!

[47] Percy Hughes, "The Technique of Philosophic Observation," *Journal of Philosophy* (1938) Vol. XXXV, 295ff.

[48] Cf. *Process and Reality*, 5.

[49] *Experience and Nature*, 92, 214.

[50] That is, God can be no more than a conceptual formula unless we directly *perceive* Him in appreciating His works.

XII. SUMMARY

Despite the critical title I have given this Chapter, my purpose is genuinely to appreciate Whitehead's doctrine of human life and thought—to realize and sense, that is, the presence in him of dynamic, creative potency in helping onward that New Reformation of which he speaks. To do this I find I must construe his esoteric terminology into words and phrases in common use, believing that the necessary transformation of meaning and thought will follow from the novel context each word thus receives. Only in this way may we hope to test whether in fact we have caught or sadly muffed his gospel.

His *Concept of Nature* (1920) imposed on Whitehead the task of finding the place of Mind in Nature. His Gifford Lectures (1927-8) presented his solution of this problem, which is embodied in *Process and Reality* (1929), especially in Part II, Chapter III, entitled *The Order of Nature*. The "key notion" of this discovery is that the flux of energy throughout Nature is continuous, from those modes of electro-magnetic energy which are the special concern of physics to the spiritual aspirations expressed in human policy and art.

The problem centers in the interpretation of the human body. In Whitehead's approach to this problem the elements of Nature are not inert, whether as infinitesimal particles or as a spatio-temporal field. These elements are *acts*, each responding to and expressing itself in other acts, in a universe of transactions, each act being unlimited in scope but effective primarily at some focus. In these terms the relations and qualities of Nature are not externally imposed on acts but are the properties that acts disclose in their transactions.

All qualities and values through Nature exist primarily as aims or, better, aimings of individual acts, which become fully actual only as they evoke response in other acts. A scale or hierarchy of acts and values exist in terms of intensity of creative emphases. The significance of the human body in Nature is that it focalizes acts of all degrees of creative emphasis, and is a mechanism achieved by Nature for subordinating acts of minimum creativity, acts of routine, to acts of maximum creativity, acts of conscious self-direction toward ideal ends. This interpretation of the human body justifies the title of the new science Whitehead proposes, *Psychological Physiology*.

The essential concept of this new science would be that of noncorporeal acts occurring within a body, each of which is effective in that medium which they collectively create as their own emplacement, namely the "empty spaces" within that body. The permissibility of this concept rests upon Whitehead's physical doctrine of space-time, upon which I can pass no judgment, except to say that at present it has no rival in making intelligible the relation of imaginative thought and feeling and action to the mechanisms of our bodies. It gives a plausible scientific status to the common belief in what has immemorially been named the Spirit.

In this account of Psychological Physiology the human body appears as furnishing the environment necessary to Spirit, evoking its activities, expressing itself in them and likewise itself responsive and expressive of them. But in this doctrine the body rather "amplifies" than governs spiritual life. Indeed the body fully *lives* only as these spiritual activities are dominant, modifying bodily routines and fixations to secure their adaptation to novelties immediately present. Moreover, such incorporeal activities are free, each in its own kind and degree, to respond to those possibilities which Nature at-large (or God) sustains, and so to direct the life of the body towards the realization and embodiment of new modes of excellence. The path of organic evolution is witness to the presence of such spiritual aspirations even in unconscious life. Conscious life appears with the power to set in contrast what is with what might be.

This doctrine of Psychological Physiology opens the way to an account, both "natural" and spiritual, of reason functioning in the enfranchisement of Man in Nature. This new science would be the exact antithesis of that "physiological psychology" which confuses modern thought. It for the first time opens, or seems to open, a way to "take up Psychology into the total body of Philosophy." Yet, as I see it, it is in certain respects quite inadequate. Without important modification it can not interpret indisputable items of every day experience.

This inadequacy I explain as due to employing in psychological study the "method of discovery" which Whitehead has defined as involving a "flight into the thin air of imaginative generalization." This method is applicable only to the study of Mathematical Relations, or to the "principles of connectedness in general." It applies to psychology only in so far as those principles are exemplified in the life-career of individuals. With Whitehead this method means the analysis of acts into processes (prehensions) and the play of thought upon all possible combinations of certain processes precisely defined *ad hoc*. This method gives almost free rein to arbitrary assumptions. It submits only on rare occasions to correction by "irreducible and stubborn fact."

Criticism and correction of such arbitrary assumptions by stubborn fact can in matters psychological be secured through presenting not "processes" but concrete acts as these occur in the life-career of persons. The entirety of such acts is best perceived when life is presented as a history of self-education, more or less successful in attaining "active wisdom." Hence the pioneers in genuine psychological research are the skilled biographers, historic or fictional, of our day; but their associates are such men as Galton, James, Binet, Dewey, Alfred Adler, and McDougall, who approach the problems of psychology from the biotic study of life-movement and life-career.[51]

The most obvious and important inadequacies of Whitehead's psychological doctrine then become apparent. In the first place, all histories portray acts as the work of some underlying agent. In physical analysis it is, I suppose, philosophically important to substitute *acts* for inert particles or fields. But to reduce a *person* to a series of acts makes nonsense not only of biography but of civil law, of ethics, of art, of religion, of friendship, and of love. The significance of the Platonic *psyche* Whitehead only begins to appreciate in *Adventures of Ideas*. This first inadequacy is the direct and disastrous result of applying physical generalizations beyond the merely physical domain.

Whitehead opposes the separation of psychology from

[51] Compare Percy Hughes, *Introduction to Psychology from the Standpoint of Life-Career* (1926-28).

epistemology, and would heal the breach by inclosing the former in the latter. Consciousness, he says, is cognition. All consciousness is cognitive, to be sure, but in most acts of life in most people the cognitive process is subordinate to the practical or to the algedonic aim of the act as a whole. A reformed psychology will embrace epistemology. It is a philosophic weakness to suppose we live in order to know.

By classing processes as either physical or conceptual, and by making conceptual and mental practically equivalent terms, Whitehead obscures the sharp contrast that exists between acts in which perceptual processes are subordinate to the conceptual aim and those acts in which conceptions are subordinate to perceptual adaptation.

Whitehead's two "pure" modes of perception are successive phases of but one type of perceptual act, which I call *explanatory*. He ignores perceptions of the "substantive" type, which usage calls *observation*, and ignores also *appreciative* perceptions, such as Croce calls "the undifferentiated unity of the perception of the actual with the image of the possible."

In consequence Whitehead's attempt to find a perceptual basis for our knowledge of causation is limited to causation of the coercive, compulsive type, in which consequences are "explained" because they are necessitated by their antecedents. He overlooks the perceptual basis of our concept of factors *observed* as essentials in coöperative, contemporary causation; nor does he recognize the perceptual basis of our concept of "final" causation, appreciated as the potential scope of an event.

None the less I entertain the hope that Psychological Physiology, as defined by Whitehead, will show the way to bring all we know as human within the scope of empirical, scientific consideration. Now, when man laments as never before his divorce of Reason from Spirit, their hands are seen to be joined. With that vision psychology is reborn as the science of the living soul. But its continued life and growth depend upon facts found and expressed in the biographies of individual persons.

PERCY HUGHES

DEPARTMENT OF PHILOSOPHY
LEHIGH UNIVERSITY

7

Wilbur M. Urban

WHITEHEAD'S PHILOSOPHY OF LANGUAGE AND ITS RELATION TO HIS METAPHYSICS

WHITEHEAD'S PHILOSOPHY OF LANGUAGE AND ITS RELATION TO HIS METAPHYSICS

I

THE many admirers of Whitehead's magnificent attempt at a synthesis of naturalism and idealism—of whom the present writer is one—will welcome the chance which this volume offers to receive definitive answers to many problems which have been troubling them. Some at least of the difficulties in his philosophy revolve about problems of language, for his metaphysics, as a whole, turns at crucial points on his philosophy of language. I for one have felt this difficulty most acutely and I look forward to further enlightenment at this point.

The problem of language plays a much larger rôle in modern philosophy than is at first sight realized, and Whitehead's philosophy is no exception to the rule. There are several reasons for this. The first is a profound scepticism of language arising out of the purely naturalistic view of its origin and nature, which followed upon the application of Darwinism to all forms of human culture. Being the cries of the forest and mountain, corrupted and complicated by anthropoid apes, how can it be expected to apprehend or express reality? The second reason is the growing depreciation of language in science and the progressive substitution of non-linguistic symbols in all the more exact sciences. This preoccupation with language is intensified in all those forms of philosophy which we may describe as process philosophies. If the ultimate character of reality is process, if to be is to change, then language, as Bergson perhaps most clearly saw, must be a fundamental problem. For how can a language designed, as he believed himself able to show, for the manipulation of the static, either apprehend or express reality which is ultimately process? In the nature of the case it cannot. It is not "moulded on reality" and can only distort its true character.

For these and other reasons Whitehead shares the modern preoccupation with problems of language and a critique of language constitutes in a sense a prolegomenon to his metaphysics. It is, therefore, not only appropriate that his philosophy of language should be included among the topics of this volume; it is absolutely necessary if the real implications of his philosophy are to be understood. In certain studies already published I discussed "The Problem of Language in *Process and Reality*" and attempted to point out certain elements of unintelligibility in his metaphysics connected with both his use and his theory of language.[1] In the present article I shall restate some of these positions emphasizing particularly the implications for his metaphysics.

II. WHITEHEAD'S NATURALISTIC THEORY OF LANGUAGE

A basal assumption of Whitehead's entire philosophy is the inability of natural language to express reality. "The language of literature," he tells us, "breaks down precisely at the task of expressing in explicit form the larger generalities—the very generalities which metaphysics seeks to express." "Metaphysics deals with those notions that are relevant to the most general aspects of experience. Ordinary language was, however, made to deal with particulars." Thus, for him "philosophy redesigns language in the same way that, in a physical science, pre-existing appliances are redesigned."[2]

This general position is the product of two tendencies in modern thought both of which have, apparently, greatly influenced Whitehead. The first of these is that of Bergson from whom, he admits, the organicist philosophy has got its main insights. Natural language was made to handle the static and can not grasp the dynamic; it is not "moulded on reality." Bergson

[1] "Elements of Unintelligibility in Whitehead's Metaphysics: The Problem of Language in *Process and Reality*." *The Journal of Philosophy*, Vol. XXXV, No. 23. Also in *Language and Reality* at various points, but especially in Appendix III.
[2] *Process and Reality*, 16. (Page references in this essay to *Process and Reality* are to the American edition, 1929.)

concludes, rightly on his premises, that we should not try to express reality in linguistic symbol, but use language only poetically to bring us to a point where we may intuit directly the Duration which escapes language. The other source is the New Logic, which tells us that ordinary language, and the natural logic derived from it, distorts reality and must therefore be abandoned for non-linguistic symbols, the ideal being mathematical description which would not be subject to the demand of retranslation into the natural language of common sense. In the words of Bertrand Russell, "logic which trusts in language to any degree is likely to lead to the verbalism of a false metaphysics."

Whitehead has been influenced by both tendencies, but is content to draw neither conclusion. He will be neither a mere poet nor a mere mathematical logician. Instead he proposes to redesign philosophical or metaphysical language and sets out blithely to carry out this Herculean task—with the result that he has created an entirely new metaphysical idiom, one which extrudes from metaphysical discourse all those concepts and categories which hitherto have made communication between mind and mind possible. He has designed an entirely new idiom which, as we shall see, turns the older idiom upside down.

The radical character of such a proposal constitutes in itself a challenge to the philosopher. Indeed, the mere suggestion that language should be redesigned as pre-existing physical appliances are redesigned comes as a shock, for it indicates a view of language wholly foreign to that which has dominated the entire history of European culture and philosophy. The tacit assumption, shared alike by both the philosophies from which Whitehead has drawn his inspiration, is the idea that language is an extension of the tool-making function of the intelligence which has developed under the influence of modern evolutionary naturalism. According to this naturalistic view, to which Whitehead apparently subscribes, the function of natural language is purely pragmatic—"a useful abstract for the purposes of life," an instrument made to manipulate matter, but one that breaks down completely when it seeks to express the ultimate nature of things.

It is this naturalistic theory of language, upon which his entire philosophy of language rests, which creates my first difficulty with this philosophy. Although unquestioned in many quarters, it must, I think, be challenged. Even in linguistic science these assumptions are being increasingly challenged. Elsewhere I have subjected this entire theory to criticism, a criticism into which I cannot enter here.[3] It is enough to realize the doubtful assumptions that underlie the proposal. Let us proceed then to the specific reasons which lead Whitehead to think that natural language must thus be completely redesigned.

III. The Specific Reasons for the Redesigning of Language

A.

"All modern philosophy," Whitehead tells us, "hinges about the difficulty of describing the world in terms of subject and predicate, substance and quality, particular and universal. The result always does violence to immediate experience."[4] For the employment of the subject-predicate notion in language and logic there is, "a sound pragmatic defense. But in metaphysics the concept is sheer error."[5] We are not surprised then to find that Whitehead's thinking proceeds upon a rather wholesale condemnation of all that has hitherto been thought and written in philosophy. Taken as a whole, we are told, his philosophy of organism goes back to Pre-Kantian modes of thought (although I have never quite understood this statement). But all these Pre-Kantians (Descartes, Spinoza, Leibniz, Locke, and Hume) are permeated with the above errors. Hume, we are told, despite his sceptical nominalism, never actually moved from the subject-predicate habits of thought. Both Locke and Hume failed to realize that their problem required a more drastic revision of the categories than they actually effected. As a result we find, especially in Hume, "a vagueness and inconsistency" arising from the fact that he proceeds "on the tacit presupposition of

---

[3] *Language and Reality*, chap. II. Also chap. VIII, sec. VIII.
[4] *Process and Reality*, 78.
[5] *Ibid.*, 122.

the mind as subject and of its contents as predicates—a presupposition which explicitly he repudiates."[6]

This is a most important passage, for it indicates how radical the position really is. Pre-Kantian, even more than Kantian modes of thought, could talk only in terms of the very categories which Whitehead deliberately extrudes. In the second place, it represents a type of "empiricism" infinitely more radical than even that of Hume. The latter, although he might talk "vaguely and inconsistently," did nevertheless talk a subject-predicate language, because experience as he understood it could not be otherwise expressed. In the name of a novel conception of experience and of a supposed new insight into the nature of reality, Whitehead is ready to do violence to the fundamental principles of language and linguistic expression—even to the verge of verbal unintelligibility. It is only when we realize the lengths to which Whitehead is willing to carry his redesigning that we realize how radical his position really is.

B.

There seem to be two specific reasons why he proposes to redesign literary language so completely. They reflect the two main sources of his philosophy and the two motives which have dominated all his thinking. The first of these is mathematics and mathematical physics; the second the concept of pure experience derived, we may suppose, from Bergson and James.

The tacit assumption underlying Whitehead's entire philosophy of language is that we somehow know the fundamental nature of things apart from language and its categories and can then turn back and see that language does not "correspond." One of the main sources of this knowledge is modern physics with its notion of events. In place of the substantial material entities persisting in time and moving in space, modern physics has substituted, as the ultimate components of reality, a very different kind of reality, and this is describable as events. We know this to be the fact, and our language, which was made to deal with supposed substantial entities, must be redesigned to correspond with the new conceptions.

[6] *Ibid.*, 81.

Now obviously I am challenging neither the new conceptions of physics nor the development of a new type of mathematical symbolism to deal with the new conceptions. It may well be that these conceptions are necessary. It may also be true that ordinary language becomes less and less usable in physics, and that it must not only be redesigned but conceivably ultimately abandoned for graphs and equations. Indeed, I should be willing to admit that, on certain theories of science and of scientific intelligibility, the categories of natural language might not only conceivably be redesigned but even completely extruded, as is actually proposed by many scientists. Granted that science is purely operational, is concerned merely with the manipulation of symbols for control—in other words seeks merely instrumental intelligibility—I see no reason, in principle at least, why we should not, if we wish, reverse completely the structure of natural language and the categories connected with it. But it does not at all follow that this would be possible in metaphysics, where the object is to understand and not merely to control.

Now I do not myself believe that this exclusively operational view of science can be maintained—there are difficulties here also, as I have pointed out. Moreover, I doubt very much whether Whitehead accepts it. But that is not the point here. What I should insist upon is that, even if it were true for physical science, it would not necessarily be true for philosophy. Intelligibility in science may consist exclusively in necessary relations—"the fact is no longer isolated and it is therefore intelligible," but intelligibility in metaphysics is something else again. What I have in mind was well expressed by Bergson in the following epigram: "Science strives towards a symbolism of relations; metaphysics towards a symbolism of things." The language and symbolisms of science are themselves a "useful abstract" for certain purposes. The more ultimate aspects of experience with which metaphysics is concerned can be expressed only in the dramatic or "literary" language of concrete experience.

C.

With this we come to Whitehead's second main reason for the redesigning of "natural" language, namely that, while this language and its categories express a useful abstract for life, such language does violence to immediate experience. This second reason has more profound implications for metaphysics; for while science, conceived as operational, might itself be a useful abstract for control, the immediate experience which lies back of both the purposes of life and the purposes of science is the ultimate thing.

The fundamental assumption here, closely related to the assumption underlying the preceding reflections, is that of the dualism of experience and expression—that immediate experience and its expression in language are two wholly different things which may, so to speak, tragically diverge. In other words, that we first have knowledge by simple acquaintance and then knowledge by description. The latter, involving as it does language, may do violence to this experience. "Language refers to presentational immediacy as interpreted by symbolic reference," and this symbolic reference may interpret the experience falsely. Indeed, according to Whitehead, it does interpret falsely. Language was, so to speak, explicitly "made to deceive the philosopher," and the only way to pure experience is by stripping off language and its symbolisms.

This assumption, no less than the preceding one, must, I feel, be challenged. Language is not an external tag or mould. It is rather a necessary condition of the experience of objects as such. The entire development of the modern philosophy of language makes it clear that intuition and expression are inseparable. Anything that can become more than a diffused awareness has language as a constitutive element. On this point I am wholly in agreement with Ernst Cassirer—namely that such a hypothetical form of knowledge—pure experience—is pure myth. One need not go to the length of Croce's axiom, that intuition and expression are identical, in order to maintain that they are inseparable. Elsewhere I have shown, I think, that without language and its categories there is no experience

in any intelligible sense.[7] We may conceivably have sense data
without language and its categories, but mere "having" is not
knowing. It is meaning that turns sense data into things or
objects, and wherever there is meaning there language enters
into mere diffused awareness as a constitutive element.

This is, I think, the crucial question with regard to Whitehead's philosophy of language. If intuition and expression are
inseparable, then the function of the relating of the moments
of experience belongs to thought and language. Another way
of stating this is that communication is itself a necessary part
of experience—communication either latent or overt; until it
has taken on communicable form it is not experience. This we
may call the linguo-centric predicament. Language can then
not ultimately do violence to immediate experience. It is true,
of course, that it may, and often does, express experience imperfectly, and correction of language is often necessary. But this
is quite a different thing from either the abandonment of natural language, as in mysticism, or a complete redesigning which
reverses all the categories of language.

D.

It is perhaps impossible to say which is the primary motive
in Whitehead's philosophy and, therefore, in his proposal to
redesign language—namely, the appeal to modern physics and
the revision of its basal categories, or the direct appeal to immediate experience. Whitehead came to philosophy from
mathematics and mathematical physics, and his recent statement
to the effect that "we must end with my first love, Symbolic
Logic," suggests that, after all, the first is the dominant motive
in all his thinking. If this is the case, as indeed I have long
suspected, the tacit assumption throughout his entire philosophy is really the primacy of science and mathematical logic. It
is not experience in all its fullness and richness which dictates
the redesigning of language which Whitehead proposes, but
modern physics—as indeed his notion of language as a pre-
existing physical appliance suggests.

It is at this point that I find my chief difficulties, not only

[7] *Language and Reality*, chap. VIII, 340 ff.

with Whitehead's philosophy of language but with his entire philosophy, and it is at this point that I especially seek light. It is more than likely that my difficulties are due to my own limitations, but they are very real and I find them shared by others. I will purposely put them rather bluntly. Does he mean what he says in *Science and the Modern World* or does he not? There, it would at least seem, the primacy is given to literary or, as I have described it, dramatic language in the expression and interpretation of reality—that it is precisely the function of an enlightened philosophy to determine the limits of science in philosophy as a whole, and of its special idiom in the language of philosophy. Yet when one seeks to penetrate to the ultimate motives of his thinking, it seems that science and its language are ultimately normative.

I can not, therefore, avoid the impression that there are two antithetical and ultimately unreconciled motives in Whitehead's thinking. As a scientist he has learned one ideal of expression, namely the impersonal ideal of mathematics. As a man, and one conversant with poets and philosophers, he has also learned another. But I think it is fair to say that he has never been able to fuse or relate the two. He is constantly vacillating between the two ideals. On the face of it, it would seem that I must be wrong here and that there must be some answer to my difficulties. I am hoping for further light on the matter.

IV. Whitehead's New Categorial Scheme. The Reversal of The Traditional Categories

A.

We have now seen the reasons for the redesigning of language as proposed by Whitehead. Our initial doubt of the feasibility of the proposal to redesign language as the pre-existing appliances of physics are redesigned is rather increased than decreased when we consider the reasons for it. In any case it is wholly clear, I think, that such redesigning of language involves also a redesigning of the categories or, as Whitehead describes it, a new categorial scheme. Before entering upon this question in detail, let us see the significance or implications of such a notion.

The inseparable relation between "natural" language and the categories is, as Whitehead would himself admit, an outstanding character of all traditional European philosophy—it is, in fact, one of the characters which make of that philosophy a continuous tradition. The categorial scheme of Aristotle uses language as the key to the categories and, although it was specifically the Greek language which formed the clue, the underlying assumption was that of a universal language implicit in the particular positive languages. Similarly Kant uses language and the logic of our language as the *Leitfaden* to the categories. The underlying reason for this procedure—and one the full significance of which is not always realized—is that the *only* way of determining being or reality is in those forms or categories in which intelligible statements about it are possible.

We know then how, on assumptions such as these, the categorial scheme of traditional philosophy would have to be constructed. "The mind" in order to grasp things "derives," as Bergson says, "three kinds of representations [or categories], namely (1) qualities, (2) forms of essences, (3) acts. To these three ways of seeing correspond three categories of words: *adjectives, substantives,* and *verbs.*" On the assumptions of traditional philosophy, these are the key to the main categories. But we can also see how, on Bergson's assumptions, assumptions in principle shared also by Whitehead, these categories would be modified. "Adjectives and substantives," we are told, "symbolize states;" they represent only the static. But if reality is not static, as both hold, nouns and adjectives can only misrepresent reality. The burden therefore falls on the verb. The verb also, according to Bergson, when used as a symbol, together with the other linguistic symbols as in the subject-predicate form, "turns movement into a state in order to apprehend and grasp it. The verb also is a name for a state." Bergson has an illustration at this point. "We say the child becomes a man." But in this proposition " 'becomes'," he tells us, "is a verb of indeterminate meaning, intended to mask the absurdity into which we fall when we attribute the state 'man' to the subject 'child'."

The truth is that, if language were moulded on reality, we should not say this, but rather "there is becoming from the child to the man."[8] For Bergson to be is to become, and language only in so far as it expresses becoming in any way represents reality. It is clear, then, in what direction a revision of the categories must, on the preceding assumptions, proceed. As we must have a language made up largely of verbs, so we must have a categorial scheme in which the categories are all primarily dynamic. It is interesting to see how differently Bergson and Whitehead, starting from the same premises, proceed at this point. Bergson, finding that language and its categories are not moulded on reality, abandons them for direct intuition and mysticism. Whitehead proceeds to redesign them. It is this that we must now examine in detail.

B.

Chapter II of *Process and Reality* is then given over to what is called a new categorial scheme. An adequate treatment of this chapter with its eight categories of existence and twenty-seven categories of explanation would require an entire book. I will consider rather the principle involved in the redesigning and the consequences which follow from it. Let us see more concretely what actually happens in Whitehead's philosophy. For the category of substance we have that of actual occasion, for the category of inherence that of ingression, and for the category of thinghood that of concrescence.

Each of these radical revisions of the categories requires some attention, but it is primarily that of the actual occasion which is significant, for it is this notion or category that is in a sense determinative of all the rest.

The ultimate of analysis for Whitehead is an event, an occasion, a drop of experience. This is the ultimate metaphysical subject of discourse about which anything that is said must be said. "Literary" language will want to talk about it as though it were an entity, but that would be to distort it. To be is to happen and one can talk about a happening only in the dynamic language of verbs. As the term for this ultimate itself is rede-

[8] *Creative Evolution* (English translation, 1911), 303-4; 312-13.

signed, so also must any quality or character applied to it be redesigned, with significant consequences, as we shall see.

The category of concrescence is almost equally fundamental in Whitehead's revision of the categorial scheme. He quite definitely looks upon it as something distinctively modern. Certain philosophers, he tells us, of the eighteenth and seventeenth centuries made a discovery which they themselves only half realized. The discovery is that there are two kinds of fluency. One is the transition from particular existent to particular existent. This transition, in Locke's language, is the perpetually perishing which is one aspect of the notion of time. The other kind, again in Locke's terms, is "the concrescence which is the real internal constitution of a particular existent." This second kind involves another aspect of the notion of time.[9] About the perpetually perishing nothing intelligible can be said, but if the temporal contains in its very nature this concrescence, then we have, as it were, a surrogate for the category of thinghood which is not only a basal category of all practical communication, but also of all natural metaphysics which, as we have seen, strives towards a "symbolism of things."

The category of ingression follows, I suppose, necessarily from the other two. For traditional thought the universals inhere in objects; for a revised categorial scheme, revised in the direction of dynamism, they must ingress. Now I myself have great difficulty with this category of ingression. It is a notion which seeks to revise the relation of the universal to the particular, the two elements of permanence and flux. But it seems scarcely to retain the essence of the "universal" and the permanent, for if the eternal objects ingress in any intelligible sense, they themselves must ultimately be in flux, and change and flux are notions applicable only to particulars. The consequence of this revision of the relation of the universal to the particular is that the entire natural metaphysics of the human mind, based as it is on a trust in natural language, and upon the traditional relation of universal to particular implied in that language, must be abandoned.

But we must not lose the forest for the trees. Enough has

[9] *Process and Reality*, 320.

been said to make clear my main difficulty. It is clear, I think, that for Whitehead all categories are categories of becoming, and the redesigning of the categories implicit in the redesigning of language turns the ordinary categories of thought and expression upside down. Well, it may be asked, what of it? Why should they not be redesigned—even out of all recognition? My answer is simply to raise the question whether, after all, this can really be done, whether such a reversal of the speech categories is really possible.

Now I would not be misunderstood here, although as a matter of fact I have already been misunderstood—and somewhat grossly. There is nothing illegal in changing names and categories in this fashion—although one sometimes wishes that there were something left of the old fear of changing God-given names. I am not crying out in the name of tradition and *philosophia perennis,* thus far and no further. There is nothing sacrosanct about the categories of either Aristotle or Kant. This is not in the least the question. The question is rather whether such a complete reversal of natural speech construction is possible and intelligible communication can at the same time remain—whether, indeed, such a reversal does not in fact itself do violence to experience as we can alone know it and express it. The entire problem comes to a head in connection with the traditional category of subject and predicate, with its substance-attribute metaphysics. In applying our argument at this point I shall be able to make clearer the sources of my difficulties, not only with Whitehead's philosophy of language but also with much of his metaphysics to which his philosophy of language is so closely related.

V. WHITEHEAD'S "DUALITY OF LANGUAGE" AND ITS CONSEQUENCES

All modern philosophy, we were told, hinges about the difficulty of describing the world in terms of subject and predicate, substance and quality, particular and universal. Undoubtedly. But this is nothing to the difficulty which the modernists in philosophy find in describing it in any other terms. We have seen what, according to Whitehead, are the sources of our difficulties when we seek to describe the world in traditional categories. Perhaps we may now see the difficulties when we extrude or even seek to revise these categories. A further study of his revision of the notions of particular and universal would be rewarding, but space will not permit and our chief interest is in the terms subject and predicate, with the corresponding categories of substance and quality.

Hume, we have seen, simply was not able to carry out completely the revision of the traditional categories which his supposed empirical analysis implied. The special point at which his difficulty appears is that, while he explicitly repudiated the presupposition of the mind as substance, he proceeded in all his discourse on the tacit assumption of the mind as subject and its contents as predicates. This difficulty is equally present in Whitehead also. Despite the fact that he has seen it in Hume, he is himself subject to the same vagueness and inconsistency as that with which he charges Hume. A more detailed examination at this point will make clear my main difficulties with Whitehead's entire philosophy of language.

The immediate experience, which for Whitehead is the determining principle, and to which ordinary language does violence, has as an ultimate of analysis the cosmic variable "feeling." Every actual occasion, every prehension has this element. Now ordinary language can not talk about feeling without implying a feeler, i.e., "one" who *has* the feeling. Substance-attribute language is here indispensable for what we may call ordinary pragmatic intelligibility. But precisely this language "does violence to immediate experience" and must therefore be redesigned—a redesigning which involves the elimination of the categories of subject and predicate, substance and attribute. For this we must substitute a language wholly of verbs.

The result of this, as I have been pointing out all along, is to turn ordinary language upside down. We are told that the feeler is the unity emergent from its own feelings. Now I do not profess to understand what this means. I understand the words, but I get no sense. But this is not my point. This failure to understand may be due to the limitations of my own intelligence, of which I am painfully aware. My point is rather this. If Mr. Whitehead actually used his redesigned language consistently—if he actually thought in terms of these new categories—we should at least understand him in a sense. But this is just what he does not do. He is constantly being tricked—by the truth, shall we say?—into another kind of language. These very feelings from which the feeler is said to emerge are constantly being given the character of the feeler—with the result that our confusion becomes twice confounded. Whitehead is subject to the same fatality which followed Hume.

I have made this same criticism in other connections and Mr. Victor Lowe has found this criticism "wholly misplaced."[10] He writes:

That an occasion of experience should be *both* these things, both feeler and emergent feeling,—in Whitehead's terminology, both a 'subject' and a 'superject'—has seemed to Professor Urban (and doubtless to many other philosophers) utterly unintelligible. I do not think it is; but if it is, so is James's doctrine of the 'passing thought' which is the thinker in his *Psychology*.

He then proceeds to develop this point, showing that radical empiricism prohibits an "antecedent subject which relates together." He rightly suggests that for me James's account of the moment of experience is intrinsically as unintelligible as is Whitehead's, for a radical empiricism in this sense can not in principle be made intelligible. But his main point has to do with my criticism of the duality in Whitehead's language, when he speaks of the occasion as the subject of its feelings (a way of talking which the critic understands, as well as their superject (an expression which I find "fantastic"). This criticism he holds is wholly misplaced, for the duality in Whitehead's language is deliberate. The duality, he holds, is "rightly introduced, since an experiential, temporalistic pluralism must assign to the drop of experience functions which other types of metaphysics can distribute among other entities."

[10] "William James and Whitehead's Doctrine of Prehensions." *The Journal of Philosophy*, Vol. XXXVIII, No. 5 (Feb. 27, 1941), 124.

Ah, but that is just the point. I do not deny that this duality is ultimately deliberate, although I doubt whether it was at first. But if it is deliberate, it seems to me to be all the more confusing. What I should be disposed to insist upon is that, on his premises, Whitehead ought not to do this. An "experiential temporalistic pluralism" does, indeed, assign to the drop of experience functions which other types of metaphysics can distribute among other entities; but it ought not to do so. That it does so is, of course, proof of my contention with regard to language and its categories. In order to express itself intelligibly Whitehead's philosophy must use the categories of the traditional categorial scheme. But it ought not to do so, for on his very premises such procedure distorts reality. A drop of experience can not be an entity, nor can it have applied to it the attributes and functions which other types of metaphysics employ.

It is said that the intelligibility of Whitehead's philosophy, and of the language in which it is expressed, turns entirely upon the question whether we experience or think that we experience what Whitehead does, namely the felt transitions embodied in the notion of prehension. If we do not experience that with him, then his language is really not understandable and all his redesigning of language is unnecessary and even perverse. If the function of the relating of the moments of experience is held to belong to thought and language, that is that intuition and expression are inseparable, then such criticism is perhaps justified. There is, I think, a partial truth here, but it is only a part of the truth. Even if we experience felt transitions within, such feelings or intuitions must be communicated; and if they are communicated in language, the traditional categories of language must come into play.

If there is any perversity in this redesigning of language, it is to be found at a still more fundamental and significant point. It is in fact here that I find my chief difficulties with Whitehead's entire philosophy. I shall try to state the point as simply as possible.

The chief notions in Whitehead's metaphysics are taken from "literary" or natural language—terms such as feeling, value and valuation, and mind, etc. In order to use them in his metaphysics, with its fundamental revision of all the categories, these too must be redesigned, as I have put it, out of all *recognition*. This we have seen in detail in the case of "feeling;" but in my earlier studies I have shown the same to be true for all the other terms or notions. Value, mind—even the notion of God itself—all must be thus completely redesigned to fit into Whitehead's "process" philosophy. It is this distortion of language—and with it, as I believe, distortion of experience which language necessarily expresses—that gives us pause. It is this primarily which makes understanding of Whitehead difficult—which creates the "elements of unintelligibility" in his philosophy.

Whitehead seems himself to sense this difficulty. He tells us:

Philosophers can never hope finally to formulate these metaphysical first principles [namely the experience categories which he assigns to all the occasions in nature]. Weakness of insight and *deficiencies of language* stand in the way inexorably. Words and phrases must be stretched towards a generality foreign to their ordinary usage; and however such elements of language be stabilized as technicalities, they remain *metaphors* mutely appealing for an imaginative leap.[11]

Now I should not question this in principle: I should simply be disposed to query whether we may not be asked to make too much of an imaginative leap. The stretching of words and phrases towards generality, the moulding of our ordinary concepts of experience, is characteristic of all metaphysics with its characteristic symbolism. The question here is solely whether these terms, taken from natural or "literary" language, can suffer this redesigning and still remain intelligible.

VI. Philosophical Intelligibility and Process Philosophies

Process and Reality belongs to the general group of modern philosophies which are called process philosophies, philosophies, which, in Bergson's terms, find more of reality in becoming than in that which becomes. They involve "temporalism, plural-

---

[11] *Process and Reality*, 6. (Italics mine.)

ism and the absolutizing of becoming." The fundamental problem with which we have been concerned all along is whether pure process, pure dynamism, can be made intelligible—or indeed can be intelligibly expressed at all.

This general movement has been described as "taking time seriously"—to my mind an obvious misnomer. Philosophy, especially traditional philosophy, has always taken time seriously, and it is precisely because it has taken time so seriously that it has constantly insisted upon the timeless and the eternal. For it has always seen that the meaning of space and time must lie outside space and time. It is only when we take the eternal seriously that we can give this obviously serious life of ours in time any real meaning.

The assumption that there is more in becoming than in that which becomes (more of reality and value) is the exact opposite of the assumption of *philosophia perennis* which is that there is more in that which becomes than in the process itself. Bergson, as I have already indicated, drew the only legitimate conclusion from a philosophy of absolute becoming, namely that reality can not be expressed.

Now it would, I think, be a misrepresentation of Whitehead's metaphysics to suggest that his is a pure process philosophy in the sense of either Bergson or Dewey. Indeed, he tells us in Part V of *Process and Reality* that the fundamental opposition in philosophy around which ideals fashion themselves are the two notions of permanence and flux. He points out rightly that the danger to philosophy lies in narrowness of selection of the facts in support of either of the two ideals. There can be no question, I think, that in seeking a solution for this fundamental opposition he also seeks a genuine synthesis of the two notions; but it seems to me equally clear that no such synthesis is really achieved. It would seem not unfair to say that at all critical points throughout Whitehead's entire philosophy time and flux are given the last word; if this is not true, I hope to be corrected. One statement makes this quite clear. The fact that it is a statement about God makes it indeed all the clearer, for if there is one place where the norm of permanence is most in evidence it is in religious experience. "Neither God nor the world reaches static completion. Both are in the grip of the ultimate metaphysical ground, the creative advance into novelty. Either of them, God and the World, is the instrument of novelty for the other." Leaving out of account the religious aspects and implications of this form of statement—which have been considered elsewhere—we shall consider only the metaphysical aspect of the question. It is clear, I think, that we have here no real solution of the opposition of the temporal and the eternal, of the permanent and the flux.

My own view is that this is inevitable. No one has been able to serve these two masters in the past, and it seems to me unlikely that any one will be able to do so in the future. For either there is really more in becoming than in that which becomes or there is not. If there is, then process is the last word. If there is more in that which becomes, then this "more" must come from participation in that which does not become—something that is there "from the foundation of the world." There is, I think, no middle ground: at least I have never been able to find one. It is not, however, so much this fact itself as its bearing on the philosophy of language which concerns us at the present moment.

Long ago—indeed from the time of Plato's *Cratylus* on—it was seen that a philosophy of pure becoming is incompatible with the validity of language. Reality so conceived can not be intelligibly expressed. Bergson saw this fully; and it is for this reason that his entire philosophy rests upon a depreciation of language. We may question his dictum that language was made wholly to deal with the static, in the sense of the spatial— for, while it began thus, it has in its development far transcended its original function—but we may quite truly say that it is impossible so to remake it as to deal with pure becoming. The reason why Bergson turned his back on traditional philosophy was because of the primacy given to permanence. If he has in principle returned to *philosophia perennis*, is it not probable that it is because he has found that only such a philosophy can make itself intelligible?[12]

[12] The conversion of Henri Bergson to Catholicism—if that report proves correct—raises many fascinating questions as to the fundamental motives of this drastic

VII. Linguistic Intelligibility and Philosophical Intelligibility

The reason why Whitehead's philosophy of language is such an important part of his philosophy as a whole is that the very condition of his expressing his philosophical insights at all is that, on his premises, he must first redesign ordinary language, create a new philosophical idiom; otherwise these insights can not be expressed. A very real, and also a very proper question, is, accordingly, whether this language can be *understood*, whether it is intelligible.

Now this may seem a strange question to ask; and unless it is properly understood the question itself may be nonsense. Obviously Whitehead's language is understandable or intelligible in one very important sense. Otherwise it would be difficult to see how innumerable followers could get so much suggestion and inspiration from his writings. It would be equally difficult to understand how the present writer, or any other critic, could apprehend his meaning sufficiently to venture to call it unintelligible. It is necessary, therefore, to make it quite clear what is understood by this notion; and this involves a distinction between linguistic and philosophical intelligibility.

Merely as philosophical *language* Whitehead's writings are not easy to read. Even in the limited sense of merely verbal intelligibility there is much to be desired in the way of understanding his peculiar idiom. Some of the main reasons for this linguistic unintelligibility have, I hope, been made clear. But, I also insisted that the difficulties in understanding *Process and Reality* lie much deeper than the linguistic and categorial level. Behind this linguistic unintelligibility lies a still more fundamental philosophical unintelligibility. Or, better expressed perhaps, the very linguistic unintelligibility itself springs from a more fundamental source.

As I see the situation, this duality of language springs from a still more fundamental duality of thought. This arises from Whitehead's own uncertainty as to what constitutes intelligibility.

revision of his thinking. The motives were doubtless many and what they were we shall possibly never know. But is it unreasonable to suppose that philosophical motives of this fundamental kind were determinative?

As a physicist and logician he has learned one ideal or norm of intelligibility, namely the impersonal ideal of mathematics. As a man and as one conversant with poets and philosophers he has learned another. But, as I have already said, it is, I think, fair to say that he has never been able to fuse or relate the two.

Elsewhere I have described these two conflicting norms in detail;[13] here I can state them only in the briefest form. The first, the "idealistic," is that which dominated the entire European tradition from Plato and Aristotle on, namely that the source of meaning and intelligibility is ultimately in the good or value. Value and mind are given the primacy in the "categorial scheme." The second, the naturalistic, springs from the notion that the impersonal is more intelligible than the personal, entities and relations from which values have been abstracted more so than the concrete wholes from which the abstractions have been made. Thus develops a categorial scheme in which mind and personality are derivative elements emerging from a substratum of impersonal reality, and values from that which is value-free.

Now I think there is no question that, in principle at least, Whitehead accepts the first ideal as primary. Thus, in his lectures on *Nature and Life*,[14] in speaking of the Newtonian physics, he says, "Newton's methodology of physics was an overwhelming success. But the forces which he introduced still left nature without meaning and value. He thus illustrated a great philosophic truth, that a dead nature can give no reasons. All ultimate reasons are in terms of aim at value." This is but one of many similar statements throughout his writings, and if it means anything at all, it means that whatever norms of intelligibility we may construct in physics, and in science in general, in philosophy or metaphysics at least rationality, intelligibility, involves reference to, or "aim at," value. But the other principle of intelligibility is constantly asserting itself and is constantly neutralizing the primary principle. The result is that in actual practice Whitehead is constantly vacillating between the two ideals, and the result is confusion.

[13] "Elements of Unintelligibility, *etc.*," 627 ff; cf. fn. 1 above.
[14] P. 9

This conflict of two principles of intelligibility in White-head's thinking is shown most completely, I think, in his latest statement of his philosophy as a whole, namely his "Remarks" at the time of the session devoted to his philosophy at the meet-ing of the American Philosophical Association in 1936. He says:

We must end with my first love—Symbolic Logic. When in the dis-tant future the subject has expanded, so as to examine patterns depending on connections other than those of space, number, and quantity—when this expansion has occurred, I suggest that Symbolic Logic, that is to say, the symbolic examination of pattern with the use of real variables, will become the foundation of aesthetics. From that stage it will proceed to conquer ethics and theology.[15]

To me this passage is as enlightening as it is staggering. It is staggering for the reason that it seems to me, in principle, to go contrary to all that Whitehead has been saying hitherto. It has always seemed to me, and I supposed that it was White-head's view also, that the very essence of the aesthetic experi-ence—to say nothing of the ethical and religious—is that it catches something in reality, qualities and values, which always slip through the meshes of our logical nets, no matter how fine we make them; and it was for this reason that the language of poet and saint can express something that science and its lan-guage can not. But the passage may also be very enlightening. For it seems to confirm the suspicion which I have had all along, that the spirit of Whitehead's philosophy is after all funda-mentally naturalistic—that his first love is really the impersonal ideal of intelligibility that has been developed in science and mathematics, and that his acceptance of the traditional ideal of intelligibility, with his reference to value, has never been more than half-hearted. Either this, or he is insensible to the es-sential conflict of the two norms. I confess that this is one of the points at which I can least follow Whitehead's thought, and one on which I am most anxious to receive light. I suspect that there are others who feel much the same way.

[15] Published in the *Philosophical Review*, Vol. XLVI (1937), 178-186; quotation on p. 186.

VIII. The Synthesis of Idealism and Naturalism

A.

At the beginning of this paper I spoke of Whitehead's philosophy as an attempt at a synthesis of naturalism and idealism and acknowledged myself as one of the many admirers of this attempt. He himself describes it as an attempt "to transform the main ideas of objective idealism unto a realistic basis." After our account of the two ideals or norms of philosophical intelligibility in Whitehead's system we shall be able both to understand and evaluate this proposal.

The crucial question, of course, is what are the main ideas of idealism which are thus to be transformed. But equally important is the further question as to what is the realistic basis unto which they are to be thus transformed.

With regard to the first question we are not left in doubt. The first essential of such an idealism is the cosmic significance of values. Deny this element and the only idealism that would remain would be indistinguishable from naturalism. "Value in its elementary non-human form is the universal feature of the connection of things," according to Samuel Alexander, and Whitehead, who shares this position with Alexander, maintains the same principle in *Process and Reality*. He conceives it as his main task to overcome the isolation between natural science and value experiences and, in order to bridge the gulf, he, like Alexander, reads value down into the elementary constituents of the universe. Value in its elementary non-human form is a universal feature of reality, a "cosmic variable." The real, the crucial issue, is, as is now apparent, what the realistic basis is unto which this idealism is to be transformed.

First of all it is evident, I think, that in this context realistic means naturalistic also. The essence of naturalism has always been the priority of the space-time world and the derivative character of mind, the primacy of the physical and non-mental categories in the categorial scheme; just as the essential of idealism has always been the primacy of value and of mental categories in the categorial scheme.

We can understand perfectly the naturalistic character of

Alexander's realism which makes space-time primary and all
other categories, including that of Deity, secondary. No less
naturalistic, I think, is that of Whitehead which makes events
primary even though space and spatialized time are secondary.
The primacy of the physical and non-mental categories in the
categorial scheme is the essential doctrine of both forms of
"realism." Now certainly the main features of idealism can
not be grafted on a realism such as that of Alexander. He has
indeed, in a sense, given value cosmic significance; but, in order
to make it a universal feature of the interconnection of things,
as he conceives things, the notion of value must be so redesigned
as to make it little more than a name for the space-time relations themselves. I do not see that the situation is in principle
different in the case of the philosophy of events. The realism
here is also naturalistic. In attempting to bridge the gulf between natural science and value experiences Whitehead has
also so redesigned the notion of value as practically to redesign
it away. The same is true of his treatment of mind.

B.

I am well aware that one must proceed here also with great
caution. It is possible to do great injustice to Whitehead's intentions, if not to the consequences of his thinking. That he
does not intend a mere naturalism, I am well aware. That the
spirit of his entire philosophy is in a sense idealistic, I would
also admit. But I can not escape the conviction that in principle
his realistic basis is essentially naturalistic. It may be argued,
as indeed it has been suggested by Professor Hoernlé, that the
fact that he attributes "subjective immediacy" to the actual
entities aligns him with the idealists, and that he *calls* his doctrine realistic merely because, while thus attributing to them
subjective immediacy, he holds them to be devoid of consciousness. But this I find to be very doubtful reasoning. The notions
of mind and value, which Whitehead thus finds it possible to
associate with his elements, are far indeed from the notions
required by objective idealism, or indeed by any other kind of
idealism. That which chiefly aligns Whitehead's philosophy
with naturalism is the fact that, in the last analysis, he, as well

as Alexander, gives to the impersonal and non-value categories the primacy in the categorial scheme.[16]

I have confessed my admiration for this attempt at synthesis even if, for the reasons given, it seems to me to have failed. Professor Whitehead, is, I think we all feel, the magnanimous philosopher *par excellence* in the modern world of "minute philosophers." Being thus large-minded, we can well understand why he should constantly want to say "both—and," that the self is both subject and superject, that reality is both permanence and flux, that God is both the ground and the outcome of process. We can understand all this; and we can understand also why such a philosopher should seek to maintain a dual ideal of intelligibility, one derived from his first love, mathematical logic, and one derived from his later loves, to which, being human, nothing human is alien. But what it is difficult for me at least to understand is how they can be held together without giving the one or the other the primary position in metaphysical interpretation. This feat has never been successfully achieved in the past, and I do not believe it can ever be in the future.

This, then, is the last question which I should like to ask of Professor Whitehead—how can this be done? Until it is answered, I do not think that I shall ever understand his philosophy.

WILBUR M. URBAN

DEPARTMENT OF PHILOSOPHY
YALE UNIVERSITY

[16] It can, I think, only confuse the issues, to place Whitehead among the idealists, as does R. F. Alfred Hoernlé in his article, "The Revival of Idealism in the United States," in *Contemporary Idealism in America*. The main ideas of idealism have not been maintained and therefore can not be transformed unto a realistic basis.

8

A. D. Ritchie

WHITEHEAD'S DEFENCE OF
SPECULATIVE REASON

WHITEHEAD'S DEFENCE OF
SPECULATIVE REASON

THERE is a widespread belief that a book which is short and easy to read must be unimportant—in spite of Descartes' *Meditations* and Berkeley's *Principles*. Perhaps this is why little notice has been taken of Whitehead's book *The Function of Reason,* though a great deal of his philosophy is to be found in it. You cannot ask a more important question about a philosopher than: "How does he conceive his task as a thinker?" Few philosophers have answered such questions as carefully and as explicitly as Whitehead has done. The following is intended simply as a statement in rather different terms of what I believe to be Whitehead's meaning and its relation to his own metaphysical position. I shall try to bring out and at least partly discuss certain difficulties that are inherent in Whitehead's views and the still greater difficulties inherent in the alternatives.

If Reason is interpreted in the narrowest possible sense, as Hume defines the term, it comes to mean simply that which calculates or sets out arguments in logical order; which does in fact the kind of thing the mathematician is popularly supposed to do in working hours and which is capable of very little else. If that is the summit of our life as cognitive and reflective beings then it has to be admitted that "Reason is, and ought only to be the slave of the passions and can never pretend to any other office than to serve and obey them." That leaves no place for philosophy as it was conceived by Socrates and has usually been conceived since. Hume realised and acknowledged the consequences of his view. Others who have made much the same estimate of Reason have been less clear headed. The consequences of Hume's view are certainly peculiar. The "passions," those processes, forces, or whatever they are, that move us to action, are a plurality. When their supposed monarch has been dethroned, they might perhaps be expected to form a republic in which all of them would be free, equal and responsible citizens. But that is just what the passions never can do, because they are an indefinite plurality, a hopeless confusion, that is not even composed of individuals capable of being recognised or counted. Moreover, Hume has to confess that there is a special kind of instinct founded upon habit, perhaps a special kind of passion, which results in what is called "belief." But we own to a plurality of beliefs and we find among them one, the most unaccountable of all, the belief that beliefs should be logically consistent, which leads us to criticize and condemn some beliefs while approving of others, and even leads us to indulge the phantasy that all our beliefs can and should be unified into a system. For the fact is that we cannot even begin to analyse and criticize beliefs except from a theoretical standpoint, which implies prior adherence to some speculative philosophy, as well as a "divine right" on the side of Reason to order or at least criticize the passions. Hume could have excused himself by saying that his standpoint was instinctive, and that, as no further philosophical enquiry could alter it, further philosophical enquiry was superfluous. A good excuse, as excuses go, but still only an excuse.

The meaning of the term Reason must then be widened, as Kant did in his more expansive moods, when he was prepared to admit that there was Theoretical as well as Practical Reason without saying at the same time that the generic term implied no common ground between the two species. If it is widened we are faced with undoubted difficulties; this one of finding common ground between apparently disparate activities and the other of excluding undesirable hangers-on such as mere *Schwärmerei* on the one side and mere low cunning on another. But these difficulties are nothing to those that result from the narrow usage of Hume.

"The function of Reason," Whitehead says,[1] "is to promote the

---
[1] *The Function of Reason,* 2.

art of life." This is as wide a definition as can well be asked for, though Hume might have accepted it apart from certain suggestions attaching to the word "promote." As Whitehead goes on to say, "the art of life is *first* to be alive, *secondly* to be alive in a satisfactory way, and *thirdly* to acquire an increase in satisfaction."[2] There are, I take it, three main points of emphasis. (1) Reason has its roots in the foundation of our being, in organic life as such, and is not solely an efflorescence, superstructure or decoration. (2) At the opposite pole it stretches out higher than we can grasp; it is not complete but contains always something struggling to be born. (3) Considered laterally, as it were, Reason has as many sides as life has. The difficulty here is to recognise that there are distinctions without making them impassable gulfs, as Kant tended to do in distinguishing between Theoretical and Practical Reason. Whitehead's Theoretical Reason, of course, includes Kant's Practical Reason; or rather, he does not recognise a purely theoretical understanding contemplating a purely phenomenal world. Such understanding would have nothing to do but acknowledge types of repetition among particular brute facts incapable of anything but "vacuous actuality." These repetitions would merely add a new set of general brute facts to the particular ones. The Kantian Theoretical Reason would be a passive onlooker at a scene intrinsically meaningless and uninteresting.

So far as the art of life "is first to be alive, secondly to be alive in a satisfactory way" Reason is required to be practical, as the plain man understands "practical." This, as Whitehead says, is the Reason of Ulysses, which is shared "with the foxes."[3] More is needed for the third condition "to acquire an increase in satisfaction," namely, theoretical realization or understanding of these things as exemplifying a theoretical system.[4] This is the Reason of Plato which is shared with the Gods. Plato and Ulysses, Gods and foxes, are sometimes at loggerheads. I rather think Whitehead exaggerates the antagonism, as Plato himself certainly did, and that point must be considered shortly. But

[2] *Ibid.*, 5.
[3] *Ibid.*, 7.
[4] *Ibid.*, 6.

there is another antagonism mentioned but perhaps hardly sufficiently emphasized by Whitehead, that between the Reason of Plato and what, as Greek names are in order, might be called the Reason of Ion. Ion, it will be remembered, thought he had scientific understanding of poetry in general and of Homer in particular, but was undeceived by Socrates, and had to admit that both he and the poet he interpreted were moved by divine inspiration without understanding, the poet directly and the rhapsody at second hand through the poet. In using these various names and in suggesting antagonism among them it is important to guard against the notion that any of them are opposites or contraries, as in a bipolar system. They are more like contrasting instruments in an orchestra which are all necessary for the full rendering of the music. If those of one kind are too loud they mar the effect, and if any are out of time or out of tune the result is a horrid noise.

Let us first consider Ulysses, because Whitehead is not always quite fair to him and even hints that he is no true ancestor of Plato. The main indictments brought against Ulysses are two. Firstly, necessity is not the mother of invention but only of futile dodges, and secondly, reason as applied to the solution of practical problems degenerates and petrifies as methodology and ultimately as mere habit, unless it is revivified by the theoretical reason; by reason "enthroned above the practical tasks of the world," seeking "with disinterested curiosity an understanding of the world."[5] This second indictment is, I believe, entirely just, the first not quite. It is possible for the theoretical reason to degenerate and petrify, not into methodology exactly, but into pure formalism, if it is too much aloof from the world, too much like the Gods of Epicurus. There is nothing to prevent reason that is too cloistered from contenting itself with the contemplation of what it happens to know, of the ideas that appeal to it as being clear and distinct, and ignoring anything else it happens not to know. We can be jolted out of complacency by disasters in the practical sphere which compel us to acknowledge ignorance, to attend to things that are obscure,

[5] *Ibid.*, 29.

and seek the causes of failure. If "the bones of his [Ulysses] companions are strewn on many a reef and many an isle,"[6] that is greatly to their credit and a reproach to those companions of Plato who died smugly and comfortably in their beds.

Whitehead, in his accounts of the rise of science in Western Europe, has admirably emphasized the importance of the theoretical and speculative side of discovery but, I think, undervalues the stimulating effect of practical wants. The men of the sixteenth and seventeenth centuries knew that the determination of longitude at sea was an urgent practical problem and knew it was soluble if certain astronomical events, like occultations of stars by the moon, could be predicted with sufficient accuracy so that the navigator could determine his distance East or West of Greenwich by observing when they occurred according to his local time.[7] The speculative reason of the Greeks had been content with relatively inaccurate astronomical predictions and crude methods of observation, because they saw no need for greater accuracy, and therefore they had no criteria for preferring a heliocentric to a geocentric planetary theory. The practical difficulties of pumping water out of deep mines and ventilating them stimulated interests that led to the barometer, the air pump, and the study of gases generally, out of which came ultimately the atomic theory and theoretical chemistry. These discoveries might have come without the practical stimulus, but hardly so soon. Other instances might be given, such as the problems of constructing accurate timekeepers, mainly for the sake of finding longitude, of finding the trajectories of projectiles, and of handling large masses of metal for making artillery. The bogus practical problems of drawing horoscopes and transmuting metals might really be cited too.

The founders of the Royal Society certainly expected practical fruits to spring from their scientific activities, and in this they were not deceived; but they were deceived if they ex-

---

[6] *Ibid.*, 8.

[7] The problem of determining the longitude of places on shore is, of course, easier because no prediction is needed. It is enough to observe the same astronomical event at Greenwich or any other known point and at the place to be fixed and then compare notes afterwards.

pected these fruits to grow quickly and easily. The technique of mechanical invention had to be learnt, more particularly a knowledge of the kind of things mechanical invention can and cannot do and of how to profit by failure. The general theoretical knowledge needed to construct a chronometer must have been available for nearly a hundred years before the first one sufficiently accurate for finding longitude was made in 1761. The delay seems to have been imposed by purely practical difficulties; the difficulty of finding the right technical dodge for an escapement mechanism which would maintain the oscillations of the balance wheel isochronous with an error less than 1 in 100,000, as well as providing for temperature compensation. In this case the reason of Plato had said all it could long before Ulysses had worked through his repertory of many wiles to find the right one. The point to emphasise is that his many wiles are a corollary of his much-endurance.

The Abbot Mendel was a follower of Plato, but Ulysses in the shape of the practical horticulturist had presented him with a problem and put in his hands a technique adequate up to a certain point. In this case the collaboration of Plato and Ulysses has been fruitful for the latter beyond his wildest dreams, and has given the former some of his most intriguing problems.

Plato himself was no personal friend of Ulysses, but he admits that contradictions produce bewilderment and bewilderment produces search.[8] Purely theoretical contradiction we can sometimes turn our backs upon, but contradiction between what we want and what we have is not so easily ignored. Though Plato and Ulysses can and do frequently quarrel, they are necessary to one another. This however is a minor point; the next is more important.

Speculative Reason, Whitehead says,

seeks with disinterested curiosity an understanding of the world. Naught that happens is alien to it. It is driven forward by the ultimate faith that all particular fact is understandable as illustrating the general principle of its own nature and of its status among other particular facts.[9] . . .

[8] *Republic* VII, 524A.
[9] *The Function of Reason*, 29.

Also so long as understanding is incomplete, it remains to that extent unsatisfied. It thus constitutes itself the urge from the good to the better life.[10]

Again:

the Speculative Reason is in its essence untrammelled by method. Its function is to pierce into the general reasons beyond limited reasons, to understand all methods as coördinated in a nature of things only to be grasped by transcending all method. This infinite ideal is never to be attained by the bounded intelligence of mankind.[11]

In considering the passages quoted we must add the point Whitehead has previously made[12] that the rejection of final causes in the interests of methodology (with the further excuse that final causes have often been misused) is a fundamental error. The disinterestedness of reason has been taken to mean that the world it contemplated was without interest, and that reason had no "status among other particular facts," or none worth mentioning.

When Plato made the apprehension of the Form of the Good the final aim of reason and chose training in scientific thought as the propaedeutic for the purpose, he was saying something very like what Spinoza said about the intellectual love of God, only he had not contradicted himself beforehand by denying final causes. The fact that the Forms are but imperfectly embodied or realised in the temporal material world Plato took to be a reproach against that world—perhaps rightly. But he did not consider it a reproach against the Forms themselves that these, though formal causes in Aristotle's sense, seem to live in a world of their own; again too much like Epicurean Gods, who "lie beside their nectar, careless of mankind." Nor had he grounds for supposing there is a Form of the Good that are not equally grounds for supposing there is a Form of the Evil.

There is a fallacy which dogs a careless Idealism. If the Ideal is eternal and is the only real, why bother about anything; everything is all right anyway, isn't it? There is also an answer-

[10] *Ibid.*, 30.
[11] *Ibid.*, 51.
[12] *Ibid.*, 7 seq.

able question. If there is an absolute or ideal Good, why not an absolute or ideal Bad? Descartes suggested that the world might be governed by a malicious demon who contrived so that the more we strive for truth the more we are deceived, and the more we strive to do right the greater our wrongdoing. These and similar nightmares are not easily disposed of except in naturalistic terms. Ideals are the product of Reason and Reason itself is the child of the environing world, material and non-material, in which it is born and bred. Mother Nature may be often puzzled at the whims of this wayward creature and suspect it to be a changeling. Nonetheless it is no changeling but her own flesh and blood, or she could never have nourished it. Reason may think itself a changeling too and sigh for a life of ease in some fabulous Garden of the Hesperides, but like all Nature's brood has to go out to work for a living. If the universe were entirely evil or utterly indifferent, then human aspirations would indeed be futile defiances of fate, but they would also be inexplicable and sheer miracle. The new difficulty of course is to avoid the Naturalistic Fallacy: to contrive to assert that human values and ideals have really sprung from the soil of the environment and yet are not the soil itself faintly disguised: to recognise that the rose grows out of the dung, is nourished by it, is quite definitely made of it, without supposing it smells of it. The spokesmen of Emergent Evolution have avoided this fallacy, but only to the extent of stating as a brute fact (to be accepted with natural piety) that in the historical sequence there was a time when something or other definitely did not exist and a later time when it did, adding the rider that this is not to be considered as a miracle but as a natural process and in fact what is meant by evolution. This acceptance of "epigenetic evolution" would have profoundly shocked the seventeenth century; but it seems inevitable. It has the important result of denying the doctrine *ex nihilo nihil fit* as a metaphysical first principle. (The doctrine still provides a useful rule of method for scientific investigation.) There remains the further task, after acknowledging creation as a fact, of trying to understand it as a principle. Whitehead's discussion of Reason is a step in this direction.

The Idealist attempt to substitute what is called a dialectical process for a historical process seems to be a failure. If it is an attempt to produce a hyper-logic, which is to be creative, to override ordinary logic, which is analytic, restrictive and critical, it is a fraud. If it is an attempt to describe how human thought does actually tend to develop, it is highly suggestive and valuable, but it is psychology, and over-simplified psychology. In any case dialectic does not do what is asked of it. However, the Hegelians have insisted on the vital point that thought is always incomplete yet always aiming at completion, and it is this that makes it thought not something else. But this can be said equally well by those who "take time seriously" and are concerned to exhibit Reason as a phase in a concrete historical process, which is itself not purely thinking.

After these preliminaries let me quote what seems to me Whitehead's most important statement.

But when mentality is working at a high level, it brings novelty into the appetitions of mental experience. In this function, there is a sheer element of anarchy. But mentality now becomes self-regulative. It canalizes its own operations by its own judgments. It introduces a higher appetition which discriminates among its own anarchic productions. Reason appears. It is Reason, thus conceived, which is the subject-matter of this discussion. We have to consider the introduction of anarchy, the revolt from anarchy, the use of anarchy, and the regulation of anarchy. Reason civilizes the brute force of anarchic appetition. Apart from anarchic appetition, nature is doomed to slow descent toward nothingness. Mere repetitive experience gradually eliminates element after element and fades towards vacuity. Mere anarchic appetition accomplishes quickly the same end, reached slowly by repetition. Reason is the special embodiment in us of the disciplined counter-agency which saves the world.[13]

The anarchic phase is the Reason of Ion. It is still a kind of reason, but because of its anarchy thought can always go wrong and frequently does so. True prophets are far fewer than false prophets. "Perhaps it is safer to stone them, in some merciful way,"[14] if we assume that safety is the first consideration.

Clearly without a phase of anarchy there can be no novelty

[13] *Ibid.*, 27f.
[14] *Ibid.*, 53.

and without novelty no Reason, except in Hume's sense of logical habit. Logical habit is part of Reason, but emphatically not the whole of it; like anything else merely orderly it is just repetition. Anarchy in the sense here intended is not *dis*order, or order that has been spoilt, but formlessness out of which new order may be born and which is tolerant of diverse kinds of order. Many voices from the eighteenth century to the present day have been raised in support of anarchic appetition to separate it off from Reason and sometimes to exalt it at the expense of Reason. This is the attitude that is at least implicit in Shaftesbury, Hutcheson and Hume himself, openly declared by Rousseau, by the leaders of the Romantic Movement in literature and in some of the religious movements of the eighteenth and early nineteenth century. In recent times Bergson has given a new turn to it on the philosophic side. (I hesitate to include Pragmatism in the same category. Certainly Pierce and his Pragmaticism are not to be included.) Altogether the supporters of anarchy are a distinguished company, and they would appear more distinguished if they had not encouraged disreputable parasites who would oust Reason altogether. If, however, we disregard the parasites, who have indeed nothing coherent to say for themselves, all these advocates of the claims of anarchic appetition are concerned to assert that "mere repetitive experience gradually eliminates element after element and fades towards vacuity," but have failed to realise that "mere anarchic appetition accomplishes quickly the same end." Their protest of course has been an important one in so far as it is a protest against what may be called the bureaucratic view, that the anarchic element is simply a nuisance that ought to be eliminated. The bureaucratic view is always powerful in human affairs and perhaps always needs to be denounced, though, as far as I know, no respectable philosopher since Parmenides has defended it. Granted that some protest is needed, it is most important that it should not separate the anarchic element from reason as something antagonistic or quite distinct. The value of Whitehead's statement is that it avoids any such separation, but treats anarchy as a phase in a total process which involves control of anarchy.

All philosophers, except extreme sceptics, have believed that somehow or other "the order and connection of ideas is the same as the order and connection of things." They differ enormously of course in what they have to say about the character of ideas and of things and about the character of the connection between them, but about this they do not differ seriously. If it were not for this, anything a philosopher had to say about the nature of thought or reason or mental life generally would be of purely sentimental interest, like the things the lady-novelists say about their heroines' complicated feelings. Thus Whitehead's account of Reason must be taken as part and parcel of his general metaphysical theory and that of course is how he states it in *The Function of Reason*, though without going into details and in particular without his special technical terminology. It is obvious at first glance that Reason embodies at the highest level known to man what in Whitehead's view is the character of all actuality, namely that anything deserving the name of a concrete or real entity is such as the result of a process of "concrescence" in virtue of which it takes up into itself all that is relevant from its environment, orders it according to its own nature and then reissues it with the stamp of its own individuality. Wherever the process produces something new and is not merely repetitive there is something recognisably akin to Reason.

Granted that Reason has a part to play in the Universe, there are two obvious types of theory about its status and its relation to actual events, which may be called (1) Supernaturalism and (2) Naturalism. It is true, the late Professor A. A. Bowman[15] put forward what may be a third alternative, but perhaps I may be excused from considering it here and may be permitted to discuss the matter in terms of these two. Either (1) Reason is an archetype and *vera causa*, as that which produces order and value. But on this view Reason is a timeless universal and the doctrine of *universalia ante rem* is implied. In that case temporal actualities sink to the level of the half real or even illusory; there are really no efficient causes in the ordinary sense, only Formal and Final Causes; existence comes to mean

[15] In *A Sacramental Universe* (Princeton and Oxford, 1939).

the non-temporal existence of universals. Or else (2) Reason is an actual existent which has become actualized in a historical spatio-temporal process and has prototypes which are in part efficient causes. Formal or final causes, though *universalia in re*, are not as such actual existing entities, for they are non-temporal. That is to say either (1) all reality is non-temporal, eternal, universal, and particulars are a sham, or (2) there are both actual temporal existents and eternal forms.

Whether or not there is a genuine third alternative, little argument I think is needed to dispose of the nominalist and conceptualist theories that explain away universals. Really the summary dismissal in Plato's *Parmenides* (132 B-C) should suffice. If anything more is needed three arguments may be briefly indicated. (1) Without universals knowledge is impossible, for knowledge is of universals, as the *Theaetetus* is intended to show. (2) As Mr. Russell points out, to say universals are words or thoughts is no solution because the words or thoughts intended are themselves a special kind of universals and are not particulars. (3) The use, value, truth or falsehood of sentences composed of words or of thoughts depend upon their reference to something else (possibly other sentences or thoughts) and this is a relation and therefore universal. Universals cannot be explained away as "nothing but" something else, which is imagined as particular, without self-contradiction. The trouble about them is to find a place for them in relation to particulars and state the relation. It is a trouble that troubles every possible philosophy. It is, I think, convenient to use the traditional names Forms or Essences as an indication that universals in the full sense are truths, patterns or ideals, that classes are doubtfully to be included and simple sense qualities probably to be excluded. Certainly many fallacies have been introduced into discussion by treating sense qualities such as colours as typical universals, whereas the typical universal is a "specification" in the engineer's sense.

The problems of the status of universals have been unnecessarily confused by something that has been included in the "Platonic" tradition. I say "Platonic" to avoid assuming that Plato himself is implicated. It is a result of the natural human desire to eat one's cake and have it, and it turns upon an ambiguous use of 'eternal' and 'eternity'. These terms as applied to the Forms should mean quite strictly non-temporal, having nothing to do with succession, change, or endurance through time. But they have been taken to mean also enduring or persisting in spite of change for a very long time or even for longer than any assignable finite length of time. It is as if non-spatial was taken to mean also larger than any assignable magnitude. There are long standing confusions underlying the notion of substance and of the immortality of the soul which come from identifying the non-temporal character of truths and ideals with long persistence in time. The identification is made for the sake of believing that any actual existent we value is going to endure for a very long time, if possible endlessly. Everything which exists or lives has a beginning and, by the same token, an end. There seems no reason why its mere ceasing to exist should condemn it in any way or why its value should bear any relation to the length of time it endures—however that is to be measured. In any case, every life-time is short relative to a longer life and long relative to a shorter one, so that value and length can hardly bear any simple relation to one another.

Some people suppose that the sting of tragedy lies in the fact that the hero dies; whereas it lies in the fact that the hero is one inherently capable of choosing right, and yet, for reasons within or outside his control, chooses wrong when opportunity comes, and suffers for his mistake. In one life opportunity comes once and never again and the past is irrevocable. If the hero chooses right, his death is no tragedy.

Could tragedy be mitigated if the hero lived again another life? If he did, either the lives would be linked by continuity of memory, or not. If not, then in the next life, either it will come about that for the same kind of person similar causes will have similar effects, or else, if they do not, there is no more genuine link between the two lives than between Queen Elizabeth's *Ark Royal* and the present ship called by the same name. If the lives are linked by continuity of memory then they are both really one life and the suggestion means that fate is averted, opportunity comes twice and the past is revocable. It is in fact the conventional "happy ending" which spoils the play but brings in the money. (Plato's ingenious combination of continuity and discontinuity of memory in the myth of the Tenth Book of the *Republic* is too ingenious.)

Popular thinking in these matters seems to be governed by the belief that we are virtuous (at least in intention) but unhappy in our lives and therefore deserve some compensation. Nobody I believe has ever thought of himself as happier than he deserved to be and therefore requiring compensatory unhappiness hereafter. That argument is always reserved for others. For that reason it can be dismissed as completely invalid, and it throws considerable doubt upon all arguments for another life to compensate for this. Finally one may ask, if it be true that our lives are "solitary, poor, nasty and brutish," is it not lucky that they are also short?

Surely the chief characteristic of life is that every life is unique, not only in the sense that each one is a different person, but even more that life is lived through once only and then finished. If immortality or eternal life is to be taken seriously, as it must be, it does not mean that life is repeated or continued; that is merely an evasion of difficulties and a refusal to face the truth. What immortality means is a certain quality or intensity, a depth or a height or a new dimension of life, but inevitably something non-temporal. Spinoza said this explicitly and I believe Plato intended to say it too, but tangled his thought with myths based on traditional belief.

To return to Whitehead after what may appear to be a digression; I am not suggesting that he agrees with Spinoza on this subject, though it is perhaps one of the few points where there is no necessary disagreement. The main issue is that the life of Reason, like life at any level, is a temporal process; it is something operating at a particular time under limitations and according to conditions, but it is that which raises processes to a higher level of operation. The height of the level of operation is to be judged in terms of Form or Essence, of that which is non-temporal but characterizes, informs, or is embodied or realized in the temporal process. The relation between forms which are non-temporal and actual processes or events can only be stated in metaphorical terms by means of verbs which normally indicate spatial and temporal relations. The metaphors are therefore misleading if taken seriously. The relation is perhaps best put in Aristotelian language by saying that the temporal process is the "matter" which the eternal essence "informs." In any case this is a difficulty, perhaps purely verbal, perhaps not, for any theory whatsoever which acknowledges genuine process in time and the equally genuine but quite different reality of forms. The difference can be expressed by saying that only events exist, that they have the characters they exhibit because of the particular place and time they occupy and have both external and internal relations. Therefore the existence of forms, if they exist, is whenever and wherever events are informed by them. The only possible alternative would seem to be to say that forms exist and nothing else; that the passage of time is illusion or time simply is not. This leaves it to be explained how we are illuded by something which is not there. (How can time be "the moving image of eternity" if the one fact we know about eternity is that it is immobile?)

The chief problem that remains to be considered is whether Formal and Final Causes (there is no need to distinguish between them for the present) can be in any sense *verae causae*. Final causes have sometimes been considered as though they were a special sort of efficient cause which operated in reverse, from future to past. This view has such curious consequences that it must be rejected by any one who believes in the reality of time. There would be no great difficulty of course for those who deny time, change and process, and therefore deny efficient cause in the ordinary sense, namely that which leads in the' historical sequence to change. On this view what we call past, present and future coexist eternally. So-called causal relations are, if anything, logical relations and operate indifferently in any direction.

On any other theory the consequences of supposing that final causes operate from future to past may be illustrated as follows. Wellington fought the battle of Waterloo for the sake of victory; that was his end and, at the time he was fighting, it was represented by a future event. If the future event, victory, somehow influenced the present events during the battle we must assume the opposite final cause, defeat, was at work also pulling the opposite (or the same?) way. Again, if the future can alter the present, the present can alter the past, and the near past can alter the earlier past. The past would then not be fixed and irrevocable but really fictitious, which is as much as to deny efficient causation and make the past unknowable. The notion of efficient causation implies that whatever exists as actual fact is as it is because of what happened before, and that what happened before was in its own day actual fact and was as it was: unalterable. It is true that information about past events and our opinions on them may alter, but we can have knowledge of them at all only because they themselves are not altered by whether we know them or not. Events after June 1815 can alter our knowledge about the battle of Waterloo, but only because the event itself was there to know about, that is to say, is unalterable.

Of course Wellington had a plan in his mind before and during the battle (as had Napoleon), and in so far as these plans were events they were part causes in the sense of efficient causes determining the course of events. In this sense, the plan, which may be considered a formal cause, is also a special kind of efficient cause. There is nothing here paradoxical or absurd, but there is the unfortunate fact that though a plan, a thought in a man's mind (or something happening in his brain, if you prefer) may be and indeed almost certainly is a kind of efficient cause; it is a kind we know little about, in fact next to nothing compared with our knowledge of the kind of causes physics deals with. We do and should use our knowledge of efficient causes as far as it will go, but when we find the information it provides is trivial we have to turn elsewhere for understanding. Sometimes the information provided by physical knowledge of efficient causes is trivial because of ignorance of relevant facts or principles, but not always. From the point of view of physical science and of efficient causes, playing the violin consists in rubbing the entrails of a dead sheep with hairs from the tail of a dead horse, and apart from the quantitative variations in the rubbing and in the length and tension of entrails rubbed there is nothing more to be said. No conceivable extension of physical knowledge in general or of the properties of entrails and hairs in particular could do more than add further details equally trivial. Triviality here is not a consequence of ignorance. If one is to say anything significant about violin playing it must be said in terms of formal and final causes, of what music is being played and how well it is being played. That kind of statement gives a kind of understanding that no statement about efficient and material causes can give and it is in virtue of that understanding that formal and final causes are *verae causae*.

We cannot escape the consequences of the past, that is what material and efficient causation means, but sometimes and in some ways we can use what we inherit from the past as a means and opportunity to make something new out of it. If that is so, there must be some aspects of future events which are in principle unpredictable because prediction is based upon repetition and can only deal with what is repeated. To put the matter in theological language, God is creating the future out of the past and even He does not know everything that is going to happen until it does happen.

There is one question which naturally arises from this discussion, that I have not dealt with. If all existence is temporal, is it also spatio-temporal? Alexander boldly maintained that it was and has been severely criticised for so doing. I should prefer to leave the discussion of this point to others more competent than I am, and merely suggest that paradoxical consequences follow the adoption of either alternative, whether it is said that all events are spatio-temporal or that some events are temporal and not spatial while others are both. It is possible that *a priori* there is no way of deciding. Empirically it seems obvious that the spatial relations of material processes are important, but the spatial relations of mental processes, if any, unimportant. In other words, the spatial extent of mental life is very minute or very difficult of observation and need not as a rule be taken into consideration.

By way of conclusion I should like to put a question in terms of the distinction between Naturalism and Supernaturalism. This distinction, I think, is a more important one than the rather similar and more usual, but more ambiguous, one of

Realism and Idealism. The latter indeed is not only ambiguous in its academic use, but suffers further from the use of these terms by the man in the street (or the man in the newspaper office) to mark the distinction between the hard boiled and the half baked.

The Naturalist is one for whom all parts of experience are parts of one whole and that whole is Nature, and whose first task is to try to understand Nature both in its parts and in their relation to the whole. He might decide that all parts were of equal importance or value, in which case they would none of them be of any importance or value, as values are comparative. Indeed, with no principle of selection he could hardly proceed at all unless he were in the position of Laplace's calculator, who could calculate the state of the whole universe at any time given its whole state at another time. But then he would have no reason for taking one date rather than another as his starting point, probably no definite knowledge whether he was calculating forwards or backwards in time, certainly no reason why he should choose to do it forwards rather than backwards. In fact, there seems no reason why the calculator should set to work at all, while incidentally there is one reason why he should not. That is, that, if he had the misfortune to choose to start from his immediate past and calculate forwards, he would have to calculate his own calculations, and might find it confusing. To avoid such troubles the Naturalist will not treat all things alike. He will select what is of greater value and neglect, or at least subordinate, what is of less value, though he will endeavour as far as he can to let Nature reveal a scale of values to him rather than impose a private scale of values on Nature. If it be objected that values are in any case the things judged to be valuable by him, he can reply that he himself is a natural object like any other and entitled to count for one, though not more than one.

Still there is a difficulty. Once the Naturalist has allowed himself the luxury of distinguishing the more and the less valuable, he does appear to have contradicted himself and abandoned the apparent clarity of his starting point, a candid recognition of all facts. He is like the "Cat that Walked by Himself" in Kipling's story. The Cat insists that all places are alike to him and yet chooses to leave the wild wet woods when he wishes to claim his place by the fire and his saucer of milk.

As against the Naturalist, the Supernaturalist starts with a radical distinction between the realm of values, of what is valuable in its own right, and the subordinate or alien realm of mere fact and mere history, which in itself has no value. Though the Naturalist, accused of inconsistency by the Supernaturalist, may retort *tu quoque*, for the present purpose the retort is beside the point, even if true. The question is, can the Naturalist be consistent? In asking the question I am assuming of course that Whitehead is a Naturalist. I am making also a more dubious assumption that there is no genuine synthesis as between thesis and antithesis of Naturalism and Supernaturalism.

A. D. RITCHIE

THE UNIVERSITY
MANCHESTER, ENGLAND

9

Arthur E. Murphy

WHITEHEAD AND THE METHOD OF SPECULATIVE PHILOSOPHY

WHITEHEAD AND THE METHOD OF
SPECULATIVE PHILOSOPHY

IN the preface to *Process and Reality*, Whitehead lists nine prevalent habits of thought which in that volume "are repudiated, in so far as concerns their influence on philosophy." The first of these is "the distrust of speculative philosophy."[1] And in his more recent works, *Adventures of Ideas* and *Modes of Thought*, he has devoted an increasing share of his attention to an exposition and defense of the aims and methods of this type of philosophy against the suspicions and attacks currently directed against them. Coming as it did at the height of the 'positivistic' and 'analytic' attacks on metaphysics, and from a thinker whose eminence as a scientist and logician is unquestioned, this reinforcement of the hard-pressed metaphysicians was naturally a welcome and formidable one. But it is not merely or mainly by the weight of his authority that Whitehead has bolstered the case for speculative philosophy. In *Process and Reality* he has given us a system of philosophy which is worthy in its scope, technical elaboration, and profundity to rank beside the classics in this field. And in *Adventures of Ideas* he was able to apply the results of this speculative venture to problems of primary philosophical concern in a peculiarly suggestive and illuminating way. We should all, I think, be tempted to become metaphysicians, if we could thereby be endowed with the wit to make such philosophically penetrating observations on the nature and value of human experience as that book contains. If the suspicion to which Whitehead has referred has in considerable measure been allayed, and the prestige of speculative philosophy largely

---

[1] *Process and Reality*, viii. (References in this essay to *Process and Reality* are all taken from the American edition, 1929.)

restored, at least in professional and academic circles, it is to these writings, I believe, more than to any other single factor, that this result is due.

In this paper I propose to investigate this reformulation of the aims and procedures of speculative philosophy, in an attempt to determine as precisely as possible what the distinctive features of this type of inquiry are and how its conclusions are substantiated. The issues raised are of fundamental importance, not only for academic philosophy but for all serious and responsible thinking about the nature of the world and the status of human beings in it. If Whitehead is right and the prevalent distrust of speculative philosophy wrong, then we have all—save for a few metaphysicians—been unwarrantably neglecting a basically important source of information about God, nature, and ourselves. If, on the other hand, Whitehead is mistaken, and if this manner of philosophizing remains, even after his ministrations, an equivocal and unreliable procedure, the animus against it can be raised from the level of mere suspicion to that of reasoned rejection of its cognitive claims. For if the genius of Whitehead cannot rehabilitate speculative philosophy, it is not likely that others will be more successful. My initial interest, however, is not in acceptance or rejection but in understanding. What, on the showing of its most distinguished contemporary exponent, *is* speculative philosophy and what reasons are there for accepting it as a trustworthy philosophical procedure? Once this question is answered we shall be in a better position than have many past controversialists to come to a decision as to its cognitive merits. What that decision ought to be I shall try to make clear in the concluding section of the paper.

It is of crucial importance to distinguish at the outset between 'speculation' as that aspect of human thought which strives to extend the boundaries of understanding beyond its previously established limits, and speculative *philosophy* as practiced by metaphysicians and exemplified, for instance, in *Process and Reality*, which claims to achieve this extension by a quite special method of its own. The latter is, of course, a species of the former, and is entitled to share in any credit which attaches to speculation as such, as an 'adventure of ideas' beyond the range of conventionally established categories and procedures. But it also involves certain features peculiar to itself; and it is on these, rather than on the more general advantages or disadvantages of imaginatively adventurous thinking, that I wish to direct attention.

It is, however, proper to notice at the outset how much of truth and wisdom there is in Whitehead's eloquent defense of speculation in this wider sense. There are scholars so intellectually imprisoned by the categorial limits of their specialization that they can see nothing but 'nonsense' in ideas of a different and wider application.

For scholars the reasonable topics in the world are penned in isolated regions, *this* subject-matter or *that* subject-matter. Your thorough-going scholar resents the airy speculation which connects his own patch of knowledge with that of his neighbor. He finds his fundamental concepts interpreted, twisted, modified. He has ceased to be king of his own castle, by reason of speculations of uncomfortable generality, violating the very grammar of his thoughts.[2]

In stressing the inadequacy of such an attitude and defending against it the reasonable demand of the human mind for an inclusive wisdom that will do justice to all aspects of experience Whitehead is speaking not merely for speculative philosophy but for any philosophy that takes itself and its responsibilities seriously.

Again, in making himself the spokesman for insights which cannot be expressed in a language dictated by accepted preconceptions, he is on the side of intellectual progress and against a sort of obscurantism which, in the past, has more than once blocked the path of inquiry. Much that was 'nonsense' in its first expression, as judged by currently accepted standards, has proved in its development and application to be very good sense indeed. The attempt to say what cannot be said in an already existing and necessarily provisional language is an essential phase in the advance of knowledge. "New directions of thought arise from flashes of intuition bringing new material within the scope of scholarly learning. They commence as the sheer ven-

[2] *Adventures of Ideas*, 137-8.

tures of rash speculation."[3] I should prefer to italicize the word 'commence' in this quotation, as it will be important for future reference. But as it stands, it says something that is true and, as a protest against the narrowness of much current positivism, important.

So much being agreed, we may proceed to the more specific issue. Some of the most important advances in the sciences have *commenced* as ventures of speculation, and valuable innovations in the arts have been similarly 'rash', when judged by the standards of their time. On the other hand, as Whitehead would no doubt agree, there have been speculative ventures which have come to nothing and which by such tests at least as we can yet apply must be pronounced failures. If works on metaphysics that lay claim to rational credence are to be reliably distinguished from those treatises on the occult which are frequently placed in disturbing proximity to them on the shelves of public libraries, we need some sort of test by which we can assure ourselves that they belong in the former category rather than the latter. And this is not (though Whitehead sometimes writes as though it were) a question of the *general* merits of daring speculation as opposed to verbal orthodoxy, but of the specific methods, claims, and performances of the type of philosophy which he recommends. What, then, is speculative philosophy?

"Speculative philosophy is the endeavour to frame a coherent, logical, necessary system of general ideas in terms of which every item of our experience can be interpreted."[4] Its method is philosophic generalization—"the utilization of specific notions, applying to a restricted group of facts, for the divination of the generic notions which apply to all facts."[5] On the hypothesis developed in *Process and Reality*, "an actual fact is a fact of aesthetic experience,"[6] and the laws applying to all facts are a generalization of those found initially applicable in our own aesthetic experience. In its emphasis on generalization the method of speculative philosophy is similar to that of the

[3] *Ibid.*, 138.
[4] *Process and Reality*, 4.
[5] *Process and Reality*, 8.
[6] *Ibid.*, 427.

sciences. There is, however, a fundamental difference between these disciplines.

It is the task of philosophy to work at the concordance of ideas conceived as illustrated in the concrete facts of the real world. It seeks those generalities which characterize the complete reality of fact, and apart from which any fact must sink into an abstraction. But science makes the abstraction, and is content to understand the complete fact in respect to only some of its essential aspects.[7] . . . The final problem is to conceive a complete fact.[8]

So far so good. There is, however, a further peculiarity of speculative philosophy which Whitehead does not so frequently discuss, but which is fully exemplified in his practice. Speculative philosophy is in search of those generalities which apply to everything that is actual, or that actually exists. But it does not reach such generalities by observing what everything that we elsewhere take to be 'actual' is like and achieving a formula which applies in the same sense to all such entities. Its generalizations apply not to all 'facts' (as we should more usually understand them) but to the *final* or *ultimate* facts, and to others insofar as they can be shown to be abstracted from, or appearances of, those taken to be fundamentally and completely real. It is for this reason that speculative philosophy can pursue, in a single hypothesis, the general and the concrete. For we are in search of what is common to all things insofar as they are 'concrete', 'finally actual', 'ultimately real', or the like, and since nothing in its final reality can be a mere abstraction we are naturally led in a different direction from that which the sciences pursue.

This difference is most fully exemplified in Whitehead's notion of an actual entity, and in the use to which he puts it.

'Actual entities'—also termed 'actual occasions'—are the final real things of which the world is made up. There is no going behind actual entities to find anything more real. . . . The final facts are, all alike, actual entities and these actual entities are drops of experience, complex and interdependent.[9]

---

[7] *Adventures of Ideas*, 187.
[8] *Ibid.*, 283.
[9] *Process and Reality*, 27f.

These actual entities occupy, as will be seen, a position of peculiar primacy. For, according to what Whitehead calls "the ontological principle,"

the reasons for things are always to be found in the composite nature of definite actual entities—in the nature of God for reasons of highest absoluteness, and in the nature of definite temporal actual entities for reasons which refer to a particular environment. The ontological principle can be summarized as: no actual entity, then no reason.[10]

It would be a mistake to suppose that this means only that what things in more usual senses 'actually' are, is the final 'reason' in which all our reasonings must terminate. Our tests of actuality or genuineness vary from one activity and aspect of experience to another. Speculative philosophy is not primarily concerned with these usages and tests in their non-speculative application. It is intent on discovering what the 'ultimate' or 'final' facts may be, and since the requirements for speculative ultimacy are different from those which we make use of in more pedestrian activities, it will not be surprising if we are impelled, in order to arrive at the full or final actuality of things, to attribute to them properties which they would otherwise hardly be suspected to possess. Thus Whitehead finds it evident that no *final* actuality can be devoid of significance for itself, or subjective immediacy. Once this is established we can go on to say that what, in the sciences, is abstractly known as physical causation, must in its inner being be an aspect of subjective experience, a drive toward aesthetic satisfaction. The following passage makes this clear. "The final actuality has the unity of power. The essence of power is the drive towards aesthetic worth for its own sake. All power is a derivative from this fact of composition attaining worth for itself. There is no other fact."[11] And, when we use this metaphysically arrived at knowledge of all actuality to supplement the abstraction of the sciences, we acquire information of a very sweeping sort.

The notion of physical energy, which is at the base of physics, must then be conceived as an abstraction from the complex energy, emotional and purposeful, inherent in the subjective form of the final synthesis in which

---

[10] *Ibid.*, 28.
[11] *Modes of Thought*, 163.

each occasion of experience completes itself.[12] . . . The creativity of the world is the throbbing emotion of the past hurling itself into a new transcendent fact.[13]

It can thus be seen that the recourse to actual entities, in their final or complete reality, which might at first have seemed a detour on the road to matter-of-fact knowledge, has actually turned into a surprisingly efficient shortcut. We are, at the end of *Process and Reality*, in a position to make statements about everything that ever did or does or will actually exist, in any cosmic epoch and in the remote interstices of interstellar space, to the effect that such an entity, in its final actuality, is a feeler of feelings, operating primarily to fuse its emotional responses to its actual world, a world felt sympathetically as a world of other feelers and their feelings, into an aesthetic harmony which will constitute a final satisfaction and, as responsively felt by later actualities, will be 'objectively immortal' in the world beyond itself. Each such actuality has conceptual as well as physical feelings, i.e., responds emotionally to ideal possibilities resident in the mind of God, and is thus susceptible to the divine persuasion. And each, in its own way, realizes its subjective aim and thus achieves self-realization. "Self-realization is the ultimate fact of facts."[14] It is actual entities *thus defined* that are the ultimate reasons, and it is in terms of them that everything else is to be understood.

This information is not got by weighing and correlating all that from various sources we find out about the world. There are clues to it in the sciences, but the sciences, by the limitations of their method, remain incurably abstract. "The experiences on which accurate science bases itself are completely superficial."[15] And this is true also of our more practical, conscious adjustments to the world. "The central organism which is the soul of a man is mainly concerned with the trivialities of human existence."[16] It is to the vague and dim, but ontologically profound,

[12] *Adventures of Ideas*, 239.
[13] *Ibid.*, 227.
[14] *Process and Reality*, 340.
[15] *Modes of Thought*, 41.
[16] *Ibid.*, 42.

background of experience that we must turn for an adumbration of the deeper facts of concrete nature. Here "in the dim recesses behind consciousness there is the sense of realities behind abstractions."[17] From the standpoint of the ultimate the various aspects of our experience must thus be revalued with respect to their capacity to disclose what actually exists. And it is, of course, only as thus revalued, that they can enter into the speculative scheme or be used either to confirm or confute a speculative hypothesis. Our clear and distinct perception in what he calls "the mode of presentational immediacy" does not directly confirm Whitehead's hypothesis; on the contrary it has served to suggest that objects like sticks and stones are without emotions—vacuously actual—since they behave so unfeelingly in our more superficial contact with them. But we should not expect such specious clarity to serve as an adequate clue to the *final* reality of things. Nor need we wait for the more abstract procedures of the sciences to verify the emotional strivings of actual entities. For we know on speculative grounds what *any* actual entity must be, and hence electrons, so far as they pretend to speculative status, must preserve the pattern. " 'Actuality' means nothing else than this ultimate entry into the concrete, in abstraction from which there is mere non-entity. In other words, abstraction from the notion of 'entry into the concrete' is a self-contradictory notion, since it asks us to conceive a thing as not a thing."[18] It is to be remembered that 'entry into the concrete' means entry into the subjective experience of an actual entity. To deny such 'entry' as an indispensable condition for everything that exists, or did or will or could exist, is to conceive a thing as not a thing—not an 'actual entity'—and that would now appear to be impossible.

Hence we come to the conclusion that actual entities, in their relation of emotional concern and aesthetic striving are "the sole reality of the universe."[19] Their casual action is a transmission of feeling—"In this vector transmission of primitive feeling—the primitive provision of width for contrast is secured by pulses of emotion, which in the coördinate division of occasions appear

[17] *Ibid.*, 170.
[18] *Process and Reality*, 321.
[19] *Adventures of Ideas*, 228.

as wave-lengths and vibrations"[20] and all that is given as stubborn fact in the world must be referred, finally, to the decision of some actual entity or entities, because "in separation from actual entities there is nothing, merely nonentity—'The rest is silence'."[21] And, most forcibly of all,

It is a contradiction in terms to assume that some explanatory fact can float into the actual world out of nonentity. Nonentity is nothingness. Every explanatory fact refers to the decision and to the efficacity of an actual thing. The notion of 'subsistence' is merely the notion of how eternal objects can be components of the primordial nature of God.[22]

Once being actual, or being anything at all, is identified with being *finally* actual, and once *final* actuality is identified with the being of sentient 'actual entities', it is evident that everything must *finally* be referent to a feeler of feelings, appearances to the contrary notwithstanding, or be just nothing at all. "The rest is silence."

So far, the procedure of speculative philosophy seems straightforward enough. It is a method of arriving at statements purporting to provide correct information about (among other things) our spatio-temporal environment, by means of an identification of what is *ultimately, finally,* or *completely* actual or real, and a consequent determination in its terms of what anything whatever must actually or really be, on pain of being demoted to complete or partial nonentity if it fails to meet these specifications. But how do we determine what *is* finally actual in this sense? This is the next important question, and it is, unfortunately, not an easy one to answer. It is notorious that speculative philosophers have differed widely, not merely about the entities which satisfied their criteria for final actuality, but about these criteria themselves. The real must be that which is intelligible or satisfies the mind, we have been told. But we have also heard, on high authority, that the intellect is condemned to deal with mere appearances, and that the mark of reality is to be irreducible to all intellectual specifications. Nothing that is *truly* real

[20] *Process and Reality*, 247.
[21] *Process and Reality*, 68.
[22] *Ibid.*, 73.

can come to be or pass away, say the devotees of the eternal. But it is a fundamental principle of Whitehead's philosophy—the "principle of process"—that "how an actual entity *becomes* constitutes *what* that actual entity *is;* so that the two descriptions of an actual entity are not independent. Its 'being' is constituted by its 'becoming'."[23] The very title of Whitehead's *magnum opus, Process and Reality,* stands as a challenge to F. H. Bradley's *Appearance and Reality*—the masterwork of British metaphysics in the preceding generation—which had purported to demonstrate that what is *ultimately* real cannot be in process of becoming, and that what appears as process within it is not ultimately real. How are we to decide between these mighty opposites? It is the essential inner nature of anything whatever that was, is, or ever shall be, that hangs upon the answer.

The issue is even more difficult of adjudication than it might at first appear. It could not be settled by producing well-authenticated instances of process and attempting to refute Bradley by pointing out that here at least processes actually occur. For Bradley does not deny that process has this common or garden variety of actuality. Processes 'actually' occur, by ordinary tests, but such occurrence does not meet his requirement for *ultimate* reality. It lacks that all-inclusiveness and self-completeness which he has speculatively identified as the prerequisite for complete actuality. Given the initial stipulation, the conclusion follows, and it applies as much to Whitehead's actual entities as to anything else. Even the God of *Process and Reality* is, by this standard, deficient in real being, for it depends on other actualities for its complete determination. But equally, if we accept Whitehead's principle of process, we must reject the Bradleyan Absolute as a mere 'abstraction', lacking that concreteness which only a process in a world of environing processes could possess. And, while both Bradley and Whitehead find it quite incredible that anything non-sentient could be fully real, their great contemporary, Samuel Alexander, discerned the *basic* reality of things in pure space-time and was confident that all more complex levels of existence were "reducible with-

---

[23] *Process and Reality*, 34f. (Italics in text.)

out remainder" to this primal source of Being. It is not the mere fact of disagreement here that is disturbing. What is wanted is some way of settling the issues raised that will not beg the question at the outset by identifying *ultimate* reality with the object of its own speculative preference and then triumphantly demonstrating that, given this stipulation, nothing but this preferential entity, or set of entities, can 'ultimately' be anything at all. I do not suggest that speculative philosophy does in fact reduce 'without remainder' to this unenlightening procedure. But if it has more substantial grounds for the speculative identification of the 'ultimate', on which so much depends, we may properly at this point, borrowing the language of Hume, "desire that they be produced."

One response to this request is easily made, but not—save for those already committed to the speculative identification in question—very helpful. It may be that, given proper capacities and training, one finally and quite directly sees that true (or final, or ultimate) Being must be of one sort or another and that this direct insight, once achieved, is its own justification. Whitehead has written at times as though he had something like this in mind. Thus, in his most recent book, he tells us that "in philosophical writings proof should be at a minimum. The whole effort should be to display the self-evidence of basic truths, concerning the nature of things and their connection." . . . "Philosophy is either self-evident or it is not philosophy."[24] If this means merely that verification in philosophy (as in all inquiry about matter-of-fact) carries us beyond mere argument to what we find directly and at first hand to be the case, it is hardly open to question. And I should myself prefer, in the light of Whitehead's procedure elsewhere, to suppose that this is what he is saying. If, however, it means that such dicta as his principle of process, or the claim that everything whatever that exists must have feelings, are self-evident, or that speculative philosophers have an insight into the nature of reality which enables them to see quite directly that these principles are true, then there is little more to be said. Those who lack such

[24] *Modes of Thought,* 66f.

insight or believe themselves possessed of one which discloses something quite opposite about the ultimate Being of things, are evidently disqualified as critics—they simply have not seen or, what is even more unfortunate, have seen what isn't there. M. Maritain, the eminent neo-Thomist, in a recent defense of metaphysics assumes this lofty position.

The problem of metaphysics reduces itself finally to the problem of abstractive intuition and to the question whether, at the summit of abstraction, being itself, insofar as it is being—permeating the world of sensible experience, yet exceeding this world on all sides—is or is not the object of such an intuition. Everybody does not have it. And if we ask why positivism old and new and Kantism ignore this intuition, we shall be bound finally to admit that it is because there are philosophers who see, and philosophers who do not see.[25]

We must, of course, add the proviso that it must be those who *really* see, not those who, like Spinoza and Hegel and Hobbes and even Whitehead—whose speculative theology violates the first principles of scholastic metaphysics—merely *think* they see and do not, to whom the less gifted must turn for guidance in these matters, if Maritain is correct. Where insights disagree the true seer will know how to decide between them. Which is the true seer will be evident to those who possess the true insight, though only *truly* evident to those who *really* see, to be sure. If they are unable to persuade competitors of the unique authority of their peculiarly privileged grasp of the ultimate, we should hardly be surprised at that. There are in these matters, as Maritain has told us, those who do not see, and their failure to discern the final truth must be expected and discounted. There, since our present concern is with examinable claims to knowledge, we must leave the matter. It may be even as the seer says. But for those of us who do not possess the special insight in question there will be no reason to believe that Maritain or Aquinas, rather than Bradley or Alexander or Whitehead is the favored recipient of speculative illumination. And those who do see will have no need of the more

[25] "Science, Philosophy, and Faith," in *Science, Philosophy and Religion* (New York, 1941), 176.

pedestrian method of inquiry by which, in this paper, I am trying to come at the meaning and testable validity of the statements of speculative philosophy.

I have referred to this proposed method of validating the basic statements of speculative philosophy, not because it seems to me at all characteristic of Whitehead's usual procedure, but because it does represent a way out for metaphysicians in difficulties and one to which they have at times been prone to resort. And it really *is* a way out. The thinker in any field who claims immediate insight into the truth of his contentions is in an impregnable position. The fact that others do not see what he sees will never prove its non-existence—they may simply lack the special faculty required for this special contact with reality. No amount of evidence that claims to insight of this sort have in other instances proved empty will disturb his position. For those were *false* claims, whereas he sees quite immediately and directly that his is true. And if he does, then he does. Whether he does or not, only those who themselves have the same true insight can finally decide. But it is a way out of the region of publicly examinable knowledge claims, and those who take it should be prepared also to take the consequences and to acknowledge their subject to be the esoteric specialty to which it thus resolves itself.

Speculative philosophers have not usually been content to rest their cognitive claims on so meager a basis. For speculative philosophy is one phase or aspect of a more inclusive philosophic enterprise, the search for comprehensive wisdom in the reasonable ordering and interpretation of the experienced world in all its humanly significant aspects and dimensions. It is concerned, therefore, not merely with 'ultimate' reality in its complete finality, but also with the use to which an insight into such reality can be put in making comprehensive sense of the world as, in the several phases of our experience and activity, we come to know it. Even the most zealous devotee of an ulterior and transcendent reality finds himself under the obligation of 'saving the appearances', however 'mere' and close to nonentity these may finally be judged to be. That means that he must show that the experienced world is most justly and adequately

understood when we take as *finally* real the object of his speculative insight and view everything else as derivative from and
dependent upon this privileged reality. When this responsibility
is accepted, the speculative identification of something-or-other,
whether God, space-time, or Whitehead's actual entities, as the
final reality of things is more than an arbitrary stipulation or a
claim to esoteric insight. It becomes a part of a reasoned interpretation of the world in all its experienced aspects, an interpretation in which each aspect is judged philosophically in terms of
its place in and contribution to what, on the whole, we find
credible, reliable, and humanly important. And it is in terms
of their capacity to further such an interpretation and to contribute to the wisdom which is its goal, that the speculative
claims of competing metaphysics can reasonably be judged.

No one has said this more eloquently than has Whitehead.
He tells us:

Philosophy is not—or at least should not be—a ferocious debate between
irritable professors. It is a survey of possibilities and their comparison with
actualities. In philosophy the fact, the theory, the alternatives, and the
ideal, are weighed together. Its gifts are insight and foresight, and a sense
of the worth of life, in short, that sense of importance which nerves all
civilized effort. . . . Philosophy is an attempt to clarify those fundamental
beliefs which finally determine the emphasis of attention that lies at the
base of character.[26]

Philosophy, then, attempts to clarify our fundamental beliefs
about the emphasis of attention which determines what is for
us to be fundamental in our response to the experienced world.
How does *speculative* philosophy, as previously described, further this undertaking, and how is its success to be judged? When
we have answered this question, we shall (finally), I think,
have found our way out of the puzzle with which the problem
of the validation of claims to the speculative identification of the
ultimate had left us.

What I want to suggest as an answer, to be tested in its
application to Whitehead's further pronouncements and procedure, is this. In the context of the philosophical interpretation

---

[26] *Adventures of Ideas*, 125.

of experience, a 'final actuality' or 'ultimate reality' is the assumed ontological underpinning for that phase or aspect of the experienced world for which the speculative philosopher wishes to claim a privileged position in his estimate of that in the world which is philosophically of basic importance. The problem that confronts him is a genuine and fundamental one. Experience comes to us from many sources; we test and interpret its deliverances by criteria appropriate to the several activities through which we have commerce with it. But these criteria are various, and the results achieved in one sort of activity will not, as a rule, directly satisfy the demands made in another. A measured quantity will be exactly what a physicist needs for his purposes, but it will not satisfy the aspirations of a poet or answer the moral questionings of a saint. It is 'real' enough, no doubt, in the context of scientific inquiry, but it is not *ultimately* real, it will not serve as a satisfactory basis for a synthesis in which all phases of experience are assigned the importance which a wise man acknowledges them to possess. What then *is* ultimate, in the sense that it will provide such a basis, clarifying our estimates of importance by reference to its own preëminent importance and thus ordering all else in relation to itself?

If 'values' seem to be of primary importance, as for human beings they obviously are, then values should, as Urban has urged, be given a privileged position in a philosophical interpretation of the world. And that means that finally, and in the end, we cannot but believe that in our value experience lies the clue to what is ultimately real in the Universe and that, in consequence, a valueless existence would be impossible, a mere non-being. If we are particularly impressed with the transitoriness of things and find it enlightening and humanly wise to view them under the aspect of mutability, it will be natural to express this insight by the dictum that becoming is no mere appearance, as past metaphysicians have wrongly claimed, but is ultimately real, is of the very stuff of reality itself. And if, on the contrary, we are led, in an understandable state of exaltation, to echo Goethe, echoing Plato, in the claim that "the things that pass are only shadows," we shall have at once the material for a metaphysics of the eternal which, while the mood persists, no amount of 'refutation' from a different philosophical standpoint will be likely to shake. This transformation of 'ultimate' *importance* for the organization of experience around humanly basic interests into ultimate *reality* as a disclosure of the true or final being of things and, at long last, into information about what everything that exists really is—appearance to the contrary notwithstanding—seems to me to be the normal procedure of speculative philosophers, insofar as they can give reasons for their ontological insight and render it intelligible to the uninitiated. There is no question of the authenticity of the 'insight' as a significant human experience. The mood in which a man can say that beauty is truth, or that love is as strong as death is humanly understandable, and may be philosophically enlightening, if it helps to show us how greatly those things matter which satisfy the heart. Compared with them, from the standpoint of human satisfaction, the physical world with all its stars and milky ways is a thing of secondary and merely instrumental significance. But when *ultimate importance* relative to human interests wisely selected as fundamental is identified with *ultimate reality* as the character anything that exists must really possess, and human importance thus expands into existential potency or pervasiveness, something has occurred which needs more warrant than the initial experience can itself provide. It has been the function of speculative philosophy to provide this warrant, and it is in its performance of this function that its claims to ontological ultimacy and finality are most accurately understood. Such, at least, is the thesis which, in the remainder of this paper, I shall try to substantiate in reference to Whitehead's version of speculative philosophy.

We return, then, to the recurrent question. How, in Whitehead's philosophy, is the speculative identification of the ultimately actual achieved, and what is the philosophical use of statements in which such ultimacy is claimed or imputed? How, for example, is it established that no entity that actually exists can be 'vacuously actual', i.e., devoid of subjective immediacy or feeling? Whitehead does not deny that there are some objects which *appear* to us as inanimate in that variety of perceptual experience which he calls presentational immediacy, on which the sciences chiefly depend for their data. Nor do the sciences give more than hints of any further pervasive animation. But we are looking not for the 'superficialities' of clear and distinct ideas nor for the abstractness of science. We want to know what a *full* or *concrete* fact is, and for this, Whitehead holds, we must look to our own experience. And there is no doubt that such 'concreteness' does include our emotional responses to the world, and that these are humanly important. A philosophy which excluded them from 'reality' and so far misplaced concreteness as to restrict what actually exists to what a mathematical physicist would include in his statements would evidently be mistaken. We cannot take account for all that, in experience, we find meaningful, genuine, and desirable, without considering events in the special aspects they take on when enjoyed, valued, and artistically arranged by a human organism intent on making the most of its experience. What is apprehended in vividness, immediacy, and fullness of satisfaction, when we stand in those special relations to our environment which enable us to sympathize with its feelings, enjoy its beauty and the like, is certainly a completer fact than anything an abstract and analytic description can give us. The 'concrete' is here a fact of aesthetic experience, and it is on such facts that philosophy, as the critic of abstractions and seeker for the concrete or total fact, is asked to base itself.

May we then go on to maintain that *any* actual fact is a fact of aesthetic experience and that the 'concrete' fact from which the sciences abstract, even when they are talking about the transmission of light in interstellar spaces, is a striving for aesthetic harmony on the part of the 'actualities' there resident? This does not seem, *prima facie*, a reasonable step to take. No doubt the knowledge the sciences give us of what is there occurring is abstract, i.e., incomplete, and it would be sheer dogmatism to limit the complete existence of electrons to what is thus known about them. But that does not convict the entities in question of metaphysical deficiency of being, to be supplemented, lest they lapse into nonentity, by what makes *our* 'being' concrete—its emotional 'concern' with a surrounding world. It merely says—apart from speculative transformation— that we do not know more completely what they are, and that, in default of further means of getting into contact with them, it is the part of prudence to acknowledge it. If I could enter into sociable communication with an electron, I could doubtless apprehend it more vividly, and with an aesthetic satisfaction which I am not now privileged to enjoy. But it would surely be rash to postulate such social relations in order to assure myself that an electron 'finally' is what I and my human associates are found to be when I know *them* most satisfyingly—a center of emotional concern. No such conclusion seems at all necessary in order to allow us to recognize that we know some physical objects incompletely or that other objects, sentient organisms, which we do know more about, have feelings and that this fact is essential to an adequate understanding of them. Yet that is all that the abstract-concrete contrast serves to establish, unless, of course, we are committed to a speculative identification of what is most humanly complete—what fills out our own experience most vividly—with what is existentially pervasive. I cannot for my own part see the slightest reason for supposing that hosts of entities in the world around me may not be as 'vacuously actual' as they appear to be. They *may* have feelings too, for all I know, but to claim that, under penalty of non-existence, they must have them in order to enjoy the type of emotional concern that renders my experience a 'complete' fact, seems a very questionable procedure.

Another type of consideration on which Whitehead lays stress in substantiating his speculative claims appeals to our rudimentary, but primary, experience of causal efficacy for basic evidence as to the nature of 'actuality'.

Our enjoyment of actuality is a realization of worth, good or bad. It is a value-experience. Its basic expression is—Have a care, here is something that matters! Yes—that is the best phrase—the primary glimmering of consciousness reveals, Something that matters.

And in this experience

the dim meaning of fact—or actuality—is intrinsic importance for itself, for the others, and for the whole.[27]

[27] *Modes of Thought,* 159.

And further,

the sense of importance is not exclusively referent to the experiencing self. It is exactly this vague sense which differentiates itself into the disclosure of the whole, the many, and the self. It is the importance of others which melts into the importance of the self. Actuality is the self-enjoyment of importance.[28]

I am not disposed to question the occurrence of such experiences; though, for my own part, I find them so very vague and dim as to be, for evidential purposes, highly inconclusive as sources of information about matters of fact in the surrounding world. I want rather to examine the process of reasoning which purports to justify the preferred status here accorded to such experiences as means of determining what actuality 'finally' is, and therefore what everything actual that has ever existed must 'finally' have been. Why should I trust my rudimentary grasp of the dim meaning of actuality as more ultimate information than physics can supply as to what is going on emotionally inside Cleopatra's Needle on the Thames Embankment? The procedure, I believe, can only be made intelligible in terms of the identification of what for some human purposes is important with what is *finally* actual and hence existentially ubiquitous.

The following passage will make the issue clear:

The deliverances of clear and distinct consciousness require criticism by reference to elements in experience which are neither clear nor distinct. On the contrary, they are dim, massive and important. These dim elements provide for art that final background apart from which its effects fade. The type of Truth which human art seeks lies in the eliciting of this background to haunt the objects presented for clear consciousness.[29]

This statement occurs in a chapter on "Truth and Beauty" and in its context has a plausible meaning. The dim background of experience is no doubt *aesthetically* important and striking effects are sometimes produced by works that appeal to it. But what is thus for immediate feeling 'profound' and 'dim' is taken by Whitehead as our best source of information about what is

[28] *Ibid.*, 16of.
[29] *Adventures of Ideas*, 348.

going on at times and places remote from our bodies, since, as immediately enjoyed, it feels massive and profound and such profundity is, in turn, our means of access to that *final* actuality from which explicit consciousness has abstracted.

Mentality is an agent of simplification; and for this reason appearance is an incredibly simplified edition of reality. There should be no paradox in this statement. *A moment's introspection assures one of the feebleness of human intellectual operations,* and of the dim massive complexity of our feelings of derivation.[30]

The italics are not in the text. I have had recourse to them to call attention to what seems to me an instructive instance of the procedure of speculative philosophy. We are asked to determine *by introspection,* by comparison of the difference in *feeling* between intellectual operations and dim awareness, the 'feebleness' of our intellectual operations. Now this is not, evidently, the sort of ground on which we should elsewhere discriminate the reliability, as information about perceived existents, of scientific description and dim feeling. Scientific statements can receive independent verification, they frequently accord with and are supported by the subsequent course of events in a way in which our dim feelings of derivation, when these are used as a basis for statements about what occurs or will occur elsewhere, are not. It is only when one has identified aesthetic importance and felt urgency with inside information as to what is finally actual and hence—once the speculative transformation is complete—with factual information as to what is going on in our bodily environment, that the cognitive preëminence of our feelings of importance as contrasted with scientific description becomes apparent. It is a procedure which, independently of such identification, would have singularly little justification.

Another instructive instance of this same type of procedure is observable when the speculative philosopher turns upon his critics and challenges them to propose any reasonable alternative to the philosophical method he has followed. Granted that he himself is taking what seems to him most important in human experience as a clue to the nature of the real world, what other

[30] *Adventures of Ideas,* 273.

course, he asks, is possible for human reason? Are not *all* our ideas, scientific as well as speculative, of human and therefore 'anthropomorphic' origin? And how else should we proceed, if we are to avoid dualism, agnosticism, and final scepticism, save by finding in experience the clue to 'reality' itself? Thus Whitehead tells us that "the philosophy of organism attributes 'feeling' throughout the actual world. It bases this doctrine upon the directly observed fact that 'feeling' survives as a known element constitutive of the 'formal' existence of such actual entities as we can best observe."[31] And why should it not? For

any doctrine which refuses to place human experience outside nature, must find in descriptions of human experience factors which also enter into the descriptions of less specialized natural occurrences. If there be no such factors, then the doctrine of human experience as a fact within nature is mere bluff, founded upon vague phrases whose sole merit is a comforting familiarity. We should either admit dualism, at least as a provisional doctrine, or we should point out the identical elements connecting human experience with physical science.[32]

This has a persuasive sound, but it does less than justice to the peculiarities of speculative philosophy. One way of "pointing out the identical elements connecting human experience with physical science" is indeed essential. It is that of indicating what it is in the behavior of perceptually observed objects and events that verifies scientific statements and thus justifies the claim that they are probably correct. In this way what we experience of the world can sometimes be reliably used as evidence of what is occurring elsewhere. But, as the history of physics has shown, this does not at all require the assumption that what is there occurring is qualitatively *like* what we most intimately observe and personally enjoy in our own experience. If that were so, Aristotelian physics would possess a far better empirical warrant than the abstractions of quantum mechanics can claim. It is one thing to use observed events as the basis for hypotheses capable of verification or of confutation by subsequent events which occur or do not occur in the manner predicted. It is quite

[31] *Process and Reality*, 268.
[32] *Adventures of Ideas*, 237.

another thing to use them in their enjoyed immediacy as samples of ultimate or final actuality, where the only available test of 'finality' is this enjoyed immediacy itself and where, in consequence, only a speculative identification of the ultimately real with the aesthetically enjoyed can bridge the gap between what is thus observed and the inner 'actuality' of existents elsewhere. To be sure, we may in this mood persuade ourselves that what we apprehend in our rudimentary feelings of emotional concern discloses the 'dim meaning of actuality'; but this too can be rationally supported only on the assumption that what is most primitively urgent for us is also existentially ubiquitous. The sciences require no such assumption and have, on the contrary, made their most impressive progress as they have departed from it.

We are justified, I think, in concluding that the rejection of the process of speculative identification of what is primitively enjoyed with what is existentially pervasive does not deprive us of all connections between 'experience' and 'nature', but only of that sort of connection which consists in generalizing the aesthetic and emotional aspect of human experience beyond the limits of the special existential conditions under which, in the case of human organisms, such experience occurs. And that sort of connection has not in the past, outside speculative philosophy, proved either necessary or on the whole very useful as a source of independently confirmable information about the world.

So again, when it is maintained that the world must be intelligible, if our reasonings are to apply to it, and that "All ultimate reasons are in terms of aim at value,"[33] we must distinguish with care between 'reasons' and 'ultimate reasons'. That the world is 'intelligible' in the sense that by processes of inquiry we can find out facts about it that we should otherwise not have known, seems moderately well established. But that the world is *ultimately* intelligible in the sense of corresponding in its structure and behavior to what speculative philosophers find peculiarly satisfying when they search for the *final* reality in their own experience, is a conclusion for which there is little inde-

[33] *Modes of Thought*, 184.

pendent evidence. The criteria for such final intelligibility are curiously shifting and conflicting as we pass from one period or school to another. Lovejoy's *The Great Chain of Being* gives a very instructive account of some of the odd and, on the basis of present knowledge, probably false conclusions to which eminent speculators have in the past, and in the name of sufficient reason and intelligibility, been led. The growth of empirical knowledge has shown little respect for the final and ultimate demands of speculative reason, save insofar as they can be substantiated by more pedestrian methods of factual inquiry. If, therefore, we insist that a denial of them, when they lack this empirical support, would leave the world unintelligible, it must be in this special sense of speculative intelligibility that the claim is made. That is to say, unless such demands were acknowledged, speculative philosophers would not be able to maintain, with a show of rational necessity, that the categories they find important in some favored area of experience—moral, aesthetic, or, if they are 'naturalists', spatio-temporal—define the ultimate structure of all that does or can exist. Thus we return once more to a now familiar line of thought.

There is one further form this argument may take that needs at this point to be considered. When critics question the necessity of assuming that everything that exists in the world is aiming at value, they are supposed by speculative philosophers to be denying that teleological process is *ultimately* actual, and hence denying that it is actual at all. But surely values are 'real' and life is earnest and what is best in human nature is not to be reduced to a mere accident in a 'dead' and 'mindless' universe. This is the process of reasoning by which one speculative philosopher destroys another, and it is highly regarded in many circles. But it is not to the point here. For it rests on the very same speculative identification of 'actual' (by contextually reliable tests) with *'ultimately'* or *'finally* actual', as the ground and basis for all existence, which is here called in question. The argument is simply working in the reverse direction: if not 'ultimately' actual, then not actual at all. Of course, the world is beautiful if in aesthetic experience we find it so, and 'meaningful' if in some measure its happenings support our hopes and strivings. Nature is not 'merely' dead if there are living organisms in it, as we know that there are, nor 'merely' blind if men can see. Nor is an 'unfeeling' nature merely chaotic, relative to human purposes, if we can sometimes make plans, as in fact we can, and count with reasonable assurance on the regularities in events to provide us with the means for their fulfillment. Such humanly important facts are 'actual' by tests appropriate to the activities in which our concern with existence passes from dim awareness to reasonably grounded belief. Nor would they be rendered dubious by a denial of Whitehead's metaphysics. I can believe that my sense of the value of existence might in some slight measure be heightened by the assurance that the minutest constituents of ostensibly inorganic objects were activated by ideals; though this satisfaction would be somewhat dimmed by the further recognition that this idealistic behavior was of such a generalized nature as to be wholly compatible with their continuing to act, in all my other commerce with them, in a characteristically inert and unfeeling manner. But to suppose that my assurance of the worth of friendship, or of courage, or of the things that are good to see and hear must be grounded on any such speculative claim, or would lose its cogency if that hypothesis were disproved, is quite incredible. That such a supposition can seriously be maintained by eminently serious men is evidence, I think, of the extent to which the requirements of speculative philosophy diverge from those which elsewhere determine the grounds and order of our beliefs.

Throughout this paper I have been concerned primarily to identify the methods characteristic of speculative philosophy and the way in which it proceeds to its conclusions. The problem that remains is to evaluate these procedures and come to some conclusions as to their appropriate place in the reasonable ordering and interpretation of experience. From what standpoint is this evaluation to be made? I have remarked at several stages in the analysis that the method speculative philosophers use is not that which *elsewhere* recommends itself to us or proves reliable. But speculative philosophy is after all a very special sort of investigation and as such is perhaps not to be bound by ordinary rules. And if its protagonists are prepared to purchase immunity from criticism by claiming for their subject a unique access to ultimate truth which only those possessed of its insights and antecedently committed to its procedures can grasp, there is little more that we can say to them, or they to us. If, however, their aim is to reach not merely 'Reality' as the appropriate object of speculative discourse, but the inclusive wisdom which an understanding of philosophic scope and penetration can sometimes achieve, we may work towards a common understanding.

It is from the standpoint of such a philosophical interpretation of the several aspects of experience—according to each its due weight and value, but allowing to none a position which narrows or distorts the rest—that the outcome of this speculative adventure can, I think, most fairly be judged. Are we able, when we apply the results of this philosophy to the world we know through all our means of commerce with it, to see more justly what is enlightening and valuable in each aspect of experience, and to estimate more judiciously the contributions that each can make to a humanly good life? What are the fruits of the speculative identification of ultimate reality in comprehensive philosophical wisdom? This is our final question, and it can be answered briefly.

Whitehead's speculative philosophy tells us that the conclusions of the more exact sciences are abstract, and that we must not 'misplace concreteness' by identifying such abstractions with the ultimate or final reality of things. This is true, and, as a counter-weight to the teachings of those who were addicted to such identification, important. It is a correction of the one-sidedness of speculative mechanism or materialism. But it achieves this insight by espousing a rival ultimate reality, to be found not at all in the 'vacuous actuality' of material process but in the inner recesses of feeling. It corrects the overstatement that nothing is 'really' purposive in behavior by the equally sweeping assertion that everything is really so. And in order to make good this contention it is forced to treat the most exactly verified statements of the sciences as 'superficial' in comparison to the dim deliverances of primitive feeling, when each is judged in respect of its capacity to provide information about the nature of what exists. This seems to me neither necessary, nor judicious, nor fruitful. Taken seriously outside the range of metaphysical dispute it would invite us to subordinate what we know most accurately to what, save as an oracle of speculative ultimacy, is a notoriously untrustworthy guide. On the level of metaphysics it invites an answering over-correction of its own overstatement from a rival metaphysics which will rediscover the merits of the exact sciences as sources of reliable information about the world and conclude in consequence that values are 'finally' unreal, since no physical test of their existence can be found. It is this unhappy conflict of thesis and antithesis, equally onesided and false, in which Hegel thought he had found the pattern of human reason. But, in fact, it is the logic not of science, or of practice, or of ordinary good sense, but only of that speculative philosophy which, by claiming ultimate and exclusively final reality for the objects of its philosophical preference, generates interminably inconclusive controversy with other pretenders as onesided as itself. It is not in this way that the store of reliable human knowledge is substantially increased.

Whitehead's philosophy gives a place of peculiar philosophical significance to aesthetic experience and to the enjoyment of beauty. This is admirable. But it achieves this result by treating a work of art as "a message from the unseen" which at its best "reveals as in a flash intimate, absolute Truth regarding the Nature of Things."[34] It thus encourages us to value aesthetic goods not 'finally' for their satisfactoriness in aesthetic enjoyment but rather, and more profoundly, as sources of information concerning the metaphysical insides, or 'formal being', of the ultimate actualities of which the world is made. The confusions to which such a procedure invites us, and the opportunities for oracular pseudo-profundities in the field of aesthetic criticism are endless, and their source is precisely that speculative identification which will not permit us to enjoy a genuine good without inflating it into a candidate for 'ultimate' reality. It is not surprising that such inflation seems at times, to those of us who have retained old-fashioned predilections for clarity and dis-

[34] *Adventures of Ideas*, 350.

tinctness, to debase our intellectual currency in a disturbing fashion.

Finally, this philosophy provides a conception of the universe "which is the justification for the ideals characterizing the civilized phases of human society."[35] And it is well, in these days of uncertainty and insecurity, that our ideals should be justified. Hence, when we read that "The basis of democracy is the common fact of value-experience, as constituting the essential nature of each pulsation of actuality,"[36] we are heartened and reassured. But the comfort is mainly verbal, and, if applied to worries about the desirability of democracy as a form of human political organization, more than a little misleading. For we have here justified the value on which democracy rests *speculatively*, i.e., by predicating it of everything that 'actually' exists, and it has naturally become a little thin when spread so widely. The value that "constitutes the essential nature of each pulsation of actuality" exists wherever anything whatever is occurring. It is realized in dictatorship as well as in democracy. It is realized in cosmic epochs in which nothing like human life as we know it could possibly exist. It is realized, in fact, wherever anything whatever is going on; for everything that exists, or did exist, or will exist has 'value' for itself and for others in this sense. If the worth which I attach to my fellow citizens had no better warrant than this speculative identification with the inner urge in everything that happens, it would be insecurely grounded indeed. It rests, in fact, on the enjoyed value of free human intercourse and coöperation and on a reasonable belief in the possibility of maintaining such goods by the governmental procedures at our disposal. To look for the justification of democracy in the emotional strivings of things in general is to do less than justice to the uniqueness of human goods. Moreover, it is as likely to lead to scepticism as to ethical idealism. For, if we persist in looking for the justification of our values where such justification is not to be found, we are tempted, when we have failed to find it there, to conclude that it does not really exist at all and that the bottom has been knocked out of our world

---

[35] *Modes of Thought*, 143.
[36] *Ibid.*, 151.

because its alleged metaphysical underpinnings are palpably insecure. That sort of scepticism is the normal response, in critical minds, to that sort of speculative justification. Values that are humanly satisfying and attainable do not need such a foundation and do not profit by its equivocal support.

In sum, then, the effect of speculative identification, when it is seriously applied to the interpretation of experience, is to 'justify' some human interests by according them a status in 'ultimate reality' which they neither require nor can reasonably maintain. Its basic fault is not that it is too philosophical—if philosophy stands for comprehensive and discriminating wisdom —but that it is not philosophical enough, for it has failed to assign to the 'ultimates' of its preferential concern a place and function which in the long run and with due regard to the whole scope of our experience, can reasonably be maintained. I conclude, therefore, that, great as Whitehead's contributions to other fields of philosophy have been, his rehabilitation of speculative philosophy is not to be accepted as successful, nor the method he recommends for it as a reliable philosophical procedure.

ARTHUR E. MURPHY

DEPARTMENT OF PHILOSOPHY
UNIVERSITY OF ILLINOIS

10

William Ernest Hocking

WHITEHEAD ON MIND AND NATURE

WHITEHEAD ON MIND AND NATURE

I. General Characters

I SHALL first put down my impression of what the salient characters of Whitehead's philosophy are, as the most concrete way of opening the questions I would now like to put to my friend and colleague. To state what I conceive his view to be is to confess what I have not grasped.

It ought to be true of a metaphysical doctrine that one's impressions of it bear some resemblance to one's direct impressions of the world. I find this true of Whitehead's metaphysics in several ways. First, it is vast enough to allow a good deal of the unfathomed to coexist with a near side allowing a sense of acquaintance if not of provisional mastery. Second, it is varied enough to present a certain qualitative adequacy: it is not stepmotherly to flesh nor to spirit, logic nor poetry, physics nor history, reason nor the non-reason of fact. In his hands, the empirical attitude becomes equivalent to breadth and candor of recognition. Third, underneath a plural and intricate surface, a disconcerting array of new categories, occasional inconsistencies (not peculiar to this system), one feels an integral character. Its complexities emerge from a scruple for justice. In working with it one acquires an intuition of its unity of view not wholly separable from one's intuition of the man himself.

i. Whitehead's philosophy undertakes to be a description of the world done in categories more adequate than we have had both to physical fact and to experience at large. In summary terms, it is an interpretation of the workings of nature on the pattern of a unit of process capable of caring for quality, rather than on the pattern of pellets or energy quanta which care for nothing. Its conceptual task is to develop the altered scheme of connections and groupings such units would exhibit. Hence it is among other things an attempt to provide exact expression for the inexactitudes of concrete happening, its degrees of freedom, its qualitative novelties.

ii. This philosophy arises not in any usual discontent with traditional frames of thought, but in a sense of scandal to intellectual conscience at some of our commonly accepted maladjustments between thought and fact. First at the violence done within geometry and physics by continuing the cracking assumptions of the Newtonian epoch, and the further violence done by the excess-revisions of Minkowski and Einstein. Second, at the violence done to experience by taking the physical world-picture as metaphysically primary, and the further violence done by those who would rectify this error at the expense of the rationality of the world. Beneath the garb of a pilgrim Whitehead hides the crusader's sword and temper. He has spread through the body of a polite professional philosophy the sense of a momentous task to be done, and has stirred a cleverly critical age to the renewed duty of constructing a metaphysics.

iii. Whitehead's construction springs from a striking freshness of impression achieved against the pressure of a 'learned tradition' which it is one of his pleasantries to put into its place. The interest of Plato comes from the fact that Plato had never read Aristotle. The advantage enjoyed by the Greek mind is that there was no Greek tradition before it. Partly with Greek aid, Whitehead overcomes the handicap of living in the 19th and 20th centuries with an incredible weight of intellectual history on his head, recovering much of that early attack and experimental boldness, and giving us rather like an era than like a single individual a flood of impulse and a gallery of inchoate conceptual forms. It is a human gift to be able to acquire naïveté; it is what Lao Tze called "returning to the root:" to do so to this extent is, in my judgment, as important a deed as to set up an impeccable list of primitive notions.

With the learned tradition Whitehead also distrusts the subtle commitments of language, which buckets along the convenient acceptances of common thought. It is characteristic that *Process and Reality* opens not with a *credo* nor a set of postulates, but with a *repudio*, whose point ii rejects confidence in language as a well of philosophy.

Of the same piece is his preference for "naïve realism" as against the sophisticated realism of Russell, which he characterizes as 'an indefensible half-way house'. 'Russell's private world is but a private dream of a public world. The naïve realist conceives mentality as adventuring amid realities, not amid dreams. Mind is inside its images, not its images inside the mind: I am 'immersed in a topic' in mathematics, not the reverse. We are actors in scenes, not the scenes inside us."[1]

I suspect that his revolt against the 'bifurcation of nature' begins with his sympathy for Greek thought,—and earlier. 'The savage sees the devil moving things. No doubt the human race begins by thinking wrong,—but not all wrong. We are still engaged in criticising and shaping discernments which have always been in the race.' 'Broad objects to getting the different lines of thought together, feeling, enthusiasm and the rest. But why not? Experience does not come in compartments. We cannot keep the sciences apart, still less their objects, such as the physical and the mental: it is almost childish to attempt it. The thing is, to *cut across in new ways;* get your religion into your physics, and your physics into your aesthetics.'

iv. A descriptive metaphysics does not come forward with a proof of its case: but it has its assumptions which constitute starting points. The philosopher's good faith consists in announcing the assumptions he makes—when he is aware of them. And since they occupy the paradoxical position of initial finalities, such assumptions should be 'intuitions' in the sense of what one 'sees' to be true with sufficient assurance to put it forward as premiss. They are points of accepted vulnerability.

[1] Much of my discussion in this paper will have reference, beyond actual quotations from Mr. Whitehead's published writings, to personal discussions and informal conversations. In such cases I shall put Mr. Whitehead's words, as I recall them, in single quotation marks, which will serve to admonish the reader to take them as illustrative, not as *ipsissima verba*.

Whitehead is peculiarly liberal in these assumptions, and although it belongs to his bent to choose them in wholly personal fashion, he commonly puts them forward as deliverances of common sense, positions which it would be a bit foolish not to take for granted. Let me draw up a few of these intuitions, such as I find carrying the main load of his argument.

(i.) Reality is becoming. 'It is passing before one,—a remark too obvious to make. You can't catch a moment by the scruff of the neck: it's gone, you know!'

(ii.) There are no primary substances. 'The notion of a static world of independent entities is baseless'.

(iii.) Flux realizes 'eternal entities'. 'Every statement with a touch of generality in it is meaningless without the eternal. ... The comparison of distinct occasions is an appeal to the eternal exemplified in each. ... All reference to possibility is a reference to something in the occasion which is not occasional. ... The fact that there are particular occasions is an eternal fact. ... Unless there is the eternal in this sense there is no science and no metaphysics.'

(iv.) Togetherness is never an external relation. 'Togetherness is not a mere abstract form: it makes a difference what the elements are. Each is something for the other, as chairs are something for the users.'

(v.) Perception deals with the actual, not with representations of the actual. 'I never could see why we should be born dreaming of another world'.

(vi.) Action intends to affect real being outside myself. (*SMW*, 126. Cf. Bergson, "*L'action ne saurait se mouvoir dans l'irréel.*")

(vii.) There is no All-One. 'All reality as one entity is nonsense'. 'Becoming is not managed from without. There is no stage manager. Becoming is its own explanation, includes its own motive and motive power.' 'I am very near to absolute idealism, when you take the finite as an abstraction; the slightest push would push me over. But where I differ is, your Absolute is a super-reality. My point is, when you try to get a ground of reality more real than the given, you get an abstraction: your super-reality is an under-reality. Reality is always emergence into a finite modal entity.'

v. It will be observed that many of these dicta are negative, expressing negative intuitions, things that cannot be true. Without strong negations, no reform. This holds true of descriptive metaphysics. As a description it is an essay in artistry,—the world sits for its portrait. But all great artists are something of the rebel, and all rebellion has to have its devil.

Whitehead has at least two such (not persons, but doctrines),—Aristotle's doctrine of primary substances, taken as an echo of Greek subject-predicate syntax, and the dualism of Descartes, which with the substance-doctrine is credited with spreading through modern times the poison of bifurcation. Absolute monism is another evil, but (for a refreshing change) not the chief culprit.

The demon of substance has the precise fault of Lucifer, self-sufficiency, implying external relation to other substances, inherent immortality, stubborn timelessness at the core, shipwrecking every attempt to account for change. 'If activity is of the essence, you have got to recast your categories, putting at the foundation that which acts, a unit urge of self-formation'.

To say that the elements of being are not self-enclosed is to say that they are permeable to each other. It is this which provides for Whitehead's philosophy the designation 'organic'. 'The entities take account of one another. What happens is an emergence, a fusion of entities, a mutuality. When I regard myself as in a real room, it is as in something beyond myself; and there is an emergent value, a unity of room and self. There is a becomingness of structure, almost a relation becoming a substance. A structural togetherness is being realized.'

vi. I have reserved for separate mention two assumptions which do not come into frequent emphasis, and which pull in somewhat contrary directions. Perhaps I should call them persuasions. One that the world is not simple. The other that it has unit beings, and of one kind.

When Copernicus and Kepler worked on the theory of planetary motions they were able to assume that the simpler solution was the truer: this premiss was essential to their argument. The formulations of Einstein have spoiled the assumption of simplicity: they have introduced a complicating term even into the laconic Newtonian synthesis. The breach between macroscopic and infra-atomic physics constitutes another violation of nature's simplicity. Prior to this, Richard's determinations of the atomic weights had already robbed the theory of chemical elements of the beauties of Dalton's law. Simplicity ceases to be a useful heuristic principle in physical investigation. The same is true in the realms of art and of law. We recall Sir Henry Maine's witty critique of the ideals which promoted equity as an appeal to principle from the crooked turns of statute law. A distrust of simple formulae seems to lie at the basis of much of Whitehead's categorial scheme.

On the other hand, he assumes that there are units to be discovered, and that these are of the same kind. To support this view, he falls back on an "ideal of cosmological theory"[2] which sounds suspiciously like a part of the learned tradition. "The presumption that there is only one genus of actual entity constitutes an ideal of cosmological theory to which the philosophy of organism endeavours to conform."[2] This ideal certainly receives a degree of recognition in the fact that most atomists, monadists, and personalists have found it sufficient to adopt a homogeneous pluralism. Some, however, have considered that they must have both material atoms and souls; and others, doubting whether the fields of the universe and the forces at play there could be derived from the unit entities, have felt themselves driven to a heterogeneous pluralism in which space, time, energy and quality appear as independent factors. The homogeneous pluralism has the advantage of simplicity. And simplicity here means theoretical power: for the greater the number of your independent assumptions, the greater the number of problems you create at the outset,—problems of the relation of one type of entity to another. The ideal of a monism-of-kind, therefore, is an ideal of all explanatory theory, and is cognate with simplicity.

I judge that the coexistence of these two contrasting persuasions is inescapable, for a realistic view of the intricacies of the world requires the one, and the business of theoretically mastering it requires the other. The drift toward some sort of monism is inseparable from the speculative enterprise.

[2] *Process and Reality,* 168.

vii. A persuasion of Whitehead's which is not wholly separable from the distrust of simplicity is the rejection of the 'clear and distinct' as a criterion of truth. And with this, the rejection both of sensation and of conscious judgment as primary aspects of reality.

Does common sense allow us to believe that the operations of judgment, operations which require definition in terms of conscious apprehension, are foundational? . . . Those elements which stand out clearly and distinctly in our consciousness are not its basic facts. . . . Late derivative elements are more clearly illuminated by consciousness than the primitive elements . . . Neglect of this law produces most of the difficulties of philosophy.[3]

viii. These several intuitions and persuasions govern the meaning which Whitehead gives to the 'real', and the character of his unit entity.

The 'real' for Whitehead is the concrete thisness of the process going on within us and before us: whatever enters into the weaving of experience is derivatively real because the weaving *is* the reality. Three current notions of the real are thus explicitly rejected: (1) that the real is permanent being in any form; (2) that the real is something irrationally believed in, behind the web of experience; (3) that the real is transcendent unity of feeling, experiential in nature but beyond those explicit shapes which are 'inconsistent if taken as real'—a phrase which for Whitehead all but summarizes Bradley.

This sharp rejection of any transcendent element in the 'real' raises the question whether the contrast of appearance and reality retains any significance. Whitehead's answer is that the term 'reality' is useful: there is a *becoming real*, ergo, a less real if not an unreal. We can perhaps best approach the meaning of the word via the notion of 'realization', which is the bringing of an idea into particular being, as the gift of a boat may 'realize' a boy's dream. I have been inclined to define 'reality' by way of the notion of dependence: the real is that independent being on which other beings depend; and the relation of dependence may, obviously, take us behind the scenes in search of the independent. Whitehead objects to definition by dependence on this account,

[3] *Ibid.*, 244ff.

and further because dependence is likely to be a one-way relation, irreversible, whereas for him the distinction between appearance and reality is relative, and what is appearance from one point of view may be real from another. The task of philosophy, as he sees it, is to "conciliate its conceptions of a real world" with what is there before us.

The unit entity, then, in which this notion of the real is embedded, is—to state it paradoxically—a unit of *becoming real*. It is not a term whose definition is self-identity, though it has self-identity. It is certainly not a term in the equations of mathematical physics. It is not a monad, though the ingredients going into a monad have a strong family resemblance to those which enter into the 'actual occasion'. Like the monad, the occasion has a mental and a physical pole and contains an image of the universe. But this image, for the occasion, is veridical, not a mirror. And unlike the monad, the occasion does not last: its essence is transition. It is, in one sense, all windows: its relations to the rest of the world are its vital spark. It is an experience; and 'an' experience is the universe from a particular point of view. But it has this in common with substance,—it is not composed of these relatednesses, it is something in itself. It is subject, and in this capacity its being is a self-enjoyment and a self-realization.

If anyone at this point were to recall a portion of the learned tradition, dated about 1807, to the effect that "Substance must be raised to subject," I think there would be a degree of assent. But there would be two modifications. (1) The dictum would be pluralized,—"Substances must be raised to subjects." (2) And we should be warned that subjectivity must not be considered to imply consciousness and thought, inasmuch as consciousness only arises "in the higher phases of concrescence."

ix. So far as Whitehead's metaphysics is descriptive, it has to be taken as one takes the report of a traveler,—not as a matter of debate, for what a man sees he sees. The intuitions are the important part of the story: the conceptual web is subservient to them. This web must indeed be considered on its own merits: it has to expound the intuitions, to display inner relevances, to show power in capturing elusive meanings. But it has chiefly to answer the questions we have to put to the intuitions themselves, by way of better grasping what they are.

These intuitions must be consistent with each other: they must cohere, even if they do not imply each other.[4] They ought to escape old difficulties and provide paths for experiment. They ought not, in the long run, to raise more difficulties than they allay; though at first all new paths are more difficult than an old road. And they ought to make the world more intelligible than before,—which is tantamount to saying that a good set of intuitions, with the categories belonging to them, will to some extent explain even while they describe.

I believe that Whitehead's method of description intends to accept these responsibilities. It is certainly not an empiricism which stalls within a supposed 'given'. It recognizes the contingency of what is there ('You can push contingency back and back, but you never seem to get rid of it. . . . You can't give a reason for history'). But the scheme moves toward rationality. To rest in the given is to rest in the opaque. Empiricism per se is the acceptance of opacity, that is to say, of mental subservience in the universe. The original cult of empiricism in modern times had a different temper: as a revolt against authority it was a call on every man to use his own eyes, a democratic note in knowledge. The latter-day cult of empiricism has been a democracy of cognitive grovel,—the stoppage of knowledge at what sense shows,—the common servility of mankind before a datum which they must accept and ask no questions. Whitehead moves out of this cul de sac.

His 'description' is the discovery of idea in the fact.[5] We cannot make descriptive judgments of universals alone—this is Bradley's failure: he cannot find *this* wolf eating *this* lamb, but only a universe characterized by wolfiness eating lambiness. But it is as great an error to ignore the universals: experience is not composed of physical particulars. 'We cannot go a step beyond experience, but we must go all the steps that experience imposes on us. . . . In each particular occasion there is to be discerned

[4] *Ibid.*, 5.
[5] Intuition iii, above.

some eternal basis for all occasions. . . . Broad seems to think that there is a certain definite observational wage-fund! But observation of nature is infinitely more delicate because of poetry (for example), which leads us to perceive associations and relevancies. The occasion is always more to us because of its significances.'

Description at this level becomes interpretation, and is a fair subject for discussion. It is to be judged not alone by its success in revealing new lines of ordering experience, and by its inner consistency, but also by its power to promote our understanding of the world, which is the true task of metaphysics.

II. MIND AND NATURE

x. I comment specifically on Whitehead's treatment of the relations between mind and nature partly because this seems to be the jumping-off place from his philosophy of nature to his general metaphysics; but chiefly because it seems to me to present his most striking contributions and his most serious difficulties.

A preliminary word is necessary on the development of Whitehead's treatment. Beginning with a recognition that no superficial revision would deal with the conceptual confusion within geometry and physics, Whitehead was little inclined to assume as data all the paradoxes which a good Einsteinian is expected to believe before breakfast. Physics is not to be merged with geometry out of hand: the world of physical events may have its regional peculiarities of structure, but geometrical space retains its absolute uniformity. Nor is psychology to be invoked to rescue physics. None of the apparent anomalies of nature are to be understood by reminding ourselves that there is a 'mind' taking cognizance of them, the observer qua mental does not affect the thing observed. This meant simply that mental occurrences have nothing to do, and never can have anything to do, with physical equations. This situation, which I believe absolutely sound, and consistent with all Whitehead's later work, is somewhat violently expressed by the noted phrase, nature is 'closed to mind'. All that is required is that mind be a non-differential factor. This is consistent with two suppositions, either that nature is 'closed to mind' or that it is uniformly open to mind.

The point which Whitehead was trying to save was not a realistic metaphysics,—he was not at that time talking metaphysics: it was the autonomy of physics, or of pan-physics. He was defining physical nature as "an assemblage of factors within fact" so far mutually inter-referring as to constitute a system complete in itself. It is, in the mathematical sense, a closed group.[6] This consideration should have spared Whitehead the criticism of inconsistency as he developed his modified subjectivism, even such inconsistency as is implied in progress toward the truth. There is no progress from earlier to later on a topic which the earlier does not treat.

Meantime, his polemic against the bifurcation of nature made increasingly insistent the question how that clean-cut physical system was to be supplemented. For the 'secondary qualities' were not entering into its equations as operators. They were certainly present in the terminal situations from which the system departed and to which it returned; but they were no part of that "assemblage of factors within the fact" with which physics was dealing. Any synoptical view of experience must include them and also the minds which are indubitably there. In some way these two supplementary elements presumably belong together. But not as represented in Berkeleian or Cartesian subjectivism. In *Science and the Modern World*, the intuitions are mentioned which lead him to reject this answer. Among them this, that "We are within a world, and not the world within us." The 'world' here means nature in its colored and sounding concreteness: it is this concrete world which surrounds me, was before me, and will be after me, and is therefore no product of my creativity.

In *Process and Reality* and all later works the solution is adopted in the form of a 'revised subjectivistic principle' supplemented by the 'objectivistic principle' which we have noted. There is no 'vacuous actuality', no *res vera* which is not self-enjoying. There is the developed theory of prehensions, which

[6] Cf. on this point, my paper on "The Group Concept in the Service of Philosophy," *Journal of Philosophy, Psychology and Scientific Method*, (Aug. 2, 1906), Vol. III, No. 16.

run the span from "blind physical perceptivity" to conceptual thought. The 'theory of strains' brings feeling and physical fact into close conjunction. In *Nature and Life* the important remark appears that in a sense I am in the world, and in a sense the world is in me.[7] This is a development.

But it is not merely the presence of quality as an integral part of nature that governs this growth of theory. It is the *history* of quality as well. It is as qualitative, and only so, that nature presents a 'creative advance'. It is this directionality, characterized by the incessant emergence of novelty and of significant togetherness, which calls for factors in some sense mental or teleological.

It is Whitehead's achievement to present the process of nature as a co-operation of causal and teleological factors, in which the strict autonomy of the causal order, so far as it can finish the description of event, is scrupulously preserved.

xi. The first comment I wish to make is that the 'actual occasion' is not a term of description in the direct sense. It is an hypothesis. It cannot be kept in place by pointing to its presence as a datum: it can only hold its own if it proves to be a valuable conceptual tool. It shares this character with the electron. But the electron is upheld by precise verification of precise prediction, whereas in the nature of the case the 'occasion' cannot secure such support. It can have at best the general support derived from the consideration that if the world were a world of 'occasions', concrete nature would be a scene of qualitative change; and it is such a scene.

xii. As an hypothesis, the 'occasion' carries us in the direction of earlier views of the world in which animation was presumed to be widespread. The direction of mental progress, broadly speaking, had been to restrict the area of nature taken as animate. The substitution of 'forces' for mental agents, and of 'laws' for forces, is indeed of no definitive philosophical meaning: it indicates an intention to examine nature by exact measurement,

---

[7] Pp. 40-42; cf. *Modes of Thought*, 224ff. esp. 227.

and for the rest a mere resignation of knowledge. The expulsion of final causes from Galileo's formulae has not expelled them from the universe. But the operative value of these dementalized formulae has given them an air of sufficiency.

Nevertheless, the hypothesis of pervasive animation recurs. Fechner and Paulsen, Verworn (*Protistenstudien*) and Haeckel, McDougall and Driesch, have all been impressed by "the insufficiency of mechanical explanations;" and (being pre-emergentists) felt obliged to trace the thus-certified mentality of organic beings genetically back into the supposed 'inanimate'. The proposal of Whitehead is far more cautious: it is not offering any universal *Beseeltheit* of nature. It links happenings by 'prehension', not by consciousness; the very word forbids identifying this function with apprehension. Yet there is a kinship in the type of hypothesis, as in the pressures which lead to it.

For Whitehead, one of these pressures is the incapacity of 'emergence' to stand as a primary principle of cosmology. Emergence is the name for a problem, not for a solution: something has arrived which is not provided for in the antecedents,—to give such events a common name is merely to signalize a recurrent mystery. Further, there is but one emergent entity: consciousness. All the others 'emerge' *for* consciousness: the properties of chemical compounds are increasingly predictable,—it is only the saltiness of NaCl as compared with the acrid tang of KCl which has to be discovered, and by the tasting tongue. Given your subjectivity, every occasion becomes unique: hence the subjective principle is prior to qualitative emergence, not itself an emergent in the same sense. This is recognized in Whitehead's theory.

I raise the question, however, whether the pervasiveness of this subjective principle, as comminuted in the unit occasion, is justified by its theoretical value.

xiii. Suppose we argue as follows:
Everywhere in nature there is a creative advance marked by the ingression or emergence of new qualities;

The 'actual occasion' with its subjectivity and prehensions is requisite for this emergence;

Hence, the actual occasion and its subjectivity are universal.

Such an argument assumes that the bifurcation of nature is dismissed, since for physical process alone there is no creative advance. If now we are dismissing bifurcation in any degree by aid of the conception of the actual occasion, our argument runs in a circle. To be sure, non-bifurcation is an intuition, and to this extent a premiss. But this is the juncture at which the intuition attempts to embed itself in the theory, each supporting the other. I ask then first whether the concept of the occasion does eliminate the scandal of bifurcation.

xiv. It belongs to the concept of the occasion that it prehends nature itself, not in representation; and therefore that the qualities it prehends are *there*. But what is meant by saying the qualities are there, in addition to the fact that I perceive them as there? To say that the red of the sunset is "in nature" is not an explanation, it is the position to be explained. It can hardly be said to be localized physically in the sunset, for the sunset is not localized. To say that it is there as enjoyed by the sunset is no better, for who is the sunset and where? To say that it is there as enjoyed by the occasions composing the sunset would appear untrue, since the redness is a function (unless physiology deceives us) of sunlight plus atmospheric siftings plus a special eye-position: as a part of a sunset it is a phenomenon involving at least three terms widely separated in space, hard to attribute to any other subject or series of subjects than the one original observer.

But assume, since this triadic situation is in nature, and its intermediate phase as a localized sheaf of red rays is also there, that the occasions subjacent to these rays are self-enjoying events or parts of such and that they enjoy themselves as red, not as rays alone. Does this save the integrity of nature? Only at the cost of denying that the experience of redness by the rays themselves is subject to the triadic relatedness required for *my* perception of redness. There must then be two kinds of red-experience, one of immediate and unconditional self-enjoyment, and one of prehension under specific conditions. The self-enjoyment of the external occasion is no part of these conditions: neither physicist nor physiologist is able to take it into account. These scientists are obliged to treat my awareness-of-red as an event which follows upon other events from which awareness-of-red is absent. If this situation is not escaped, bifurcation is not escaped.

For bifurcation *arises solely from the view that perception results from conditions which are non-perceptual*, whether this view takes the form of a transmissive theory in which (as for Galileo) the activity emanates from the object, or the form of a prehensive theory in which the activity emanates from the subject. For in either case, nature as perceived cannot be identical with nature as the totality of the conditions of perception. We must count two, and separate the two in quality.

If to escape this result, perception is made direct and unconditional, the physical context is repudiated as part of the real. That Whitehead intends no such sacrifice is to be inferred from his "theory of strains:" here he points out that "the present perception is strictly inherited from the antecedent bodily functioning, unless all physiological teaching is to be abandoned."[8] And were we to make this sacrifice, still perception is unveridical. For while we perceive the qualities, presumed there, we do not perceive those external occasions which are (or were) entertaining them. If we only perceive the qualities and not the qualities-as-enjoyed, we are not, according to the theory, perceiving them as they are;—the appearance lifts away from the reality.

xv. If then the theory of occasions cannot save the world of nature from that double aspect which is called bifurcation, it becomes a live question whether it can hold its own as a theory.

Without it we have a simpler situation. The sunset is red for me, and for others similarly situated: it is not red 'in itself' and certainly not 'for itself'. In itself it is at least, whether for Whitehead or for Galileo, the physical-mathematical system of events which includes in its seamless mesh the brain-events subserving perception. In any theory, that system must be given some kind

[8] *Process and Reality*, 475.7.

of ontological status, and it must be different from the status of perception. There is then no need on any theory to duplicate my experience of red-sunset in its qualitative character, by assuming a galaxy of preceding prehenders or self-enjoyers. They are theoretically otiose.

And without them, nature is *not* bifurcated in the strict sense of the word. Bifurcation can hardly mean anything but a two-forking in which what goes into one fork does not go into the other, neither fork being complete. If the whole were on one side and a part on the other, the fork-image ceases to apply. But this is the situation: nature is complete *for me*, and what is abstracted off into the set of physical conditions is a part of the whole. It was Berkeley who first felt the scandal of bifurcation, and to cure it reunited the primary with the secondary qualities in the same ontological plane. It was not the right plane, that of 'ideas', but it did achieve an integration of nature, without that piecemeal duplication which complicates Whitehead's picture and yet does not save the principle of objectivity.

xvi. But there are also positive reasons against the theory of actual occasions. They derive from that field of value in which, as Whitehead rightly observed, the metaphysical conspectus which can bring together mind and nature has to be sought. They come particularly from a consideration illustrated in cosmic history in its broadest phases.

Whitehead justly remarks that the direction of change is toward a more structural togetherness. This, I presume, is what Herbert Spencer was driving at under the name of 'integration' with a wholly different set of illustrations in mind. But Spencer, Hegel, and to some extent Charles Peirce, recognized that integration was always attended by an accentuation of differences, and of the gulfs between types. Continuities are plowed across by deep-going furrows, and the species become islands of determinate form. Now this gap-making process has held as between the organic and the inorganic aspects of nature, with their different types of response. The inorganic limits not the range but the kinds of entity to which it responds: the organic with far less range extends its response to kind without limit. The tugs pulling at a steamer take account of its momentum, its stream-bearing and the like: they care nothing for the anxieties and urges animating captains and crews, and are unable to respond to them. Now the point is, that this *selective and limited response of the inanimate is valuable* to the captains and crews. They rely on the emotional insensitivity of ropes and propellers: they must be able to add or subtract horse-power and to ignore the emotions of laboring engines. It has a definite meaning that whole aspects of nature shall be devoid of self-felt meaning, and thus be open to exploit without compunction.

These considerations touch primarily on facts of cosmology, but also broadly on the field of ethics. It belongs to the teleology of the world to clear a part of the world forest of all trace of teleology, except in its total drift. If we insist on endowing nature with microcosmic livingness, we inject an ethical scruple into all action. So far as occasion merely prehends occasion there is no intrusion of being on being; but occasions do not limit themselves to prehending: there is clash, interruption, occlusion, suppression. An entity capable of self-realization and self-enjoyment must be capable of frustration, of calamities of position. If all is organism, no organism can act without affecting organism; and what is ignorant and crude in our molar relations to the infinitely sensitive galaxies of elementary occasions about and within us can only be conceived as blindly destructive. A voluntary rigor mortis would be the requirement of realization: a voluntary *unsympathy* a condition of survival. In brief, the ethical requirement upon cosmology is that beings capable of affecting one another for better or for worse must live within range of possible communication. Organicity must be able to draw itself into a society, which however vast, must be small in comparison with its inorganic environment.

Otherwise natural piety is destroyed at the root; for the inner working of things can hardly be accidentally beneficent when the unit occasions must accept as their destiny whatever fate the including masses unknowingly impose on them.

xvii. The original error, I believe, is in an unwritten assumption of Whitehead's method. Observing rightly that one cannot derive (for example) change from changelessness, he assumes that the alternative must be taken of deriving change from change. It is this which requires him to bring into his initial set-up all the fundamentally diverse ingredients of the world. But what he fails to observe is that if you derive change from change you do not derive it at all,—you assume it. If this principle is consistently followed, your theory assumes everything it has to account for, and therefore deals only in circles.

We seem to be in the presence of a perfectly good dilemma: We must either explain things by what they are or else by what they are not. If we explain them by what they are, we leave them unexplained. If we explain them by what they are not, our explanation is fallacious. (The same dilemma exists if instead of 'explain' we read 'describe in terms of'.) This brings all metaphysical effort to so sudden a halt that we must examine the case farther.

I shall call one of these procedures 'homeotypal explanation', the other 'heterotypal explanation'. Seeing that heterotypal explanation, in the case of change, attempts to derive the fluent from the static, Whitehead renounces it, as did Bergson, Bradley, and Zeno. Whitehead and Bergson adopt homeotypal explanation, process shall be understood by event not by substance,— and thereby, though with much greater subtlety, fall back on the old metaphysical device of explaining a phenomenon by an 'essence' of the same sort. What physics has discovered is the *non-fertility of homeotypal explanation:* heat is not motion; but it is better to explain heat by motion than to refer it to the calorific principle, for while we leave a mystery we get a fertile correspondence, which is part of what is wanted.

The same holds good in metaphysics. We do not account for change by introducing an atom of process into our first principles, nor for creation by a principle of creativity, nor for the arrival of any quality by the presence in the universe of an eternal entity of that sort which, under proper circumstances, can realize existence. Nor do we account for mind as we know it by disseminating through the universe germs of mentality in a comminuted and diminished condition.[9]

[9] The failure of the principle of 'emergence' is on a similar ground. It has to account for the new and different. It sees the futility of accounting for the new by the old, which was the ancient fallacy of evolution. But it also feels dimly that

But if homeotypal explanation is empty, heterotypal explanation is absurd. From the discrete we can get no continuity, from number no extension, from the point no magnitude, from matter no mind, from mind no matter, from the static no change (and from the flux no endurance?). In the matter of points and magnitudes, the method of "extensive abstraction" arises from perceiving and rejecting this absurdity. If the point is in truth a zero of extension, you have in hand precisely nothing and you can do nothing with it. If we are to have a geometry based on exactitude, and exactitude based on the point, then points must be somehow pregnant with lines, areas, and volumes. Then they must have bowels: let them be classes, pointed classes, classes of areas shooting toward an inner nothingness, but never putting finger on the limit nor knowing what they are shooting at. From such points we can derive geometry, for we have packed geometry into these interminable vestibules of postponed punctuality.[10] From something we can derive something.

Now Whitehead is not afraid of Hume; but such analyses as these, with their boundless ingenuity, still seem to me to exhibit the sort of palsy which Hume has spread over the analysts of the last century. Hume's dictum is—no heterotypal explanation: there can be no rational passage from something to something else. Then, since all passage is passage to something else, including causal passage, all passage is irrational.

I should like to join in the general praise of Hume's acuity, and I will: but Hume's mental conscience was, I fear, more

---

accounting for the new by the new is uninstructive. It therefore signalizes the fact of novelty, and ascribes to the world a tendency for novelty to arrive in unpredictable fashion! This is homeotypal explanation not in respect to what arrives, but in respect to its novelty. On such a scheme, underivableness acquires a sort of positive scientific merit of a perverse sort. Naturally the wisdom of the emergence principle has to be retrospective, for it has no power to exclude anything whatever from arriving and therefore no power to account for anything that arrives.

[10] Of course, 'postponed' is a bad word, because the vestibule is said to be the very point we are seeking, as though infinite deferment were punctuality itself. However,

> If, limping, we are told
> The journey to the rainbow's foot,—
> It *is* the pot of gold,

we have to anticipate a collapse: the journey has lost its point!

tricky than candid. Like Zeno, he was more interested in making a neat point than in telling as much truth as he knew. That passage is always to something else, and that the logic of identity will never get you across,—that is an observation worth making. But Hume knew very well that the something else is not 'anything else whatever': it is always a related otherness. Having made the first observation, he should have made the second one, to point out the relevance of B, the second state, to A, the first one. Whitehead has done this, and in doing so has come to the verge of solving the dilemma of heterotypal explanation.

When Aristotle spoke of 'potentiality', he was not falling back on homeotypes. He was saying that if A is something quite definite (let us avoid the word substance) and yet capable of development or of response, it will change not in general but in a specific manner, just because it is itself: it belongs to its being A that it entertains the conditional possibility of becoming B. Let us generalize this and say that there are beings of which it is true that "the more they change the more they are the same thing": and in such cases heterotypal explanation ceases to be absurd. The hope of metaphysics is to find such cases and to consider whether they belong among our primary data. If we find them, the complexity of our structure will evidently be much relieved; for if one being may become another, that one accounts for two, and the ideal of simplicity may again take courage.

xviii. It is this purely logical consideration which gave rise to the demand of 1807 that substance must be raised to subject. Neither Aristotle's primary substances nor Spinoza's one substance could satisfy the heterotypal requirement. Physical entities, whether material or energetic, had as their prime merit a calculable identity; even in respect to the incessant motion of nature, principles of conservation in one form or other enabled the observer to treat nature-process as an identical whole,—a most valuable trait for those who propose to change things, since all intelligent action must assume that the universe in other respects holds sufficiently steady while this act occurs! That is one reason why physics moves away from the realm of quality and value: it must consider change not as the arrival of novelty but as the translocation of the same thing. Matter and energy do not afford heterotypal explanations. With mentality the situation is reversed: mind is the sort of thing which has to change in order to be itself, and which is heterotypal to all its objects. It is for this reason that subjectivity is metaphysically fertile as physical nature is not. And we have here an added reason for holding to the non-subjectivity of the detail of physical nature.

xix. In these remarks I have but touched the fringe of great subjects which Whitehead has so greatly treated. He has reversed the trend which expelled final causes from nature on the mistaken assumption that their presence must sully the purity of scientific method. This fight for expulsion had for its aim to secure for the objects of physical science a group cleanness, closed to mind. I share with Whitehead a jealous regard for that cleanness. I would prefer to secure it by considering nature as uniformly, that is to say non-differentially, open to mind. The final causes inseparable from mentality will then assume what seems to me their actual relation to the mesh of physical happening.

It is not that causes and purposes *mix* in this mesh, so that an uncertain problem of the resolution of components has to decide what part is due to each. Neither do causes lose their measured perfectness, nor purposes account for deviations from the strict line. *Telos* ($\tau\acute{\epsilon}\lambda o\varsigma$) ought not to be identified with aberration. Rather, *telos* is the whole, and causation is its instrument and organ. The causal picture of the world must be an integral picture, calculable and impersonal, in order that it may be a fit tool for the purposes of *telos*.

But if there is a complete causal story of the world and at the same time a complete purposive story which is history, we have a dual record of the same process. Bifurcation in this sense cannot be escaped, nor should it be avoided in a world in which we have two views of every mental fact, that of self-awareness and that of the exterior physical apparition. The unity of nature in its reality lies in the fact that what conscious beings are aware of *is* its reality. The physical version of happening, in abstraction from quality and meaning, is not a denial of the purposive version, nor vice versa: the physical is the external language of the purposive, that is to say, its symbol.

These are my questions, put with renewed gratitude for the content and spirit of Whitehead's knightly adventure of ideas. From no man have I received so wide a sense of the dignity of the human calling to think the world; from no man have I learned so much.

WILLIAM ERNEST HOCKING

DEPARTMENT OF PHILOSOPHY
HARVARD UNIVERSITY

II

Roy Wood Sellars

PHILOSOPHY OF ORGANISM AND
PHYSICAL REALISM

PHILOSOPHY OF ORGANISM AND PHYSICAL REALISM

THE purpose guiding this essay is to assist in the clarification of the philosophy of organism by means of queries and contrasts. It is my understanding that the editor of this volume, in asking me to contribute, was led to do so by his belief that the postulates, or principles, which have, rightly or wrongly, dominated my philosophical outlook differ rather sharply from those operating in Professor Whitehead's thought. These basic differences do, I am persuaded, exist and a rather detailed indication of their presence in both epistemology and ontology should be stimulating. I confess that such confrontation of basic differences has been challenging to me and has led me to feel the need for more adequate analysis and more precision in statement. Needless to say, I shall look forward to Professor Whitehead's comments with the greatest of interest. They should enable me to see more clearly just where and why our paths diverge.

The general ingredients of the position developed in *Process and Reality* are indicated in the running historical commentaries which furnish one of the delightful features of the book. It is evident that Plato's teaching is integrated with that of Descartes and Locke. Leibniz's attack upon the Cartesian idea of *res extensa* is in the background while, coming to more recent times, the influence of Bradley, Bergson, and Alexander is acknowledged. Modern physics has obviously exerted its effect in the stress upon events, rhythms, process and relativity. One quickly notes the rejection of the category of substance interpreted as simple endurance. Such simple endurance is held to be the illusion supporting what may be called the tradition of eleatic materialism with its stress upon changelessness and simple location. The alternative adopted to such simple, or undifferentiated, endurance is an endurance explained in terms of something more ultimate. Appeal is made to the more subjectivistic Cartesian category of *res vera* as given a reformed, realistic extension along lines suggested by neorealism and confirmed, in his opinion, by later passages in the writings of Locke. The result is a massive movement of construction from the microscopic to the macroscopic, from minute, rhythmic beats of becoming to a semi-Platonic, immanent and supervenient God. The reader is always aware that it is the mind of a present-day thinker that he is observing in operation. He is, I think, conscious of the basic choices being made all along the line and of the motivations, scientific, epistemological, logical and ontological, dominating the perspective.

Suppose we begin with certain admittedly generic labels to indicate these basic choices. The following immediately occur to one: Platonism, panpsychism, neorealism, eventism, atomism, relativism. Of course, qualifications and specifications must immediately be introduced. His Platonism is more theistic than Plato's, his eternal objects more tinged with the quality of feeling. Cartesian subjectivism points in the direction of modern idealism. Again, his panpsychism does not emphasize consciousness or, perhaps, even sentiency; so that "feeling" becomes a technical term expressive of his rejection of the idea of vacuous actuality. It may here be pointed out that his assignment of consciousness to a high-grade actuality savors of C. A. Strong's form of panpsychism in his book, *The Origin of Consciousness*. Finally, Whitehead's neorealism of prehension seems at the level of sense-perception to prepare the way for something akin in certain respects to critical realism.

It is not long before one realizes that there is here working a daring and persistent mind, aware of the need for subtle distinctions and challenging novelties and ready to throw overboard traditional categories. Almost offhand I note such features as the aforementioned rejection of the category of substance. I cannot help querying whether it could not have been reformed; whether he is not intimidated by a conception bound up with what I have called eleatic materialism, as this appeared in Newtonian physics. Philosophical thought with respect to the category of substance has been much richer than this implies. It must not be forgotten that Aristotle formulated his concept of substance in an attempt to meet the *impasse* of Megarian eleaticism. And, in our own day, Johnson continued this effort at development and clarification. I merely mention this point here for I shall take it up at more length later. Suffice it to say, that eventists have made a basic choice in their rejection of substance, and I am not convinced that it has been a wise one. Again, I note a reaction against Humian sensationalism and scepticism, a reaction with which I am largely in agreement. There is the attempt to justify the causal category in an objective eventist fashion. And here comes his recognition that induction must have an ontological basis, a position with which, again, I sympathize. In fact, I find myself quite exhilarated by this philosophy in the grand manner. Continuing this enumeration of outstanding features, I would call attention to the thesis that sense-perception is a superficial mode of knowing as against the more basic intuition of process.

Yet, curiously, for all his apparent radicalism, Professor Whitehead turns out to be a conservative in many matters. He is opposed to naturalism in any of its forms; he is a theist; he flirts with the idea of immortality; he believes in religious and moral intuitions as significant guides in ultimate matters; he accepts universals and hardly considers it worth while to examine nominalism; he holds that potentiality must be explained in terms of eternal objects envisaged by God and ingredient in actual occasions and not by the activation of dispositions in natural, material systems. In all this I take him to be logical. Having made his basic choices he abides by them and clear-sightedly grasps their implications; yet all of this gives a physical realist, who has defended evolutionary naturalism, critical realism, ontological nominalism and humanism, much pause for thought.

Professor Whitehead has been a coiner of phrases to express his rejections. I take two of the most effective to have been the "fallacy of simple location" and the "bifurcation of nature." The first I shall consider in my defense of substance. There I shall argue for an adjectival view of space and time and real connections in nature, a development which also rejects the schematism of classical physics. But I have never been quite certain as to the precise meaning of the phrase, "bifurcation of nature." Does it mean merely a rejection of Cartesian dualism? In that case the evolutionary naturalist with his notion of the emergence of mindedness and consciousness would agree with him. Does it mean that the traditional distinction between primary qualities and secondary qualities does not fit in with neo-realism, prehension and idealism? Then I would assent; but I would reply that critical realism can reform the distinction by asserting that we intuit sensory presentations but abstractly describe physical things in terms of quantity, structure and behavior, a description which by no means exhausts the being of the objects so described, as we know in the case of ourselves as organic things known in two ways.

Since epistemology will play a considerable part in the contrasts which I wish to indicate and comment on, it may be well to point out that critical realism is, in its essentials, an attempt to reform representative realism by doing justice to the factors and distinctions which reflection elicits in a careful study of perceiving. Its primary thesis is that perceiving is denotative, depictive and judgmental and that sensory presentations are used as guides, symbols and bases of judgmental characterization. Now, it was long the fashion to deride any such attempt to reanalyze and reform representative realism. I well remember how impatient such a kindly man as S. Alexander was at the very idea of such a project. And, in this country, Woodbridge and Dewey were convinced that epistemology was something of a monstrosity resulting from Cartesian dualism. How can ideas in a purely mental realm know things in a physical domain?

Now critical realism, as I interpret it, is free from Cartesian dualism for the simple reason that the knower is the embodied self which is concerned with and characterizes the things around it in the same world with itself. I shall have something more to say about this situation when, later, I discuss Whitehead's comparison of his position with that of Santayana. At present I merely want to suggest that he seems to me to start from a neo-realistic modification of idealism. Sensory presentations are thought of as continuations of the just past. It might be called a unique development of *an eventist kind of neorealism.* There are successive intuitions of past feelings. Here we have the doctrine of objective immortality and the functioning of one species of eternal objects in a sort of conserved and substantial-istic fashion, that is, if resort is not had to God. Such a line of procedure seems to me entirely logical within its perspective. I would only point out that, since I do not believe in Platonic universals, this construction is precluded for me. But I might well query whether eternal objects are Platonic or Aristotelian. Are they only *in* actual occasions? Or do they have a status in-dependent of them, though in God? I have already suggested that I am even to the left of Aristotle in this matter. But I should like to know the existential relation between eternal objects and feeling. I have, myself, always thought of feelings as particulars and in no sense reducible to universals. The naturalistic panpsychism of men like Strong and Drake did take this view but, then, for them feelings had the status of sub-stance, that is, of mind-stuff. And, since Whitehead relinquishes any kind of stuff, it would seem that an actual occasion is con-stituted out of universals; only, as I see it, a sentient kind of universal, a concrete and not an abstract, universal. Such uni-versals would seem to function almost like a stuff, that is, to possess a kind of undifferentiated duration. They are *eternal objects.*

Because this alignment is important it must be explored and contrasts made. I take it that the whole doctrine of prehension, so far as it has a cognitive and not a dominantly causal meaning, stems from the perspective of neorealism, that is, presentational-ism. I remember how a Korean student of mine, who was very much of a mystic, felt drawn to the organic philosophy because it meant a kind of direct participation in things. The best the critical realist could do was to claim that sense-data were so causally conditioned that things *appeared* in them, that is, that they were *such that* they could properly be used as materials for knowing. To know a thing did not involve any literal participation in it. At least this was my form of critical realism which stressed similarity and representationalism. I take it that Santayana with his theory of essences which makes possible a literal identity, or participation, is really nearer to Whitehead's view and to neorealism than I am. These points will come up for discussion later. Mr. Whitehead writes:

Actual entities involve each other by reason of their prehensions of each other. There are thus real individual facts of the *togetherness of actual entities*, which are real, individual, and particular, in the same sense in which actual entities and the prehensions are real, individual and particular. Any such particular fact of togetherness among actual entities is called a 'nexus' (plural form is written 'nexūs'). The ultimate facts of immediate actual experience are actual entities, prehensions, and nexūs. All else is, for our experience, derivative abstraction.[1]

This *togetherness*, which covers both the togetherness within any actual entity and among actual entities, is important for Whitehead's thought. He has difficulty, however, in extending it to contemporary actual occasions because of his temporalism, with its backward glance so far as the physical pole is concerned, and because of his acceptance of relativity. This latter point had best be taken up in connection with the mode of presentational immediacy, that is, with what is ordinarily called sense-perception. It is in this mode that some critics have thought to note a position more akin to critical realism interpreted as an indirect, or nonapprehensional, kind of knowing. But it seems to me to be mainly a more hypothetical form of neorealism. The interesting feature of it to me is the acknowledged presence of symbolism and of categories such as endurance. It is his thesis that sense-perception fosters illusions leading to eleatic materialism.

Although this is not a novel thesis, it deserves consideration. Certainly any one who wishes a reformed conception of substance must bear it in mind.

In our perception of the contemporary world via presentational immediacy, nexūs of actual entities are objectified for the percipient under the perspective of their characters of extensive continuity. In the percep-

---

[1] *Process and Reality*, 29f. (Italics mine.) (References to *Process and Reality* throughout this essay are to the American edition, 1929.)

tion of a contemporary stone, for example, the separate individuality of each actual entity in the nexūs constituting the stone is merged into the unity of the extensive plenum, which for Descartes and for common sense, *is* the stone. . . . Thus the immediate percept assumes the character of the quiet undifferentiated endurance of the material stone, perceived by means of its quality of colour. . . . The stone, thus interpreted, guarantees the *vera causa,* and conjectural explanations in science and philosophy follow its model.[2]

I do not doubt that there has been a great deal of picture thinking of this sort and that conceptions of substance off the main line of philosophic thought have been dominated by them. Classic physics and Locke in his substratum schematism are instances. It will be my endeavor to show how a more critical form of epistemology can unite with a more activistic ontology to escape the eleatic and Cartesian picture-thinking which is a theoretical restatement of the illusions of naïve perception. The problem, as I see it, is to reform the category of substance without following Leibniz into spiritualistic pluralism.

Whitehead is rightly emphatic in his recognition of the interplay of epistemology and ontology on this point. It is by means of his conception of togetherness as combined with a neorealistic idea of participation that he hopes to avoid traditional pitfalls. The accent is upon internal relations of a felt, or psychologistic, type. Hence his neorealism swings in the direction of idealism. Relations are internal and not external. I stress this point because critical realism in the form I developed sought to meet the problem by distinguishing between different species of relations, so-called; some of them not really being relations but facts whose discovery was made possible by mental relatings or comparisons.

Perhaps a few words should be said about these species of relations, for I regard the clarification as tremendously important for both epistemology and ontology. Thus, I would distinguish between (a) physical connections, which I take to be a *togetherness* of physical substances in a field or neighborhood which is a condition of transeunt causality, (b) logical or ideal

---

[2] *Process and Reality,* 119f.

relations such as similarity and equality, and (c) relational feelings and felt compresence in consciousness. These relational feelings are, in my opinion, a partial disclosure in a privileged case of the unity and togetherness intrinsic to substance. In *Evolutionary Naturalism* I made these distinctions and indicated their relevance to epistemology and ontology. Thus I pointed out that logical, or ideal, relations are of the nature of facts about the compared terms to the effect that they are equal or alike and are not expressive of literal connections between the terms compared. The mental relating makes the act of judging possible; but the declared facts are about the objects. I use this idea in my denial of the literal existence of a cognitive relation between my knowledge-claim and a transcendent thing made a denoted object. I take this analysis to be quite essential to critical realism, and I wonder how far Whitehead would allow it in knowledge of contemporary occasions in the mode of presentational immediacy.

The last on my list are relational feelings and felt compresence in consciousness. Here, I take it, we have the species corresponding to his ·experiential togetherness with its aesthetic or psychological note. I judge that he would deny relations of the type of physical connections between reformed substances which I, as a physical realist, accept. Perhaps I can best illustrate what I have in mind by saying that I regard the human organism as an emergent substance having an integrated wholeness and powers and dispositions going with that wholeness. It is not a mere society or nexus. It has a unity expressed in its actions. It and its powers involve a substantial integration resting upon physical connections.

We have here a basic divergence which demands exploration. As an emergent evolutionist working on a realistic basis, I have been led to stress organization and integration as ontological facts and therefore to reject eleatic materialism of the billiard-ball type. But this meant, to me, not a plunge into subjectivism but a basic challenge to extreme atomism. It signified that togetherness in nature meant a synthesis in which components entered into new and intimate relations such that a genuinely novel unity emerged with characteristic capacities and properties. I was led to think of an emergent causality, transitional between transeunt and immanent causality, an emergent causality creative of a new and differentiated substance. And, in a sort of Aristotelianism of the left, this meant to me that the substantial reality was a formed material system, an emergent "real essence"—to use Locke's term—in which internal relations were of the degree and kind made possible by the energies involved. In this fashion I hoped to get rid of the vitalistic, nonevolutionary element in Aristotelianism, with its stress upon forms as dominant entities, and to recover an emergent causality closely linked with the ideas of process and integration. This line of reasoning seemed, as time went on, to agree with developments in physics, chemistry, biology and psychology, which emphasized fields and *Gestalten*.

Now the curious implication of this emphasis upon organization is that it seems to me that mine is more a philosophy of organism than is Professor Whitehead's. In the microscopic cross section of the contemporary world of actual occasions, he is an atomist, even though these atomic occasions participate in a common past. I, on the other hand, as a reformed substantialist, hold that there are coëxistent substances, expressive of different levels of evolution, which are the scenes of transeunt, emergent and immanent causality. For such a setup relational propositions become as significant as subject-predicate propositions.

As I understand his position, Mr. Whitehead believes that this perspective is precluded by basic epistemological and ontological principles. It is my impression that we here run up sharply against the deadlock between neorealism and critical realism. Mr. Whitehead writes:

All metaphysical theories which admit a disjunction between the component elements of individual experience on the one hand and on the other hand the component elements of the external world, must inevitably run into difficulties over the truth and falsehood of propositions, and over the grounds of judgment. The former difficulty is metaphysical, the latter epistemological. But all difficulties as to first principles are only camouflaged metaphysical difficulties. Thus also the epistemological difficulty is only solvable by an appeal to ontology. The first difficulty poses the question as to the account of truth and falsehood, and the second difficulty poses the question as to the account of the intuitive perception of truth and falsehood. The former concerns propositions, the latter concerns judgments. There is a togetherness of the component elements in individual experience. This 'togetherness' has that special, peculiar meaning of 'togetherness in experience'. *It is a togetherness of its own kind, explicable by reference to nothing else.* . . . In either case, there is the unique 'experiential togetherness'. The consideration of experiential togetherness raises the final metaphysical question: whether there is any other meaning of 'togetherness'. *The denial of any alternative meaning, that is to say, of any meaning not abstracted from the experiential meaning, is the 'subjectivist' doctrine.* This reformed version of the subjectivist doctrine is the doctrine of the philosophy of organism.[3]

In this passage we have, packed together, all the essentials of the divergence between physical realism and reformed subjectivism. It is clear that the quotation emphasizes the rejection of representative realism as involving all the difficulties confronting the correspondence theory of truth. If there is a disjunction between a proposition and what it is about; and if what it is about consists of a state of affairs in an external world which transcends the component elements of individual experience—how are you going to pass judgments and test them? Whitehead argues that you are confronted here with a basic metaphysical problem. The point to note is that he takes his side with the critics of the correspondence theory of truth, so far as this involves transcendence or, as he calls it, disjunction.

I must confess that I do not like the term, disjunction, which savors of Cartesian dualism with its separate domains. The critical realist is not a Cartesian dualist; at least, the physical realist is not. I would hold that sensory presentations are events which are in causal continuity with the things which we are concerned about in perception. They are employed as indices and guides in both denotation and predication. Instead of a Cartesian dualism we have a setup in which a minded organism is responding to the things around it which impinge upon it through the sense organs. As I see it, the divergence, correctly grasped, involves the existential status of sensory presentations. I would hold them to be of the nature of events in the knowing organism,

[3] *Process and Reality,* 288. (Italics mine.)

generated therein as a result of transeunt causality from the environment and apprehended and used by the said organism in its high-level, conscious, cognitive response. There is no existential disjunction here; it is rather a case of organic selves in responsive contact with their environment. Consciousness and mind are regarded as adjectival to such organic selves, and appeal is made to evolution in terms of emergent causality. But it is quite clear that such a view had to work out a revolutionary conception of the so-called cognitive relation, that is, it had to deny that guided denotational reference meant any literal transcendence of the conscious field of the knowing self. In perceiving this book before me, I am guided both indexically and predicatively by the sensory presentation aroused causally in me; but what I am concerned with and judge about is the book, something which I regard as in my environment, a substantial complex other than myself and not produced by my perceiving it. It is my opinion that many who deny this kind of intentional reference do not see that it is entailed by any recognition of selfhood. It implies that my sensory presentations, meanings, and acts are mine, and that I do set myself, my activities and data, sensory or propositional, over against what I am dealing with and concerned with. There seems to me nothing mystical or mysterious in this quite empirical and empirically verifiable meaning of an intentional reference based on organic response.

Now, as I understand his position, Whitehead gives up such a self as savoring of substantialism. Hence this epistemology and metaphysics are closed to him. It is fascinating to see how thoroughly logical he is here as els ˜where. Thus he avowedly takes the path of reformed subjectivism, in which there is a realistic overlapping of prehended occasions and no substantive self, in preference to the path which physical realism takes, which recognizes a substantive self and is a reformation of representative realism. The decision is basic. From it will flow his Platonism and his rejection of naturalism and humanism. Let us get it clear. The philosophy of organism rejects a substantive, though emergent and differentiated, organic self with powers, dispositions, constitution and functions, aroused sensory activities, transcendent reference, the correspondence theory of the meaning of truth in such a context, any significance to substantial connectedness as within and between physical things. If this interpretation is correct, the lines of the debate are set.

On the whole, I would say that neorealists, pragmatists, and idealists are logically on his side but are less intransigent and a little more flabby. Thus, the majority of the new realists simply weakened before the facts of illusion and error; while the pragmatists rested their case upon a blanket experience which never faced up to reformed subjectivism or never realized the categorial complexity of the self which is the empirical source of the meanings used in perception. Whitehead hardly does full justice to an enduring self. Idealism is so protean in shape that a brief characterization in this context is difficult. One would, however, be justified in saying that it rested upon a rejection of the correspondence theory of truth and upon the postulate that physical categories are either unthinkable or phenomenal.

Yet, whereas it is clear that Whitehead's epistemology expresses an attempt to get back to presentationalism in terms of prehensions and the becoming of the subject-superject, it is undeniable that, at the level of sense-perception which is less hypothetical, his analysis of symbolic reference has a surprising amount of material in common with the theories of critical realism. For instance, I know that Strong, Drake, and I had for years emphasized the importance of motor, organic response for the explanation of denotative, symbolic reference. I suppose the chief difference between our interest and Whitehead's was, first, that he was primarily interested in the element of causal efficacy in seeing with the eye and touching with the hand; and, second, that he did not regard the mode of presentational immediacy, with the categories which seemed to go with it, as significant as it was to us. I hope to take up both of these points later.

But, to come back to the passage quoted: Am I right in assuming that Professor Whitehead was basically convinced that any form of representationalism faced insuperable difficulties? That was a natural assumption, but, in my opinion, an unfortunate one. Yet I am personally glad he made it; for in no other way would we have had a mind of the first order devote itself to the exploration of a "reformed subjectivism."

Since the chief purpose of this essay is to clarify contrasts, I shall dwell a little longer on this primary decision. As I see it, the metaphysical theories he is rejecting are of the type called Cartesian dualism. And what he says about them would be echoed by Dewey, Bradley, and Woodbridge. And yet I would distinguish. I have always rejected Cartesian dualism and yet maintained critical realism as against idealism, pragmatism, and neorealism. This has meant for me an "under-the-hat theory of mind" and the kind of denotative symbolism and representationalism I have indicated. I think Professor Whitehead is quite right when he asserts that epistemology always is ultimately inseparable from ontology. To me a person's conscious experience is intrinsic to his organism—and I think that, in a somewhat different fashion, it is so for him.

I must postpone the task of presenting the chief elements in any reformed substantialism until later. At this point a few words upon the correspondence theory of truth are in order.

Professor Whitehead is persuaded, as are so many others, that there can be no testing of the truth of propositions about denoted things to enable us to decide whether we judge correctly when we assert that such propositions are true. It is a metaphysical difficulty, he asserts, entailed by a *disjunction* between the component elements of individual experience and component elements of the external world. So put, the difficulty would be insurmountable. But the critical realist would not admit the validity of this formulation. There is no such complete disjunction. Any adequate theory of truth must assign a basic rôle to sensory presentations as indexical or referential guides and as verificatory or evidential grounds. As I see it, the divergence between his position and mine is that he turns away from the mode of presentational immediacy to the, to him, far more interesting mode of causal immediacy. The stress is upon extreme temporalism. I, on the other hand, emphasize the status of sensory presentations in the setting of perception, regarding them as causally mediated, and as generated in the organic self, and yet as furnishing the raw material for a directed cognition of things co-real with the organic self. I have no doubt that it is a fact about our constitution and situation that sensory presentations are so used.

But what does this imply? Simply that, *if* we do attain knowledge about our environment—and I think that we clearly do—our sensory presentations must be in some fashion iconic, or appearances of the things which they are used to indicate. I doubt that much sense can be given to sense-perception without such an implication. It is for reflection to work out the proper theory of the status of sensory presentations and the reason for their cognitive value.

Now Whitehead, as well as the critical realist, accepts a causal theory of data. The doctrine of objective immortality of actual occasions is a principle used to account for a causal reproduction or conformity of an almost conservational type. Now, the nearest I would come to this would be in the theory that memory images depend upon the activation of brain-patterns established by past perception. The concern of the critical realist lies with the functioning of sensory presentations at the level of presentational immediacy. And here he would argue for a causal control of such presentations, such that they are in some measure conformal to, and appearances of, their causal control. Hence, there is here no such complete existential disjunction as Whitehead seems to regard as the opposite of his position. A correspondence theory of truth of a realistic sort, accordingly, holds that particular perceptual propositions denote and make predications about things correlative to the organic and responding self; and that such denoting and predications are guided and verified by sensory presentations used by the responding and cognizing organic self. So responsibly connected and referred, a perceptual proposition makes a claim to denote and disclose the characteristics and location of things. To say that a proposition is true is to assert that this claim is, on the evidence, justified; and that the denoted thing *is* as it is characterized. Such assertion of trueness *implies* that the propositional content corresponds to the characteristics which it is used to disclose. In other words, verification always rests upon empirical evidence; but the whole operation works within the almost automatic operational assumption that sensory presentations are significant for the things the organic self is responding to. I take some pride in pointing out that, for this view, guided intentional reference involves no literal transcendence of consciousness nor a mythological "relation of similarity" between the proposition and the denoted thing. That things are similar is a fact about them. In short, knowledge *implies* similarity and such similarity *implies* that sensory presentations are appearances of things. As I see it, we must either be agnostics or accept this assumption, which is a working assumption of the organic self. It is, however, a working assumption which can be given a rational foundation in a causal theory of sensory presentations. Such is the critical realist's reformed version of representative realism.

I am now ready to put general agreements and differences, as I see them, in the following fashion: Both Whitehead and I hold to a causal theory of sensory presentations and both of us supplement them at the level of sense-perception by insistence upon a background of bodily and interpretative response; but Whitehead is inclined to belittle sense-perception and its accompanying categories and to be suspicious of the substance-predicative perspective, while I seek to explore a more critical development of sense-perception and its categories. The consequence is that he turns inward to a reformed subjectivism with its empirical complexities and suggestions and proceeds to speculate in terms of prehensions, process, teleology and ingredience. The physical realist, on the other hand, presses back of any superficial Lockian substratum to a reformed materialism which stresses such categories as endurance, organization, behavior, dispositions and potentialities; that is, he would lay emphasis upon the development and use of categories in external cognition from sense-perception onward and would hold that self-awareness assists in the comprehension and clarification of such categories.

Thus we come back once more to the really basic problem of categories and their implications. The physical realist thinks in terms of categorial meanings of an objective sort. The organic self is just one thing among other things, in commerce with them. Hence, sense-perception is reanalyzed to bring out the element of thinghood operating within it. Judgment is made explicit, and the scientific conception of the world replaces the schematism of sensuous qualities stuck on an undifferentiated substratum. This point is important and signifies that sensory qualia, as such, are considered subjective and intra-cerebral. Emphasis is placed upon abstract indications of structure and behavior which can fit into and explicate the categorial scheme of self and things. This categorial scheme demands an enrichment in terms of spatial and temporal and causal connections, all conceived in harmony with a substantival matrix.

Now, as I study Whitehead, I am more than ever convinced that our paths diverged in large part because of our different analysis of sense-perception. While, following neorealism, he thought of it as an affair of sensing, I regarded it as a rather confusing mingling of sensing and judging. The more I traced the implications of the judgmental phase, the more I felt the projective, but validated, operation of the organic self. Things perceived are as real as ourselves and we are in commerce with them. Such a perspective involved an objective togetherness conceived in terms of categories. He, on the other hand, did not have this categorial matrix which is only possible for an epistemological position akin to critical realism. The result was that he fell back upon psychologism, that is, upon a togetherness conceivable only on the experienced foundation of felt, aesthetic compresence.

We should by now at least be aware of the basic assumptions and decisions dividing the two philosophies we are engaged in examining and contrasting. In the one, there is the rejection of any reform of representative realism and categorial substantialism and the adoption of a subjectivism reformed along the lines of a daring eventist form of neorealism. It is a magnificent endeavor, and one should expect terminological novelties and conceptual obscurities. If the direction taken is the correct one, philosophy will gradually make it its own and slowly achieve clarity. In the other perspective, which is admittedly less novel and more in line with a *naturalistic philosophia perennis,* there is the attempt to reanalyze perception to elicit its judgmental categorial ingredients and to develop a *Kategorienlehre* which will link such an epistemology with a naturalistic ontology. This basic divergence manifests itself quite logically and definitely in the varying theses about "togetherness." While the physical realist distinguishes between the objective, categorially conceived togetherness expressive of, and relevant to, the texture and behavior of things and selves and the subjective, aesthetic compresence involving relational feelings, Whitehead, quite logically, plumbs for a complete rejection of the first and a concentration on the second.

In order that the reader may see that the basic decisions discussed above are central, I shall permit myself again to quote:

The contrary doctrine, that there is a 'togetherness' *not derivative from experiential togetherness*, leads to the disjunction of the components of subjective experience from the community of the external world. This disjunction creates the insurmountable difficulty for epistemology. For intuitive judgment is concerned with togetherness in experience, and there is no bridge between togetherness in experience, and togetherness of the non-experiential sort.[4]

He then proceeds to assert that subjectivism, when combined with sensationalism, involves either a retreat to Leibniz or an advance to Bradley. It is by the doctrine that one actual occasion can be objectified in another that he believes he can escape. Each actual entity is a throb of experience including the actual world in its scope.

Here is the watershed between physical realism and the philosophy of organism. The first takes the path of objective, denotative reference and employs carefully elicited categories, such as things, causality, structure, function; while the other, as I see it, introspects and takes the path of a monadism with windows, a monadism of atomic occasions expressive of an ultimate creativity operating under the control of God. All of Whitehead's doctrines follow quite logically from this rejection of physical realism; and no one can doubt the imaginative daring of his metaphysics. But it may well still be queried whether he did not take a path involving something of a *tour de force*. Certainly, a thinker like myself who does not possess his type of moral and religious intuitions—or shall we say traditions?— is more inclined to reanalyze the categories of common sense

[4] *Process and Reality*, 288f. (Italics mine.)

and science. I shall, therefore, in the main leave it to other panpsychists to query his treatment of the intricacies of the subject-superject, and devote myself to a clarification of the status of the category of substance and intrinsic duration in relation to objective togetherness. Whitehead's challenge is explicit.

Descartes' discovery on the side of subjectivism requires balancing by an 'objectivist' principle as to the datum for experience. Also, with the advent of Cartesian subjectivism, the substance-quality category has lost all claim to metaphysical primacy; and, with this deposition of substance-quality, we can reject the notion of individual substances, each with its private world of qualities and sensations.[5]

Let us try to bring these difficulties to a head. As I see it, Whitehead is convinced that the category of substance in its Aristotelian form is misleading and superficial, for it neglects relations and does not furnish a basis for scientific induction. Also, it reflects the rather superficial knowledge emphasized by sense-perception, to wit, the assignment of qualities to things, as in the judgment: This stone is grey. The traditional assumption that substances require nothing outside themselves in order to exist makes them unable to tell a tale about the survival of order in their environment. Furthermore, Hume was unconsciously dominated by this tradition, even though he had accepted the subjectivism of Descartes. His minds were, to all intents, isolated mental substances.

Now a reformed materialist like myself recognizes the validity of these criticisms. If we are to keep the category of substance it must be profoundly modified and reinterpreted. Stress must be laid upon connections and fields and causality and change. This much I have already indicated. But these modifications are not, I take it, difficult to make. The truth is, that Aristotle had begun to crystallize science along the lines of natural kinds and vital forms. Modern science finds the Ionian perspective more open and less specialized. And, as a matter of historical fact, the science of the seventeenth century got much of its philosophic inspiration from Democritean and Pythagorean

---

[5] *Process and Reality*, 243.

sources. Professor Aaron makes out a good case for the influence which Gassendi, an Epicurean, had upon Locke, a view which, as he points out, was entertained by Leibniz. The query, therefore, is inevitable: Why must it be assumed that things are *not* connected up with their environment? A fresh eye and an acquaintance with scientific facts concerning adjustment and equilibrium lead to a reintroduction of connections, integrations, and functional dependence. The intriguing thing, of course, is that the philosophy of organism is seeking to do by means of windowed monads what the physical realist is trying to accomplish by a less eleatic conception of matter.

Having adopted different principles, our paths diverge more the farther we go. Starting in both epistemology and ontology, the divergence continues into religion and theology. The category of substance, it should be noted, has always been in unstable equilibrium. Decrease the amount of vitalism and formal teleology in it and the trend in it was always toward the left, that is, toward naturalism. It may be recalled that even St. Thomas was accused of giving too much encouragement to the devotees of nature. Now physical realism represents in essentials a line of development to the left of Aristotle and more continuous with Ionic thought. Professor Whitehead turns back to Platonism. Eternal objects in some measure point beyond the actual occasions in which they are ingredient; in some sense they are other than their instances. I, as a critical materialist, argue for what is loosely called nominalism and might better be called particularism with similarity. But more of this contrast later.

To me the high value of Whitehead's thought is ontological. It is a serious alternative to any form of materialism. In this respect it is far more stimulating than any traditional form of experientialism, such as Dewey's, which never really grapples with ontology. Perhaps this aspect of his thought comes to a head in the treatment of duration. Is duration an ultimate characteristic of physical being? Or is duration something secondary to be derived from rhythmic becoming plus objective immortality? These are the topics we must next consider.

It seems to me that, for Whitehead, God and eternal objects give the foundation for endurance and thus make rhythmic becoming possible. In other words, becoming is never a creation *de novo*. At the best, it is a sort of integration of eternal objects of the two types, an organic integration symbolized by the term feeling. Feeling becomes here a sort of relational term indicating the birth of something akin to what the idealists call a concrete universal. It indicates the rejection of abstract universals which have not had in them the breath of life and creativity. Now I can understand the logic of this construction, even though I am sceptical of the building stones.

The substantialist approach has been determined by different material. By its logic it has sought to explain events in terms of active changes within a physical system involving both intrinsic duration and a capacity for alteration. Such categorial thought has, I admit, been tantalizingly difficult. Misconceive intrinsic duration and you get eleaticism. And those who have been dominated by picture-thinking, that is, as Whitehead argues, by naïve realism of the searchlight variety, have tended to fall back upon a billiard-ball conception of matter. But the critical realist escapes from this temptation by his emphasis upon the judgmental use of the data of observation in the light of categories such as structure, behavior, and substance. In the light of this more critical approach, endurance does not entail passivity and the absence of such traits as connections, organization, dispositions, constitution. Certainly, modern science, as it moves from the world of the evolved and integrated downward, never arrives empirically at isolated particles of an eleatic type. What we always have is a field, a relational complex, elements in their domain, something coëxistential, dynamic and productive of change. But such change is an alteration of constitution and not a loss of endurance. In other words, as I see it, change is adjectival, that is, it must be conceived as applying not to the constituents of being but to their constitution. Another way of putting it is to hold that the base of change is activity and that activity involves an alteration of constitution but not, in any sense, a lapse of that which is active. In scientific language energy-changes do not conflict with the conservation of energy; being does not use itself up. To me, this means that duration is intrinsic to nature.

As I have suggested, the proper alignment of the categories is not an easy matter. But I am convinced that the critical materialist can so order his categories that for him, too, reality can include process. There must be constituents which are never intrinsic, eleatic isolates, but whose very nature it is to be tensionally connected in a system. Any such system has a constitution which is subject to change; but such change does not impugn the intrinsic durational character of the constituents.

And, when all is said, does not Whitehead arrive at an analogous analysis? Does he not postulate eternal objects as the constituents which lend themselves to the event of becoming? Does he not have the antecedent nature of God with its envisagement of essences? Here we have operative the tradition of transcendentalism, of emanation, of a conserving cause. All I would suggest is that naturalism has an intelligible alternative. It must rethink substance in terms of basic categories. In the context of subjectivism Whitehead has defended much that I also would defend. For example, he backs the realistic insights of Locke against Berkeley and Hume and stresses the importance of an objective, or real, causality for ontology and induction. Here, again, I am impressed with the fact that his demands are essentially those of the physical realist and that we are in league against logical positivism. And yet he ultimately takes the high Platonic road, whereas I take the route of a re-thought naturalism. The divergence rests in part upon different epistemological and ontological analyses.

It will be recalled that Descartes rejected the intrinsic endurance of both *res extensa* and *res cogitans*. Both were secondary and dependent substances. Hence, he was led to introduce the traditional notion of a conserving cause, namely, God. This theory had old roots in theology and went with the distinction between a necessary being and a contingent being. It would seem that Descartes adopted this principle in part because of theological bias, in part because of a confusion between mathematical time and physical duration. Like many others since, he read the mathematical atomism of seconds into nature. In our day C. A. Strong has done likewise. But to do so is to rob nature of endurance and self-conservation. It has always seemed to me that time rests upon events and that events presuppose active endurance.

Very few eventists have faced up to the problem as well as Whitehead. Russell does not; for he takes refuge in a rather mystical conception of law. Hume appealed to habits but actually gave no ontological status to them. It can be said of Whitehead that he does not avoid the question. He frankly takes the Cartesian path.

It will be remembered that in his *Principles of Philosophy* [Part I, Principle XXI; also *Meditation* III] Descartes states that endurance is nothing else than successive re-creation by God. Thus the Cartesian conception of the human soul and that here put forward differ only in the function assigned to God. Both conceptions involve a succession of occasions, each with its measure of immediate completeness.[6]

I have indicated in a sketchy fashion the categorial scheme of the critical materialist to the left of Aristotle in order to bring out the contrast. It is evident that I am sceptical of the ability of the theistic panpsychist to derive from feeling the categorial traits I find in our thinking. Feeling seems to me something to be correlated with events, with functioning, something by its very nature adjectival to an active substance such as the organic self.

Here we are in the very heart of ontology as I understand it. In Whitehead's case I am not certain that I see clearly the status of feeling. It is a feeling that feels, a feeling that enables the subject to pass to the phase of being a superject, a feeling somehow intrinsic to eternal objects. To me, a feeling is an empirical feature of the consciousness of a functioning organic self and must be given the status of an event. It is, however, not the whole of an event but merely that qualitative feature of the cerebral event in which we consciously participate. It is what I have elsewhere called the only natural isolate or abstract. There is *more* to the cerebral event; but *this more* can not be given. As I see it, this is just the ultimate situation.

These basic queries are brought to a head by the famous denial of "vacuous actuality." I take this expression to be a very clever formulation of Bradley's famous challenge to give an instance of existence which is not a bit of experience. I remember how long

[6] *Adventures of Ideas*, 263.

I brooded over this challenge in the early days, when I was trying to think through a critical form of realism. It forced me to distinguish between *knowing about* facts and intuiting or being *acquainted with*. Let us see what precisely it is that haunts any realistic materialism. Are we in a position to think in terms of categories and facts what we cannot in a more literal sense experience? But, first, what is meant by "vacuous" here? The answer is, "The term, 'vacuous actuality' here means the notion of *res vera* devoid of subjective immediacy." It is further pointed out that the notion of vacuous actuality is closely allied to the notion of the inherence of quality in substance.

In the first place, the critical realist maintains that we can denote and characterize what we cannot intuit. Thus I take this book to be a domain of substances connected together directly and indirectly; and I believe that I know many facts significant for this state of affairs. And yet I hold that we have no participative acquaintance with it. Here is where reformed subjectivism conflicts with critical realism. Nevertheless, I maintain that all existents must have an existential content, that they cannot be vacuous. Relative opaqueness and un-get-at-ableness—to use Eddington's expression—does not involve existential vacuity. Knowledge, mediated by the sensory presentations generated in an organic self, achieves so much that it is ungenerous to say that actuality must be considered vacuous if it is not lit up on the inside with feeling or constituted by feeling.

In the second place, I feel that Professor Whitehead is, like all the neorealists, unfair to the category of substance. His substance is a wraithlike affair related to representative perceptionism, the sort of thing parodied by Berkeley. Now I hold that in the concept of substance we have the fructifying resultant of both self-knowledge and external knowledge. The organic self is *that which* expresses itself in activities such as perceiving, feeling, deliberating, desiring, willing, learning, growing, digesting, moving about, etc. It is known through these activities disclosed through experiences. Such a self is not vacuous nor is it some blank substratum to which entities called properties are attached. I suppose that the basic claim of the realist here is that knowing does comprehend its object but does not exhaust it. To know an object is not to be it. Even in self-knowledge there is, I think, this lack of equivalence between knowing and being. I would not call this agnosticism but reflective awareness of what knowledge is. Consequently I would not hold that actuality is ever vacuous; I would merely assert that knowledge presupposes a determinate and contentful reality. Of course, no experientialist, idealist, or subjectivist is ever satisfied with this element of *moreness* which is demanded by our categories but transcends sentient experience.

I cannot help but feel that Cartesian dualism has led to a belittlement of the concrete internal reality of the things we perceive, making them into something like abstract space onto which sensory qualia are splashed or stuck. Now I would reject such an outlook as heartily as does Whitehead. The real crux is with respect to the organic self. If it is *that which* perceives, wills, and experiences but is ontologically *more than* the pulses of experience, then the same must be said of the things perceived which are empirically independent of it, though less highly evolved. How does Professor Whitehead account for such characteristics as structure, dispositions, abilities? I find myself unable to reduce the self to a "route" of high-grade subjects. All of which means, again, that I do not think he has done justice to the possibilities in the concepts of organization and substantive togetherness.

Suppose we examine in the light of the above analysis his comment on Santayana.

Now the exact point where Santayana differs from the organic philosophy is his implicit assumption that 'intuitions themselves' cannot be among the 'data of intuition', . . . This possibility is what Santayana denies and the organic philosophy asserts. In this respect Santayana is voicing the position which, implicitly or explicitly, pervades modern philosophy. He is only distinguished by his clarity of thought. If Santayana's position be granted, there is a phenomenal veil, a primitive credulity associated with action and valuation, and a mysterious symbolism from the veil to the realities behind the veil. The only difference between such philosophers lies in their reading of the symbolism, some read more and some less. *There can be no decision between them, since there are no rational principles which penetrate from the veil to the dark background of reality.*[7]

[7] *Process and Reality*, 216. (Italics mine.)

While my own epistemology differs on certain points from Santayana's, especially, perhaps, in stressing the particularity of sensory presentations used in the denotative and interpretative act of perception and in rejecting a realm of essences, the basic realism remains. And we have already indicated that there is a suggestion of such realism in Whitehead's mode of presentational immediacy. In fact, the stress upon the whole bodily background as giving the sense of existence and of bodily responsive participation is somewhat shared. It seems to me clear that the causal order of stimulus and directed response functions to give structure to perception and to lift it beyond passive sensationalism. So would, I believe, Whitehead hold. And yet I think that unitary response brings up again the question of unitary, organized, substantial wholeness, a wholeness historically achieved through emergent causality. I find difficulty in grasping the equivalent in his position of such macroscopic holism. Now, remembering that Santayana is a poet, I do not take too seriously his phrase 'animal faith'. Surely, it merely stands for the fact of living response. Even human belief has been defined by Peirce and other pragmatists in terms of operative habits of response. And now we come to the question-begging epithet of "veil." The meaning of veil is that of something to obscure or shut out from view. As I see it, there is every reason to hold that sensory presentations are aids to disclosure rather than veils. Ask any blind man what he thinks about it. He knows that he lacks guidance of the kind visual presentations would give. And, as a matter of fact, does not every empiricist hold that sensory data are points of departure for knowledge? And are there no rational principles which justify a critical use of sensory presentations as iconic for indexically denoting and predicatively characterizing external things? I think there are.

I believe that the strategic thesis of critical realism is that sensing is not the same as perceiving. Sensing is by itself essentially subjective and eventist, whereas perceiving is denotative, interpretative, and objective in its reference as expressing a directed response of the organic self. This would mean a causal theory of sensory presentations as the terminus *ad quem* of a causal process and a counter referential theory of perceptual claims. Is not this a rational theory which agrees with the facts of psychology and of logic? And when Professor Whitehead concerns himself with unveridical perception in the mode of presentational immediacy as, for instance, in the case of the distant star, does he not have much the same analysis in mind? But the significant point is that, for the critical realist, knowing, from the first, concerns itself, not with this hypothetical veil, but with things regarded as co-real with agent and knower. As a matter of fact, this metaphor of veil is historically connected with Locke's representative perceptionism, that is, with the view that we first cognitively intuit ideas and then infer, or postulate, that they resemble things not given.

There is just one final point of divergence which I want to consider, that of nominalism as against eternal objects. It is obvious that a nominalist cannot be a Platonist and that what may be called the mechanism of Whitehead's system is closed to him.

It will be recalled that I argued that ideal relations, such as similarity and equality, are not really relations at all. They are really facts about objects, facts evidenced by relevant data and accompanied by relational feelings in consciousness. Now I hold that sensations are events which are qualitied, but that the qualia are as particular as the sensations. One reason is that they seem to me to be given that way; another is that I cannot conceive of a particular which is not in some fashion qualitied. In sensation, then, the ultimate is a this-here-now-what.

But why consider this particular *what* a universal? I take it that this is an operational fiction, due to discrimination and cognitive use, quite analogous to the corresponding distinction between a word and an instance of a word. In perceiving and knowing in general we are not concerned with a particular sense-datum for its own sake but as an indexical guide to the denoted thing. Again, we build up conceptual habits which are ready to make use of both sensations and images in a generic, predicative way. So-called universals are, then, really expressions of operations and discriminations made possible by the similarity of things. Were all things unique, such operations would have had no relevance. Our tendency is to read such *abstracta* into things and call them universals. Both language and calculational formulae conspire to mislead us.

Now the import of such a position is obvious. If universals are not factors in sensory experience, Whitehead's Platonic construction has no fulcrum. As we saw, it assumes that the physical pole of an actual occasion consists of universals which constitute what causally perdures and is repeated. These eternal objects are the factors which make possible the participation of one actual occasion organically in others. They give the windows to his monadic events. If there are no such eternal objects, but only sensations of a similar sort generated in organic selves, critical realism displaces neorealism; and evolutionary naturalism with its stress upon substantive organization must be substituted for the philosophy of organism. Nor is this all. Nominalism would eclipse Platonism, and religious humanism be in a position to defend itself against theism.

I know of no other philosophy that has the dynamic power to press upon one such fundamental alternatives. In my years of philosophizing I have persistently explored the naturalistic route, hoping to get clearer insight as I moved back and forth between epistemology and ontology. No other writer of recent times has so forced me to ask second questions as has Professor Whitehead.

ROY WOOD SELLARS

DEPARTMENT OF PHILOSOPHY
UNIVERSITY OF MICHIGAN

12

John Goheen

WHITEHEAD'S THEORY OF VALUE

WHITEHEAD'S THEORY OF VALUE

I

ONE OF Whitehead's most interesting statements concerning the problem of value is to be found in a previously unpublished paper entitled "Mathematics and the Good."[1] As its Platonic title suggests, this paper emphasizes the function of form and the conditions of its presence in events as fundamental in the analysis of value. Reasons internal to Whitehead's philosophy make it impossible to give a complete account of value by reference to form or the conditions of its function in nature. It is necessary as well to consider the character of the event itself as an experiencing organism if the analysis of value is to be complete. There are times, however, when Whitehead finds it convenient to separate form and the conditions of its presence in events from the description of the event as a process of feeling. In the discussion which follows this distinction will be observed only in so far as it is useful in the exposition of Whitehead's views. It is after all the event exemplifying form which is the ultimate object of Whitehead's analysis of value.

In a very general sense Whitehead characterizes value as a function of limitation. In "Mathematics and the Good" this doctrine receives the following formulation: "All value is the gift of finitude which is the necessary condition for activity."[2] Finitude is derivative from the form or pattern which is exemplified in the event in process. Pattern, whether simple or complex, imposes limitation on existence, and with the limited event

[1] The writer is indebted to Professor Whitehead for his permission to consult the manuscript of this essay. The essay will be found constituting a part of Professor Whitehead's "Reply" on pp. 666-681 of the present volume.
[2] "Mathematics and the Good."

value emerges. It is in this sense that Whitehead interprets mathematics as yielding some of the most general patterns which may or do qualify events. As realized in natural occurrences mathematical relations confer value. An event has value because it has a finite structure.

There are two ways in which this doctrine might be interpreted. First, it might be held that form or pattern is itself "good" in some way or other. This would be a Platonic view which is not, explicitly at least, Whitehead's doctrine. However, there is some justification for this interpretation in the emphasis on form or pattern and the importance it has throughout Whitehead's writings (cf. the doctrine of "unity" and the "achievement of definiteness" discussed later). Form seems to have some peculiar value significance in itself. To define exactly this element is one of the difficulties in discussing Whitehead's theory of value. Second, form or pattern might be held to be one of the factors making for value. If something exists, according to Whitehead, it possesses value. To exist implies form or pattern. Hence, form or pattern is one of the most obvious (and in Whitehead's view the most significant and important) conditions of value. This interpretation serves to clarify the first interpretation, for the emphasis on form or pattern, which is a condition of existence (and, hence, value), is an arbitrary selection among the various factors which constitute the event in Whitehead's theory. The reasons for Whitehead's selection of form as peculiarly significant in the discussion of value, either as having value in itself or as the most important and most "valuable" factor in the event, will be discussed later.

It is perhaps of some explanatory importance to note that Whitehead's conception of value under the second interpretation above approximates the views of certain philosophers of the older European tradition.[3] To exist is to possess some form (as one ontological condition), and though it be a "low" form, a thing exists in virtue of a given form and derives whatever value it has (whether good or evil) from that form. When this conception is coupled with the notion of form as the universal object of appetition, as it is for some of the traditional

---

[3] Augustine's theory is perhaps the most typical of this approach to value.

European philosophers, form takes on all the characteristics of the Good. As such this is not Whitehead's view, but it will serve the reader as a point of reference in the discussion which follows.

This emphasis on the rôle of pattern as a condition of value must be corrected by reference to the concrete event. The true locus of value in Whitehead's philosophy is most adequately expressed by the following statement from *Science and the Modern World*: " 'Value' is the word I use for the intrinsic reality of an event."[4] In the passage from which this statement is taken Whitehead uses such expressions as "definite finite entity" and "matter-of-fact entities" in order to make it perfectly clear that he views events throughout nature as centers of value. Every event functions under some pattern, but it is the event itself which is "valuable." It is for this reason that pattern can be said to be the necessary, but not the sufficient, condition of value. "Realization therefore is in itself the attainment of value."[5]

Thus activity itself (and not just pattern) is also a necessary condition for value as the substratum of pattern. Pattern and activity, the most general ontological conditions, are at the same time the sufficient and necessary conditions of value. Every event in fulfilling these general conditions is *ipso facto* "valuable." This is not to assert that every event is *Good* in meeting these general ontological conditions, according to Whitehead. Further conditions must be present or absent if the event is respectively Good or Evil. The following passage states the most general conditions of Good:

The notion of the importance of pattern is as old as civilization. Every art is founded on the study of pattern. Also the cohesion of social systems depends on the maintenance of patterns of behaviour; and advances in civilization depend on the fortunate modification of such behaviour patterns. Thus the *infusion* of pattern into natural occurrences, and the *stability* of such patterns, and the *modification* of such patterns, is the necessary condition for the realization of the Good.[6]

[4] *Science and the Modern World*, 136.

[5] *Ibid.*, 136.

[6] "Mathematics and the Good." (Italics mine.)

The good is realized when all of these conditions are met by the event or "unit of feeling." "Infusion of pattern" alone, or "stability" of pattern alone, or "modification" of pattern alone would give rise to value, since the most general conditions of pattern exemplified in an event would be fulfilled, but the necessary conditions of the good would be absent. In *Process and Reality* the "low-grade" organism is said to illustrate the mere repetition of pattern.[7] The "low-grade" organism has "stability" of pattern but undergoes little if any "modification" of pattern. "Modification" of pattern, on the contrary, without some degree of "stability" would produce sudden, revolutionary change. In the ideal process the already attained pattern of functioning must be conserved in the pattern of functioning of the future. These general conditions of the good will be recognized as guiding Whitehead's analysis of social change in *Adventures of Ideas*. The good society finds some degree of "stability" in the face of innovation or "modification" of its form.[8]

This is perhaps sufficient comment to suggest that all of Whitehead's ontology is relevant, more or less, to his analysis of value and the Good. Many of his views on value, such as those just considered, refer solely to the metaphysical structure. Others involve what might be called the "psychology" of the event as a process of feeling. In the passage quoted above it will be noted that Whitehead speaks of the "fortunate modification" of pattern. There are, therefore, further conditions governing "infusion," "stability" and "modification" of pattern which distinguish fortunate from unfortunate change. As the following passage shows, these conditions are stated first of all in terms of the event as a process of feeling:

And you cannot discuss Good or Evil without some reference to the interweaving of divers patterns of experience. The antecedent situation may demand depth of realization, and a thin pattern may thwart conceptual expectation. There is then the evil of triviality—a sketch in place of a full picture.[9]

[7] *Process and Reality*, 364. (All references to the American edition.)
[8] *Adventures of Ideas*, 331 ff.
[9] "Mathematics and the Good."

The notion of "conceptual expectation" is introduced by Whitehead to make explicit one of the relationships which may hold within the general framework of "infusion," "stability" and "modification" of pattern. It is clear from the example given that Whitehead has in mind the experience of a "high-grade" organism, man. Since, however, every event has its psychological side, some form of anticipation and satisfaction holds throughout nature. There is the "demand" for a certain satisfaction, which, when attained, is the "fortunate modification" of pattern.

The psychological relationship of "demand" and satisfaction refers to the concrete event as an experiencing organism. Form or pattern are the way in which this experience is had. If "infusion," "stability" and "modification" of pattern are the general structure of Good, it is as a structure of experience that this is the case. The Good rests ultimately in the "unit of feeling" (or experiencing organism) in just this sense. Value, whether Good or Evil, is the character of feeling which is experienced under a certain pattern of activity. The real burden of Whitehead's conception of value must, therefore, be borne by his analysis of the event as a "unit of feeling."

Following Whitehead's insistence that all philosophical discussion must have its origins in experience, it can be assumed that he looks upon the general pattern of the Good as an inference from the experience itself of Good. Value of any sort is a quality of experience, but it is not for that reason any more hidden to scientific or philosophic consideration than any other experience. Nor is it more "subjective" than any other experience which the organism "feels." It is for this reason that Whitehead undertakes to indicate the most general pattern of the Good in "Mathematics and the Good." Within this general pattern arises the question of the analysis of the psychological relationships such as "demand" and satisfaction.

These psychological relationships as such are not analyzed in "Mathematics and the Good." Whitehead chooses instead to treat them under the general notion of "adjustment." It is "adjustment" which explains, presumably, the relation between "demand" and satisfaction, and, consequently, the difference between fortunate and unfortunate "modification" of pattern. In the passage just quoted the evil of triviality is a form of maladjustment of pattern within the event. "Conceptual expectation" requires the satisfaction of seeing the "full picture," and must be regarded as a form of "adjustment" among the "infusion," "stability" and "modification" of patterns within the event. "Adjustment," therefore, governs the most general conditions of the Good.

The conception of "adjustment" plays an equally important rôle in *Adventures of Ideas*. In this latter work Whitehead introduces the terms "Beauty" and "Harmony" to indicate certain general conditions which characterize some events. "Beauty" is defined as "the perfection of Harmony." "Harmony," in turn, is defined as "the perfection of Subjective Form."[10] The "perfection of Subjective Form" is a form of "adjustment" within the complexity of feelings or "prehensions" composing the event. Beauty itself involves a complex set of adjustments within the event. In this respect Beauty is similar to, if not identical with, the notion of Good of the previous analysis. "Conformation," the influx or infusion of pattern, finds a degree of unification within the feeling subject which unites the "prehended" patterns of the past with new patterns for the future. If the anticipated pattern is compatible with the event, its realization would correspond exactly with the "fortunate modification" of "Mathematics and the Good."

Adjustment (or adaptation), however, is the basic notion in this analysis as the following passage shows:

"Adaptation" implies an end. Thus Beauty is only defined when the aim of the 'adaptation' has been analysed. This aim is twofold. It is in the first place, the absence of mutual inhibition among the various prehensions, so that the intensities of subjective form, which naturally and properly—or in one word, conformally—arise from the objective contents of the various prehensions, do not inhibit each other. . . . In the second place, there is the major form of Beauty. This form presupposes the first form, and adds to it the condition that the conjunction in one synthesis of the various prehensions introduces new contrasts of objective content with objective content.[11]

[10] *Adventures of Ideas*, 325.
[11] *Ibid.*, 324.

"Adjustment" governs both of these forms of Beauty. In the first case, the absence of inhibiting patterns implies the adjustment of the many patterns within a complex whole. In the second case, the presence of an anticipated pattern implies the adjustment or appropriateness of that pattern to the present "demand." In both forms of Beauty the meaning of "adjustment" is closely linked with the "end" or purpose of the event. Since every event has an "end," according to Whitehead, "adjustment" dominates all process. Thus the notion of "adjustment" finds its significance for the analysis of Beauty and the Good not in any formal properties which can be said to be the nature of "adjustment," but in the relation which holds between the striving organism and the end sought.

The importance of the notion of "adjustment" is apparent as well in Whitehead's discussion of "Harmony" and "Discord." ". . . Discord—in itself destructive and evil—is the positive feeling of a quick shift of aim from the tameness of outworn perfection to some other ideal with its freshness still upon it."[12] As the opposite of Harmony, Discord is the clash of feelings composing the event. In the positive sense Discord is the essence of Adventure. In this sense it is the appropriate change in feeling for the future. Analogous to the manner in which Discord is in one relation the opposite of Harmony and in another relation part of the meaning of Harmony itself, Harmony has two forms. "A mere qualitative Harmony within an experience comparatively barren of objects of high significance is a debased type of Harmony, tame, vague, deficient in outline and intention."[13] This form of Harmony is to be contrasted with the Harmony where there is the introduction of an aim "with its freshness still upon it."

These doctrines serve to illustrate two distinct ways in which Whitehead qualifies the general structure of Beauty and the Good. In the first place, the relations holding among "infusion," "stability" and "modification" of pattern are interpreted through the notion of "adjustment," which, in turn, derives its meaning from such notions as "demand," "conceptual expecta-

[12] *Ibid.*, 330-1.
[13] *Ibid.*, 339.

tion," and "end" or "aim." In this respect both "adjustment" and the general conditions of the Good could be interpreted as purely descriptive of certain patterns of change. They may be viewed, therefore, as presumably indicating where experience of the Good is to be found. But it is questionable that they really serve this function at all. In the first place, "infusion," "stability" and "modification" of pattern is so general in its formulation that it would seem to hold in some degree for any change whatsoever. In this sense it hardly serves to designate anything sufficiently specific to serve as a guide to the Good. "Adjustment," as a general condition governing the relation among "infusion," "stability" and "modification" of pattern, adds little to relieve this situation.

Furthermore, "adjustment" is a term open to suspicion: it is not always a purely descriptive term. Like "Perfection" and "Harmony," "adjustment" often possesses connotations of "good." And "adjusted" change would be, *ipso facto*, a good change. Such terminology is not only likely to mislead, but, as such, throws no light on the nature of those processes in which the good experience occurs.

As suggested above, Whitehead's intention in the use of the term "adjustment" is to indicate that certain patterns of behavior issue in satisfaction. In so far as "adjustment" is confined to this usage it has a legitimate meaning. The study of Good would then be concerned with the description of those patterns of experience in which satisfaction occurs. In part, at least, this is Whitehead's purpose in *Adventures of Ideas*, and to some degree in other writings. In this respect his view is like that of Hume, who held that knowledge of value can be had by setting down the likes and dislikes of men. But, unlike Hume, Whitehead attempts to state the general formula for all such experience.

In the second place, it will be noted that Whitehead qualifies certain relations holding among the general conditions of Beauty and Good by such evaluative expressions as "debased," "tame" and "vague." Such qualifications specifically concern a low type of "Harmony" (*AI*, 339). According to the present interpretation, Whitehead does not mean (though this may not be too clear) that the pattern of process is itself "debased," but rather that the pattern of such experience is "felt" as disagreeable. It then becomes a question in Whitehead's theory of appealing to common experience for justification in applying such derogatory terms to any given form of experience. Whitehead, for one, feels a certain way about a given pattern of activity. However, in view of Whitehead's very decided condemnation of this sort of Harmony, it is clear that he expects some degree of acceptance among organisms which have experienced this "Harmony." A catalogue of the "passions" is the result of this sort of procedure in which varying degrees and kinds of satisfaction and dissatisfaction are listed and described.

To the degree that Whitehead undertakes this analysis of the various forms of Beauty and Good in terms of the most general conditions such as "infusion," "stability" and "modification" of pattern, his discussion hardly indicates more than that certain arrangements of pattern where *change* occurs give rise to Good, and certain others, especially *static* patterns, produce the "low" or Evil. In the case of Good this is analogous to the common contention that Beauty is to be found in an ordered pattern with some variety. In fact this means very little until specific patterns and variations are indicated. And this more specific analysis has not been supplied by Whitehead.

This is especially striking if one raises the simple question: What *degree* of "infusion," "stability" or "modification" of pattern is required in order to distinguish those experiences which are Good? Some degree of "stability" of pattern, for example, is indicated by Whitehead as necessary for such experience. But what degree, and over what time, remains obscure in Whitehead's discussion of this problem. In general, a sudden, constantly changing experience is unpleasant (under certain circumstances), and an unchanging experience is equally unpleasant (under certain circumstances). More precise knowledge than this must be secured before the general formulation can be viewed as successful.

In respect to the first set of qualifications mentioned above, it can be seen that Whitehead's discussion of value takes on a different dimension altogether. "Demand" and "conceptual expectation" characterize the organism in the act of "valuing" or anticipating an end. The example given in the quotation on page 440 above shows this very clearly. Whitehead refers to an individual prepared by antecedent experience to see a "full picture." To be presented with a sketch is a disappointment under the circumstances. To see the "full picture" is to attain the desired end. As will be clear later, Whitehead himself treats this relation as basic in his discussion of value, for Beauty and the Good are, at best, only partially explained by reference to the general conditions which control the way pattern impinges on events. Neither the notion of "adjustment" nor the relation of "infusion," "stability" and "modification" of pattern, which is the general framework in which "adjustment" presumably operates, have any significance apart from the analysis of value in terms of "demand" and satisfaction.

II

These last remarks lead naturally to Whitehead's analysis of the actual entity itself. A few of the major distinctions from his "theory of feelings" will serve the purpose of the present discussion.[14] A fundamental relationship is that of the feeling subject and what is felt. This relationship, holding throughout nature, is interpreted by Whitehead to mean that the subject is not only what it is now (in view of its past), but it is more than its immediate inheritance from the past. It is also its final cause, i.e., transcendent of the present. As final cause the subject is said to be *"causa sui."*[15] Every entity involves the activity of self-creation.

The relevance of this doctrine to the views already discussed is obvious. It is the subject which feels its experience to be Good under the "infusion," "stability" and "modification" of pattern. This experience, however, is not "suffered," for the subject is active and self-creative in its pursuit of satisfactory

---

[14] Particular attention will be paid to two theories, i.e., the theory of "unity" and the theory of "valuation." It is, of course, impossible to undertake a complete account of the theory of feeling, even where it is relevant to theory of value, in this paper.

[15] *Process and Reality,* 339.

experience. Thus, the subject is not only conditioned by its past, but attends as well to its future. Though this view of the subject is derived from what would commonly be called "animal psychology," all events are "units of feeling" in this sense. The experiences of satisfaction and dissatisfaction are found on all levels of existence, according to Whitehead's theory of feeling.

Two aspects of self-creation are particularly important for the discussion of value: (1) "unity," which is the ultimate end guiding the self-creative entity; (2) "novelty" or uniqueness, which every phase of the creative activity involves. ". . . the attainment of a *peculiar definiteness* is the final cause which animates a particular process; . . ."[16] The "finitude" which was previously said to be the "gift" of definite pattern must now be looked at in terms of the activity to achieve "unity." At any stage the event is finite, but that "unity" which is the final stage is the "peculiar definiteness" mentioned above. This does not imply that an event has one constant end. Though the end of many events in nature may be fairly constant, the purpose of Whitehead's analysis is to allow for events in which the end is subject to the changing conditions of experience. In the case of man, for example, the end may be in terms of some ideal suggested by the present context of experience, and this end may change in the light of further experience.[17]

It is not Whitehead's intention to argue from the presence of attained "unity" in nature to the presence of purpose in natural events. He asserts initially that every event is essentially appetitive. Events "feel" not only their environments (the immediate past), but "feel" some end, as well. The feeling of an end involves appetition or "purpose" in this sense. The subject is constituted by its feeling of its own past together with the appetition for an end as part of the present.[18] "This final cause is an inherent element in the feeling, constituting the unity of that feeling."[19] Appetition for "unity" controls the present formation of the organism as well as directing its future.

[16] *Ibid.*, 340. (Italics mine.)
[17] *Ibid.*, 342.
[18] *Ibid.*, 130; 390.
[19] *Ibid.*, 339.

The subject's aim at "unity" determines every feeling to be compatible with that "unity."[20] It is an ultimate aesthetic "unity" (not a logical "unity") which dominates the development of the organism.[21] This is referred to as the "pre-established harmony" of the organism. It is in this sense that Whitehead makes every event in nature thoroughly teleological. It is not the purpose of the present discussion to raise the question of the propriety of this analysis for physical events. If the relation of subject and end-unity exists throughout nature, then it is essentially this same structure which holds on the plane of human conduct.

Partial explanation of this doctrine of final "unity" lies in Whitehead's conception of the event, composed of many feelings (ultimately feelings of the entire universe), as attaining the individuality which makes it this event and not any other. As far as theory of value is concerned this view implies the selection or elimination of certain "influences" or feelings to which the organism is subject. (This is explained later under "valuation.") This selection of feelings, which later become the essential constituents of the organism's nature, must be guided by some end. Otherwise, according to Whitehead, there is no explanation of why organisms achieve certain definite patterns rather than others. The end in view of which all selection is made is called "unity."

Quite apart from the implications of this view for the interpretation of natural occurrences, the activity of man is essentially "ethical" under this doctrine. The activity of the individual is dominated by a desire for some form of existence which is viewed, consciously or unconsciously, as the resolution of all present conflict (or dissatisfaction). Resolution of conflict is a form of existence which will "feel" better than the present state of conflict. Since feeling is the ultimate nature of value, "unity" is best explained as the feeling of a form of activity which resolves the present conflict of "interests." As pointed out elsewhere, conscious intelligence may dominate and guide

[20] *Ibid.*, 39.
[21] *Adventures of Ideas*, 336.

the resolution of conflict, but this is the rare instance. "Trial and error" is a better example of the kind of activity which Whitehead would interpret in this way.

It is in this light that Whitehead uses the term "compatibility" to describe the "unity" of feeling which is the result of the resolution of conflict. The disagreeable, the unpleasant are all forms of feeling which find their resolution in "unity" or the harmony of feeling. Since the organism is constantly undergoing pressure from and changes in the environment, it is constantly meeting new needs and difficulties which present themselves for resolution. The "compatibility" of feeling thus stands always as something more or less urgent and desirable to the organism. In this sense it is the final aim of all activity.

When cast in terms of conflict and its resolution Whitehead's theory of value is close to that of Dewey. According to Whitehead, a path of conduct or activity may be undertaken as a resolution for a previous difficulty and the success or failure of this path of conduct lies in the kind of feeling which issues from it. The emphasis on feeling is perhaps the element here which Dewey would reject, for he insists on more overt, objective grounds for the determination of what is good. The same difference carries through in Whitehead's emphasis on the individual. As a center of feeling the individual is the arbiter of all value. There is no other source of judgment with respect to satisfactory and dissatisfactory feeling. It is in this sense that the "uniqueness" of the individual is stressed throughout Whitehead's writings. This does not preclude the influence of the environment on what the individual feels as satisfactory, but it is the individual's private feeling which is final.

In Whitehead's theory of feeling there is another element, which, though present throughout nature to some degree, rises to preëminent importance in the case of man. This is the element of "conceptual feeling." The "datum" of the conceptual activity of the organism is a pattern or "eternal object." The way in which the organism feels an eternal object is called "valuation."[22] "Valuation" involves primarily the act of determining what rôle the "ideal" will play in the development of the

[22] *Process and Reality*, 367-9.

organism. This act is subject to compatibility with other feelings (both physical and mental) which compose the event, as well as the feeling for the end-unity itself. Consequently, a conceptual feeling may play a major or minor rôle, as the case may be. Whitehead refers to this as valuation "up or down."[23]

Conceptual feeling may merely reproduce the eternal object exemplified in the physical feeling of an event. But conceptual feeling may also give rise to the entertaining of eternal objects which are not merely duplicates of the form of physical feeling. Though compatible with the ideas derived from the physical feeling, some conceptual feelings may be concerned with eternal objects which are different from those derived directly from physical feeling, and thus constitute a genuinely ideal source of stimulation for the organism. This function is the source of origination throughout nature.[24]

This doctrine is especially important for any consideration of Whitehead's theory of feeling as a theory of value. Mental activity (which always involves the feeling for pattern) may play the relatively passive rôle of reflecting the forms of physical activity. Mind in this sense merely knows how its body is acting. Such mental activity allows no departure from the fixed patterns of behavior already performed. Thus the form of realized activity is continued (reënacted), and controls the future. But where mental activity occurs in the form of "valuation" the future activity of the organism is subject to change, for it is through sensitivity to new patterns that modification of the future is possible. This is the major condition of "moral responsibility," as Whitehead interprets it.[25] The individual determines his own future through the act of "valuation."

This is not, however, a simple act of free choice. The individual is already a complex entity whose physical form of existence and whose mental life are functioning under definite patterns. Besides, the individual is imbedded in a social pattern to which he is subject. Part of the "freedom" which Whitehead

---

[23] Ibid., 369.

[24] Every successive stage of an event is novel, but conceptual feeling introduces new ideas into process, constituting another kind of novelty.

[25] Process and Reality, 390.

has in mind is the power of the individual to "think of" other possible forms of existence. Some of these forms will be rejected in the act of "valuation" by the very fact that the form of the individual's past renders them impossible for him to achieve. There will remain certain alternative forms of activity which are "compatible" with his past. It is within this sphere that changes may occur, whether for Good or Evil, for the pattern chosen becomes the form of future activity. It is in this sense that the individual is "self-caused."

The striving of the organism towards "unity" is in terms of integration of both physical and mental feelings. In an organism where "valuation" takes place in any marked degree purposive action results. Though conscious purpose arises under very exceptional conditions, according to Whitehead, it is sufficient to remark here that in the act of valuation the subject transcends the causal determinates of its past and "entertains" eternal objects (or patterns) which are ultimately synthesized with (and thus realized in) its total nature.[26]

The act of "valuation" itself takes the form of "adversion" or "aversion." Like or dislike characterizes the subject (or subjective form) as it entertains the eternal objects which offer themselves, so to speak, as alternative forms for the future. If the conceptual feeling, derived as it may be in a very simple case from the physical aspect of the organism, is entertained under the form of "adversion" the subsequent physical feelings of the organism are enforced or enhanced. There is a strengthening of that form of physical existence. If "aversion" prevails, the physical feelings are transmitted to the next moment of existence with "attenuated intensity."[27] Through "valuation" the organism constitutes both its present nature and its future nature.

The liking of some form of activity or possible activity, as in the case of an ideal, serves to strengthen it so that it tends to be repeated or striven for, as the case may be. This function

---

[26] *Ibid.*, 387-8.

[27] *Ibid.*, 388, 422; *Adventures of Ideas*, 330. This is close to Spinoza's doctrine of the active and passive emotions and their effect on the existence of the individual.

could well be called the habit forming activity of the emotions. Dislike has the opposite effect; it tends to disrupt the form of activity, and even destroy it. The positive enjoyment of a certain pattern is thus a form of the feeling of satisfaction, and, as such, a form of the Good.

In organisms where "propositional feelings" (a species of conceptual feeling) take place the notions of truth or falsity are secondary to the valuation of the subject. ". . . it is more important that a proposition be interesting than that it be true."[28] It is how a proposition is valued by the organism which determines the future of the proposition either as a purely abstract entity or in its application to the control of experience. A proposition sufficiently "liked" may determine the direction of the organism towards research and pursuit of scientific knowledge, for example.

The subject attains increasing "intensity" of feeling in terms of the contrast between eternal objects. Contrast may exist between an eternal object (or pattern) at present realized and an eternal object which is still a possibility, or between two eternal objects both of which are possibilities, etc. As complexity of conceptual feeling increases, the subjective feeling is intensified so long as the act of "valuation" is able to achieve balance among the various feelings.[29] "Contrast under identity" is the phrase Whitehead uses to indicate that the emphasis or choice of the act of "valuation" is conditioned by the subjective aim at "unity."

These basic doctrines from the "theory of feeling" reveal Whitehead's conception of value itself as identical with feeling. Two dimensions of this feeling are suggested: first, the organism's feeling of satisfaction or dissatisfaction, and, second, the degree of intensity of this experience. It will be noted that the complexity of the organism is essentially a question of the capacity for complex feelings. Any organism may have the satisfaction of its wants, but only the more complex organism enjoys

[28] *Process and Reality*, 395-6. Cf. also 402.
[29] *Ibid.*, 424-5; cf. *Modes of Thought*, 10-27 (for a discussion of "importance" which is relevant here).

the intensity of feeling which issues from the consideration or actual enjoyment of new patterns of activity.

It is on the most complex levels of experience, as in the case of man, that new patterns of activity emerge as purely ideal ends. Thus Whitehead's doctrine of value as feeling finds its most important application in the sphere of activity where planning and intelligent action occur. This capacity to entertain new, unrealized ends makes possible the change which is necessary for the "modification" of pattern, which is one of the primary conditions for the experience of the Good. It explains as well why Whitehead often uses Platonic language in discussing the Good, Ideas are, in view of their importance for the new (and interesting) forms of experience, genuine objects of pursuit; they are felt as Good in certain circumstances. It is difficult, therefore, in view of Whitehead's conception that ideas have no reality apart from some center of feeling, to separate the ideas or patterns from the character of the feeling.

This type of feeling is relatively rare. The mere repetition of pattern which we have seen characterizes the "low-grade" organism is to be considered, according to Whitehead, as the feeling of an inherited pattern. No new patterns intrude themselves into that feeling; the traditional form of activity is followed. But this notion is not limited to organisms where there is little if any possibility of change through new patterns. Certain societies, according to Whitehead, illustrate this function of feeling where a given form of activity is repeated through successive generations.

Whitehead sometimes uses the term "concern" or interest to designate the essential activity of the organism. "Concern" is, in fact, often synonymous with "feeling" in Whitehead's writings. Like and dislike color the "concern" of the organism, making for experience which is respectively Good or Evil. This view (if the present interpretation is correct) involves one difficulty which is especially relevant to this doctrine of "valuation." If the function of "valuation," which is the forming of the likes and dislikes, which determine in turn the activity of the organism, has a positive character ("valuation up," or liking) in the organisms which merely repeat old patterns (for example, the static society), the theory of feeling seems to imply that the resultant activity is felt as Good. It is conceivable, therefore, that the liking for the *status quo* may be more intense (and hence the form of that activity prolonged) than for some form of experienced change ("modification").

This is the basis in the theory of feeling for the former objection to the notion of "adjustment" in so far as this term seemed to imply change. The same objection holds for the general formula of the Good where "modification" of pattern is said to be essential. If there is in the factual situation some question of the positive "valuation" of change by higher organisms, it then appears doubtful that the general pattern of the Good experience as formulated by Whitehead is an adequate generalization. A philosophy of change is perhaps initially disposed to find in change something universally desirable.

It is clear from Whitehead's conception of "valuation" that his view of value is a form of "interest" theory. But it is an interest theory which is governed, as has been pointed out, by the notion of "unity." In this sense the Good is any appropriate unifying "end" under the given circumstances of need or "demand." Thus there is a strong emphasis in Whitehead's treatment of value on the function of choice or selection of "ends." Once selected, these "ends" or values control and define activity.[30] In *Modes of Thought* this aspect of value is discussed under the notion of "Importance." The individual, immersed in society, is subject in part to the directive character of the "values" prevalent in his group. Morality controls the "ends" which find their realization in the life of the individual as "satisfactions." In this way the act of "valuation" is subject to control, for the likes and dislikes, adversions and aversions of the individual are directed to certain ends as appropriate under the circumstances involved. But even ". . . morality is always the aim at that union of harmony."[31]

[30] In this respect Whitehead's view has affinities to that of certain contemporary writers. Cf. Stevenson, C. L., "The Emotive Meaning of Ethical Terms," *Mind*, vol. XLVI, no. 181, Jan., 1937.

[31] *Modes of Thought*, 19.

Thus, it is Whitehead's intention to subject the entire doctrine of "valuation" to the demands of aesthetic "Harmony." This is strikingly indicated by his extension of "Harmony" and "perfection" to cover the situation of organic needs, "valuation" and the end "valued." More specifically, this takes the form of extending the aesthetic notion of the part-whole relation to the need-end relation. Following his observations that the part-whole relation in aesthetic experience often involves some element of discord, Whitehead treats the need-end relation as a form of "Harmony" where some clash of parts aids or enlivens the whole. But this is an extension which risks losing sight of the very nature of the relations in which "valuation" takes place. The existence of organic needs is commonly a situation where the entertainment of an end (even an "appropriate" end) does not constitute a "Harmony," except in such an extremely vague or general way that all the meaning which the term may have in aesthetics (and it is of dubious character even there) is lost.

The attainment of "unity" gives rise to the organism's "satisfaction" (sometimes called "contentment").[32] The term "aesthetic" is peculiarly applicable to this final achievement in view of Whitehead's conception of the final event as divers "feelings" under some principle of unification. The "satisfaction" is just this feeling of unification. This is the notion of "aesthetic" in the ultimate sense. Whitehead, however, extends the term "aesthetic" to cover various kinds of experience. In *Adventures of Ideas* it is stated that ". . . imperfection aiming at a higher type stands above lower perfections."[33] This means that attained "satisfaction" can be inferior in the character of its feeling to the feeling for a higher type of unity. Thus the subjective form of every event is under the guise of some kind of aesthetic feeling. If the feeling is too discordant, it is termed "aesthetic destruction" (evil). "Aesthetic" in the positive sense is made to cover two general cases: (1) where "unity" is attained ("satisfaction"); (2) where an "end" entertained in the complex of immediate feeling is an appropriate end.

[32] *Process and Reality*, 129, 323, 335. Also, *Adventures of Ideas*, 248.
[33] *Adventures of Ideas*, 330.

In both cases the immediate feeling can be said to have positive "value." Presumably both of these cases fall under the general conditions governing all value, i.e., definite pattern of "finitude," though it is difficult to see how the second case meets the demand for definite pattern. Moreover, the two cases must meet the requirement of Good and Beauty in some sense, though it is difficult to see how these general conditions are met by the first case where the end is attained. The term "aesthetic" makes it clear, however, that Whitehead thinks of both of these kinds of feeling as forms of satisfaction. In this sense Whitehead is in agreement with established usage among aestheticians.[34]

It is in accordance with the view that value is the gift of definite pattern that Whitehead makes "unity" the end guiding all organic development. But if "infusion," "stability" and "modification" of pattern are the necessary conditions of Good, the attainment of definite pattern is not itself Good. Strictly speaking, Good applies to a *process* of feeling. Yet, in *Adventures of Ideas*, Beauty covers both the case of attained "unity" (a finished process) and the case where some element of Discord is present (as in the striving for an unrealized end), and the latter case is said to be, in some instances, a "higher type" than the former.[35] Thus the "final satisfaction" of the organism, which is the achievement of "unity," has the position of being an end which in itself is not the highest form of Beauty or Good. This creates a curious situation in Whitehead's theory of value. If, as we have seen, the resolution of conflict in the form of satisfactory feeling is the aim of every organism, and it is conflict of feeling which the organism seeks to avoid, the Good seems clearly indicated. On the other hand, it appears that to resolve a given conflict may not be the Good; indeed, it may be better to have conflict than to resolve it. It may well be the case that a feeling of change (as in the recognition of a problem and the interest in its future solution) is more satisfactory than the feeling of the resolution of the difficulty. In that

---

[34] Cf. Santayana, G., *Sense of Beauty*, 24. Like Whitehead, Santayana treats the moral values as not essentially different from aesthetic values.

[35] *Adventures of Ideas*, 330.

case the notion of "definite pattern," as the correlate of satisfactory feeling, is inadequate. Or, if the notion of "definite pattern" covers both cases, its ambiguity is such that any and every pattern may give rise to "satisfaction."

There is no question that Whitehead aligns "definite pattern," "unity" and "order" with satisfactory feeling throughout his writings. This has been stressed previously, but the following statement is striking in this respect: "The intensity of satisfaction is promoted by the 'order' in the phases from which concrescence arises and through which it passes; it is enfeebled by the 'disorder'."[36] But the interpretation of satisfaction as the experience of "definite pattern" is open to serious question. The resolution of conflict is not necessarily any more a pattern than the conflict itself. This is not to question Whitehead's assertion that certain patterns of activity "feel" better than others; but it is another thing to assert that "definite pattern" is the source of satisfactory feeling.

This criticism reflects as well on the notion that value is the "gift of finitude." Pattern or form, in the ordinary sense of defining or limiting an event, may well be a condition of existence, but, as such, throws no light on the nature of value or the Good. This is clear from Whitehead's analysis of value in terms of feeling, for it is satisfaction which distinguishes the Good from all other experiences. The individual may then find satisfaction in certain forms of activity rather than others. "Definite pattern," or the greatest degree of "finitude" is designated by Whitehead as that which holds the greatest degree of satisfaction for the organism. As such it acquires a worth above all other forms of experience. It is then an easy transition to read into this greatest degree of "finitude" the qualities which it has as a universal object of appetition and satisfaction. The Platonic tendencies in Whitehead may very well spring from this transition.

The conflict which exists between the conception of "definite pattern" and the general formula of the Good is also illuminating with respect to the interpretation of "definite pattern." In accordance with the doctrine of "achievement," the organ-

---

[36] *Process and Reality*, 129-30.

ism can be viewed as attaining more and more "definite pattern" in its progressive solution of conflict (on the side of feeling, more and more satisfactory experience). Thus Whitehead views satisfaction as arising in the approximation of the goal of "definite pattern." This view throws into relief the difficulty with the doctrine of "unity." Presumably indefinite pattern is as much a source of satisfaction as "definite pattern" or "unity" itself.

III

It has been one of the purposes of this paper to point out that Whitehead's theory of value is divisible into two distinct parts, i.e., (1) the doctrine of pattern or form (the general formula of the Good, "finitude," "unity"), and (2) the doctrine of feeling. It is the first of these two doctrines to which most of the objections raised in the previous discussion apply. As has been suggested, there is no objection to describing the patterns or forms under which satisfactory experience occurs. There may be some very general formula (such as the general condition of the Good in Whitehead's theory) which governs the experience felt as satisfactory. If this is so, there will be need of "middle principles" which will bridge the gap between the general formula itself and the actual experiences of value. Whitehead's formal treatment of these experiences is so general that it fails as an instrument of discrimination among the various forms of value. He has not supplied the "middle principles."

The theory of feeling, on the contrary, which is psychology from the introspective point of view, is immediately relevant to the actual situations in which value arises. On this level Whitehead has offered many doctrines (some of which have only been mentioned here) which are important in the consideration of the nature of value. As has been pointed out, the basic situation in the analysis of value is the organism reacting favorably or unfavorably to the stimuli around it. These stimuli may be derived from the body and its environment, or they may be purely theoretical ideas. In either case the likes or dislikes of the organism disclose the feeling tone of the present and determine the feeling tone of the future. It is within the general framework of want and satisfying of want that likes and dislikes operate as the sign of Good or Evil, as the case may be. Thus the theory of feeling, which is developed by Whitehead as a description of the nature of events, may find its most important application in the interpretation of value.

JOHN GOHEEN

DEPARTMENT OF PHILOSOPHY
QUEENS COLLEGE OF
THE COLLEGE OF THE CITY OF NEW YORK

13

Bertram Morris

THE ART-PROCESS AND THE AESTHETIC FACT
IN WHITEHEAD'S PHILOSOPHY

THE ART-PROCESS AND THE AESTHETIC FACT
IN WHITEHEAD'S PHILOSOPHY

FEW philosophies are as congenial to an understanding of art as that of Alfred North Whitehead. This is not sheer accident, for Professor Whitehead definitely approaches philosophy from the aesthetic point of view. Some commentators have even called his philosophy an aestheticism. Quite apart from the epithets, much too cavalierly tossed about in philosophic circles, Professor Whitehead has unquestionably made a persistent effort to understand the nature and to set forth the principles of experience. From the most rudimentary restlessness of so-called inorganic things to the refined cultural activities of human beings the categories involved are primarily aesthetic, found at low as well as at high emotional temperatures. His philosophy of organism zealously rejects half-hearted empiricism, which plays favorites with certain types of data to the exclusion of others. Philosophy must envisage all types of data, and ascertain those which are genuinely stubborn, irreducible facts. Whether we call the philosophy of organism empiricism or rationalism is of no significance; what matters is its allegation that philosophy is descriptive of experience.

We are told by Professor Whitehead that "an actual fact is a fact of aesthetic experience."[1] Though he finds much that commends itself in British empiricism—especially in Locke—he

---

[1] *Process and Reality*, 427. (Page references to *Process and Reality* in this essay are to the American edition, 1930.) *Religion in the Making*, 115; cf. also 104f.: "The metaphysical doctrine, here expounded, finds the foundations of the world in the aesthetic experience, rather than—as with Kant—in the cognitive and conceptive experience. All order is therefore aesthetic order, and the moral order is merely certain aspects of aesthetic order. The actual world is the outcome of the aesthetic order, and the aesthetic order is derived from the immanence of God."

refuses to accede to Hume's oversimplification of experience as constituted of mere sequences of impressions and ideas. The intrinsic order in experience is aesthetic. Despite its emphasis upon the aesthetic, the philosophy of organism is not advisedly pronounced an aestheticism. One of Whitehead's own statements seems to express a more balanced judgment. Philosophy, he says, must start "from some section of our experience," and he believes that:

at present the most fruitful, because the most neglected, starting point is that section of value-theory which we term aesthetics. Our enjoyment of the values of human art, or of natural beauty, our horror at the obvious vulgarities and defacements which force themselves upon us—all these modes of experience are sufficiently abstracted to be relatively obvious. And yet evidently they disclose the very meaning of things.[2]

Regardless of its starting-point, certainly his philosophy is more than aesthetics. Even though we consider aesthetic order to be the essence of organic mechanism, we are wise to look more specifically to that aspect of his philosophy which comes under the rubric of aesthetics proper. There is, of course, the danger of considering separately things inseparably related. We can only take precaution to make our selections as little arbitrary as possible. Through this inevitable simplification we may further the purpose of this volume, in the hope that Professor Whitehead will help us to distrust our simplification and to point out the errors.

I

Philosophy, I assume, is basically analysis directed towards understanding. We may suffer passions and we may engage in activity quite apart from philosophy, but we come to philosophical understanding only through analysis. Whitehead makes analysis the primary function of philosophy, and recognizes two divergent modes. One is logical analysis directed towards completed things; the other is historical analysis directed towards the process by which things attain their completed (or provisionally

[2] *Proceedings and Addresses*, The American Philosophical Association (1936). 185, in *The Philosophical Review*, XLVI:2 (March 1937).

completed) status in the world. Logical analysis is of secondary import for aesthetics. It is, however, not unrelated to the subject, as we shall later have occasion to see. Of signal importance to aesthetics is the historical process through which the aesthetic fact comes into being. Whereas logical analysis is the method of mathematics or coördinate division, historical analysis is the method of aesthetic or genetic analysis, an actual entity in its growth from phase to phase.[3]

The least arbitrary aspects of genetic process are those of beginning, middle, and end—even though there may be neither absolute beginning nor absolute end. The end has a more or less determinate status, which Whitehead calls satisfaction, actual entity, concrescent, unity, individuality, etc. But its essence is determinacy as the real stubborn fact. For aesthetic purposes, it is wise to distinguish as clearly as possible the process from the end at which it is aimed: the achievement resulting in "satisfaction." There is some warrant for distinguishing between the process as art, conceived fundamentally as an activity, and the end as beauty, the satisfaction aimed at.[4] The two together constitute what we may call the aesthetic situation. Analysis of the situation, by which the process of art issues into beauty, is the task of aesthetics, to which Whitehead has greatly contributed.

Beauty is defined as "the mutual adaptation of the several factors in an occasion of experience. Thus in its primary sense Beauty is a quality which finds its exemplification in actual occasions: or put conversely, it is a quality in which such occasions can severally participate."[5] The far-reaching problem of aesthetics is how to understand individuality. Experientially, one of the clearest realizations of individuality is the aesthetic situation, rather clearly marked off as one which is its own justification and its own value. And the pregnant meaning of perception resides in its disclosure of individuality as the ultimate

[3] *Process and Reality*, 433f.

[4] *Science and the Modern World*, 279-280 (page references to *Science and the Modern World* in this essay are to the American edition, 1925); *Adventures of Ideas*, 341: "The teleology of the Universe is directed to the production of Beauty."

[5] *Adventures of Ideas*, 324.

concrete fact.[6] It comes to fulfillment in immediate experience. To understand it as the aesthetic fact, we must see it as the result of process whose essence is creativity or advance into novelty. The peregrinations of this advance constitute the richness and fullness prehended in the aesthetic whole. Whitehead has called this the "principle of process," the ninth category of explanation: "That *how* an actual entity *becomes* constitutes *what* that actuality *is;* so that the two descriptions of an actual entity are not independent. Its 'being' is constituted by its 'becoming'." In aesthetic terms as above used, this means that beauty is the art-process come to realization. For "realization" is "a gathering of things together into the unity of a prehension."[7]

We have suggested that process may be least arbitrarily analyzed according to its three phases, beginning, middle, and end. Whitehead himself has referred to them as the responsive phase, the supplemental stage, and satisfaction, respectively.[8] These distinctions are only relative, but they are sufficiently discriminable that we can treat each in turn.

The beginning of the art-process is constituted by the phase of "receptivity." Actually, the reception is an extremely complex situation, evolved from the relation of an organic body to the so-called physical world. The inner constitution of the matrix from which the art-process emerges need not now detain us. But, we are told, the data from which the process takes its course are comparable to Locke's "ideas." Since the aesthetic process cannot occur vacuously, it presupposes crude subject-matter—the welter of data—from which aesthetic order derives. In some sense this subject-matter is external, and appears to be more or less passively received from without. As it issues into the supplemental stage it becomes enmeshed in the privacy of originative powers, which mark the throes of art-creation. In the case of music we may consider that the theme of a composition is rather passively received. The genius of the composer is less

[6] Cf. *Religion in the Making*, 100f, and *Science and the Modern World*, 131.

[7] *Science and the Modern World*, 98.

[8] *Process and Reality*, 323ff. Also cf. his division in *Science and the Modern World* into: substantial activity, conditioned potentialities for synthesis, and achieved outcome, 247.

in evidence in the theme, which is a statement of the material, more or less external, than in the way in which he treats it; that is, in its development. This phase marks the genuine advance into novelty. For the composer can do little more than accept or reject the theme, and the recapitulation is scarcely more than the determinate restatement of the theme as developed. Between the primary and the final stages the composer exhibits his true genius, or lack of it. Similar illustrations might be given from the various arts, though one recognizes, even in the above, the danger involved in illustrating philosophical theory, especially Whitehead's.

To repeat, creativity belongs primarily to the supplemental stage, which on the one hand does not and must not lose its germs of appetition, and which on the other carries the "intellectual" development towards satisfaction. Satisfaction results from labor pains, and those pains are engendered in the process of creation, from which aesthetic order emerges. The artist is not free to act capriciously. The essence of his freedom is restraint, self-imposed, by virtue of which intensity of quality appears in the final phase. Thus, the intellectual elaboration must conform with the original appetition involved in the data, whose definite satisfaction becomes the capstone of the aesthetic structure. Here is achieved the stage of determinacy which is the aesthetic fact. It is the consummatory object whose value is its own being. Having achieved definiteness of prehension for high-grade experience, it is now ready for dissolution, save insofar as its value has objective immortality for a further occasion of experience. Beauty is achieved at the end of the process, but since process is everywhere primary, beauty itself is doomed to perish. As Sandburg laments: "I cried over beautiful things, knowing no beautiful thing lasts." But in the perishing of beauty, we are saved from romanticism, and are again prepared to face the new world of the present.

We are in need of further analysis and clarification concerning the art-process. To be sure, in almost all of Whitehead's writings the theme of creativity, together with its modes of manifestation, is an ever-recurring topic. In general, we may say that he is taking seriously the reality of past, present, and future, and trying to understand the essential continuity of the consummatory process. For only as the beginnings of process are carried over into the present and anticipate the future is it possible to effect "order entering upon novelty." However sympathetic we find ourselves with the project, it nevertheless raises some crucial issues. Though we must slur over the details, we cannot but review the general movement of thought in which these issues arise.

II

Of prime importance to aesthetic theory are Whitehead's nine categorial obligations. Extended comment on each is neither desirable nor feasible, but to follow through some of the leading ideas is indispensable. Whitehead's problem is to give articulate account of the principle of value. His analysis has due regard for the complexity of high-grade experience, involving the real togetherness of the physical matrix with subjective processes issuing into the objective unity of an actual entity. Apart from the "physical" underpinning, the art-process has no significance for man as a person within a culture. Apart from process, creativity is meaningless. And apart from unity, value is frustrated and concrescence unrealized. Accordingly, five factors are involved in interpreting the situation: "(i) the 'subject' which feels, (ii) the 'initial data' which are to be felt, (iii) the 'elimination' in virtue of negative prehensions, (iv) the 'objective datum' which is felt, and (v) the 'subjective form' which is *how* the subject feels that objective datum."[9] The further analysis of these five factors is apparently intended to account for the integral interconnection between the "inorganic" world and conscious experience, for only as they are transmuted in higher phases do they acquire consciousness.[10]

Since all entities are dipolar, both physical and conceptual, they all seem necessarily to involve at least the germs of consciousness, come to full fruition in higher phases of experience. In higher life the physical pole is reproduced, and the conceptual pole is rudimentary appetition, containing a drive towards reali-

[9] *Process and Reality,* 337f.
[10] *Ibid.,* 362.

zation, which is reënacted in the subjective form. Obviously, the doctrine insists upon a principle of potentiality, whose agency is effected by what Whitehead calls the eternal object. The eternal object functions processually at two levels, though with emphases varying from triviality, in a feeling which is primarily physical, to one of utmost import, in conscious experience mediated by propositions. Once the physical feelings are reënacted in subjective form the office of eternal objects becomes increasingly dictatorial. For the reënactment of subjective forms leaves us with the multitudinous welter of impressions demanding concrescence in an actual entity. Hence the first three categorial obligations of subjective unity, objective identity, and objective diversity. Primarily aesthetic categories, they all insist in one way or another upon unity in diversity, upon organic interrelation in which each aspect must contribute to the integrity of the whole. The further analysis as to how this is attained is extremely complex: it seems to suppose a kind of architectonic mill in which category is superadded upon category. We may mention a few of the leading ideas.

The subjective forms must somehow be integrated. Now high-grade experience demands that physical feelings be comprehended in a nexus, in which the lowly feelings become transmuted. The *petites perceptiones* take on a massive appearance in apperception. This is accounted for by an elaborate mechanism in which subjective forms are effected through conceptual valuation, conceptual reversion, and especially transmutation. Thus, the characteristic of a nexus becomes the datum from which creativity proceeds. The subjective forms must consequently be integrated in the creative process. Teleology is the principle by which integration is achieved. This Whitehead calls the subjective aim. "The relation between their [the prehensions'] subjective forms is constituted by the one subjective aim which guides their formation."[11] Obviously, the subjective form and subjective aim cannot be separate, and it is necessary to connect them. Not one but two ways of connecting form and aim are suggested: one through the intermediary of subjective

[11] *Ibid.*, 359.

unity, and the other through eternal objects. "The actuality is the totality of prehensions with subjective unity in process of concrescence into concrete unity." And ". . . the eternal object is functioning relationally between the initial data on the one hand and the concrescent subject on the other."[12] Whitehead is somewhat apologetic for his analysis. He concedes, "There is some arbitrariness in taking a component from the datum with a component from the subjective form, and in considering them, on the ground of congruity, as forming a subordinate prehension." And he adds, "The justification is that the genetic process can be thereby analysed."[13] Presently, we shall observe some important problems that arise from this analysis, but before turning to them, we may to advantage emphasize some of the many productive aspects of Whitehead's analysis in its bearing upon aesthetic matters.

III

Perhaps Whitehead's greatest contribution to aesthetic analysis stems from his relentless insistence upon the primacy of process. Actual facts have a natural history in which their essence consists. This being the case, we must take potentiality seriously; and we reify that which is not intrinsically concrete only at the cost of confusion, error, ugliness, and general moral debilitation. When we recognize the facts of potentiality and teleology, we approach experience stubbornly and realistically. We must not reject final causes simply because they are currently unpopular. Few philosophers since Aristotle have more boldly grounded potentiality in philosophy than has Whitehead. His recognition of the widespread fallacy of misplaced concreteness underwrites his own approach, and the insistence upon process is his way of correcting the fallacy.

Process signifies continuity, with both change and permanence. Whitehead's doctrine of actual entities as "a concrescence of prehensions, which have originated in its process of becoming" marks an attempt to make experience intelligible, from its lowliest urgencies to its highest realizations. Sensationalism is a

[12] *Ibid.*, 359, 364.
[13] *Ibid.*, 360.

misreading of experience, precisely because it is atomic in a way which repudiates continuity. Experience is more than focal clarity; for clarity is "interconnected vaguely and yet insistently with other items in dim apprehension, and this dimness shading off imperceptibly into undiscriminated feeling."[14] In *Modes of Thought* Whitehead severely criticizes pseudo-atomism, criticism which is emphasized by what he calls the "fallacy of the perfect dictionary." And again, "A young man does not initiate his experience by dancing with impressions of sensation, and then proceed to conjecture a partner."[15] The charge appears to be that the sensationalist is blind to the continuity of experience, in which novelty is not an impression come out of the blue, with no causal relations, but is a continuous advance, intrinsically ordered in its genetic development.

Whitehead bolsters his position by asserting that all actual entities are dipolar. Their physical must not be shorn from their conceptual aspect, and it is the latter which makes possible the development of a thing in prehension. It constitutes the lure for feeling which becomes determinate. "We enjoy the green foliage of the spring greenly: we enjoy the sunset with an emotional pattern including among its elements the colours and the contrasts of the vision. It is this that makes Art possible." This potentiality for becoming is no mere abstract concept, for:

in the intuition of a mere multiplicity of three or four objects, the mere number imposes no subjective form. It is merely a condition regulating some pattern of effective components. In abstraction from those components, mere triplicity can dictate no subjective form. . . But green can. And there lies the difference between the sensa and the abstract mathematical forms.[16]

The potentiality of art issues into beauty only through the process of becoming determinate. We feel yellowy, sheepishly, or heroically as a prelude to the *feeling* of yellow, or of sheep, or of the Eroica. The conceptual feeling is an appetite towards a new possibility. In such fashion the eternal object functions in

[14] *The Function of Reason*, 62f.
[15] *Process and Reality*, 481.
[16] *Adventures of Ideas*, 321f.

direct appreciation. And the yellowy or heroic feel appears to be Whitehead's interpretation of empathy—which partakes more of creation than of imputation. In the final analysis the feel must be aimed at satisfaction, in which determinacy occurs: the yellowy must be expressed as this determinate yellow.

Expression thrives on the continuity of the past brought into the present as acceptable form. The process is subjective and the actuality achieved is objective. It is the "process of transition from indetermination towards terminal determination."[17] Satisfaction is brought about through the real potentiality of the eternal object ingressing in the actual occasion.

Eternal objects in and of themselves are pure potentials, which determine nothing. This follows from their definition as "any entity whose conceptual recognition does not involve a necessary reference to any definite actual entities of the temporal world."[18] The analysis of an eternal object as a pure potential discloses only other eternal objects. The experiential import of eternal objects is found in *real*, as opposed to general potentiality.[19] In real potentiality we come face on to the vital problems of finite existence, what Whitehead calls decision. Decision is the principle of selectivity, which is the ground of finitude. In themselves eternal objects are not selective, though they enter into—ingress into—finite situations. Decision is then that grading of eternal objects which ingress into actual situations. The aesthetic synthesis is the grading of eternal objects by which the decided individuality of the occasion becomes relevantly determined.[20]

Real potentiality is effected only in the settled world, in which freedom of decision is determined by actualities confronting us. On the one side there are the eternal objects relevant to the situation, and on the other is the subjective aim or lure for feeling to bring about a higher and more inclusive concrescence. All concrescence is effected through decision—even that pertaining

[17] *Process and Reality*, 72.
[18] *Ibid.*, 70.
[19] *Ibid.*, 102.
[20] Cf. *Science and the Modern World*, 226ff.

to God. Moreover, decision is always double-barrelled, involving both inclusion and exclusion. Art is made possible only by reason of finite decision.[21] The principle of spontaneity is that originality of decision which belongs to the essense of an occasion. Art can thrive only as finite realization, for decision can emerge only in social relationships, in which there is genuine novelty and not mere repetition. To be sure, Whitehead thinks the "importance" of art traces to the immanence of the infinite in the finite, but precisely because art is expression, it reveals the pluralistic and finite character of things. By reason of its selectivity art achieves not the "large average effects" of science, but the individual expression whose intense quality overcomes impersonality of science.[22] The zest of art is nothing short of the creative advance into novelty in which individuality comes into determinate being.

The principles of art are identity and contrast. "The novel consequent must be graded in relevance so as to preserve some identity of character with the ground," and "The novel consequent must be graded in relevance so as to preserve some contrast with the ground in respect to that same identity of character."[23] The principles are elementary and indispensable. Unity in diversity is the compelling principle in all aesthetic theory. What is called for is its proper interpretation. For Whitehead the meaning of unity and diversity is largely the meaning of the philosophy of organism, and more specifically the creative advance issuing into intensity of quality. In the more limited aesthetic context, this means that, "The canons of art are merely the expression, in specialized forms, of the requisites for depth of experience."[24] The theme is developed according to a kind of Hegelian triad: triviality, vagueness, and massive simplicity.

Triviality arises from lack of coördination in the factors of the datum, so that no feeling arising from one factor is reinforced by any feeling arising from another factor. . . . Incompatibility has predominated over con-

---

[21] *Ibid.*, 247.
[22] *Modes of Thought*, 28ff.
[23] *Process and Reality*, 427.
[24] *Ibid.*, 483.

trast. . . . Triviality is due to the wrong sort of width. . . . Harmony is this combination of width and narrowness.[25]

Vagueness, on the other hand, is due to "an excess of identification." Intense quality does not emerge because contrast is not present to make quality definite. Narrowness may give depth to experience, but heightened experience requires a breadth span, along with depth. Triviality and vagueness find their proper rôles in the synthesis, massive simplicity. "The right chaos, and the right vagueness, are jointly required for any effective harmony."[26] Happy decision, which is the principle of genius, brings about that massive simplicity, which is the consummatory stage of the aesthetic process.

Decision has two other aspects we may briefly consider: exclusion and frustation. The first is only the corollary of decision as the productive side of the lure for feeling consummated in finite individuality. The exclusive is determined by the indefinite number of eternal objects irrelevant to the realization of the actual entity. These are constituted by the negations implied by the affirmations of finite realization. They are, moreover, not insignificant, for they contribute further richness to the aesthetic object and enhance its quality. Positive knowledge is gained when the artist knows what is excluded by his decision. And usually this is learned the painful way, through making mistakes and correcting them, though Mozart comes close to being an exception. In contrast to Mozart, Beethoven's production bears the marks of frustration and continued revisions, the fruits of which are intensified quality. There is a sense in which exclusion and frustration are integral to the art-process.[27]

Art thrives in dissonance, but a dissonance ultimately resolved in consonance. Where it is unresolved, we have frustration or discord. Discord is aesthetic destruction, and results in anaesthesia; not that which is merely exclusion, but that which is a positive fact of evil.[28] The destructive which does not lead on

[25] *Ibid.*, 170.
[26] *Ibid.*, 171.
[27] Cf. *Modes of Thought*, 116.
[28] Cf. *Adventures of Ideas*, 329.

to the production of new aesthetic wholes is that frustration or evil which is the ineradicable loss of value. This is the "slow relapse into general anaesthesia, or into tameness which is its prelude. Perfection at a low level ranks below Imperfection with higher aim."[29] In *Religion in the Making*, Whitehead again speaks of this principle of evil as the loss of positive values that might have been. With Mill he thinks it better to be a Socrates dissatisfied than a pig satisfied, not because pigs are intrinsically evil, but only because value that might have been fails of realization. In general, we may say that ugliness is simply the inhibiting of higher values that might have been achieved.

We are here in a position to recognize a cardinal tenet of Whitehead's aesthetic: aesthetic value is fundamentally a principle of action, which may be everywhere present. Because of this fact, aesthetics must not be limited to the fine arts or even to them plus appreciation of nature. Art is not passive reception of fine feelings. It is not mere sensitivity, but is through and through activity. "Sensitiveness without impulse spells decadence, and impulse without sensitiveness spells brutality."[30] This aesthetic theory bears the imprint of the protest of the author in his preface to *Aims of Education*, "the protest against dead knowledge, that is to say, against inert ideas." Art is achieved through moving ideas, and by sensitive action, it scorns triviality and sterility, and leads one through "the throbbing emotion of the past hurling itself into a new transcendent fact." This is the immediate pregnant world of the present, through which alone any further resolution is possible. The process involved we may call the teleological-immanent. It is the lure for feeling coming to greater and greater determinacy. Its end, the specious-immanent, is achieved when aesthetic purpose has been realized in the unity of the whole. Thus, final causation is implicit in the fulfilment of experience. For only as subjective aim—may we not say, the artist's intent?—threads the teleological process does the work of art make sense. The unifying

[29] *Ibid.*, 339.
[30] *Science and the Modern World*, 280.

principle is implicit throughout the process, by reason of which alone the ultimate unity as the specious-immanent comes into being.

This immanence is what Whitehead further treats of as symbolism. For symbolic relations are the real internal togetherness of things, in virtue of which experience develops its own intrinsic meaning. The emotional component is essential to the rush of experience, through which expression comes to fulfilment. "Mankind, it seems, has to find a symbol in order to express itself. Indeed 'expression' is 'symbolism'."[31] This immanent process is the past brought into the present, and the present anticipating the pregnant future; and the realism of the art-process resides in its coming to grips with the present, in which alone all reconstruction occurs. "The good of the Universe cannot lie in indefinite postponement. The Day of Judgment is an important notion: but that Day is always with us. Thus Art takes care of the immediate fruition, here and now; . . ."[32] The here and now constitutes the real world in which anticipation and purposiveness in immediate enjoyment overcome the fallacious abstraction of completely passive contemplation.

Teleology resides in the present, considered as the link between its caused status from the past and its causing status toward the future. It is the art-process generated from the gross data with its "given" character and being forced on towards its own inevitable conclusion, because "the present bears in its own essence the relationships which it will have to the future." The process is the same in principle for both appreciation and creation. Appreciation, like the sympathetic vibration of a string, involves an immensely lower degree of creativity, yet it signifies a participation in the creative advance. So we may say with Coleridge, we know a man is a poet because he makes poets of us. In participating in the process, we enjoy the richness of experience and the urgency of emotion leading on towards concrescence. "Each little emotion . . . refuses to accept its status as a detached fact in our consciousness. It insists upon its symbolic

[31] *Symbolism*, 62.
[32] *Adventures of Ideas*, 346.

transfer to the unity of the main effect."[33] The fullness of the effect is the confluence of the many elements finally merging with their total effect in the specious-immanent, which is presentational immediacy. The immediate is barren, save in its relation to antecedent teleology, for the appearance has its roots in the process of coming to be.

Thus Whitehead's theory is one of self-expression. Expression is a process of the imagination grounded in the data of our world, leading to true understanding. The self is in a genuine sense unknown, save as the process comes to an adequate conclusion. The subject is developed out of objective data and comes to be known for what it is in the satisfied imagination. Having its roots in crude sense-data, beauty finally emerges out of a process as individuality, which is immediate insight. The process is not limited to the rarefied atmosphere of the fine arts, but is commonly engaged in by all high-grade organisms. On fortunate occasions the process issues into determinate beauties; on less fortunate occasions, where there is frustration and inhibition, it issues into ugliness. Thus although the Greeks preëminently embodied the aesthetic attitude in their culture, to imitate their ideals is to distort the Greek spirit. Historical mindedness must not lead us to substitute the culture of another epoch for that of our own. However much the past is brought into the present, the present is nevertheless an adventure into a new world. The aesthetic attitude is in essence an orientation towards the new. Copyists and imitators are sheer sentimental romantics.

Only a philosophy which takes process seriously can square with experience. In this respect the philosophy of organism commands high respect. Our statement of Whitehead's analysis has purposely remained close to the text, even though to a large measure it has been necessary to construct from his various writings what appears to be the aesthetic theory of the philosophy of organism. Perhaps Professor Whitehead has consciously refused to develop an aesthetic theory as such. Certainly he has opposed again and again bifurcations, which signify the ultimate defeat of metaphysics. Because the philosophy of organism refuses to

[33] *Symbolism*, 86.

separate causal, perceptive, emotional, and purposive facts, it may be that aesthetic theory as such is uncalled for and misleading. Whatever Professor Whitehead's attitude towards aesthetics as such may be—and we could profit by having it clarified—we may to advantage pause to raise some critical questions, the answers to which he may be willing to suggest. Our questions may be centered around each of the three phases of the aesthetic situation previously distinguished; the receptive, the supplemental, and the consummatory, respectively.

IV

At the first stage we ask primarily for clarification. The aesthetic situation is ordinarily considered to be one which intrinsically involves consciousness, where the qualitative facts are such as to be unintelligible save in terms of some form of direct and immediate conscious experience. The problem is complicated in Whitehead's philosophy, for he continually speaks in a language which ordinarily connotes conscious activity—e.g., the mental, conceptual purpose, feeling, etc.—and then we are brought up short by his occasional statements that these do not involve consciousness. A natural suggestion might be that there is continuity from the simplest physical and mental feelings to the high-grade feelings of human beings, and perhaps even to God. But if it is only a matter of degree, then there is no point in denying that consciousness belongs to the lowly forms. Whitehead continually emphasizes the fact that consciousness is selective, and that it belongs to the finite, but still it is the selectivity and finitude of high-grade experience. Even if non-conscious elements appear in experience, it is not conscious *because* of them—that is, they do not produce consciousness. Since the subjective form is a reiteration of the datum, not the datum itself, it would seem as though there could be no non-conscious elements in experience.

On the one hand Whitehead suggests that consciousness is the development of the mental pole of an object, and on the other that it supervenes or emerges. He says,

Of course consciousness, like everything else, is in a sense indefinable. It is just itself and must be experienced. But, also like other things, it is

the *emergent quality* illustrated in the essence of a conjunction of circumstances. . . . Consciousness is that *quality which emerges* into the
objective content as the result of the conjunction of a fact and a supposition about that fact.[34]

Now an emergent depending on a *conjunction* marks a situation
the essence of which is discontinuity. Here the notion of continuous process gives way to discontinuity, and the art-principle
which is organic is discontinuous with the scientific principle of
conjunction, which is not organic, but emergent. In other words,
to understand discontinuity we need a kind of operational logic,
for an emergent cannot be truly explained, whereas art, which
is purposive and continuous, involves an integrating teleological
principle. Thus we question whether we can get along without
bifurcation, namely, that which is apparently necessary to distinguish between science and art.

In the supplemental stage Whitehead seems correctly to suggest the principle we have called the teleological-immanent, the
principle of conscious appetition coming to fulfilment in art. Yet
he has analyzed this according to a host of faculties and categories
reminiscent of Kant's superstructure of machinery: physical feelings transformed in subjective form, further transmuted through
reversion, having a subjective aim, leading to subjective unity,
all of which must somehow be analysis of the objective individuality which beauty is. However suggestive Whitehead's statements are, one suspects that determinate things cannot come out
as finished products on the belt line. His simple original postulate has a clarity and a ring to it significant of what seems to be
the art-process, namely, the "principle of process." But division
into prehensions and prehensions of prehensions seems to yield
an atomism at odds with aesthetic experience. Even though we
recognize that prehensions are not absolute—the grounding of
his "provisional realism"—we may well ask whether provisional
realism clarifies a genetic analysis, which by his own admission
has an element of arbitrariness.[35] Most significant of all is his
attempt to make eternal objects intrinsic to the aesthetic process.

[34] *Adventures of Ideas*, 347. (Italics supplied.)
[35] Cf. supra, *Process and Reality*, 360.

Eternal objects are the most troublesome of Whitehead's categories. No doubt other essays in this volume will consider the problem in some detail. In the context of aesthetics one question is uppermost: do eternal objects help us understand individuality? Unquestionably the claim is that Whitehead needs eternal objects to explain the creative advance.[36] He seems to suppose this himself when he writes: "In this two-way rôle, the eternal object is functioning relationally between the initial data on the one hand and the concrescent subject on the other."[37] Now it looks as if Whitehead needs eternal objects to relate two things put asunder, namely, subjective form and subjective aim. Hence, the office of eternal objects to relate them. Once these are sundered they cannot be related again, and for reasons similar to those Whitehead advances against Bradley.[38] Eternal objects, which may be conceived apart from matter, are said to "ingress" or "participate" in matter. When the problem is so cast, it leads to the host of insoluble difficulties Plato raised in *Parmenides*.

If I am not mistaken, the problem from the aesthetic, though probably not from the metaphysical, point of view is largely verbal. Whitehead must—and I think properly—consider the aesthetic process as the potential becoming the actual; that is, the indeterminate becoming the determinate. Call this ingression of eternal objects or what we will, it does not alter the matter. But this potentiality is what is called *real* potency. "Pure potentiality" never created anything, nor does it participate in anything.[39] Whitehead goes to some pains to distinguish two species of eternal objects, which he tries to make two sides of the same

[36] Everett Hall in his "Of what Use are Whitehead's Eternal Objects," *Journal of Philosophy*, Vol. 27, no. 2, Jan. 16, 1930, has considered other aspects of the problem. Cf. Emmet, *Whitehead's Philosophy of Organism*, 127-128fn.

[37] *Process and Reality*, 364.

[38] Cf. *ibid.*, 350.

[39] There is an unfortunate ambiguity in "pure potency." On the one hand it is independent of "any" occasion, and "its analysis only discloses [discloses only] other eternal objects." (*Process and Reality*, 34.) On the other hand, the eternal object can never be apart from at least one instance; ". . . the general principle [i.e., the eternal object] does not involve the realization of any particular instance, though it does necessitate the realization of *some* instance," (*Process and Reality*, 295f.) all of which casts doubt upon the possibility of a realm of pure eternal objects, and makes questionable the possibility of pure, formal analysis.

fact; but to make the universal, which exists independently of things, a side of the ingression, which exists only in things, is to carry metaphor a bit far. To treat individuality as the "grading" of universals is to end by denying the existence of individuals, for which there can be no principle of individuation. "Grading" may help for analysis in logic; it cannot define an individual, save through a confusion of individuality with particularity.

If ingression of universals signifies only that real potentiality becomes actuality, then we have a basis for understanding individuality. Whatever problems such a view might raise for interpreting the realm of pure possibility, the aesthetic situation becomes clarified. Possibility in art is real possibility become actualized. For I suppose it doesn't quite make sense to speak of knowledge of a possible work of art which is not actual. To know a possible work of art is to create it, and then it is no longer a possible but an actual. Otherwise, since the individual is unique and determinate, we should have to invent *ad hoc* a new eternal object for each individuality. One wonders whether Whitehead, through a verbal identification, unwarranted and unjustified, has confused individuality with particularity, by which he further tries to bring the logical and the genetic together. The "principle of process" is necessary in aesthetics, but its confusion with logical analysis leads us astray.

Finally, there is a question with respect to the last stage—satisfaction. This is border-line theory between aesthetics and theology. Art is finite. Ultimate concrescence is infinite. Hence, art is the ground of "provisional realism." Satisfaction is incurably atomic, yet it has relations beyond, as "Eros urging towards perfection." Individuals die, yet they have objective immortality in God, who is the poet of the world. That beauties die is well enough attested. Yet there is the lingering suspicion that the assumption of an infinite poet explains no facts we could not equally well explain without that assumption. The ground for concrescence is experience itself. Since God's nature is also one in process, "incomplete," one wonders whether it is anything more than an hypostatization of the concrescences of finite experience writ large. Whitehead seems not to have resolved the issue of monism and pluralism. The fact of genuine

ugliness—actual frustration—suggests a pluralism that even
God cannot resolve. The destruction of positive values, unre-
placed by anything higher, is much too vivid and widespread to
be glossed over by the supposition of an ultimate concrescence.

Whitehead holds challenging ideas as to the nature of the
aesthetic process, but further clarification is desirable. Does the
art-process begin with a kind of emergent, in some genuine
sense disjointed from and discontinuous with the non-conscious
processes of the physical world? Does the ingression of eternal
objects refer to anything more than the real determination possible of and implicit in actual occasions, together with its exclu-
sions by reason of decision? And if so, must we not distinguish
scientific analyses concerned with particulars from aesthetic analysis concerned with individuals? Finally, if art is genuinely and
intrinsically finite, are we referred on to the infinite, when the
essence of understanding process is its own self-evidence of attainment—a satisfaction which is also satisfactory? Can we, as
Warner Fite has asked, make a single poem of *L'Allegro* and
Il Penseroso? Must we not take ugliness quite as seriously as
beauty? These are legitimate questions that may well give us
pause. Aesthetic theory, it seems, gains in significance as we are
able to contrast it with other types of theory. A synthesis of all
problems in aesthetic terms leads to an arcadian paradise, lovely
if one can afford it.

V

Our review of Whitehead's aesthetic has followed the genetic
method by which the art-process leads on to the aesthetic
fact. To stop here is to omit the other adventurous path of the
philosophy of organism, namely, the place of coördinate analysis. In emphasizing the genetic, we have emphasized the more
important aspect for aesthetic purposes. Coördinate analysis,
with its insistence upon morphology is primarily the way of
science, rather than the way of art. As we have suggested, however, morphological analysis is not unrelated to aesthetic matters. We can do little more than suggest some points of contact
and perhaps raise a question or two.

Whereas genetic analysis is properly thought to be the art-

process in which individuality emerges, coördinate analysis applies to the division of regions. Coördinate analysis is of morphological structures, and of necessity refers to the physical pole.
For only the physical is divisible into regions. Since the mental
pole is "incurably one," it cannot be understood coördinately.
Hence, "In dividing the region, we are ignoring the subjective
unity [,] which is inconsistent with such division. But the
region is , after all, divisible, although in the genetic growth it
is undivided."[40] These divisions are then to be considered not
as what is separate, but as "what might be separate." Apparently, such analysis is important for determining the physical
nature to which any concrescence must conform. The physical
region is logically prior to the concrescence, inasmuch as it is
presupposed by but does not presuppose the concrescence.[41] Since
this type of analysis makes subjective unity irrelevant to the
divisibility of the region, it cannot properly account for either
art or beauty. Nor does it appear that Whitehead means that
it should.

Coördinate analysis does not give the essence of the art-process. Coördinate analysis applied to art is technique, for it is that
aspect of the aesthetic situation which constitutes the physical
region, or that which is a necessary but not a sufficient condition
of art. Technique can be—and often is—subjected to morphological analysis ad nauseam. It represents the more mechanical
aspect of art, in which the method of extensive connection can
be followed out in detail. Since it is independent of the mental
pole and separated from subjective unity, there is no urgency
by which it intrinsically demands realization in art-production.
Thus the draftsman qua draftsman is the mechanical embodiment of the technician at the opposite pole from the artist.

However good a draftsman the artist may be, his art consists
not in mechanical manipulation according to set patterns, but in
advance beyond them. Coördinate analysis yields patterns, and
patterns which may be repeated or reënacted indefinitely, but
such reënaction does not help us to understand art. The point
at which pattern becomes mechanical repetition is the point at

[40] *Process and Reality*, 435.
[41] Cf. *ibid.*, 434.

which art lapses into the physical. When this occurs, we are no longer called upon to analyze the situation aesthetically, but only scientifically, in which the individual gives way to the particular, and the universal refers not to an individual thing, but to a *class* of things. In a somewhat different context, Whitehead has recognized the problem as the relationship between the proposition and the judgment, in which the former emerges in the analysis of the latter. Judgment is through and through synthesis; the proposition is abstracted from the judging subject and from the subjective form. "The judgment is a decision of feeling, the proposition is what is felt; but it is only part of the datum felt."[42] Whereas the proposition is true or false, the judgment is correct or incorrect. We may suggest that judgments refer primarily to art and aesthetic phenomena and that propositions refer to technique. The correctness of judgment is grounded experientially, the truth of propositions is grounded factually. Aesthetic criticism is judgment; scientific analysis is propositional.

Pattern is ambiguous: it may be thought of as order achieved in the growing determinacy of an actual occasion, or it may be thought of as propositional contents repeated in the physical context. The latter is technique, and as such is devoid of aesthetic value, precisely because it is unqualified, and hence not individualized. The former is the principle of value; the principle of intelligibility, which accounts for the uniqueness of a thing. In a word, it is style. To confuse technique with style is to lose track of the principle by which art becomes intelligible. This seems to suggest a kind of bifurcation which is essential to an understanding of our culture. It is the platitude that science is science and art is art, and neither is the other.

To synthesize science with art is to shear science of its "practical" value in our contemporary world. In its application science treats not of individuals, but particulars; and, as has often been pointed out, the virtue of science is its "middle-sized principles," by which it can be effective in innumerable situations. Let science become art, and the laboratory becomes the atelier. However much one might welcome the shift, it would close the gap be-

[42] *Ibid.*, 293.

tween science and art through a blindness to the peculiar function which science serves in solving a kind of problem that art
cannot today solve. Large-scale production, and in general the
mechanization of the industrial world would have to go by the
board. We seem to be led to the conclusion that the rift between
science and art is with us today, and that by reason of the
peculiarities of science and of art each to deal with its own
kind of problem, we cannot synthesize the scientific and aesthetic
points of view without what seems to be the remote and merely
wishful resolution of culture and civilization, of life and industry.[43]

Finally, we may raise the question whether the mathematical
method can be ultimately synthesized with the aesthetic. Insofar
as mathematical forms are pure forms abstracted from content,
they can dictate no subjective form for prehension.[44] Pure forms,
or pure eternal objects dictate no contents whatsoever; and
Whitehead has suggested that mathematical symbols differ from
ordinary language in that, provided the rules are kept, they do
the reasoning for one.[45] I am aware of a number of his statements which seem to controvert this thesis. But one of the questions we may ask is whether we must give divergent descriptions
of mathematical reasoning and aesthetic process. Again, like art
and science, no doubt mathematics and art have points of contact, but is it proper to assume that because there are points of
contact, that they are therefore synthesized? That this is not
now the case is implied by Professor Whitehead when he says
that perhaps in the distant future symbolic logic "will become
the foundation of aesthetics."[46] If symbolic logic, as appears to
be the case, deals with elements of a class and abstract relations
between them, is it conceivable that such analysis can take the
place of the genetic analysis of advance into novelty, where what

[43] Professor Whitehead has himself pointed out this same dualism, it seems, in the
divergence between speculative and practical reason. Can we genuinely synthesize
the "god-like" reason of Plato with the "fox-like" reason of Odysseus? Where blind
force and stupidity prevail, the synthesis can be only a romantic ideal.

[44] Cf. *Adventures of Ideas*, 322.

[45] Cf. *Symbolism*, 2.

[46] *Proceedings and Addresses*, The American Philosophical Association (1936),
186, in *The Philosophical Review*, XLVI:2 (March 1937).

a thing is, is constituted by its becoming, and where the process of becoming cannot be divided into discrete elements with relations? Does it not seem as though this substitutes coördinate division, analyzing technique, for genetic analysis, in which we discover in immanent experience the real relations constituting the aesthetic fact?

How far we can resolve the dualism of philosophy is largely controversial. It does seem, however, that Professor Whitehead has made genuine contributions towards a solution of the old dualisms. Perhaps most important is his treatment of process and actuality, and among other dualisms, he has helped us to understand transcendence and immanence, the temporal and the present, symbolic reference and meaning, to mention only a few. But whether we have an adequate resolution of the problem of analysis and synthesis seems, to me at least, highly questionable. Perhaps it is because I have misread Professor Whitehead's philosophy. Perhaps Professor Whitehead is willing to clear up some of the misunderstandings, which may at the same time be the misunderstandings of others as well.

BERTRAM MORRIS

DEPARTMENT OF PHILOSOPHY
NORTHWESTERN UNIVERSITY

14

Julius Seelye Bixler

WHITEHEAD'S PHILOSOPHY OF RELIGION

WHITEHEAD'S PHILOSOPHY OF RELIGION

PROFESSOR WHITEHEAD once remarked in conversation that the real greatness of William James lay in the fact that, instead of offering a stereotyped definition of truth, he had left with his readers a sense of the need for a receptive mind and heart, and a readiness to find significance in new experiences from whatever direction they might come. One feels that the remark might be applied to Professor Whitehead himself. Like James he has taught not so much by offering formal definitions, which might too easily become instances of "misplaced concreteness," but rather by helping his students to be responsive to the rich variety of the changing pattern of events. It seems fair to say, also, that nowhere does his appeal for sensitiveness to emergent novelty come into sharper relief than in the part of his philosophy which deals with religious subjects. It is the religious aspect of the changing world which haunts the readers of Whitehead's books. With Windelband, Whitehead would agree that we become most aware of what religion means as we ponder the endless succession of drops of time passing into eternity, and with Schleiermacher he would point to the religious quality of moments of transition, as when we stand in the presence of birth or death.

Because he dwells so much on the overtones of our experience and refers to the fringes of consciousness which resist verbalization, he is a philosopher who inquires about the meaning of religious intuitions rather than a theologian who offers proofs for the existence of a divine being. Perhaps it is on this account that the editor has asked for a sketch of his philosophy of religion in addition to an essay on his idea of God. Whitehead is more sympathetic than many to the view that our religiously significant experiences include more than can be conveyed by our formal statements and that their loss in definiteness is offset by their richer quality. Whether we like it or not, we are more sure that we have religious moments than we are that we know how God should be defined. Like James, Whitehead is a defender of these moments in spite of their inarticulate nature and even, one feels, because precision in some cases may distort the truth. "It is characteristic of the learned mind to exalt words. Yet mothers can ponder many things in their hearts which their lips cannot express. These many things, which are thus known, constitute the ultimate religious evidence beyond which there is no appeal."[1]

It is worth noting, also, that not only the topics he selects but the forms of expression Whitehead uses adapt themselves easily to the religious point of view. Scientific as it is, and notable in its contributions to logic, his philosophy can yet be said to face in the religious direction. His interest in "togetherness" is not only metaphysical but religious in its stress on the need for fellowship with other living centers of experience and with the mysterious universe as a whole. His eagerness that we refrain from "bifurcating Nature" and that we look for final as well as efficient causes reflects a willingness to explore religious aims. His use of the Quaker word "concern" to explain what "prehension" means, his emphasis on growth, on the rhythm of life both human and cosmic, on value and quality, as well as on the penetrating nature of non-sensuous insights shows a tendency to grant religious considerations the first place. In *Process and Reality* when he wishes to characterize what he calls "the deepest problem of metaphysics," he quotes the lines of the hymn: "Abide with me, fast falls the eventide." Above all his insistence on "relevance," the relevance of idea not only to fact but to emotion, purpose, and practical outcome, indicates a sympathy with what is basic in the religious attitude. Both his cosmology and his psychology, that is to say, have a religious flavor. We have no right to use this for partisan purposes; but we should not neglect it, if we seek to understand what he is after.

Whitehead is thus a philosopher of religion, and especially of

[1] *Religion in the Making,* 67.

religion in its sensitiveness to the creative quality in the passing flux of events. He urges us to become aware of the significance of the deeper currents of emotion at work in our own time and to cultivate the sense of importance of contemporary events without which civilization must perish. He asks us also to study the productive elements in the great epochs of the past. A special insight developed in one great creative period interests him particularly. This is the period of roughly twelve hundred years from the appearance of the Hebrew prophets to the death of Augustine. In the chapter on "The New Reformation" in *Adventures of Ideas* Whitehead remarks that in this period a great insight went through three phases. First came the discovery by Plato that the divine element in the world is to be conceived as a persuasive and not a coercive agency. Then this idea was embodied in the lowly man of Nazareth with his message of peace and love. The third phase included the effort of Christian theologians to combine Plato's insight and Jesus' life in a metaphysical theory of divine immanence.

Whitehead argues that Plato failed to bring God completely into the world. Only a derivative image of God and only imitations of the real Ideas entered the world of flux. The Christian theologians brought the eternal into the temporal by finding God immanent in Christ and in the third person of the Trinity. But, after making this start in the right direction, they invalidated their own solution by refusing to apply to God the conditions which regulate temporal process. Like the God of the Old Testament he became an Oriental despot, internally complete and supreme in his omnipotence. The theologians were quite ready to say that God was necessary to the world, but they could not see that the world was also necessary to God. Actually, although they did not recognize it, the old dualism of eminent and derivative reality remained on their hands in aggravated form.

It thus becomes the business of philosophical theology, says Whitehead, to show how the lure of persuasive reason arises in a world which seems to be based on the clash of senseless compulsions. Plato, like a man "dazed by his own penetration," never really got the forms into flux. Christianity made a start, but went on to describe a God of power rather than of love.

How then shall we attack this problem? As all readers of Whitehead know, he himself attacks it as a problem of cosmology. That he takes this approach is itself significant, since what it means, in effect, is that we cannot understand the hopes and fears of our own inner life until we understand the world of which they are a part. As we look at the cosmos which produced us we see that its nature and ours are alike in that both are, so to say, made of the same stuff to operate in the same way. What is basic in human experience can be described in the same terms which science uses to describe the flow of electrical energy. Instead of saying with the Hindus that "Atman is Brahman" and that we should look within ourselves to discover what obtains outside, Whitehead urges us to formulate first a theory of the world based on scientific observation and metaphysical reflection. It is true that we must also look within, but we understand our own inner life as we see that it is our way of taking the outer world. The subject neither creates nor prescribes the laws for the object, but takes the object as it presents itself and interprets it by its own "subjective aim."

The central feature of his cosmological theory is of course the fact of process. As he expresses it, we have to reckon not with a procession of forms or succession of instantaneous configurations of matter but with a "form of the process." Actuality in its essence is process-with-relations. The process itself has internal relations which, together with the individuality or "subjective form" of each event, constitute the reality of the on-going world. Instead of separate entities in space and time, or a bifurcated Nature, with colorless and soundless bits of matter set against colorful, sound-creating minds, the world shows a creative forward movement where each event exists for the prehension or inclusion of all the others, and where each in its turn is the growth of a new way of feeling the rest of the universe. The older theory, with its bits of matter in simple location and its divorce between nature and life, furnished no basis for induction, for a theory of efficient causation, or for a belief in final causes and objective values. To see the kind of relationships the world exhibits we should look within our own experience and observe, for example, how the past of a quarter of a second ago maintains itself with differences in the present moment. The same kind of unity-in-difference is found throughout nature. In Whitehead's words, the creativity of the world is the throbbing emotion of the past hurling itself into a new transcendent fact. Each event is dipolar with a physical inheritance from the past and a mental reaction which drives it on to its own self-completion. The physical inheritance or physical pole is the real antecedent world as taken up into that event. It is thus actuality or what is given, whereas the mental pole is the spontaneous expression of the life of the occasion for itself. By means of the action of the mental pole actuality differentiates itself into the appearances which mark conscious and perceptive experience. In an act of concrescence each event receives the past and it achieves its own subjective aim by the way it envisages future possibility.

In this passage we may distinguish, for purposes of analysis, three aspects. *First* is the process of creation by which the actual world has the character of temporal passage into novelty. Creativity, like the Aristotelian matter or the modern neutral stuff, is without a character of its own, since it is itself the utmost in generality. It is what goes on, but, although we cannot characterize it in general, it is true that where we find it at work, under conditions of our observation, we always find it active. We can at least say that it is not mere passive receptivity. *Second* are the eternal objects, qualities or essences, including secondary qualities like colors and sounds, and also value qualities. These are not actual but become concrete and therefore real as they are "ingredient" in events. By this ingredience they contribute definiteness to the events. *Finally*, there is God, the actual, non-temporal entity who in his primordial nature is the principle of concretion, bringing a definite outcome from a situation "otherwise riddled with ambiguity," and who in his consequent nature receives the creative advance of the world and saves what in it is of worth.

If we keep in mind the essential "togetherness" of this creative process we may guard against errors into which Whitehead believes that theologians are prone to fall. The modernists, for example, have made God into an idea. To do this is to set up a false abstraction. Though non-temporal, God is an actual entity, making a difference in events as all actual entities must. In the same way we should emphasize to ourselves the binding, prehending, actively creative quality of all the relationships found in the on-going process. We see it in the creative relevance of an actual occasion for every other actual occasion, in the projection of the object itself into the subject as the subject prehends it, in the activity of the subjective form by which the subject recreates the object, as also in the work performed by the idea which does not passively mirror or reflect, but actively fashions the object. In the creative process everything suffuses and is suffused by everything else. The environment seeps into the occasion and the occasion extends itself into the environment. Each event is what it is both because the others are what they are and present themselves to it in their own way, and also because it has its own special activity of taking them into its subjective aim and influencing them in turn.

The whole creative process is characterized by a peculiar kind of twoness-in-one such that permanence and passage become two aspects of one reality, each needed not only for the totality but for the other's actuality. This twoness affects the nature of God himself. In his primordial nature God limits the infinite possibilities of the eternal objects so that they can become actual, whereas in his consequent nature he envisages the perfection which acts as a norm for each event. The temporal passage "exhibits an order . . . and a self-contrast with ideals, which show that its creative passage is subject to the immanence of an unchanging actual entity."[2] God as this actual entity enters into each creative phase not as the Creator but rather as the principle of limitation. He is not responsible for the evil. He does not create the world but saves it. In Whitehead's words he is "the poet of the world, with tender patience leading it by his vision of truth, beauty, and goodness."[3] He is the Principle of Concretion[4] or the Supreme Ground for limitation, "dividing the Good

[2] *Religion in the Making*, 99.
[3] *Process and Reality* (American edition), 526.
[4] *Science and the Modern World*, 243. (American edition, 1925.)

from the Evil and establishing Reason 'within her dominions supreme'.["5] For us the world passes into a veiled background because the various occasions develop destructive incompatibilities. "But God so receives the world that there is nothing obstructive in it, therefore the past remains unveiled in his nature."[6]

It is on this fact of creative togetherness that Whitehead's argument for teleology is based. In asking us to consider the evidences for final causes, as in directing us to the discovery of relationships, Whitehead suggests that we look within our own experience and then consider whether we really can abstract what happens there from what happens in nature. We see that we are driven by our thoughts as well as by the molecules in our bodies. At each moment of our conscious life we are controlled by purposes. Body influences mind, but mind affects what the body does. If you wish to understand history would you weigh the statesmen who control events or plot their temperatures?, Whitehead asks in *Modes of Thought* (p. 25f.). Men try to put aside the checkered history of morality and religion for the stable generalities of science. But, he goes on, unfortunately for this "smug endeavour" to view the universe as the incarnation of the commonplace, the impact of aesthetic, moral, and religious notions is inescapable. They are the disrupting and energizing forces of civilization. Molecules, Whitehead says elsewhere, may blindly run in accordance with general laws. But molecules differ in their intrinsic character according to the general organic plan of the situations in which they find themselves. An electron within a given body is different from an electron outside, by reason of the plan or mental state which the body develops. Yet such modification through plan is common in nature and not confined to living bodies. Each event must be understood in terms of a plan or unity which, as Whitehead says, points to meaning and value.

It is therefore the teleological intuition of religion which gives our view of nature the necessary completeness. Apart from the religious vision human life is but a flash of occasional enjoy-

[5] *Ibid.,* 251.
[6] Quoted from a lecture.

ments lighting up a mass of pain and misery, a bagatelle of transient experience, as Whitehead calls it. Without some transcendental aim civilization either wallows in pleasure or relapses into barren repetition. But the aim at social harmony is plainly discernible as resident in Nature. Nature has a tendency to be in tune, an *eros* toward perfection. Why has the trend of evolution been upwards? Because there is a factor in experience called Reason which "directs and criticizes the urge toward the attainment of an end realized in imagination."[7] Opposed to decay there is a disturbing element, a "noble discontent," a tropism to the beckoning light, a flight after the unattainable. In the universe there is a unity enjoying value and by its immanence sharing value. We call this unity God. God is that by which there is importance, value, and ideal beyond the actual; he is that which sustains the aim at vivid experience.

Two fairly detailed definitions of the religious vision should be given here. The first is from *Science and the Modern World.*[8] "Religion" Whitehead says

is the vision of something which stands beyond, behind, and within, the passing flux of immediate things; something which is real, and yet waiting to be realised; something which is a remote possibility, and yet the greatest of present facts; something that gives meaning to all that passes, and yet eludes apprehension; something whose possession is the final good, and yet is beyond all reach; something which is the ultimate ideal, and the hopeless quest.

And from *Religion in the Making,*[9]

The religious insight is the grasp of this truth: That the order of the world, the depth of reality of the world, the value of the world in its whole and in its parts, the beauty of the world, the zest of life, the peace of life, and the mastery of evil, are all bound together—not accidentally, but by reason of this truth: that the universe exhibits a creativity with infinite freedom, and a realm of forms with infinite possibilities; but that this creativity and these forms are together impotent to achieve actuality apart from the completed ideal harmony, which is God.

---

[7] *The Function of Reason,* 5.
[8] Pp. 267f.
[9] Pp. 119f.

Both these quotations emphasize the "togetherness" and the harmony characteristic of religion. Whitehead has much to say of the completed ideal harmony; but we should note clearly that he does not say that there is no disharmony, and he emphatically repudiates the idea of one divine event to which the whole creation moves. The passing flux contains altogether too much incompatibility of individual aims and too much instability for any such characterization. There is a forward and upward trend, the universe does have a tendency to be in tune; but we recognize these characteristics by comparison with others which are less harmonious. Evil is the force of fragmentary purposes which disregard the eternal vision. It is not enough to say that evil is negative or privative. Evil is a brute motive force on its own account. It is positive and destructive, where good is positive and creative. It arises from a fundamental incompatibility in the aims of the individual occasions. Yet the hopeful feature is that it is itself unstable. Indeed, "the fact of the instability of evil is the moral order of the world."[10] In all creative advance there must be loss and decay, and especially with the emergence of consciousness there must be frustration and tragedy. Whitehead would have us remember, however, that where we have genuine tragedy we have not merely loss but the disclosure of an ideal. Tragedy reveals what might have been or what was, and often it points to what still can be. The difference between gross evil, which is sheer obstruction or action at cross purposes, and tragic evil is that tragedy points to the permanent above the flux. Tragedy, therefore, is not evil unrelieved.

It is obvious that this view of evil affects the nature of God. God's nature is founded on what is infinite and eternal, but is itself being completed by advancing reality. The temporal passage of the world, that is to say, marks a real advance in his nature. In Whitehead's terms, on the "primordial" side God is the conceptualization of the eternal objects and is free, infinite and eternal, but deficient in actuality. On the "consequent" side, in relation to the advancing world, he is determined, incomplete, and conscious. Thus while, as Professor Hartshorne says, it is

---

[10] *Religion in the Making*, 95.

difficult to apply the word "limitation" to Whitehead's God, if we mean that some other conceivable Being might have what he lacks, it is also true that Whitehead interprets God as not in all respects infinite. If he were, Whitehead says, he would be evil as well as good. In this sense he is "decided and is thereby limited," the limitation being imposed by his goodness.[11] It is perhaps more strict to say that God is the supreme ground for limitation, and in this capacity distinguishes good from evil. But, in whatever sense we take the word "limitation," Whitehead is clear on the score that the traditional notion of omnipotence is both meaningless and harmful. "A happy God" he once remarked, "would be horrible." As the ground of limitation God exists in the midst of the flux. It is not that we have a flux upon which God imposes order as the Demiourgos imposed measure and number, or a flux which happens to possess an order of its own, but that the actual world of process exists because there is an order. The presence of order is necessary for the existence of the world at all. Thus we can as truly say that the world creates God as that God creates the world. God and the world are the contrasted opposites in terms of which the creative process works to bring unity out of the manifold and at the same time to allow new individuals to emerge from the total passage.

We observe at this point that the problem is stated rather than solved when we say that there is order in the flux of events. The real problem is—what kind of order? Is it the order of efficient or final causation, of events externally determined or self-determined? Obviously, for Whitehead it is both, and his whole philosophy may be described as the attempt to show why it is both and how efficient and final causes interact. If our interpretation is correct, he does it by suggesting that one grows out of the other in the process by which the past is taken up into each event and transformed into a subjective aim which refers to future possibility, but is not completely dominated by it or at least is not held down to one way of taking it. Here we have another instance of the twoness-in-one so characteristic of White-

[11] *Ibid.*, 153.

head's work. He insists that reality is one process, yet he insists also that each event is dipolar. Each is many yet one, bearing the content of the past yet open to the future, within the chain of efficient causes yet purposeful, determined by its relation to others yet possessing its own uniqueness, born of actuality yet reaching out into appearance, transient and fleeting yet having a hold on the permanent, seeking its own yet at times immersed in the common good.

The crux of the problem appears to lie in the conception of freedom, since Whitehead is definitely of the opinion that each occasion makes its spontaneous contribution to the on-going passage. We remarked above that the internal relations among events are binding up to a point. Each event receives the entire past and is internally related to each event in the past. Yet it reacts to the future in its own way and this is possible because it is independent of its contemporaries. Its companions of the moment leave it to work out its own destiny so that Creativity itself is ever determined afresh by its own creatures. God tries to persuade the world at each occasion to such perfection as is possible for it. But the extent to which each occasion surrenders is not for him to determine. Spontaneity and originality of decision belong to the essence of each occasion.

We notice two elements in this freedom. First, it is the sign of individuality. Freedom is the claim of the individual to vigorous self-assertion. As such it colors the harmony to which Whitehead so often refers. This harmony is not insipid or monotonous, but is the harmony of enduring individuals which retain their uniqueness in their common relationship. In the second place, freedom means a certain kind of independence of the flux and ability to hold fast to the permanent. It is this characteristic of the freedom of each occasion which enables Whitehead to say that the world is both passing shadow and final fact, where the shadow passes into the fact and constitutes it while yet the fact is prior to the shadow. There is a Kingdom of Heaven prior to the actual passage of actual things, and there is the same Kingdom finding its completion through the accomplishment of this passage. The Kingdom is in the world, yet not of the world.

The problem of how freedom arises in a process where the past is dominant and how, once it has appeared, it yields its individuality and fixes its attention on the eternal good is thus another form of the problem how an ideal order can be influential in a world of natural causation. Whitehead attacks the question from a different angle in his discussion of value. Value in the first instance means individuality. Value is the expression of a perfection proper to our own nature. Value, Whitehead says again, "is the word I use for the intrinsic nature of an event." To be an actual entity is to have self interest, which means to have a feeling of evaluation, an emotional tone. Whitehead here appears to be talking about subjective value, that is, natural living psychological value, the feeling of the organism for itself. Yet value has also its objective side and its relation to the eternal. In *Religion in the Making*[12] Whitehead says: "The peculiar character of religious truth is that it explicitly deals with values. It brings into our consciousness that permanent side of the universe which we can care for." Thus value means not only "self-enjoyment" and "realization of subjective aim" but realization of "a meaning which flows from the nature of things."

Obviously we have here the familiar dualism of that which satisfies and that which is rightly satisfactory, and the question is, how two experiences so different from each other in quality can be made parts of the same process. Whitehead offers an answer in his comment on the nature of religion. In the religious moment, he says, there is a merging of three types of value—the value of the individual for himself, the value of diverse individuals for each other, and the value of the objective world which is both derivative from the relations of its individuals and also necessary for them. If our interpretation is correct, Whitehead is here saying that we cannot make any final distinction between subjective and objective value or between psychological and metaphysical justification for value. In the case of value, as in the case of efficient and final causes, experience and thought, actual physical inheritance and apparent possibilities, we are

[12] P. 124.

confronted with a single process with two aspects which literally grow out of each other. Each is derivative from the other and necessary for it. If we protest that we obscure the difference between the two, such as the ethical difference between living for one's self and living for a cause, by merging them in this way, Whitehead replies that we cannot understand the difference or account for it unless we see the unity in the difference. In the case of freedom, for example, we have a quality that emerges in the natural course of events and changes this course in a way which is none the less natural because it is unpredictable and allows for possibilities that are genuinely new. Putting it in abstract terms which are necessary for analytic thought, although they fail to reflect the flowing nature of reality, we may say that it is characteristic of each occasion, first, to develop from the past, second, to attain an individuality of its own, third, to find an *eros* toward social harmony such that, in the case of many, it is discovered that true individuality is won through absorption in what is super-individual. In the case of many, we must repeat, this is true, since there is a tendency for the universe to be in tune. In the natural course of events freedom is rightly used. But it would not truly be freedom were it not subject to abuse; so that it is not true in the case of all. Another way of stating it is to say that evil is a positive disruptive force. This may look like dualism, but Whitehead would have us remember that he is only directing our attention to the richness of the unity which is actually there. After all, neither good nor evil, order, value, nor flux exist apart as separate entities. We may stress their distinctness for special purposes of our own; but we raise problems instead of solving them when we press the separation too far. It is probably true that we have not yet learned how to do justice to this unity in our verbalized thought; but this is simply another instance of the way our thought lags behind our basic intuitions. And in this case thought itself has its special reasons for desiring unity.

As we follow this problem through in Whitehead's work we see how large a part of the burden is borne by the notion of development. Freedom is itself a certain kind of development, where influences from the past issue into a new concrescent awareness of future possibility. As creation develops, that is to say, certain things take place which would be inexplicable if the world or its parts were static, but which are natural, given the passage of events. Let us take the case of religion. It begins when men find that in the regular process of development they turn from self-preserving activities to play, and from play to ritual. Ritual provokes emotions and thoughts which draw men still further away from concern with self-centered, immediate need. When thought appears religion loses its unreflective, ritualistic, social character and seeks solitariness. In a famous passage Whitehead observes that religion is "what the individual does with his own solitariness."[13] He goes on to say that "the great religious conceptions which haunt the imaginations of civilized mankind are scenes of solitariness: Prometheus chained to his rock, Mahomet brooding in the desert, the meditations of the Buddha, the solitary Man on the Cross."[14] But those who quote such passages do not always observe that Whitehead does not refer to complete detachment—either from the passing or from the permanent—and does not here run afoul of the fallacy of misplaced concreteness. The religion of solitary moments is the religion of rationality. It offers detachment from immediate social and routine interests in order that there may be attachment to the universal. It brings not escape from the flux but an appeal to the general character which gives meaning to the flux. The development is from concern with self-preservation to self-forgetfulness in play and ritual, then to deeper awareness of the universal. Whitehead makes this clear when, further on, he writes: "In its solitariness the spirit asks, What, in the way of value, is the attainment of life? And it can find no such value till it has merged its individual claim with that of the objective universe. Religion is world-loyalty."[15] In the normal course of events we are taken out of ourselves and into the presence of perfection. In love, for example:

the potentialities of the loved object are felt passionately as a claim that it

---

[13] *Religion in the Making*, 16.
[14] *Ibid.*, 19f.
[15] *Ibid.*, 60.

find itself in a friendly Universe. Such love is really an intense feeling as to how the harmony of the world should be realized in particular objects. It is the feeling as to what would happen if right could triumph in a beautiful world, with discord routed. It . . . involves deep feeling of an aim in the Universe, winning such triumph as is possible to it.[16]

Intrinsic value thus is actually realized through the desires of finite beings. This does not always happen, for freedom is real. Yet the fact that it does happen must be construed to mean that intrinsic like instrumental values are part of the creative passage. We should now observe that for examples of intrinsic value Whitehead turns most frequently to the aesthetic experience. Aesthetic order is the highest type of order because it is the most concrete. Logical order is important, but aesthetic harmony is more than mere consistency. Logicians, Whitehead says, are not called in to advise artists. Like logic, aesthetics is concerned with the enjoyment of self-evidence.[17] But aesthetics pays more attention to the individuality of the parts, without losing its sense for the totality. Therefore the lure of aesthetic relevance is both more concrete and more inclusive than the lure of logical relevance. This consideration leads to the extreme statement that all order is aesthetic order, moral like logical order being but an aspect of aesthetic order, so that the "foundation of the world" is in aesthetic experience. Or, as Whitehead says elsewhere, the teleology of the universe is directed to the production of Beauty. Beauty is the one aim which by its nature is self-justifying.

It will be observed from the foregoing that Whitehead is as intent as is Plato on making clear the difference in quality between eternal and temporal, intrinsic and instrumental, spiritual and natural. But he is much more sure than Plato about the limits to this dualism. Plato knew that the two members must be brought together; yet he found that when he did unite them they had a tendency to split apart again. Whitehead, recognizing the difficulty and allowing for the distinction, yet emphasizes the fact that unity has the first and the last word. His is a phi-

---

[16] *Adventures of Ideas*, 373.
[17] *Modes of Thought*, 83.

losophy of organism. The teleological self-creation, which is characteristic of reality, is itself the form and therefore one aspect of the unity of the process itself. The grandeur of truth arises, he says, from the very nature of the order of things. "The life aim of survival is modified into human aim at survival for diversified worth while experience."[18] The excellent grows out of the concrete experience of decision to become the permanent.

It seems fair to compare this (as has been done by Dr. W. P. McEwen in an unpublished manuscript) with Faust's sublimation of his will-to-power and will-to-romance in his final discovery that his own will could be merged in a socially creative endeavour which brought dignity and peace. Or we may compare it with Schweitzer's assertion that his sensitive exploration of the natural will to live brought an awareness of the will to love. Or, on the plane of social experience, we may find an example in Pundit Nehru's comment that the desire of the Indians for national independence is gradually being transformed into a desire for world socialism and justice for all men. The discovery in each case is of a more inclusive and more reasonable ideal which grows out of the actual concrete situation with the decisions it requires.

And yet, as an indication of the fact that no amount of stress on the unity, the naturalness, the concreteness of the process can blur the distinctions which must be made within it, we should notice that Whitehead closes what is in many ways his most impressive religious book, *Adventures of Ideas*, with a dualism that is not wholly resolved. Temporal and eternal have been joined together in the creative process; but, when the discussion turns to practical attitudes and actual beliefs and hopes, they break apart again as adventure on the one hand and peace on the other. Adventure gathers up into itself the virtues of the eager searching quest, characteristic of the transient decisive moment. Peace expresses the values of permanence as they are found, not in anaesthesia or soporific contentment, but in the synthesis of a rich harmony of individualities. They have much in common. Yet they are not the same, and our thought can never wholly

[18] *Ibid.*, 43.

recapture the distinctiveness with which they present themselves in experience.

Philosophies and religions seem to divide as emphatically on this issue as on any. With all his yearning for the assurance of salvation, and his sympathy with the sentiment of rationality, James was primarily a philosopher of adventure, just as, in spite of his emphasis on the will and his assertion that the Absolute was a man of war, Royce offered a philosophy of peace. The interest of the Jews in their own origin and destiny and in the effective decisions of a Divine Will in history marks the religion of the Old Testament as one of adventure; whereas the craving of the Hindus for a release from temporal responsibilities forced them to seek a religion of peace. Whitehead tries to do justice to both, insisting that "Both—And" offers a better means of handling the situation than the sharp disjunction of "Either—Or."

Adventure is what saves civilization from staleness, boredom, and orthodoxy. A civilization with the adventurous spirit is free, vigorous, and creative. Where adventure is lacking we have literature without depth, science concerned only with the elaboration of details, art busy with comparatively unimportant shades of distinction, religion devoted to dogma. Only the adventurous can understand the past, for what was great in the past was itself adventurous. On the other hand, peace stands not so much for safety as for steadiness, especially steadiness in the conviction that fine action is treasured in the nature of things. Peace saves adventure from cruelty and ruthlessness. So construed peace does not inhibit action but releases it. It removes the stress of acquisitive feeling arising from the soul's preoccupation with itself. "One of its fruits," says Whitehead, "is that passion whose existence Hume denied, the love of mankind as such."[19]

Thus we may say that adventure is actuality with its own inherent freshness and vigor. Vitality is of the essence of each occasion and contributes to its value as well as to its natural effectiveness. When it leads to conflicts it should be sublimated

[19] Cf. *Adventures of Ideas*, 47.

rather than thwarted. Peace is the disclosure of the ideal harmony toward which each occasion may tend without the vitality being lost. It supervenes upon actuality as the future supervenes in idea upon the present. Yet, as if he thought the word itself savored too much of static conformity, Whitehead seems unwilling to conclude with peace. His final emphasis is on the "Unity of Adventure," where individuals retain their freedom yet share in a common quest.

The foregoing sketch, incomplete as it is, should yet be sufficient to suggest that Whitehead offers us a philosophy of religion notable for its grasp of the salient features in the religious attitude and especially for its awareness of the particular needs of the present time.

In the first place it furnishes religion with a much needed defense against the attacks of a scientific positivism. Never before in the history of thought was there so aggressive an eagerness as we see today to show that knowledge comes only through sense experience and by the methods of the laboratory. Without disparaging the senses Whitehead claims that we have other organs of receptiveness and then, instead of emphasizing their complete separation, greatly strengthens his argument by saying that the two kinds of knowledge enter into one coherent scheme. "Sense-data and value data," he says in *Religion in the Making*,[20] "are dealt with by the same mode of thought." But there are some things that the senses cannot do. We watch a humming bird's wings and see a patch of color where really there are thousands of vibrations. We hear one note instead of the great variety in nature's tone. The senses simplify, and it is well for us to seek simplicity; but we should distrust it when it is found. Reflective thought, which puts experiences into words, has also its danger of over-simplification. Language is a tricky instrument which does only partial justice to our deepest intuitions. The prominent facts of consciousness are the superficial facts; those that are important are on the fringe. Therefore we mistakenly criticize the mystic when he attaches importance to experiences he cannot explain. Some experiences are significant

[20] *Vide* Chap. IV.

in the highest degree, even though it takes us a long time to tell what they are significant of. The present enthusiasm for the scientific method in religion is thus based on a misconception. Art and poetry offer nearer analogies since, like religion, they direct us to the inarticulate and incommunicable quality of the vivid flash of insight.

In the second place, at a time when dogma is again coming into the forefront of theological thought, Whitehead makes both a direct and an indirect attack upon dogmatism. The direct attack is based on the obvious truth that dogmatism means staying put instead of moving forward. The religion which stays in one place is "the last refuge of human savagery." The more indirect attack is part of Whitehead's analysis of the subject-object situation. We should not think of a subject as engaged in copying an object but as incorporating in its own subjective aim the objects which present themselves. In the religious situation this means that special dignity as objects of loyalty should not be given to items of belief. To do this is to abstract ideas from their living emotional context and to make them unresponsive to the march of events. Our religious experience should center not in questions weighted on the intellectual side, such as "Is there a God?" or "What do you believe?", but in our own aspirations toward value and our awareness of what value implies. As Whitehead puts it in *The Aims of Education,* our problem is to fit the world to our perceptions, not our perceptions to the world. Truth is not something set apart for our ideas to copy, and a belief has no special sanctity of its own. Our religious ideas arise out of the situation where we creatively apprehend the data given, especially the data derived from the currents of emotion which relate us to our fellow men, the historic passage of events, and the creative process itself where God as the principle of actualization is implied in all we feel and do.

Third, Whitehead's attack on dogmatism is one with his appeal for the quality which the world today craves above all others, the quality of tolerance. If religion is to minister to the desperate need of our tragic era by binding up humanity's wounds it must forget its partisan strife and become, as Whitehead says, World-loyalty. Whitehead's revolt against authority and his stress on the rights of the individual are part of his appeal for tolerance. The unity we require must emerge from below as part of our immediately felt yearning for fellowship, instead of being imposed from above in the form of beliefs bequeathed by another generation and crystallized in an institution. We require our own way of expressing our loyalties, and we must remember that others are like us in this respect. Thus Whitehead would have the Bible find its climax in the funeral oration of Pericles with its plea for tolerance and for the rule of persuasiveness rather than in the book of Revelation with its picture of a God of power. God is the spirit of reason and love, the great companion, a fellow-sufferer who understands. Those who worship him must have a religion based on the companionship of all free participants in the unity of adventure.

In the fourth place, Whitehead in an age of self-assertiveness offers us a religion which, to use an ancient phrase, could be called "natural piety." The purpose of religious education, he says, is to teach duty and reverence. Duty arises from our potential control over the course of events. The foundation of reverence is the "perception that the present holds within itself the complete sum of existence, backwards and forwards, that whole amplitude of time, which is eternity."[21] Philosophy, as he says elsewhere, begins in wonder. It teaches humility in the presence of the ultimate mystery. We should note especially that he means not the mystery stressed in some movements of contemporary theology which makes of the worshipper a cringing, fearful suppliant, but the mystery which by its fascination lures men on to action and to further speculation. It is the mystery not of an abstract alien Deity who stands aloof from human need and desire, supreme in the sovereignty of a will which knows no other laws than its own, but of the creative process at which we do not cease to wonder when we find that we share its work.

Finally, Whitehead invites us to think of religion and of history itself as essentially an experience of growth. We should

[21] *The Aims of Education*, 23.

not be misled by those who cry that there is no health in us or that progress is an idle dream or that our present failures have the last word. It is the nature of reality to move forward, and it is the essence of each occasion to have the opportunity for creative advance even though the opportunity may be abused by reason of freedom. The Greek sculptors were right in taking their standards of beauty and their ideas of what is most deeply real from the dynamic symmetry exemplified by the growing body. The ideal is in the process, yet the process never wholly attains the ideal. Life shows a "noble discontent" which refuses to allow it to rest with present achievement but stimulates to further effort.

In all this Whitehead makes an emphasis of supreme importance today, when he shows that religion is the fruition and not the denial of culture. God is not, as some theologians would claim, the "Wholly Other" or an arbitrary sovereign will, or a despot in whose presence "all our righteousnesses are as filthy rags." God needs the world as much as the world needs God. We reach association with him by following the path that our reason, conscience, and aesthetic perceptiveness point, not by any leap into the dark or denial of the worth of our rational and cultural life. We see him when we see the "rightness in things" and when we cultivate and find the implications of our sensitiveness for that which is of good report. The new insights emerging today in the best of our art, literature, and philosophy are indications of a creative process which is not pagan but religious, and we must discover the holy in that which, instead of denying those insights or minimizing their worth, brings them into harmonious synthesis.

Nor does Whitehead allow us to forget that the ideas of culture or of theology when abstracted from the living currents of personal experience are futile. Of education, for example, he has said expressly that the spoken word and personal influence of the teacher can never be supplanted by lectures set down on paper or recorded for the phonograph. Words emerge from felt situations and contribute to them in turn. Teaching means sharing overtones of emotion as much as stating mere facts. Anyone who has observed Whitehead's own students in the classroom is not surprised to find that they have learned from him not so much a system of philosophy as a method of philosophizing. Instead of repeating his phrases they have been stimulated to productive work on their own account. In this connection it is perhaps not inappropriate to refer to what at present writing was his latest public appearance, the delivery of the Ingersoll Lecture on "Immortality" in April, 1941.[22] The problem of personal immortality, he said in this lecture, is part of the wider topic of realized value. Value is that which emphasizes persistence. Value judgments point beyond the immediacy of historical fact. But values have a passion for realization in the world of action and when, through the creative process, they enter this world they endow the fleeting moment with the significance of the permanent. The large audience which greeted Professor Whitehead on this occasion and which received the lecture with the tribute of complete silence was perhaps reminded of another famous discourse on immortality with its indirect exemplification of the idea it sought to convey. Plato in the *Phaedo* supplemented his arguments with a picture of the way a brave man meets death. Professor Whitehead, in the simplicity of his personal persuasiveness as he spoke out of the maturity of his experience, gave his audience not arguments alone but an impression of the entrance of eternal quality into the fleeting moment.

So we return to the theme with which we began. Like James, Whitehead has given us not a new stereotype of truth, or God, or immortality, but a new eagerness to receive intimations of what these words may mean. He has made us more responsive to the fact of passage and more ready to perceive its creative aspect. Our age is not likely to yield to boredom but it could easily be overcome by fear. Whitehead teaches us to look below the surface of political events and to become aware of the massive emotional currents which are working to produce a new life for society. In the same way he teaches us to look below the superficialities of sense experience that we may become aware of the deeper relationships which bring security to the individual because they bind him to his fellow men and to his God. Ours

---

[22] Cf. for the entire content of this lecture pp. 682-700 in Professor Whitehead's "Summary" below. (Ed. Note.)

is an age of transition, and transition brings pain. But "at the heart of the nature of things there are always the dream of youth and the harvest of tragedy. The Adventure of the Universe starts with the dream and reaps tragic Beauty."[23] Yet suffering attains its end in harmony and the experience of this harmony, "with its union of Youth and Tragedy, is the sense of Peace. In this way the World receives its persuasion toward such perfections as are possible for its diverse individual occasions."[24]

JULIUS SEELYE BIXLER

HARVARD DIVINITY SCHOOL
CAMBRIDGE, MASSACHUSETTS

[23] *Adventures of Ideas,* 381.
[24] *Ibid.*

15

Charles Hartshorne

WHITEHEAD'S IDEA OF GOD

WHITEHEAD'S IDEA OF GOD

I. Whitehead and the Theistic Tradition

FROM Plato, Aristotle, and Philo to Spinoza, Leibniz, and Schleiermacher, the great metaphysicians and theologians of over twenty centuries tried to find a rational meaning in the religious idea, the idea of God. And from Carneades to Hume, Kant, Dewey, Santayana, and Russell, some of the acutest philosophical minds have pronounced the effort a failure. Whitehead, for his part, holds the definite and carefully considered opinion that the classical versions of theism are one and all unsound, collectively a "scandalous failure." His idea of God is consequently an intentional departure from most of the philosophical past.[1] Not that he is claiming to be the only philosopher who has understood God! What he offers us is rather the most technically adequate version of a conception of God which a score of philosophers and theologians of great distinction, and hundreds with humbler attainments, have been working out since the fifteenth century, and especially during the last one hundred years. Whitehead is following a trail blazed by some great and many able predecessors (among them Fechner, Pfleiderer, Bergson), but it is only in his thought that their work (much of which may be known to him only indirectly, if at all) comes to fruition in an elaborately systematized philosophy in which the conception of God and the other philosophical conceptions seem as if made for each other, and nothing is mere *ad hoc* concession to some interest or evidence which the general system is not properly adapted to cover. Whitehead's is not the first philosophy to

---

[1] Cf. *Process and Reality*, 519f., 526; *Modes of Thought*, 92-95, 111f., 164. (Page references in this essay to *Process and Reality* are to the American edition, 1929.)

lead naturally and consistently to the religious idea of God, for
Fechner's and Ward's philosophies did that; but it is, I think,
the first great systematic philosophy to do so.

One must note, however, that Whitehead does not simply
brush aside as valueless the work of the classical theists, but
rather he sets forth a higher synthesis of the more extreme
tendencies of recent theism (as seen, for example, in James) and
the older conceptions. According to Whitehead these older conceptions, in spite of their differences, nearly all involve much
the same fundamental error. This is the error into which philosophy generally has tended to fall with regard to most of its
problems, the "fallacy of misplaced concreteness." The fallacy
takes two forms in relation to God. (1) We may identify God,
conceived in terms of value, with sheer "perfection," defined
as completeness or maximality of value such that nothing conceivably *could* be added to it, and from which therefore every
form of self-enrichment, every aspect of process, and of potential
but unactual value, is absent. This means that the temporal
character of value and all contrast between purpose and achievement, as well as all mutual exclusiveness among values (which
seems of their very essence[2]) and all relationship to beings
whose value is not perfect, must be *abstracted from*, omitted
from consideration, in order to conceive the perfect, which must
not be contaminated, it is held, by containing any of these things.
(2) We may also identify God, conceived in terms of causality,
with sheer power or activity, a "cause of all," which is in no
aspect of its being the effect of any, an agent which acts but is
not acted upon. In this case, too, God is arrived at by abstracting from or omitting one pole of a categorical contrast (or trying
to omit it, for unconsciously is it not still asserted?).

A similar abstractness is involved in the concept of God as the
"most real being," or "pure actuality;" for of the two polar
aspects of reality, actuality and potentiality, only the first could
be present in an absolutely maximal reality.[3] Potency must be
simply omitted. This is only feebly disguised by the quibbling

---

[2] Cf. *Process and Reality*, 225; *Adventures of Ideas*, 356; *Modes of Thought*,
72-75.

[3] *Ibid.*, 93-97.

distinction between internal and "external" potency, as when it is said that, though God is all that he could be, he may not produce all the effects "outside" himself that he could produce. Here is simply another abstract or one-sided idea, this time that of *being* as wholly independent of *doing*. The conception leads to interesting paradoxes, such as that though God actually knows his potential external acts as potential, potentially he knows them as actual (for they are capable of actuality, and *were* they actual he would know that they were so). In short, his knowledge has a contingent aspect, but his being has no such aspect—as though anything could be more intimately part of a knower than his knowledge and its immediate contents (or does omniscience know indirectly, hence, surely, imperfectly?)!

The two ideas of sheer absolute perfection and sheer causality or actuality represent extremes to which there is in each case an opposite extreme. It is clear that the doctrine, God is the World-Cause as capable of being considered in complete abstraction from his effects, or from the world, has as its logical contrary—*not* merely contradictory—the doctrine, God is the world as capable of being grasped entirely apart from any supreme and independent cause. Between the two opposites there lies a median position which contradicts the extremes only in so far as they contradict each other and retains the characteristic positive features of both. This is the doctrine that God is both a supreme causal factor which can be abstracted from the world of its effects and, in another aspect of himself, the supreme totality of all his effects, and of their effects. That is, God may be conceived (1) as the mere creator, (2) as the creator-with-the-creatures, or (3) as the mere total of creatures (as not really such). The advantage of (2) is not only that it includes the positive factors of (1) and (3), but that it thereby enables these factors really to be themselves. A creator without creatures is nothing *as* creator, and similarly, the creature as such is nothing without creator. The history of thought seems to show that for every defense of an extreme position such as (1) or (3), there will be a defense, roughly equal in sincerity and ability, of the contrary extreme; so that, unless we can get above the conflict and accord some part-truth to each of the embattled opposites, there is no sane hope of progress toward agreement. Consequently, the burden of proof should be considered as falling primarily upon the extremists, in this case, upon those who assert either radical and complete absolutism or radical and complete relativism, radical and complete independence of God from the world, or his complete identity with it—or even with a part of it, say, with a dream in the mind of man.

Let us symbolize the doctrine of sheer independence as CC, meaning not only that there is an independent or purely causal aspect of God, C, but that there is no other aspect, that independent power describes all aspects of the divine being. Then the opposite extreme may be indicated by WW, meaning not only that there is a world-aspect of God, W, but that there is nothing independent of the world in God, nothing but W. Then obviously the median position is CW, indicating that there is an independent factor, which is cause but not effect, and also a dependent or, as Whitehead calls it, a "consequent" factor, which itself has causes. Now if God is sheer absolute perfection, a doctrine which we may symbolize as AA, nothing but absolute perfection, then there is no basis, from the standpoint of perfection, for the distinction, from the standpoint of causality, which CW involves. Simple perfection is—simple, as theologians have nearly all agreed. But suppose perfection has two aspects, one absolute, or A, the other not absolute and hence in some sense relative, or R. Then the C in CW might be the A in AR, and the W might be the R. (In general the partisans of sheer perfection favored CC as against WW.) It is also apparent that as CW is to CC and WW, so is AR to AA and RR. In each case we have a positive synthesis which excludes only the negative or abstract aspect of the extremes.

How can we define R? Very simply. In its generic meaning, perfection, whether as A or as R, is an excellence such that its possessor *surpasses all other conceivable beings*. But A-Perfection means the property of surpassing all others *while not surpassing self* (growth or improvement being thus excluded from whatever aspects of a being are A); while R-Perfection means surpassing all others *while also surpassing self* (permitting, if not requiring, growth in the R aspects of a being). Thus R is a richer conception than A, since it includes the relation of universal superiority to others, which is the only positive feature of A, and includes also the equally positive relation of self-superiority or self-enrichment. The "un-self-transcending transcender of all others" is A, the "self-transcending transcender of all others" is R.[4] Now there is no obvious reason why a being might not *in some aspects* transcend all others but *not* itself, whereas in other aspects it transcended all others than self *and self as well*. More than that, just as cause-with-effect is more intelligible than mere cause or mere contingent phenomena alone, so to transcend self in some respect and others in all respects, to be AR, is more intelligible than to transcend others in all respects and *self in none*, to be AA, or than to transcend *both self and others in all respects*, to be RR. For, as to RR, if self is transcended in all respects, then self has no identity and no meaning; and as to AA, if self cannot surpass itself then it can in no valuable sense involve self-contrast, and without self-contrast self-identity is also meaningless. In still other terms, if there were no abiding standard of growth, growth would be meaningless, and the standard must involve an aspect (A) which does not itself grow but measures all growth, including growth of standards. But, at the opposite extreme, were there no growth there would be nothing for the standard to measure. Measure of growth and growth belong together, in one reality, the perfect which is both absolute and relative, both static and dynamic, though not in the same aspects of its being. It is this last qualification that has been most sadly lacking in the tradition. It has been too lightly assumed that God's perfection must be all of one kind, without contrast or categorical distinction.

Of course it may be objected that perfection means primarily completeness, the absolute realization of value, and only secondarily and in consequence of this absoluteness the impossibility of self-improvement as well as of being surpassed or equalled

[4] Whitehead says that every actual entity transcends its actual world, even including God. But this means it adds itself as a new value to existence, and since God and God alone *fully possesses* or prehends every such addition, God "transcends" or excels others in a special or preëminent sense, and that is the sense in which I am using the term.

by others. But this way of formulating the matter leads to the same outcome. For it cannot be that all dimensions of value admit of absoluteness, and it equally cannot be that none of them do. For some of the dimensions of value are neutral to the contrast between actual and possible reality, and some are not, and the former dimensions imply an absolute maximum, whereas the latter exclude such a maximum; and each of these types of dimension involves the other, so that AR is required if value is to have any meaning at all. Let us take an illustration. The accuracy and adequacy of knowledge to its objects, its truth, is independent of which among these objects are actualities and which are mere possibilities, provided only that the actual things be known as actual and the potencies be known as potencies, that is, in each case, provided that things be known as they are. But the joy, the aesthetic richness, of the knowledge depends in part upon just what things are actualized. For instance, it depends upon the wealth of harmonious contrasts which the objects involve; it also depends, so far as what is known is sentient or perhaps even conscious, upon the degree of joy or sorrow felt by the sentient individuals known, since knowledge of feeling is irreducibly sympathetic, is "feeling of feeling."

Now there can be no absolute maximum of harmonious contrasts, since possible contrasts are inexhaustible and mutually exclusive by the very meaning of possibility as a field of open alternatives.[5] Similarly there can be no "greatest possible happiness of all things other than God." Hence the aesthetic value, and the sympathetic joy, of God's knowledge cannot be absolute. Yet its accuracy and adequacy, its truth, to what is actual and what is possible, at a given stage of cosmic development certainly can be complete, by the very meaning of knowledge. It cannot be that the whole of *de facto* reality could not be known, such an unknowable whole being meaningless. Indeed, as we shall see, the cosmic whole must actually be known. Hence God's knowledge must be A in its cognitive perfection or truth, and R in its concrete self-value as enjoyment or bliss.

Similar reasoning supports the view that there must be an independent causal factor which, like cognitive adequacy, is

[5] Cf. *Adventures of Ideas*, 330; *Process and Reality*, 69.

abstract and neutral to the distinction between potential and actual, and that there must also be a dependent or consequent factor which is concrete and varies with *de facto* actualization of potency. In other words, AR-CW [or better perhaps, A(C)-R (W), to show that A and C, R and W, are the same factors considered from two points of view, those of value and causality] is the most promising formula for the divine nature, although the idea it defines is one whose possibilities have only recently been explored.

There is an important ambiguity to be removed from the foregoing analysis. In the assertion that the A (C) factor is independent of or abstractable from the world, "world" is to be taken to mean: this actual world which does exist with just the particular things it contains. C is involved in each and every one of these particulars but itself involves none of them. Yet C, as interpreted through CW, implies nevertheless that there is *some* world, some set of particulars, or other. The world could, so far as C is concerned, and so far as anything is concerned, have been different from what it is, but some sort of world must have been "there," that is, must have been content to the divine knower and effect of the divine cause. Accidents must needs happen, though this or that particular accident need not have happened. Contingent existences form a class which must have members, but not any members you choose to point to. W as the generic factor in all particulars is essential to C, as R is to A, or as variety is to unity. What is contingent is a special form or case under W, say Wm or Wn (really CWm or CWn), the *de facto* world that now or at some other specified time happens to exist. W requires that there be *some* Wm or other, but not that there be this or that Wm.

We are now ready for the crucial question: Is Whitehead's idea of God a case of AR-CW, or is it one more abstract extreme (such as AA-CC, or AA-CW, or RR-WW, or some other of the eight logically possible cases), involving the fallacy of misplaced concreteness which Whitehead has been at pains to avoid? Certainly his intention is to conceive God in a balanced or concrete way, for he lays down the methodological principle that "God is not to be treated as an exception to all the metaphysical principles, invoked to save their collapse." Rather "he is their chief exemplification."[6] And the metaphysical principles form a set of contraries or "ideal opposites."[7] Every actual entity, including God, is dipolar, and that in several ways. Nothing concrete or actual is merely one or merely many, or a mere cause which is in no way effect, or a completeness which is in no way incomplete or subject to addition, or an activity which is in no way passive, or the mere contrary of these. Of course, neither God nor anything else is in the same sense and respect cause and effect, or active and passive, or good and evil, or simple and complex; but to grant this is not to admit that there either can or must be something actual which is in no genuine sense and respect effect, passive, complex, or evil (God is the "fellow-sufferer," he suffers evil,[8] though he does not commit it[9]). Yet all these unqualified, or not consistently and clearly qualified, negations had been commonplaces, indeed almost automatic reflexes, in theological discussions. They are all explicitly rejected in Whitehead's philosophy, and this is the first time, to the best of my knowledge, that this rejection has been so systematically worked out. (Nicolaus of Cusa affirms both poles of the polarities with respect to God, but scarcely shows by what distinctions contradiction is to be avoided. Rather he glories in contradictions.)

According to Whitehead, God and the World may be compared through

. . . a group of antitheses, whose apparent self-contradiction depend on neglect of the diverse categories of existence. In each antithesis there is a shift of meaning which converts the opposition into a contrast.

It is as true to say that God is permanent and the World fluent, as that the World is permanent and God is fluent. . . .

It is as true to say that God creates the World, as that the World creates God.[10]

The classical procedure was to affirm that God is "above the

[6] *Process and Reality*, 521.

[7] *Ibid.*, 529.

[8] *Ibid.*, 532.

[9] *Science and the Modern World*, 251; *Religion in the Making*, 153, 155. (Page references in this essay to *Science and the Modern World* are to the American edition, 1925.)

[10] *Process and Reality*, 528.

categories," while at the same time, in order not to have to admit that God is for our thought simply nothing at all, giving certain categories (called "transcendentals") a preferred status as incomparably more true of God than their contraries, or as, in abstraction from their contraries, applicable at least "analogically," though not "univocally," to God and to other beings. Thus, for example, actual being or form as opposed to potency or matter, and one as opposed to many, were held to be descriptive of God. According to Whitehead, the distinction between God and other things (the totality of which he calls the World) is to be treated in a manner at once less equivocal and more complex and subtle. It is less equivocal, for Whitehead commits himself to the application of all contrary categories to God, and in my opinion faithfully carries out this undertaking. (Moral evil is not a category, being absent not only from God but from the lower creatures; yet aesthetic evil is a category and is entirely absent nowhere.) The Whiteheadian procedure is more complex and subtle than the traditional one because God is contrasted with inferior beings not by the simple method of deciding which among the categories are to have the privilege of applying (even though not univocally) to God, but by showing in what way each of the categories, the entire complexity of ultimate contraries, has its "chief," that is, supreme, instance in God. It is the unrivalled excellence of the activity-*and*-passivity, the unity-*and*-complexity, the being-*and*-becoming, yes the joy-*and*-suffering, of God which elevates him above all others, actual or conceivable. Whitehead's God is as much, nay more, the supreme being as is the God of the Thomists. The difference is that Whitehead so conceives being that it can really have a supreme instance, without equivocation, and if by analogy, then an analogy that does not play favorites among the irreducible dimensions of existence upon which all analogy depends.

It might be objected that at least "supremacy," or being the "chief" instance of the categories, is itself a category which, *rather* than its contrary, "inferiority," or "being surpassed by another," must be favored in relation to God. But this is the exception that our rule is able readily to account for. The contrast between the being that is better than all others and these others is the contrast between a by definition unique individual, and a mere class of individuals. Of course to be the supreme being is peculiar to God. But by the same token supremacy is not a category, analogous to actuality as opposed to potency, or unity as opposed to complexity, or being as opposed to becoming. Moreover, we shall find that in a real sense even the supreme being includes inferior being, though it is not any the less supreme over it for that.

It is true that Whitehead objects to "metaphysical compliments"[11] to God, and thus appears to suggest that God has been too highly thought of, is not really "supreme" over all conceivable beings. Nevertheless, I think his position is better expressed by saying that in the attempt to praise God people have unwittingly talked nonsense (emptied their categories of meaning) and nonsense is doubtfully classified as praise. Only in one sense is it possible, according to Whitehead's philosophy as I understand it, to overpraise God. At any stage of the cosmic process there may be possibilities of value for that stage greater than those actually achieved in it, because of the unlucky or even perverse actions of the creatures. All does not occur for the best. This means that God's concrete being is not all that it might have been as "inheriting" that stage. But on Whitehead's principles no God is conceivable who would not thus depend for part of his value upon the actions of the creatures. Thus, though God is at any time less than he (but only he) might have been, he is not in his generic property (as he is at all times) less than he generically might be; for, to be subject to being sometimes less than is, at those times, possible is implied in the only generic nature that any God *could* have. In still other terms, God's realization is less than it might have been, because all realization, realization as such, is essentially social, and hence in its concrete degree dependent upon other beings. Thus there are no "limitations" in God except those the general possibility of which in the perfect being is part of the meaning of any conceivable perfection.

We have already implied an affirmative answer to our ques-

[11] *Science and the Modern World*, 250.

tion, Is the God of *Process and Reality* describable as AR-CW? We have now to document this answer.

II. PRIMORDIAL AND CONSEQUENT NATURES

That Whitehead's God is not AA is easy to prove. For "all realization is finite, and there is no perfection which is the infinitude of all perfections."[12] Moreover, the Consequent Nature of God is said to be relative, incomplete, and in flux.[13] Nor is God CC, for he is to be conceived "as requiring his union with the world," and Whitehead criticizes the classical theologians for supposing that though God is necessary to the world, the world is not necessary to God.[14] On the other hand, Whitehead's God, taken in one aspect, really is A and is C. For the Primordial Nature is "limited by no actuality which it presupposes," and is complete, perfect, infinite.[15] That is, God is unequivocally A and C, though not AA and CC. Is he AR and CW? He is certainly A plus a relative aspect, and he is C plus the world as internal to his complete nature.[16] Thus to show that he is AR-CW we need only prove that the relativity ascribed to him is relative perfection and not ordinary, imperfect relativity. Now since God contains in "everlasting imperishableness" all actual values, from the moment of their actualization, and combined in the utmost harmony of which they are capable,[17] there is no conceivable way in which any individual (personal-order society) other than God could equal, not to mention surpass, him. For the content of the other individual, if and when it exists, must be fully contained in God, so that the two could not be distinguished except as the other failed to contain some value that was contained in God. Thus God is the self-surpassing being who in all possible circumstances surpasses all others, that is, he is R-Perfect.

When it is said that the Primordial Nature is complete, yet "deficient" in actuality,[18] the apparent inconsistency is only ap-

[12] *Adventures of Ideas*, 330, 333, 356.
[13] Cf. *Process and Reality*, 523-27.
[14] Cf. *Adventures of Ideas*, 215, 217; also *Process and Reality*, 529.
[15] Cf. *Process and Reality*, 521, 523f.
[16] Cf. *Modes of Thought*, 128.
[17] Cf. *Process and Reality*, 524f., 530.
[18] *Ibid.*

parent. For "the unlimited conceptual realization of the absolute wealth of potentiality,"[19] *as* such realization of the potential, is superior to any conceivable conceptual realization or awareness of potency that could be distinguished from God's. It is complete in its kind or dimension, the dimension of "mentality" or abstract realization of value. But it does not at all follow, a long tradition to the contrary notwithstanding, that God must be complete in concrete dimensions as well. Nay, it follows that he cannot be. For potentiality could be neither complete nor incomplete, it could be nothing, were there a complete actuality, a full realization of potency. Inexhaustibleness is of the essence of potency and the presupposition of actuality. Possibilities are in part mutually incompatible, they are not always compossible, and, as Whitehead says, theologians have been strangely reluctant to face the implications of this truth.[20]

It might be thought that if God is CW, both the supreme cause and the supreme totality of effects, he must be the pantheistic, all-inclusive substance, responsible for all evil, the "supreme author of the play," and the "foundation of the metaphysical situation with its ultimate activity," against which Whitehead protests.[21] Does he not say that God is "in the grip of the ultimate metaphysical ground,"[22] the "creativity," which is repeatedly distinguished from God and never identified with him? In all these ways it seems to be implied that there is a causal factor, a C, which is beyond God. This is a delicate point, but I think the answer is, No. First, the creativity is not an actual entity or agent which does things; it is the common property or generic name for all the doings. Second, the internality of the world to God's concrete or consequent nature has nothing to do with a reduction of all activity, all creative "decision," to God's own activity or decision. For there are two ways in which activity may be contained in a given actuality, (1) as self-decided by that actuality, and (2) as contributed by the self-decisions of others. "Recipience," "patience," tolerant prehen-

[19] *Ibid.*
[20] Cf. *Adventures of Ideas*, 357.
[21] *Science and the Modern World*, 250f.
[22] *Process and Reality*, 529.

sion of the activity of others, is essential to concrete being, whether that of God or of anyone else. God has all activity within himself only because he accepts the activity of others as such and enjoys it within his own "immediacy." God appropriates the actions, the decisions, of others, he does not decide just what they are to be. We are told in the most unequivocal language that God's influence upon others is not decisive to the last degree of determination.[23]

This solution of the problem of evil is the oldest of all (cf. the Book of Genesis), except for the fact that scarcely anyone before Whitehead ever made an adequate and honest place for it in a comprehensive metaphysical system (Varisco, Ward, and Fechner are perhaps exceptions to this statement). The problem is how a genuine *division of power*, hence of responsibility for good and evil (implying a possibility at least that *all* of the evil, as well as *some* aspects of the good, may derive from creaturely decisions) can be reconciled with the ascription of all the wealth of actuality to God. To do this we must have general metaphysical principles whereby actualities can be *contained in other actualities yet retain their own self-decisions*. Now, according to Whitehead, it is true that every actuality as a whole is an act of self-decision. But it contains parts which are decided by others, indeed are constituted by the self-decisions of others (in the first-mentioned actuality's past). The synthesis is free, but the content synthesized is in part derived from others. In Aristotelian language (but not in Aristotelian doctrine), actualities are, through their form, matter for each other's form. This is the social nature of reality. To be decided in part by others is essential to being as such.[24] To enjoy a decision it is not necessary to make it, but only to make a further decision as to just how the first decision is to be enjoyed in relation to other actualities, that is, it is only necessary to "objectify" the first decision within one's own immediacy. If God were "pure actuality" in the sense of simple perfection, AA, then to enjoy a decision he would have to make it. The *actus purus*, the form containing no others as matter, the activity without recipience, was a precise

[23] Cf. *Religion in the Making*, 94f; *Process and Reality*, 343f., 525f.

[24] Cf. *Process and Reality*, 68.

way of denying the social nature of God, of denying absolutely that God is love, as Spinoza almost consistently perceived and the schoolmen made it a point of honor not consistently to perceive. Also, as Whitehead points out,[25] the notion—which theologians first hit upon in the doctrine of the Trinity—that personalities can be literally immanent in each other can be at least as validly applied to relations among the creatures and between the creatures and God; though of course the creatures' receptivity for each other and for God is subject to certain imperfections, involving particularly the relegation of most of the included content to a low or negligible level of awareness, or distinctness of consciousness.

When Whitehead says that creativity in general is wider than God, he is simply pointing out, as I take it, that not all decisions are God's self-decisions. He is not denying that all decisions are in some manner enjoyed, possessed, by God. Even we enjoy many decisions that we do not make, particularly the radically subhuman and, in our awareness, not individually distinguishable decisions of the bodily members, such as cells or molecules. Creativity is thus, I suggest, the abstraction which leaves out of account the duality of decisions as self-made and as made by others. Thus all creativity belongs to God *either, but not both,* as his self-decision *or* as his uniquely adequate way of being decided by others. All this only amounts to saying that existence is social and that there is a supreme, hence supremely social, existent—in which double assertion all great truths are contained with a fullness from which men (apparently dazzled, in Plato's image, with excess of light) have fled as though it were the most baneful of errors.

We have now to ask how far the distinction between A (or C) and R (or W) coincides with Whitehead's distinction between Primordial and Consequent Natures, or as I shall say, PN and CN.

PN is described as the conceptual envisagement of eternal possibilities, and as such is absolutely perfect, A. But this is not the only A aspect of God which Whitehead recognizes. For the

---

[25] Cf. *Adventures of Ideas,* 216.

divine awareness of all actual occasions as so far occurrent, his enjoyment of the total past of the universe, is perfect in its adequacy to that past, and equally and unsurpassably so at all times. With each new stage of the universe, there is more for God to know, but he knows each and every stage, as it is actualized, quite perfectly, or "without the qualification of any loss either of individual identity or of completeness of unity."[26] Is then God simply omniscient in the old-fashioned sense? Yes, on two conditions.

(1) "Knowledge of all things" means, of each thing as it is, of the actual as actual, of the merely possible as merely possible, of the future as future, of the past as past. For Whitehead there is a future, even for God, not because God is in advance ignorant of future events, but because, so long as they are future, objects of knowledge are not events, are not fully individual and determinate entities. There is nothing in the future for anyone to be ignorant of, except those more or less determinate outlines of probability or possibility, those impure potentials, which distinguish the future both from the determinate past and from the pure undecidedness of the eternal potencies. These outlines of the future are known to God just as they, at any time, are, so that he is entirely without error or ignorance in regard to them. This doctrine is at least five hundred years old, but apparently no great philosopher saw its importance before Whitehead.

(2) Though God's knowledge is at all times, and so primordially, free from error and ignorance, and thus cognitively absolute, A, yet there is a sense in which it perpetually improves upon itself, namely in richness of content and so in aesthetic value. As future possibilities gain determinacy and become actual events, God's knowledge, without the slightest increase in adequacy to its content, realizes the aesthetic value involved in the *new contrasts* which the new content presents, both in itself and in relation to the old. For Whitehead, the value of truth consists in its contribution to harmony, unity in variety, but the harmony due to the truth correspondence between knower and known is only one dimension upon which the harmony of knowl-

---

[26] *Process and Reality,* 532.

edge must be measured.[27] There is also the unity-in-variety of the object itself, which becomes, through the correspondence, the possession of the subject. Furthermore, there is no such thing as absolute or maximal unity in variety, since every definite variety excludes others. Apart from process, there would be but one out of all possible over-all aesthetic patterns for the content of God's knowledge. Through process, the wealth of patterns can be inexhaustibly increased, though it can never become absolute.

But not only is God at all times unsurpassably perfect in the accuracy and adequacy of his knowledge, both of the possible and of the *de facto* or actual (though he is ever growing in the resultant aesthetic enjoyment), but he is also at all times unsurpassably perfect in the adequacy (goodness, wisdom) of his purposes and decisions. He "saves all that can be saved," and he exerts a "particular providence for particular occasions"[28] (James's "piece-meal supernaturalism"), by furnishing all but the last element of determinateness to the subjective aims of the actual entities. Now we are given no suggestion that any other conceivable being could surpass the quality of these divine functions, or that God himself is any more adequate in discharging them at one time than another. Thus there is aesthetic but not ethical or cognitive improvement in God, aesthetic R-Perfection and ethico-cognitive A-Perfection.

It follows that if the PN is that which God primordially or at all times is—and otherwise it seems a confusing phrase—then the description of PN as "conceptual" is inadequate. PN is at once conceptual, volitional, and perceptual. It is in fact the *common element of all the successive conceptual, perceptual, and appetitive states of the divine life*, abstracting from the differences between these states. This common element is abstract, and so it is *known* by conception, but it is equally a quality of perception and of will.

With non-divine individuals no literally primordial character is possible, since these individuals have had a genesis. But there is a quasi-primordial feature of every enduring individual, the

---

[27] Cf. *Adventures of Ideas*, 342, 344.
[28] *Process and Reality*, 525, 532.

individual quality which a man, say, has had during all his life as a person. This seems to involve a relatively fixed style of both conceiving and perceiving, as well as of volition. Only God has an absolutely fixed and ungenerated general style or self-identical character, an abstract element of strict invariance individual to him. The PN is this element of mere identity, apart from all differences in the Divine Life. It is true that identity has meaning only in relation to difference, and really includes difference; but we may distinguish between difference as such, as a generic and hence identical abstract factor, and this or that individual, concrete difference. Now the CN is this peculiar identity of difference or change as such. It and the PN mutually require each other. But there is a third something which contains both of these abstractions with a contingent addition, the *de facto* individual difference, the concrete partly novel divine state of the given now. Thus we have (1) the static perfection of PN, which is a definite quantum of value, namely, absolute or maximal value, and, as necessary to this perfection but applying to other dimensions of value, (2) the dynamic perfection of CN, which is not a definite degree or quantum of value, but the *generic property* of (3) a *class* of possible values, this property consisting in the values' being always superior to those possessed by any being other than God, and also superior to those possessed by God himself at any earlier time, as well as inferior to any values that he may possess in the future. The primordial or static perfection includes the law that there shall be a consequent or dynamic perfection. The law that there shall be change in the form of enrichment is itself unchanging, unenriched. We have, then, to distinguish between the generic property of having a consequent state, and the particular state that God in any given now may have. It is to be remembered also that when we refer to God we ourselves are always in some consequent state, say CNm, which contains not only the entire generic or abstract divine nature, PN-CN, but also some individual *de facto* concrete phase of that nature, PN-CNm. The impossibility of deducing any particular PN-CNm from the PN-CN is thus no difficulty. The only use it could have would be to enable a non-actual something to know actuality by a knowledge which was itself non-actual. But we can deduce the necessity that there be *some* concrete state, PN-CNm or PN-CNn or PN-CNo, etc., and that each such state be followed by a successor; and this deduction is not useless, for it guarantees that there will be a future, that planning is not futile. The deduction consists in drawing the consequences from the negative outcome of the effort to find any basis of meaning in experience, however imaginatively extended, for the notion of the mere abstract or generic factors as entities simply apart from any instances. One may abstract from *each* instance but not from *all* instances. Another instance will always do, but none at all will not do. (This was Aristotle's insight, I take it.)

Abstraction from the concrete proceeds backward in time and depends upon memory, as Plato saw. Today need not have followed yesterday, although *some* today must have followed yesterday, and similarly with yesterday in relation to its predecessor. Thus we can abstract from any finite slice of the past, however large, but not from all the past. As Whitehead says, the primordial nature is not before or apart from but *with* all process, every stage of which is a contingent successor to its presupposed predecessor.

Thus we have the following structure of the divine life:

PN-CNn as containing PN-CNm, its predecessor, as containing . . . etc.
PN-CNo as containing PN-CNn as containing PN-CNm . . . etc.
PN-CNp . . . etc.
etc.

Each stage is the cumulation of the earlier, and contains of the later only an approximate outline, plus the law that there shall be *some* individual event or other of which the outline will be approximately descriptive. (See below, section iv.) The certainty that this law will be fulfilled is based on the omnipotence of God, if by this old term is meant that he is absolutely equipped with the power and the will to bring the fulfillment about somehow, to prevent the world from collapsing into chaos or empty monotony.

Since any given PN-CNm state could have been otherwise, we must conceive a disjunctive series, PN-CNm1 or PN-CNm2 or PN-CNm3 . . . , as the total set of things PN-CNm might have been, granting its predecessor. Suppose, then, PN-CNm1 has actually occurred; it is an interesting question whether PN-CNm2 and so on are to be regarded as individually determinate or definite, *or* as more or less indeterminate segments of a range of possibilities in which, as possibilities, nothing quite so definite in quality as an actual event is present. Of course there must be the possibility that the indeterminate may become determinate, as well as the law that *some* indeterminate segment of possibility shall be individually determined. But the possibility of further or individual determination need not itself be individually determinate. This is the question of the definiteness or otherwise of eternal objects or pure potentials. (See section viii.) It has a certain bearing on the question of the conceptual character of the PN. If eternal possibilities are fully definite items, then God's concepts need never change, and his entire conceptual being is fixed forever. All that can change (or give place to new ones) are his physical prehensions and with them his hybrid prehensions of the impure potentials as relevant to a given state of the cosmos. The hybrid prehensions will change, however, only in their physical constituents, and the impure potentials will be simply identical with certain eternal objects as selected for a given occasion by the physical prehensions. If, on the other hand, impure potentials are more definite than anything to be found in eternal possibility, then God's concepts must become more determinate with time, and thus it will not be true that the conceptual aspect of his being is completely primordial, just as it is not true that the physical aspect of his being is completely derivative. (What is not derivative is the law, the general how, of his derivations, his unique style, whose functioning had no beginning, of *adequately* prehending actualities.)

It is to be understood of course that any PN-CNm implies a set of world-members, of creatures, as existing in it. Since in this fashion PN-CNm embraces ordinary imperfect things, there is no need to attribute ordinary imperfection or ordinary relativity, r, to God himself, except precisely as properties of *his* parts. Just as a small part can belong to a large whole, so it is clear that the imperfections of the parts are not as such and identically imperfections of the whole. What *is* true is that the whole must be R- and not merely A-Perfect. (For there can be no greatest possible whole of imperfect parts, any more than there can be a greatest possible number, or an absolute variety.) Consequently, we need not consider the ideas of God which are derivable by adding r to A and R. AR makes room for all the r's there may be, whereas mere A would make any r factor strictly superfluous, irrelevant, meaningless.[29] The interesting thing is that whereas so many writers have seen that there might be difficulty in conceiving finite evils to exist as such, if there be an in all ways simply perfect or best being (in the best or only possible state of itself), far fewer have seen that it is equally difficult to make sense out of finite good as out of finite evil, assuming AA. Neither finite good nor finite evil can have anything to do with sheer maximal good. God as AA could not impart significance to finite values, whether positive or negative. The problem is to enable the finite to contribute to the "best" being, without demanding, what is impossible, that the contribution should, either alone or with whatever supplementation you please, effect an absolute sum. No sum of finites can be absolute or can intelligibly contribute toward making anything absolute. It can very well, however, contribute toward making something R-Perfect, superior to all that is not itself, and through progress superior even to itself.

There is a relation of this to the Russellian theory of types. There can be no "all" which is absolute being, the all of all possible totalities. But there can be an all which nothing other than itself can surpass since anything other than itself will, to exist, belong to the "itself." The cosmos must be such an all, if we admit that any possible entity is possible only because the cosmos might produce it, either within and as a part of itself, or as a state of itself as a whole. The unity of this whole is involved in its parts, since their very existence is their rôle in the cosmos as one, as *the* cosmos. Thus the correct treatment of

[29] This is sometimes admitted by neo-scholastics. See for instance E. I. Watkin, *A Philosophy of Form* (1938), 47. This writer tries to mitigate his admission by reasoning which I am prepared to show is fallacious.

all avoids the two extremes of AA and rr or mere relativity. As at all times the complete possessor of all that at those times exists, the cosmos must have an A aspect, for there are no degrees of complete possession. But since there will be more to possess at one time than another there is, also, an R factor. AA and rr (or atheism) are the twin absurdities between which philosophy has tragi-comically swung for over two millennia.

III. ARGUMENTS FOR GOD'S EXISTENCE

It is Whitehead's contention that "metaphysics is a descriptive science," that direct experience, intuition, is basic, and proof is secondary. So far, Whitehead agrees with Bergson. The groundwork of all existence is present in all instances of existence, hence in all experience, and the task is to see it there. Argument can only rest upon some part of the groundwork that happens to be more clearly discriminated. Still, in so far as some aspects of the metaphysical situation are more readily observed than others, at least in a given state of culture, personal or social, argument may be in order. And Whitehead does offer what might with some qualification be called "proofs for God," even though he also declares that "nothing like proof" is possible. God is, according to him, that aspect of the metaphysical situation which, though involved in the other aspects, is less immediately apparent and obvious (at least to ordinary non-religious experience) than they, and in so far is in need of indirect evidence.

To the question, Why after all is there a conception of God in Whitehead's philosophy? the answer is two-fold. First, Whitehead is not without religion. Second, his categories, adopted at least as much for other purposes, require God as their "chief" and indispensable exemplification. In saying that God must not be invoked to save the collapse of the categories by making him an exception to them, Whitehead is not denying that the categories, however well chosen, would collapse without God, but he is saying that they must require God, if at all, as their supreme instance, not as an exception or a violation of their requirements. There can be no obligation upon categories to render God superfluous, unless the possibility of atheism is

axiomatic. (Since Whitehead believes in the unconsciousness of
much that is in experience in the form of feeling and impulse,
he is not committed to accept at face value the claims of various
persons to "believe" in a godless world.) Categories are obligated to describe the world in terms of their exemplifications,
and if they can only do this on the admission that there is a
chief example of their meaning, that fact is in so far a proof
that such an example, a God, exists, unless another set of
categories, at least equally adequate for other purposes, will
function without a supreme example.

How do Whitehead's categories require a supreme example?
There are as many answers as there are categories; for they all
require God. (1) Possibility implies a supreme and primordial
ground, (2) actuality an all-inclusive actual entity, (3) the
transition (creativity) from possibility to actuality a supreme
creative agent, (4) memory a highest type of retention of
elapsed events, (5) purpose and love a highest or perfect type
of purpose and love, and (6) order a supreme ordering factor.
(3) is Whitehead's well-known argument for a principle of
limitation or concretion. (1) is the argument from the "ontological principle," (2) is found particularly in *Modes of
Thought,* and is given no title, (4) is the doctrine of everlastingness, not presented so much as an argument for God as a consequence drawn from accepting his existence, but capable of becoming an argument; (5) and (6) are found here and there
throughout his writings.

(1) Possibility is either a property of existent things, or it is
independent of all existence, a self-sufficient realm of essence, as
Santayana says it is—though at the same time substituting
essence for possibility and thereby advertising that he is not
really solving or even facing the question of possible quality,
any more than of actual quality, but is talking about something
nobody ever encountered, that is, a quality as it would be were
it neither actual (a datum in a real experience) nor even capable
of being actual. Only qualities that at least *might* get into existence concern us, and the only more than verbal notion anyone
has ever set forth as to what would make non-actual things
possible is the notion of "power," the "I can," as an unde-

termined but determinable aspect of an existent. Only what exists has the power to create further existence, and it has this power because what exists is not complete in all aspects but has an element of futurity, or a principle of self-transcendence, of being potentially what it as yet is not. But if the only existents are ordinary imperfect things, and if, as it seems reasonable to suppose, these things have not always existed, then when they came into existence they did so as determinations of determinables already existing, and the ultimate power involved must lie back of all such non-primordial and secondary things. "The general possibility of the universe must be somewhere" is the summary of this line of argument.[30] If possibility is meaningless without existence, then it cannot be that all existents are contingent, for this is to say that the being of possibility also is contingent, that it might have been that nothing was possible —precisely the implication of Santayana's doctrine, since had nature not existed (and its existence is said not to be necessary) there would have been nothing capable of actualizing essences, which are not self-actualizing. The conclusion of the argument is that there is a primordial power *whose non-existence is not a possibility, since possibility presupposes its existence.* Its reality being the ground of alternatives, its non-reality is not an alternative. This is the old argument from contingent being to necessary being, with the difference that it is *not* concluded that the necessary being is necessary in all its aspects, but only that any contingent aspects it or other things may have presuppose one aspect of itself which in all possible times, places, and instances necessarily is. What can this necessary aspect be? We experience potentiality as the way in which experience involves the future in the present, in the form of more or less determinate purposes, undecided as to the precise value which is to be actualized, but determined to actualize some value or other. This involves universals, ranges of value, and a function of deciding at a given moment upon *a* value within such a range. Personality is the only clear case we know of such a combination of universals and decisions. To say the necessary, primordial power is a primordial personality, in its essential character an ungenerated, indestructi-

---

[30] *Process and Reality*, 73.

ble unity of subjective aim, appetitions, mentality, and acts of fiat, is simply to give the only answer we can to the question, what is the non-contingent basis of contingency? In the last few remarks we have expanded (1) to include (3), the argument for a principle of limitation.

As to (2), what can it mean to say of an occasion that it actually occurs in a world in which other actualities also exist? To stand outside the occasion and say, "it exists," is to refer it to a *common measure or register of existence* by reference to which other things also exist.[31] This measure cannot be the thing's own solipsistic or private self-awareness; for then existence would have no common or public meaning, and to say many things exist would be to say nothing.[32] Nor can the measure be the imperfect sort of social awareness that ordinary things may have of each other, for then there is no criterion to decide between the imperfections of their views of themselves and each other. To refer to "existence" as a public meaning is to refer to a register on which, with infinite exactitude, everything is recorded just as it "really is," on pain of its not being really anything. Since actuality is essentially, for Whitehead, an affair of value and feeling, the register of existence must be something infinitely sensitive to shades and varieties of feeling.[33] All is clear if we assume an all-embracing "tenderness," or sympathy, which appropriates all feeling as soon as occurrent, not by robbing it of its selfhood, its self-decisive character, but by enjoying this character with infinite "patience" or tolerance. The standard of existence must also be the standard of value, for nothing can really measure what we are that cannot measure what we are worth to ourselves and to each other. It must be fully conscious, for the unconscious cannot answer, point for point, quality for quality, to the conscious, or even to the contrast between the conscious and the un- or semi-conscious.

As to (6), it is perhaps Whitehead's favorite argument. The only empirical basis for order, the only answer to Hume, that Whitehead finds is in such factors as immediate memory, an-

---

[31] Cf. *Modes of Thought*, 149ff.
[32] *Ibid.*, 140ff.
[33] *Ibid.*, 151, 159, 162-65.

ticipation, the sense of conformation to past emotions and purposes and to the feelings flowing to us from the body, and the necessity for aesthetic harmony among these factors if the en during self or personal society is to have any richness of content. Order is drive toward harmony in the relations of past, present, and future, of self and others immanent in self. It is aesthetic teleology. Now if there is no cosmic seeker of harmony, there can be no reason why the various seekers for harmony should have the pure luck to succeed in assisting rather than thwarting each other in the search. They have only limited knowledge of each other's needs, or of their own needs, and indeed, they would have no standard by which to recognize each other as realities. Local order can in some minor way be in the hands of local orderers, local aesthetic drives; but cosmic order, presupposed by all lesser orders, can only be safe, or anything but doomed, if there be a unitary cosmic aesthetic drive, that is, a cosmic love which seeks beauty everywhere it can be attained, and guides the general direction of cosmic change so that the right balance of novelty and repetition shall in general be secured. The laws of nature are not merely "imposed" upon dead matter, nor merely immanent trends in local agencies, nor mere descriptions of uniformities observed (they would then give no assurance as to the future).[34] They are immanent, but this immanence is given a cosmic reference by an element of imposition, of interfusing of ideals more or less unconsciously derived from the one whose subjective aim effectively surveys the cosmic whole. This is not the usual argument from design. For it holds, not merely that the order of the world is so superior that it must have a superior orderer, but that if we did not take a cosmic order unconsciously for granted we would not be able even to say "world" or to know anything at all, even about disorder. To believe that there is a cosmos is to believe in a cosmic individual whose content of integration is in part the variety we see.

That the general trend of physical nature seems to be toward

---

[34] *Adventures of Ideas*, Chap. VII. See also *Symbolism, Its Meaning and Effect*, Chap. II, for Whitehead's "answer to Hume," an answer which, however, cannot be understood apart from the doctrine of God. See also *Modes of Thought*, 162f., and *Religion in the Making*, 104f.

a state of minimal activity or "running down" (second law of thermo-dynamics) shows that the ultimate creative aspect of reality is not accessible to the physicist, not that there is no such aspect. Moreover, the running down of a type of order is a familiar aesthetic phenomenon, as we see in the history of the arts. Each general style has its day in art, and then undergoes decline, loss of appeal and zest, until some new order, through exploration "along the borders of chaos" as Whitehead says, is arrived at. It *ought* not to be that the present style of natural activity, the pattern of the present cosmic epoch, should last forever. With the inexhaustible realm of possibilities not utilized in that pattern to draw upon, why should the cosmic artist adhere forever to one design?[35]

And if the physical world in general is running down, life on this planet is a partial exception, there being no evidence that the ascent of life is a mere example of the laws of quantum mechanics, but every reason to think it is partly contrary to those laws (though not in gross physical degree, the issues of life involving small amounts of energy, physically regarded). In life we see a creative force—Whitehead agrees with Bergson here—of which low-grade physical realities are only a sort of minimal and in a manner retrograde expression. They are there chiefly to serve, and to pass away when their service is done.

(5) Since the basic structure of reality for Whitehead is the social integration of occasions, it is not surprising that he argues for a cosmic, supreme, and in certain senses perfect sociality. Only because there is a cosmic society with personal order (though Whitehead does not use this expression in this connection), a supreme love, whose integrity is presupposed as the measure of all lesser orders and of all disorder, can we conceive the various societies as more or less integrated, or as in any way comparable to each other, or able in general to survive in each other's presence.

When a society disintegrates, this is not a disintegration of the cosmos, but a rearrangement of its integrity, without which nothing would have any definite character in relation to anything

---

[35] Cf. *Religion in the Making*, 160; *The Function of Reason* (1929), 21-23, 72.

else. Integrity is not indeed the only value, since richness of content is also a value. God seeks richness of enjoyment in his creatures generally so far as guidance of their free decisions (by determining the limits within which the freedom is to exist) can produce such richness. For his own richness of content is the total richness of theirs. He loves them quite literally as himself, for they furnish parts of himself and his happiness through their own happiness.[36]

The argument from everlastingness I shall consider in the next section.

IV. EVERLASTINGNESS AND FUTURITY IN GOD

Whitehead has not always written as though the principle of process applied to God. He has called God "non-temporal," and has contrasted him with "the temporal world." He has never, I think, said that God has a past, present, or future. And in one passage he has stated that for God there is no past.[37] The context of this last remark, however, indicates that what is meant is that the primordial conceptual awareness of eternal objects is not derivative from any antecedent concrete awareness, since the divine conceptual awareness must have been already involved in any concrete awareness. As for "non-temporal," the definitive declaration is surely the passage which describes God as in one sense non-temporal and in another sense temporal.[38] We must, I think, also emphasize the fact that it is in Whitehead's three most recent books that the temporal aspect of God is most clearly and vigorously affirmed, so that there may have been a change in Whitehead's belief since he wrote *Science and Religion*, a change in the direction of greater consistency with the Principle of Process.

Is there a past for God? It is said that in God occasions never "perish," and in *that* sense nothing is past, is gone, for God.

[36] Cf. *Process and Reality*, 161; *Religion in the Making*, 158. For an analysis and defense of the doctrine, ancient in religion, but almost unexplored in philosophy, that God is love (in a non-Pickwickian sense) see my book, *Man's Vision of God and the Logic of Theism* (Willett, Clark and Co., 1941). In this book many of the problems dealt with in the present essay are given a more detailed treatment.

[37] *Process and Reality*, 134.

[38] *Adventures of Ideas*, 267.

But it does not follow that there is no order of succession in the
divine life, which is most expressly stated to be "fluent." It is
indeed not the case that succession depends essentially upon
perishing, upon the fading of immediacy as events cease to be
present events. As twenty centuries overlooked, and Bergson
was one of the first to realize—though only in his somewhat
cloudy, "intuitive" fashion—the order of succession depends
rather upon the logical difference between retrospective and
prospective relationships.[39] The later event prehends the earlier
and so contains it, but the converse is not true; and this one-way
relationship remains even when both earlier and later events are
in the past (or when—it is all the same—there is a new present),
no matter how fully their original immediacy is preserved.
Obviously, it is not because of fading or perishing that earlier
is contained in later, though later is not contained in earlier. It
is rather *in spite of perishing*. Were loss of immediacy the last
word, how could the faded event in its non-faded vividness, as
it was when present, be contained in the new present? Yet such
containing is the theory of succession under discussion. It is the
reality of the new *as added to that of the old*, rather than the
unreality of the old, that constitutes process. The denial of
perishing in God, so far from removing succession, is required
to rescue it from partial if not complete destruction. For us,
much of the past, that which has been, is "as though it had never
been," except for profoundly unconscious prehensions, and these
cannot be construed unless there is some consciousness whose
clarity registers and measures their content. It is adequate awareness which measures inadequate, not vice versa. Thus for instance the Primordial envisagement of eternal objects is necessary to make our inferior envisagement of them possible. And
similarly, in the CN, "succession does not mean loss of immediate unison," and this preservation of events as they are
when they occur is just what gives them a definite status in the
"past," as *x* has a definite place in "*x* as a part of *y*," where *y*
is the later, richer, more determinate entity. This is that higher
mode of becoming which men have tried vainly for centuries to

[39] Cf. *ibid.*, 247, 251; *Process and Reality*, 363.

conceive when they held that all is together in God, yet not static or inactive or dead.

The poetic majesty of the conception of unfading everlastingness of all occasions in God (down to the *de facto* present) should not blind us to the simple, cogent reason for the idea. It is almost comical to see critics (including Santayana) object to the immortality of the past as a fantastic, incredible, gratuitous idea, while these same persons—Mead being almost the only exception known to me—light-heartedly assume the immortality of truth, however detailed and trivial, about the past. Indeed, they usually go further and assume the eternity of truth, its completeness above time altogether, thus rendering time an illusion of which the real content is timeless. Such critics substitute for the simple and consistent idea of Whitehead and Bergson the following paradoxes: (a) They suppose a world of truth which is, item for item, an exact duplicate of the past, in one-to-one correspondence with its determinations, however detailed. This duplicate or truth world lacks of the actual past no determinate character, but only an ineffable something called actuality. (b) They suppose that truth is *real now* as involving a relation of correspondence with an object which is not real now. Relation-to-the-past is there—save for the past. Relation-to is there, we should say. If we add to these paradoxes the almost universally accompanying one that (c) truth about past, present, or future is said to be timelessly complete in all eternity, although that which it is about is either incomplete or at least seems to lose its distinctive character of process if it be supposed complete, we have three appalling demands upon credulity, or ability to believe nonsense. It was indeed partly to avoid such absurdities that Bergson adopted his view of the cumulative character of time.

But perhaps it will be thought a paradox that the past should, in present experience, be still immediately given. I have elsewhere on several occasions explained this to mean that the past involves universals of which later events are instances, and in such fashion that the instances imply their universals but not the converse. Every event contains more or less determinate desires, expectations, fears, purposes, hopes, and these involve generality, indetermination as to the exact details which may fulfill or disappoint or somehow be relevant to them. The planned or feared event as outlined in the plan or fear is never so individually definite as the event which comes to pass at the time in question, and this greater definiteness of the subsequent event remains exactly that, no matter how complete the preservation of the earlier event. Indeed, it is only if the preservation is complete that the precise indeterminations of the past in its hopes and fears can be retrospectively seen for what they were when present. On the other hand, the fulfillment or disappointment, felt as such, of a purpose or hope includes the memory of the purpose or hope, plus details not foreseen in the anticipatory state and not contained in it as preserved in memory, as to how things actually "came out." Clearly logic allows the asymmetrical relationship required. A can be in B although B is not in A. In fact, there would otherwise be no distinction between general and particular; for the general is that which does not imply other things (unless they are of equal generality), whereas the particular contains the general as an abstractable feature. Why should not this asymmetrical structure of universal-particular be essentially an aspect of the structure of time? Time either is or is not essential to existence and to all being. Many who think it is thus essential reject the only theory of time that does justice to its basic place in being as the key to the interrelations of the categories.

The foregoing doctrine can be expressed as the contention that the cause is *never* "equal to the effect," the latter always being the richer; the former, seen retrospectively, being a reduction of the latter to an abstract or incomplete version of itself. The subject is always "superject," always an enrichment of existence, even of God, and it involves that which is enriched, but not conversely. This *is* succession. When Whitehead views PN as a causal factor implied by all actual entities but requiring none of them in particular, he is consistent with his first principles. But those are deceiving themselves who, like Spinoza and Jonathan Edwards, wish to conceive God as C, as existing and intelligible in himself alone, and at the same time hold that all things follow without qualification from his nature (Spinoza in a sense makes a qualification, but it is equivocal), or that it is the function of a cause to necessitate its effect. Independence *means* asymmetrical contingency (or asymmetrical determinism, it is the same thing), the non-involvement of the effect in the cause, or it means nothing. There are no degrees of necessity. If my hat requires God and God requires my hat (at least as an illusion or "appearance"), the logical status of the one is as dependent or independent as that of the other. Whitehead has escaped this old trap, and has done so by "taking time [and freedom and memory] seriously."

There are three questions concerning the temporal structure of God which I should like to put to Professor Whitehead. In doing so I am in danger of revealing my lack of scientific knowledge, but I hope at least that the questions will have a definite meaning.

1. Must there not be a cosmic present, in spite of relativity physics, the *de facto* totality of actual entities as present in the divine immediacy? As Parker and Bergson have said, the inability of human beings, by signalling methods, to determine a unique cosmic present or simultaneity need not prevent God, who knows things directly, from experiencing such a present. Since God is not spatially localized, it appears that he must intuit all occasions wherever they are as they occur in one state of experience. But then can it be without qualification true that contemporaries are causally independent, non-immanent in each other? Since they are all immanent in God, and he in turn immanent in them, must they not be immanent in each other? For, since God is not spatially separated from things, it seems no definite lapse of time can occur either between his prehension of them or theirs of him. There can be no transmission with the velocity of light from an event to the divine observer, or from the divine process itself to the creaturely events. (There is a somewhat similar problem about the relation of the human consciousness to brain-cell events.)

2. If there is a divine present, distinguishable from both the divine past and the divine future, it will, I take it, be an "epochal" affair, not a mathematical instant, nor yet containing

infinite divisions, but a unit actually undivided yet potentially divisible (such that it might have been divided, or might have been part of a longer undivided epoch). What will be the length of this epoch? I should suppose it would be identical with that of the shortest creaturely unit or specious present, since the perfect perception (physical prehension) will make whatever discriminations are necessary to follow the distinctions in the things perceived, no more and no less. The longer units will then be experienced by God as overlapping several of the shorter, and therefore not absolutely undivided, taking account of the immanence of the shorter in their prehensions. But this involves problems of synchronization that inevitably baffle my lay mind.

Whitehead says that the consequent nature shares with each actual entity its actual world, that is, the totality of things definitely in its past. But God shares worlds not just with each but with all actual entities not definitely in the cosmic future, that is, with all really "actual" entities, since future entities are nonactual, indeterminate, potential.

3. Is the world-process, as everlasting in God, without beginning? Then the totality of actual occasions is an actual infinite. I have no objection to this, provided, as I hope—and in spite of Kant, Renouvier, and Parker—the idea of the actual infinite is meaningful. If the totality of immortalized actualities is infinite, then the enrichment of God through each new occasion is the addition to a realization already infinite. This too, I take it, is not fatal, since either (a) the order of the infinity might increase, or (b) if the number of elapsed events did not increase, the class would, since new members are added and none lost. (a) is, as I understand from mathematicians, not compatible with the epochal theory of time. It seems that (b) must be the solution. And I suppose the addition of new contrasts to everlasting reality can enrich it aesthetically without effecting a numerical increase in the contrasts already there.

V. Personality, Substance, and Event in God

The Absolute-Relative or AR conception of divine perfection is that God is the self-transcending transcender of all others except self. Self-transcendence presupposes the notion of self.

But the unit of reality in Whitehead's thought, it might be objected, is not self or enduring individual or substance but the occasion or event. Self is apparently a secondary notion, in fact a certain sort of "society" of "its" occasions or states. It seems to follow that the self-transcending selfhood of God must also be a secondary matter, whereas in consistency Whitehead is bound to assert that God, at least as PN, is an absolute necessity of existence.

The difficulty is, I believe, largely verbal. Whitehead is not essentially or without far-reaching qualifications committed to the view that occasions are more fundamental than enduring individuals.[40] First of all, nothing is more fundamental than the unvarying totality of eternal possibilities; and these would be nothing apart from the self-identity of God as PN. Secondly, to belong to a society with personal order, that is, an enduring individual or substance, is one of the two chief ways in which an occasion is enabled to possess richness of contrast in its content, the other consisting in its enjoying social relations with members of personally ordered societies other than its own. Mere occasions which did not belong, directly or indirectly, to any person or substance would be the impossible case of occasions with no significant content, a case excluded absolutely by the necessarily existent goodness of God, the cosmic orderer.[41] In addition, occasions that failed to belong to at least one personal society, namely God, would have no place in temporal order, would not really be occasions, events. For the unity of time is immanent in occasions, which are successive to each other only because each contributes to the value of the next, and substantiality is constituted by the particularly prominent strands of this contributiveness or immanence, and the divine substantiality is the only adequate or perfect measure and ground of temporal unity.

What Whitehead definitely rejects in substantialism is: (1) the idea that it is merely an accidental property of some kinds of substances that they involve accidents, occasions, process; (2) the idea that substances cannot (or at least, need not) have each

---

[40] Cf. *Modes of Thought*, 132, 133f.

[41] Cf. *Religion in the Making*, 103ff., 119, 156; *Process and Reality*, 142; *Adventures of Ideas*, 362f.

other as accidents, cannot or need not be immanent in each other;[42] and (3) the idea that the unity of substance is an absolute, all-or-none affair. (1) would imply that there might be a substance which had no accidents and was not in process; (3) would make the most fragile and imperfectly integrated self as much a self as God. According to Whitehead, (2) is, as he once remarked, the foundation of immorality. Those who accuse Whitehead of dissolving personal identity[43] (and thus damaging our ethical conceptions) might bear in mind that what he really does is to assert the *equal* importance of inter-personal relations, and also to assert the absolute meaninglessness of substance apart from change.

I wish, however, to go farther, and to maintain that Whitehead can more truly conceive God, at least, as a self-identical substance than the old substantialisms could. For when it was a question of God, traditional doctrines really came closer to the idea of a state without substance than of a substance without states. Where all distinction between substance and state is eliminated, if any meaning survives it is more like the idea of a single occasion, which as Whitehead points out is "immutable," than it is like an enduring individual which identifies itself in the midst of successive states, which is therefore precisely *not* immutable but changing, and therefore remains also itself as that same changing individual or endurer of accidents. On the other hand, Whitehead, who seems to take states more seriously than substance, really does view God as an enduring individual with a unique and indeed perfect form of self-identity. God is the self-transcending transcender of all, not the mere state of complete value. In other words, he is a self-contrasting and therefore in a significant sense self-identical subject with an ever partly new superject, not just a single non-self-related or barely "simple" state of being. Without self-contrast, self-identity is meaningless and substance degenerates into a mere state, subject into a mere object. So far from true is it that Whitehead fails to do justice, in relation to God, to the real meaning of substance.

But, some will ask, is Whitehead's God personal? A person

---

[42] Cf. *Religion in the Making*, 107f.
[43] On this question, see also below, sec. viii.

in ordinary language is at least what is in some degree *conscious* and *individual*. Now Whitehead makes it very plain that his God is conscious, taking CN as well as PN into account. The individuality of God is also evident enough. The individual is the *determinate* or decided (except as to its future, and even that is relatively decided) in contrast to the multiple indecisiveness of mere potentiality, and it is the *integrated* in contrast to the "democracy" or even looser organization of a society of societies when the former society is without personal order. Now the concrete being of God is definite and is *not* the equivalent in actuality of the entire realm of possibilities. [The absolute God (AA) of the tradition was, on the other hand, more or less admittedly non-individual, for it was the complete actualization of potency, or it was a completeness "beyond" potency and actuality.] Also the concrete being of God is asserted by Whitehead to have preëminent unity, surpassing that of any other individual. So what is there of personality that God could fail to possess, and possess in a superlative degree?

Is God, then, the "personal order" of the inclusive society of societies, implying that the universe is God's body? Whitehead does not say these things in so many words, but he says things from which they are deducible, by his own definitions of the terms of the above question. Personal order is raised to the highest potency in the immediacy of the past as unfadingly everlasting in God, and in this order the cosmos is contained. Moreover, the definition of body applies literally to God, if suitably generalized to cover a supreme case. For the body is simply that much of the world with which the mind, or personal society, has effective immediate interactions of mutual inheritance, and over which its influence is dominant.[44] Such is God's relation to all of the world, and therefore all of it is his body. This has none of the degrading effects that giving God a body is supposed to have; indeed, it is only a way of saying that God's social relations with all things are uniquely adequate, that he really and fully loves all of them, and that they all, however inadequately or unconsciously, love him. It scarcely needs say-

---

[44] Cf. *Modes of Thought*, 30, 32f, 157; *Process and Reality*, 182f.

ing that to have a body is not to be connected with lumps of mere dead insentient matter, "vacuous actuality," there being no such thing for Whitehead, or perhaps for any philosopher who competently and honestly faces the destructive analysis of this concept which modern philosophy has effected. Nor is it true for Whitehead that lesser organisms within a mind's organism are absolutely controlled by that mind, deprived of all decisions of their own, or that what the parts of the body decide for themselves the dominant mind decides for itself. Hence creaturely freedom and God's non-responsibility for evil are compatible with the view that God is the personality of the cosmic body, the totality of societies inferior to that personal-order society which is the mind and life of God.

VI. The Principle of Concretion

It is somewhat unfortunate that Whitehead's view of God was chiefly associated, for some years, with the phrase "principle of limitation" (or of concretion). This is an inadequate description of his view, and that in three ways. (1) God is at once the principle of abstraction, of unbounded possibility, *and* of concretion, of limited realization of possibility. The eternal possibilities which require limitation by divine fiat are themselves divine concepts.[45] (2) God is not merely a principle or set of principles; he is the concrete actual entity whose importance has the universality of first principles. (3) God is not the only agent of abstraction or of concretion, but he is the "supreme" agent,[46] the only agent equal to a principle in the scope of its action. Every subject-superject is an effector of concretion and contains the envisagement of possibilities. But God is the only such agent whose functioning is presupposed by all existence throughout all time, the only strictly cosmic agent.

Possibilities do not themselves decide which of them is to be actual.[47] This would be a contradiction, since it would make the unselected possibilities impossible. Further, actuality cannot in advance decide upon its future stages, since futurity in its

[45] Cf. *Religion in the Making*, 153.
[46] *Ibid.*, 152.
[47] Cf. *Science and the Modern World*, 244.

distinctive difference from pastness means a certain indecisiveness in what is future so long as it is so.[48] Hence the "selection" of a given possibility for realization can only be a free act in the present occasion, which is self-creative.[49] No reason can be given from which such a free act can be deduced, although that there be some such act or other following upon any given moment of process is a deducible necessity from the nature of reality as process.

Thus we understand when Whitehead says of God:

> His existence is the ultimate irrationality. For no reason can be given for just that limitation which it stands in His nature to impose. . . . No reason can be given for the nature of God, because that nature is the ground of rationality. . . . There is a metaphysical need for a principle of determination, but there can be no metaphysical reason for what is determined.[50]

This is the metaphysical basis of the methodological truth that matters of fact are not knowable *a priori*. Metaphysically necessary truth is abstract, and embraces of concrete facts only the requirement that there be some such facts. The whole truth is metaphysical plus empirical, and this is so even for God. Whitehead is denying Spinoza's notion that all things follow from the necessary essence of Substance, and Leibniz's notion that all things follow from God's goodness plus the superiority of this world over all possible worlds. Leibniz never did tell us intelligibly how some one set of possibilities could be better than all others. Deduction must assume something more definite and particular than a mere "what is possible is possible." Creation is the dance of Shiva, of which the Hindus speak, not the drawing of a conclusion. There is an unbridgeable gulf between reasoning, which turns upon universals, and action, which is always individual. By reasoning upon universals some conclusion as to the *sort* of thing to be done may be reached, but what is done will be an individual instance, not a sort, and the leap from the sort to the instance will not be reasoning but sheer fiat.

---

[48] Cf. *Adventures of Ideas,* 249, 250f.
[49] *Ibid.,* 328.
[50] *Science and the Modern World,* 249f.

After the instance is given, then the next decision will have to take account of it. Thus, as Whitehead says, reason presupposes creation. What is reasonable depends upon what has been done, including that in what has been done that is more than reasonable.

When Kant said that artistic rules are deduced from genius, not the acts of genius from artistic rules, he was unwittingly suggesting a theory of process superior to that furnished by his own philosophy, according to which events must conform to absolute rules. It is rather events that furnish the basis for the particular, approximate rules that are relevant at a given time.[51] The cosmic creative genius is the ground of all definite laws, and no antecedent law implies the particular laws which the creative acts from time to time express and, for some limited period, establish.[52]

It is true that in *The Function of Reason* Whitehead says that reason is the organ by which orderly novelty is introduced into the world. Reason balances the need for contrast and the unexpected against the need for harmony of the new with the old. But "reason" here refers, I take it, to the total act which includes reasoning in our human case and in the cosmic or divine case includes that part of reason which is the awareness of possibility as such. But it is clear that the particular orderly novelty is not as it were deduced or necessary.

VII. Evil and God's Power

Is God an efficient or a final cause? He is an efficient cause because he is a final cause, and vice versa. He furnishes their subjective aims to the creatures (open to their further determination as to details). This furnishing is effected by the hybrid prehensions which the creatures have of God's conceptual prehensions.[53] (This is a return to the doctrine of Augustine, Matthew of Aquasparta, Malebranche, and Spinoza, that we see truth in the divine ideas.) Now prehensions, whether physical or hybrid, are the bridge over which efficient causality is trans

[51] Cf. *Process and Reality*, 140.
[52] Cf. *Modes of Thought*, 196.
[53] Cf. *Process and Reality*, 343, 532.

mitted. But what is transmitted in the hybrid prehensions which we have of God is an aim, that is, a final cause. God controls by "persuading." The persuasion is, up to a certain point, irresistible, but only because we love God with an immediate love or sympathetic prehension which is our very being, and can therefore at most be distorted rather than destroyed, while we persist at least.

God's persuasion of us is balanced by our persuasion of him. He prehends our prehensions, and the particular subjective aims which he furnishes us are made what they are partly by his participation in our own previous decisions.[54] God literally feels our feelings, our desires become elements of desire in him. Our decisions indeed cannot become his decisions, as though he decided them; and this means that our ethical evil cannot be made God's ethical evil. Ethical evil prehended in another becomes aesthetic evil in the other. God suffers our evil acts (he also enjoys them, so far as we do) and he suffers their consequences in others, as we often do not.

But is God positively righteous? No, if this means, Does he reward and punish with mathematical exactitude, "though the heavens fall." And the heavens would fall, for it is not possible that God should serve any absolute law of reward and punishment and also get on with the business of cosmic prosperity and beauty.[55] God is perfectly good, but with the goodness of love, not of legalistic justice, which is a secondary device of goodness. And love, as Whitehead reminds us, is "a little oblivious as to morals," if, that is, by morality is meant a set of rules for determining the distribution of sweet and bitter according to "desert." Existence is social, and it cannot be that what an individual enjoys or suffers should follow exclusively from his own good or evil acts or be exactly fitted to these. The goodness of God consists in this, that he never thwarts any desire, however perverse or trivial, without himself sharing fully in every quality of feeling of pain or sorrow that the thwarting involves in the creatures. Thus God is the "fellow-sufferer who

---

[54] *Ibid.; Religion in the Making,* 159.
[55] Cf. *Process and Reality,* 373f., 520; *Religion in the Making,* 104f.

understands."[56] He does what has to be done to maintain the social beauty of the cosmic system, and its enjoyableness for most of the creatures; and he does not do it coldly or from without, but as one who is within the tragedy as well as within the triumph of life.

To such a view Santayana has objected that it is strange that God, who has been working through all the past, should have brought the world at last to the state it is now in.[57] This writer even suggests that the devil could as well say that he tolerates good for the sake of evil as God can say that he tolerates evil for the sake of good. Now, first, there can for Whitehead be no question of gradually eliminating evil from the universe, for the causes of ever-new evil must be operating in the present as in the past, since they lie in the same element of free-decisions-plus-social-interdependence upon which all good also depends. Increased opportunities for good also mean increased opportunities for evil, as all can see in human history and in any conceivable history. What counts is the surplus of good, the good of existence on the whole, not only for God but, as part of his good, for the creatures generally or in the main. Now the total value which the travail of the past has harvested, and the deepest meaning of "progress," is not to be seen by taking a cross section of the present, in attempted abstraction from the immortal past. It is the total or real present as in God, all existence down to the latest increment, that is metaphysically progressing toward ever new and greater richness of contrast and harmony. The rate of this progressing is not fixed by fate or deity, but is always something to be decided, in part, by each and every creature. What is not to be decided, even by God, is that progress, in the sense and direction explained, there shall be, for this is the "necessary goodness" and perfection of power of God, which lie beyond the "accidents of will." The rate of progress is greatest when the creatures (a) do the best they know or can guess as to how to contribute to it (avoid ethical evil), and (b) are lucky in their guess. It is a question of luck,

[56] *Process and Reality*, 532.
[57] *The Philosophy of George Santayana*, Paul A. Schilpp (ed.), (Northwestern University, Evanston and Chicago, 1940), 594.

for each is largely ignorant of what others are doing, and God can only set limits to the amount of harm which bad guesses can do, he cannot rigorously eliminate the harm while leaving the creatures their essential measure of freedom.

In the second place God does not "secretly commission the evil to appear, in order that the good may assert itself." Evil is not primarily there so that the good may have something to vanquish. Evil arises automatically in connection with the pursuit of good. Evil requires no contriving, just as to miss the target requires no skill. But is God's skill then limited? No, but the target is a self-moving one, and the exact direction of its movement is incalculable, hence the outcome of the shot depends partly upon chance. This lies in the conditions of existence, any possible existence, and does not limit God by comparison with any conceivable being.

Granting that evil does arise, God does wring some good out of it.[58] Yet it is good that is to be pursued, not evil, even as means to good. Monotony and suffering are the two rocks which the ship of being, aiming at beauty and love, must ever seek to avoid, and the only reason for steering toward either rock is to correct a drift toward the other. The destruction of interest through monotony is just as great a danger as suffering and hatred. It is part of Whitehead's insight that he sees this so clearly.

VIII. God and Eternal Objects

Occasions are ingredients of process that are immutable but not primordial; eternal objects are ingredients of process that are both immutable and primordial. Enduring societies are ingredients of process that are neither immutable nor, with one exception (God's life as a personal society of divine occasions), primordial (although primordially there are some societies or other). Societies are mutable factors in process. But there seems to be a fourth type of entity, the impure potentials, the selection of pure potentials or eternal objects which are realizable in a given society, which conform to the style of feeling and subjective aim characterizing such a society. Like their societies,

[58] Cf. *Religion in the Making*, 155.

impure potentials belong not to all time, either forward or backward, but to a certain stretch of time. It is true that like societies they are immortal in the sense that their having been belongs to the everlasting content of being, but if their societies cease to add to the series of occasions constituting them, then the impure potentials are no longer capable of further actualization in the manner peculiar to these societies.

Now there are two ways of conceiving the relation of impure to pure potentials. Either the former are mere selections among the latter, or mere arrangements of them with respect to gradations of relevance and with respect to positive or negative prehensions, or the mixed potentials are really creative determinations without which potencies would be determinable rather than determinate or wholly definite. If all the "forms of definiteness," each perfectly definite in itself, are eternally given to God, it is not altogether clear to me what actualization accomplishes. True, it removes contradictions among possibilities; but if contradiction does not interfere with definite envisagement, again there is some difficulty to see what need there is to remove it.

Whitehead does say that the eternal objects have indeterminacy as to their mode of ingression, but there is perhaps some obscurity as to what this qualification involves.[59] Granting that there must be some eternal measure of quality, some set of ultimate variables or dimensions, such as "intensity," "complexity," "joy," "suffering," is it necessary that these variables involve all possible values as distinct items, for instance all the possible "lines" or "points" on the color-solid, all possible ways of *subdividing the continuity* of quality? Or is there a process of "extensive abstraction," or something analogous, by which subdivisions are inexhaustibly created in the course of the creative advance of the world? Then, though any actual set of qualities would be infinitely far from exhausting possibility, for it would have reached no limit of subdivision and would be confined also to certain portions of the dimensions subdivided, yet no item of the actual qualities would be antecedently contained in possi-

---

[59] Cf. *Process and Reality*, 72, 225f.; *Science and the Modern World*, chap. x.

bility, and thus actualization would really add something, namely, definiteness.[60] Whitehead would doubtless insist, with Santayana, that mathematical ideas at least must be regarded as definite prior to any particular embodiment.[61] (The very idea of "*continuity* of quality" seems to imply this.) But mathematical ideas, as Whitehead has often remarked, are abstract or general. We say that every pair is, as pair, equivalent to every other— pair of apples, pair of virtues; but a determinate color is not a class name in such fashion. "All the reds I could not tell from this red" may yet as reds all be slightly different, in saturation, hue, or tint (meaning by these terms attributes of sensation, not of physical stimuli, conceived quantitatively), and it is not clear to me why these differences must be eternally given to God as distinct items.

It would not follow, as Santayana has suggested, that choice between alternatives would no longer be possible.[62] For such choice need not operate among eternal possibilities exclusively, but can involve those determinations of the ultimate determinables which have already been achieved in the past. A painter can decide between using red and green in a given part of his picture, since he has seen red and green before, but it follows neither that red and green are eternal nor that the exact red-sensation which his painting will give him, or someone else, will duplicate perfectly any previously experienced quality. Each moment of time will add a little to the definiteness of qualities, even as envisaged by deity, but only a little.

On any showing there is a division of potentialities into two radically different levels: the level which contains the categories, those utterly general dimensions of reality of which Whitehead's philosophy gives the most complete description yet set forth, and without which as at least implicitly involved nothing at all can be conceived; and the level of specific qualities, from which it seems possible really to abstract entirely and still have meaning. Whitehead seems to be trying to deduce the specific from the

[60] See my essay, "Santayana's Doctrine of Essence," in *The Library of Living Philosophers*, Vol. II.

[61] *The Philosophy of George Santayana* (*op. cit.*), 535.

[62] *Ibid.*, 592.

generic, to show that the primordial nature of existence involves all species of quality. Is this any more credible than that all things follow from the nature of substance? It seems that either "red" is a category, as general as "process," or it is not completely general, and then we have to consider whether or not it is the law of generality that the less general should be contingent, should be external to the more general.

Of course, that there be some species or other must itself be a category. Specificity in general may be eternal, though no given species is so.

There is this advantage in restricting the eternal to the categorical universals[63] (and to God as envisaging and always *somehow* applying them). This is that the enduring subject of states (or self-identical individual) might then be given a somewhat more secure status. The enduring self might be constituted, in one aspect, by its impure potential, its own peculiar potency of becoming as a type of quality not to be found in eternal objects. (The other aspect of self-identity would be the immanence of a thing's history in its present being, by which the Whiteheadian enduring individual has a *concrete* identity woefully lacking in the older substantialist philosophies.) It sometimes seems to me that the semblance of not having enough substantiality in his societies of occasions is due to Whitehead's ascription of so much specific identity to the eternal objects as belonging to the divine self primordially, leaving only "selection" among these for the identities of lesser selves.

If arithmetic and pure geometry follow from the categories of logic, as *Principia Mathematica* seems to show, then mathematical ideas must be regarded as eternal objects, even if my suggestions be accepted. As a mathematician, Whitehead may perhaps have been unduly influenced, as in a somewhat analogous connection he thinks Plato was,[64] by the atypical character of mathematical properties, their extreme abstractness and generality. It also does not appear to me that his idea of God, or of most other subjects, would be injured—perhaps it would be

---

[63] This restriction was first suggested by Dorothy Emmett. See her book, *Whitehead's Philosophy of Organism* (Macmillan Co., Ltd., London, 1932), chap. v.

[64] Cf. *Modes of Thought*, 126-127.

clarified and strengthened—if one eliminated the idea of *eternal species*, while retaining that of eternal highest genera, including the genus of specificity as such.[65]

I should like to close by expressing the conviction that the chief obstacle to a more general appreciation of the greatness and truth of Whitehead's philosophy is not any defects it may contain, but that greatness and truth itself. Most of us, to think with any clearness, must drastically over-simplify reality. Every page of Whitehead shows that his power to grasp complex relationships and his familiarity with diverse aspects of life and the world as disclosed in science and experience are greatly superior to that of most of us teachers and writers in philosophy.

CHARLES HARTSHORNE

DEPARTMENT OF PHILOSOPHY
THE UNIVERSITY OF CHICAGO

[65] The difficult chapter on "Abstractions" in *Science and the Modern World* (chap. x) is the basic text for the doctrine of eternal objects. It seems clearly to affirm the eternity of specific as well as generic properties (see *op. cit.*, 232).

16

Paul Arthur Schilpp

WHITEHEAD'S MORAL PHILOSOPHY

WHITEHEAD'S MORAL PHILOSOPHY

I. Introduction

PROFESSOR WHITEHEAD has never written a systematic treatise on moral philosophy. This is well known to everyone at all familiar with his writings. There are reasons for this fact. Professor Whitehead was a mathematician for a long time before he became a philosopher. Moreover, when he did turn his major attention to philosophy, it was first to the twin-brother of mathematics, namely to logic, that he turned, and from there—quite naturally—to the philosophy of science and to metaphysics. Even his constant and never-subsiding interest in aesthetics is not out of line with this general development of his interests. For, almost from the very beginning, Professor Whitehead seems to have been almost as much impressed by the beauty and harmony of mathematical forms as by the purely mathematical or scientific meanings expressed in (mathematical) relationships. So that his predilection for the theory of beauty and for the philosophy of art is by no means out of line with his general position.

At the same time it would be absurd to assume that Professor Whitehead has been oblivious to the problems of morals. Unless, indeed, by "morals" be meant merely the existing and unquestionably accepted general 'mores' of any specific community or social group. In this latter sense, it is true, Mr. Whitehead has been quite unconcerned, if in fact he has not been an actual rebel in such matters.[1]

[1] The following four quotations from *Adventures of Ideas* will abundantly bear out this statement: ". . . the defence of morals is the battle-cry which best rallies stupidity against change. Perhaps countless ages ago respectable amœbæ refused to migrate from ocean to dry land—refusing in defence of morals." (345-346) ". . . stagnation is the deadly foe of morality. Yet in human society the champions

One need merely read in the lines—or, perhaps still better, between the lines—of Professor Whitehead's "Autobiographical Notes"[2] to see that he has been tremendously concerned with the good of human society and that he has always been willing to spend himself in all important issues having to do with the welfare and improvement of that society. Specifically the reader may be referred to such instances as Mr. Whitehead's confession that his "political opinions were, and are, on the liberal side, as against the conservatives;" that in England now his "vote would be given for the moderate side of the Labour party;"[3] to the fact that, during his life in London, he served on over a score of different commissions and committees; and so forth.

This ethical interest is attested by his books as well. It is doubtful, for example, whether any other contemporary philosopher has been more concerned with the nature, problems, and future of civilization. Both Whitehead's *Adventures of Ideas* and his *Modes of Thought* might very well be called "Critical Essays on Civilization." Part IV of the former book is, indeed, entitled "Civilization;" and the Preface to the book frankly tells us that "The book is in fact a study of the concept of civilization."[4] Chapter IV in *Modes of Thought* is headed "Civilized Universe." As "a general definition of civilization" Whitehead advances the idea that "a civilized society is exhibiting the five qualities of Truth, Beauty, Adventure, Art, Peace."[5] Moreover, "in every civilization at its culmination we should

---

of morality are on the whole the fierce opponents of new ideals. Mankind has been afflicted with low-toned moralists, . . ." (346) "The pure conservative is fighting against the essence of the universe." (354) "Moral codes have suffered from the exaggerated claims made for them. The dogmatic fallacy has here done its worst. Each such code has been put out by a God on a mountain top, or by a Saint in a cave, or by a divine Despot on a throne, or, at the lowest, by ancestors with a wisdom beyond later question. In any case, each code is incapable of improvement; and unfortunately in details they fail to agree either with each other or with our existing moral intuitions. The result is that the world is shocked, or amused, by the sight of saintly old people hindering in the name of morality the removal of obvious brutalities from the legal system." (374)

[2] Cf. pp. 3-14 above.
[3] *Ibid.*, 13.
[4] *Adventures of Ideas*, vii.
[5] *Ibid.*, 353.

find a large measure of realization of a certain type of *perfection*."[6] And, finally, "civilization in its aim at fineness of feeling *should* so arrange its social relations, and the relations of its members to their natural environment, as to evoke into the experiences of its members Appearances dominated by the *harmonies of forceful enduring things*."[7] If, nevertheless, "the concept of Civilization . . . remains inherently incomplete" and vague, this is due to the fact that "no logical argument can demonstrate this gap."[8] And, in *Modes of Thought*, Whitehead adds: "Civilized beings are those who survey the world with some large generality of understanding,"[9] since "Civilization involves the understanding of the given world in respect to its *quali*fications."[10] Expressions like these are, after all, those of a moralist. For Professor Whitehead is never satisfied with mere statements of "matters-of-fact;" he always estimates, evaluates, passes judgment, in brief, is concerned with the purpose, value, meaning, and worth of situations and events. These, as everyone will admit, are the procedures—*not* of the mere fact-finding and describing scientist,[11] but—of the judgment-passing, moral philosopher and philosopher of history.[12]

[6] *Ibid.*, 357 (italics mine).
[7] *Ibid.*, 363 (italics mine).
[8] *Ibid.*, 380.
[9] *Modes of Thought*, 5.
[10] *Ibid.*, 162 (italics mine).
[11] The present writer does not, in fact, know of a more clear-cut and, in its finality, more devastating characterization of mere "matter-of-fact" than the following three-sentence paragraph, the content of which would seem to be important enough to justify committing the entire paragraph to memory:
"Matter-of-fact is an abstraction, arrived at by confining thought to purely formal relations which then masquerade as the final reality. This is why science, in its perfection, relapses into the study of differential equations. The concrete world has slipped through the meshes of the scientific net." *Modes of Thought*, 25.
Also: "The notion of a mere fact is the triumph of the abstract intellect. . . . There is no such fact." *Ibid.*, 12-13.
[12] At this point, for example, Whitehead's exceedingly keen insight into the real nature of history is beautifully attested by a brief paragraph of six sentences in which incisiveness of statement vies with importance of content for honors: ". . . the study of history as mere sequence wears itself out. It is a make-belief. There are oceans of facts. We seek that thread of coördination derived from the special forms of importance prevalent in the respective epochs. Apart from such

However, even in his very first lecture in *Process and Reality*, delivered in 1927 in the University of Edinburgh, we already find this quite explicit statement:

The selectiveness of individual experience is moral so far as it conforms to the balance of importance disclosed in the rational vision; and conversely the conversion of the intellectual insight into an emotional force corrects the sensitive experience in the direction of morality. The correction is in proportion to the rationality of the insight.

Morality of outlook is inseparably conjoined with generality of outlook. The antithesis between the general good and the individual interest can be abolished only when the individual is such that its interest is the general good, thus exemplifying the loss of the minor intensities in order to find them again with finer composition in a wider sweep of interest.[13]

Nor is this quotation (to comments on the content of which we shall return) the only reference to morality in Professor Whitehead's Gifford Lectures. For the present it will suffice, however. Enough has already been quoted[14] to establish the fact that Mr. Whitehead, in theory as well as in practice, is in the best sense of the word a moral philosopher, in spite of the fact that he has never found time to write an independent treatise on morality.[15]

II. Exposition

1. *Introductory.*—Only a critical moralist would assert that "The simple-minded use of the notions 'right or wrong' is one

---

interests, intrinsic within each period, there would be no language, no art, no heroism, no devotion. Ideals lie beyond matter-of-fact, and yet provide the colour of its development." *Modes of Thought*, 25.

[13] *Process and Reality* (American edition of 1929), 22-23.

[14] Moreover, the many additional quotations from Mr. Whitehead's works which will be used in the following sections of this discussion will bear such added witness to our present contention that further enumeration at this point would be a work of supererogation.

[15] However, the present writer is inclined to agree with the judgment of Dr. Victor Lowe (cf. pp. 116f above) that the tasks of Professor Whitehead have largely been those of a specialist, whose far-reaching contributions to the fields of the philosophy of science and metaphysics have justifiably kept him from a detailed incursion into certain other philosophical areas. So that we ought, perhaps, to be thankful for the fact that no independent treatise on the subject of moral philosophy from Whitehead's pen exists.

of the chief obstacles to the progress of understanding."[16] Yet this assertion is not merely true, but needs very much to be stated and to be brought out into the open. However, the statement—even though it is located at the close of a section which, as such, is not at all concerned with moral issues but is given to a critical analysis of "the notion of a mere fact,"[17]—is a splendid demonstration of the fact that Whitehead has been (1) an accurate observer of so-called "moral behavior" and "moral judgment," (2) a mind engaged in thoughtful reflection on the problems of the nature of real morality, and (3) devoted to the welfare of human society, to the "progress of understanding."[18]

2. *The general nature of morality.*—What, then, is Mr. Whitehead's view of the nature of morality? "Morality," he writes,[19] "consists in the control of process so as to maximize importance." Now, brief as this statement is, it is thoroughly characteristic of Whitehead, and it also offers as good an initial insight into his conception of the nature of morality as could possibly be found in many paragraphs or even pages of material. In the first place, it locates morality within Whitehead's metaphysical scheme: it "consists in [a certain] control of *process.*" Therewith it points to the dynamic nature not only of the universe as such, but also to the further assumption that a signifi-

---

[16] Modes of Thought, 15.

[17] Ibid., 12-15.

[18] It may be wise to say a few words here about procedure. This would seem to be all the more called for because of the fact that the reader will very shortly find himself burdened with what may seem like an endless number of quotations from Whitehead. The very fact that we have no independent treatise on the subject of ethics from the pen of Mr. Whitehead makes it necessary, not merely to cite occasional quotations in order to establish a particular point but rather, to bring together (as much as space will permit) as wide a variety of statements from the pen of Mr. Whitehead (in this particular area) as possible. This will, indeed, be our aim. In order, however, to break up what would otherwise appear to be a monotonous barrage of quotations, the attempt will be made to arrange the quotations under different sectional heads, which latter will in themselves indicate something of the ideational procedure with which Whitehead attacks the problem of ethics. The reader will still need to be warned, however, not to take the sectional divisions too seriously or to treat their respective content too independently. For it must never be forgotten that all the ideas to be treated under *all* of the sectional heads are closely interwoven and must all be regarded as part and parcel of one general structure and scheme.

[19] In *ibid.*, 19.

cant interpretation of morality must be equally "processive" and dynamic, rather than substantive or static. And, secondly, the statement locates the nature of morality as subsumed under the more general—and, as we shall find later on, ultimate—category of "importance." Both of these assertions are basic for any understanding of Whitehead's conception of the nature of morality. Let us, therefore, look at them somewhat more closely.

Fortunately the significance of *process* in the philosophy of Whitehead is already so well established, that at this point a basic understanding of the notion of *process* (in Whitehead's sense and use of the word) may be taken for granted. "Nothing," Mr. Whitehead tells us,[20] "is finally understood until its reference to process has been made evident." For *process* is, to put it in the briefest possible fashion, the on-going of the universe. Now, says Mr. Whitehead, the nature of morality consists "in the control of process" in such a fashion "as to maximize importance." Something of what is meant by "maximizing importance" is stated in the very next sentence by Mr. Whitehead himself, when he adds: "It is the aim at greatness of experience. . . ."[21] This helps, but by itself it is hardly sufficient. For, as I have already intimated, *importance* is a basic category for Mr. Whitehead.

3. *Importance.*—" 'Importance'," we are told, "can be inadequately defined as 'Interest, involving that intensity of individual feeling which leads to publicity of expression'."[22] Moreover, ". . . there are two aspects to Importance; one based on the unity of the Universe, the other on the individuality of the details. The word 'Interest' suggests the latter aspect; the word 'Importance' leans towards the former. In some sense or other interest always modifies expression." In fact, "for the sake of reminding ourselves of this aspect of 'Importance', the word 'Interest' will occasionally be used as a synonym."[23] And this "sense of importance (or interest) is embedded in the very being of animal experience."[24] Moreover,

[20] *Ibid.*, 64.
[21] *Ibid.*, 19.
[22] *Modes of Thought*, 11.
[23] *Ibid.*, 11.
[24] *Ibid.*, 12.

. . . one characterization of importance is that it is that aspect of feeling whereby a perspective is imposed upon the universe of things felt. . . . The two notions of importance and of perspective are closely inter-twined . . . perspective is the dead abstraction of mere fact from the living importance of things felt.[25]

And again:

Importance is a generic notion which has been obscured by the over-whelming prominence of a few of its innumberable species. The terms 'morality', 'logic', 'religion', 'art' have each of them been claimed as exhausting the whole meaning of importance. *Each of them denotes a subordinate species.* But the genus stretches beyond any finite group of species. . . . No one of these specializations exhausts the final unity of purpose in the world. *The generic aim of process is the attainment of importance,* in that species and to that extent which in that instance is possible.[26]

At the same time, "*Morality is always the aim at that union* of harmony, intensity, and vividness which involves *the perfection of importance* for that occasion."[27] ". . . our action is moral if we have thereby *safe-guarded the importance of experience* so far as it depends on that concrete instance in the world's history."[28] ". . . the necessity for investigation of the peculiar char-acterization of that sense of importance which is current in the thought of each age. All classification depends on the current character of importance."[29] "Importance arises from this fusion of the finite and the infinite."[30] "Importance," moreover, "re-veals itself as transitions of emotion. My importance is my emotional worth now, . . ."[31] And, "Actuality is the self-enjoyment of importance . . . the concept of actuality as some-thing that matters, by reason of its own self-enjoyment, which includes enjoyment of others and transitions towards the fu-ture."[32] "The sense of importance is a function of the analysis

[25] *Ibid.,* 15.
[26] *Ibid.,* 16 (italics mine).
[27] *Ibid.,* 19 (italics mine).
[28] *Ibid.,* 20 (italics mine).
[29] *Ibid.,* 21-22.
[30] *Ibid.,* 108.
[31] *Ibid.,* 160.
[32] *Ibid.,* 161.

of experienced quality."[33] But: "The variations of importance are beyond our weak imaginations; . . ."[34] If, in addition to these assertions concerning the nature of "importance," anything more were needed to bring out the centrality of the concept in Whitehead's philosophy and more particularly for his value-theory, the following two quotations certainly would meet such need. In the former of the two Mr. Whitehead differentiates his own use of the term "importance" sharply from its "common use." In the second he insists that "Importance" is an ultimate category, which, as such, can never be expected "to be fully explained." "Of course," he writes, "the word 'importance', as in common use, has been reduced to suggest a silly little pomposity which is the extreme of trivialization of its meaning here."[35] And, finally, " *'Importance' is a fundamental notion not to be fully explained* by any reference to a finite number of other factors."[36] In connection with this last statement it is interesting to note that, in his Ingersoll Lecture, Professor Whitehead makes a similar claim for the notions of 'better' and 'worse'. There he writes: "This activity of internal adjustment is expressed by our moral and aesthetic judgments. *Such judgments involve the ultimate notions of 'better' and 'worse'.*"[37] And, in *Modes of Thought,* we read: "*Our intuitions* of righteousness *disclose an absoluteness* in the nature of things, and so does the taste of a *lump of sugar.*"[38]

Whatever else these quotations may mean, they certainly furnish incisive evidence that Professor Whitehead has much to say and has thought deeply on questions and problems of morals and that his views in that field are rooted in the procedures and processes of physiological and psychic conduct and behavior. In other words, morals for him are, after all, certain kinds of judgments passed and conduct experienced by certain kinds of

---

[33] *Ibid.,* 162.

[34] *Ibid.,* 165.

[35] *Ibid.,* 16.

[36] *Ibid.,* 11 (italics mine).

[37] Cf. p. 685 below (italics mine).

[38] *Modes of Thought,* 165 (italics, except for the *"lump of sugar"* where they are Whitehead's own, are by the present writer).

organisms, such as men. When he says, therefore, that "morality consists in the control of process so as to maximize importance," he is not spinning a new rationalistic theory out of his (i.e., out of another philosopher's) head, nor is he engaging in mere wish-thinking. Rather, he proceeds to broaden and deepen the meaning of the word "Importance" so greatly that the sentence—which, at first sight, looks like a considerable exaggeration of the importance of "Importance"—takes on a good deal of specific meaning.[39]

There are, however, three specific points in these quotations to which particular attention needs to be called. The first of these is the subordination not merely of morality, but of logic, religion, and art as well, under the generic notion of 'importance'. Mr. Whitehead actually complains of the fact that the importance of 'importance' has been obscured by what he calls "the overwhelming prominence of a few of its innumerable species," such as morality, logic, religion, and art. This, certainly, is a unique protest, unless, indeed, it be shared by what might be called the "psychological moralists." For it is perfectly clear from most of the quotations that 'importance' is fundamentally a part of the psychic processes of value-judgments, which latter are themselves largely emotionally dominated and controlled. This becomes particularly clear in the passage where Mr. Whitehead frankly, although in only a partial fashion, identifies the notions of 'importance' and 'interest'. It also appears, however, in any number of other passages. The obviously emotional and subjective content of such words as "transitions of emotions," "self-enjoyment," and "emotional worth"—all words and phrases employed in the above quotations as characterizing or revealing or even constituting 'importance'—simply cannot be explained away. Nor need one

---

[39] Within the limited confines of this paper it is impossible to give either an exhaustive interpretation or a sufficiently detailed critique of this fundamental concept of 'Importance' in Whitehead's thought. In view of the prominence given to this concept, especially in *Modes of Thought* (in which the opening Lecture, pp. 1-27, is entitled "Importance"), a thorough-going treatment of the subject would require an independent treatise, for which there is here no room. For another brief discussion of the concept the reader is referred to the essay on "Whitehead's Theory of Value" by Mr. Goheen in this volume (see chap. 12 above).

think that Mr. Whitehead himself would want them explained away. These words and phrases were undoubtedly deliberately and reflectively chosen. In other words, Mr. Whitehead does intend to give to the notion of 'Importance'—even in his much broader and profounder sense of the word than it bears in ordinary language—a definitely emotional and subjective flavor. So that, from this particular vantage-point Professor Whitehead's moral philosophy could well be classed among the so-called "moral interest theories." In any case, however, I should say that the subordination of morality to 'importance' is not merely highly interesting, but is likely to play a determinative rôle in the final interpretation of Whitehead's moral philosophy.

It must, nevertheless, be said that the 'interest'-side is by no means the *only* constitutive aspect of Mr. Whitehead's notion of 'importance'. He himself has told us that "there are *two aspects* to Importance;" the aspect which is best represented by 'Interest' is said to be based "on the individuality of the details;" whereas the second aspect—which Whitehead really names first—is "based on the unity of the Universe." So that, quite in harmony with Mr. Whitehead's general metaphysical position, 'importance' arises as a process of interaction between a perspective of things felt (i.e., interest) and the ultimate unity of the universe, as a "fusion of the finite and the infinite." In this connection it ought also to be kept in mind, however, that it is, after all, not merely 'importance' which arises out of that fusion of the finite and the infinite. Actualized value arises in the same way, according to Mr. Whitehead, and so does any other actual entity. Some philosophers may take this fact to be a demonstration of the internal unity of Mr. Whitehead's thought. Others, however, will find it difficult to make clear distinctions among entities and notions, which differ so widely in common sense understanding and ordinary usage, if they are all to be reduced to the identical type of genesis and appearance. Although, from a standpoint of either logic or experience, there would seem to be no intrinsic reason why differing objects, entities, and notions might not all arise in similar or even identical fashion. In fact, in a universe which really *is* a *uni*verse, such identity of process might well be expected.

The third point which deserves special consideration is, one may suppose, a direct outcome of the position discussed under the first point, the fact, namely, that Mr. Whitehead makes of 'importance' an ultimate category. Over against the finality, ultimacy, and irreducibility of the Good of Mr. G. E. Moore, Mr. Whitehead places the ultimacy and finality of 'importance'. Perhaps even this early in our discussion it may be suggested that 'Importance', as we have seen, is largely, though not exclusively, reducible to personal reactions in terms of interest. This possibility of partial reduction would seem to render it not quite as ultimate or as final as might be desired. This is a point worth keeping in mind in connection with Whitehead's moral philosophy.

4. *Ideal aims.*—In *Adventures of Ideas* we find Mr. Whitehead stating that "the business of morals" is "the effect of the present on the future."[40] And this remark is followed (on the same page) by the claim: "There is a paradox concerning morals. . . . Morals consists in the aim at the ideal, and at its lowest it concerns the prevention of relapse to lower levels."[41] In *Modes of Thought* we read: "Thus morals and religion arise as aspects of this human *impetus towards the best* in each occasion. . . . Morality emphasizes the detailed occasion; while religion emphasizes the unity of ideal inherent in the universe."[42] In Mr. Whitehead's essay, "Mathematics and the Good," he writes: "Our exact conceptual experience is a mode of emphasis. It vivifies the *ideals* which invigorate the real happenings. It adds the perception of worth and beauty to the mere transition of sense-experience . . . the *transformation of the real experience into its ideal limit.*"[43] And in his Ingersoll Lecture we find him saying:

The confusion of variety is transformed into the coördinated unity of a dominant character [or 'style']. The many become one, and by this miracle achieve a triumph of effectiveness—for good or for evil. *This achievement is the essence of* art and of *moral purpose.* The

[40] *Adventures of Ideas*, 346.
[41] *Ibid.*
[42] *Modes of Thought*, 39 (italics mine).
[43] "Mathematics and the Good," cf. p. 674 below (italics mine).

World of Fact would dissolve into the nothingness of confusion apart from its modes of unity derived from its preservation of dominant characters of Value.[44]

In other words, the books and essays of the past decade are all saying that "morals consists in the aim at the ideal," that it is concerned with "effecting the future" by commitment to ideals now, that it is an "impetus towards the best," that it is interested in "transforming the real experience into its ideal limit," and that the achievement of "the coördinated unity of a dominant character," which is also called by Whitehead "a triumph of effectiveness," is "the essence of moral purpose."

5. *Process, transition, finite-infinite, past-present-future.*— When it comes to Whitehead's emphasis on process, transition, and the generally dynamic character of morality (or, perhaps more accurately, of the conditions of morality), we find the following. Mr. Whitehead begins by saying that "no static maintenance of perfection is possible. This axiom is rooted in the nature of things." He then goes on to say:

Advance or Decadence are the only choices offered to mankind. The pure conservative is fighting against the essence of the universe. This doctrine is founded upon three metaphysical principles. [1] One principle is that the very essence of real actuality—that is, of the completely real—is *process*. Thus each actual thing is only to be understood in terms of its becoming and perishing . . . process is itself the actuality, and requires no antecedent static cabinet. . . . [2] I now pass to the second metaphysical principle. It is the doctrine that *every occasion of actuality is in its own nature finite*. There is no totality which is the harmony of all perfections. Whatever is realized in any one occasion of experience necessarily excludes the unbounded welter of contrary possibilities . . . [the] synthesis of the ideal with the real is just what happens in each finite occasion. . . . [3] The third metaphysical principle may be termed *the principle of Individuality*. It concerns the doctrine of Harmony; . . . Sense-perception, despite its prominence in consciousness, belongs to the superficialities of experience. . . . The great Harmony is the harmony of enduring individualities, connected in the unity of a background.[45]

---

[44] "Immortality," cf. p. 690 below (italics mine).

[45] *Adventures of Ideas*, 354-362 (italics mine, except in the one instance of the word *process*).

In *Modes of Thought* Mr. Whitehead says that "All forms of realization express some aspect of finitude. Such a form expresses its nature as being *this*, and not *that*. In other words, it expresses exclusion; and exclusion means finitude."[46] And again: "The full solemnity of the world arises from the sense of positive achievement within the finite, combined with the sense of modes of infinitude stretching beyond each finite fact."[47] And this (already cited above): "Importance arises from this fusion of the finite and the infinite."[48] And finally:

Process and individuality require each other. In separation all meaning evaporates. The form of process (or, in other words, the appetition) derives its character from the individuals involved, and the characters of the individuals can only be understood in terms of the process in which they are implicated . . . every individual thing infects any process in which it is involved, and thus any process cannot be considered in abstraction from particular things involved.[49]

In "Mathematics and the Good" we read: "The infinite has no properties. All value is the gift of finitude which is the necessary condition for activity."[50] "Infinitude is mere vacancy apart from its embodiment of finite values."[51] And: "Creativity involves the production of value-experience, by the inflow from the infinite into the finite. . . ."[52]

And in his Ingersoll Lecture we find Mr. Whitehead saying: "The World which emphasizes the multiplicity of mortal things is the World of Activity . . . of Origination . . . the Creative World. It creates the Present by transforming the Past, and by anticipating the Future."[53] And again:

The World which emphasizes Persistence is the World of Value. Value is in its nature timeless and immortal. Its essence is not rooted in any passing circumstance. The immediacy of some mortal circumstance is only valuable because it shares in the immortality of some value. The

[46] *Modes of Thought*, 107.
[47] *Ibid.*, 108.
[48] *Ibid.*, 108.
[49] *Ibid.*, 133.
[50] Cf. p. 674 below.
[51] *Ibid.*, 675.
[52] *Ibid.*, 681.
[53] Cf. p. 684 below.

value inherent in the Universe has an essential independence of any moment of time; and yet it loses its meaning apart from its necessary reference to the World of passing fact. Value refers to Fact, and Fact refers to Value . . . value-judgment points beyond the immediacy of historic fact.[54]

To the reader unfamiliar with Professor Whitehead's general philosophy it may not be immediately obvious what the quotations cited in this section have to do with ethics or with moral philosophy. Not one of these quotations seems so much as to refer to morals or morality. Nevertheless, if it will be kept in mind that, according to Whitehead, "morality consists in the control of process so as to maximize importance,"[55] and that "the effect of the present on the future is the business of morals,"[56] it should not be so difficult to see some vital and immediate connection between these quotations and Whitehead's theory of morals. For, in Whitehead's philosophy, the moral judgment is no more an isolated judgment than moral purpose is an isolated purpose or the moral act an isolated act. These judgments, purposes, and acts must all be seen and understood in their larger setting, "connected in the unity of a background," themselves all integral parts of the on-going 'process', and controlling the process in such a fashion as to produce an effect upon the future which will "maximize importance" by "aiming at the greatness of experience."[57] Purely verbally, however, the presence of such words as 'perfection', 'importance', 'process', 'individuality', 'value', 'value-experience', etc., in most of the quotations, should show, on even a superficial view, how closely implicated is the connection (with morals).

In the first of our present series of quotations, Mr. Whitehead seems to be saying that the impossibility of any static maintenance of perfection is axiomatic, because "rooted in the nature of things." And the three metaphysical principles upon which this doctrine is said to be founded are all dynamic (not static) conceptions, viz., 'process', 'the finite character of every

[54] *Ibid.*, 684.
[55] *Modes of Thought*, 19.
[56] *Adventures of Ideas*, 346.
[57] *Modes of Thought*, 19.

occasion of actuality', and 'the principle of individuality', which latter is said to "concern the doctrine of Harmony;" and the great Harmony, in its turn, is said to be "the harmony of enduring individualities, connected in the unity of a background." The applicability of these assertions and principles to such matters as the aim at moral perfection, the finite nature of each and every moral judgment and act, etc., etc., should certainly be obvious. The same should hold for the principle that it is the "fusion of the finite and the infinite" from which "Importance arises;" since 'Importance', like anything else actual or potential, is, of course, an aspect of 'process', sharing with 'process' in the eternal fusion of the finite and the infinite. And values too take on concrete embodiment in the finite-infinite connectedness. And it is by "the inflow from the infinite into the finite" that the World of Activity "creates the Present by transforming the Past, and by anticipating the Future." Even the "essential independence" of the "immortality of values inherent in the Universe" "loses its meaning apart from its necessary reference to the World of passing fact." And moral values obviously share in this nature of values in general.

6. *Unity, coördination, connectedness.*—The connection from the preceding section to the present one must already have become obvious. For the principle of connectedness has already appeared in some of our last series of quotations. It will be interesting nevertheless,—and of considerable importance for an understanding of the total problem here under discussion,— to see more particularly how strongly Mr. Whitehead stresses this specific aspect. "The notion of a mere fact," Whitehead writes in *Modes of Thought*, "is the triumph of the abstract intellect. . . . A single fact in isolation is the primary myth required for finite thought, . . . *there is no such fact. Connectedness is of the essence of all things of all types.* . . . No fact is merely itself."[58] In "Mathematics and the Good" we read: "*The notion of the essential relatedness of all things* is the primary step in understanding how finite entities require the unbounded universe, and how the universe acquires meaning and value by

---

[58] *Modes of Thought*, 12-13 (italics mine).

reason of its embodiment of the activity of finitude."[59] And again: "Plato's Dialogues . . . are suffused with implicit suggestion of the *concrete unity of experience,* whereby every abstract topic obtains its interest."[60] And in his Ingersoll Lecture he says: "judgment is a process of unification. It involves the necessary relevance of values to each other."[61] And: "values require each other. *The* essential character of the World of Value is coördination."[62] And, finally:

> . . . the reality inherent in the World of Value involves the primary experience of the finite perspectives for realization in the essential multiplicity of the World of Activity. But the World of Value emphasizes *the essential unity of the many;* whereas the World of Fact emphasizes the essential multiplicity in *the realization of this unity.* Thus the Universe, which embraces both Worlds, exhibits the one as many, and the many as one.[63]

It is perhaps hardly necessary either to discuss these statements at length or do more than point to their obvious implications. The connectedness which is said to be "of the essence of all things," and which makes of mere "single facts in isolation" a sheer—though for the abstract intellect sometimes a quite necessary and often certainly useful—"myth," is the obvious metaphysical pre-condition of "the concrete unity of experience."[64] Without this both the world of value and the world of activity would be unthinkable and meaningless. For, judgment itself is a "process of unification" and "involves the necessary relevance of values to each other." In fact, "the essential character of the World of Value is [precisely] coördination." Indeed, this interconnectedness is of the very essence of the universe itself, since the universe embraces both, the World of Value and the World of Fact; the World of Value emphasizing "the essential unity of the many," and the World of Fact em-

---

[59] "Mathematics and the Good," cf. pp. 674f below (italics mine).
[60] *Ibid.,* 680 below (italics mine).
[61] "Immortality," cf. p. 685 below.
[62] *Ibid.,* 692 below (italics mine).
[63] *Ibid.,* 693 below (italics mine).
[64] Which phrase, by the way, is as much an essential part of the philosophy of John Dewey as of that of Whitehead.

phasizing "the essential multiplicity in the realization of this unity." The applicability of these doctrines to *moral* judgments, *moral* values, and to the *moral* unity of experience hardly requires separate mention.

7. *Pattern, structure, order, system, form, mathematics.*— We come here to that aspect of Whitehead's thought in which much of his uniqueness resides. "My topic," Whitehead writes, in *Modes of Thought,* "is the relation of Order to The Good, and the relation of mathematics to the notion of Order."[65] Even Professor Whitehead himself sufficiently realizes the rather startling nature of this statement, for he adds: "At first sight, the notion of any important connection between the multiplication table and the moral beauty of the Sermon on the Mount is fantastic."[66] However, such a connection seems "fantastic" only "at first sight." For Mr. Whitehead proceeds: "And yet, consideration of the development of human clarity of experience from its foundation of confused animal satisfactions discloses mathematical understanding as the primary example of insight into the nature of The Good."[67] Furthermore, in a 1941 essay, whose very title, "Mathematics and the Good," already tells the story, he gives his reasons for such an assertion. "All value," he writes,

is the gift of finitude which is the necessary condition for *activity*. Also activity means the origination of *patterns* of assemblage, and *mathematics is the study of pattern.* Here we find *the essential clue which relates mathematics to the study of the good, and the study of the bad.*[68]

Nor is this all. A few pages further on we are told:

Mathematics is now being transformed into the intellectual analysis of types of patterns. . . . *The infusion of pattern* into natural occurrences, and *the stability of* such *patterns,* and *the modification of* such *patterns, is the necessary condition for the realization of the Good.* [In fact,] *Mathematics is the most powerful technique for the understanding of pattern,* and for the analysis of the realationships of patterns . . . in the next two thousand years the overwhelming novelty in human

[65] *Modes of Thought,* 104.
[66] *Ibid.*
[67] *Ibid.*
[68] "Mathematics and the Good," cf. p. 674 below (italics mine).

thought will be the dominance of mathematical understanding. . . . Applied mathematics is the transference of this study to other examples of the realization of these patterns.[69]

Modes of Thought also aims to clarify this position. There Mr. Whitehead says: ". . . *the rise* in vivid experience *of the Good and of the Bad depends upon* the intuition of *exact forms of limitation. Among such forms Number* has a chief place."[70] And:

Mankind enjoys a vision of the function of form within fact, and of the issue of value from this interplay. That day in the history of mankind when the vague appreciation of multitude was transformed into the *exact observation of number,* human beings made a long stride in the comprehension of *that interweaving of form necessary for the higher life which is the disclosure of the Good.*[71]

We are reminded that "Man understands structure. . . . He constructs distant objectives. . . . He can aim at the best. But *the essence of this human control of purposes depends on the understanding of structure* in its variety of applications. To be human requires the study of structure."[72] "System," too, "*is essential* for rational thought. But . . . the closed system is the death of living understanding . . . our primary insight is a mixture of clarity and vagueness."[73] "We must be systematic; but we should keep our systems open. In other words, we should be sensitive to their limitations."[74]

On the other hand, "In itself a pattern is neither good nor bad. . . . I am emphasizing *the function of pattern in the production of Good or Evil* in *the finite unity of feeling* which embraces the enjoyment of that pattern."[75]

Unquestionably, the functions of mathematics, of mathematical patterns (forms, structures), and of mathematical relationships have played a very important part in the develop-

---

[69] *Ibid.,* 677f below (italics mine).
[70] *Modes of Thought,* 107 (italics mine).
[71] *Ibid.,* 106 (italics mine).
[72] *Ibid.,* 105 (italics mine).
[73] *Ibid.,* 114 (italics mine).
[74] *Ibid.,* 8.
[75] "Mathematics and the Good," cf. pp. 679, 680 below (italics mine).

ment of human civilization and culture; and that means, obviously, in the development of human understanding. There are, moreover, few human beings alive today who are as basically qualified and equipped to understand and appreciate the far reaching nature of this contribution of mathematics to human thought and understanding as is Professor Whitehead. In calling our attention to the vast significance of the "exact observation of number," he is emphasizing an important truth. Furthermore, it is perhaps true that "Mathematics is the most powerful technique for the understanding of pattern" known to mankind today. It is also true, moreover, that the understanding of structure and system "is essential for rational thought." Nor can Mr. Whitehead be accused of having permitted his predilection for mathematics and his fondness for structure and pattern to close his eyes to the dynamic and always structure-breaking nature of "process." For, after all, it is "process" which is the first metaphysical category of Mr. Whitehead's philosophy. Even in the midst of his stressing the structural, formal, systematic, and pattern-aspect of value, of activity, of experience, and of good and evil, it is doubtful whether he allows himself, even for a moment, to forget the fundamentally dynamic and processive character of the universe and of human life and thought. For, it is precisely in the midst of his discussion of the relationship of mathematics to the Good and of pattern, structure, and system that he warns us that "the *closed system* is the death of living understanding."[76]

Mr. Whitehead is, furthermore, right in calling attention to the close connection between order and the good. For example, one certainly can not but agree when one reads the following two statements: "There is a natural affinity between Order and Goodness. . . . There can be no excellence except upon some basis of order."[77] And:

It is natural to associate Clarity and Order with the attainment of the Good; and to associate Vagueness and Disorder with the Bad. For example, in writing a testimonial, the phrase 'Her mind is clear and

[76] *Modes of Thought,* 114 (italics mine).
[77] *Ibid.,* 103.

orderly' would be taken as praise; while the phrase 'Her mind is vague and disorderly' would read as condemnation.[78]

One must, moreover, agree fully with the reason Mr. White-head adduces for such judgment. "The reason for such judgment," he goes on to write, "is based upon the fact that clarity and orderliness enable the possessor *to deal with foreseen situations*. They are *necessary* foundations *for the maintenance of existing* social situations."[79] At the same time, Mr. Whitehead does not stop there. He proceeds:

And yet they are not enough. Transcendence of mere clarity and order is *necessary for dealing with the unforeseen,* for progress, for excitement. Life degenerates when enclosed within the shackles of mere conformation. A power of *incorporating* vague and *disorderly elements* of experience *is essential for the advance into novelty.*

The understanding of the universe is rooted in the implications of this advance. Apart from it, Creation is meaningless, divorced from change. Time has then no application to the static nature of things. Existence is meaningless. The universe is reduced to static futility—devoid of life and motion.[80]

8. *Disorder, conflict, frustration.*—The last quotation quite definitely leads us over to a consideration of these categories of disorder, conflict, and frustration. On first sight these seem to be the precise contradictories of the categories of order, system, and form. How, then, can anyone successfully use *both* types in explanation and justification of moral (or, for that matter, of any other kind of) experience? Mr. Whitehead is, indeed, well aware of this difficulty. For, in the passage from which we have just quoted, he goes on to say:

In the history of European philosophic thought, in the history of great thinkers, a curious wavering can be detected on this question. The appeal to life and motion is interwoven with the presupposition of the supreme reality as devoid of change. Changeless order is conceived as the final perfection, with the result that the historic universe is degraded to a status of partial reality, issuing into the notion of mere appearance.

[78] *Ibid.*, 108 (italics mine).

[79] *Ibid.*, (italics mine).

[80] *Ibid.*, 109 (italics mine). A critical discussion of the doctrine of the close connection between mathematics and the good must be postponed to Part III of this essay.

The result has been that the most evident characteristic of our experience has been dismissed into a subordinate role in metaphysical construction. We live in a world of turmoil. Philosophy, and religion, as influenced by orthodox philosophic thought, dismiss turmoil. Such dismissal is the outcome of tired decadence. We should beware of philosophies which express the dominant emotions of periods of slow social decay . . . civilizations rise as well as fall. We require philosophy to explain the rise of types of order, the transitions from type to type, and the mixtures of good and bad involved in the universe as it stands self-evident in our experience. Such a universe is the locus of importance.[81]

In fact, according to Mr. Whitehead, "The *essence of life* is to be *found in* the *frustrations of established order.* The Universe refuses the deadening influence of complete conformity."[82] But this is only one side of the story. For,

. . . there is necessity that the importance of experience requires adequate stability of order. Complete confusion can be equated with complete frustration. And yet the transitions of history exhibit transitions of forms of order. Epoch gives way to epoch. If we insist on construing the new epoch in terms of the forms of order in its predecessor we see mere confusion. Also there is no sharp division. There are always forms of order partially dominant, and partially frustrated. Order is never complete; frustration is never complete. There is transition within the dominant order; and there is transition to new forms of dominant order. Such transition is a frustration of the prevalent dominance. And yet it is the realization of that vibrant novelty which elicits the excitement of life.[83]

Realizing the difficulties involved in these apparent contradictions, Mr. Whitehead summarizes his discussion at this point by saying that "What we have to explain is the trend towards order which is the overwhelming deliverance of experience. What we have also to explain is the frustration of order, and the absence of necessity in any particular form of order."[84]

Earlier in the same book,[85] moreover, Mr. Whitehead had

[81] *Ibid.,* 109-110.
[82] *Ibid.,* 119 (italics mine).
[83] *Ibid.,* 118-119.
[84] *Ibid.,* 120.
[85] I.e., *Modes of Thought.*

insisted upon the same fundamental character of both order and disorder or confusion. "There is no reason to hold that confusion is less fundamental than is order. Our task is to evolve a general concept which allows room for both."[86] And, in answer to the query as to how that is to be done, Whitehead replies:

My suggestion is that we start from the notion of *two aspects of the Universe*. It includes *a factor of unity*, involving in its essence the connexity of things, unity of purpose, and unity of enjoyment. The whole notion of *importance* is referent to this *ultimate unity*. There is also equally fundamental in the Universe, *a factor of multiplicity*. There are many actualities, each with its own experience, enjoying individually, and yet requiring each other.

Any description of the unity will require many actualities; and any description of the many will require the notion of the unity from which importance and purpose is derived. By reason of the essential individuality of the many things, *there are conflicts of finite realizations*. Thus the summation of the many into the one, and the derivation of importance from the one into the many, involves the notion of *disorder*, of *conflict*, of *frustration*.

These are the primary aspects of the universe which common sense brooding over the aspects of existence hands over to philosophy for elucidation into some coherence of understanding. Philosophy shirks its task when it summarily dismisses one side of the dilemma. *We can never fully understand. But we can increase our penetration.*[87]

Whatever one may think about it—and the reader will remember that, in general, we are reserving our critique for Part III of this essay—it certainly cannot be denied that, despite his closing admission of the inability to "understand fully,"[88] Mr. Whitehead has stated his position on this point quite emphatically. He has called attention to the obvious presence of order, structure, system, form, and pattern in the universe. And he has been equally as insistent upon stating the presence of conflict, disorder, frustration. More than that: he has pointed

---

[86] *Ibid.*, 70.

[87] *Ibid.*, 70-71 (italics mine).

[88] And who, in his good sense, would attempt to gainsay this admission? It is, in fact, quite refreshing to have a major philosopher frankly state this, otherwise after all rather obvious, fact. Too often philosophers are prone to give at least the *impression* of something like omniscience.

out the essential character of both, and insisted that both are equally necessary. He has tried, moreover, to give *reasons*— and good reasons they are—for the necessity of both. He has recognized the dilemmatic character of the problem, but has, at the same time, indicated at least the general direction in which one would have to move to solve the difficulty, in so far as it can be solved. And then he has finally admitted that a complete solution of this problem is not (at present at least) given to man.

That the problem calling for solution in this connection is particularly aggravated by the basic nature of Whitehead's own way of looking at and dealing with the universe, I am inclined to admit. Since Mr. Goheen has, however, made it a special point to raise and discuss this issue in his own essay,[89] there is no call for doing so either here or in my critical discussion (in Part III); and this all the less so because I find myself in practically complete agreement with the way in which Mr. Goheen has stated the issue.

9. *Perspective, selection.*—The relationship of 'selection' to 'importance' is rather clearly brought out in the following Whiteheadian passage:

The notion of 'importance' also refers to grades of importance and types of importance. . . . There is no importance in a vacuum. Thus 'importance' leads us back to matter-of-fact. But the multiplicity of matter-of-fact requires for a finite intellect *selection* in dealing with it. Now 'selection' requires the notion of '*this rather than that.*' Thus intellectual freedom issues from selection, and selection requires the notion of relative importance in order to give it meaning. Thus 'importance', 'selection', and 'intellectual freedom' are bound up together, and they all involve some reference to matter-of-fact.[90]

And in his Ingersoll Lecture Mr. Whitehead insists that "every entity involves an *indefinite array of perspectives,* each perspective expressing a finite characteristic of that entity."[91] If this be so, one need not be surprised to find that "In the absence of

[89] Cf. his essay on "Whitehead's Theory of Value" on pp. 437-459, and especially pp. 456-458 above.

[90] *Modes of Thought,* 9-10 (italics mine).

[91] "Immortality," cf. p. 682 below (italics mine).

perspective there is triviality."[92] The act of 'evaluation' is, according to Mr. Whitehead, also one of selection. For, "Evaluation . . . means the analysis of particular facts in the World of Activity to determine the values realized and the values excluded."[93]

The close connection between perspective and importance on the one hand, and perspective and feeling on the other, is brought out very precisely in the following two quotations:

. . . perspective is gradation of relevance; that is to say, it is gradation of importance. Feeling is the agent which reduces the universe to its perspective for fact. Apart from gradations of feeling, the infinitude of detail produces an infinitude of effect in the constitution of each fact. And that is all that is to be said, when we omit feeling. But we feel differently about these effects and thus reduce them to a perspective. 'To be negligible' means 'to be negligible for some coördination of feeling'. Thus *perspective is the outcome of feeling;* and feeling is graded by the sense of interest as to the variety of its differentiations.[94]

. . . one characterization of *importance* is that it is *that aspect of feeling whereby a perspective is imposed upon the universe of things felt.* . . . The two notions of importance and of perspective are closely intertwined . . . perspective is the dead abstraction of mere fact from the living importance of things felt. The concrete truth is the variation of interest; the abstraction is the universe in perspective; the consequent science is the scheme of physical laws which, with unexpressed presuppositions, expresses the patterns of perspective as observed by average human beings.[95]

In a world acknowledgedly consisting of a vast multiplicity of things it is perhaps not necessary to justify Mr. Whitehead's position at this point. That such a world calls for "selection," and that even any specific finite entity "involves an indefinite array of perspectives," may be taken to be so obvious that we can spare ourselves additional words here. Nor need anyone act surprised at the close inter-connection between 'feeling' and 'perspective'. If "perspective is gradation of relevance" (or, of

[92] *Modes of Thought,* 115. And 'triviality', we shall discover under Sec. 13 below, is, according to Whitehead, one of the worst of evils.

[93] "Immortality;" cf. p. 685 below.

[94] *Modes of Thought,* 13 (italics mine).

[95] *Ibid.,* 15-16 (italics mine).

'importance'), and if 'importance' (or relevance) still has any recognizable relationship to the word in ordinary every-day usage, then, obviously, the emotions are definitely implicated in 'perspective', because importance has no recognizable meaning without reference to feelings.

10. *Feeling, emotion, interest, self-enjoyment, worth, evaluation.*—Once again our attention is called to the close interconnection and over-lapping of the different aspects of Whitehead's position. For, in a discussion of Whitehead's treatment of the place of emotions in the moral life, the very two quotations with which we closed the preceding sections need to occupy first place.[96] We shall, however, spare ourselves idle repetition of passages so closely at hand.[97]

As early as in his Lowell Lectures (1926) Mr. Whitehead wrote: "Value is inherent in actuality itself. To be an actual entity is to have a *self-interest*. This self-interest is a *feeling of self-valuation; it is an emotional tone*."[98] And in his Gifford Lectures, in enumerating and discussing his twenty-seven "Categories of Explanation," Mr. Whitehead stressed—as the twenty-fifth such category—the element of a "fully determinate feeling," i.e., what he calls, the 'satisfaction'. There we are told that "The final phase in the process of concrescence, constituting an actual entity, is one complex, fully determinate feeling. This final phase is termed the 'satisfaction'."[99] And three hundred pages further on in the same work we find that "The 'satisfaction' is the contentment of the creative urge by the fulfilment of its categoreal demands."[100]

In his Ingersoll Lecture Mr. Whitehead adds: "Evaluation functions actively as incitement and aversion. It is Persuasion,

[96] Cf. the quotations in the text in connection with footnotes 91 and 92.

[97] As everyone knows, of course, *Process and Reality* has practically its entire Part III, entitled "The Theory of Prehension" (pp. 331-428 in American edition of 1929), dealing with the subject of "feeling." It is entirely beyond the scope of the present paper to enter into a discussion of this exceedingly technical subject and problem. Although it ought at least to be said that, according to Mr. Whitehead's philosophy of organism, every actual entity, whether living or inanimate, is a center of feeling.

[98] *Religion in the Making,* 100 (italics mine).

[99] *Process and Reality,* 38.

[100] *Ibid.,* 335.

where persuasion includes 'incitement towards' and 'deterence from' a manifold possibility."[101] In *Modes of Thought* he writes that "Consciousness is the first example of the selectiveness of enjoyment in the higher animals."[102] And it is there also that we read that "At the base of our existence is the *sense of 'worth'*. Now 'worth' essentially presupposes that which is 'worthy'. . . . It is the sense of existence for its own sake."[103] Since, moreover, "our experience is a value-experience,"[104] "Everything has some value for itself, for others, and for the whole. This characterizes the meaning of actuality. *By reason of this character, constituting reality, the conception of morals arises.*"[105] In fact, "Our *enjoyment of actuality is a realization of worth*, good or bad. It is a value-experience. Its basic expression is—Have a care, here is *something that matters!* Yes—that is the best phrase—the primary glimmering of consciousness reveals, Something that matters."[106] "Importance," as we have already seen, "reveals itself as transitions of emotion. My importance is my emotional worth now."[107] Also, "Actuality is the self-enjoyment of importance. But this self-enjoyment has the character of the self-enjoyment of others melting into the enjoyment of the one self."[108] And, according to Mr. Whitehead's own emphatic statement, "The main point of this description is the concept of actuality as something that matters, by reason of its own self-enjoyment, which includes enjoyment of others and transitions towards the future."[109] "The ego enjoys an importance stretching beyond itself."[110] "The sense of reality is the sense of effectiveness, and *the sense of effectiveness is the drive towards the satisfaction of appetition*. There is a past, real in its own right, satisfying itself in the present." [111] And finally,

[101] "Immortality." Cf. p. 687 below.
[102] *Modes of Thought*, 40.
[103] *Ibid.*, 149 (italics mine).
[104] *Ibid.*, 150.
[105] *Ibid.*, 151 (italics mine).
[106] *Ibid.*, 159 (italics mine).
[107] *Ibid.*, 160; cf. also footnote 31 above.
[108] *Ibid.*, 161.
[109] *Ibid.*
[110] *Ibid.*, 165.
[111] *Ibid.*, 167 (italics mine).

Fact includes in its own nature something which is not fact, although it constitutes a realized item within fact. This is the conceptual side of fact. But, as usual, the philosophic tradition is too abstract. There is no such independent item in actuality as 'mere concept'. *The concept is always clothed with emotion*, that is to say, with hope, or with fear, or with hatred, or with eager aspiration, or with the pleasure of analysis. The variations in the quality of appetition are infinite. But the notion of 'mere concept', or of 'mere realization', apart from *a relevant emotional derivation, which is its emotional origin,* is fallacious.[112]

The emphasis in Mr. Whitehead's moral theory on the rôle which the feelings and emotions play in the characterization and description of some of the most fundamental terms is thoroughly apparent in all of these quotations, including the last two in Sec. 9. "Perspective is the outcome of feeling." ". . . importance . . . is that aspect of feeling . . ." "Evaluation functions actively as incitement and aversion." "Importance reveals itself as transitions of emotion." "Actuality is the self-enjoyment of importance." ". . . the sense of effectiveness is the drive towards the satisfaction of appetition." Any "concept is always clothed with emotion." The near-identification of 'importance' with interest:[113] all of these statements would appear to be clear enough and to offer a very real justification for the proposal[114] that Whitehead's moral philosophy is classifiable among the "moral interest theories." The ordinary "moral interest" philosopher needs, however, to be warned at this point, lest he count Professor Whitehead as a full-fledged member of his camp without having counted the balance of the cost. For there certainly are aspects of Mr. Whitehead's moral theory which would not fit at all into the frame of thinking and of position occupied by the usual "Moral interest" group.

11. *Personal identity, personality as center of value-experience.*—Although Mr. Whitehead's most careful and most detailed analysis of the problem of self-identity is to be found in *Modes of Thought,*[115] our quotations on this subject will all

---

[112] *Ibid.,* 167 (italics mine).
[113] Which we have noted several times before. Cf. pp. 568 and 572 above.
[114] Already mentioned on p. 572 above.
[115] *Modes of Thought,* 218-228.

be taken from his latest written statement, viz., from his Inger-soll Lecture of 1941.[116] For, whereas the analysis in *Modes of Thought* proceeds largely along scientific and common-sense lines, the discussion in the lecture on "Immortality" is almost wholly from the standpoint of value-theory and is therefore much more closely related to moral considerations. Having posed the question: "Can we find any general character of the World of Fact which expresses its adjustment for the embodi-ment of Value?", Mr. Whitehead retorts: "The answer to this question is the tendency of the transitory occasions of fact to unite themselves into sequences of Personal Identity. Each such personal sequence involves the capacity of its members to sustain identity of Value."[117] It is, in fact, "This problem of 'personal identity' in a changing world of occasions [which] is the key example for understanding the essential fusion of the World of Activity with the World of Value."[118]

Each single example of personal identity is a special mode of coördination of the ideal world into a limited rôle of effectiveness. This maintenance of character is the way in which the finitude of the actual world em-braces the infinitude of possibility. In each personality, the large in-finitude of possibility is recessive and ineffective; but a perspective of ideal existence enters into the finite actuality. . . . The essential coördina-tion of values dominates the essential differentiation of facts.[119]

Once more: "Apart from some mode of personality there is trivialization of value."[120] And finally, and also most emphati-cally: "Personality is the extreme example of the sustained reali-zation of a type of value."[121]

In other words, personality is the highest example of the sustained realization of certain types of value; and this is so because in the sustained fact of personal identity those particular types of value find their most exemplary embodiment in the world of fact; because it is in persons that "the finitude of the

[116] "Immortality," published for the first time in the present volume. Cf. pp. 682-700 below.
[117] "Immortality," p. 688 below.
[118] *Ibid.*, p. 689 below.
[119] *Ibid.*, p. 691 below.
[120] *Ibid.*, p. 693 below.
[121] *Ibid.*, p. 690 below.

actual world embraces the infinitude of possibility" in a peculiarly effective fashion; because "in each personality . . . a
perspective of ideal existence enters into the finite actuality;"
because "each . . . personal sequence involves the capacity of its
members to sustain identity of Value." Persons, though by no
means the only bearers of value, are therefore the most sustained bearers of at least certain types of value. However, even
such "sustained personal identities" are no more isolated events
or processes than are any other actualities in the universe. In the
first place they are themselves made up of an uncounted and
innumerable multiplicity of events and processes. In the second
place they are inextricably related to, connected with, and a part
of Nature itself. And, in the third place, they are part of a
society of persons, a further relationship which enters con-
stitutively into the essence of their being. It is to a brief consideration of this third factor that we shall turn next.

12. *Social self-transcendence.*—This idea finds admirable
expression in *Adventures of Ideas*. There Whitehead remarks
that "Transcendence begins with the leap from the actuality of
the immediate occasion to the notion of personal existence, which
is a society of occasions. . . . It is in the nature of the present
that it should thus transcend itself by reason of the immanence
in it of the 'other'."[122] "The general health of social life" finally
rests back on the doctrine that "the perfection of life resides in
aims beyond the individual person in question."[123] And earlier:
". . . its [the immediate subject's] own constitution involves
that its own activity in *self*-formation passes into its activity
of *other*-formation."[124] In *Modes of Thought* we read: "This
clarity of human vision both enhances the uniqueness of each
individual occasion, and at the same time discloses its essential
relationships to occasions other than itself. It emphasizes both
finite individuality and also the relationship to other individualities."[125] Finally, "these [moral] codes . . . aim at a social
perfection. . . . Such conformation of purpose to ideal beyond
personal limitations is the conception of that Peace with which

[122] *Adventures of Ideas*, 375-376.
[123] *Ibid.*, 373.
[124] *Adventures of Ideas*, 248.
[125] *Modes of Thought*, 105.

the wise man can face his fate, master of his soul."[126]

These few sentences, which could of course be duplicated many times over, will suffice to indicate (1) that Mr. Whitehead does not take personality or individuality in a restricted sense, but realizes, in fact, that "the perfection of life resides in aims beyond the individual person;" and (2) that he is not merely concerned with "the general health of social life," but with the "aim at social perfection," without thinking of such social perfection either as a static and unchanging goal or as something which could ever be fully realized. Besides, if it could be fully realized, one must surmise that Mr. Whitehead would be the first one to insist that such fact would indicate a mistake in the conception of the ideal in the first instance. Nor is it, I take it, necessary to point out here that Professor Whitehead's moral and social conceptions at this point are thoroughly in harmony with and rooted in the general nature of his metaphysics, both as concerns the doctrine of 'process' and also that of a thorough-going relativism.

13. *The Good (and evil)*.—After all those considerations we are ready, at last, to look at Mr. Whitehead's conception of *The Good*. It ought, perhaps, to be said, in this connection, that neither the word 'good' nor 'goodness' is to be found in the index of *Process and Reality*.[127] *Adventures of Ideas*, which, as we saw very early in this essay, "is in fact a study of the concept of civilization,"[128] and which contains independent chapters on "Truth" and on "Beauty," but none on "Goodness," contains two references to the word 'goodness', in the index, but the two references are to two successive pages. On the other hand, although neither 'good' nor 'goodness' appears in the index, *Modes of Thought* actually contains quite a number of references to and discussions of 'The Good', in one form or another.[129] Moreover, the title of one of the last two essays, available at the time of this writing, from the pen of Professor Whitehead is,

---

[126] *Adventures of Ideas*, 375.

[127] Although in the text the word does appear; for example, on p. 50, where we read: "A conceptual prehension is a direct vision of some possibility of good or evil—of some possibility as to how actualities *may* be *definite*." PR

[128] *Adventures of Ideas*, vii.

[129] Cf. *Modes of Thought*, 103, 104, 106, 107, 108, 112, 116, etc.

"Mathematics and the Good."[130] Although, in all fairness to the reader, it ought to be said at once that, outside of Mr. Whitehead's point of departure in this essay—which is a reference to Plato's famous lecture on "The Notion of the Good"—, the references to 'The Good' are more incidental than the title of the essay would lead one to suspect.[131]

"Goodness," according to Whitehead, "is a qualification belonging to the constitution of reality, which in any of its individual actualizations is better or worse. Good and evil lie in depths and distances below and beyond appearance. They solely concern inter-relations within the real world."[132] We have already seen, moreover, that "consideration of the development of human clarity of experience from its foundation of confused animal satisfactions discloses mathematical understanding as the primary example of insight into the nature of The Good." But when we quoted this passage before,[133] we omitted the immediately following sentence, which admonishes us to "remember that *morals constitute only one aspect of The Good, an aspect often overstressed.*"[134] And just one page before these remarks Mr. Whitehad suggests "three principles of division expressed by the three pairs of opposites—Clarity and Vagueness, Order and Disorder, The Good and the Bad" as "fundamental characterizations of our experience."[135] In "Mathematics and the Good" we learn that "mathematical concepts and ideals of the Good" are "ideals which stretch beyond any immediate realization."[136] And it is in the same essay that we read:

. . . you cannot discuss Good and Evil without some reference to the interweaving of divers patterns of experience. The antecedent situation

---

[130] This will be found on pp. 666-681 below.

[131] This relative dearth of references to 'the good' in even an essay, entitled "Mathematics and the Good," may account for the fact that one of the present writer's correspondents, who himself is an ardent disciple of Whitehead, upon hearing that the writer was engaged in writing on "Whitehead's Moral Philosophy," wrote in a letter: "I suggest that you take as a model for your essay on 'Whitehead's Moral Philosophy' a well-known treatise on the Snakes of Ireland."

[132] *Adventures of Ideas*, 345.

[133] Under Sec. 7 above.

[134] *Modes of Thought*, 104 (italics mine).

[135] *Ibid.*, 103.

[136] "Mathematics and the Good," p. 673 below.

may demand depth of realization, and a thin pattern may thwart conceptual expectation. There is then the evil of triviality—a sketch in place of a full picture. Again, two patterns eliciting intense experience may thwart each other. There is then the intense evil of active deprivation. . . .

There may be other types of evil. But we are concerned with the maladjustment of patterns of experience. . . . In itself a pattern is neither good nor bad. . . . The point that I am emphasizing is the function of pattern in the production of Good or Evil in the finite unit of feeling which embraces the enjoyment of that pattern.[137]

Many years before these last quotations Mr. Whitehead had already written that "There is a self-preservation inherent in that which is good in itself."[138] And: ". . . the creativeness of what can without qualification be termed good. Evil is positive and destructive; what is good is positive and creative."[139] And again: "The contrast in the world between evil and good is the contrast between the turbulence of evil and the 'peace which passeth all understanding'."[140] And it was in those same Lowell Lectures (of 1926) that Mr. Whitehead has given what are perhaps his clearest delineations of what he means by evil. Viz., "The fact of the instability of evil is the moral order in the world."[141] "Evil . . . is . . . a destructive agent among things greater than itself."[142] "Evil promotes its own elimination by destruction, or degradation, or by elevation. . . . But in its own nature it is unstable."[143] "There is evil when things are at cross-purposes."[144] To this should be added a few telling remarks about 'evil' from Mr. Whitehead's Gifford Lectures (of 1929). "The ultimate evil in the temporal world is deeper than any specific evil. It lies in the fact that the past fades, that time is a 'perpetual perishing'."[145] "The nature of evil is that the characters of things are mutually obstructive."[146] "The struggle

[137] *Ibid.*, pp. 679f below.
[138] *Religion in the Making*, 98.
[139] *Ibid.*, 96.
[140] *Ibid.*, 97.
[141] *Ibid.*, 95.
[142] *Ibid.*
[143] *Ibid.*, 96.
[144] *Ibid.*, 97.
[145] *Process and Reality*, 517.
[146] *Ibid.*

with evil is a process of building up a mode of utilization by the provision of intermediate elements introducing a complex structure of harmony."[147] In *Adventures of Ideas* Mr. Whitehead adds that "Evil is the half-way house between perfection and triviality."[148] It will, I think, have to be admitted that the intent of these quotations from the middle and the late nineteentwenties is quite in line with that of the quotations from the thirties and early forties which we have already given.

In the light of Whitehead's general position certain important features emerge from these statements which need to be emphasized. In the first place, the Good seems to be always something concrete: this is why it always has a feeling-aspect. And, secondly, any concrete moment of experience must be revealed in a pattern of events, it must, in other words, take its place within a system. Specific value seems to attach only to concrete events in concrete experience. And the real concrete is the infinite-finite uniqueness of each event. The highest possible value, moreover, seems to mean the highest possible order. And, since mathematics is the subject *par excellence* concerned with order and pattern, mathematical understanding is "the primary example of insight into the nature of The Good." Good and evil—like two other pairs of opposites, viz., like Clarity and Vagueness, and Order and Disorder—belong to the "fundamental characterizations of our experience." As concerns "evil," Mr. Whitehead stresses the evils of "triviality" and of "active deprivation." He admits, however, that there may still be "other types of evil." But he is not interested in such "other types;" for, he writes, "we are only concerned with mal-adjustments of patterns of experience." Now it stands to reason that, if there may also be "other types of evil" (besides those which are "evil" in the sense of being "mal-adjustments of patterns of experience"), there may also be other types of good. In other words, it is questionable whether there is anything in what has yet been said by Mr. Whitehead to demonstrate the proposition that the good must be patterned. Nor has he proved the proposition that "pattern is good." In fact, he himself writes: "In itself a pattern is neither good nor bad." The only reason, however, why one should not take this

[147] *Ibid.*
[148] *Adventures of Ideas*, 355.

last statement too much to heart lies in the fact that "in itself" a pattern is nothing anyway; so that, obviously, "in itself" it can also not be either good or bad. One wonders whether Mr. Whitehead's statement at that point means to assert anything more than just that proposition which, in the light of his entire notion of 'process', etc., is self-evident. In any case, however, Mr. Whitehead admits categorically that the point which he is emphasizing throughout is "the function of pattern in the production of Good or Evil in the finite unit of feeling which embraces the enjoyment of that pattern." He admits, in other words, that he is looking at the entire problem of the production of Good or Evil *only from the standpoint of the function of pattern.* One is, therefore, forced to ask: Is this way of looking at the problem one of intentional and purposeful self-limitation, or is this way of looking at it inherent in the nature of the problem itself? If it should be the former, then one would be forced to continue the original question by asking: Are the intent and purpose held in view purely idiosyncratic with Mr. Whitehead, or are there additional reasons in the nature of the problem itself which have driven Mr. Whitehead to attack the problem from this peculiar standpoint? Should it, on the other hand, be the latter of the two alternatives mentioned, then it will be incumbent upon Mr. Whitehead—in one fashion or another— to demonstrate the thesis that the function of pattern intrinsically inheres in the very nature of the Good. As things stand at present, I do not think that Mr. Whitehead has clearly answered either of the original questions; nor do I think that his words permit a definite conclusion on the part of the interpreter and critic.

One more point should be emphasized here. "Morals," Mr. Whitehead says, "constitute *only one aspect* of The Good, an aspect often overstressed." It is, of course, a mere platitude to say that the word "good" has many meanings aside from its specifically moral connotations. I suppose, for example, that we shall always use such language as "This is good soup," and "We have had exceptionally good weather," etc. It is, however, greatly to be doubted whether it is this sort of thing that Mr. Whitehead had in mind when he wrote the sentence just quoted.

The fact that he speaks of "The Good" adds weight to this presumption. Perhaps the whole idea should be considered as part of the idea which we met in Sect. 3 above, namely that morals, *et al.*, are all subordinate to 'importance'; so 'moral goodness' is subordinate to a much broader concept of 'The Good'. Be that as it may, one certainly cannot help being struck by the closing clause of the sentence, asserting that the moral aspect of The Good "is often overstressed." One wonders, moreover, whether at this point Mr. Whitehead's claims are so close to those of Plato as one is led to believe. For, although it is true, of course, that Plato's concept of The Good is an exceedingly broad and wide one, it is probably also true that, first and fundamentally, that concept with Plato was a *moral* concept.

14. *Perfection.*—Although the concept of 'perfection' in Whitehead is largely concerned with the aesthetic field, there is evidence—in a few isolated instances in Whitehead's writings—that the notion also carries over into the moral field. In no case, however, is the notion a static concept. Here too Mr. Whitehead is thoroughly consistent with his major philosophical position and emphasis. This is so true in the case of his ideas on 'perfection' that, in his chapter on "Beauty" in *Adventures of Ideas*, Mr. Whitehead writes:

. . . we shall find that always there are imperfect occasions better than occasions which realize some given type of perfection. There are in fact higher and lower perfections, and an imperfection aiming at a higher type stands above lower perfections. . . . Progress is founded upon the experience of discordant feelings. The social value of liberty lies in its production of discords. There are perfections beyond perfections. All realization is finite, and there is no perfection which is the infinitude of all perfections. Perfections of diverse types are among themselves discordant. Thus the contribution to Beauty which can be supplied by Discord . . . is the positive feeling of a quick *shift of aim from the tameness of outworn perfection to some other ideal with its freshness still upon it.* Thus the value of Discord is a tribute to the merits of Imperfection.[149]

In this passage we have an interpretation of perfection as far removed from the notion of a static and unchanging perfection

---

[149] *Adventures of Ideas*, 330-331 (italics mine).

as anything possibly could be. Here perfection and imperfection, harmony and discord, lower and higher perfections are all brought into such relationship that, despite the superficially apparent contradictions, a unitary view emerges. In this view perfection is basically a not-yet-reached-ideal, and an ideal which is everything but perfect the moment it is reached or one has come at all close to reaching it.

This notion is, moreover, thoroughly in agreement with the following remark, occurring a little later in the same volume: ". . . no static maintenance of perfection is possible. . . . Advance or Decadence are the only choices offered to mankind."[150] And this in turn is quite in harmony with the following statement, from "Mathematics and the Good":

Any practical experience of exactness of realization is denied to mankind: Whereas mathematics, and *ideals of perfection*, are concerned with exactness. It is the difference between practice and theory. All theory demands exact notions, somewhere or other, however concealed. In practice exactness vanishes: the sole problem is: 'Does it Work?' But the aim of practice can only be defined by the use of theory; so the question 'Does it Work?' is a reference to practice. The vagueness of practice is energized by the clarity of ideal experience.[151]

Ideals of perfection are concerned with exactness; but exactness is never actually realized by mankind; nevertheless, without the ideal nothing of significance is ever realized. There *is* a difference between theory and practice. But the difference between them does not mean that either can actually get along without the other; each is, in fact, indispensable to the other. This idea is one from which many a too perfectionist moral philosopher could learn much.

Perfection, moreover, just because it is relative to the practice of actualization, is always a different concept under different circumstances. In other words, there is no such thing as a concept of 'perfection' which can be filled with identical content and be applicable under any and all circumstances. Perfection, then, is always relative to its setting. This comes out clearly in

---

[150] *Ibid.*, 354.

[151] "Mathematics and the Good," cf. p. 673 below (italics mine).

the following statement: "The moral code is the behaviour-patterns which in the environment for which it is designed will promote the evolution of that environment towards *its proper perfection*."[152] "The evolution of the environment towards its *proper* perfection," this is the way Mr. Whitehead puts it. And this is in complete agreement, not merely with the general notion of 'perfection' which we have seen emerging here, but also with the general moral and aesthetic position of Mr. Whitehead's thought. For each type of environment has its own proper "perfection," a perfection differing from any other by precisely the specific nature of this particular environment. These statements should suffice to indicate how far Mr. Whitehead's theory of perfection is from the usual type of ethical perfectionism.

15. *Abstraction.*—Abstraction, which is an important concept in both the epistemology and the metaphysics of Whitehead's thought, also has particular significance in the realm of moral values. For: "Our conscious thought is an abstraction of entities from the background of existence. Thought is one form of emphasis."[153] And: "Abstraction involves emphasis, and emphasis vivifies experience, for good, or for evil."[154] Moreover, "Every abstraction derives its importance from its reference to some background of feeling. . . ."[155] And such abstraction is possible because "Human intelligence can conceive of a type of things in abstraction from exemplification. The most obvious disclosures of this characteristic of humanity are mathematical concepts and ideals of the Good—ideals which stretch beyond any immediate realization."[156] Here Mr. Whitehead specifically mentions that "ideals of the Good"—together with mathematical concepts (which latter, as a matter of fact, are never far away anyway when Mr. Whitehead speaks of ideals or of abstraction)—are "the most obvious disclosures of this characteristic of humanity": namely the ability to conceive of certain types of things "in

---

[152] *Adventures of Ideas,* 377 (italics mine).
[153] "Mathematics and the Good," cf. p. 672 below.
[154] *Ibid.,* cf. p. 681 below.
[155] *Ibid.,* cf. p. 679 below.
[156] *Ibid.,* cf. pp. 672f below.

abstraction from exemplification." Abstraction is a unique human capacity, which animal intelligence does not share with men. And the process required for abstraction is nowhere more obvious than in the abstractions of mathematics[157] and of "ideals of the Good." At the same time, however, it must not be forgotten that, although "No entity is *merely* characterized by its individual character, or merely by its relationships," "no entity can be considered in abstraction from the universe, and no entity can be divested of its own individuality."[158] Also: "There is no self-contained abstraction."[159] "Evaluation," Mr. Whitehead tells us in the Ingersoll Lecture, "always presupposes abstraction from the sheer immediacy of fact."[160] Thus here again we have the finite-infinite, the appearance-reality, the content-form, the actual-ideal and all the other relationships of that type coming to the fore. It is again the eternal 'process' of the interconnection and interrelationship of value and activity which lies at the bottom also of Whitehead's notion of 'abstraction' and which makes the notion of 'abstraction' of importance for his ethical outlook.

The whole point is put perhaps most concisely and at the same time most clearly and emphatically in two famous paragraphs of *Modes of Thought,* viz.,

. . . this possibility of abstraction, whereby individuals and the forms of process constituting their existence can be considered separately, brings out a fundamental intuition which lies at the basis of all thought. This intuition consists in the essential passage from experience of individual fact to the conception of character. Thence we proceed to the concept of the stability of character amidst the succession of facts. Thence we proceed to the concept of the partial identity of successive facts in a given route of succession. Thence we proceed to the potentiality of the facts for maintaining such partial identity amid such succession.

In other words, *as soon as we abstract*, so as to separate the notions of serial forms and of individual facts involved, *we necessarily introduce the*

[157] For example: According to Mr. Whitehead, "the fundamental notion at the base of Algebra" is: "Any example of a given sort, in abstraction from some particular exemplification of the example or of the sort." ("Mathematics and the Good," p. 672 below.)

[158] "Mathematics and the Good," cf. p. 678 below.

[159] "Immortality," cf. p. 685 below.

[160] *Ibid.,* cf. p. 685 below.

notion of potentiality: namely, the potentiality of facts for the series and of the series for the facts. All our knowledge consists in conceiving possible adjustments of series and of individual facts to each other. . . . The mere immediate exemplification is only one aspect of our experience.[161]

It is perhaps hardly necessary to call specific attention to the direct bearing of a passage like this to the problems of morality. For anyone who holds at all to a dynamic interpretation of morality will see at once the significance of the notion of 'potentiality', especially when 'potentiality' is described as Mr. Whitehead has done it here. This kind of potentiality would seem to me to be of the very essence of any concept of morality which can stand up under critical scrutiny.[162] It is in this sense that the moral life is the adventurous life. And certainly no one has broken more or stronger lances in behalf of the far reaching meaningfulness of Adventure for the significant living of life than has Professor Whitehead.[163]

16. *Universal (general) principles.*—Under this head we come to that aspect of the ethical problem which has been perhaps most controversial in nature throughout the long history of ethical reflection. It is no wonder, therefore, that Professor Whitehead also speaks on the subject, despite the fact that he has nowhere treated the ethical question systematically. As a matter of fact, Mr. Whitehead very nicely escapes between the horns of the dilemma as it is usually (though probably incorrectly) stated. Although he does not admit the existence of universal moral laws which can automatically be applied in every instance of the necessity for moral choice or decision,[164] he is by no means blind to the need for general guidance, and therefore for something like general principles. In *Adventures of Ideas* he writes:

[161] *Modes of Thought*, 135-136 (italics mine).
[162] Although I do not remember having used the term 'potentiality', the sort of thing Mr. Whitehead seems to me to be having in mind here I have discussed in some detail in my paper, "On the Nature of the Ethical Problem" (*International Journal of Ethics*, Vol. XLVII, No. 1, October 1936, pp. 57-69).
[163] His chapter on "Adventure" (Chap. XIX) in *Adventures of Ideas* is certainly a classic. I shall not attempt to despoil it by venturing to quote from it here. The chapter should be read in its entirety.
[164] We shall turn to a specific discussion of this in our next section, viz., 17.

Although particular codes of morality reflect, more or less imperfectly, the special circumstances of social structure concerned, *it is natural to seek for some highly general principles* underlying all such codes. Such generalities should reflect the very notions of the harmonizing of harmonies, and of particular individual actualities as the sole authentic reality. These are *the principles of the generality of harmony*, and of *the importance of the individual*. The first means '*order*', and the second means '*love*'. Between the two there is a suggestion of opposition. For 'order' is impersonal; and love, above all things, is personal. The antithesis is solved by rating types of order in relative importance according to their success in magnifying the individual actualities, that is to say, in promoting strength of experience.[165]

And in *Modes of Thought* he adds that morality "does concern *the general ideal* which should be the justification for any particular objective."[166] In other words, Mr. Whitehead not merely admits the "naturalness" of "seeking for some highly general principles" underlying all types of moral codes, but he specifically indicates the general direction in which one should go to look for such "general principles." And he finds the answer to the demand in two principles, viz., (1) the "principle of the generality of harmony," and (2) the "principle of the importance of the individual." The former of these two principles is the principle of "order," and the second one is that of "love." Here, says Mr. Whitehead, lie the only two "highly general principles" which, on the one hand, can satisfy the perfectly "natural" demand for a "general ideal," and, on the other, leave room for the wide variety and divergency of individual situation, need, interest, understanding, or, what have you, to allow the individual moral agent to make his own creative approach to and decision in every specific situation which calls for moral choice or decision. This is an ethical judgment which comes fairly close to that of Kant.[167] Reminiscent of Kant also is Professor Whitehead's insistence upon the principle of "the importance of the individual."

---

[165] *Adventures of Ideas*, 376 (italics mine).
[166] *Modes of Thought*, 20 (italics mine).
[167] Provided Kant is not interpreted in the customary—absurd—fashion. Cf. the present writer's *Kant's Pre-Critical Ethics* (Evanston and Chicago, 1938).

Mr. Whitehead's second "general principle" (that of "the importance of the individual") is, moreover, not merely a sop thrown here to man's natural inclination to look for such "general principles." This is proved by the fact that, in an earlier chapter,[168] he had already asserted that the doctrine of the impossibility of a static maintenance of perfection "is founded upon three *metaphysical principles*," those of (1) process, (2) the finite nature of every occasion of actuality, and (3) the principle of Individuality, which latter was said to "concern the doctrine of Harmony." This last metaphysical principle of "Individuality, which concerns the doctrine of Harmony," certainly comes close to containing within itself *both* of the "general principles" of the "generality of harmony" and of the "importance of the individual." These two "general principles," therefore, are actually of the nature of metaphysical principles.

17. *No universal moral laws.*—Does the admission of general and even metaphysical principles in connection with moral behavior, then, imply the existence of universal moral laws, everywhere and always the same? Mr. Whitehead gives a clear and unequivocal negative answer to this question. He writes: "There is *no one* behaviour-system belonging to the essential character of the universe, as the *universal moral ideal*."[169] Again: ". . . the notion that there are certain regulative notions, sufficiently precise to prescribe details of conduct, for all reasonable beings on Earth, in every planet, and in every star-system, is at once to be put aside."[170] And again: "The notion of the *unqualified stability* of particular laws of nature and of *particular moral codes is a primary illusion* which has vitiated much philosophy."[171] Certainly it would not have been possible for Mr. Whitehead to state his views on this particular subject more pointedly than they are stated in these three passages. But he is not satisfied with merely making these categorical assertions. He insists that it lies in the very nature and essence of morality that there can be no specific moral codes of universal applicability. Here is

---

[168] *Adventures of Ideas*, 354-360; cf. the first cited quotation under Sec. 5 above.
[169] *Modes of Thought*, 20 (italics mine).
[170] *Adventures of Ideas*, 375.
[171] *Modes of Thought*, 18 (italics mine).

the way he puts it: "*If there were a necessary conformation* of Appearance to Reality, then *Morality would vanish.* There is *no morality about the multiplication table,* whose items are necessarily linked."[172] *Necessary conformation,* in other words, belongs only to *completely abstract* systems of thought; and, although we have seen that "ideals of the Good" together with "mathematical concepts" are the "most obvious disclosures" of the distinctly human capacity for abstraction, morality itself is always a *combination* of the abstract and the concrete, whereas mathematics is a purely abstract system of patterns and necessarily determined relationships. The moral life has, after all, to be lived; it is an actualized life, even though the moral ideal (the general "ideal of the Good") is itself largely an abstraction (like any other ideal concept). And actualization takes place in the realm of concrete experience.

There are, then, according to Mr. Whitehead, two very good reasons why there can be no definite universal moral laws. First, because the moral life is part of the realm of finite actualization, of the realm of concrete activity, where no two things, situations, events, or processes are ever entirely identical or alike, and change—process—is therefore of the very essence of this realm. And, secondly, although the moral life—because it is *influenced* by the patterns of "ideals of the Good" (which is, in fact, what makes it in the best sense moral)—is in a sense a patterned life and shares therefore with mathematics in the partaking of ideal (abstract) patterns, its concrete life of activity and actualization makes the moral ideals applicable in any specific concrete instance of need for moral choice and decision *relative* to the total then existing situation and to its specific needs and requirements. In this, I think, Professor Whitehead is entirely right.

18. *Emphasis on the temporal relativity in morality.*—What we have just been saying is, of course, an essential aspect of Mr. Whitehead's insistence upon the fact that moral codes, behavior-patterns, and morality in general are always "dated." They are, that is to say, always relative to a particular cultural epoch and concrete situation. This is brought out quite specifically in the following passages. "Morality is always the aim at that union

---

[172] *Adventures of Ideas,* 378 (italics mine).

of harmony, intensity, and vividness which involves the perfection of importance *for that occasion.*"[173] "... the necessity for investigation of the *peculiar* characterization of that sense of importance which is *current in the thought of each age.* All classification depends on the *current character* of importance."[174] "The moral code is the behaviour-patterns which *in the environment for which it is designed* will promote the evolution of that environment towards its proper perfection."[175] "Each society has *its own type of perfection,* and puts up with certain blots, *at that stage inevitable.* ... All realization of the Good is finite, and necessarily excludes certain other types."[176] And again:

There is no one behaviour-system belonging to the essential character of the universe, as the universal moral ideal. What is universal is the spirit which should permeate any behaviour-system *in the circumstances* of its adoption. Thus *morality does not indicate what you are to do in mythological abstractions.* It does concern the general ideal which should be the justification for *any particular objective* ... our action is moral if we have thereby safe-guarded the importance of experience so far as it depends on *that concrete instance in the world's history.*[177]

Even logic and mathematics, when used as processes of induction, lose their absolute generality, according to Mr. Whitehead. Viz., "... the absolute generality of logic and mathematics vanish. Also induction loses any security. For, *in other circumstances, there will be other results.*"[178]

It should be kept in mind, in this connection, that this temporal relativity does not apply merely to actually existing so-called "moral codes"—that is too obvious a fact and one far too nearly universally recognized than that Mr. Whitehead would taste either breath or ink on it—but to "ideals of the Good" and to "general ideals" as well. In other words, even "abstract concepts," such as ideals, are dated or datable. For, after all, they too grow out of the cultural epoch and milieu of which they are a part.

[173] *Modes of Thought,* 19 (italics mine).
[174] *Ibid.,* 21-22 (italics mine).
[175] *Adventures of Ideas,* 377 (italics mine).
[176] *Ibid.,* 375 (italics mine).
[177] *Modes of Thought,* 20 (italics mine).
[178] *Ibid.,* 134 (italics mine).

19. *The Good as beautiful, etc.*—I do not think that it is too much to say that, for Professor Whitehead, beauty and the beautiful is second only in personal interest (to him) to mathematical pattern. It would be unthinkable, therefore, that this strong sense of beauty should not crop out in Mr. Whitehead's considerations of morals and of the Good. We are not so surprised, then, when we read that "The real world is good when it is beautiful;"[179] or that ". . . beauty, moral and aesthetic, is the aim of existence."[180] Such statements would, in fact, indicate that goodness is subordinate to beauty. This would seem to be borne out also by the fact that, in the passage in which Mr. Whitehead subordinates morality, logic, religion, and art to 'importance',[181] the concept of beauty is notable by its absence. One is also driven to the same conclusion by the whole of Part IV of *Adventures of Ideas*. For there we are informed that "Truth and Beauty are the great regulative properties in virtue of which Appearance justifies itself to the immediate decision of the experient subject."[182] Goodness, it will be noted, is again absent from this list of "regulative properties." And the chapters constituting this Part IV are as follows: "Truth," "Beauty," "Truth and Beauty," "Adventure," and "Peace." Here again one feels a strange absence: that of Goodness. That this absence is not unintentional is proved, moreover, by a specific statement in the chapter on "Truth and Beauty," where Mr. Whitehead— evidently himself conscious of the strange absence of Goodness from all this discussion—writes: "Goodness is the third member of the trinity which traditionally has been assigned *as the* complex *aim of art*—namely, Truth, Beauty, and Goodness. With the point of view here adopted, *Goodness must be denied a place* among the aims of art."[183] In this last sentence I have purposely italicized those six words, without completing the italicizing of the rest of the sentence, even though this may do violence to Mr. Whitehead's actual statement. For, with the sentence in its entirety I can find no fault. I too should deny to goodness a

---

[179] *Adventures of Ideas*, 345.
[180] "Autobiographical Notes," cf. p. 8 above.
[181] *Modes of Thought*, 16.
[182] *Adventures of Ideas*, 309.
[183] *Ibid.*, 345 (italics mine).

place among the aims of art; I should agree, moreover, entirely with the reasons Mr. Whitehead adduces[184] for this assertion. But I cannot agree that the famous trinity of Truth, Beauty, and Goodness is primarily famous for its having been assigned as "the complex *aim of art*." I rather imagine that Plato would be horrified if he were to hear such a claim being made in all seriousness. The trinity of these values is traditionally famous for quite other reasons, of which Mr. Whitehead is, of course, as much aware as is anyone else. Nor can it be said that the meaning and significance of Goodness has been rescued by Mr. Whitehead's next two sentences, to the effect that ". . . Goodness is a qualification belonging to the constitution of reality, which in any of its individual actualizations is better or worse. Good and evil lie in depths and distances below and beyond appearance."[185] For it is, after all, just one sentence beyond that we find the sentence already quoted: "The real world is good when it is beautiful." No, I think it is undeniable that Mr. Whitehead finds no place for Goodness *alongside* of Truth and Beauty, but subordinates Goodness to Beauty; and that quite aside from the relationship of each of the three values to art or to the aims of art. It is intentional, therefore, that Part IV of *Adventures* contains no separate chapter on "Goodness."

The reader of *Adventures of Ideas* might have entertained some hope that perhaps the closing chapter of the book, on "Peace," might turn out to be a discussion of 'Goodness' under another name. Such readers, however, were destined to be disappointed. The chapter does, indeed, contain perhaps as many passages referring to 'Goodness' or to morals as does any other chapter in any of Mr. Whitehead's more recent books.[186] But it cannot be said that the chapter supplants one on 'Goodness' or on morality. In fact, the preceding chapter, on "Adventure," comes, in the judgment of the present writer, far closer to doing so; and this despite the fact that there are many less actual references to either goodness or morality in it than there are in the chapter on "Peace." It comes closer, none the less, because the very notion of 'adventure' as treated by Mr. Whitehead

---

[184] At the same place.
[185] *Ibid.*
[186] Most of these references have already been quoted in this essay.

seems to approximate a profoundly ethical idea: the idea of the basic human requirement for creative effort in novel directions. Mr. Whitehead himself, however, does not seem to make the specific connection between 'adventure' and a reasonable interpretation of the ethical good. Whether this connection was in his mind or not, I would not undertake to guess.

20. *Summary and conclusion of Part II.*—A summary of the content of the last eighteen sections would practically require a re-writing—even though in different words—of what has been said. In fact, each of the sections is itself at best only a mere summary of the subject it intends to treat. Nothing more has been possible within the space-limitations of the present undertaking. One may nevertheless express the hope that what has been done will have accomplished the primary purpose of laying before the reader the passages—brought together from Mr. Whitehead's major works of the past fifteen years—in which he expresses himself on any aspect of the broad subject of ethics and moral philosophy. One thing ought to be clear above everything else: in the light of the almost innumerable references to moral codes, morality, moral goodness, moral purpose, *et al.*, it ought forever to be impossible to assert that Professor Whitehead has no interest at all in the issues and problems of moral philosophy. Instead, it should be repeated[187] that Mr. Whitehead's particular choice of devotion to particular aspects of mathematics, science, and philosophy by no means precludes any and every interest in other fields. He may not be an ethicist, but neither is Mr. Dewey a mathematician. Yet Mr. Whitehead has real interest in and some profound insights into certain aspects of the moral problem; as, indeed, Mr. Dewey has in mathematical issues. The absence of specific treatises in the respective field or fields makes neither man less great as a philosopher.

III. Critique

We turn now to a brief critical discussion of the ethical ideas found actual or latent in Mr. Whitehead's written work. Such a discussion is also, quite obviously, handicapped by the lack of any systematic treatment of the problems of ethics on the part

[187] What I have already suggested in footnote 15 above.

of Mr. Whitehead. But the reader who has been patient enough to follow the discussion thus far, will be aware of this handicap and will, therefore, peruse any criticisms which may be offered with this fact in mind.

This concluding Part will be divided into four sections, as follows: 1. Points which seem to require no critical comment; 2. Points which stand in need of critical discussion; and 3. Points which appear objectionable; to be followed 4. by a final few words in conclusion.

1. *Points which seem to require no critical comment.*—A number of points emerge from our previous discussion which seem to require no critical comment since there will be fairly general agreement on most of these points among contemporary ethicists. These points will merely be enumerated in sequence with no comment, in order that space may be saved for the necessary discussion under Sections 2 and 3 of this division. It must always be kept in mind, however, that the correctness of these points is contingent upon the correctness of the interpretative exposition of the preceding section.

Fairly general agreement might be had upon each of the following points, with all of which the present writer certainly finds himself in agreement:

a) Professor Whitehead's generally negative attitude towards most accepted "moral codes" as at best only approximations towards real morality and, at worst, definite hindrances to human progress;

b) his denial of the existence of absolutely valid universal moral laws, valid regardless of time, place, or circumstance;

c) his insistence that real morality aims at the actualization (realization) of ideals, which ideals may be based on "general principles" which are "universal" only in the sense that "the spirit which should permeate any behaviour-system in the circumstances of its adoption" is universal;[188]

d) his notion that ideals are aims at 'perfection', which ideals are nevertheless "dated" (with regard to a specific cultural epoch and setting), and his resulting refusal to acknowledge any absolute perfection;

[188] Cf. *Modes of Thought*, 20.

e) his notion that morality itself is also 'processive', *not* substantive;

f) his acknowledgment that morality has deep roots in interest and feeling;

g) his insistence that in morality man is aiming at the achievement of unity, both within himself and for society;

h) his acknowledgment that real morality needs to be based on rational (*not* ratiocinative) perspective and selection;

i) his realization that morality is a creative, adventurous function, instead of being a passive acceptance of existing moral codes;

j) his admission that "personality is the extreme example of the sustained realization of a type of value," that type of value being essentially such as is possible for a creature capable of abstract idealization, i.e., a moral spiritual being; and, finally,

k) his insistence that true morality aims at social perfection and that the perfection of life resides in aims beyond the individual person in question.

2. *Points which stand in need of critical discussion.*—The points to be raised under this head are not numerous, but most of them are fundamental in Mr. Whitehead's position.

a) The first question concerns the subordination of morals under the notion of 'importance'. As has already been indicated,[189] this peculiar relationship between 'importance' and morality is beset by difficulties which do not seem to be overcome even by the broad connotation which Mr. Whitehead gives to 'importance'. Even if one were to agree to what seems to be Mr. Whitehead's proposal, namely that 'importance' is fundamentally made up of a combination of 'interest' and 'unity', it still does not seem plausible—and it is certainly far from established—that morality should be a species of the genus constituted by that combination. Unless the essential meaning of Whitehead's notion of 'importance' has been missed,[190] there have appeared no sufficiently adequate reasons for accepting this doctrine of the subordination of morals under 'importance'.

---

[189] Under Sec. 3 of Part II above.

[190] It would be absurd to assume that such misunderstanding or misreading of Mr. Whitehead's notion of 'importance' is an impossibility. Cf. footnote 39 above.

b) The second question concerns the use of 'importance' as itself an ultimate category. This point can be dealt with very briefly indeed. For it would seem that the very fact that 'importance' is itself constituted by the still more fundamental (and therefore more truly 'ultimate') emotional-toned 'interest' and the category of 'unity' would prove—at least from a standpoint of logic—that 'importance', being the combination of 'interest' and 'unity', is not itself an *ultimate* category. But, obviously, the question here also turns finally on whether or not we have been able to grasp Whitehead's precise meaning of 'importance'.

c) The third question concerns what appears to be too close an identification of morality with 'interest' and with the resultant large founding of morality upon the emotions in general. It has been brought out in Part II above[191] that there is sufficient evidence in Mr. Whitehead's statements to make it possible to class his ethical theory—in so far as one is apparent in his remarks—among the "moral interest theories." And—as has also been indicated at the same place above—there are some evidences which might cause one to believe that Professor Whitehead would, as a matter of fact, quite welcome being counted as one of that group, so far as his moral philosophy is concerned. At the same time it would seem that the founding of real morality upon the quicksand of largely emotional reactions provides a treacherously thin foundation for morals. It would hardly seem possible that Mr. Whitehead could be satisfied with such a flimsy and all too shifty foundation. But, again, only Mr. Whitehead himself can answer this question.

d) The fourth question concerns Mr. Whitehead's recourse to (moral and other) 'intuitions' as absolutes. When Mr. Whitehead writes that "Our intuitions of righteousness disclose an absoluteness in the nature of things, and so does the taste of a *lump of sugar*,"[192] I must confess that I am sorely troubled by such a statement. On first sight it would seem that the "absoluteness" refers only to "the nature of things," a metaphysical doctrine with which one might not be disposed to pick fault. But a closer look at the sentence completely changes that first

[191] Cf. Sec. 10.
[192] *Modes of Thought*, 165 (italics in the original text).

impression. For, the "taste of a lump of sugar" hardly can be said to "disclose an absoluteness in the nature of things;" rather the sense of "absoluteness" is *in the taste itself*. It is the immediacy and apparent finality of the taste itself which gives the sense of an "absolute." I doubt whether "the taste of a lump of sugar" has ever given anyone a sense of the "absoluteness *in the nature of things*." But the taste-intuition may be felt as an absolute, certainly as a final factual experience. Now, if this interpretation is correct, then the meaning of the sentence ascribes similar finality and absoluteness to "our intuitions of righteousness;" that is to say, to the intuition itself, and *not* to "the nature of things" which is disclosed in the intuition. Neither the time nor the space required to analyze and discuss the validity or plausibility of this doctrine on its own merits can be taken here. It must suffice merely to point out that— whatever the merits of the doctrine itself in its own right—the doctrine definitely conflicts with the many times reiterated statements by Mr. Whitehead, to the effect that there are no such things as universal moral laws or universally identical moral intuitions. It does not, therefore, seem to me that he can have it both ways. If moral intuitions are real absolutes or finalities, then they are also universal and universally valid. Yet Mr. Whitehead is not merely repeatedly, but also insistently, denying this position.

In all fairness to Professor Whitehead it ought to be said, however, that it is at least possible that all he means by the quoted sentence is the following: There is *a sense of* immediacy and finality about our moral intuitions which is very much akin to *the sense of* finality in the taste of a lump of sugar. Both *appear* to be immediate intuitions which are just had, felt, sensed as what they are had, felt, and sensed. There *seems to be* no further accounting for them by recourse to anything behind or beyond them. If this is all that Mr. Whitehead means to assert in this connection, I can see no reason for any argument. In that case, however, it would still need to be pointed out that what *seems* and *feels* very immediate and final may—especially in the case of the "intuitions of righteousness"—upon closer analysis and inspection turn out not to be either actually immediate or truly final. Such intuitions, upon inspection, not merely may, but in most cases will be capable of being traced back to early training, indoctrination, education, or up-bringing. What I am trying to say is just this: Our intuitions of righteousness, when closely inspected and analyzed seem to me to disclose *neither* any absoluteness in the nature of things themselves *nor* even about the intuitions themselves. What *appears* as absolute is due to the immediate feeling-tone connected with the experience, *not* either to the nature of things or to the nature of the intuition —unless, indeed, the intuition itself is finally reduced to its mere feeling-tone. If this latter is what is meant, then the sentence under discussion says nothing more or less profound than that "feelings are what they are, and are felt as what they are felt." Even though one might not be disposed to quarrel with such a statement, one is bound to ask of what particularly informative value such a statement would be.

e) Finally, under this general head, the question must be raised, as to whether or not Whitehead's metaphysical predilections would leave room for a coherent ethical theory. Any serious attempt to answer this question on the basis of all the given facts would, however, require an independent treatise of considerable length. All that can be done at this point, therefore, is to indicate, in a few lines, some of the facts in Mr. Whitehead's metaphysical theory which necessitate raising the question at all. On the negative side, grave doubts may be expressed about the possibility of erecting a coherent ethical theory upon the substructure of a position which, at almost every point, is mathematical, if it is anything. Despite Mr. Whitehead's repeated heroic efforts to get both mathematics and The Good, so to speak, out of the same pail, the present writer remains unconvinced by any and all of those attempts. I fear that Mr. Whitehead's philosophical thought has become so saturated by his first intellectual love for and by his life-long interest in mathematics that—instead of with Spinoza seeing all things *sub specie aeternitatis* or with the naturalists' *sub specie naturae*—Mr. Whitehead simply cannot help seeing all things *sub specie mathematicae*. And, as the next section will indicate, a coherent and rationally justifiable ethical theory hardly seems capable of growing out of sheer mathematics. Mr. Whitehead's most recent attempt in that direction[193] appears to be only the best and most conclusive demonstration of the futility and impossibility of any such undertaking. "Mathematics and the Good" is still a profound and philosophically helpful paper on certain aspects and implications of mathematics. I have learned much from it. But it is decidedly *not* a paper on "The Good," despite its opening comparison with Plato's famous lecture on "The Nature of the Good."

As over against these considerations, on the positive side of the account, it is to be said that Mr. Whitehead's fundamental metaphysical reduction to process in place of substance and to events in place of things seems to be all not merely to the good of his metaphysics but to the good of an intelligent and intelligible modern ethical theory as well. His insistence and interpretation of relativity is also a definite asset in this same general direction. In fact, by far the most of Mr. Whitehead's metaphysical axioms and principles—with the single exception stressed in the preceding paragraph—would appear to adapt themselves admirably to a far more rational moral philosophy than are most current ethical theories. Nevertheless, I repeat that the question here raised cannot be adequately answered without a much more detailed analysis and discussion than is possible here.

3. *Points which appear objectionable.*—To the extent to which Whitehead's position in the area of moral philosophy has been set forth here, there would seem to be only two points to which serious objection is taken. As concerns the first of the two points, I shall do little more than simply state it. The second one, however, which is far more important, will need some discussion.

a) Professor Whitehead's theory of the close connection between morality and beauty, so that at times it looks like an actual identification, does not seem to be able to stand up under critical analysis. Granted, there are points of possible comparison, such as the fact that both areas fall into the field of value-judgments and value-experience, and that both make use of

---

[193] Viz., "Mathematics and the Good," cf. pp. 666-681 below.

ideal abstractions. There would, nevertheless, appear to be sufficient differences, both of kind and in number, between the two types of value-judgment and value-experience to warrant a rather precise method of differing analysis, procedure, and conclusion for the two areas. A reduction of ethics to aesthetics would appear to be just as disastrous as would a reduction of aesthetics to ethics. This latter point Mr. Whitehead sees clearly; but the former, which he does not seem to see, would appear to be just as obvious. After all, morality is not beauty, though the moral life—like a lot of other things—may be beautiful; but it is not the fact that it is beautiful which makes it moral.

b) However, still greater and more fundamental objection is taken to Mr. Whitehead's close identification of morality with (mathematical) pattern. Suppose that, following Mr. Whitehead, we were to say that the "good life" is the "patterned life." Immediately the question arises: What *kind* of pattern? For, certainly, it could not be just any kind of pattern. Mr. Whitehead himself says that "in itself a pattern is neither good nor bad." Moreover, the "bad life"—if there be such (and if not, the "good life," obviously, would have no meaning)—must have a pattern also. Consequently we are still confronted with the need for an answer to the question: What kind of pattern? Where do we get the criterion for the choice of pattern? So far as the present writer has been able to make out, Mr. Whitehead offers no specific answer to this question whatsoever.

Furthermore, even if there be an answer to this question, we are still far from having an answer to our difficulties. For in that case we find ourselves confronted by the fact that, if the "good life" has a specific kind of pattern, this may mean that the good life ceases to be the dynamic sort of thing all life is supposed to be. In other words, in that case, pattern (form, structure) may become a fence, an act of limitation; whereas the "good life" should be spacious, broad, dynamic, adventurous, open to growth, to change, in brief: wide open to new creation. Now I realize, of course, that the mere fact of pattern does not, *eo ipso*, necessarily imply limitation; such an assumption would be absurd. On the other hand, it does seem that the more specific and definite is the specific nature of the pattern, the greater is the likelihood of such limitation. And, as was pointed out in the preceding paragraph, it is precisely a specific type of pattern which seemed to be required. So that, from the present argument we seem to arrive at the following dilemma: either the moral life has no specific type of pattern at all, in which case it is not identifiable from the point of view of patterns or form; or else, if it does have a definite and specific kind of pattern, then it would seem to be far more limited in nature than the basically 'processive', dynamic, and adventurous point of view of Whitehead's general philosophical position would permit. Nor, so far as the present writer can see, does there seem to be any way out between the horns of this dilemma.

Now if, by the connection between mathematics and the Good, Mr. Whitehead means mainly to call attention to the fact that—just as "even the simplest notion of arithmetic" can not escape "this inescapable condition for existence" to the effect that every item of finite knowledge "derives its truth, and its very meaning, from its unanalyzable relevance to the background which is the unbounded Universe,"[194] so—the conception of 'the Good' must derive its meaning and its truth from its own (analyzed or unanalyzed) relevance to the background which is —again—the unbounded Universe at every level of experience: I say, if this is the major connection Mr. Whitehead has in mind here, then one can not only find no fault in the connection or in the analogy, but it probably could be said that most modern ethicists would be likely to be in complete accord with this thesis. It is, however, greatly to be doubted that this is all that Mr. Whitehead has in mind in his insistence upon the major (philosophical) connection between morality and mathematics. For when, in his most recent discourse on this subject,[195] he calls the doctrine "of mathematics elucidating the notion of The Good" "a basic truth of philosophy," which has been sadly neglected by philosophers ever since Plato's original intuition in this field "failed to make [it] evident to future generations,"

---

[194] Cf. "Mathematics and the Good," p. 670 below. In his next section (V) Mr. Whitehead categorically repeats this assertion: "Even in arithmetic you cannot get rid of a sub-conscious reference to the unbounded universe." (*Ibid.*, 672.)

[195] "Mathematics and the Good," cf. pp. 666-681 below, esp. p. 666.

it is certainly evident that for Mr. Whitehead the relationship between mathematics and the Good is far more immediate, vital and definite than the mere analogy suggested in the early sentences of this paragraph. As a matter of fact, Professor Whitehead, after frankly admitting that Plato's lecture on this subject "was a failure," just because "he did not succeed in making evident to future generations his intuition of mathematics as elucidating the notion of The Good," adds: "It is the purpose of the present essay to investigate this topic in the light of our modern knowledge. . . . My topic is the connection between modern mathematics and the notion of the Good." At least *one* earnest and serious reader of this latest (Platonic?) attempt feels it necessary to record it as his deliberate judgment that this latest attempt "to make evident" the doctrine of "mathematics as elucidating the notion of The Good" has succeeded no better than, according to Mr. Whitehead, did that of Plato twenty-three centuries ago. Even yet the doctrine is neither "made evident" nor even sufficiently "elucidated" to say what it is supposed to mean.

We may be permitted a final suggestion in this connection. It would seem that it would be possible for Mr. Whitehead to find a way out of all the difficulties and problems we have been mentioning, if by 'pattern' he were to mean the 'formal *method*'; that is to say, the process of rational reflection, creative adventurous construction, and transition as the only *method* capable of coping successfully with the exigencies of human experience and with the needs of moral obligation; in other words, a procedural conception of form and pattern. It is, however, questionable whether Mr. Whitehead's present strong emphasis on 'importance' and on its constituents, viz., 'interest' (emotional) and 'unity', make such an interpretation of his ethical position admissible.

There can probably be no question that, in all this work, Professor Whitehead is, more or less consciously, looking for something, without finding it quite possible to put his finger very precisely on it. This is nothing to be ashamed of. There is, certainly, much to be said in favor of the philosopher who remains throughout his life a diligent *seeker* after truth. He comes far closer to being a truly wise and wisdom-loving man than does the philosopher who claims to have arrived. It should be said, in fact, that in this sense Professor Whitehead's ethical position is far more honest than are most theories of ethics claiming, as they do, to have a substantive and final solution to the problem of ethics, but being found, on careful examination and analysis, to have nothing of the kind.

4. *Conclusion.*—The upshot of this discussion can be stated very briefly. Professor Whitehead's position in the field of moral philosophy is largely determined by the following four factors: first, and foremost, by the nature of his metaphysics; secondly, by his predilection for mathematics and mathematical patterns; thirdly, by his universalizing of feeling as the basic reaction of every actual entity, even in the inorganic realm; and, finally—and derived from (3)—by his taking "aesthetic experience" as an ultimate category (and "foundation of the world"[196]).

It only remains to leave with the reader one more word of warning. It is a warning Professor Whitehead himself gives on the closing page of his most recent utterance, his Ingersoll Lecture. Perhaps Mr. Whitehead will permit the present writer to make use of the identical warning with reference to the present paper, especially since the warning applies, of course, to all human discourse of any kind and at any time. "There is not a sentence," writes Mr. Whitehead, "which adequately states its own meaning. There is always a background of presuppositions which defies analysis by reason of its infinitude. . . . In fact, there is not a sentence, or a word, with a meaning which is independent of the circumstances under which it is uttered. . . . My point is that *we cannot rely upon any adequate analysis.*"[197] How nearly adequate the above interpretation and criticisms are will, therefore, also depend largely upon the background and intention with which the reader comes both to the works of Whitehead and to the present discussion.

PAUL ARTHUR SCHILPP

DEPARTMENT OF PHILOSOPHY
NORTHWESTERN UNIVERSITY

[196] *Religion in the Making,* 104-105.
[197] "Immortality," cf. p. 699 below (italics mine).

17

Henry W. Holmes

WHITEHEAD'S VIEWS ON EDUCATION

WHITEHEAD'S VIEWS ON EDUCATION

"EXACTNESS is a fake." These words, the concluding sentence of Professor Whitehead's latest public utterance, the Ingersoll Lecture on "Immortality," delivered at Harvard in May, carry something essential in his philosophy —the ring of it, the flavor of its ripened fruit. He builds his view of the universe on bases deeper than exact discriminations among sense perceptions, broader than the clarities of intellectual discourse. "I contend that the notion of mere knowledge is a high abstraction, and that conscious discrimination itself is a variable factor only present in the more elaborate examples of occasions of experience. The basis of experience is emotional."[1] Logic does not give us reality in its fullness nor do the sciences reveal the fundamental elements of nature. Philosophy must indeed include and understand the sciences, their logic and their facts, as it includes experience of every sort; but it cannot be maintained that all the sciences put together succeed in picturing the ultimate structure of things or provide a satisfactory interpretation of experience as a whole. Philosophic generalization requires an "imaginative penetration" which goes beyond "pinning down thought to the strict systematization of detailed . . . antecedent observation. . . ."[2] Logical perfection and coherence are inescapable requirements of a philosophic system; but the satisfaction of these requirements does not guarantee that a philosophy has either covered all the facts to be interpreted or penetrated to the ultimate and universal character of fact itself. Whitehead's own conclusion as to what those actual entities are from which the whole of things is built gives to them a living

[1] *Adventures of Ideas*, 225-226.
[2] *Process and Reality*, 7.

quality and an inherent connectedness: the world is not a junk-
yard of dead stuff, known from without by consciousness, either
human or divine—or both; it is a dynamic process creating itself
and uniting itself in a continuum to which it gives a real and
differentiated content. But this process is the movement and
adventuring, the never-ending birth and death, of entities far
simpler than the human soul; and it finds its unity in modes of
being quite beyond our finite consciousness. Our sharp decisions
about meanings, values, causes, and the future, as we draw them
from the carefully distinguished facts of science, are less definitive than we suppose. "Exactness is a fake."

It is not my task to estimate the value or success of Whitehead's metaphysics. But I cannot write about his views on education without reference to his vision of the broader shape of
things. For his general philosophical position has a bearing on
some theoretical perplexities which vaguely trouble education
in America and which may yet become of much importance in
the educational thinking of the world. What Whitehead has
said about education itself is memorable, and it is my chief
purpose in this chapter to write about the views of education
which he makes explicit; but he has not written about education
extensively and it is not unlikely that his influence on education
will have to come in part by indirection—through interpretation
of his general theory. Of such interpretation I should like to
make a modest and a brief beginning. The limitations Whitehead assigns to the precisions of scientific thinking provide me
with a starting point.

I

In American education the word "philosophy" is used with
much frequency, but it is seldom used to designate the kind of
thinking recognized philosophers engage in or the completed
system of any particular philosopher. The word is commonly
employed in a loose popular sense, as indicating the broader
views about education held by a person or a group. Such views
may be of a rather low order of generality; if they transcend
the processes of education itself, they seldom go further than
a few conclusions about the nature and function of intelligence

or the meaning of democracy. It is altogether clear that determined meditation on intelligence or democracy, or on education *per se*, leads inevitably in the end to basic philosophic questions; but educational discussion seldom presses on to views about the meaning of human freedom, the interpretation of nature, or the problem of consciousness. This is not unnatural, and it may not even be regrettable, for philosophy in the proper sense is not a field for easy exploration or popular discussion. Yet clearly it would be a gain for education if there could be widespread recognition of the fact that there is a technical field of thought and inquiry properly known as philosophy, with a history of its own and persistent problems, and that educational theory has something to learn from it. This amounts to a plea that educational theory, in its own technical development, should take philosophy seriously. If persons who start to think comprehensively about education want to rule out metaphysics, they ought at least to know what they are ruling out.

A philosophy of education worthy of the name can hardly rule out metaphysics—or some position on its problems. It is possible, indeed, to think of the relation between educational and philosophical thinking as an interaction—philosophy deriving some of its insights from educational experience and reflection upon educational issues, and educational theory deriving some of its generalizations from broader philosophical conclusions. Of the former trend there are but few examples in America—one, however, which is notable: John Dewey. The philosophic thought of William James developed in some part, no doubt, from what he had to say to teachers; but James spoke as a psychologist and never gave to education any comprehensive study. G. Stanley Hall had philosophic notions which derived from what he thought and wrote on education; but his philosophizing was not systematic. Dewey's whole philosophy draws deeply on his earlier thinking about education.

In an autobiographical essay, Dr. Dewey states that for many years *Democracy and Education* was the book in which his philosophy 'was most fully expounded'. In this essay he raises the question as to why so many philosophers, although themselves engaged in educational work, 'have not taken education with sufficient seriousness for it to occur to them that any rational person could actually think it possible that philosophizing should focus about education as the supreme human interest, in which, moreover, other problems, cosmological, moral, logical, come to a head'.[3]

The fact that Dewey developed his philosophy out of serious and consistent thinking about education—and the further fact that he early established and directed an educational institution of a novel character and wrote persuasively about it in his *School and Society*—account for his being accepted as *the* philosopher of education in America.

Thus Dewey's philosophy derives from education and becomes also the chief example of that other and opposite process, the application of a philosophic theory to educational thinking and hence to educational practice. If ever a philosophy has received a pragmatic test through education, it is Dewey's philosophy. No doubt New England transcendentalism affected American education; and to some extent the idealism of W. T. Harris did so. But Dewey's systematic thought, developing the central strain in Pierce and James, has come to be an educational gospel in America—not always understood, of course, but dutifully instanced. I doubt if any period or country can provide a more complete example of philosophy in action—not even Germany beneath the dominance of Hegel. Yet naturally there are misunderstandings and divisions in the ranks, and some reactions more or less rebellious. And at the present moment, when all faiths are shaken and all thinking challenged to go deeper into its foundations, there is a noticeable tendency to ask for something more than Dewey's philosophic theories offer. I do not say that this implies abandonment of Dewey's chief corrections of the older schools of thought or his additions to our educational insights; it is more like a feeling of dissatisfaction with the limitations of his method and his scope—in part articulate in philosophic thinking, in part a vague suspicion in the public mind.

[3] *The Philosophy of John Dewey* (*The Library of Living Philosophers*, Vol. I, 1939), chapter on "The Educational Philosophy of John Dewey," by John L. Childs, 419

For Dewey is not a constructive metaphysician. He offers us no systematic account of reality other than the account of it which we can get from the sciences and from common sense, duly criticized and generalized by philosophic reflection. He does not indulge in speculation as to the nature of any supposed or conjectured being—God, or any self-moved entity below the bounds of human recognition, or any harmony of harmonies uniting "the dream of youth and the harvest of tragedy" which lie "at the heart of the nature of things."[4] Dewey's naturalism defines a cosmos; but as Santayana justly says, his metaphysics finds no place for "realities or powers deeper than obvious objects."[5] A paragraph from Whitehead may be quoted as an illustration of the difference between naturalism as a basis for metaphysical thought and the more daring or imaginative way of thinking which Whitehead himself exemplifies. The point is that Dewey could not have written in this vein. The quotation is from the final section of *Adventures of Ideas:*

> The concept of Civilization, as developed up to this stage, remains inherently incomplete. No logical argument can demonstrate this gap. Such arguments are merely subsidiary helps for the conscious realization of metaphysical intuition. *Non in dialectica complacuit Deo salvum facere populum suum.* This saying, quoted by Cardinal Newman, should be the motto of every metaphysician. He is seeking amid the dim recesses of his ape-like consciousness and beyond the reaches of dictionary language, for the premises implicit in all reasoning. The speculative methods of metaphysics are dangerous, easily perverted. So is all Adventure; but Adventure belongs to the essence of civilization.[6]

It is not difficult to see how Dewey's philosophy, derived in no small part from education, should flow back upon it and be seized to justify and guide it. Has the more adventurous— if you will, the more poetic or indeed the mystic—mode of thinking, which the quoted paragraph describes, a bearing upon education? In particular, has Whitehead's general philosophic theory, being of this type, a value for the educational theorist?

[4] *Adventures of Ideas*, 381.
[5] *The Philosophy of John Dewey*, 247.
[6] *Adventures of Ideas*, 380.

Neither *Process and Reality* nor *Adventures of Ideas* contains direct references to education as a process, although the latter book contains an important passage on the development of professional competence in education. In any case, I am about to advance an argument which might, I suppose, attach to all systems of truly speculative philosophy, not alone to Whitehead's. For various reasons it seems to me to have peculiar force as applied to Whitehead's metaphysics, but I should have to go beyond the space I have at my command to demonstrate this special application. My contention is that the basic notion of speculative thinking, as opposed to naturalistic or empirical thinking on the one hand and to dogma on the other, has importance for a theory of education.

Its first importance lies in ridding education of the dreary thought that science has the only answers to its questions and the only satisfaction of its hopes. This statement might itself be "easily perverted." Imaginative insights cannot stand if scientific findings and experiment have shown them to be false —or even lacking in the general interest which enthusiastic speculation first attaches to them. Nor is this a plea for poetry in philosophic thinking or for fancy as a method of escape from fact in education. We have not yet begun to realize all the benefits that science has in store for educational theory and practice; its possibilities are almost limitless. And speculative thinking has its rigors, too—and nowhere better stated than in *Process and Reality*. But something will not yield in human minds which grants the possibility of apprehensions, feelings, intimations which are neither scientific in their primary character nor subject in the course of any future we can think of to experimental test. Spontaneous insights have a place in thinking about any human interest.[7]

The second way in which a speculative method may enfranchise education is in adding to the range of objects educational theory includes. "No man hath seen God;" and unless thinking beyond the bounds of science in the ordinary sense is pertinent

---

[7] Chapter IV of *Adventures of Ideas* contains so many passages which support and illustrate this point and lift it into a larger context, that I could hardly choose one for quotation, even if my space permitted.

to education, nothing religious (except the vaguest optimism and humanitarian feeling) can find place within the educational program. It is hard, indeed, to see how anything of cosmic import—such as Whitehead's notion of the universal process of adventure in the world, substantiating human freedom in a metaphysical construction; or the vision of a beauty or a rationality in universal nature, quite beyond the manufacturing enterprise of artful human beings—can come within a purely naturalistic theory of education. Nor can such things come within dogmatic teaching of a creed, except in name. If speculation must be charged with supernaturalism, the answer is that limiting our thought to what is natural is a curiously contradictory process; for common sense and all the testimony of determined systematic thinking are in accord with Hamlet—"There are more things in heaven and earth, Horatio, than are dreamed of in your philosophy." To recognize the mystery of things is very natural. But this is not magic, nor superstition, nor what Hall termed "transmundane irruption." If objects beyond scientific verification are to be brought within the compass of education, speculative philosophy would not introduce them as idols, or as objects to be accepted as defined, or as fearful symbols to be used for purposes of institutional authority. Freedom of worship is a fundamental freedom not because it gives religious sects (or schools of philosophic thought) the right to regiment their followers, but because it makes whatever is worshipful also subject to thought.

For speculative philosophy renders to education this supreme service—that it lays before the soul the universal scope of things —its natural objects and events and its mysterious deeps—and will not let a creed shut off from contemplation or inquiry anything whatever. Speculative philosophy invites speculation. Naturalism calls some of the objects of speculation derogatory names and makes all speculative thinking seem unimportant or impertinent. Dogmatism crushes speculation—but it may be noted that dogmatic philosophies do not always shut off scientific inquiry. Naturalism and dogmatic supernaturalism may indeed unite against the broadest speculative inquiry; for naturalism rules some of its objects out as being unknown to science, and supernaturalism (in the form of dogmatic religion) rules out further thought about them. What is thus shut off from human thinking is the possibility of any novel insight into the nature of things, and with it that source of hope in human reason which is a chief support of human courage—"here in this web of strangeness caught, and prey to troubled thought."

In Whitehead's *The Function of Reason* there is an analysis of these matters profounder and more comprehensive than the one put forward in these paragraphs of mine; but Whitehead does not speak specifically of education. Yet this one statement about the relations of speculation and reason seems to me to imply educational consequences:

Thus when . . . [a] novel speculation is produced a threefold problem is set. Some special science, the cosmological scheme, and the novel concept will have points of agreement and points of variance. Reason intervenes in the capacity of arbiter and yet with a further exercise of speculation. The science is modified, the cosmological outlook is modified, and the novel concept is modified. The joint discipline has eliminated elements of folly, or of mere omission, from all three. The purposes of mankind receive the consequential modification, and the shock is transmitted through the whole sociological structure of methods and of institutions.[8]

To keep speculative thinking active, not to limit its scope in any way whatever, and to make its place and possibilities apparent to every person who can grasp in the simplest terms the idea of free thought about anything beyond the practical necessities of life—surely this is not an indifferent service. Education can take its cue from speculative thought or from some type of thinking of more limited character. The number of persons who can (or should) attempt constructive thinking of the speculative type is so infinitesimally small that no claim can be made on their behalf for educational opportunity. The recruitment of philosophic genius must be left to fate. But general receptivity to the idea that human thinking is neither sinful nor wholly incompetent in the face of the mysteries of life is one of the

[8] *The Function of Reason*, 70.

guarantees of tolerant and hopeful living on the part of multitudes.

II

I have found certain aspects of Whitehead's general philosophy especially suggestive for educational policy. His doctrine of freedom in relation to the functions of professional organizations, on the one hand, and to the limits of power in the modern state, on the other, seems to me so important that it ought to be set forth here, and largely by quotation. I shall draw from this doctrine one conclusion for present practice which seems to me to have wide support in Whitehead's writing but for which I cannot quote chapter and verse.

Speaking of social tolerance "as a requisite for high civilization," Whitehead[9] makes the observation that the "first explicit defence" of such tolerance—the setting of this special argument being an account of human freedom in its historic growth as an idea—"is found in the speech of Pericles as reported by Thucydides. It puts forth the conception of an organized society successfully preserving freedom of behavior for its individual members." Whitehead at once leads this notion back to Plato's views of the spiritual elements in the universe. These, Whitehead says, are "deeper notions, from which all claims for freedom must spring." It is because the psychic factors in the cosmos are, as Plato asserts, "the ground of all life and motion" and "the source of all spontaneity," that we can draw such conclusions as that "human psychic activity thus contains the origins of precious harmonies within the transient world," and that "the end of human society is to elicit such (human) psychic energies," and that there is a basis in the nature of things for "the importance of social tolerance."

In the paragraphs which follow the phrases I have quoted, there is the most compact and inspiring account of the idea of freedom of thinking it has ever been my privilege to read. But I must pass it by, to turn to Whitehead's exposition of the mod-

---

[9] The quotations in this paragraph will be found on p. 64 of *Adventures of Ideas*.

ern machinery by which social progress through tolerance and free thinking is achieved.

I quote parts of Section V of Chapter IV of *Adventures of Ideas*.[10]

Political philosophy can claim no exemption from the doctrine of the golden mean. Unrestricted liberty means complete absence of any compulsory coördination. . . . Unfortunately . . . a few men in the whole caste of their character, and most men in some of their actions, are anti-social in respect to the peculiar type of any society possible in their time. There can be no evasion of the plain fact that compulsion is necessary. . . . It follows that a doctrine as to the social mingling of liberty and compulsion is required.

The doctrine Whitehead proposes centers in

a wide distribution of institutions founded upon professional qualifications and exacting such qualifications. Obviously the canalization of a variety of occupations into professions is a prerequisite. Here the term Profession means a vocation whose activities are subjected to theoretical analysis and are modified by theoretical conclusions drawn from that analysis. This analysis has regard to the purposes of the vocation and to the adaptation of the activities for the attainment of those purposes [and to the nature of the facts in view]. . . . Thus foresight based upon theory, and theory based upon the nature of things, are essential to a profession. . . . The organization of professions by means of self-governing institutions places the problem of liberty at a new angle. For now it is the institution which claims liberty and also exercises control. . . . Also, the sovereign state of modern legal theory has its sphere of action and its limitations. . . . The rôle of the state is a general judgment on the activity of the various organizations. It can judge whether they welcome ability, whether they stand high among the kindred institutions throughout the world. But where the state ceases to exercise any legitimate authority is when it assumes to decide upon questions within the purview of sciences or professions. . . . Of course, whoever at any moment has physical power, has [control] of physical compulsion, whether he be a bandit, a judge, or a political ruler. But moral authority is limited by competence to attain those ends whose immediate dominance is evident to enlightened wisdom. Political loyalty ceases at the frontiers of radical incapacity.

[10] *Ibid.*, 71 ff.

Thus from a metaphysical doctrine of the universal significance of the spirit, Whitehead's thought leads into the modern development of self-organized professional groups. In the course of his argument he refers specifically[11] to the professional organization of education. This argument for institutional autonomy among the members of a united and qualified educational profession is broader and deeper than any I have elsewhere encountered.

I find support in it—and in the general tenor of Whitehead's thought on other problems—for the conclusion that teachers should not ally themselves with other groups in our present social order—with labor unions, for example, any more than with managerial groups; or with political parties, or one authoritative state "party;" or with the church or any sect thereof. Whitehead's metaphysics is pluralistic and dynamic; many actual, living entities compose the universe. His social views correspond: through the action of many "societies," human life is seeking to weave itself "into a texture of persuasive beauty analogous to the delicate splendor of nature." This is not the activity for further activity, growth for more growth, which is the ultimate vision presented for education by Dewey. It has in view a progress toward harmony, but the harmony is forever active and alive. Meanwhile, in our own day, we are moving through a revolutionary period, the outcome of which—unless the recrudescent doctrine of the dominant nation and the dominant race, together with the power of brute force, should temporarily again command our lives—will be the organization of a world society diversely governed by groups of competent professionals controlled by a democratic political body to which all men belong.

The overwhelming importance of education, both for professional competence and for general civic competence, is obvious. And education must have a selective character and a pervasive vocational reference, but with important general elements. Whitehead's views on education are nowhere narrowly "cultural." He is interested in technical education—in the direction of which, in England, he had much experience; he has

[11] *Ibid.*, 78.

taken special interest at Harvard in the development of the
Graduate School of Business Administration—perceiving the
possibility of making business (as the Harvard Commencement
ritual puts it) "one of the oldest of the arts, the newest of the
professions." His views of general education look toward the
training of youth in civic, political, and philosophic understanding. But I cannot find that he has faced squarely the inclusive
problem of providing an education either adequately selective
with reference to vocations or general with respect to social
intelligence and character for the young of an entire nation—
America, for example, with its thirty million pupils of school
and college age. Perhaps this problem, or this group of problems, could not come within the natural bounds of philosophic
thinking such as his: these are the immediate issues of an educational profession which is mastering all too slowly its own difficult techniques.

III

Most of Whitehead's explicit educational theory is contained
in about one hundred and fifty pages of a book published in
1929, *The Aims of Education*. These seven chapters are repub-
lished addresses and essays written at various times between
1912 and 1928. They refer in the main (so far as they have
reference at all to specific and particular conditions) to English
schools and the English educational situation. Although the
ideas set forth in *The Aims of Education* have been supplemented by the ideas presented in a few other essays of an educational character (see bibliography in this volume), one who is
interested in Whitehead's general views on education should
turn first to his philosophic books, especially *Adventures of
Ideas, Religion in the Making, Symbolism*, and *The Function
of Reason*, and then read his *Aims of Education*. There is no
book of Whitehead's which does what Dewey's *Democracy and
Education* did—expound the author's general philosophy in
its bearing on educational issues and problems. One cannot gain
a just appreciation of what Whitehead has to say on education
by reading *The Aims of Education* plus all his educational
articles outside that volume. Viewed in the light of his con-

structive philosophic thought, that book is the only statement of his educational theory; but it must be taken as reflective of his general theory of life. And this is true in spite of the fact that his greater systematic works followed after his essays on education. When he wrote on education, his more general interpretation of life and nature must have been at work in his mind: at any rate, I can discover no inconsistency between the two.

The wit, the common sense, the penetration of the essays in *The Aims of Education* commend them so decisively to teachers that it would be an impertinence for me to exhibit these merits by quotation. There is so much to be learned from the compact wisdom of these pages that they justify repeated reading. But they have one grave defect—or rather, they are subject to one grave misunderstanding. Being brief, and being in effect the application of a philosophic outlook, they may seem to settle many problems and provide a kind of outline for a general plan of action. Again and again Whitehead warns his readers that his broad distinctions must be used as starting-points for further thought and for the careful working out of many problems of detail. But there is a type of mind which will resist all admonitions not to be content with general notions—but to complete them and correct them by attention to the facts, to bring to bear upon them findings of experiment, to use them chiefly as criteria for judgment on the meaning and importance of research. Professor Whitehead makes no reference at all to educational research, either English or American; and his references to the literature of education are limited to the mention of one or two British reports. No one should go to him for critical reaction to previous or current studies or experiments in education. What he offers is of quite a different character—and I should call it all the more important: the thinking of a man of genius on the general ordering and significance of education, based on his own experience and learning.

But those who are building up theories or programs in education have need to cover much besides, and every properly trained teacher must also know something about these other things—I mean, for example, the facts as to individual differences in intelligence, as revealed by the work of psychologists from Binet to Terman; the facts as to the nature of learning in general and in particular subjects, as set forth by Thorndike and a host of others; the history, status, and administrative problems of schools, as studied in this country by Cubberley, Judd, Suzzallo, and many of their fellow workers; the facts as to the economic and social issues implicit in educational policy, as presented by such contemporary reports as those of the American Youth Commission, the Education Policies Commission, and the New York Regents Inquiry. Not to turn from the insights of a Whitehead to these very different materials would be to study education by the intermittent flashes of one powerful light alone.

In saying this, I use a metaphor which is in one respect misleading. What Whitehead writes on education is above all things connected. There is nothing discontinuous in his educational thinking. He does not give us discrete insights, but a total pattern. And the pattern of his view of education fits into the pattern of his view of life; nor does it seem to me a pattern anywhere unsound. I think of it as simply not completed, in its educational phase, by fuller study of the facts, especially the facts of individual differences in human powers. Whitehead's views of what "even an average child" can get out of French and Latin[12] are not to be accepted as a basis for action in the schools. But the general argument Whitehead advances as to the character and order of learning and the meaning of education for civilization is trustworthy, coherent, and (more important) powerful. His way of looking at the whole educational enterprise has the clarity and sting of a northwest wind after a murky morning. But it is more than inspiring. It is workable, if one will make some necessary exceptions and some further discriminations and certain (sometimes very difficult) dispositions.

To the difficulty of some of the dispositions which must be made before education can do its full work, Whitehead's own words can attest:

[12] Cf. chap. V of *Aims of Education*.

When one considers in its length and in its breadth the importance of this question of the education of a nation's young, the broken lives, the defeated hopes, the national failures, which result from the frivolous inertia with which it is treated, it is difficult to restrain within oneself a savage rage.[13]

There are certainly times (I think we live in one of them) when it would be well for us all to think less of exceptions, discriminations, and details, and to go at our business on the main lines Whitehead and others have pointed out with the vigor he implies we ought to show.

The main lines of Whitehead's educational vision I should call four. They are not even as separate as the four sides of a square—but perhaps they are as distinguishable as the strands in a rope. To name them (and therefore to do them an immediate injustice), I might call them the Living Process of Education, the Living Utility of Education, the Living Rhythm of Education, and the Living Quality of Final Educational Ends. Such names are mere hooks, and they will add nothing to what any reader can get from *The Aims of Education;* but I can present more handily what I have to say about Whitehead's constructive thought in my field of interest by using some such group of headings.

1. *Education ceases, denies its own ends and its essential nature, rots what it should keep alive and sweet, the moment it forgets that children are living, growing, active organisms making their way into a world whose only valid meanings are achieved within the living present.*

This is the fundamental strand in the rope of Whitehead's educational doctrine. The idea of self-activity as a basis for education is of course not new. It is almost the whole of Froebel's theory and is far older than Froebel; it is of the essence of Dewey's educational thought and central in the Progressive Education movement which is based on Dewey's views. But I have never found outside of Whitehead (because no philosophy gives the same metaphysical emphasis to the adventurous movement of reality—a movement which *makes* time and space in

[13] *The Aims of Education,* 22.

their concreteness as it goes) such clear insistence on the *consummation* of the educative process in the present. And I would point out (and wish I might elaborate with greater emphasis) that Whitehead's theory also saves *largeness* in the character of education, as Dewey's often fails to do—perhaps, I hasten to admit, because his views have been too hastily applied.[14] I mean by "largeness" the full sweep of history and the full scope of organized thinking in science and mathematics. Whitehead's views on the Classics (Chapter V of *The Aims of Education*) show both his emphasis on making the meaning of Rome a part of the meaning of present life and his emphasis on the importance of a content, a character, a firm, extensive *texture* in the educative process. A "project" in school may be active enough, but it may not carry much more meaning than the making of a hut in the child's back yard at home. This criticism of "learning by doing" has been leveled times without number against practice based on Dewey. It cannot be leveled at practice based on Whitehead. The latter's views may be adversely criticized on another ground—that he overestimates the power of average minds to penetrate historical and scientific meanings: but his doctrines are admittedly concerned with education "on its intellectual side,"[15] and he makes quite clear his admission (cf. his treatment of Mathematics in Chapter VI of *The Aims of Education*) that he is concerned at certain points with "the more intelligent pupils." But for all pupils and in all subjects Whitehead emphasizes the importance of dealing *with a few large ideas actively considered, constructively used.* "Inert ideas," "scraps of information," "mere knowledge" have nothing to do with education. "A merely well-informed man is the most useless bore on God's earth."

2. *Education becomes and remains a living process, and it*

---

[14] The philosophic difference between Dewey and Whitehead seems to me, however, to have much to do with this difference in their educational doctrines. The exchange of views between Dewey and Whitehead on the relation between fact and principle in experience, as reported in the *Proceedings* of the American Philosophical Association, Vol. X, 1936 (*Philosophical Review*, March, 1937, 170-186), is illuminating.

[15] *The Aims of Education*, Preface, first sentence.

has personal and national importance, only as it is useful in some way at every point in personal growth and only as it eventuates in specialized power, conscious of its own inherently demanded "style," in a form of work which is socially valuable.

There is a prating theory of education which makes all usefulness in learning mean and self-regarding. This is a slavish doctrine, against which Whitehead sets his face. As he traces the history of freedom in *Adventures of Ideas* and envisages a democracy in which no man is a slave and yet in which that "natural aristocracy of intellect and character" of Thomas Jefferson's vision of the state is brought to leadership and power, Whitehead spreads before us general views which give this doctrine of utility in education a firm basis and a wide horizon. His sense for practical necessities comes out in his insistence in *The Aims of Education* on the shortness of the time we have for education and the immediacy of the national demands upon democracy. Technical education is immensely important; but it must be living, too, and never disconnected from the life of science or of art. What Whitehead does not see (or does not emphasize) is the enormous difficulty of making education for the duller minds and slower-moving bodies what it can be (and clearly should be) for the rest—an active process leading to broad understandings and to special competence without the slightest rending "of the seamless cloth of learning."

The problem of adjusting individual talents to the national tasks would be fraught with the gravest difficulties in a competitive economy in any case; in capitalistic democracy at war (and afterwards in reconstruction) the problem is terrific. Guidance is a central function of the schools; and Whitehead's double emphasis on active social understanding and on special competence in chosen forms of usefulness is eminently sound. But our economy needs vast revisions if the human cry for work to do is to be answered; and our education of the less constructive and ambitious among children must be infinitely more skilful than it is at present. In war or peace we must be "total, not totalitarian" (Professor R. B. Perry's phrase): but the "ends whose dominance is evident to enlightened wisdom" are not evident to everyone; and natural limitations make intelligent participation in the maintenance of a classless society which is fully mobile[16] an immensely difficult educational task for schools and industry and government. Whitehead is absolutely right in asserting that "the antithesis between a technical and a liberal education is fallacious," and that "education should turn out the pupil with something he knows well and something he can do well"[17] but step this argument down to the needs of "the other fifty per cent" of American children under present conditions and the problem becomes staggering.

3. *Education must take account of the periodic character of growth, and of the rise and fall of energy in interest and the power of attention, and of the balance between the need for immediacy of active understanding and the need for grasp of the external and unyielding essentials both of the organized thought to be mastered and the social demands to be met.*

Whitehead's doctrine of rhythm in education is both striking and sound. It partakes of his antagonism to fallacious distinctions in all education and in all interpretations of life and nature. It is consonant with his views on the "social mingling of liberty and compulsion." The novelty and the practicality of his divisions of intellectual progress—both in general as children grow and in particular as they advance in learning any subject—make this particular notion a highly suggestive contribution to educational psychology. Some one ought to compare Whitehead's three stages—the stage of romance, the stage of precision, and the stage of generalization—with the older views of G. Stanley Hall and with more recent and more factual studies of individual development. It should be noted that no one can misinterpret Whitehead as advocating sharp divisions and a saltatory theory of growth. I venture to say that the most competent students of child development will find something refreshing in Whitehead's doctrine of rhythm; and further, that much futile discussion on the conflicting claims of freedom and discipline (*pace* Montessori, for example) would be avoided by asking the disputants to read the chapter on "The Rhythmic Claims of Free-

[16] Cf. President Conant's "Education for a Classless Society," Occasional Pamphlet IV of the Harvard Graduate School of Education.
[17] Chap. IV of *The Aims of Education*.

dom and Discipline" in *The Aims of Education*. The reading of that chapter should be followed by the reading of *The Function of Reason* and the short (but difficult) book on *Symbolism, Its Meaning and Effect*. At a certain risk of touching on the profundity of Whitehead's doctrine of rhythm too lightly, or at a tangent, I quote from the final paragraphs of *Symbolism*:

Thus mankind by means of its elaborate system of symbolic transference can achieve miracles of sensitiveness to a distant environment, and to a problematic future. . . . It is not true, that the mere workings of nature in any particular organism are in all respects favorable either to the existence of that organism, or to its happiness, or to the progress of the society in which the organism finds itself. . . . No elaborate community of elaborate organisms could exist unless its systems of symbols were in general successful. Codes, rules of behaviour, canons of art, are attempts to impose systematic action which on the whole will promote favourable symbolic interconnections. . . . Free men obey the rules which they themselves have made. . . . The art of free society consists first in the maintenance of the symbolic code; and secondly in fearlessness of revision, to secure that the code serves those purposes which satisfy an enlightened reason. Those societies which cannot combine reverence to their symbols with freedom of revision, must ultimately decay either from anarchy, or from the slow atrophy of a life stifled by useless shadows.[18]

The advocates of the child-centered school should read Whitehead. So should the advocates of a fixed common culture derived from the past.

4. *The ultimate ends of education are living religion, living aesthetic enjoyment, and a living courage which urges men toward new creative adventure.*

A religious education is an education which inculcates duty and reverence. Duty arises from our potential control over the course of events. Where attainable knowledge could have changed the issue, ignorance has the guilt of vice. And the foundation of reverence is this perception, that the present holds within itself the complete sum of existence, backwards and forwards, that whole amplitude of time, which is eternity.[19]

The ultimate motive power, alike in science, in morality, and in religion, is the sense of value, the sense of importance. It takes the various

[18] *Symbolism*, 87f.
[19] *The Aims of Education*, 23.

forms of wonder, of curiosity, of reverence, or worship, of tumultuous desire for merging personality in something beyond itself. This sense of value imposes on life incredible labours, and apart from it life sinks back into the passivity of its lower types. The most penetrating exhibition of this force is the sense of beauty, the aesthetic sense of realized perfection. This thought leads me to ask, whether in our modern education we emphasize sufficiently the functions of art.[20]

The second of these two quotations is followed by an argument for art in national education and art for popular consumption which implies an economic situation in which relative poverty is a fixed character and art becomes a source of morale to "herded town populations, reared in a scientific age" and a bulwark against "some savage outbreak of defeated longings" in the future. There seems to me to be more economic hope than Whitehead here admits; and passages in *Adventures of Ideas* lead me to believe that he himself now holds to a more optimistic view with respect to the spread of material prosperity. If standards of living do advance for all, both religion and art become less necessary as means of inducing contentment on the part of vast numbers "in the stations to which it has pleased God to call them." But there are frustrations deeper than those of poverty. Technocracy may rescue the whole race from want, yet the dream of youth will forever face its harvest of tragedy, and maturity will turn for comfort to the worship of God and the enjoyment of beauty. These uses for religion and the arts are permanent, but I cannot think they represent the fundamental reason for conceiving education as directed toward aesthetic and religious ends. I feel sure there is in Whitehead's educational writings some passage I have missed; he must have said that beauty sends us back to life more bent to use our powers in creation, and that from worship we bring out of sensing God within us and beyond us a more vital feeling of His presence in the moving flame of life. The philosophic statement which would support this view may be found in the concluding paragraphs of *Process and Reality*.

HENRY W. HOLMES

GRADUATE SCHOOL OF EDUCATION
HARVARD UNIVERSITY

[20] *Ibid.*, 62f.

18

John Dewey

THE PHILOSOPHY OF WHITEHEAD

THE PHILOSOPHY OF WHITEHEAD

I

IT was long the fashion for philosophers to base their doctrines upon what each one happened to regard as "first principles," the latter being "premises" in their capacity of coming logically first. When the principles were regarded, under the influence of Aristotelianism, as axioms or self-evident truths, apart from which there was no demonstration of other truths (and without demonstration no "science"), they seemed to descend directly via pure intellect, out of the ether of reason, situated next to God or perhaps in his own intrinsic abode. Even if there were some special occasion in virtue of which they were humanly noted, there was nothing beyond them or outside of them from which, as truths, they arose or upon which they depended. One might as well suppose that the stars, and not simply the view of them, were dependent upon the ladder by which one, perhaps, mounted to see them as to give attention to the setting in which "principles" were formulated. When the latter were called postulates, in place of premises, there was gain in candor and in knowledge by philosophers of what they were about. But the change did not of itself ensure recognition and statement of the background out of which postulates arise and which determines the function they perform.

It cannot be said, even yet, that explicit attention is given as a matter of course to the background which sets the special problems with which a given philosopher is occupied. This failure is partly due to the persistence of the tradition according to which it derogates from the purity of philosophy to doubt its immaculate conception. But it is also due, I think, to the fact that a philosophic thinker is much more explicitly aware of what lies ahead and of being urged forward than of the background from which he derives his push. And, as I write these words, I am painfully aware of the inadequacy of the word "background" to convey what I have in mind—the words "place" or "point of departure" being even more inadequate, if they suggest anything narrower than the home and regional environment from which a traveller sets out.

Whitehead, it seems to me, has come closer than most philosophers have done to stating the nature of the region from which he sets out. It is for that reason I have engaged in these introductory remarks. I am thinking especially of a passage in which, after saying that philosophy "can deal only with things in some sense experienced," he goes on to say,

The living organ of experience is the living body as a whole. Every instability of any part of it—be it chemical, physical, or molar—imposes an activity of readjustment throughout the whole organism. In the course of such physical activities human experience has its origin. The plausible interpretation of such experience is that it is one of the natural activities involved in the functioning of such a high-grade organism. *The actualities of nature . . . must be explanatory of this fact. . . .*

Such experience seems to be more particularly related to the activities of the brain. But . . . we cannot determine with what molecules the brain begins and the rest of the body ends. Further, we cannot tell with what molecules the body ends and the external world begins. The truth is that the brain is continuous with the body, and the body is continuous with the rest of the natural world. Human experience is an act of self-origination including the whole of nature, limited to the *perspective* of a focal region, located within the body, but not necessarily persisting in any fixed coördination with a definite part of the brain.[1]

If I had a right to assume on the part of the reader acquaintance with my own writings on the topic of the reciprocal connections of nature and experience, and the bearing of these connections

---

[1] *Adventures of Ideas*, 289-90. (Italics not in original text.) The fact that my further references and quotations are limited to this particular book of Whitehead's is partially due to the limitations under which this essay is written. But in view of the simplicity and completeness with which the gist of Whitehead's doctrines is set forth in this book, I do not regard this limitation as of especial importance in respect to my interpretation and criticism.

upon the problems and task of philosophy, I would add that it will also be obvious why I cite this particular passage. For what I have called the background and point of departure seems to be the same for both of us, no matter what deviations may occur later. And such a community of backgrounds is so rare that I make no apology for dwelling upon it at the outset. In any case, the reader is entitled to the warning that my belief in the fundamental significance of the ideas set forth in the passage quoted controls what I have to say about the tenor of Whitehead's philosophy. If I am wrong in attributing central importance to the ideas that experience is a manifestation of the energies of the organism; that these energies are in such intimate continuity with the rest of nature that the traits of experience provide clews for forming "generalized descriptions" of nature—the especial business of philosophy according to Whitehead—and that what is discovered about the rest of nature (constituting the conclusions of the natural sciences) provides the organs for analyzing and understanding what is otherwise obscure and ambiguous in experiences directly had— if, I say, I am wrong in this view, then there will be no particular point to what I have further to say.

Whitehead is of course well aware that "experience" has often been restricted, both by those who called themselves empiricists and by their opponents, to certain arbitrarily selected activities of the organism to which a privileged rôle is assigned. For experience has, notoriously, been limited to the activities of sense-organs—or rather to their products, called sensations, or, better, sensa. In the light of the history of culture, one can find reasons for this peculiar arbitrary selection. But, viewing the matter impartially, the limitation can only be regarded as one of the most extraordinary and uncalled for errors human belief has ever indulged in—especially since, if one really began there and stuck, in the conclusion, solely to what the beginning justifies, one would never know even that he had sense-organs or that the sense-organs are organs of a creature engaged in living in an environment partly friendly and partly hostile to its activities. Whitehead expressly repudiates this restriction:

We must appeal to evidence relating to every variety of occasion. Nothing can be omitted, experience drunk and experience sober, experience sleeping and experience waking, experience drowsy and experience wide-awake, experience self-conscious and experience self-forgetful, experience intellectual and experience physical, experience religious and experience sceptical, experience anxious and experience care-free, experience anticipatory and experience retrospective, experience happy and experience grieving, experience dominated by emotion and experience under self-restraint, experience in the light and experience in the dark, experience normal and experience abnormal.[2]

Those who profess belief in empirical philosophy can hardly be other than grateful for emancipation from chains which, after all, were self-imposed. Artists, poets, prophets may be drawn to a philosophy that sees "experience" to be rich beyond the possibility of exhaustion and subtle beyond the reach of human wit.

II

I am not sure that the denial of "the bifurcation of nature" found in Whitehead's earlier writings was connected, consciously, with the enlarged and deepened idea about experience which is expressed in the passages quoted from his later writings. I imagine the denial had its source in Whitehead's reflections upon the new science; a mathematical strain dominates his cosmological account. But I have no doubt the denial has its completion in the express sense that physical nature must be such as to account for the specialized peculiarities of human experience, while the latter provides clews to be used in expanding to their full significance that which physical science discovers. "Neutral monists" have denied the existence of a gulf between physical and "mental" experience. Indeed, thoroughgoing materialism and spiritual idealism have at all times denied its existence. But as long as Newtonian physics was the accepted authority about the constitution of nature in its physical aspects, such theories seemed forced. Dualism was not so much an inferential conclusion as it was a frank recognition of the difference between the traits marking the objects of (Newtonian) physics and the un-

[2] *Op. cit.*, 290f.

deniable features of immediate experience. The genius of White-head is exhibited in the earliness of his perception that the new mathematical physics did away with the supposedly scientific foundations, upon the physical side, which gave obvious point to the separation. Given this initial move, continued reflection could hardly do other than develop a less abstract, a more vital, sense of the essential community of the less and the more specialized occasions of experience.

In any case we have such a passage as the following: "All final individual actualities have the metaphysical character of occasions of experience;" a passage to be read and understood in connection with the thesis that, granted this view, "the direct evidence as to the connectedness of one's immediate present occasion of experience with one's immediately past occasions can be validly used to suggest categories applying to the connectedness of all *occasions in nature*."[3] If the meaning assigned to this sentence is not entirely clear, the following sentence should render it definite: "An occasion of experience which includes a human mentality is an extreme instance, at one end of the scale, of those happenings which constitute nature"[4]—a sentence which shows, I believe, the sense in which propositions like the following are to be understood: "It is a false dichotomy to think of Nature *and* Man. Mankind is that factor *in* Nature which exhibits in its most intense form the plasticity of nature."[5]

This doctrine that all actual existences are to be treated as "occasions of experience" carries and elaborates, it seems to me, the significance contained in the propositions I quoted earlier about the depth and width of scope of experience. The idea that the immediate traits of distinctively human experience are highly specialized cases of what actually goes on in every actualized event of nature does infinitely more than merely deny the existence of an impassable gulf between physical and psychological subject-matter. It authorizes us, as philosophers engaged in forming highly generalized descriptions of nature, to use the traits of immediate experience as clews for interpreting our

[3] *Op. cit.*, 284. (Italics not in original text.)
[4] *Op. cit.*, 237.
[5] *Op. cit.*, 99.

observations of non-human and non-animate nature. It also authorizes us to carry over the main conclusions of physical science into explanation and description of mysterious and inexplicable traits of experience marked by "consciousness." It enables us to do so without engaging in the dogmatic mechanistic materialism that inevitably resulted when Newtonian physics was used to account for what is distinctive in human experience. That which on the negative side is simply an elimination of the grounds of the metaphysical dualism of physical and mental, material and ideal, object and subject, opens the road to free observation of whatever experience of any kind discloses and points toward:—free, that is, from a rigid frame of preconceptions.

For the generalization of "experience" which is involved in calling every actual existence by the name "occasion of experience" has a two-fold consequence, each aspect of this dual consequence being complementary to the other. The traits of human experience can be used to direct observation of the generalized traits of all nature. For they are intensified manifestations, specialized developments, of conditions and factors found everywhere in nature. On the other hand, all the generalizations to which physical science leads are resources available for analysis and descriptive interpretation of all the phenomena of human life, personal and "social." It is my impression that in his earlier writings Whitehead started preferably from the physical side, and then moved on to a doctrine of nature "in general" without much explicit attention to what may be called experience from the psychological point of view, while in his later writings he supplements and extends the conclusions thus reached by adoption of a reverse movement:—that from specialized human experience through physical experience to a comprehensive doctrine of Nature. The "events" of his earlier treatises thus become the "occasions of experience" of later writings. But whether or not this impression is well-founded is of slight importance compared with the fact that Whitehead proceeds systematically upon the ground indicated in the following passage: "The world within experience is identical with the world beyond experience, the occasion of experience is within the world and the world is within the occasion. The categories have to elucidate this paradox of the connectedness of things:—the many things, the one world without and within."[6]

In putting forward this particular mode of approach to interpretation of Whitehead's philosophy, I am doubtless deliberately emphasizing the things with which my own way of philosophical thinking most agrees. I would not deny that Whitehead's philosophy is so comprehensive that there are other ways of approach that other commentators and critics may find more significant than the one I have taken. None the less it cannot be denied that the path I have chosen is explicitly indicated (with increasing plainness) in Whitehead's own writings, so that what I say is legitimate if not inclusive. And if it is legitimate then I am entitled to my personal, and perhaps private, view that the consistency and sensitivity with which Whitehead follows the method thereby determined is the source of the originality and fecundity of his writings. For I believe that only by means of a view of the same general nature as is involved in this position can philosophy escape the road it has been following, a road which demonstrably has led to a dead end, where virtuosity of academic technique may flourish, but which cannot save philosophy from the sterility that is the Dead Sea fruit of academicism.

III

The passage already quoted to the effect that experiences involving human mentality are but extreme instances of the happenings constitutive of nature, is directly followed by the sentences:

Any doctrine that refuses to place human experience outside nature, must find in the description of experience factors which enter also into the description of less specialized natural occurrences. If there be no such factors, then the doctrine of human experience as a fact within nature is mere bluff, founded upon vague phrases whose sole merit is a comforting familiarity. We should either admit dualism, at least as a provisional

[6] *Op. cit.*, 293.

doctrine, or we should point out the identical elements connecting human experience with physical science.[7]

That my interpretation is justly open to the charge of over-simplifying the philosophy of Whitehead is true in the sense in which it is an oversimplification to exhibit the skeleton of an organism without reference to flesh, blood, and the muscles with which it performs its actions. But I do not claim to be here concerned with anything but the skeleton of Whitehead's system, and even so only with its backbone. Any reader of his writings who keeps an open mind does not have to be reminded of the profound suggestiveness that marks the pages of such a book as *Science and the Modern World* and *Adventures of Ideas,* and of the extraordinarily wide field to which these suggestions refer. My particular theme compels me to be content with only this indefinite reference to everything in his books that does not have to do with what I take to be the general structural condition of his thinking. Accordingly, I now pass to consideration of the treatment given two historic problems of philosophy, confining myself in respect to them to matters that exemplify the principle of procedure I have taken to constitute the originality of Whitehead's thought, and that mark the direction in which he has made a contribution to subsequent philosophizing the surest to grow in scope and fruitfulness.

IV

In speaking of Whitehead's doctrine of the identity of elements in human and physical subject-matter of experience, I quoted a sentence in which the general view took on a special concrete form. The sentence was to the effect that the connectedness of present conscious experience with experience immediately past "can be validly used to suggest categories applying to the connectedness of all occasions in nature." I propose to apply this statement to an account of what follows with respect to the problem of the subject-object relation, and the problem of the discrete-continuous, or individuality and relativity. That is to

[7] *Op. cit.,* 237.

say, I wish to give in condensed form an outline of how Whitehead, starting from the *prima facie* fact that every temporally
present immediate experience contains within itself elements
of what is passing (which will soon *be* the past) and what is
coming (which will be itself the immediately present as soon as
the passing has become the past), goes on to derive from the
fact an explanation both of the subject-object relation and the
individuality-continuity relation, as universal traits of all the actualities of Nature.

The fact as to human experience is stated as follows: "Each
moment of experience confesses itself to be a transition between
two worlds, the immediate past and the immediate future. This
is the persistent delivery of common sense. Also this immediate
future is immanent in the present with some degree of structural
definition." In a previous passage, after speaking of "the immanence of past occasions in the occasions which are future,
relatively to them," he goes on to say:

It is evident that the future certainty is something for the present. The
most familiar habits of mankind witness to this fact. Legal contracts, social understandings of every type, ambitions, anxieties, railway time-
tables, are futile gestures of consciousness apart from the fact that the
present bears in its own realized constitution relationships to a future
beyond itself. Cut away the future and the present collapses, emptied of
its proper content. Immediate existence requires the insertion of the future
in the crannies of the present.[8]

The immanence of the immediately past in the immediately
present is with equal assurance a direct fact of observation.
Otherwise we should be always starting anew and never getting
anywhere. Life would be unceasing interruptions with nothing
to interrupt. As Whitehead acutely remarks, Hume was forced,
in order to procure even a semblance of plausibility, to balance
his extreme atomization with recognition of cumulative continuity in the force he attributes to habit and to anticipation.
Without the presence of the past in the immediate present there
would be no keeping track of what we are doing (including
thinking), and no power of selecting and adapting means to

[8] *Op. cit.*, 246.

effectuation of the plans which are the future in the present. We should not even be aware, I add on my own account, that what is called "consciousness" is in flux, unless the past somehow lingered in the present so that we are aware of change and contrast.

The influence of the new physics, with its theories of space-time, relativity, vectors and world-lines, paths of energy, differentiates the identification of actual entities with processes, asserted by Whitehead to exist, from everything of the kind traditionally ascribed to the Heraclitean river:—a point, it seems to me, not always taken into consideration by critics of his position. For instead of our not being able to step into the same river twice, we can step in twice—and many times, as we do whenever we make statements about an *object*—because the river or process exhibits temporal immanences. But even if the new physics was the original source of the idea, it does not seem probable that the idea of "prehension" would have acquired the broad sweep now marking it without explicit observation of the facts of immediate experience. The interpretation given by Whitehead of the subject-object structure is a fundamental instance of the peculiar kind of "prehension" which is seen in the presence of past and future in every immediately present experience.

For he agrees with the view of (modern) philosophy that the relation of subject-object "is the fundamental structural pattern of experience . . . but not in the sense in which subject-object is identified with knower-known." The ground of his dissent from this identification (which has so controlled modern epistemology as to make it impossible for any one view to win general acceptance over against other views) is suggested in the sentence after the one just quoted: "I contend that the notion of mere knowledge is a high abstraction, and that conscious discrimination itself is a variable factor only present in the more elaborate examples of occasions of experience."[9] However, the next sentence reads, "The basis of experience is emo-

[9] *Op. cit.,* 225f.

tional," and the context indicates that Whitehead is chiefly interested in showing that the fundamental connection of actual occasions is that of taking over "affective tone," or a connection in which things have "concern" one for another. Although this aspect of his doctrine tends to dominate his interpretation of that temporal immanence which is manifested in determination of a present experience by retention and anticipation, nevertheless the latter is so involved in Whitehead's account of the "subject-object" structure, that I confine my account to this point, reserving what I have to say about its subordination to a superior emphasis upon emotion and affection till later. Anticipating here the gist of my later critical remarks, I would say his emphasis upon the emotional seems to be the result of the failure to adopt and carry through consistently his interpretation in terms of *active energies*. For this procedure would have resulted in a *functional* interpretation of "identical elements," while as it is, Whitehead seems to fall back upon identity of *contents*.

The chapter in which the subject-object structure of experience is discussed is clothed in language not readily understandable when it is taken in isolation from the system which gives words their technical meanings. However, I shall quote a passage and then venture upon an interpretation through a paraphrase.

An occasion of experience is an activity, analysable into modes of functioning which jointly constitute its process of becoming. Each mode [of experience] is analysable into the total experience as [an] active subject, and into the thing or object with which the special activity is concerned. ... An object is anything performing this function of a datum provoking some special activity of the occasion in question. Thus subject and object are relative terms. An occasion is a subject in respect to its special activity concerning an object; and anything is an object in respect to its provocation of some special activity within a subject.[10]

Any difficulties that attend grasp of the meaning of this

[10] *Op. cit.*, 226f. This passage taken by itself would justify interpretation of Whitehead's doctrine in terms of a connection of active energies, or what I just called the functional interpretation.

passage will be mitigated, if not dissipated, I think, if one bears in mind a certain duality of relationship. We begin with the fact that every occasion or actual existence is a temporal process. When we observe, without preconception, the nature of the becoming which forms the process, we see that it is aroused or provoked by some other actual and active occasion. In so far, the latter is object, and the process is subject, which started but which is carried forward to *special* or distinctive activity only by the stimulation it receives from another process. A process as subject does not merely undergo or experience the object. Its own actualization, as the single special process it is, is conditioned upon the nature of the provocation it receives.

If the account stopped at this point, it would, however, be defective. For the process which in the account just given forms the subject, and which is so to speak on the receiving end, is also an active factor in evoking the special activities of other things. In other words, occasions that are objects with respect to being things already given, and hence can function to provoke the special activities that determine other processes as subjects, are themselves subjects, having their own qualitative immediacy of being with respect to some other processes or given objects. Indeed, a process may achieve its own special forms of activity, and become thereby a subject in the full sense of the term, in the very interaction in which it operates as object in reference to some other process as subject. Reciprocally, it is true that the process which, from the standpoint first mentioned, is subject, becomes, as the process which it is moves forward, that which provokes the distinctive energies of other processes;—it takes on, that is to say, the function that defines an object. These considerations provide what I call the "duplicity"—though not a rigid dualism—in the subject-object structure. It follows that the subject-object relation in cases of deliberate or conscious knowledge is a specialized case of this general form of inter-connectedness of the energies constituting processes as actual entities.

In discussing the subject-object relation we have, of necessity, trenched upon considerations which are pertinent to determination of the meaning of the discrete-continuous, individual-associational, relation. Indeed, at times I am not sure but that it was the problem in this latter form that was the primary factor in initiation of the distinctive elements in Whitehead's system. In any event, the need for reconstructing the doctrine of independent Newtonian atoms, which was forced by the doctrine of relativity as well as by that of quanta, brought the problem of atomicity-continuity into the foreground. Hence we have the intimate connection of this problem with the subject-object problem, a closeness that is contained in the passage in which it is said that "subject" is a name for "an actual entity in its immediacy of self-attainment when it stands out for itself alone. . . ."[11] It constitutes atomicity in physical occasions as it determines what we call individuality in human occasions. As in the latter we find both "distinguishable individualities" and continuity in the form of "personal identity," so in the former "we should expect a doctrine of quanta, where the individualities of the occasions are relevant, and a doctrine of continuity where the conformal transference of subjective form is the dominating fact."[12]

The meaning of the last clause of the sentence just quoted may not be readily understandable apart from reference to the places in which the phrase "conformal transference" is explained. For the purpose of the present theme, however, it may suffice to identify its meaning in terms of the immanence of the past in the present, thereby involving the way in which the present, in spite of its relative novelty as present, is subordinated to what the past inserts in it. The meaning could then be paraphrased as follows: The process of self-attainment is durational and, in its dependence upon given "objects," extensional. It is not so much a name for the process as a whole as for its "decisive moment." Although in a certain sense "self-originating," it is not literally self-achieving, since the latter is a matter of connectedness. When the special activities are relatively complete, the subject (a functional term, be it recalled) takes on that function which defines an object, and thereby it gives direction

[11] *Op. cit.*, 227.
[12] *Op. cit.*, 239.

to other occasions which, like itself, would remain aborted potentialities unless given direction from what, in a certain sense, is external and "objective." The self-attainment of qualitative immediacy and finality (of individuality) is then a phase, though a decisive and outstanding one, of a process having continuity. Or, in Whitehead's own words, "The individual immediacy of an occasion is the final unity of subjective form, which is the occasion as an absolute reality. This immediacy is its moment of *sheer individuality, bounded on either side by essential relativity.*"[13]

<h1 style="text-align:center">V</h1>

I recall the fact that my discussion is limited to statement of what I take to be that which provides the most direct clew for entering into the system of Whitehead, so that the special points brought up are by way of illustrating the central theme. The new philosophical departure initiated by deep reflection upon the general significance of the new physics in its contrast with Newtonian cosmology was, as I have said, carried through by taking human experience to be a specialization of the traits of nature thus disclosed. When so taken, it was possible, indeed, was necessary, to turn around and use the specialized traits in interpretation of physical occasions. This procedure is the source, in my opinion, of the immense provocative and directive power of Whitehead's thought in the present critical juncture of philosophy. This opinion is the reason I limit my discussion to it, omitting reference to the multitude of special themes upon which Whitehead has shed abundant light. I turn now to certain matters in which Mr. Whitehead's treatment has aroused queries and uncertain misgivings. I begin with the following question: What, after all, does he take the task and office of philosophy to be? If, in discussing this question, I quote passages which seem to indicate two different views about this matter, it is not for the cheap purpose of pointing out inconsistencies—which in any case may be verbal rather than actual. It is for the sake of the possible

---

[13] *Op. cit.*, 227. (Italics not in original text.)

bearing of what can be looked upon as two different strains upon an issue that is discussed later.

What may be called the official view of philosophy is set forth in a passage in which, after saying that the business of philosophy is to frame "descriptive generalization" (a statement in itself neutral to the problem I am raising), he goes on to say that the generalizations should be such as to form "a *coherent, logical, necessary system of general ideas* in terms of which every element of our experience can be interpreted. Here 'interpretation' means that *each element shall have* the character of a particular instance of the general scheme."[14] The italicized words of this passage suggest the kind of structure exhibited in pure mathematics. It seems to go much further than the mere statement—to which no exception can be taken—that the different portions of any philosophical scheme must hang together. For it makes, if I understand it aright, an assertion about what the constituents of nature itself *must* be in and of themselves. This conception of the nature and office of philosophy is in line with the classic tradition, according to which philosophy is that branch of theory which tells, in the theoretical form appropriate to knowledge as knowledge, the story of the ultimate metaphysical or ontological structure of the universe. In connection with Whitehead's frequent recurrence to the "Seven Notions" of Plato,[15] he expressly states that all philosophy is in fact "an endeavour to obtain a coherent system out of some modification of these notions" (p. 354). Again, it is expressly said that "The order of nature expresses the characters of the real things which jointly compose the *existences* to be found in nature. When we understand the *essences* of these things, we *thereby know* their mutual relations to each other."[16]

Assignment of ontological priority to general characters and essences, and subordination to them of the existences actually observed in nature accords, to all appearances, not simply with the Platonic point of view, but with the assimilation of the

[14] *Op. cit.*, 285; cited there from p. 4 of the author's *Process and Reality*. (Italics not in original text.)

[15] *Op. cit.*, 171-2, 188, 203, 241-2, 354, 366.

[16] *Op. cit.*, 142. (Italics not in the original text.)

proper subject-matter of philosophy (the constitution of nature)
to that of mathematical theory. Hence it is legitimate to quote
in this connection the following passage:

The general science of mathematics is concerned with the investigation
of patterns of connectedness in abstraction from the particular relata and
the particular modes of connection. . . . The essential connectedness of
things can never be safely omitted. This is the doctrine of the thorough-
going relativity which infects the universe and which makes the totality of
things as it were a Receptacle uniting all that happens.[17]

Such passages seem to be intended to convey the meaning implied in the expression that it is the business of philosophy to
frame a system in which "each element shall have the character
of a particular instance of a general scheme." Thereby they
seem to warrant the conclusion that the phrase saying that general characters or *essences* constitute natural *existences* is to be
taken literally. Deficiency of my own intellectual grasp may be
the cause of my belief that this entire strain of thought substitutes abstract logical connectedness for the concrete existential
temporal connectedness upon which I have based my interpretation of Whitehead's system. It is enough, in any case, to make
me wonder whether I am on the right track when I make that
interpretation.

Yet there are passages that give a freer and perhaps looser
view of the office of philosophy, passages in which it is affirmed
that the "gifts of philosophy" are "insight and foresight, and a
sense of the worth of life, in short, that sense of *importance
which nerves all civilized effort* . . . ," a passage which ends by
saying that "Philosophy is an attempt to clarify those fundamental beliefs [connected with fears, hopes, judgment of what
is worth while] which finally determine the emphasis of attention that is the base of character."[18]

A philosophy of experience that is thoroughgoing and systematic in its treatment of experience will, it seems to me, treat
philosophy itself as a form of experience. It will realize that
this statement is true not only of the philosophies put forward

[17] *Op. cit.*, 197.
[18] *Op. cit.*, 125. (Italics not in original text.) Cf. what is said on pp. 203-4 of
op. cit.

by others but of the philosophy one is now and here engaged in putting forth. It will realize that philosophies, itself included, are not outside intellectual reports upon subject-matters of experience that are complete and finished in themselves, but that that philosophy is an experimental effort at purification, continuation and extension of those elements of things already experienced that commend themselves to critical judgment as worthy, while it operates upon the basis of knowledge as wide and accurate as possible. It will necessarily look to what is known for clews and for means of testing. But it will not take itself to be a kind of knowledge. It will not be concerned with just reporting and "explaining" in a coherent way the things that are valid in past experiences. It will concern itself with the conditions under which they have arisen for the sake of being better able to form plans by which they may be reinforced and expanded. It will be in so far a genetic account of experience. When a new mode and object of experience is anticipated or actually brought into being it will ask, without ceasing, after its *consequences*. It will be a *functional* account of experience. Report, even in the most systematic fashion, of subject-matters and contents, of even the most "universal" and "essential" characters will be subordinated to determination of what will follow in consequence of them:— as a result, namely, of the way in which existential incarnations operate for good and for evil.

I may appear to have abandoned the philosophy of Whitehead to set forth my own idea of what philosophy is. But what I am actually trying to do is to state my uncertainty, when all is said and done, of just what course is followed by Mr. Whitehead. Of one thing I am quite sure. He has opened an immensely fruitful new path for subsequent philosophy to follow, and has accomplished this task by wedding observable facts of physical experience to observable facts of human experience. The result is an almost incomparable suggestiveness on all sorts of topics—in case a mind is not closed to suggestion from a new source. But I am not sure that he does not frequently block and divert his own movements on the road he is opening by subjecting his conclusions to a combination of considerations too exclusively derived from a combination of mathematics with excessive piety toward those historic philosophers from whom he has derived valuable suggestions.

I have little sympathy with most of the criticisms that are passed upon Mr. Whitehead on the score of the terminology he uses. I find myself in complete agreement with what he has said about the limitations the inherited state of language places upon development of new ideas. And I fail to see how anyone who has struggled to get beyond restatement, in slightly changed verbal form, of old ideas can fail to sympathize with White-head's struggles to find words to convey ideas which have not been previously fixed in conventional modes of expression. Consequently, if I mention by way of adverse criticism his use of a mentalistic vocabulary, illustrated by such words as emotion, enjoyment, etc., etc., in his description of what are usually called physical phenomena, it is only because that usage seems to me to arise from that aspect of his philosophy in which cognitive report of existing subject-matter gets the better of a *genetic-functional* account made in behalf of possibilities of experience not yet adequately realized.

It is one thing, marking to my mind a great advance, to see and say that there must be something homologous in the material of physical science and that of feeling, ideas, emotion and enjoyment as they occur in human experience. But for the purpose of discovery of better possibilities and the criticism of what exists all that is needed in the way of homology is correspondence of *functions*. Insistence upon identity of content tends, I believe, to obscuration of what is philosophically important. One can thoroughly agree with Whitehead when for example he says: "The mere phrase that 'physical science is an abstraction', is a confession of philosophic failure. It is the business of rational thought to describe the more concrete fact from which that abstraction is derivable." But one may unite such agreement with deep regret that a previous sentence reads: "The notion of physical energy, which is at the base of physics, must then be conceived as an abstraction from the complex energy, *emotional and purposeful*, inherent in the subjective form of the *final* synthesis in which each occasion completes itself."[19] That the

[19] *Op. cit.*, 239. (Italics not in original text.)

statement does not appear to be in harmony with his own theory according to which attainment of a subjective form is not final but marks a selected moment in an ongoing process may be only a technical matter. But in what the passage stands for, it appears to repeat that conversion of moral idealism, the idealism of action, into ontological idealism or "spiritualism," a conversion which the history of thought demonstrates to be the fatal weakness of the whole movement initiated by Plato and Aristotle. It is doubtless true, as Mr. Whitehead has said, that the reaction against dogmatic and imposed systematizations marking so many historic philosophies, has led other thinkers to undue neglect of the kind of system that is important. But the abstract formalization that defines systematization upon the model provided by mathematics does not shut out the possibility of that kind of system in which what is known about Nature, physical and human, is brought to bear upon intelligent *criticism* of what exists (and hence is capable of being *known*) and upon construction of alternatives, of possibilities, which the play of free critical intelligence indicates to be better worth while. The substance of Whitehead's system I find to be of the latter sort; its formal statements seem to me often to lean in the former direction.

JOHN DEWEY

NEW YORK CITY

Alfred North Whitehead

THE PHILOSOPHER'S SUMMARY

To my great regret bad health, culminating in a serious illness, has prevented study of the chapters in this book, ~~previous to~~ before publication By taking my writings as a text for discussion, the authors of these chapters have done me an honour which I fully appreciate.

/ The absence of any direct expression of my reaction to these chapters is but a slight loss. The progress of philosophy does not primarily involve reactions of agreement or dissent. It essentially ~~depends~~ consists in the enlargement of thought, whereby contradictions and agreements are transformed into partial aspects of wider points of view. Thus my own reaction to this book should consist in devoting many years to rewriting my previous works. Unfortunately this is impossible.

/ The two chapters which follow were delivered as lectures in Harvard in the years 1940, 1941, respectively. They summarize

FACSIMILE OF EXPLANATORY NOTE FROM ALFRED NORTH WHITEHEAD TO INTRODUCE "THE PHILOSOPHER'S SUMMARY" basic ideas from which my philosophic thought has developed, and which became more clear in the course of that development.

= Finally, I wish to ~~express~~ state my sense of the energy and zeal with which Professor Schilpp is editing a series of volumes, each volume expressing the points of view of a large group of writers. He is producing a display of contemporary thought, unified in each volume by its reference to ~~some~~ contemporary writer as providing a common text. In this enterprise the function of the text is to produce a unity in the thoughts of the authors of the chapters. Professor Schilpp deserves our gratitude for discovering a new mode of exhibiting contemporary thought.

My thanks are also due to Dr Victor Lowe and Dr Robert Baldwin for their unremitting zeal in discovering ~~my~~ miscellaneous publications extending over sixty years,

Cambridge, Mass.
September 20, 1941

Alfred North Whitehead

1. MATHEMATICS AND THE GOOD

I

ABOUT two thousand three hundred years ago a famous lecture was delivered. The audience was distinguished: among others it included Aristotle and Xenophon. The topic of the lecture was The Notion of The Good. The lecturer was competent: he was Plato.

The lecture was a failure, so far as concerned the elucidation of its professed topic; for the lecturer mainly devoted himself to Mathematics. Since Plato with his immediate circle of disciples, the Notion of The Good has disengaged itself from mathematics. Also in modern times eminent Platonic scholars with a few exceptions successfully conceal their interest in mathematics. Plato, throughout his life, maintained his sense of the importance of mathematical thought in relation to the search for the ideal. In one of his latest writings he terms such ignorance 'swinish'. That is how he would characterize the bulk of Platonic scholars of the last century. The epithet is his, not mine.

But undoubtedly his lecture was a failure; for he did not succeed in making evident to future generations his intuition of mathematics as elucidating the notion of The Good. Many mathematicians have been good men—for example, Pascal and Newton. Also many philosophers have been mathematicians. But the peculiar associations of mathematics and The Good remains an undeveloped topic, since its first introduction by Plato. There have been researches into the topic conceived as an interesting characteristic of Plato's mind. But the doctrine, conceived as a basic truth of philosophy, faded from active thought after the first immediate Platonic epoch. Throughout the various ages of European civilization, moral philosophy and mathematics have been assigned to separate departments of university life.

It is the purpose of the present essay to investigate this topic in the light of our modern knowledge. The progress of thought and the expansion of language now make comparatively easy some slight elucidation of ideas which Plato could only express with obscure sentences and misleading myths. You will understand, however, that I am not writing on Plato. My topic is the connection between modern mathematics and the notion of The Good. No reference to any detailed mathematical theorems will be essentially involved. We shall be considering the general nature of the science which is now in process of development. This is a philosophic investigation. Many mathematicians know their details but are ignorant of any philosophic characterization of their science.

II

Within the period of sixty or seventy years preceding the present time, the progressive civilization of the European races has undergone one of the most profound changes in human history. The whole world has been affected; but the origination of the revolution is seated in the races of western Europe and Northern America. It is a change of point of view. Scientific thought had developed with a uniform trend for four centuries, namely, throughout the sixteenth, seventeenth, eighteenth, and nineteenth centuries. In the seventeenth century, Galileo, Descartes, Newton, and Leibniz elaborated the set of concepts, mathematical and physical, within which the whole movement was confined. The culmination may be placed in the decade from 1870 to 1880. At that time Helmholtz, Pasteur, Darwin, and Clerk-Maxwell were developing their discoveries. It was a triumph which produced the death of the period. The change affects every department of thought. In this chapter I emphasize chiefly the shift in the scope of mathematical knowledge. Many of the discoveries which were effective in producing this revolution were made a century earlier than the decade which is here chosen as the final culmination. But the wide realization of their joint effect took place in the fifty years subsequent to 1880. May I add, as an aside, that in addition to its main topic of mathematics and The Good, this chapter is also designed to illustrate how thought develops from epoch to epoch, with its slow half-disclosures? Apart from such knowledge you cannot understand either Plato, or any other philosopher.

III

In order to understand the change, let us conceive the development of an intellectual life which initiated its growth about the year 1870, at the age of about nine or ten years. The whole story reads like a modern version of a Platonic dialogue—for example, the *Theaetetus* or the *Parmenides*. At the commencement of his intellectual life the child would have known the multiplication table up to twelve-times-twelve. Addition, subtraction, multiplication, and division had been mastered. Simple fractions were familiar notions. The decimal notation for fractions was added in the next two or three years. In this way, the whole basis of arithmetic was soon mastered by the young pupil.

In the same period Geometry and Algebra were introduced. In Geometry, the notions of points, lines, planes, and other surfaces are fundamental. The procedure is to introduce some complex pattern of these entities defined by certain relationships between its parts and then to investigate what other relationships in that pattern are implicitly involved in these assumptions. For example, a right-angled triangle is introduced. It is then proved that—assuming Euclidean Geometry—the square on the hypotenuse is equal to the sum of the squares on the other sides.

This example is interesting. For a child can easily look on a figure of a right-angled triangle—as drawn on the black-board by his teacher—without the notion of the squares on the various sides arising in his consciousness. In other words, a defined pattern—such as a right-angled triangle—does not disclose its various intricacies to immediate consciousness.

This curious limitation of conscious understanding is the fundamental fact of epistemology. The child knew what his teacher was talking about, namely, the right-angled triangle quite evidently suggested on the board by the thick chalk lines. And yet the child did not know the infinitude of properties which were implicitly involved.

The primary factors in the boy's concept of a right-angled triangle—as he looked at the black-board—were points, lines, straightness of lines, angles, right-angles. No one of these notions has any meaning apart from the reference to the all-enveloping space. A point has definite position in space, but does not (as then explained) share in any spatial extension. Lines and straight lines have position and also do share in spatial extension with definite limitations. Angles are certain spatial relations between straight lines. Thus no one of the notions involved in the concept of a right-angled triangle has any meaning apart from reference to the spatial system involved.

IV

At that date, apart from a small selection even among eminent mathematicians, it was presupposed that there was only one coherent analysis of the notion of space; in other words, that any two people talking about space must refer to the same system of relations, provided that you expressed a full analysis of every ramification of their meanings. The aim of mathematics, according to their belief, and according to Plato's belief, and according to Euclid's belief, was the adequate expression of this unique, coherent notion of spatiality. We now know that this notion, which had triumphed for about two thousand four hundred years as the necessary foundation for any physical science, was a mistake. It was a glorious mistake: for apart from the simplification thus introduced into the foundations of thought, our modern physical science would have had no agreed simplification of presuppositions by means of which it could express itself.

Thus, the error promoted the advance of learning up to the close of the nineteenth century. At the close of that period, it obstructed the proper expression of scientific ideas. Luckily the mathematicians—at least some of them—had got ahead of the sober thoughts of sensible men of science, and had invented all sorts of fantastic variations from orthodox geometry. At the turn of the centuries, that is, between 1890 and 1910, it was discovered that these variant types of geometry were of essential importance for the expression of our modern scientific knowledge.

From the faint beginnings of geometry, in Egypt and Mesopotamia, up to the present is a stretch of time extending for almost four thousand years. Throughout the whole period this error of a unique geometry has prevailed. Our notions of today have a history of about one hundred to a hundred and fifty years. We enjoy the pleasurable satisfaction that "Now we know."

We shall never understand the history of exact scientific knowledge unless we examine the relation of this feeling "Now we know" to the types of learning prevalent in each epoch. In some shape or other it is always present among the dominant group who are preserving and promoting civilized learning. It is a misapplication of that sense of success which is essential for the maintenance of any enterprise. Can this misapplication be characterized? We may complete the phrase "Now we know" by an adverb. We can mean "Now we know —*in part;*" or we can mean "Now we know—*completely.*" The distinction between the two phrases marks the difference between Plato and Aristotle, so far as their influence on future generations is concerned. The notion of the complete self-sufficiency of any item of finite knowledge is the fundamental error of dogmatism. Every such item derives its truth, and its very meaning, from its unanalyzed relevance to the background which is the unbounded Universe. Not even the simplest notion of arithmetic escapes this inescapable condition for existence. Every scrap of our knowledge derives its meaning from the fact that we are factors in the universe, and are dependent on the universe for every detail of our experience. The thorough sceptic is a dogmatist. He enjoys the delusion of complete futility. Wherever there is the sense of self-sufficient completion, there is the germ of vicious dogmatism. There is no entity which enjoys an isolated, self-sufficiency of existence. In other words, finitude is not self-supporting.

The summarized conclusion of this discussion is that geometry, as studied through the ages, is one chapter of the doctrine of Pattern; and that Pattern, as known to finite discrimination, is a partial disclosure with an essential relevance to the background of the Universe. Also the term "Geometry" refers to a genus of patterns; and this genus includes a variety of species.

V

We now turn to the discussion of Number, considered as a fundamental mathematical notion. This section can be shortened, because many relevant reflections have already been expressed in the previous examination of Geometry.

The doctrine of number from the Greek period onwards has always included queer little contradictions which thoughtful people disregarded. In the last quarter of the nineteenth century, a more thorough examination of the whole subject, initiated by Georg Cantor and Frege in Germany and Austria, and by Peano and Pieri in Italy, and in England by students of symbolic logic, disclosed a number of awkward questions. Finally Bertrand Russell produced a peculiarly glaring self-contradiction in the current reasoning. I well remember that he explained it to Frege in a private letter. Frege's answer commenced with the exclamation, "Alas, arithmetic totters!"

Frege was correct: Arithmetic tottered and still totters. But Bertrand Russell was equal to the occasion. We were then in the midst of writing a book entitled, *Principia Mathematica*. Russell introduced the notion of "types" of entities. According to that doctrine, the notion of number should only be applied to a group of entities of the same type. Thus the number "three" as applied to entities of one type has a different meaning to the number "three" as applied to entities of another type. For example, if we are considering two different types, there are two different meanings of the number "three."

Russell was perfectly correct. By confining numerical reasoning within one type, all the difficulties are avoided. He had discovered a rule of safety. But unfortunately this rule cannot be expressed apart from the presupposition that the notion of number applies beyond the limitations of the rule. For the number "three" in each type, itself belongs to different types. Also each type is itself of a distinct type from other types. Thus, according to the rule, the conception of two different types is nonsense, and the conception of two different meanings of the number three is nonsense. It follows that our only way of understanding the rule is nonsense. It follows that the rule must be limited to the notion of a rule of safety, and that the complete explanation of number awaits an understanding of the relevance of the notion of the varieties of multiplicity to the infinitude of things. Even in arithmetic you cannot get rid of a sub-conscious reference to the unbounded universe. You are abstracting details from a totality, and are imposing limitations on your abstraction. Remember that a refusal to think does not imply the non-existence of entities for thought. Our conscious thought is an abstraction of entities from the background of existence. Thought is one form of emphasis.

VI

Finally in this survey of mathematical notions we come to Algebra. Who invented Algebra? It was invented "in Arabia" or "in India," you all want to tell me. In one sense that is true —namely, the useful symbolism for the algebraic ideas started in one or other, or in both, of those countries. But there is a further question, which, I am sure, would have interested Plato if he had known about Algebra. Who invented the fundamental idea which is thus symbolized?

What is the fundamental notion at the base of Algebra? It is the notion of "*Any* example of a given sort, in abstraction from some particular exemplification of the example or of the sort."

VII

The first animal on this Earth, who even for a moment entertained this notion, was the first rational creature. You can observe animals choosing between *this thing* or *that thing*. But animal intelligence requires concrete exemplification. Human intelligence can conceive of a type of things in abstraction from

exemplification. The most obvious disclosures of this characteristic of humanity are mathematical concepts and ideals of the
Good—ideals which stretch beyond any immediate realization.

Any practical experience of exactness of realization is denied
to mankind: Whereas mathematics, and ideals of perfection,
are concerned with exactness. It is the difference between practice and theory. All theory demands exact notions, somewhere
or other, however concealed. In practice exactness vanishes: the
sole problem is, "Does it Work?" But the aim of practice can
only be defined by the use of theory; so the question "Does it
Work?" is a reference to theory. Also the importance of theory
resides in its reference to practice. The vagueness of practice
is energized by the clarity of ideal experience.

No one has ever observed in practice any exact mathematical
notion. Consider the child as he learnt his geometry. He never
observed an exact point or an exact line, or exact straightness, or
an exact circle. Such things were unrealized ideals in the child's
mind. So much will be conceded by the man of practical good
sense. But when we pass to arithmetic he stalls. You can hear
him saying—perhaps you are saying it yourselves—"I can see
one chair, two chairs, three chairs, four chairs, and five chairs,
and I can observe that two chairs and three chairs when assem-
bled together form a group of five chairs." In this way, our
sensible friend has observed exactly exemplifications of arithmetical notions and of an arithmetic theorem.

Now the question is—Has he observed exactly, or, Has he
had exact notions elicited in his conceptual experience? In what
sense did he observe exactly one chair? He observed a vague
differentiation of the general context of his visual experience.
But suppose we pin him down to one billionth of an inch.
Where does the chair end and the rest of things begin? Which
atom belongs to the chair, and which atom belongs to surrounding space? The chair is perpetually gaining and losing
atoms. It is not exactly differentiated from its surroundings, nor
is it exactly self-identical as time slips by. Again, consider
the chair during long periods. It gradually changes, even
throughout its solid wooden parts. At the end of a million

years in a cave, it becomes fragile, and dissolves at a touch. A slow, imperceptible change is always in progress.

Remember that the human concepts of one inch in length, and of one second in time, as being reasonable basic quantities, are purely relevant to human life. Further, the modern discoveries of physicists and astronomers have disclosed to us the relevance of minute, and of immense, happenings. Our exact conceptual experience is a mode of emphasis. It vivifies the ideals which invigorate the real happenings. It adds the perception of worth and beauty to the mere transition of sense-experience. It is by reason of the conceptual stimulus that the sunset displays the glory of the sky. By this statement, it is not meant that a feeble train of explicit thoughts works the miracle. It is the transformation of the real experience into its ideal limit. Our existence is invigorated by conceptual ideals, transforming vague perceptions.

We cannot understand the flux which constitutes our human experience unless we realize that it is raised above the futility of infinitude by various successive types of modes of emphasis which generate the active energy of a finite assemblage. The superstitious awe of infinitude has been the bane of philosophy. The infinite has no properties. All value is the gift of finitude which is the necessary condition for activity. Also activity means the origination of patterns of assemblage, and mathematics is the study of pattern. Here we find the essential clue which relates mathematics to the study of the good, and the study of the bad.

VIII

You will notice that earlier in this essay we have emphasized that there are no self-existent finite entities. The finite essentially refers to an unbounded background. We have now arrived at the converse doctrine, namely, that infinitude in itself is meaningless and valueless. It acquires meaning and value by its embodiment of finite entities. Apart from the finite, the infinite is devoid of meaning and cannot be distinguished from nonentity. The notion of the essential relatedness of all things is the primary step in understanding how finite entities require the unbounded universe, and how the universe acquires meaning and value by reason of its embodiment of the activity of finitude.

Among philosophers, Spinoza emphasized the fundamental infinitude and introduced a subordinate differentiation by finite modes. Also conversely, Leibniz emphasized the necessity of finite monads and based them upon a substratum of Deistic infinitude. Neither of them adequately emphasized the fact that infinitude is mere vacancy apart from its embodiment of finite values, and that finite entities are meaningless apart from their relationship beyond themselves. The notion of "understanding" requires some grasp of how the finitude of the entity in question requires infinity, and also some notion of how infinity requires finitude. This search for such understanding is the definition of philosophy. It is the reason why mathematics, which deals with finite patterns, is related to the notion of the Good and to the notion of the Bad.

The great religions illustrate this doctrine. Buddhism emphasizes the sheer infinity of the divine principle, and thereby its practical influence has been robbed of energetic activity. The followers of the religion have lacked impulse. The doctrinal squabbles of Christianity have been concerned with the characterization of the infinite in terms of finitude. It was impossible to conceive energy in other terms. The very notion of goodness was conceived in terms of active opposition to the powers of evil, and thereby in terms of the limitation of deity. Such limitation was explicitly denied and implicitly accepted.

IX

The history of the science of algebra is the story of the growth of a technique for representation of finite patterns. Algebra is one chapter in the larger technique, which is language. But, in the main, language indicates its meanings by means of casual associations as they arise in human history. It is true that language strives to embody some aspects of those meanings in its very structure. A deep sounding word embodies the deep solemnity of grief. In fact, the art of literature, vocal or written, is to adjust the language so that it embodies what it indicates.

But the larger part of what language physically presents is irrelevant to the meaning indicated. The sentence is a sequence of words. But this sequence is, in general, irrelevant to the meaning. For example, "Humpty-Dumpty sat on a wall" involves a sequence which is irrelevant to the meaning. The wall is in no sense subsequent to Humpty-Dumpty. Also the posture of sitting might have been realized simultaneously with the origination of the sitter and the wall. Thus the verbal order has the faintest reference to the idea conveyed. It is true that by exciting expectation, and by delay, the verbal order does work on the emotions of the recipient. But the sort of emotion, thus aroused, depends on the character of the recipient. Algebra reverses the relative importance of the factors in ordinary language. It is essentially a written language, and it endeavours to exemplify in its written structures the patterns which it is its purpose to convey. It may not be always wholly successsful in this endeavour. But it does invert the ordinary habits of language. In the usage of Algebra, the pattern of the marks on paper is a particular instance of the pattern to be conveyed to thought.

Also there is an enlargement of the notion of "any." In arithmetic we write "two plus three" equals "three plus two." We are considering two processes of assemblage. The type of assemblage is indicated by the word—or sign—"plus," and its meaning is restricted by the reference to number. The two procedures are asserted to issue in groups with identical number of members. This number is in fact "five;" but it is not mentioned.

Now in algebra, the restriction of thought to particular numbers is avoided. We write "$x + y = y + x$," where x and y are any two numbers. Thus the emphasis on pattern, as distinct from the special entities involved in the pattern, is increased. Thus algebra in its initiation involved an immense advance in the study of pattern. Relationships of diverse patterns, such as that involved in the Binomial Theorem, entered into human thought. Of course, algebra grew slowly. For centuries it was conceived as a mode of asking for the solution of equations. Somewhere in medieval times, an unfortunate emperor, or other bigwig, together with his court, had to listen to a learned Italian expounding the solution of a cubic equation. Poor men—a lovely Italian afternoon was wasted! They would have yawned if their interest had not been sustained by the sense of magic.

X

At the beginning of the nineteenth century, Algebra was the study of patterns involved in the various ways of assembling numbers, so that each assemblage issued in the indication of one number, conceived as the outcome of that assemblage. The relation of equality between two assemblages meant that both assemblages indicated the same number. But the interest was directed to the two patterns of assemblage, with their identical indications. In this way, certain general characteristics of patterns of number as realized in the evolving universe were identified with characteristics of patterns of marks on two-dimensional surfaces—usually sheets of paper. Such identities of pattern of meaning with pattern of written marks, or sound variation, are a subordinate characteristic of ordinary language, though of some importance in respect to spoken language. But this identity is the major characteristic of algebraic language.

Today, surveying the first half of the twentieth century, we find an immense extension of algebra. It has been extended beyond the field of number, and applies to a large group of patterns in which number is a subordinate factor. Very often when number is explicitly admitted, its major use is to provide names, as it is employed for the naming of houses. Thus mathematics is now being transformed into the intellectual analysis of types of pattern.

The notion of the importance of pattern is as old as civilization. Every art is founded on the study of pattern. Also the cohesion of social systems depends on the maintenance of patterns of behaviour; and advances in civilization depend on the fortunate modification of such behaviour patterns. Thus the infusion of pattern into natural occurrences, and the stability of such patterns, and the modification of such patterns, is the necessary condition for the realization of the Good.

Mathematics is the most powerful technique for the understanding of pattern, and for the analysis of the relationships of patterns. Here we reach the fundamental justification for the topic of Plato's lecture. Having regard to the immensity of its subject-matter mathematics, even modern mathematics, is a science in its babyhood. If civilization continues to advance, in the next two thousand years the overwhelming novelty in human thought will be the dominance of mathematical understanding.

The essence of this generalized mathematics is the study of the most observable examples of the relevant patterns; and applied mathematics is the transference of this study to other examples of the realization of these patterns.

XI

Pattern is only one factor in our realization of experience, either as immediate value or as stimulus to activity for future value. For example in a picture, the geometrical pattern may be good, but the relationship of colours may be horrible. Also each individual colour may be poverty-stricken, indeterminate, and feeble. This example elicits the truth that no entity is merely characterized by its individual character, or merely by its relationships. Each entity possesses essentially an individual character, and also is essentially a terminal of relationship, potential or actual. Some of the factors of individual character enter into the relationships, and conversely the relationships enter into the character. In other words, no entity can be considered in abstraction from the universe, and no entity can be divested of its own individuality. The traditional logic overstressed the notion of individual character. The notion of "any" frees us from individual character: but there is no entity which is merely "any." Thus when algebra is applied, factors beyond algebraic thought are relevant to the total situation. Returning to the picture, mere geometry is not the whole tale. Colours are relevant.

In a picture colour (including black and white) may be reduced to a minimum, as in a pen-and-ink sketch. But some differentiation of colour is necessary for the physical presentation of geometrical design. On the other hand, colour may be dominant in some glorious work of art. Again, the drawing may be good, and colour effect may be a failure. The whole topic of Good and Evil arises. And you cannot discuss Good and Evil without some reference to the interweaving of divers patterns of experience. The antecedent situation may demand depth of realization, and a thin pattern may thwart conceptual expectation. There is then the evil of triviality—a sketch in place of a full picture. Again, two patterns eliciting intense experience may thwart each other. There is then the intense evil of active deprivation. This type has three forms: a concept may conflict with a reality, or two realities may conflict, or two concepts may conflict.

There may be other types of evil. But we are concerned with the mal-adjustment of patterns of experience. The total pattern has inhibited the insistent effect of either of its parts. But this notion is meaningless except as a reference to the background of feeling—namely emotional and analytic experience —within which that total pattern arises. Every abstraction derives its importance from its reference to some background of feeling, which is seeking its unity as one individual complex fact in its immediate present. In itself a pattern is neither good nor bad. But every pattern can only exist in virtue of the doom of realization, actual or conceptual. And this doom consigns the pattern to play its part in an uprush of feeling, which is the awakening of infinitude to finite activity. Such is the nature of existence: it is the acquisition of pattern by feeling, in its emphasis on a finite group of selected particulars which are the entities patterned—for example, the spatial arrangements of colours and sounds. But the particulars concerned are not necessarily purely qualitative. A human being is more than an assortment of colours and sounds. The notion of pattern emphasizes the relativity of existence, namely, how things are connected. But the things thus connected are entities in themselves. Each entity in a pattern enters into other patterns, and retains its own individuality in this variety of existence. The crux of philosophy is to retain the balance between the individuality of existence and the relativity of existence. Also each individual entity in one pattern may be capable of analysis, so as to display itself as the unity of achieved pattern. The point that I am emphasizing is the function of pattern in the production of Good or Evil in the finite unit of feeling which embraces the enjoyment of that pattern. Also the essential characterization of mathematics is the study of pattern in abstraction from the particulars which are patterned.

XII

When Plato in his lecture connected mathematics with the notion of the Good, he was defending—consciously or unconsciously—the traditional ways of thought spread through all races of mankind. The novelty was the method of abstraction which the Greek genius was gradually emphasizing. Mathematics, as studied in his own Academy, was an abstraction of geometrical and numerical characterizations from the concrete facts of Athenian life. Aristotle was dissecting animals, and was analysing political constitutions. He conceived of genera and species. He thus abstracted the logical characters from the full-blooded experience. The new epoch of scientific abstractions was arising.

One danger in the use of this technique is the simple-minded use of Logic, whereby an erroneous proposition is merely discarded. All propositions are erroneous unless they are construed in reference to a background which we experience without any conscious analysis. Every scientific proposition which the great scientists of the mid-nineteenth century entertained, was erroneous in the sense in which it was then construed. Their doctrine of space was wrong: their doctrine of matter was wrong: their doctrines of evidence were wrong. The abiding interest of Plato's Dialogues does not lie in their enunciation of abstract doctrines. They are suffused with the implicit suggestion of the concrete unity of experience, whereby every abstract topic obtains its interest.

XIII

Abstraction involves emphasis, and emphasis vivifies experience, for good, or for evil. All characteristics peculiar to actualities are modes of emphasis whereby finitude vivifies the infinite. In this way Creativity involves the production of value-experience, by the inflow from the infinite into the finite, deriving special character from the details and the totality of the finite pattern.

This is the abstraction involved in the creation of any actuality, with its union of finitude with infinity. But consciousness proceeds to a second order of abstraction whereby finite constituents of the actual thing are abstracted from that thing. This procedure is necessary for finite thought, though it weakens the sense of reality. It is the basis of science. The task of philosophy is to reverse this process and thus to exhibit the fusion of analysis with actuality. It follows that Philosophy is not a science.

ALFRED NORTH WHITEHEAD

2. IMMORTALITY*

PREFACE

IN this lecture the general concept of Immortality will be stressed, and the reference to mankind will be a deduction from wider considerations. It will be presupposed that all entities or factors in the universe are essentially relevant to each other's existence. A complete account lies beyond our conscious experience. In what follows, this doctrine of essential relevance is applied to the interpretation of those fundamental beliefs concerned with the notion of immortality.

I

There is finitude—unless this were true, infinity would have no meaning. The contrast of finitude and infinity arises from the fundamental metaphysical truth that every entity involves an indefinite array of perspectives, each perspective expressing a finite characteristic of that entity. But any one finite perspective does not enable an entity to shake off its essential connection with totality. The infinite background always remains as the unanalysed reason why that finite perspective of that entity has the special character that it does have. Any analysis of the limited perspective always includes some additional factors of the background. The entity is then experienced in a wider finite perspective, still presupposing the inevitable background which is the universe in its relation to that entity.

For example, consider this lecture hall. We each have an immediate finite experience of it. In order to understand this hall, thus experienced, we widen the analysis of its obvious relations. The hall is part of a building; the building is in Cam-

* Ed. Note: This second part of Professor Whitehead's "Summary" was originally delivered on April 22, 1941, as the Ingersoll Lecture at the Harvard Divinity School. It is printed here by special permission of the Dean of the Divinity School and at the suggestion of Professor Whitehead himself.

bridge, Mass.; Cambridge, Mass., is on the surface of the Earth; the Earth is a planet in the solar system; the solar system belongs to a nebula; this nebula belongs to a spatially related system of nebulae; these nebulae exhibit a system with a finite temporal existence; they have arisen from antecedent circumstances which we are unable to specify, and will transform into other forms of existence beyond our imagination. Also we have no reason to believe that our present knowledge of these nebulae represents the facts which are immediately relevant to their own forms of activity. Indeed we have every reason to doubt such a supposition. For the history of human thought in the past is a pitiful tale of a self-satisfaction with a supposed adequacy of knowledge in respect to factors of human existence. We now know that in the past such self-satisfaction was a delusion. Accordingly, when we survey ourselves and our colleagues we have every reason to doubt the adequacy of our knowledge in any particular. Knowledge is a process of exploration. It has some relevance of truth. Also the self-satisfaction has some justification. In a sense, this room has solid walls, resting upon a stationary foundation. Our ancestors thought that this was the whole truth. We know that it embodies a truth important for lawyers and for the University Corporation which manages the property. But it is not a truth relevant beyond such finite restrictions.

Today, we are discussing the immortality of human beings who make use of this hall. For the purposes of this discussion the limited perspectives of legal systems and of University Corporations are irrelevant.

II

"The Immortality of Man"—What can this phrase mean? Consider the term "Immortality," and endeavour to understand it by reference to its antithesis "Mortality." The two words refer to two aspects of the Universe, aspects which are presupposed in every experience which we enjoy. I will term these aspects "The Two Worlds." They require each other, and together constitute the concrete Universe. Either World considered by itself is an abstraction. For this reason, any ade-

quate description of one World includes characterizations derived from the other, in order to exhibit the concrete Universe in its relation to either of its two aspects. These Worlds
are the major examples of perspectives of the Universe. The
word "evaluation" expresses the elucidation of one of the abstractions by reference to the other.

III

The World which emphasizes the multiplicity of mortal
things is the World of Activity. It is the World of Origination:
It is the Creative World. It creates the Present by transforming
the Past, and by anticipating the Future. When we emphasize
sheer Active Creation, the emphasis is upon the Present—
namely, upon "Creation Now," where the reference to transition has been omitted.

And yet Activity loses its meaning when it is reduced to "mere
creation now:" the absence of Value destroys any possibility of
reason. "Creation Now" is a matter-of-fact which is one aspect of the Universe—namely, the fact of immediate origination. The notions of Past and Future are then ghosts within
the fact of the Present.

IV

The World which emphasizes Persistence is the World of
Value. Value is in its nature timeless and immortal. Its essence
is not rooted in any passing circumstance. The immediacy of
some mortal circumstance is only valuable because it shares in
the immortality of some value. The value inherent in the
Universe has an essential independence of any moment of time;
and yet it loses its meaning apart from its necessary reference
to the World of passing fact. Value refers to Fact, and Fact refers to Value. [This statement is a direct contradiction to Plato,
and to the theological tradition derived from him.]

But no heroic deed, and no unworthy act, depends for its
heroism, or disgust, upon the exact second of time at which it
occurs, unless such change of time places it in a different sequence of values. The value-judgment points beyond the immediacy of historic fact.

The description of either of the two Worlds involves stages which include characteristics borrowed from the other World. The reason is that these Worlds are abstractions from the Universe; and every abstraction involves reference to the totality of existence. There is no self-contained abstraction.

For this reason Value cannot be considered apart from the Activity which is the primary character of the other World. Value is the general name for the infinity of Values, partly concordant and partly discordant. The essence of these values is their capacity for realization in the World of Action. Such realization involves the exclusion of discordant values. Thus the World of Values must be conceived as active with the adjustment of the potentialities for realization. This activity of internal adjustment is expressed by our moral and aesthetic judgments. Such judgments involve the ultimate notions of "better" and "worse." This internal activity of the World of Value will be termed "Valuation," for the purpose of this discussion. This character of Valuation is one meaning of the term Judgment. Judgment is a process of unification. It involves the necessary relevance of values to each other.

Value is also relevant to the process of realization in the World of Activity. Thus there is a further intrusion of judgment which is here called Evaluation. This term will be used to mean the analysis of particular facts in the World of Activity to determine the values realized and the values excluded. There is no escape from the totality of the Universe, and exclusion is an activity comparable to inclusion. Every fact in the World of Activity has a positive relevance to the whole range of the World of Value. Evaluation refers equally to omissions and admissions.

Evaluation involves a process of modification: the World of Activity is modified by the World of Value. It receives pleasure or disgust from the Evaluations. It receives acceptance or rejection: It receives its perspective of the past, and it receives its purpose for the future. This interconnection of the two Worlds is Evaluation, and it is an activity of modification.

But Evaluation always presupposes abstraction from the sheer immediacy of fact: It involves reference to Valuation.

If you are enjoying a meal, and are conscious of pleasure
derived from apple-tart, it is the sort of taste that you enjoy.
Of course the tart has to come at the right time. But it is not
the moment of clock-time which gives importance; it is the
sequence of types of value—for instance, the antecedent nature
of the meal, and your initial hunger. Thus you can only express what the meal means to you, in terms of a sequence of
timeless valuations.

In this way the process of evaluation exhibits an immortal
world of coördinated value. Thus the two sides of the Universe are the World of Origination and the World of Value.
And the Value is timeless, and yet by its transformation into
Evaluation it assumes the function of a modification of events
in time. Either World can only be explained by reference to
the other World; but this reference does not depend upon
words, or other explicit forms of indication. [This statement
is a summary of the endeavour throughout this chapter to avoid
the feeble Platonic doctrine of "imitation" and the feebler
modern pragmatic dismissal of "immortality."]

V

To sum up this discussion:—Origination is creation, whereas Value issues into modification of creative action. Creation
aims at Value, whereas Value is saved from the futility of abstraction by its impact upon the process of Creation. But in
this fusion, Value preserves its Immortality. In what sense does
creative action derive immortality from Value? This is the
topic of our lecture.

The notion of Effectiveness cannot be divorced from the
understanding of the World of Value. The notion of a purely
abstract self-enjoyment of values apart from any reference to
effectiveness in action was the fundamental error prevalent in
Greek philosophy, an error which was inherited by the her-
mits of the first Christian centuries, and which is not unknown
in the modern world of learning.

The activity of conceptual valuation is in its essence a persuasive force in the development of the Universe. It becomes
evil when it aims at an impossible abstraction from the com-

munal activities of action. The two worlds of Value and of Action are bound together in the life of the Universe, so that the immortal factor of Value enters into the active creation of temporal fact.

Evaluation functions actively as incitement and aversion. It is Persuasion, where persuasion includes "incitement towards" and "deterrence from" a manifold of possibility.

Thus the World of Activity is grounded upon the multiplicity of finite Acts, and the World of Value is grounded upon the unity of active coördination of the various possibilities of Value. The essential junction of the two Worlds infuses the unity of the coördinated values into the multiplicity of the finite acts. The meaning of the acts is found in the values actualized, and the meaning of the valuation is found in the facts which are realizations of their share of value.

Thus each World is futile except in its function of embodying the other.

VI

This fusion involves the fact that either World can only be described in terms of factors which are common to both of them. Such factors have a dual aspect, and each World emphasizes one of the two aspects.

These factors are the famous "Ideas," which it is the glory of Greek thought to have explicitly discovered, and the tragedy of Greek thought to have misconceived in respect to their status in the Universe.

The misconception which has haunted philosophic literature throughout the centuries is the notion of "independent existence." There is no such mode of existence; every entity is only to be understood in terms of the way in which it is interwoven with the rest of the Universe. Unfortunately this fundamental philosophic doctrine has not been applied either to the concept of "God," nor (in the Greek tradition) to the concept of "Ideas." An "Idea" is the entity answering questions which enquire "How?" Such a question seeks the "sort" of occurrence. For example, "How did it happen that the motor-car stopped?"; the answer is the occurrence of a "redness of lighting" amid suitable surroundings. Thus the special entry of the Idea "Redness" into the world of fact elucidates the special transition of fact which is the stoppage of the car.

A different functioning of "Redness" is the enjoyment of a glorious sunset. In this example, the realized value is evident. A third case is the intention of an artist to paint a sunset. This is an intention towards realization, which is the basic character of the World of Value. But this intention is itself a realization within the Universe.

Thus each "idea" has two sides; namely, it is a shape of value and a shape of fact. When we enjoy "realized value" we are experiencing the essential junction of the two worlds. But when we emphasize mere fact, or mere possibility we are making an abstraction in thought. When we enjoy fact as the realization of specific value, or possibility as an impulse towards realization, we are then stressing the ultimate character of the Universe. This ultimate character has two sides— one side is the mortal world of transitory fact acquiring the immortality of realized value; and the other side is the timeless world of mere possibility acquiring temporal realization. The bridge between the two is the "Idea" with its two sides.

VII

Thus the topic of "The Immortality of Man" is seen to be a side issue in the wider topic, which is "The Immortality of Realized Value:" namely, the temporality of mere fact acquiring the immortality of value.

Our first question must be, Can we find any general character of the World of Fact which expresses its adjustment for the embodiment of Value? The answer to this question is the tendency of the transitory occasions of fact to unite themselves into sequences of Personal Identity. Each such personal sequence involves the capacity of its members to sustain identity of Value. In this way, Value-experience introduces into the transitory World of Fact an imitation of its own essential immortality. There is nothing novel in this suggestion. It is as old as Plato. The systematic thought of ancient writers is now nearly worthless; but their detached insights are priceless. This statement can be referred to as expressing the habits of Plato's thought.

The survival of personal identity within the immediacy of a present occasion is a most remarkable character of the World of Fact. It is a partial negation of its transitory character. It is the introduction of stability by the influence of value. Another aspect of such stability is to be seen in the Scientific Laws of Nature. It is the modern fashion to deny any evidence for the stability of natural law, and at the same time implicitly to take such stability for granted. The outstanding example of such stability is Personal Identity.

Let us consider more closely the character of Personal Identity. A whole sequence of actual occasions, each with its own present immediacy, is such that each occasion embodies in its own being the antecedent members of that sequence with an emphatic experience of the self-identity of the past in the immediacy of the present. This is the realization of personal identity. This varies with the temporal span. For short periods it is so overwhelming that we hardly recognize it. For example, take a many syllabled word, such as "overwhelming" which was employed in the previous sentence: of course the person who said "over" was identical with the person who said "ing." But there was a fraction of a second between the two occasions. And yet the speaker enjoyed his self-identity during the pronunciation of the word, and the listeners never doubted the self-identity of the speaker. Also throughout this period of saying that word everyone, including the speaker, was expecting him to finish the sentence in the immediate future beyond the present; and the sentence had commenced in the more distant past.

VIII

This problem of "personal identity" in a changing world of occasions is the key example for understanding the essential fusion of the World of Activity with the World of Value. The immortality of Value has entered into the changefulness which is the essential character of Activity. "Personal identity" is exhibited when the change in the details of fact exhibits an identity of primary character amid secondary changes of value. This identity serves the double rôle of shaping a fact and realizing a specific value.

This preservation of a type of value in a sequence of change is a form of emphasis. A unity of style amid a flux of detail adds to the importance of the various details and illustrates the intrinsic value of that style which elicits such emphasis from the details. The confusion of variety is transformed into the coördinated unity of a dominant character. The many become one, and by this miracle achieve a triumph of effectiveness—for good or for evil. This achievement is the essence of art and of moral purpose. The World of Fact would dissolve into the nothingness of confusion apart from its modes of unity derived from its preservation of dominant characters of Value.

IX

Personality is the extreme example of the sustained realization of a type of value. The coördination of a social system is the vaguer form. In a short lecture a discussion of social systems must be omitted. The topic stretches from the physical Laws of Nature to the tribes and nations of Human Beings. But one remark must be made—namely, that the more effective social systems involve a large infusion of various sorts of personalities as subordinate elements in their make-up—for example, an animal body, or a society of animals, such as human beings.

Personal Identity is a difficult notion. It is dominant in human experience: the notions of civil law are based upon it. The same man is sent to prison who committed the robbery; and the same materials survive for centuries, and for millions of years. We cannot dismiss Personal Identity without dismissing the whole of human thought as expressed in every language.

X

The whole literature of the European races upon this subject is based upon notions which, within the last hundred years, have been completely discarded. The notion of the fixity of species and genera, and the notion of the unqualified definiteness of their distinction from each other, dominate the literary traditions of Philosophy, Religion, and Science. Today, these presuppositions of fixity and distinction have explicitly vanished: but in fact they dominate learned literature. Learning preserves the errors of the past, as well as its wisdom. For this reason, dictionaries are public dangers, although they are necessities.

Each single example of personal identity is a special mode of coördination of the ideal world into a limited rôle of effectiveness. This maintenance of character is the way in which the finitude of the actual world embraces the infinitude of possibility. In each personality, the large infinitude of possibility is recessive and ineffective; but a perspective of ideal existence enters into the finite actuality. Also this entrance is more or less; there are grades of dominance and grades of recessiveness. The pattern of such grades and the ideal entities which they involve, constitute the character of that persistent fact of personal existence in the World of Activity. The essential coördination of values dominates the essential differentiation of facts.

We do not adequately analyse any one personal existence; and still less is there any accuracy in the divisions into species and genera. For practical purposes in the immediate surroundings such divisions are necessary ways of developing thought. But we can give no' sufficient definitions of what we mean by "practical purposes" or by "immediate surroundings." The result is that we are confronted with a vague spread of human life, animal life, vegetable life, living cells, and material existences with personal identity devoid of life in the ordinary usage of that word.

XI

The notion of "character," as an essential factor in personal identity, illustrates the truth that the concept of Ideas must be conceived as involving gradations of generality. For example, the character of an animal belongs to a higher grade of ideas than does the special taste of food, enjoyed at some moment of its existence. Also for art, the particular shade of blue in a picture belongs to a lower grade of ideas than does the special aesthetic beauty of the picture as a whole. Each picture is beautiful in its own way, and that beauty can only be reproduced by another picture with the identical design of the identical colours.

Then there are grades of aesthetic beauty, which constitute the ideals of different schools and periods of art.

Thus the variation in the grades of ideas is endless, and it is not to be understood as a single line of increasing generality. This variation may be conceived as a spread involving an infinitude of dimensions. We can only conceive a finite fragment of this spread of grades. But as we choose a single line of advance in such generality, we seem to meet a higher type of value. For example, we enjoy a colour, but the enjoyment of the picture—if it is a good picture—involves a higher grade of value.

One aspect of evil is when a higher grade of adequate intensity is thwarted by the intrusion of a lower grade.

This is why the mere material world suggests to us no concepts of good or evil, because we can discern in it no system of grades of value.

XII

The World of Value contains within itself Evil as well as Good. In this respect the philosophic tradition derived from classical Greek thought is astoundingly superficial. It discloses the emotional attitude of fortunate individuals in a beautiful world. Ancient Hebrew literature emphasizes morality. Palestine was the unhappy battle-ground of opposing civilizations. The outcome in the gifted population was deep moral intuition interwoven with barbaric notions. Hebrew and Hellenic thought are fused together in Christian theology, with considerable loss to the finer insights of both. But Hellenic and Hebrew literature together exhibit a genius of aesthetic and moral revelation upon which any endeavour to understand the functioning of the World of Value must base itself.

Values require each other. The essential character of the World of Value is coördination. Its activity consists in the approach to multiplicity by the adjustment of its many potentialities into finite unities, each unity with a group of dominant ideas of value, mutually interwoven, and reducing the infinity of values into a graduated perspective, fading into complete exclusion.

Thus the reality inherent in the World of Value involves the primary experience of the finite perspectives for realization in the essential multiplicity of the World of Activity. But the World of Value emphasizes the essential unity of the many; whereas the World of Fact emphasizes the essential multiplicity in the realization of this unity. Thus the Universe, which embraces both Worlds, exhibits the one as many, and the many as one.

XIII

The main thesis in this lecture is that we naturally simplify the complexity of the Universe by considering it in the guise of two abstractions—namely, the World of multiple Activities and the World of coördinated Value. The prime characteristic of one world is change, and of the other world is immortality. But the understanding of the Universe requires that each World exhibits the impress of the other.

For this reason the World of Change develops Enduring Personal Identity as its effective aspect for the realization of value. Apart from some mode of personality there is trivialization of value.

But Realization is an essential factor in the World of Value, to save it from the mere futility of abstract hypothesis. Thus the effective realization of value in the World of Change should find its counterpart in the World of Value:—this means that temporal personality in one world involves immortal personality in the other.

Another way of stating this conclusion is that every factor in the Universe has two aspects for our abstractions of thought. The factor can be considered on its temporal side in the World of Change, and on its immortal side in the World of Value. We have already employed this doctrine in respect to the Platonic Ideas:—they are temporal characterizations, and immortal types of value. [We are using, with some distortion, Plato's doctrine of Imitation.]

XIV

The World of Value exhibits the essential unification of the Universe. Thus while it exhibits the immortal side of the many persons, it also involves the unification of personality. This is the concept of God.

[But it is not the God of the learned tradition of Christian Theology, nor is it the diffused God of the Hindu Buddhistic tradition. The concept lies somewhere between the two.] He is the intangible fact at the base of finite existence.

In the first place, the World of Value is not the World of Active Creativity. It is the persuasive coördination of the essential multiplicity of Creative Action. Thus God, whose existence is founded in Value, is to be conceived as persuasive towards an ideal coördination.

Also he is the unification of the multiple personalities received from the Active World. In this way, we conceive the World of Value in the guise of the coördination of many personal individualities as factors in the nature of God.

But according to the doctrine here put forward, this is only half the truth. For God in the World of Value is equally a factor in each of the many personal existences in the World of Change. The emphasis upon the divine factor in human nature is of the essence of religious thought.

XV

The discussion of this conclusion leads to the examination of the notions of Life, Consciousness, Memory, and Anticipation.

Consciousness can vary in character. In its essence it requires emphasis on finitude, namely some recognition of 'this' and 'that'. It may also involve a varying extent of memory, or it may be restricted to the immediacy of the present, devoid of memory, or anticipation. Memory is very variable; and except for a few scraps of experience, the greater part of our feelings are enjoyed and pass. The same statement is true of anticipation.

Our sense-experiences are superficial, and fail to indicate the massive self-enjoyment derived from internal bodily functioning. Indeed human experience can be described as a flood of self-enjoyment, diversified by a trickle of conscious memory and conscious anticipation. The development of literary habits has directed attention to superficial sense-experiences, such as sight and hearing; the deeper notions of "bowels of compassion," and "loving hearts" are derived from human experience as it functioned three thousand years ago. Today, they are worn out literary gestures. And yet today, a careful doctor will sit down and chat, while he observes the types of bodily experiences of the patient.

When memory and anticipation are completely absent, there is complete conformity to the average influence of the immediate past. There is no conscious confrontation of memory with possibility. Such a situation produces the activity of mere matter. When there is memory, however feeble and short-lived, the average influence of the immediate past, or future, ceases to dominate exclusively. There is then reaction against mere average material domination. Thus the universe is material in proportion to the restriction of memory and anticipation.

According to this account of the World of Activity there is no need to postulate two essentially different types of Active Entities, namely, the purely material entities and the entities alive with various modes of experiencing. The latter type is sufficient to account for the characteristics of that World, when we allow for variety of recessiveness and dominance among the basic factors of experience, namely consciousness, memory, and anticipation. This conclusion has the advantage of indicating the possibility of the emergence of Life from the lifeless material of this planet—namely, by the gradual emergence of memory and anticipation.

XVI

We now have to consider the constitution of the World of Value arising from its essential embodiment of the World of Fact.

The basic elements in the World of Fact are finite activities; the basic character of the World of Value is its timeless coordination of the infinitude of possibility for realization. In the Universe the status of the World of Fact is that of an abstraction requiring, for the completion of its concrete reality, Value and Purpose. Also in the Universe the status of the World of Value is that of an abstraction requiring, for the completion of its concrete reality, the factuality of Finite Activity. We now pass to this second question.

The primary basis of the World of Value is the coördination of all possibility for entry into the active World of Fact. Such coördination involves Harmony and Frustration, Beauty and Ugliness, Attraction and Aversion. Also there is a measure of fusion in respect to each pair of antitheses—for example, some definite possibility for realization will involve some degree of Harmony and some degree of Frustration, and so on for every other pair of antitheses.

The long tradition of European philosophy and theology has been haunted by two misconceptions. One of these misconceptions is the notion of independent existence. This error has a double origin, one civilized, and the other barbaric. The civilized origin of the notion of independent existence is the tendency of sensitive people, when they experience some factor of value on its noblest side, to feel that they are enjoying some ultimate essence of the Universe, and that therefore its existence must include an absolute independence of all inferior types. It is this final conclusion of the absoluteness of independence to which I am objecting. This error haunted Plato in respect to his Ideas, and more especially in respect to the mathematical Ideas which he so greatly enjoyed.

The second misconception is derived from the earlier types of successful civilized, or half-civilized, social system. The apparatus for preserving unity is stressed. These structures involved despotic government, sometimes better and sometimes worse. As civilization emerged, the social system required such modes of coördination.

We have evidence of the Hebrews feeling the inefficiency of casual leadership, and asking for a king—to the disgust of the priests, or at least of the later priests who wrote up the story.

Thus an unconscious presupposition was diffused that a successful social system required despotism. This notion was based on the barbaric fact, that violence was the primary mode of sustaining large-scale social existence. This belief is not yet extinct. We can see the emergence of civilized concepts in Greek and Hebrew social systems, and in the emphasis of the Roman Empire upon the development of a legal system, which was partially self-sustaining. The Roman legions were mainly stationed on the borders of the Empire.

But in later Europe the great example of the rise of civilized notions was set by the monasteries in the early middle ages. Institutions, such as Cluny in its prime, upheld the ideal of social systems devoid of violence, and yet maintaining a large effectiveness. Unfortunately all human edifices require repair and reconstruction; but our immense debt to mediaeval monasteries should not be obscured by their need of reform at the end of that epoch. The clever men of the eighteenth century expressed in words ideals enacted centuries earlier. In the modern world the activities of Cluny have been reproduced by the work of convents in regions such as Brittany and New England, but rarely in places where religion is associated with wealth.

Sociological analysis at the present moment is concentrated upon those essential factors which presented the easiest field. Such a factor was the economic motive; it would be unfair to ascribe this limited outlook to Adam Smith, although it certainly dominated his followers in the later generations. Then Idealism was in the background: the abolition of slavery was its final effort. The primary example, in the civilization of Europe after the fall of the Western branch of the Roman Empire, was afforded by the Christian monasteries in their early period.

XVII

The conclusion of this discussion is twofold. One side is that the ascription of mere happiness, and of arbitrary power to the nature of God is a profanation. This nature conceived as the unification derived from the World of Value is founded on ideals of perfection, moral and aesthetic. It receives into its unity the scattered effectiveness of realized activities, transformed by the supremacy of its own ideals. The result is Tragedy, Sympathy, and the Happiness evoked by actualized Heroism.

Of course we are unable to conceive the experience of the Supreme Unity of Existence. But these are the human terms in which we can glimpse the origin of that drive towards limited ideals of perfection which haunts the Universe. This immortality of the World of Action, derived from its transformation in God's nature is beyond our imagination to conceive. The various attempts at description are often shocking and profane. What does haunt our imagination is that the immediate facts of present action pass into permanent significance for the Universe. The insistent notion of Right and Wrong, Achievement and Failure, depends upon this background. Otherwise every activity is merely a passing whiff of insignificance.

XVIII

The final topic remaining for discussion opens a large question. So far, this lecture has proceeded in the form of dogmatic statement. What is the evidence to which it appeals?

The only answer is the reaction of our own nature to the general aspect of life in the Universe.

This answer involves complete disagreement with a widespread tradition of philosophic thought. This erroneous tradition presupposes independent existences; and this presupposition involves the possibility of an adequate description of a finite fact. The result is the presupposition of adequate separate premises from which argument can proceed.

For example, much philosophic thought is based upon the faked adequacy of some account of various modes of human experience. Thence we reach some simple conclusion as to the essential character of human knowledge, and of its essential limitation. Namely, we know what we cannot know.

Understand that I am not denying the importance of the analysis of experience: far from it. The progress of human thought is derived from the progressive enlightenment produced thereby. What I am objecting to is the absurd trust in the adequacy of our knowledge. The self-confidence of learned people is the comic tragedy of civilization.

There is not a sentence which adequately states its own meaning. There is always a background of presupposition which defies analysis by reason of its infinitude.

Let us take the simplest case; for example, the sentence, "One and one make two."

Obviously this sentence omits a necessary limitation. For one thing and itself make one thing. So we ought to say, "One thing and another thing make two things." This must mean that the togetherness of one thing with another thing issues in a group of two things.

At this stage all sorts of difficulties arise. There must be the proper sort of things in the proper sort of togetherness. The togetherness of a spark and gunpowder produces an explosion, which is very unlike two things. Thus we should say, "The proper sort of togetherness of one thing and another thing produces the sort of group which we call *two things*." Common sense at once tells you what is meant. But unfortunately there is no adequate analysis of common sense, because it involves our relation to the infinity of the Universe.

Also there is another difficulty. When anything is placed in another situation, it changes. Every hostess takes account of this truth when she invites suitable guests to a party; and every cook presupposes it as she proceeds to cook the dinner. Of course, the statement, "One and one make two" assumes that the changes in the shift of circumstance are unimportant. But it is impossible for us to analyse this notion of "unimportant change." We have to rely upon common sense.

In fact, there is not a sentence, or a word, with a meaning which is independent of the circumstances under which it is uttered. The essence of unscholarly thought consists in a neglect of this truth. Also it is equally the essence of common sense to neglect these differences of background when they are irrelevant to the immediate purpose. My point is that we cannot rely upon any adequate explicit analysis.

XIX

The conclusion is that Logic, conceived as an adequate analysis of the advance of thought, is a fake. It is a superb instrument, but it requires a background of common sense.

To take another example: Consider the "exact" statements of the various schools of Christian Theology. If the leaders of any ecclesiastical organization at present existing were transported back to the sixteenth century, and stated their full beliefs, historical and doctrinal, either in Geneva or in Spain, then Calvin, or the Inquisitors, would have been profoundly shocked, and would have acted according to their habits in such cases. Perhaps, after some explanation, both Calvin and the Inquisitors would have had the sense to shift the emphasis of their own beliefs. That is another question which does not concern us.

My point is that the final outlook of Philosophic thought cannot be based upon the exact statements which form the basis of special sciences.

The exactness is a fake.

Alfred North Whitehead

DEPARTMENT OF PHILOSOPHY
HARVARD UNIVERSITY

19

C. I. Lewis

THE CATEGORIES OF NATURAL KNOWLEDGE

19

THE CATEGORIES OF NATURAL KNOWLEDGE

IN accepting our editor's invitation to undertake an additional
essay for this collection of studies on the philosophy of Whitehead, I am aware of my temerity. Already the volume is complete and balanced in the scope of its topics and admirable in
detail: attempted addition is likely to be mere intrusion, tres-
passing on ground already covered. And in addressing myself
to Whitehead's base-concepts for the philosophy of nature, I see
in advance that I can satisfy none of the usual desiderata. This
reformulation of the categories, set forth in *An Enquiry Concerning the Principles of Natural Knowledge*, *The Concept of
Nature*, and *The Principle of Relativity*[1] is such as defies any
effort to summarize, being already succinct to that point beyond
which further compression must be mere omission. Nor can one
readily facilitate the reader's comprehension or render any point
more clear by alternative formulation. To attempt that is to risk
falling into those errors of common misconception and un-
guarded expression which are precisely what the author is engaged in pointing out and avoiding. And if one be minded to
bring perspective upon the conceptions presented, by comparison
of them with others which are outstanding in the history of philosophic thought, then one finds that Whitehead has already done
that too, either in the pages we study or in later writings, and in
a fashion discouraging of all attempts to imitate. My one excuse
for this choice of subject must be that these three books represent
that part of Whitehead's thought to which I have oftenest been

---

[1] These three books will hereafter be cited by the last word in the title, i.e., as
Knowledge, *Nature*, and *Relativity* respectively.

drawn back for further study and reflection. And with respect to this topic, I cannot expound, save fragmentarily, nor can I elucidate unless at some sacrifice of adequacy and of precision. What I can justly do is simply to call attention, hoping by some characterization to emphasize what I take to be the radical novelty and the permanent significance of this philosophy of natural knowledge. But if I can in any measure perform that office then I shall not be withheld by any foresight of unavoidable limitations in so doing.

The three books mentioned have a common subject-matter and intent, with respect to which they are mutually supplementary statements. It is in *The Principles of Natural Knowledge* that their common project is most comprehensively surveyed and the new and precise concepts on which Whitehead builds are so introduced that their place in the whole scheme may be most clearly seen. *The Concept of Nature* might, in comparison, be taken to emphasize the enforced transition from older but still dominant conceptions—in terms of which the gap between common understanding and current physical science has now become so difficult to bridge—to categories of thought which will allow the world of our everyday knowledge to be viewed once more as that same world of which contemporary science also gives account. That project requires the profoundest philosophic re-examination of those terms in which common sense, inheriting as it does from the whole stream of western philosophy from Plato down, has come to think of the world of nature. It likewise and at the same time requires attention to those challenging features of the new physics which accentuate this necessary revolution in our thinking. The two sides of this project, and their essential connection, are stressed in the opening chapter of *The Principle of Relativity:*

> To expect to reorganize our ideas of Time, Space, and Measurement without some discussion which must be ranked as philosophical is to neglect the teaching of history and the inherent probabilities of the subject. On the other hand no reorganization of these ideas can command confidence unless it supplies science with added power in the analysis of phenomena.

The evidence is twofold, and is fatally weakened if the two parts are disjoined.[2]

In this third book Whitehead also makes evident his conviction that relativity physics, in the prevailing form, calls for certain amendments of its basic procedures, rendering them less paradoxical to common sense and less divergent from the older physics. And after summary statement of premises already presented in the earlier books he here proceeds to the fundamental equations for mathematical physics in that form which he would give to this subject.

Let it be said at once, however, that I must here disjoin what Whitehead has said should not be put asunder. Both my own preponderant interest—perhaps the reader's also—and my illiteracy in the mathematical language of relativity physics dictate restriction to what concerns revision of the categories of antecedent philosophies and prevailing common sense, leaving aside that corroboration of the value of the revised concepts which comes from the demonstrated adequacy of them for the new physics. That any set of philosophic concepts should be submitted to a test so stringent, and indeed developed with that as one end in view, is unprecedented in the history of thought; and we shall do well to pause in appreciation of that fact. But the categorial conceptions whose importance is thus strikingly signalized are bound to have a wider significance, independent of this technical import of them, however impressive that may be. And plainly that accords with Whitehead's own conception and intent. What he here presents to us is in no sense a set of concepts and principles devised for the sake of a physical theory, as one may devise definitions and postulates for a predetermined mathematical system. The validity and power of this philosophy is attested by its adequacy to technical use; but the adequacy derives from the validity, not the validity from the adequacy. Even if the orientation toward physics should be supposed to dominate, there would still be a pertinent remark which we can extract from his own writings: "The . . . philosophic generaliza-

[2] P. 4.

tion will, if derived from physics, find applications in fields of experience beyond physics. It will enlighten observation in those remote fields, so that general principles can be discerned as in process of illustration. . . . In other words, some synoptic vision has been gained."[3] It is to Whitehead's synoptic envisagement of the world of nature, as expressed in these three books, that attention will be directed here.

We can, however, begin with that generality which most closely relates to what is technical and connects with the discussion of physical theory; namely, with space-time as the general structure of events. That topic is basic; it runs through the whole discussion, affecting every other aspect of this conception of nature. The form which the account of space-time eventually assumes is highly complex. But the root of the matter is in something which is more simple—and may be more readily grasped. That is, it may be so grasped if we understand at the beginning what it is which is to be achieved by such a theory, and those requirements which, as Whitehead conceives it, are to be met by any concept validly introduced in any systematic account of natural knowledge or in any scientific theory. He demands that every such concept shall be validated by identification of what it denotes in terms of factors of observable fact. It is sense-awareness which discloses such fact, and the factors so disclosed are entities for thought.

Thus there are three components in our knowledge of nature, namely, fact, factors, and entities. Fact is the undifferentiated terminus of sense-awareness; factors are termini of sense-awareness, differentiated as elements of fact; entities are factors in their function as termini of thought . . . Evidently the relations holding between natural entities are themselves natural entities, namely, they are also factors of fact, there for sense-awareness.[4]

These are slightly cryptic sayings, not to be fully grasped without some further understanding of Whitehead's procedures. Let us first illustrate:

[3] *Process and Reality*, 8.
[4] *Nature*, 13 f.

Instantaneousness is a complex logical concept . . . For example we conceive of the distribution of matter in space at an instant. This is a very useful concept in science, especially in applied mathematics; but it is a very complex idea so far as concerns its connexions with the immediate facts of sense-awareness. There is no such thing as nature at an instant posited by sense-awareness. [The least that we perceive involves always some duration.] What sense-awareness delivers over for knowledge is nature through a period. Accordingly nature at an instant, since it is not a natural entity, must be defined in terms of genuine natural entities. Unless we do so, our science, which employs the concept of instantaneous nature, must abandon all claim to be founded upon observation.[5]

What this complex logical concept of the instantaneous is, does not so far appear. Whitehead is, in fact, preparing here to introduce it; and we shall likewise mention it later. But the present point is that even a concept of a property or character which does not present itself to sense—is not 'posited by sense-awareness'—must be definable in terms of factors of what does present itself to sense, if its introduction in a scientific account of nature is to be justified. Even the instants of time and the points of applied geometry, as well as the point-particles of kinematics, the molecules and electrons of physical science and all other entities which are not to be identified in our perception of the macroscopic, must be conceptually reducible to terms, ultimately, of what can be disclosed in sense-presentation. Otherwise the concepts in question will be empty and require abandonment of all claim that the science which uses them is founded on observed fact. "The constructions of science are merely expositions of the characters of things perceived."[6] This is what I shall call Whitehead's radical empiricism.

We shall do well to pause briefly upon the character of this empiricism, because it is like no other in history, and the confusion of it with that of Locke, Berkeley and Hume, or with that empiricism for which objects are Kantian appearances in a mind, would mislead us no end. In the first place, although Whitehead is not a naturalist in the sense of regarding nature as the whole

[5] *Ibid.*, 56 f.
[6] *Ibid.*, 148.

of reality, but tells us instead that nature is an abstraction from something more concrete, he confines himself in these three books to the discussion of nature. And he defines nature in terms of sense-awareness. "Nature is that which we observe in perception through the senses."[7]

Second, the deliverances of sense are not for Whitehead findings of subjective immediacy in a mind which cognizes the world only mediately and through inference. The observer is one enduring entity and the object is another enduring entity; but perception is a relation between a percipient *event* and another event in which the object is situated. The percipient event is itself in nature, being merely the relevant state of the observing organism. Hence perception is a natural relation between entities in nature. The bifurcation of nature into a phenomenal appearance in mind and an object which is inferred as the cause of it, or constructed from immediate data by the necessities of mind in thinking an object, is wholly unacceptable to Whitehead. In the first place, the attempt to explain knowledge as the interplay between a mind which is outside of or above the world of objects in nature and a stuff which never enters mind but appears to it only through a surrogate and with 'psychic additions'; this attempt at 'metaphysical' explication of the fact of knowledge is no part of the business of natural philosophy, which legitimately concerns itself only with the relations of factors *within* knowledge. And in the second place, admitting the problem, this manner of explanation by dividing nature into two kinds, one apparent but ineffective and the other causal of the appearance but only inferable by the mind which knows it, must fail by its inability to explain our way of knowing about these two parts into which reality is so partitioned. Though Whitehead does not in so many words acknowledge it, he repudiates the whole problem of knowledge in that form which attempts a Cartesian defense against skepticism in view of the predicament of a mind which has no direct contact with the natural world except through the pineal gland. And that problem, posed by 'bifurcation,' dominates the history of theory of knowledge from Descartes to Kant,

[7] *Ibid.,* 3.

if not down to the present day. A good part of our difficulty in understanding Whitehead arises, I think, from our being historically conditioned to revert to that problem in almost every philosophic context, and to confront every answer to every philosophic question with the challenge, "But how do you know that?" So far as it is our knowledge of nature which is in question Whitehead is, so to say, prepared to rebut this skeptically motivated challenge with the answer; "You know it by observation—finally, by the deliverances of sense-awareness." When the sensibly disclosed is no longer subject to suspicion by interpretation of it as mere datum in a mind shut off from every immediate contact with reality, this skeptical approach has lost its point. This is Whitehead's realism; it is even, if you please, that form of realism commonly called 'naive'—though a word less appropriate to Whitehead's thinking, it would be hard to find; and he by no means repudiates or ignores the problems set by delusive apprehension and the other relativities of perceptual knowledge. That we shall see later on.

For similar reasons, he repudiates as invalid that watered-down form of bifurcation-theory which would interpret the scientific realities of points and instants, point-particles, electrons, molecules, and so on, as useful fictions, or merely logical constructions which, instead of being definable in terms of actual and perceptible entities of nature, enter as 'mathematical models,' or are introduced by stipulation, or though not in terms of actual entities of nature and apprehended fact, are supposed justified by intellectual convenience à la Poincaré, or otherwise savor of the pragmatic in the bad sense of pseudo and as-if.

The current answer to these objections [made by Whitehead to this attenuated form of bifurcation-theory] is that though atoms are merely conceptual, yet they are an interesting and picturesque way of saying something which is true of nature. But surely if it is something else that you mean, for heaven's sake say it.[8]

To 'say it' in terms that are traced back to the deliverances of sense-awareness, is a highly complex business; but Whitehead will not settle for less.

[8] *Ibid.*, 45.

In a highly subtle way, it is just this repudiation of concepts by stipulation and principles by convention which prevents Whitehead's full acceptance of the Einstein conception of space-time; though he always acknowledges his indebtedness to, and his deep respect for, the innovations of Einstein and Minkowski. He objects to the Einstein 'signal theory' of light, which is introduced by the stipulation (defining simultaneity of events at a distance) that, e.g., if lightning strikes the railroad track at two places, the two strokes are simultaneous just in case an observer situated midway between the two places and provided with mirrors for observing both at once would observe these two strokes simultaneously.[9] Whitehead does not object to, but accepts, simultaneity of observation as the primitive criterion for, e.g., barking both shins at once. And of course he does not object to defining simultaneity for distant events in a manner dependent on such simultaneity here and now. He does, however, object to the favored position so accorded to deliverances of one sense; and when, in his own equations, he introduces the constant c, characteristic of special relativity theory, he does so with the remark: "There is however this difference that the critical velocity c has [here] no reference to light, and merely expresses the fact that a lapse of time and a stretch of spatial route can be congruent to each other."[10]

He also objects to interpreting the component measurements, in that expression of a field of force which is constant for all frames of reference, as indicating a curvature of the space-manifold. "I do not allow that physical phenomena are due to oddities of space."[11]

His most fundamental objection, however, is that the Einstein account contains no 'antecedent theory of measurement'—a lack which Whitehead would make good by his theory of congruence. "Einstein, in my opinion, leaves the whole antecedent theory of measurement in confusion, when it is confronted by the actual conditions of our perceptual knowledge. . . . Measure-

[9] See Einstein, *The Meaning of Relativity*, 27 f.
[10] Whitehead, *Relativity*, 76.
[11] *Ibid.*, 184.

ment on his theory lacks systematic uniformity and requires a knowledge of the actual contingent physical field before it is possible."[12] It is this objection which, if we can grasp the import of it, may lead to understanding of the fundamental connection between Whitehead's interpretation of space-time and the basic position he assigns to the category of events. Why should the theory of measurement be 'antecedent'; and antecedent to what? The answer is: antecedent to the application of measurement to any dimension of physical objects or physical properties, and to any phenomenon it is the business of physical science to investigate. And antecedent because, unless some basis of measurement is so involved in the structure of nature as to be independent of the contingent properties of physical objects investigated and measured, there will be a circle in the very conception and definition of such measures.

All physical things are in process and any physical property of them may become altered. And all such properties of objects which physical science would determine are contingent properties which are indeterminable save by observation and experiment. If, then, measurements are *defined* by stipulated operations with yardsticks and clocks and other physical instruments, then our yardstick may turn out too rubbery or shorten if it is moved (and shorten with respect to what?); our clocks may run slow or fast or be affected by a magnetic field. And if we determine the simultaneity of distant events by means of observations in a mirror at the midpoint between them, then mirrors, or *this* mirror, could have physical peculiarities affecting the matter. And in spite of what Einstein says to the contrary—in the context above referred to—our determination of simultaneity, so made, must either assume that the velocity of light is uniform in opposite directions, or this operation will be utterly unsuited to any disclosure of a property significantly correlated with the occurrence of other properties as found in nature. Concepts arising by stipulation must be forever at the mercy of contingent natural facts for any status other than that of triviality. Defining our concepts for the discovery of order amongst contingent

[12] *Ibid.*, 83.

facts in terms of contingent characteristics of the same general kind as those to be determined, is like defining elasticity by reference to an elastic standard of the rigid.

For physical science, and indeed for any knowledge of the physical, the basic presumption is that the spatio-temporal characteristics of physical things are contingent properties of them; no physical object, or kind of object, has its particular and discoverable spatio-temporal properties *a priori*. But if all physical description and determinations of physical properties are not to become relative in a sense which philosophy and science have so far spared us, then there must be *something* which stands fast and provides a norm not itself subject to the contingencies of fact we would unravel.

The point here is not to avoid such assumptions as that something or other is a sufficiently rigid body, or a sufficiently reliable clock, to serve as an instrument of measurement; the point is to avoid circularity in the very conception of the various spatial and temporal equivalences (spatio-temporal congruences) which constitute our measures; to escape, for example, the absurdity of saying that because, by stipulation or convention, the platinum bar in Washington is the standard yardstick, it could not by any physical contingency become elongated or shortened, and so fail to be, at one place and time, congruent with itself at another place and time. At the very least it will be granted that it is desirable to avoid, if that can be managed, this manner of confusion between space-time itself and the contingent space-time properties of physical objects which it is the business of science to determine.

I have presented this point in my own way, and perhaps in a manner which Whitehead would not approve. But it is to this kind of problem that his conception of 'event' and of space-time as the general structure of events, is addressed. The fundamental consideration here is that events, and the relations of events, unlike physical objects and their contingent relationships, are not subject to change. Space-time as the comprehensive order of events can provide a kind of ultimate frame of reference for the processes of physically changing things precisely because an event, unlike a material object, is inalterably just what it is and related to other events just as it is.

This contrast between event and object, and the precise significance of this category of 'events,' can at first be puzzling; especially since, e.g., Mr. Blank throughout his lifetime is both a complex object and a complex event. But the basic distinction between an event which we may apprehend and an object which we may at the same time be perceiving, is one which is at bottom simple and is capable of clear statement in common-sense terms. An event is a happening; it happens just when it does and where it does; and the notion of just this event as happening elsewhere or at another time is simply a contradiction in terms. By contrast, an object may be in one place at one time and in another place at another time. It is the kind of entity which endures, and by that fact may become altered.

Events have always some spatio-temporal spread. They 'occupy' time and space, because that manner of speaking is merely an inaccurate way of saying that spatio-temporal order is an abstraction from the comprehensive relations of events to one another. One event 'extends over' (includes as a proper part) any other event which can be marked off within it. The event of the clock striking three extends over the events of the separate strokes, and extends over them as parts having just that relationship to the whole event and to one another which they do. Mr. Blank eating breakfast at seven-thirty and Mr. Blank running for the train at eight are likewise events, and both are extended over by the event which is the life of Mr. Blank from seven to nine. If we see Mr. Blank at eight o'clock, we may recognize the object Mr. Blank, but what is directly delivered to our sense-awareness is the happening, Mr. Blank running for the train. This is a particular space-time piece out of nature in its passage, delineated as what takes place then and there within our observation. But what is so observed, Whitehead takes to be, not a subjective phenomenon 'within our minds,' but just this event now happening, and happening in relation to a percipient event which is our seeing Mr. Blank run. Also, these two events stand in their specific spatio-temporal relations as parts of the more comprehensive event which is the neighborhood of the railroad station from seven-fifty to eight-ten.

We describe events as 'in' space and time, that is, by indicating their spatial and temporal bounds, or we describe them by reference to objects like Mr. Blank which are ingredient in them, or we use both methods at once in specifying what event is spoken of. But it is neither the space and time which the events are said to occupy, nor the objects ingredient in them, which are the primordial constituents of nature. These ultimate constituents are the events themselves. "There is time because there are happenings, and apart from happenings there is nothing."[13] It could likewise be said that there is space because there are happenings; because events have separate parts related as one here and one simultaneously there. As for objects, that is a story we shall come to shortly.

First, however, let us pause to observe those distinctive features of this conception of space-time as the structure of events by reason of which it avoids that confusion of spatio-temporal relationships with the contingent physical properties of changeable physical objects, and to note, in most general terms, the possibility so afforded for the introduction of concepts requisite to measurement in a manner which is free of the difficulty mentioned above.

In spite of the multiplicity and variety of theories of space and time, historical conceptions exhibit three general patterns. There is the primitive notion of space and time as 'absolute'; of space as the 'empty bowl,' partially or wholly occupied by bits of matter, but in which, and independently of what occupies and moves in it, there are absolute positions, directions, and the characters of measureable extent. With this goes the notion of time as the equable flow of nothing whatever or of everything in general, which is independent of and provides the basis for measuring the particular rates of motion of things which move and the rate of change of other processes.

This conception of space and time as absolute never really satisfied anybody. Even amongst the ancients who first recorded it we likewise find record of the unanswerable objection to it: this view ascribes a kind of being to that which is not, and assigns

---

[13] *Nature*, 66.

to this nothing a character antecedent to all characters, fixing the measures of things. The notion of the ether as the physically ultimate frame of reference is the last relic of this theory; and with the Michelson-Morley experiment it passed into history.

Second, there is the type of theory called 'relative' before the advent of relativity physics made that designation confusing; the conception namely that there are no such entities as space and time apart from what occupies them; that space is constituted by those relations of material objects which are called 'spatial,' and that time is constituted by the order and relations of the processes which objects undergo. In spite of that iconoclastic confinement to the palpable which gives this theory its plausibility, it fails to cover that sense of temporality which is reflected in the eternal flitting away of life and all states of things, even when relationships observed appear most stable. It also arouses some sense of having tucked the spatio-temporal order under things to start with, in order to be able to discover later this *general* order amongst their contingent and particular and unanticipatable relationships to one another. Specifically there is a difficulty here which affects all measurement, by making all measures relative to some contingent and alterable character of some material object or set of objects, or to some particular relationship amongst objects which could change with time. What measures time-lapse must *ipso facto* be accepted as suffering no alteration in that character of it which provides this measure; and what measures space must *ipso facto* be immune to alteration of its spatial characters. But there are no material objects thus immune to alteration of their spatial and temporal properties. Antecedent to physical investigations, involving measurements of the space-time characteristics of objects, there can be no guarantee that any of them will endure unaltered in that respect relied upon to provide a standard applicable to other objects. But until there is such an unchanging standard, physical measurement of changing things cannot proceed.

Unless space and time are in some sense antecedent to and independent of those properties of material objects which are recognized to be contingent and discoverable only by empirical observation and empirical generalization with respect to their spatio-temporal characteristics, then all scientific measurement is, theoretically at least, involved in a vicious circle, even if we refuse, practically, to be frightened lest the stars should change in their courses—thus falling back, in point of fact, on the absolutistic theory we supposedly have repudiated.

The currently fashionable method of cutting this Gordian knot, is by stipulation of operational criteria. This is as much as to say, *e.g.;* "We refuse to recognize any alteration of those material objects which provide our standard measures, in those characteristics of them which constitute this accepted criterion." But either this is justified by antecedent empirical investigations, showing this object, or kind of object, to be reliably correlated with other processes in nature, so that appeal to it will not make chaos of our attempted discovery of some general order and law amongst the processes of things at large—and in that case we are back in our vicious circle once more—or else it is a mere counsel of despair.

The third type of theory, of which Kant is the clearest representative, seeks to recover the antecedent and independent character of spatial and temporal order and its clear distinction from contingent spatial and temporal characters of particular things, by superimposing on the relativistic conception an epistemological distinction of the *a priori* from the empirically learned. For earlier theories which might be classed as of this type, space as the essence of extension may be taken as knowable *a priori* by *reason*. But Kant observes that geometry depends on steps of proof which cannot be justified by rules of logic simply, and the *a priori* status of our knowledge of space and time is attributed to the fact that space and time are forms of intuition, within which alone phenomena can appear to the mind. Taking mathematics (applied geometry, and arithmetic as generated by the time-order of counting) as indubitably valid, he seeks to establish this *a priori* character of them by showing that we know fundamental characters of space and time which could not possibly be learned by any generalizing from particular experiences.

Bergson's theory of space and time might be included as representing a fourth type; and Bergson is supposed to have influenced Whitehead. But Bergson's conception is hardly co-ordinate with the above three, and it offers nothing pertinent to the point to which I would direct attention here. Whitehead's conception of the 'passage of events' as 'creative advance' suggests Bergson, and there are other recognizable points of approximation. But Whitehead's conception of time in nature as measureable, and of a lapse of time as possibly congruent with some stretch of spatial route, directly contravenes the Bergsonian conception on these same points.

Whitehead's theory of space-time repudiates the absolutistic . notion: he takes space-time order to represent an abstraction, though an abstraction of something which is there in nature to be abstracted. He accepts not only the general relativistic conception above but the further relativity involved in the new physics. Also he repudiates any manner of apriorism, making no doubt that we discover this space-time structure of nature in the same general manner that we discover other natural facts—eventually through the deliverances of sense. His theory rejects Kantian phenomenalism and any intuition of form independent of sense-content. But it nevertheless preserves a distinction between the space-time structure of nature and the contingent relations of physical objects. And by preserving this distinction, it makes possible a theory of measurement which avoids that circularity of conception pointed out above. The space-time structure of nature is independent of and 'antecedent' to spatio-temporal characteristics of material objects which, by being involved in the natural process, can undergo some alteration, and whose reliability as possible standards of the measurable must first be attested by some empirical investigation and generalization about the physical properties of these material objects. If I may here use 'necessary' merely as the suggested antonym to 'contingent,' then I may say that on Whitehead's theory the 'geometry' of space-time expresses necessary relationships in the space-time structure of nature. (Whitehead does not use the term 'necessary' in this connection, and he uses 'antecedent' somewhat incidentally—as in the quotation above. The usage of these terms here is mine, though in what I use them to express, I believe that I am accurate to his thought.)

Whitehead's theory of space-time is historically unique because his category of 'events' is historically unique. Space-time is the general structure of *events* in nature. Thus in accepting the relativistic conception, he does so with a difference; and this difference is profoundly important. The relationships which constitute the abstractable space-time structure of nature are not here the contingent relations which material objects exhibit in the course of their adventures in the natural process. Objects have no space-time relationships except through their connection with events. And the relations of events, constitutive of that abstractable structure which is space-time, are 'necessary' in the peculiar sense that they could not be other than in fact they are. This 'necessity,' however, is not one of logic; and in spite of other differences Whitehead is at one with Kant on just this point.

Every event has spatio-temporal extension, and extension in both respects. Every event extends over other events which are its parts, and every event is in turn extended over by others. In terms of 'extending over,' further relations of events are definable. Two events having a common part 'intersect.' Two which do not intersect are 'separated.' In terms of these, other relations are definable. (I omit the further designated relationships and their definitions.) On the basis of relationships so defined, Whitehead proceeds to the 'Method of Extensive Abstraction,' to be mentioned later; and on the basis of concepts so determined he indicates the whole 'geometry' explicative of space-time as the structure of relations of events. In this 'geometry,' the metrical concepts are introduced by his theory of congruence. Durations, moments, time-systems (essential to relativity physics), the various types of spatial entities, motion, and the basic concepts of physics, all receive their consequent explication.

But to return to what belongs in a synoptic view: It will be evident without explanation in detail that just as the when and where of an event are of the essence, and its having any other locus in space-time would be a contradiction, so also its extending over just those events which in fact are parts of it, and its being extended over by just those events in which it is a part, as well as its intersecting or being separated from another event, or its having any other relationship, definable in terms of these, to another event—all these facts of relationship can only be just what they are, and follow from the events so related being just the events that they are. These relations of events are, thus, 'internal.' The whole order of space-time as the structure of events in such relationships, is fixed and 'necessary' in this sense that it could not be otherwise than in fact it is, even though our awareness of what is so contained in nature is highly fragmentary, and in our grasp of its structure, abstractly taken, we could be mistaken in ways which may not reflect any failure of cogency. There is no guarantee of certitude beyond what is implied in this nature of events, and in their universal involvement with others as being parts and as containing parts, and so on.

If now one wishes to know what difference, after all, this makes as to the distinction of the spatio-temporal from the contingent properties of material things, then the answer can be suggested briefly. The practicalities of measurement may be unaffected, and in any case the choice of a metrical unit is arbitrary. But we now have a 'geometry' of space-time, including parallels; though it also allows for different time-systems in accord with the new physics. We have also a developed and precise meaning of 'congruent with.' If we have our yardstick before us, the length of it can be 'projected' throughout the space-time system; and the *meaning* of 'one yard long' is 'congruent in length with the length of this here and now yardstick,' regardless of any vicissitudes which this physical yardstick may undergo in its adventures in time and space. That circularity in the meaning of the metrical concepts which is involved in the definition of spatio-temporal entities by stipulated relation to material objects in process, is thus obviated. Space-time itself is not constituted by the relations of material objects but by reference to events which, by their nature *as* events, can undergo no change. And if under certain physical conditions all material

objects should be systematically 'shortened,' the explanation to
be sought must be physical, and is not to be found in any attribution of curvature to the space-time manifold.

> This doctrine leads to the rejection of Einstein's interpretation of his
> formulae, as expressing a casual heterogeneity of spatio-temporal warping,
> dependent upon contingent adjectives.
>
> The case of the yard-measure illustrates my meaning. It is a contingent
> adjective of the events where it is situated. Its spatio-temporal properties
> are entirely derived from the events it qualifies . . . The yard-measure is
> merely a device for making evident obscure relations between those events
> in which it appears.[14]

Already the reader has been disturbed by the obscurity of
referring to objects, in a conception in which it appears that
what is ultimate in nature does not include objects but is constituted by unalterable events in an order of relations to one
another which is likewise unchanging and intrinsic to them. But
that is the fault of my having disarranged the order of Whitehead's exposition in my comments here. Let us now proceed,
belatedly, to this topic of the nature of objects and their connections with events.

Objects are derivative and 'adjectival' entities which *are* by
being ingredient in events, and are elicited by recognition in or
through those same deliverances of sense which are also our
direct apprehensions of events. Events happen only once, and
are spoken of as 'apprehended'; objects are the kind of entities
which can 'be again'; and are said to be 'recognized.' It follows
that the same object can be ingredient in, or 'situated' in, more
than one event. Apart from events (happenings) there is nothing whatever; but without the recognition of objects in events
in which they are situated, we could not discern or mark off the
events themselves, within the continuity of space-time. Ingredient objects are thus certain *characters* of the events which are
their situations.

The simplest kind of recognition of an object is recognition
of some permanence within the specious present; of some in-

[14] *Relativity*, 65.

gredient character which characterizes both the before-part and the after-part distinguishable in even the smallest event that we can apprehend. And the simplest objects so recognized are qualia or sense-data; tastes, colors, shape-size, and so on. Whitehead calls these 'sense-objects.' Merely as now presented and situated in the directly apprehended event, such a sense-object is concrete or individual, and it could in no sense share that kind of abstractness which characterizes universals like goodness and triangularity. But sense-objects have a kind of duality by being entities for thought as well as for direct awareness. Recognition of an object is significant of it as something recollectable, and the same in more than one event. As such as entity for thought it loses something of the individuality which it has as just this object, ingredient in this event now apprehended, retaining only the individuality of character. It is thus a kind of universal, though Whitehead does not here apply that word.

Both these references are involved in recognition—since that requires cognizance of something both as given now and as being 'again.' The distinction is relative to this duality of the factors in recognition: as characterizing this occasion, the given sense-object shares the individuality of this present sense-awareness; as recognized from one occasion to another, it constitutes an abstractable entity for thought.

For other theories, sense-objects, or sense-data, are assigned their metaphysical home in experience or in the mind, and perhaps are allowed no status as constituents in objective reality, even though recognized as *ratio cognoscendi* of some physical object. But this manner of conception leads to or presupposes the bifurcation of nature which Whitehead will not allow. There are such sense-objects as vague sounds or odors which may be given without apprehension of their situation in any specific event. But apart from such vagrant items, and in those cases in which the sense-awareness finds its place in some full perception of a physical thing, awareness of the sense-object as situated in an event is basic for authenticity of the perception. On this point he says: "The situations of sense-objects form the whole basis of our knowledge of nature, and the whole structure of natural knowledge is founded on the analysis of their relations."[15]

So long as we deal with sense-objects (or sense-data), White-head's conception of them as merely adjectival entities charac-terizing events (or occasions of experience) may not affect our common sense with any feeling of paradox. But when we come to the next category of 'perceptual objects'—the stones, trees, tables and other objects commonly recognized—then I think that the conception of such entities as adjectival and merely permanences of character, characterizing certain passages of events, does arouse some sense of paradox; and we may not be able to follow Whitehead with full understanding unless at this point we exercise our metaphysical imagination a little. We are so wedded to the notion of perceptible physical objects as ultimate realities, and of the world as that big barrel in which the whole collection of them is thrown together, that we have difficulty in envisaging nature as the continuum of happenings in their total relatedness, within which objects present them-selves as lesser and included continuities, elicited by their rela-tive preservation of continuing characters, in patterns the inter-connections of which constitute their intelligible relationships.

If I may use a distant analogy, events in their all-pervading continuity constitute that ocean of nature in which perceptual and physical objects are waves which we may discern. If there were no recognizable shapes and high-lights (sense-objects) here and there, then the whole ocean would be characterless and could not be marked off into distinguishable parts (separate events). And if there were no waves, recognizable as propagated continuities of these sensible characters, then there would be no relatively permanent objects at all. The permanence of the association of sense-objects *is* the perceptual object which is recog-nized.[16] My analogy fails most notably in that nature is no ocean all there for apprehension at one time but is the continuum of happenings in their all-pervasive passage and creative advance.

What it is most essential to observe, in turning from sense-objects to the category of perceptual objects, is that sense-aware-

---

[15] *Knowledge*, 85.
[16] Cf. *ibid.*, 88.

ness by itself does not constitute perception. Normally, however, sense-objects are apprehended as associated in some perceptual object. For example, we seldom see the color of the horse without also 'seeing the horse,' though what we *see*, in the strict sense of the term, is only a shape-size-color complex in a situation. What we do not thus strictly see, or otherwise directly sense, in perceiving an object, is 'conveyed' by the sense-object (or associated sense-objects) given in sense-awareness. This distinction between the sensed element in the perceptual object and the element which is conveyed, illustrates the distinction between 'cognition by adjective' and 'cognition by relatedness.' What is cognized by relatedness—the unseen side of the horse, or of the moon, and the closet behind the door—is known by way of the space-time relations of events, in which what is sensed is situated, to other events which are not apprehended by sense at the time in question. What is thus conveyed by what is cognized by adjective is, characteristically, determinate as to locus but relatively vague in other aspects—as *e.g.*, we are a little vague about the color of the other side of the horse. However, without this significance of the conveyed which attaches to the element directly sensed, there would be no distinction of objects as normally perceived from sense-objects—from sense-data merely.

That normally we see houses, trees, and so on, and not merely some patch of color in a situation, Whitehead recognizes by saying that perception is primarily the positing of an object in sense-awareness, rather than a judgment. But he adds: "Judgments quickly supervene and form an important ingredient in what may be termed 'completed recognition.' "[17] What such perceptual judgments particularly concern is the situation of the object perceived in events. When this judgment of situation is correct, the object perceived is not only a perceptual object but a 'physical object.' When the judgment is incorrect—when what we see is not there where we see it—the perceptual object as perceived is a delusion. It is obvious, though Whitehead does not remark it in this context, that not only perceptual judgment but also the positing of an object in sense-awareness which does not rise

[17] *Ibid.*, 89.

to the level of conscious judgment, may on occasion have this delusive character.

It will also be sure to occur to us in this connection that the possible validity of perceptual judgment—the possibility that certain disclosures of sense may *validly* convey physical objects situated in those events to which perceptual judgment, or the habitual positings of sense-awareness, normally assigns them—depends upon some lawfulness of nature. The rest of the horse must normally be there on those occasions when the deliverances of sense, constituting what we strictly see, thus conveys an unseen side. The same will obviously be true for *any* cognition by relatedness unless what is so cognized should be *completely* vague except as to its space-time relationship with what is directly sensed.

We shall further observe that the kind of lawfulness of nature which is so called for, is not satisfied by the 'necessary' laws of space-time by which whatever has a given situation in events must stand related to *something* in the space-time relationships of 'continuous with,' 'temporally before' or 'after,' and so on. What is required is some further and contingent lawfulness; that order of nature by which, in Berkeley's terms, one deliverance of sense is 'sign of another which is to come'—*e.g.*, of something we should see if we decided to walk around the horse. In this connection, let us also remark the importance of that continuity of events and of what characterizes them which Whitehead's theory prescribes. Whatever is given is given as itself having some space-time spread, and also as 'necessarily' continuous with *something* further. Thus the atomic character of Berkeleian ideas and Humean impressions is avoided, and with it the inevitable debacle of historical empiricism in the skepticism of Hume. Whitehead's conception of the 'relatedness of nature,' correlative with 'cognition by relatedness,' is integral with his whole doctrine of 'significance.' But plainly the laws expressive of the general space-time structure of events are not enough for this. It is further required that such space-time continuities must exhibit also some more specific type of continuity; some preservation of character, or some relatedness of character, formulatable by some contingent law, if perceptual knowledge and other forms of cognition are to be brought into this account.

There are likewise further problems; not only those set by delusive perception and other forms of error, but such questions as concern the star seen now though it may have exploded two centuries ago; and what is seen as in front of us and behind the mirror, though really located behind us. Whitehead by no means ignores such questions; in fact those here alluded to are the ones he mentions. Consideration of these problems must bring us to topics more complex and difficult than those so far covered; but they are also such as will lead us to our final topic of 'scientific objects' and the nature of science itself.

First, however, let us observe what *kind* of account it is which Whitehead will offer us concerning such matters. He does not attempt to explain the fact of knowledge, or the fact of the phenomena which we observe, by any metaphysical appeal to entities more ultimate in their nature and not themselves discoverable within knowledge and by perception. Any such account of knowledge explains the known by the unknown, and can give no account of *itself*. Thus he refuses that manner of explanation which supposes objective realities, beyond what appears, as causes of the appearances in mind, which appearances are then the bases of mental 'constructions' miraculously corresponding to those objects which operate as the initial causes of these mental phenomena. He likewise repudiates the myth of a transcendent mind confronting an *an-sich* reality, whose appearances it informs by its own modes of receptivity and by imposing relations reflecting its own essential modes of understanding. Any account of knowledge he would attempt must, by his radical empiricism, be in terms of the factors of fact which are knowable as *in* nature, and not in terms of entities which, by being antecedent to natural fact in general, are incapable of being known in that manner of knowledge they are invoked to explain. Nor would he attempt to explain or justify the validity of knowledge in general in that manner which could only be done if, miraculously, we had some premises of fact antecedent to all knowledge, from which the validity of it is deducible. The fact that things exist to be known, and the fact that there is perception and things perceived, are ultimate and incapable of any explanation. The only manner of their explanation to be given is one by reference to the factors of fact *in* nature and the structure of relations of factors in constituting both nature as known and our knowledge of it. In the following he speaks of science, but what he says extends also to natural knowledge generally: ". . . science is not discussing the causes of knowledge, but the coherence of knowledge. The understanding which is sought by science is an understanding of relations within nature."[18]

First, let us observe that, as is evident already, the fact that there are any perceptible and physical objects at all, is the fact of contingent continuities in events. That there is anything identifiable to sense-awareness, and hence anything for our knowledge to be 'about,' lies in the fact of some permanence of character pervading some space-time region and recognizable from moment to moment. Without that manner of continuity there would not even be sense-objects. Second, and connected with this, there is that manner of continuity which holds between the side of the horse which we see and the unseen side. Without this further kind of continuity, there would be for us no perceptual objects as distinct from mere sense-data. Let us also note the fundamental similarity between these two modes of continuity by reason of which events present to us enduring objects, and that kind of temporal continuity of events by which they constitute a causal chain. That kind of continuity of events by which they present to us the same object may in fact be regarded as a particular kind of causal chain; a character of events, so to say, propagating itself, or more accurately, pervading a certain historical route in space-time.

Incidentally, however, and lest we fall into confusion here, let us digress for a moment to observe that it is inaccurate to speak of an object as having parts. It is a consequence of this conception of objects as constituted by the persistence of character in events that, except derivatively and through their relation

[18] *Nature*, 41.

to events in which they are situated, objects can have no parts. But if this be paradox, then the paradox is mainly linguistic, and the incurring of it is incident to the explanation of certain common-sense facts. The point is that, for example, the *disjecta membra* of a chair do not constitute a chair. The leg of the chair is 'part of the chair' only when and where it adjoins the rest of the chair; that is, only within those events which can be spatially partitioned into one part in which the leg is situated and an adjoining part which is the situation of the rest of the chair. This easily adds up to the common-sense notion that there is a chair only when and where there is the whole of the chair. The part-whole relation is a space-time relation of events involved in any situation of the chair as a whole. This also illustrates rather well that 'this chair' is an adjectival qualification of events, and designates a certain uniformity of character pervading that particular continuum which is the historical route in space-time presenting the life-history of the chair. The life-history of the leg may be longer in both directions; but while the chair endures—and the leg adjoins the rest—the situation of the leg is part of any situation of the chair. That is precisely what it means to say, "The leg of the chair is part of the chair," and this does not leave open the puzzling question whether the chair, having lost one leg after another, and finally the back, is still the same chair, or whether one leg on the woodpile is still part of the chair. An object is a permanent recognizable character of its various situations.

Let us now return to the considerations which are essential for dealing with those problems of perceptual knowledge which still remain. Another point to note is that an object may be discoverable not only by sensing it directly in its situation but also by other typical manifestations; by characters which 'reflect' its presence in the neighborhood. The cook in the kitchen is typically manifested in the dining room when dinner is before us. And the star's crossing the meridian, as observed from Washington, is typically manifested throughout the United States wherever people hear the time-signal on the radio. Indeed, if we ask here, "How big is a neighborhood",? we already know

the answer: "When I drop this chalk I shake the farthest stars"
—though beyond a limited region, a particular type of manifestation may be neither detectable nor of any importance. We here
stand in the presence of that fact which Whitehead speaks of
as the 'relatedness of nature'; that fact by reason of which objects are not merely 'cognizable by adjective' in direct perception, but 'cognizable by relatedness' through their manifestations as modifications of the characters of events distinct from,
but spatio-temporally related to, those events within which they
are situated for our direct sense-observation. This manner of
fact, Whitehead speaks of as the 'ingression of the object' into
an event. An object is said to have this relation of 'ingression
into' any event if the character of the event in question typically
manifests the existence and character of this object or—in my
own language rather than Whitehead's—if the character of the
event is evidence of the object; if the event reflects the existence
and nature of the object. It is obvious that we may say, in a sense
which is intelligible, that the object is present wherever and
whenever it manifests itself; and to overlook this fact is to risk
committing the 'fallacy of simple location.' Indeed 'situation'
is only a special and simpler type of 'ingression,' whose peculiar
character is illustrated by the cook who stays in the kitchen
though her presence there is made manifest elsewhere.

However, we must not forget here—because 'ingression of
the object' suggests the object *doing* something—that even as
restricted to its situation, 'the object' is only a character characterizing this and other events, and perhaps then and there
observable to sense. If that manifestation of an object which is
a modification of the character of an event be thought of as an
'effect' of an object, not situated in this event but in some other,
then this modification of character, perhaps observed, is 'really
due to' some other *event*; the event whose character the object
peculiarly 'is.' "The conditions which determine the nature of
events can only be furnished by other events, for there is nothing
else in nature."[19] As for the object, its situation, and the variety
of its ingressions throughout the rest of nature; we must be re-

[19] *Knowledge*, 73.

minded of the occasionalists' explanation of Cartesian doctrine: the soul is present throughout the body but peculiarly present in the mid-brain, just as God is present throughout the universe but peculiarly present in the temple of Solomon. The object is somehow present in every event whose character it qualifies— and that includes, in some manner or another, the whole manifold of events in their total relatedness—but it is peculiarly present in that event (if any) in the apprehension of which it may be 'cognized by adjective' in our sense-awareness.

In considering this manner of the relationship of events, and of objects as the characters pervading certain continuities of events in space-time, we are, obviously, considering nature in its 'causal' aspect. The event of the stone dropping into the pond manifests itself in widening circles; eventually throughout the universe. But this 'causally' propagated manifestation, is, in contrast to relation of this event to the rest of simultaneous nature, one whose 'direction' determines that dimension of nature which is *time*, and is significant of passage and becoming. As we move outward in space, following this manifestation of the dropped stone, we are coincidentally moving forward in time. And if it were a scientific 'particle' of kinematics, P, instead of a dropped stone, what we should be so concentrating upon would be 'P's kinematic future,' the 'tube of force' associated with it. It is on such a point that we find the closest affinity of Whitehead's doctrine to that of Bergson: the direction of creative advance as the time-dimension, in contrast to relations with the simultaneously enduring, as spatial dimensions of matter as inert. "There are two sides of nature, as it were, antagonistic the one to the other, and yet each essential. The one side is development in creative advance, the essential becomingness of nature. The other side is the permanence of things, the fact that nature can be recognized."[20]

Just one more point, and then we shall be ready to complete the picture of perceptual knowledge. In that qualification of an event which is the ingression of an object into it, and represents the conditioning of this event by the character of some other,

[20] *Ibid.*, 98.

there will be differences in the manner in which this event may so reflect the other event. There will be events so conditioning the one in question that they may, in this relation, be classed as 'active conditioning events.' They qualify or modify or manifest themselves in this event in a manner typical of their own character; as *e.g.*, the cook's cooking in the kitchen later modifies or is manifested in events in the dining room; or as the emission of light from the star modifies the event of the image approaching the cross-hair of the telescope; or as that event in turn modifies the events in which the time-signal is heard. Amongst such active conditioning events of the one in question, we can perhaps select one as the 'generating event' whose character is 'transmitted' as successive modifications through some series of events. (But when I here speak of one event, A, as 'modifying' another event, B, this must be understood as meaning only that the *character* of A manifests itself, in some degree or manner, in the character of B. Events cannot *do* anything to one another.) There will also be events which are passive conditions of the one in question; if they were not there, when and where they are, then the event in question would not be as it is, but they account for no modification of this event which peculiarly reflects their character. Amongst such passive conditioning events, some may be called 'transmitting events'; when the emission of light from the star conditions the event of observation at the telescope, all the events of surrounding nature are also, in some degree and manner, relevant for the final happening—since, owing to the total relatedness of events in nature, if they were not as they are, then this event would be subtly, and perhaps unobservably, different—but the events spatio-temporally intervening in the causal chain between the emission of the light and the observation at the telescope will constitute an obvious illustration of this class of transmitting events. Whitehead hardly supplies any more precise criteria for these classifications than are suggested here: it appears likely that he thought of them as suggestive for our contemplation of the different modes of significance grounded in the relatedness of events in nature, and manifested as the cognizable ingressions of objects into events in their constitution of the order of nature itself. These are factors of fact which are there to be elicited for thought. But the total order of events is all there, independently of our thinking: 'nature is closed to mind.'

The broader category of the 'ingression of objects into events,' as contrasted with the narrower category of 'situation,' which is a simpler instance of it, affords possible explanation of certain facts of perception which would otherwise offer difficulty. It is obvious that any perception of an object is an instance of the ingression of the object into the event of perception. Although Whitehead points out the impossibilities of that type of theory which would explain perception as cause-effect relation of stuff inhabiting space to a mind not itself in nature, he nevertheless does bring perception under the rubric of 'ingression,' which category includes—though it is not confined to—various modes of 'causal' relationship. In order to apply this manner of explanation, however, we must observe that the mind thus causally related to an event which is 'external to it,' must be itself some entity in nature, standing in some natural relationship to the event it apprehends. First remarking then, that Whitehead nowhere implies that mind is confined to nature but often explicitly states the contrary, we must remember that it is not mind as thus transcending its implication in the natural, but the percipient event, which figures in the account of perception. And, "The percipient event is the relevant bodily state of the observer."[21]

It thus becomes possible to explain the distinction of veridical from delusive perception, and to deal with otherwise puzzling questions about the situation, in events, of the star seen now though it no longer exists, and with the problem set by the objects perceived in a mirror. Whitehead always speaks of sense-objects as situated when and where they are sensed as being. But perception has, as we have seen, two phases, one as a primary positing in sense-awareness and another when perceptual judgment supervenes in completed recognition. Difficulty could so arise over the situation of perceived objects—seen now, or seen in a mirror—as assigned by the sense-positing of some

[21] *Nature*, 152.

primitive savage, let us say, and as assigned in the observation of a scientist. But reference to the various modes of ingression can cover all such facts.

In the first place, we must recognize that perception is not a simple relation of the percipient event to that event in which the object perceived is situated, but is subject to various conditioning by other events, such as those which spatio-temporally intervene and are transmitting events for this relationship. Thus perception represents a polyadic relation of the percipient event to others, variously and complexly conditioning the ingression into the percipient event of that character recognized as the perceptual object.

So far as the distinction of veridical and non-veridical is the question, the criterion can be given as follows:

The definition of delusiveness and non-delusiveness is sufficiently obvious, namely a perceptual object is non-delusive when it is the apparent character of an event which is itself an active condition for the appearance of that character as perceptible from all percipient events . . . The situation of a physical object is its 'generating event.'[22]

Remembering that a physical object is defined as a non-delusive perceptual object, we may note that the above passage specifies two, concurrent, criteria of veridical perception; (1) the situation of a veridically perceived object is an active, generating event for the appearance of it to, or in, the percipient event—*i.e.*, for the ingression of that object in the bodily state of the observer; and (2) a veridically perceived object has the same situation for all percipient events.

Let us further remind ourselves that the awareness of *sense-*objects is simple cognition by adjective, but that perception arises by the addition to this—whether by that positing which is primary and antecedent to judgment, or by a judgment which quickly supervenes—of something conveyed and cognized by relatedness. Looking back now to condition (1), above, of the veridical character of perception, and remembering the various modes of the ingression of objects and the conditioning of

[22] *Knowledge*, 184.

events, it seems justified to rewrite that condition as follows: For perception to be veridical, it is essential that the given appearance be ascribed (by positing or by judgment) to an object actually situated in an event which is an active and generating condition of the event of this appearance; where event O is an active condition of event A just in case the character of A typically manifests a character of O; and O is a generating condition of A just in case the character of A manifests a character of O transmitted through any series of events intervening between O and A.

I have here been a little more explicit than can fully be warranted from Whitehead's pages. But if this interpretation is correct, then the kind of account to be given of such matters as the star seen now though it no longer exists, and objects viewed in the mirror, is fairly obvious. The image of the star *is* seen now passing the cross-hair of the ocular lens of the telescope. For the further phenomena such as radio time-signals, that event is generative, and the consequent apprehension of the terrestrial time of day is veridical. But for the observer whose object of apprehension is a happening in the heavens (the star emitting the light) and not a happening in the situation of the telescope, the event in the locus of the telescope is a transmitting event, spatio-temporally intervening between the event where the star is and the percipient event. For valid perception of the star, what is cognized by adjective in looking through the telescope is correctly situated in that event which is generative for the whole series terminating in the event of this perception. Some character of the initial event is typically manifested through the series for which it is the generating event, and though typically further modified by the intervening active condition of the event in the telescope, still conditions the event of its perception in a manner constituting a manifestation of it to, or in, the percipient event.

If we should be inclined to rebel against the vocabulary of this type of explication and perhaps to consider explanation by reference to such categories as in some part verbal, then let us ask ourselves if substitution of the ambiguous terminology of

causation would suit us better. It is 'causal nature' which is here
dealt with in these categories of the relatedness of events in
nature, cognition by relatedness, significance, and the ingression
of objects into events. At least this Whiteheadian account does
not end by confronting us with the debacle of causal knowledge
in Humean skepticism, nor with the insoluble puzzle of
correspondence between appearances in minds which have no
genuine contact with external objects and objects having no
actual ingress into minds. Nor does it, as less complex forms of
direct realism characteristically do, leave us with no plausible
or even possible explanation when confronted with the facts of
delusive experience and error. Let us also remind ourselves of
the methodological character of this account. It does not attempt
—as epistemology since Descartes has persistently attempted—
to explain how knowledge is possible by some 'deduction' of the
validity of knowledge, starting from no premises of objective
fact as given, or allowing itself only such initial premises as are
vouchsafed to reason by the natural light. Instead it seeks to
elicit those relations of factors of fact which are there to be
elicited in the relatedness of nature, and are implicit in the deliverances of sense because the relation of an object perceived
to a percipient event is one instance of the general relation
objects have to events in general; and because the relation of a
percipient event to other events is likewise homologous with
relations which events within our apprehension have to one
another. There is no 'problem of knowledge' here, because there
is no inner experience which is an initial datum but not a datum
of fact, and self-consciously may doubt its own status as knowledge. Fact is the terminus of sense-awareness; until there is
sense-awareness, there is nothing to be doubted; and there is
no better kind of fact to be called knowledge.

There is, however, the distinction of 'causal nature' from
'apparent nature,' as there is the correlative distinction of cognition by relatedness from cognition by adjective.

Natural science peculiarly concerns itself with knowledge by
relatedness though, as Whitehead everywhere insists, it has no
other data than the data of perception. Specifically, its business

is to elicit those connections which obtain between continuities in the apparent character of events—continuities of sensed character, constitutive of objects ingredient in these events—and space-time relationships of the events exhibiting these sensed characters.

This long discussion brings us to the final conclusion that the concrete facts of nature are events exhibiting a certain structure in their mutual relations and certain characters of their own. The aim of science is to express the relations between their characters in terms of the mutual structural relations between the events thus characterized.[23]

Whitehead also phrases this by saying that the project of science is to explain apparent nature in terms of causal nature.

But science has also two further essential characteristics—essential to its going beyond our common and perceptual knowledge. First, it moves in the direction of simplicity and uniformity of the factors of fact which are the terms of its formulations, and toward a corresponding comprehensiveness in the laws expressing their relationships. And second, in this progression to simplicity, it is obliged to discard, as its recognized objects, the vaguely bounded and relatively impermanent physical objects identifiable by their character as apparent, in favor of permanences of character identifiable through the *relationships* of such perceptual objects.

. . . physical objects fail to satisfy the requirements of science. They lack definiteness and permanence, and are not adequate for the purposes of explanation. Now the characters of their mutual relations disclose further permanences recognizable in events and among these are the scientific objects . . .

If we follow the route of the derivation of knowledge . . . molecules and electrons are the last stage in a series of abstractions. But a fact in nature has nothing to do with the logical derivation of concepts. The concepts represent our abstract intellectual apprehension of certain permanent characters of events, just as our perception of sense-objects is our awareness of qualities of nature resulting from the shifting relations of these characters. [24]

[23] *Nature*, 167 f.
[24] *Knowledge*, 187 f.

Whitehead is primarily concerned with the objects of *physical*
science—quite naturally so since the presentation of fundamental principles of mathematical physics is one objective of this
whole account; and what we here review provides the basis of
that. The scientific objects here in mind are the physical entities
affording approximation to these scientific ideals of the permanence of objects related and the comprehensiveness of laws expressing their relationships. Whitehead speaks of the electron
as representing such a scientific object for that stage of science
in which he wrote. But the analyses he gives are, characteristically, of scientific objects in an even more elemental sense—such
entities as instants and mass-particles.

For the most part, the discussion of scientific objects belongs
to that technical part and bearing of the content of the three
books which is, perforce, omitted here. And already this essay
runs beyond appropriate length. But one topic I shall further
mention briefly because it concerns the epistemological question
how the scientific formulation of laws in terms of imperceptible
scientific objects can escape that status of the fictional and as-if
to which Whitehead has objected, saying "If it is something
else that you mean, for heaven's sake say it." This point is also
the same one raised in another quotation above, in which it is
acknowledged that 'nature at an instant' is *not* an entity in
nature, but that if this concept is to have standing in a science
which acknowledges no other basis than observable fact, it must
be *definable in terms of* entities which *are* observable factors of
fact and disclosed in deliverances of sense. An additional reason
for some brief consideration of this problem is that the general
procedure of Whitehead's attack upon it—his Method of Extensive Abstraction—is one of his signal contributions to the
theory of scientific knowledge.

Let us try to discover in advance the sailent points here, by
reference to the notion of instantaneousness already mentioned.
The scientific concept of an instant is one which arises through
the attempt to achieve a general, and generally adequate, manner of answering any question 'When?' Since such a question
may relate to an event which happens anywhere, an appropriate

form for the general type of answer will be to locate this event within a duration taken as a temporal slab of all nature. If this is the period of one day, all events so specified will be determined within twenty-four hours; and that degree of precision is adequate for many purposes. But for other purposes, it would be insufficiently precise. A more accurate determination will be to locate the event within a slice of that duration, an hour. As our questions call for greater and greater precision, we can determine progressively more precise answers by specifying a slice within the slice, and then a slice of that, and so on. We can determine the time of an event to the day, to the hour, to the minute, to the second, to the thousandth of a second . . . But in order to allow for perfect generality, we cannot admit any limit to such progressively further steps in answering questions as to exact time. And if any protagonist of an operational theory of the meaning of concepts tells us that there is a limit nevertheless, set by the necessity of some actual physical operation for determining the answer, then we may reply to him that we (or scientists) are inventive people; and when we find a pressing need for greater precision in time-determination, we shall invent an operation and devise the apparatus to determine it. We shall so indicate that it is the meaningfulness of the question which is antecedent to the operational answer, and not the other way about.

What we so observe, however, is that our concept of 'when' will never be assured of the requisite generality if we stop with any specified degree of precision; with determination of the event as within any time-slice of nature, however small. So we proceed to the limit, with the scientific ideal of an instant; of a time-slice so thin that it has no time-extension. But now we have arrived at a paradox. Our successively specified time-slices, each thinner and included in the preceding ones, are still, however small, actual entities in nature. But the limit proceeded to is no longer an actual slice and is not a natural entity, though definable as just the limit approached by this series of approximations.

This crudely suggests the Method of Extensive Abstraction,

by which Whitehead defines, first, entities which figure as elements in the 'geometry' of space-time; its 'levels,' 'rects,' 'puncts,' as well as durations and motions in their relativity to time-systems; and then proceeds to conceptual delimitation of entities more obviously connected with the scientific expression of physical facts in mathematical equations, such as 'event-particles' and 'mass-particles.'

Any adequate account of this Method of Extensive Abstraction could not be included here; that would require another essay of comparable length to this one.[25] Let us here confine ourselves to what directly concerns the epistemological status, in an account like Whitehead's, of those scientific 'idealities' which are thus definable as limits of some series of approximation the members of which are themselves identifiable as natural entities and factors of natural fact. Particularly we shall be interested in what concerns the paradox above, which in one or another form affects the definition of all scientific idealities. It is to resolution of that paradox that the method is addressed.

In understanding this, I think we may help ourselves out by reference to another matter which surely was in Whitehead's mind and could, perhaps, be regarded as a sort of mathematical model of the Method of Extensive Abstraction; namely, Dedekind's conception of the nature of numbers. Let us remind ourselves that, prior to Dedekind, the natural numbers in series, and the rational fractions, definable as pairs of natural numbers (a/b) in the dense or compact order of their fractional values, were recognized as numbers in good standing, intrinsically intelligible to mathematicians. Irrationals, however, did not share this intrinsic intelligibility, but had stood since the time of Pythagoras as a conceptual puzzle and mathematical anomaly. The illuminating discovery of Dedekind, since recognized by mathematicians as dispelling that puzzle, was that the irrationals, like $\sqrt{2}$, can be specified in terms of the series of rational num-

---

[25] The best succinct outline of it which I know of (outside of Whitehead himself) is that of Professor Nathaniel Lawrence, "Whitehead's Method of Extensive Abstraction," *Philosophy of Science*, vol. 17 (1950), 142-163. Professor Lawrence there proceeds also to a discussion of matters affecting the point to which attention is directed here.

bers alone. They can be so specified since, for every rational number, there is a corresponding 'cut' in the total series of rationals; *i.e.*, a specifiable manner of dividing the whole series into two segments such that (*a*) every member of the one segment precedes every member of the other segment, and (*b*) every member of the series belongs to one segment or the other. For any rational number, a/b, the corresponding cut divides the series into a fundamental (earlier) segment comprising all rationals preceding or 'less than' a/b, and the segment comprising the remainder of the series. No two such cuts correspond to the same rational number. But there is also such a 'cut' in the series of rationals corresponding to each irrational number; for $\sqrt{2}$, the division into a fundamental segment comprising all rational numbers whose square is less than 2, and a segment comprising all rationals the square of which exceeds 2. This cut, corresponding to $\sqrt{2}$, does not coincide with the cut corresponding to any rational number. For any rational number, a/b, there will be members of the fundamental segment approaching a/b as a limit which are not members of the series approaching $\sqrt{2}$, or *vice versa*. Each such cut is therefore uniquely determined by the series of rational numbers which approaches the limit specified by the cut. It thereupon becomes possible to *define* the real numbers, in series, as the *series of cuts* in the series of rational numbers. It is obvious that one can, alternatively, define the real numbers as the series of fundamental segments of the series of rationals. The logical structure of the concept is the same, or equivalent on all logical points, whether you speak of the limits approached — and *as* approached by the specified series — or whether you speak of the corresponding series which approaches the limit in question.

The one point to which I would direct attention—and the important point for analogy with Whitehead's method—is that if a series of natural entities (in terms of the analogy, some series of natural numbers) approaches some extra-natural and scientifically ideal entity (in terms of the analogy, an irrational number) as a limit, then you can, in the conception of this 'scientific object,' regard that particular series which approaches or converges to it as a limit as being in some sense logically equivalent to this limit which it so defines in the sense of uniquely determining.

This general mode of logical equivalence—the relation namely which holds between a series which so approaches a limit as to determine it uniquely, and the limit so approached—is one which, perhaps, awaits the attention of logicians and might profitably receive such attention. Whitehead's Method of Extensive Abstraction involves a further specification of this general type of relationship; in fact it involves more than one such further specification of it, as may be seen by examination of his particular applications of the method. If we do not altogether understand its logical character and import, at least the following point, which is the crucial one for Whitehead's theory, seems clear; the concept of the series approaching the limit gives us the concept of the limit, and there is no need to reify the limit itself as anything over and above those entities in terms of which it is so constituted for our thought.

It is in this sense of determining uniquely as a limit, that a series of durations, which are entitities in nature, may define an instant, which is no natural entity, as that entity to which they converge.

I will use the term 'moment' to mean 'all nature at an instant.' A moment . . . has no temporal extension [and hence is no natural entity], and is in this respect to be contrasted with a duration which has such extension . . .

A moment is a limit to which we approach as we confine attention to durations of minimum extension.[26]

In the context just quoted, Whitehead explains the main reason for thus progressing to limits and formulating our laws of mathematical physics in terms of such ideal scientific objects: "Natural relations among the ingredients of a duration gain in complexity as we consider durations of increasing temporal extension. Accordingly there is an approach to ideal simplicity as we approach an ideal diminution of extension."

If Whitehead speaks in conflicting ways about such scientific idealities—and I think he does; sometimes speaking, as in quota-

[26] *Nature*, 57.

tions above, so as to exclude them from nature and natural fact, insisting only that they are definable in terms of natural entities, but sometimes making other statements which imply, if they do not assert, that they are nevertheless factual ingredients in nature —then I think the resolution of the puzzle so set is suggested in the following passage concerning durations and instants:

It is evident that an abstractive set [of durations] as we pass along it [in the order from including to successively smaller and included] converges to the ideal of all nature with no temporal extension, namely, to the ideal of all nature at an instant ... Now the whole point of the procedure [the Method of Extensive Abstraction] is that the quantitative expressions of these natural properties do converge to limits though the abstractive set does not converge to any limiting duration ... Thus an abstractive set is effectively the entity meant when we consider an instant of time without temporal extension ... The difficulty is to express our meaning in terms of the immediate deliverances of sense-awareness, and I offer the above explanation as a complete solution to the problem.[27]

That is to say; the set of natural entities (the finite durations considered in their order of diminishing extent) determines and defines and '*is effectively*' the ideal limit (the instant) so determined and defined; although the durations are all of them entities in nature, however small those later in the series may be, whereas the instant is an ideal entity which is nothing in nature.[28] What so determines and defines, is in some sense equivalent to and substitutable for what is determined and defined. (The correlative point may be observed in the 'mathematical model' I have suggested above.) What is scientifically said by speaking of the ideal limit could, in some manner or another (and allowing a sufficiently horrendous complexity of statement), be said in terms of the natural entities forming the abstractive set, in the order considered. And whatever is scientifically said in terms of the limit approximated to, determines

---

[27] *Ibid.*, 61 *f*.

[28] The set of durations successively considered do not, of course, literally converge to anything; they merely are what they are, and stand in those natural relations of inclusion in which they do. It is the quantitative measure of them which literally converges to zero as a limit. On this point compare *Nature*, 81.

something correlative which can be said of natural entities in the degree of their approximation to it.

In this manner—which I have attempted to suggest though I have given no full and proper account of it—Whitehead forges the final link in the chain of connection between science and its ideally simple scientific objects on the one hand, and on the other the objects of perceptual knowledge and those deliverances of sense-awareness which are the ultimate and only possible basis of all knowledge of nature. Thus he demonstrates his thesis that the world of our sensible apprehension and common knowledge is likewise that same natural world of which science also gives account. Likewise, and at the same time, he establishes the mutual relevance of his most technical formulations of fundamental principles of physics in tensor equations, and his philosophical prolegomena which we have here reviewed and which provide both the basis for and the rigorously accurate interpretation of such technical and scientific formulations affording confirmation of them.

In conclusion, I should like to say two words concerning the relation between the conceptions set forth in these three books belonging to Whitehead's 'middle-period' and those presented in such later writings as *Process and Reality*. There is, first, that kind of difference which reflects his self-imposed restriction of topic in these earlier writings. He confines himself here to the metaphysics, or 'pan-physics,' of nature; and he defines nature by reference to sense-awareness, in contradistinction to all other modes of apprehension, including the evaluative and any discernment of that more comprehensive and more concrete reality from which nature is an abstraction. So much, he says explicitly.

There is also, comparing later with earlier, much new vocabulary, making it difficult to determine whether what the earlier categories cover is still there, under some new designation or included in some different classification, or whether the older conceptions have been displaced, in whole or in part. That there is in the later an enrichment of his thinking, goes without saying. For a mind like Whitehead's that must be the case over any lapse of time.

It is, however, my opinion that divergence of his conceptions in these two periods could easily be exaggerated. I venture to think that there is little, if anything, basically important in the earlier, which is merely abandoned in the later. But what I would particularly suggest is that the prominence of conceptions, in *Process and Reality*, which cannot be found explicitly expressed in the three books we study, would hardly substantiate the inference that these later-formulated conceptions were simply not in his mind in the earlier period. There are frequent, though usually brief, references in the three books here discussed which would seem to indicate that it is the restriction of their topic which is the principal consideration affecting this kind of difference of the earlier from the later writings. The following are amongst them:

Nature is nothing else than the deliverance of sense-awareness.[29]

I also take the homogeneity of thought about nature as excluding any reference to moral or aesthetic values whose apprehension is vivid in proportion to self-conscious activity. The values of nature are perhaps the key to the metaphysical synthesis of existence. But such a synthesis is exactly what I am not attempting.[30]

Nature is an abstraction from something more concrete.[31]

. . . memory is an escape from transience . . . memory is a disengagement of the mind from the mere passage of nature; for what has passed for nature has not passed for mind . . . We may speculate, if we like, that the alliance of the passage of mind with the passage of nature arises from their both sharing in some ultimate character of passage which dominates all being.[32]

Finally there are the words with which Whitehead concludes the first of these three books, *The Principles of Natural Knowledge:*

So far as direct observation is concerned all that we know of the essential relations of life in nature is stated in two short poetic phrases. The obvious aspect by Tennyson.

[29] *Nature,* 185.
[30] *Ibid.,* 5.
[31] *Relativity,* 63.
[32] *Nature,* 68 f.

"Blow, bugle, blow, set the wild echoes flying,
And answer, echoes, answer, dying, dying, dying."

Namely, Bergson's élan vital and its relapse into matter.
And Wordsworth with more depth,

"The music in my heart I bore,
Long after it was heard no more."

C. I. LEWIS

DEPARTMENT OF PHILOSOPHY
HARVARD UNIVERSITY

BIBLIOGRAPHY OF THE WRITINGS OF
ALFRED NORTH WHITEHEAD

Published through January 3, 1951
(With Selected Reviews)

Compiled by
VICTOR LOWE
and
ROBERT C. BALDWIN

PREFATORY NOTE

THE entries in this Bibliography are arranged chronologically; except that, within every year, books are listed before articles.

We have endeavored to adapt to the particular circumstances of a Whitehead bibliography the general plan followed in the preceding volume of this *Library*. The chief departure consists in including under the entries for Whitehead's books a list of selected reviews. Such a list by its utility amply justifies itself. But, to keep the list in its proper place as part of a Bibliography of *Whitehead's* writings, it has been necessary to exclude all discussions and critical articles on Whitehead, however valuable. Their compilation must be another project. Among reviews, only those obviously possessing either a substantial general utility or a special significance have been included. Their arrangement is alphabetical.

The unusual character of a bibliographical project concerned with Whitehead's writings consists in the relatively small number of short pieces to be found. It is by shunning, for the most part, the writing of such pieces that Whitehead has been able to produce books like the *Universal Algebra, Principia Mathematica, Process and Reality*. During his life in England he delivered many political and educational speeches, usually extemporaneous and not recorded. We have nevertheless made an effort to find records of Whitehead's speeches, as well as we could during wartime and from this side of the Atlantic. We shall appreciate having omissions brought to our attention, or to that of the editor of this *Library*.

We are grateful first of all to Professor Whitehead and to Mrs. Whitehead for their kindness in answering question after question; then to their daughter, Miss Jessie M. Whitehead, of the Harvard College Library, who advised us on innumerable points and herself uncovered her father's earliest writings. Dr.

Homer Halvorson, also of the Harvard College Library, various members of the staff of the Yale University Library, and, in England, Miss Dorothy Emmet of the University of Manchester, gave invaluable assistance. Our first knowledge of some items and reviews came from the "Bibliography of Symbolic Logic," compiled by Professor Alonzo Church and published in Vol. I of the *Journal of Symbolic Logic*. We cannot begin to thank the large number of persons who responded to our inquiries; but we must specifically acknowledge the coöperation received from Professor Whitehead's publishers here and abroad.

VICTOR LOWE
ROBERT C. BALDWIN

SYRACUSE UNIVERSITY
THE UNIVERSITY OF CONNECTICUT
November 1, 1941

NOTE TO THE REVISED EDITION

PROFESSOR WHITEHEAD WROTE little in the six years between the first publication of this Bibliography and his death on December 30, 1947. His widow has informed me, through Professor W. V. Quine, that all the unpublished manuscripts which existed at that time were destroyed at his own request. They probably represented, in the main, work done from ten to fifty years earlier. Concerning his work on a fourth volume of *Principia Mathematica*, which was to have been written by him alone, Professor Whitehead seems to have felt that the results of most value were either sufficiently contained in or superseded by the published writings which are listed below as 1916-2, 1919-1, 1920-1, 1922-1, and 1929-1 (Part IV).

The differences between the Bibliography of 1941 and the present revision consist, then, chiefly—though not entirely—in the listing of new editions, translations, and partial reprints. Reprints of less than a whole Section of a Whitehead chapter have not been included.

Without the help of two of my graduate students, Harry M. Bracken and H. Lynn Womack, this edition of the Bibliography could not have been completed. Mr. Womack did so much research at the Library of Congress, and collaborated so much in the final revision, that he should really be considered co-compiler. Among those who answered my inquiries, I am particularly grateful to Professor Paul Weiss of Yale, Mr. Emerson Buchanan of the Columbia University Library, and Professor Whitehead's publishers. I have also to thank Mr. W. Edward Cushen of the University of Edinburgh for information volunteered; and Professor Quine and Mrs. Whitehead for the facts about the disposition of unpublished manuscripts.

VICTOR LOWE

Johns Hopkins University
January 4, 1951

749

WRITINGS OF ALFRED NORTH WHITEHEAD
TO NOVEMBER, 1941 (With Selected Reviews)

1879-1880

1. EDITORIALS, in the *Shirburnian Magazine*. (A. N. Whitehead, editor during the school year 1879-80: Sherborne School, Dorset, England.) Unsigned.

1886

1. A CELEBRITY AT HOME. The Clerk of the Weather. *Cambridge Review*, v. 7, no. 167, Feb. 10, 1886, pp. 202-203.
Signed "W."

2. DAVY JONES. *Cambridge Review*, v. 7, no. 174, May 12, 1886, pp. 311-312.
Signed "W."

1888

1. ON THE MOTION OF VISCOUS INCOMPRESSIBLE FLUIDS. A Method of Approximation. *Quart. Jour. of Pure and Applied Math.*, v. 23, 1888, pp. 78-93.

2. SECOND APPROXIMATIONS TO VISCOUS FLUID MOTION. A Sphere Moving Steadily in a Straight Line. *Quart. Jour. of Pure and Applied Math.*, v. 23, 1888, pp. 143-152.

1895

1. PROPOSED EXTENSION OF THE PADDOCKS. By A. N. Whitehead, J. Ward, and R. J. Glazebrook, 4 March, 1895, and R. St. J. Parry, 7 March, 1895. 3 pieces. Cambridge, 1895.
Concerns land owned by Trinity College, Cambridge.

The bibliographers have not seen this item. The evidence indicates that, though printed, it was probably not published.

1898

1. A TREATISE ON UNIVERSAL ALGEBRA, with Applications. V. 1, 1898 (no others published). Cambridge, Cambridge University Press. xxvi, 586 pp.

751

Contents: Preface—*Bk. I. Principles of Algebraic Symbolism.* I. On the Nature of a Calculus—II. Manifolds—III. Principles of Universal Algebra.

Bk. II. The Algebra of Symbolic Logic. I. The Algebra of Symbolic Logic—II. The Algebra of Symbolic Logic (cont.)—III. Existential Expressions—IV. Application to Logic—V. Propositional Interpretation.

Bk. III. Positional Manifolds. I. Fundamental Propositions—II. Straight Lines and Planes—III. Quadrics—IV. Intensity.

Bk. IV. The Calculus of Extension. I. Combinatorial Multiplication—II. Regressive Multiplication—III. Supplements—IV. Descriptive Geometry—V. Descriptive Geometry of Conics and Cubics—VI. Matrices.

Bk. V. Extensive Manifolds of Three Dimensions. I. Systems of Forces—II. Groups of Systems of Forces—III. Invariants of Groups—IV. Matrices and Forces.

Bk. VI. Theory of Metrics. I. Theory of Distance—II. Elliptic Geometry—III. Extensive Manifolds and Elliptic Geometry—IV. Hyperbolic Geometry—V. Hyperbolic Geometry (cont.)—VI. Kinematics in Three Dimensions—VII. Curves and Surfaces—VIII. Transition to Parabolic Geometry.

Bk. VII. Application of the Calculus of Extension to Geometry. I. Vectors—II. Vectors (cont.)—III. Curves and Surfaces—IV. Pure Vector Formulae.

Reviews: L. Couturat: *Revue de Métaphysique et de Morale,* v. 18, 1900, pp. 323-362; A. MacFarlane: *Science,* n.s., v. 9, 1899, pp. 324-328; G. B. Mathews: *Nature,* v. 58, 1898, pp. 385-386.

2. The Geodesic Geometry of Surfaces in non-Euclidean Space. *Proc. London Math. Soc.,* v. 29, 1897-98, Part I, pp. 275-324.

Pp. 322-324 are an Appendix by W. Burnside.

Noticed in: *Jahrbuch über d. Fortschritte d. Math.,* v. 29, 1898, p. 413.

1899

1. Sets of Operations in Relation to Groups of Finite Order. Abstract only published: *Proc. Royal Soc. of London,* v. 64, 1898-99, pp. 319-320.

"Communicated by Prof. A. R. Forsyth, F.R.S. Received Jan. 19,—read Feb. 2, 1899."

Constructs an Algebra of Groups of Finite Order, which has many affinities with the Algebra of Symbolic Logic set forth in the *Treatise on Universal Algebra* (1898).

1901

1. Memoir on the Algebra of Symbolic Logic. *Amer. Jour. of Math.,* v. 23, no. 2, 1901, pp. 139-165; and no. 4, pp. 297-316.

Captions: Preface—Part I: The Theory of Primes—Part II: The Theory of Substitutions.

1902

1. ON CARDINAL NUMBERS. *Amer. Jour. of Math.*, v. 24, no. 4, 1902, pp. 367-394.

Captions: Preface—Sect. I. Account of Peano's Logical Symbolism—II. Russell's "Logic of Relations"—III. On Finite and Infinite Cardinal Numbers—IV.—V. On Powers, Combinations and Permutations.

Preface states: "Section III is entirely due to Russell,* and is written by him throughout."

1903

1. THE LOGIC OF RELATIONS, LOGICAL SUBSTITUTION GROUPS, AND CARDINAL NUMBERS. *Amer. Jour. of Math.*, v. 25, no. 2, 1903, pp. 157-178.

Captions: Preface—Sect. I—Sect. II. The Cardinal Numbers of Various Classes—III. Orders of Various Logical Substitution Groups—IV. The Group of Primary Prime Substitutions.

Dated July 4, 1901.

1904

1. THEOREMS ON CARDINAL NUMBERS. *Amer. Jour. of Math.*, v. 26, no. 1, 1904, pp. 31-32.

Dated January, 1903.

1905

1. NOTE. *Revue de Métaphysique et de Morale*, v. 13, 1905, pp. 916-917.

Written in correction of Boutroux's interpretation (*ibid.*) of Whitehead's views on the relation of Logic to Analysis.

1906

1. THE AXIOMS OF PROJECTIVE GEOMETRY. Cambridge, Cambridge University Press, 1906. (*Cambridge Tracts in Mathematics and Mathematical Physics*, No. 4) viii, 64 pp.

Contents: Preface—I. Fundamental Considerations—II. Axioms of Classification—III. Projectivity—IV. Order—V. Quadrangular Involutions—VI. Linear Numeration Systems—VII. Coördinates—VIII. Existence Theorems.

Translation: French: Chap. I only, under the title, "Introduction logique à la géométrie," *Revue de Métaphysique et de Morale*, v. 15, 1907, pp. 34-39.

REVIEWS: See 1907—*1.*

---

* A note at the beginning of Sect. III adds: "With the exception of some of the notes."

2. On Mathematical Concepts of the Material World. *Philos. Transactions, Roy. Soc. of London,* series A, v. 205, 1906, pp. 465-525.

"Received Sept. 22,—Read Dec. 7, 1905."

Captions: Preface—Part I. (i) General Considerations. (ii) Explanation of Symbolism—II. The Punctual Concepts—III. (i) General Explanations of Linear Concepts. (ii) The Theory of Interpoints. (iii) Concept IV—IV. (i) The Theory of Dimensions. (ii) Concept V.

Reprint: Preface only (with one sentence omitted), as "Abstract," in *Proc. Royal Soc. of London,* series A, v. 77, 1906, pp. 290-291.

1907

1. The Axioms of Descriptive Geometry. Cambridge, Cambridge University Press, 1907. (*Cambridge Tracts in Mathematics and Mathematical Physics,* No. 5.) viii, 74 pp.

Contents: Preface—I. Formulations of the Axioms—II. The Associated Projective Space—III. Ideal Points—IV. General Theory of Correspondence—V. Axioms of Congruence—VI. Infinitesimal Rotations—VII. The Absolute—VIII. Metrical Geometry.

Preface states: "This tract is written in connection with the previous tract, . . . on Projective Geometry" [1906—*1*].

Reviews: (with *The Axioms of Projective Geometry*) F.S.M.: *Math. Gazette,* v. 4, pp. 287-290.

1910-1913

1. (With Bertrand Russell) Principia Mathematica. Cambridge, Cambridge University Press, 1910-1913; v. I, 1910; v. II, 1912; v. III, 1913.

Ed. 2, Camb. Univ. Press, 1925-1927.

Cf. analyzed entries under 1910, 1912, 1913.

Reviews: (Of ed. 1, v. I) M. R. Cohen: *Philos. Rev.,* v. 21, 1912, pp. 87-91; (Of the same) P. E. B. Jourdain: *Cambridge Rev.,* v. 33, 1911, pp. 7-9; (Of the same) C. J. Keyser: *Science,* n.s., v. 35, 1912, pp. 106-110 (reprinted in Keyser, *The Human Worth of Rigorous Thinking,* pp. 215-217); (Of ed. 1, v. I, II) Henri Dufumier: *Revue de Métaphysique et de Morale,* v. 20, 1912, pp. 538-566; (Of the same) G. Peano: *Bollettino di bibliografia e storia delle scienze matematiche* (Turin), v. 15, 1913, pp. 47-53, 75-81; (Of ed. 1, v. III) P. E. B. Jourdain: *Jahrbuch über d. Fortschritte d. Math.,* v. 44 (for 1913, published 1918), pp. 68-71; (Of ed. 2, v. I) B. A. Bernstein: *Bull. Amer. Math. Soc.,* v. 32, 1926, pp. 711-713; (Of the same) F. P. Ramsey: *Nature,* v. 116, 1925, pp. 127-128, and *Mind,* n.s., v. 34, 1925, pp. 506-507; (Of the same) H. M. Sheffer: *Isis,* v. 8, 1926, pp. 226-231; (Of ed. 2, v. II, III) Alonzo Church: *Bull. Amer. Math. Soc.,* v. 34, 1928, pp. 237-240; (Of the same) C. H. Langford: *Isis,* v. 10, 1928, pp. 513-519;

(Of ed. 2, v. I-III) Rudolf Carnap: *Erkenntnis*, v. 2, 1931-32, pp. 73-75; (Of the same) C. I. Lewis: *Amer. Math. Monthly*, v. 35, 1928, pp. 200-205.

1910

1. (With Bertrand Russell) PRINCIPIA MATHEMATICA, v. I. Cambridge, Cambridge University Press, 1910. xiii, 666 pp.

Ed. 2, Camb. Univ. Press, 1925. xlvi, 674 pp. Pp. xiii-xlvi comprise "Introduction to the Second Edition." Pp. 635-666 are new Appendices (App. A: The Theory of Deduction for Propositions containing Apparent Variables; App. B: Mathematical Induction; App. C: Truth-Functions and others).† "Except as regards misprints and minor errors," the text itself is unchanged from the First Ed.

Contents: Preface—*Introduction*. Chap. I. Preliminary Explanations of Ideas and Notations—II. The Theory of Logical Types—III. Incomplete Symbols.

Part I. Mathematical Logic. Sect. A. (*1-*5) The Theory of Deduction—B. (*9-*14) Theory of Apparent Variables—C. (*20-*25) Classes and Relations —D. (*30-*38) Logic of Relations—E. (*40-*43) Products and Sums of Classes.

Part II. Prolegomena to Cardinal Arithmetic. Sect. A (*50-*56) Unit Classes and Couples—B. (*60-*65) Sub-Classes, Sub-Relations, and Relative Types —C. (*70-*74) One-Many, Many-One, and One-One Relations—D. (*80-*88) Selections—E. (*90-*97) Inductive Relations.

Translation: German: Introduction only, as *Einführung in d. math. Logik (die Einleitung d. 'Principia Mathematica')*. Übertr. v. Hans Mokre. Munich (now Berlin), Drei Masken Verlag, 1932. viii, 167 pp.

For reviews, see entry under 1910-1913.

2. (With Bertrand Russell) NON-EUCLIDEAN GEOMETRY. Division VI of article, "Geometry," *Encyclopædia Britannica*, ed. 11, v. 11, pp. 724-730. (Cambridge, Cambridge University Press, 1910.)

3. AXIOMS OF GEOMETRY. Division VII of article, "Geometry," *Encyclopædia Britannica*, ed. 11, v. 11, pp. 730-736. (Cambridge, Cambridge University Press, 1910.)

1911

1. AN INTRODUCTION TO MATHEMATICS. (No. 15 in the *Home University Library of Modern Knowledge*.) London, Williams and Norgate; New York, Henry Holt and Co., 1911. 256 pp.

Published in England from 1932 to 1937 (date of last impression) by Thornton Butterworth, Ltd. Now published in England by Oxford University Press.

Contents: I. The Abstract Nature of Mathematics—II. Variables—III. Methods of Application—IV. Dynamics—V. The Symbolism of Mathematics—VI.

† Concerning the authorship of this Introduction and these appendices, see 1926-2, below.

Generalizations of Number—VII. Imaginary Numbers—VIII. Imaginary Numbers (cont.)—IX. Co-ordinate Geometry—X. Conic Sections—XI. Functions—XII. Periodicity in Nature—XIII. Trigonometry—XIV. Series—XV. The Differential Calculus—XVI. Geometry—XVII. Quantity—Bibliography——Note on the Study of Mathematics.

Translation: Icelandic: *Stærdfrædin.* Tr. by Gudm. Finnbogason. Reykjavik, Ísafoldarprentsmidja H. F., 1931.

REVIEWS: Unsigned: *Athenaeum,* v. 2, no. 4367, 1911, pp. 48-49.

2. MATHEMATICS. *Encyclopædia Britannica,* ed. 11, v. 17, pp. 878-883. (Cambridge, Cambridge University Press, 1911.)

Captions: Critical Questions—Definition of Mathematics—Applied Mathematics—Synopsis of Existing Developments of Pure Mathematics—Synopsis of Existing Developments of Applied Mathematics.

Reprint: With very slight omissions, under the title, "Mathematics, Nature of," in ed. 14, v. 15, pp. 85-89. (*Encycl. Brit.,* London and New York, 1929.)

1912

1. (With Bertrand Russell) PRINCIPIA MATHEMATICA, v. II. Cambridge, Cambridge University Press, 1912. xxxiv, 772 pp.

Ed. 2. (unaltered): Camb. Univ. Press, 1927. xxxi, 742 pp.

Contents: Prefatory Statement of Symbolic Conventions—*Part III. Cardinal Arithmetic.* Sect. A. (*100-*106) Definition and Logical Properties of Cardinal Numbers—B. (*110-*117) Addition, Multiplication and Exponentiation —C. (*118-*126) Finite and Infinite.

Part IV. Relation-Arithmetic. Sect. A. (*150-*155) Ordinal Similarity and Relation-Numbers—B. (*160-*166) Addition of Relations, and the Product of Two Relations—C. (*170-*177) The Principle of First Differences, and the Multiplication and Exponentiation of Relations—D. (*180-*186) Arithmetic of Relation-Numbers.

Part V. Series. Sect. A. (*200-*208) General Theory of Series—B. (*210-*217) On Sections, Segments, Stretches, and Derivatives—C. (*230-*234) On Convergence, and the Limits of Functions.

On p. viii is a list of Additional Errata to Vol. I.

For reviews, see entry under 1910-1913.

2. (With Bertrand Russell) PRINCIPIA MATHEMATICA, v. III. Cambridge, Cambridge University Press, 1912. x, 491 pp.

Ed. 2 (unaltered) Camb. Univ. Press, 1927. viii, 491 pp.

Contents: *Part V. Series (cont.).* Sect. D. (*250-*259) Well-ordered Series— E. (*260-*265) Finite and Infinite Series and Ordinals—F. (*270-*276) Compact Series, Rational Series, and Continuous Series.

Part VI. Quantity. Sect. A. (*300-*314) Generalization of Number—B.

(*330-*337) Vector-Families—C. (*350-*359) Measurement—D. (*370-*375) Cyclic Families.

On p. x, a list of Additional Errata to Volumes I and II.

For reviews, see entry under 1910-1913.

3. THE PRINCIPLES OF MATHEMATICS IN RELATION TO ELEMENTARY TEACHING. *Proc. of the Fifth International Congress of Mathematicians* (Cambridge, England, Aug. 22-28, 1912), v. 2, pp. 449-454. (Cambridge, Cambridge University Press, 1913.)

A communication to Sect. IV (Philosophy and Didactics) of the Congress.

Reprints: *L'Enseignement Math.*, v. 15, 1913, pp. 105-111, followed by a résumé in French, pp. 111-112; as Chap. V in *The Organisation of Thought* (1917). The reference to this address in the Preface to *The Aims of Education and Other Essays* (1929) is an error. It is not reprinted in that volume.

4. THE PLACE OF MATHEMATICS IN A LIBERAL EDUCATION. *Jour. of the Assn. of Teachers of Mathematics for the Southeastern Part of England*, v. 1, no. 1, 1912.

Presidential address at the inaugural meeting at Tonbridge, Nov. 27, 1911.

[The bibliographers have not seen this item. It is probably available only in the library of the British Museum.]

1913

1. PRESIDENTIAL ADDRESS TO THE LONDON BRANCH OF THE MATHEMATICAL ASSOCIATION. *Math. Gazette*, v. 7, no. 104, March, 1913, pp. 87-94.

Reprints: As Chap. IV, with the title, "The Mathematical Curriculum," in *The Organisation of Thought* (1917); as Chap. VI, also with that title, in *The Aims of Education and Other Essays* (1929).

1914

1. REPORT OF THE COUNCIL OF THE ROYAL SOCIETY OF LONDON. (A. N. Whitehead, member of the Council.) *Year-Book of the Royal Soc.*, 1914, pp. 177-187.

Presented to the Society at the Anniversary Meeting, Dec. 1, 1913.

1915

1. REPORT OF THE COUNCIL OF THE ROYAL SOCIETY OF LONDON. (A. N. Whitehead, member of the Council.) *Year-Book of the Royal Soc.* 1915, pp. 176-185.

Presented to the Society at the Anniversary Meeting, Nov., 1914.

2. SPACE, TIME, AND RELATIVITY. *Proc. of the Aristotelian Soc.*, n.s., v. 16, 1915-16, pp. 104-129.

Read before Sect. A (Mathematical and Physical Science) of the Manchester meeting of the British Assn. for the Advancement of Science, 1915; and later, with an appended Commentary, before the Aristotelian Society.

Reprints: As Chap. VIII, in *The Organisation of Thought* (1917); as Chap. X, in *The Aims of Education and Other Essays* (1929), with omissions.

1916

1. THE AIMS OF EDUCATION. A Plea for Reform. *Math. Gazette*, v. 8, Jan., 1916, pp. 191-203.

Presidential Address to the Mathematical Assn. [England], Jan., 1916.

Reprints: As Chap. I, in *The Organisation of Thought* (1917); as Chap. I, in *The Aims of Education and Other Essays* (1929), with omissions; *New Republic*, v. 58, 1929, pp. 244-246, with omissions.

2. LA THÉORIE RELATIONNISTE DE L'ESPACE. *Revue de Métaphysique et de Morale*, v. 23, May, 1916, pp. 423-454.

Read at Le Premier Congrès de Philosophie mathématique, Paris, April 8, 1914. A notice of the discussion appears in *L'Enseignement Math.*, v. 16, 1914, pp. 55-56, 375-376.

3. THE ORGANISATION OF THOUGHT. *Report of the 86th Meeting of the British Assn. for the Advancement of Science* (held at New-castle-on-Tyne), 1916, pp. 355-365.

Presidential address to Sect. A (Mathematical and Physical Science) of the Assn.; also read subsequently before the Aristotelian Society (Dec. 18, 1916).

Reprints: *Proc. of the Aristotelian Soc.*, n.s., v. 17, 1916-17, pp. 58-76; *Nature*, v. 98, Sept. 28, 1916, pp. 80-81, abridged by omission of the "outline" of "relevant features of modern logic"*; *Science*, n.s., v. 44, Sept. 22, 1916, pp. 409-419; *Scientific American Supplement*, v. 83, June, 1917, pp. 338-339, 366, with sub-title, "The basis of organized action"; as Chap. VI in *The Organisation of Thought* (1917); as Chap. VIII in *The Aims of Education and Other Essays* (1929), with slight omissions.

1917

1. THE ORGANISATION OF THOUGHT, EDUCATIONAL AND SCIENTIFIC. London, Williams and Norgate, 1917. viii, 228 pp.

Published in America by J. B. Lippincott Co., Philadelphia, 1917.

Contents: Preface—I. The Aims of Education (reprint of 1916-*1*)—II. Tech-

---

* In *The Organisation of Thought*, this is pp. 116-131; in *The Aims of Education and Other Essays*, pp. 163-177.

nical Education and Its Relation to Science and Literature (1917-2)—III. A Polytechnic in War-Time (Address at the Prize Distribution, Borough Polytechnic Institute, Southwark, Feb., 1917)—IV. The Mathematical Curriculum (1913-1)—V. The Principles of Mathematics in Relation to Elementary Teaching (1912-3)—VI. The Organisation of Thought (1916-3)—VII. The Anatomy of Some Scientific Ideas—VIII. Space, Time, and Relativity (1915-2).

Reprints: Chaps. I, II, IV, VI, VII, VIII, as Chaps. I, IV, VI, VIII, IX, X, in *The Aims of Education and Other Essays* (1929), with some omissions.

REVIEWS: P. E. B. Jourdain: *Mind*, n.s., v. 27, 1918, pp. 244-247. C. J. Keyser: *Science*, n.s., v. 47, Feb. 15, 1918, pp. 171-173.

2. TECHNICAL EDUCATION AND ITS RELATION TO SCIENCE AND LITERATURE. *Technical Jour.*, v. 10, Jan., 1917, pp. 59-74.

Presidential address to the Mathematical Assn. [Eng.], January, 1917.

Reprints: *Math. Gazette*, v. 9, no. 128, March, 1917, pp. 20-33; as Chap. II, in *The Organisation of Thought* (1917); as Chap. IV, in *The Aims of Education and Other Essays* (1929), with very slight omissions.

3. LETTER TO THE EDITOR. *Mathematical Gazette*, v. 9, no. 127, Jan., 1917, p. 14.

Signed on behalf of the Mathematical Assn. by A. N. Whitehead, President, and A. W. Siddons, Chairman of the Teaching Committee. Dated Nov., 1916.

1918

1. GRAPHICAL SOLUTION FOR HIGH-ANGLE FIRE. *Proc. of the Royal Soc. of London*, series A, v. 94, 1918, pp. 301-307.

1919

1. AN ENQUIRY CONCERNING THE PRINCIPLES OF NATURAL KNOWLEDGE. Cambridge, Cambridge University Press, 1919. xii, 200 pp.

Ed. 2, Camb. Univ. Press, 1925. xiv, 207 pp.

Contents: Preface—*Part I. The Traditions of Science*. I. Meaning—II. The Foundations of Dynamical Physics—III. Scientific Relativity—IV. Congruence.

Part II. The Data of Science. V. The Natural Elements—VI. Events—VII. Objects.

Part III. The Method of Extensive Abstraction. VIII. Principles of the Method of Extensive Abstraction—IX. Durations, Moments, and Time-Systems—X. Finite Abstractive Elements—XI. Points and Straight Lines—XII. Normality and Congruence—XIII. Motion.

Part IV. The Theory of Objects. XIV. The Location of Objects—XV. Material Objects—XVI. Causal Components—XVII. Figures—XVIII. Rhythms.

Preface to Second Edition is as follows: "Since the publication of the first edition of this book in 1919, the various topics contained in it have been also considered by me in *The Concept of Nature* (Camb. Univ. Press, 1920) and in *The Principle of Relativity* (Camb. Univ. Press, 1922). I hope in the immediate future to embody the standpoint of these volumes in a more complete metaphysical study. A few notes have been appended to this edition [pp. 201-207] to elucidate obscurities, and a few slips in the text have been corrected."

REVIEWS: C. D. Broad: *Hibbert Jour.*, v. 18, 1920, pp. 397-406, and *Mind*, n.s., v. 29, 1920, pp. 216-231; H. T. Costello: *Jour. of Philos.*, v. 17, 1920, pp. 326-334; G. D. Hicks: *Nature*, v. 105, June 10, 1920, pp. 446-448; T. de Laguna: *Philos. Rev.*, v. 29, 1920, pp. 269-275.

2. ADDRESS ON FOUNDER'S DAY. Stanley Technical Trade School, South Norwood, London. Feb. 1, 1919. Coventry and Son, South Norwood, S.E., England. 8 pp.

"Printed for private circulation only."

3. SYMPOSIUM:—TIME, SPACE, AND MATERIAL: ARE THEY, AND IF SO IN WHAT SENSE, THE ULTIMATE DATA OF SCIENCE? By A. N. Whitehead, Sir Oliver Lodge, J. W. Nicholson, Henry Head, Mrs. Adrian Stephen, and H. Wildon Carr. *Aristotelian Soc., Supplementary Vol. 2*, "Problems of Science and Philosophy," 1919, pp. 44-108.

Whitehead's contribution comprises pp. 44-57.

4. A REVOLUTION IN SCIENCE. *Nation* (London), v. 26, Nov. 15, 1919, pp. 232-233.

Reports and discusses the announcement by the Astronomer Royal that the photographs of the eclipse of the sun, taken by the British expeditions, confirm Einstein's prediction as to the path of light rays in a gravitational field.

Reprint: *Educational Rev.*, v. 59, Feb., 1920, pp. 148-153.

5. FUNDAMENTAL PRINCIPLES IN EDUCATION. *Report of the 87th Meeting of the British Assn. for the Advancement of Science* (Bournemouth), 1919, p. 361.

An abridgment of the address with which Whitehead opened a discussion of this subject before Section L (Education) of the Association.

1920

1. THE CONCEPT OF NATURE. Tarner Lectures delivered in Trinity College, November, 1919. Cambridge, Cambridge University Press, 1920. viii, 202 pp.

Described in the Preface as a companion volume to 1919—1.

Contents: Preface—I. Nature and Thought—II. Theories of the Bifurcation of Nature—III. Time—IV. The Method of Extensive Abstraction—V. Space and Motion—VI. Congruence—VII. Objects—VIII. Summary—IX. The Ultimate Physical Concepts—Note: On the Greek Concept of a Point—Note: On Significance and Infinite Events.

REVIEWS: G. D. Birkhoff: *Bull. Amer. Math. Soc.*, v. 28, 1922, pp. 219-221; H. Wildon Carr: *Philos. Magazine*, 6th Series, v. 40, 1920, pp. 389-392; Hans Driesch: *Kantstudien*, v. 26, 1921, pp. 204-205; E. B. McGilvary: *Philos. Rev.*, v. 30, 1921, pp. 500-507; A. E. Taylor: *Mind*, n.s., v. 30, 1921, pp. 76-83.

2. EINSTEIN's THEORY; An Alternative Suggestion. *The* (London) *Times Educational Supplement*, Feb. 12, 1920, p. 83.

1921

1. REPORT OF COMMITTEE: Appointed by the Prime Minister to Inquire into the Position of Classics in the Educational System of the United Kingdom. London, His Majesty's Stationery Office, 1921. xxii, 308 pp.

The Marquess of Crewe, Chairman. A. N. Whitehead, as a member of this Committee, contributed to the Report.

2. SCIENCE IN GENERAL EDUCATION. *Proc. of Second Congress of Universities of the Empire* (London, G. Bell & Sons, 1921), pp. 31-39.

1922

1. THE PRINCIPLE OF RELATIVITY, With Applications to Physical Science. Cambridge, Cambridge University Press, 1922. xii, 190 pp.

Contents: Preface—*Part I. General Principles.* I. Prefatory Explanations—II. The Relatedness of Nature—III. Equality—IV. Some Principles of Physical Science (reprint of 1922-4).

Part II. Physical Applications. V. The Equations of Motion—VI. On the Formula for dJ^2—VII. Permanent Gravitational Fields—VIII. Apparent Mass and the Spectral Shift—IX. Planetary Motion—X. Electromagnetic Equations—XI. Gravitation and Light Waves—XII. Temperature Effects on Gravitational Forces—XIII. The Electrostatic Potential and Spectral Shift—XIV. The Limb Effect—XV. Permanent Directions of Vibration and the Doubling Effect—XVI. Steady Electromagnetic Fields—XVII. The Moon's Motion.

Part III. Elementary Theory of Tensors. XVIII. Fundamental Notions—XIX. Elementary Properties—XX. The Process of Restriction—XXI. Tensors of the Second Order—XXII. The Galilean Tensor—XXIII. The Differentiation of Tensor Components—XXIV. Some Important Tensors.

REVIEWS: C. D. Broad: *Mind*, n.s., v. 32, April, 1923, pp. 211-219; C. P. S. [Charles Percy Sanger]: *New Statesman*, v. 20, Feb. 10, 1923, pp. 546-548; Unsigned: *Nature*, v. 111, May 26, 1923, pp. 697-699.

2. THE RHYTHM OF EDUCATION. An address delivered to the Training College Association. London, Christophers, 1922. 30 pp.
Reprint: As Chap. II, in *The Aims of Education and Other Essays* (1929).

3. DISCUSSION: THE IDEALISTIC INTERPRETATION OF EINSTEIN'S THEORY. By H. Wildon Carr, T. P. Nunn, A. N. Whitehead, and Dorothy Wrinch. *Proc. Aristotelian Soc.*, n.s., v. 22, 1921-22, pp. 123-138.
Whitehead's contribution, which is a criticism of Carr's, comprises pp. 130-134.

4. SOME PRINCIPLES OF PHYSICAL SCIENCE. A lecture dedicated to Professor Charlotte Angas Scott and read before a meeting held in her honor by her former students. Bryn Mawr College, April 18, 1922. 21 pp.
Reprint: As Chap. IV, in *The Principle of Relativity* (1922).

5. THE PHILOSOPHICAL ASPECTS OF THE PRINCIPLE OF RELATIVITY. *Proc. Aristotelian Soc.*, n.s., v. 22, 1921-22, pp. 215-223.

6. UNIFORMITY AND CONTINGENCY. *Proc. Aristotelian Soc.*, n.s., v. 23, 1922-23, pp. 1-18.
An address delivered upon A. N. Whitehead's inauguration as President of the Society, Nov. 6, 1922.

1923

1. THE PLACE OF CLASSICS IN EDUCATION. *Hibbert Jour.*, v. 21, Jan., 1923, pp. 248-261.
Reprint: As Chap. V, in *The Aims of Education and Other Essays* (1929).

2. LETTER TO THE EDITOR. *New Statesman*, v. 20, Feb. 17, 1923, p. 568.
Replies to Sanger's review of *The Principle of Relativity*.

3. THE FIRST PHYSICAL SYNTHESIS. Chap. VI, pp. 161-178, in: *Science and Civilization*, essays arranged and edited by F. S. Marvin (The Unity Series, v. VI). London, Oxford University Press, 1923. (Cheap ed., 1926.)

"The volume is based on lectures given at the Sixth Unity History School held at Woodbrooke near Birmingham in August 1922."—Pref.

4. THE RHYTHMIC CLAIMS OF FREEDOM AND DISCIPLINE. *Hibbert Jour.*, v. 21, July, 1923, pp. 657-668.

Reprint: As Chap. III, in *The Aims of Education and Other Essays* (1929).

5. SYMPOSIUM:—THE PROBLEM OF SIMULTANEITY: IS THERE A PARADOX IN THE PRINCIPLE OF RELATIVITY IN REGARD TO THE RELATION OF TIME MEASURED TO TIME LIVED? By H. Wildon Carr, R. A. Sampson, and A. N. Whitehead. *Aristotelian Soc., Supplementary Vol. 3*, "Relativity, Logic and Mysticism," 1923, pp. 15-41.

Whitehead's contribution comprises pp. 34-41.

1925

1. SCIENCE AND THE MODERN WORLD. Lowell Institute Lectures, 1925. New York, The Macmillan Company, 1925. xii, 296 pp.

Published in England by the Cambridge University Press, 1926.

Contents: Preface—I. The Origins of Modern Science—II. Mathematics as an Element in the History of Thought—III. The Century of Genius—IV. The Eighteenth Century—V. The Romantic Reaction—VI. The Nineteenth Century—VII. Relativity—VIII. The Quantum Theory—IX. Science and Philosophy—X. Abstraction—XI. God—XII. Religion and Science (reprint of 1925-3)—XIII. Requisites for Social Progress. (The Lowell Lectures as delivered consist of Chaps. I, III-IX, XIII. Chaps. II, X, XI, XII are additions.)

Reprints: By Macmillan, 1926 and later years, xii, 304 pp.; by Cambridge, 1926, xii, 304 pp.; 1927 and later years, xii, 266 pp.; cheap re-issue, 1932, xii, 266 pp.; by Penguin Books, London, 1938 ('Pelican Series'), 246 pp.; Talking Ed. for the Blind, by the National Institute for the Blind, London, 1938; chap. II, "Mathematics as an Element in the History of Thought," as chap. III, in G. P. Adams and others, comp., *Selected Writings in Philosophy*, New York, D. Appleton-Century Co., 1939, pp. 33-51.

Translation: French: *La Science et le Monde Moderne*. Trad. par A. d'Ivéry et P. Hollard. Paris, Payot (Bibliotèque scientifique), 1930. 271 pp.

Translation: Spanish: By Srta. María Rosa Lida, is to be published by Editorial Losada, S. A. (Buenos Aires), in their "Panorama" series.

REVIEWS: S. Alexander: *Nature*, v. 117, June 19, 1926, pp. 847-850; R. B. Braithwaite: *Mind*, n.s., v. 35, 1926, pp. 489-500; John Dewey: *New Republic*, v. 45, Feb. 17, 1926, pp. 360f; L. J. Henderson: *Quart. Rev. of Biology*, v. 1, 1926, pp. 289-294; Herbert Read: *New Criterion*, v. 4, 1926, pp. 581-586; Bertrand Russell: *Nation and Athenaeum*, v. 39, May 29, 1926, pp. 206-207; L. S. Stebbing: *Jour. of Philos. Studies*, v. 1, 1926, pp. 380-385; W. C. Swabey: *Philos. Rev.*, v. 35, 1926, pp. 272-279.

2. THE IMPORTANCE OF FRIENDLY RELATIONS BETWEEN ENGLAND AND THE UNITED STATES. *The Phillips Bull.*, v. 19, no. 3, April, 1925, pp. 15-18.

An address delivered on Feb. 22, 1925, at Phillips Academy, Andover, Mass.

3. RELIGION AND SCIENCE. *Atlantic Monthly*, v. 136, August, 1925, pp. 200-207.

An address delivered in the Phillips Brooks House of Harvard University.

Reprint: As Chap. XII, in *Science and the Modern World* (1925).

1926

1. RELIGION IN THE MAKING. Lowell Institute Lectures, 1926. New York, The Macmillan Co., 1926. 160 pp.

Published in England by the Cambridge University Press, 1926. Cheaper re-issue, Cambridge, 1936, x, 146 pp.

Contents: Preface—*Chap. I. Religion in History*—1. Religion Defined, 2. The Emergence of Religion, 3. Ritual and Emotion, 4. Belief, 5. Rationalism, 6. The Ascent of Man, 7. The Final Contrast—*Chap. II. Religion and Dogma* —1. The Religious Consciousness in History, 2. The Description of Religious Experience, 3. God, 4. The Quest of God—*Chap. III. Body and Spirit*—1. Religion and Metaphysics, 2. The Contribution of Religion to Metaphysics, 3. A Metaphysical Description, 4. God and the Moral Order, 5. Value and the Purpose of God, 6. Body and Mind, 7. The Creative Process—*Chap. IV. Truth and Criticism*—1. The Development of Dogma, 2. Experience and Expression, 3. The Three Traditions, 4. The Nature of God, 5. Conclusion.

Reprint: Chap. I, sec. 1, "Religion Defined," in Margaret M. Bryant, comp., *Essays Old and New*, pp. 189-190 (New York, F. S. Crofts & Co., 1940).

Translation: French: *Le Devenir de la Religion*. Trad. et préface par Philippe Devaux. Paris, Montaigne (Collection Philos. de l'Esprit), 1939. 192 pp.

REVIEWS: A. E. Taylor: *Dublin Rev.*, v. 181, July, 1927, pp. 17-41; F. R. Tennant: *Mind*, n.s., v. 36, 1927, pp. 221-228.

2. NOTE TO THE EDITOR. *Mind*, n.s., v. 35, Jan., 1926, p. 130.

Dated Nov. 5, 1925. Printed by the Editor under the heading, "Principia Mathematica."

"The great labour of supervising the second edition of the *Principia Mathematica* has been solely undertaken by Mr. Bertrand Russell. All the new matter in that edition is due to him, unless it shall be otherwise expressly stated. . . . I had been under the impression that a general statement to this effect was to appear in the first volume of the second edition."

3. THE EDUCATION OF AN ENGLISHMAN. *Atlantic Monthly*, v. 138, Aug., 1926, pp. 192-198.

Deals with Whitehead's years at Sherborne School, 1875-1880.

4. Time. *Proc. Sixth International Congress of Philos.*, held at Harvard University, Cambridge, Mass., 1926. New York & London, Longmans, Green & Co., 1927, pp. 59-64.

An address to Sect. I (Physics and Metaphysics, with special reference to the problem of time) of Division A (Metaphysics) of the Congress.

Captions: I. Supersession—II. Prehension—III. Incompleteness—IV. Objective Immortality—V. Simultaneity—VI. Time as Epochal.

1927

1. Symbolism, Its Meaning and Effect. Barbour-Page Lectures, the University of Virginia, 1927. New York, The Macmillan Co., 1927. x, 88 pp.

Published in England by the Cambridge University Press, 1928, viii, 104 pp.

Contents: Preface—*I.* 1. Kinds of Symbolism—2. Symbolism and Perception—3. On Methodology—4. Fallibility of Symbolism—5. Definition of Symbolism—6. Experience as Activity—7. Language—8. Presentational Immediacy—9. Perceptive Experience—10. Symbolic Reference in Perceptive Experience—11. Mental and Physical—12. Rôles of Sense-Data and Space in Presentational Immediacy—13. Objectification.

II. 1. Hume on Causal Efficacy—2. Kant and Causal Efficacy—3. Direct Perception of Causal Efficacy—4. Primitiveness of Causal Efficacy—5. The Intersection of the Modes of Perception—6. Localization—7. The Contrast Between Accurate Definition and Importance—8. Conclusion.

III. Uses of Symbolism.

Reviews: Charles Hartshorne: *Hound and Horn*, v. 1, 1927, pp. 148-152; A. E. Murphy: *Jour. of Philos.*, v. 26, 1929, pp. 489-498; Joseph Ratner: *New Republic*, v. 55, May 23, 1928, pp. 23f; L. J. Russell: *Jour. of Philos. Studies*, v. 3, Oct., 1928, pp. 527-530; Paul Weiss: *Nation* (N.Y.), v. 126, Feb. 1, 1928, pp. 128f.

2. England and the Narrow Seas. *Atlantic Monthly*, v. 139, June, 1927, pp. 791-798.

Sub-title on cover: *History, personal and racial.*

1928

1. Universities and Their Function. *Atlantic Monthly*, v. 141, May, 1928, pp. 638-644.

An address delivered in May, 1927, to a meeting of the Amer. Assn. of the Collegiate Schools of Business.

Reprints: *Harvard Business School Alumni Bull.*, v. 5, no. 1, Nov. 1, 1928, pp. 9-14; as Chap. VII in *The Aims of Education and Other Essays* (1929).

1929

1. PROCESS AND REALITY. An essay in cosmology. Gifford Lectures delivered in the University of Edinburgh during the session 1927-28. New York, The Macmillan Co., 1929. xii, 547 pp.

Published in England by the Cambridge University Press, 1929, xxiii, 509 pp.

Contents: Preface—*Part I. The Speculative Scheme.* I. Speculative Philosophy —II. The Categoreal Scheme—III. Some Derivative Notions.

Part II. Discussions and Applications. I. Fact and Form—II. The Extensive Continuum—III. The Order of Nature—IV. Organisms and Environment—V. Locke and Hume—VI. From Descartes to Kant—VII. The Subjectivist Principle—VIII. Symbolic Reference—IX. The Propositions—X. Process.

Part III. The Theory of Prehensions. I. The Theory of Feelings—II. The Primary Feelings—III. The Transmission of Feelings—IV. Propositions and Feelings—V. The Higher Phases of Experience.

Part IV. The Theory of Extension. I. Co-ordinate Division—II. Extensive Connection—III. Flat Loci—IV. Strains—V. Measurement.

Part V. Final Interpretation. I. The Ideal Opposites—II. God and the World. —Corrigenda [printed on p. 426 in English ed.]

REVIEWS: Montgomery Belgion: *Criterion,* v. 9, 1929-30, pp. 557-563; M. H. Moore: *Philos. Rev.,* v. 40, 1931, pp. 265-275; Ernest Nagel: *Symposium,* v. 1, June, 1930, pp. 392-398; F. S. C. Northrop: *Saturday Rev. of Literature,* v. 6, Jan. 4, 1930, p. 621; L. S. Stebbing: *Mind,* n.s., v. 39, Oct., 1930, pp. 466-475.

2. THE FUNCTION OF REASON. Louis Clark Vanuxem Foundation Lectures delivered at Princeton University, March, 1929. Princeton, Princeton University Press, 1929. 72 pp.

Published in England by Oxford University Press.

Contents: Three untitled chapters.

REVIEWS: R. I. Aaron: *Mind,* n.s., v. 39, Oct., 1930, pp. 488-492.

3. THE AIMS OF EDUCATION AND OTHER ESSAYS. New York, The Macmillan Co., 1929. vi, 247 pp.

Published in England by Williams & Norgate, London, 1929; cheaper re-issue, 1936.

Contents: Preface—I. The Aims of Education (reprint of 1916-*1*, with omissions)—II. The Rhythm of Education (1922-*2*)—III. The Rhythmic Claims of Freedom and Discipline (1923-*4*)—IV. Technical Education and its Relation to Science and Literature (1917-*2*, with very slight omissions)—V. The Place of Classics in Education (1923-*1*)—VI. The Mathematical Curriculum (1913-*1*)—VII. Universities and their Function (1928-*1*)—VIII. The Organisation of Thought (1916-*3*, with slight omissions)—IX. The Anatomy of Some Scientific Ideas (Chap. VII of 1917-1)—X. Space, Time, and Relativity (1915-2, with omissions).

REVIEWS: H. A. L. Fisher: *Nation and Athenaeum*, v. 45, June 22, 1929, p. 401; Christian Gauss: *New Republic*, v. 59, June 26, 1929, pp. 157f.

1930

1. AN ADDRESS. Delivered at the Celebration of the Fiftieth Anniversary of the Founding of Radcliffe College. *Radcliffe Quarterly*, v. 14, no. 1, Jan., 1930, pp. 1-5.

2. PREFATORY NOTE. To: Susanne K. Langer, *The Practice of Philosophy* (N.Y., Henry Holt & Co., 1930), p. vii.

1931

1. ON FORESIGHT. Introduction to W. B. Donham, *Business Adrift* (N.Y., McGraw-Hill Book Co., 1931; published in London by George Routledge & Sons, 1931), pp. xi-xxix.

An address delivered at the Harvard Graduate School of Business Administration.

Reprint: As Chap. VI, in *Adventures of Ideas* (1933), with additions.

1932

1. OBJECTS AND SUBJECTS. *Philos. Rev.*, v. 41, March, 1932, pp. 130-146.

Presidential Address to the Eastern Division of the Amer. Philos. Assn., New Haven, Conn., Dec., 1931.

Reprint: *Proc. & Addresses, Amer. Philos. Assn.*, v. 5, 1931, pp. 130-146; as Chap. XI, in *Adventures of Ideas* (1933).

2. SYMPOSIUM IN HONOR OF THE SEVENTIETH BIRTHDAY OF ALFRED NORTH WHITEHEAD. Cambridge, Mass., Harvard University Press, 1932. 29 pp.

Whitehead's response comprises pp. 22-29.

1933

1. ADVENTURES OF IDEAS. New York, The Macmillan Co., 1933. xii, 392 pp.

Published in England by the Cambridge University Press, 1933; cheaper reissue, 1938.

Contents: Preface—*Part I. Sociological.* I. Introduction—II. The Human Soul—III. The Humanitarian Ideal—IV. Aspects of Freedom—V. From

Force to Persuasion—VI. Foresight (reprint of 1931-*1*, with slight alterations and the addition of pp. 110 and 111)—Epilogue.

Part II. Cosmological. VII. Laws of Nature—VIII. Cosmologies—IX. Science and Philosophy—X. The New Reformation.

Part III. Philosophical. XI. Objects and Subjects (reprint of 1932-*1*)—XII. Past, Present, Future—XIII. The Grouping of Occasions—XIV. Appearance and Reality—XV. Philosophic Method.

Part IV. Civilization. XVI. Truth—XVII. Beauty—XVIII. Truth and Beauty —XIX. Adventure—XX. Peace.

Note from Preface: "Use has already been made of some parts of the book in response to invitations which I had the honour to receive. The main substance of Chapters I, II, III, VII, VIII was delivered as the four Mary Flexner Lectures at Bryn Mawr College, during the session 1929-1930: they have not been hitherto published. Also Chapter IX, 'Science and Philosophy'— not previously published—was delivered as the Davies Lecture in Philosophy, at the Institute of Arts and Sciences, Columbia University, March, 1932. . . . Some unpublished lectures, delivered at Dartmouth College, New Hampshire, in 1926, embodied a preliminary sketch of the topic of this book." (p. viii)

Reprint: Chap. IV, with slight omissions. In: Ruth Nanda Anshen, ed., *Freedom, its Meaning* (N.Y., Harcourt, Brace & Co., 1940), pp. 42-67.

REVIEWS: Carl Becker: *Amer. Historical Rev.*, v. 39, Oct., 1933, pp. 87-89; C. D. Burns: *Internat. Jour. of Ethics*, v. 44, 1933, pp. 166-168; Morris R. Cohen: *Yale Rev.*, n.s., v. 23, Sept., 1933, pp. 173-177; John Dewey: *New Republic*, v. 74, April 19, 1933, pp. 285-286; Dorothy Emmet: *Hibbert Jour.*, v. 32, 1934, pp. 175-183; Sydney E. Hooper: *Philosophy*, v. 8, 1933, pp. 326-344; Julian Huxley: *Spectator*, v. 150, April 28, 1933, pp. 611f.

2. THE STUDY OF THE PAST—ITS USES AND ITS DANGERS. *Harvard Business Rev.*, v. 11, July, 1933, pp. 436-444.

An address delivered at a meeting held in commemoration of the 25th Anniversary of the founding of the Harvard Business School, April 13, 1933.

Captions: The Present a Turning Point in Western Civilization—The Preceding Trend from Mediaevalism to Individualism—The New Forces at Work: the Passing of Individualism—The Increasing Pressure of General Unemployment—The Mistaken Policy of Modern Salesmanship and Production—The Need for Economic Statesmanship—The Educational Problem.

Reprint: *Educational Record*, v. 14, Oct., 1933, pp. 454-467.

1934

1. NATURE AND LIFE. Chicago, The University of Chicago Press, 1934. 46 pp.

Published in England by the Cambridge University Press, 1934 (Cambridge Miscellany, no. 13), 96 pp.

Contents: Two untitled lectures (delivered at the University of Chicago in 1933).

Reprint: In *Modes of Thought* (1938): Lecture I as Chap. VII, with title, "Nature Lifeless"; Lecture II as Chap. VIII, with title, "Nature Alive."

REVIEWS: A. E. Murphy: *Jour. of Philos.*, v. 31, 1934, pp. 329f; F. C. S. Schiller: *Mind*, n.s., v. 44, April, 1935, pp. 245-246.

2. INDICATION, CLASSES, NUMBERS, VALIDATION. *Mind*, v. 43, July, 1934, pp. 281-297; "Corrigenda," *ibid.*, Oct., 1934, p. 543.
An address to the Amer. Math. Assn.

Abstract: by W. V. Quine, in *Amer. Math. Monthly*, v. 41, March, 1934, pp. 129-131.

3. FOREWORD. In: Willard van Orman Quine, *A System of Logistic* (Cambridge, Mass., Harvard University Press, 1934; published in London by Oxford University Press), pp. ix-x.

1935

1. MINUTE ON THE LIFE AND SERVICES OF PROFESSOR JAMES HAUGHTON WOODS. *Harvard University Gazette*, v. 30, May 18, 1935, pp. 153-155.
By a Committee of the Faculty of Arts and Sciences of Harvard University; Ralph Barton Perry, Chairman. Contributed to by A. N. Whitehead.

2. THE AIM OF PHILOSOPHY. *Harvard Alumni Bull.*, v. 38, Nov. 15, 1935, pp. 234-235.
"This is an address which Professor Whitehead delivered on October 25 at the annual reception to graduate students in the Department of Philosophy."

Reprint: As the Epilogue, pp. 233-238, to *Modes of Thought* (1938); with the omission of the first and the addition of a final paragraph.

1936

1. MEMORIES. *Atlantic Monthly*, v. 157, June, 1936, pp. 672-679.

2. HARVARD: THE FUTURE. *Atlantic Monthly*, v. 158, Sept., 1936, pp. 260-270.
Occasioned by the tercentenary celebration of Harvard College.

1937

1. REMARKS. *Philos. Rev.*, v. 46, March, 1937, pp. 178-186.
Read before the Eastern Division of the Amer. Philos. Assn., as a response to the Symposium* on Whitehead's Philosophy, Cambridge, Mass., Dec. 29, 1936.
Reprint: *Proc. & Addresses, Amer. Philos. Assn.*, v. 10, 1936, pp. 178-186.

* Participants: John Dewey, A. P. Ushenko, Gregory Vlastos.

1938

1. MODES OF THOUGHT. Six lectures delivered in Wellesley College, Massachusetts [1937-38] and two lectures in the University of Chicago [1933]. New York, The Macmillan Co., 1938. viii, 241 pp.

Published in England by the Cambridge University Press, 1938.

Contents: Preface—*Part I. Creative Impulse.* I. Importance—II. Expression —III. Understanding.

Part II. Activity. IV. Perspective—V. Forms of Process—VI. Civilized Universe.

Part III. Nature and Life (reprint of 1934-*1*). VII. Nature Lifeless—VIII. Nature Alive.

Part IV. Epilogue. IX. The Aim of Philosophy (reprint of 1935-*2*).

Translation: Spanish: By Sr. Joaquín Xirau, is to be published by Editorial Losada, S. A. (Buenos Aires), in their "Biblioteca Filosófica."

REVIEWS: W. G. de Burgh: *Philosophy,* v. 14, 1939, pp. 205-211; R. A. Tsanoff: *Philos. Rev.,* v. 49, 1940, pp. 264-265.

1939

1. AN APPEAL TO SANITY. *Atlantic Monthly,* v. 163, March, 1939, pp. 309-320.

Sub-title on cover: *A World-Wide View.*

A discussion of English foreign policy with special reference to Central Europe and Palestine.

2. JOHN DEWEY AND HIS INFLUENCE. In: Schilpp, Paul Arthur, ed., *The Philosophy of John Dewey,* Evanston & Chicago, Northwestern University, 1939 (*The Library of Living Philosophers,* v. 1·), pp. 477-478.

1940

1. LETTER TO THE EDITOR. *The Boston Daily Globe,* Dec. 24, 1940, p. 12. Headed, "The Issue: Freedom."

1941

1. AUTOBIOGRAPHICAL NOTES. In: Schilpp, Paul Arthur, ed., *The Philosophy of Alfred North Whitehead,* Evanston and Chicago, Northwestern University, 1941 (*The Library of Living Philosophers,* v. 3), pp. 1-14.

This volume published in England by the Cambridge University Press, 1943;

2nd Amer. ed., Tudor Publishing Co., New York, 1951.
Reprinted in Part I of 1947-*1*.

2. MATHEMATICS AND THE GOOD. In: Schilpp, Paul Arthur, ed., *The Philosophy of Alfred North Whitehead*, Evanston and Chicago, Northwestern University, 1941 (*The Library of Living Philosophers*, v. 3), pp. 666-681 (Part I of "The Philosopher's Summary").
This volume published in England by the Cambridge University Press, 1943; 2nd Amer. ed., Tudor Publishing Co., New York, 1951.
A lecture delivered in Harvard University, Dec. 15, 1939.
Reprinted in Part II of 1947-*1*.

3. IMMORTALITY. The Ingersoll Lecture for 1941. In: Schilpp, Paul Arthur, ed., *The Philosophy of Alfred North Whitehead*, Evanston and Chicago, Northwestern University, 1941 (*The Library of Living Philosophers*, v. 3), pp. 682-700 (Part II of "The Philosopher's Summary").
This volume published in England by the Cambridge University Press, 1943; 2nd Amer. ed., Tudor Publishing Co., New York, 1951.
Delivered in the Harvard Memorial Church, April 22, 1941.
Published also in *The Harvard Divinity School Bulletin*, v. 39, 1941-42, pp. 5-21.
Reprinted in Part II of 1947-*1*.

1942

1. STATESMANSHIP AND SPECIALIZED LEARNING. *Proc. of the American Academy of Arts and Sciences*, v. 75, 1942, pp. 1-5.
Read before the Academy in Boston, October 8, 1941.
Partial Reprint: With the omission of the first two pages and the addition of a new opening paragraph, as "The Problem of Reconstruction," *Atlantic Monthly*, v. 169 (February, 1942), pp. 172-175.

1945

1. PREFACE. To: William Morgan, "The Organization of a Story and a Tale," *Jour. of American Folklore*, v. 58, no. 229, July-September, 1945, p. 169.
Dr. Morgan's article uses the concepts and terminology of *Process and Reality* to explain the growth of a folk-tale.

1946

1. THE WIT AND WISDOM OF WHITEHEAD, by A. H. Johnson, *Philosophy of Science*, v. 13, July, 1946, pp. 223-251.
Pp. 224-251 consist of short quotations from Whitehead arranged under these

headings: The Nature and Function of Philosophy—Critical Comments Concerning Philosophers and Philosophy, Thought, Science, Morality, Social Philosophy, Philosophy of History, Religion, Education.

1947

1. Essays in Science and Philosophy. New York, Philosophical Library, 1947. vi, 348 pp.

Published in England by Rider & Co., London, 1948. 255 pp.

Contents: *Part I. Personal.* Autobiographical Notes (reprint of 1941-*1*) — Memories) 1936-*1*) — The Education of an Englishman (1926-*3*) — England and the Narrow Seas (1927-*2*) — An Appeal to Sanity (1939-*1*).

Part II. Philosophy. Immortality (reprint of 1941-*3*) — Mathematics and the Good (1941-*2*) — Process and Reality (pp. 22-29 of 1932-*2*, with the last paragraph and references to other speakers at the Symposium omitted) — John Dewey and his Influence (1939-*2*) — Analysis of Meaning (1937-*1*, with the first paragraph omitted) — Uniformity and Contingency (1922-*6*).

Part III. Education. The Study of the Past—Its Uses and Its Dangers (reprint of 1933-*2*) — Education and Self-Education (1919-*2*) — Mathematics and Liberal Education (1912-*4*) — Science in General Education (1921-*2*) — Historical Changes (1930-*1*) — Harvard: The Future (1936-*1*).

Part IV. Science. The First Physical Synthesis (reprint of 1923-*3*) — Axioms of Geometry (1910-*3*) — Mathematics (1911-*2*, with one slight omission) — Non-Euclidean Geometry (1910-*2*) — Indication, Classes, Numbers, Validation (1934-*2*, *without* the *Corrigenda*) — Einstein's Theory (1920-*2*).

Acknowledgments.

Reviews: Sydney E. Hooper: *Philosophy*, v. 23, 1948, pp. 89-93; Victor Lowe: *Cronos*, v. 1, no. 2, 1947, pp. 36-38.

2. The Wit and Wisdom of Whitehead, Edited, with an Introductory Essay, by A. H. Johnson. Boston, Beacon Press, 1947. (Published in Canada by S. J. Reginald Saunders & Co., Ltd., Toronto, 1947.)

Pp. 35-102 consists of a slightly revised form of 1946-*1*, with a few additions and omissions.

ADDENDA TO THE
WRITINGS OF ALFRED NORTH WHITEHEAD
as published to January 3, 1951
(With Selected Reviews)

1910

2. (With Bertrand Russell) NON-EUCLIDEAN GEOMETRY. Division VI of article, "Geometry," *Encyclopedia Britannica*, ed. 11, v. 11, pp. 724-730. (Cambridge, Cambridge University Press, 1910.)
Reprinted in Part IV of 1947-*1*.

3. AXIOMS OF GEOMETRY. Division VII of article, "Geometry," *Encyclopedia Britannica*, ed. 11, v. 11, pp. 730-736. (Cambridge, Cambridge University Press, 1910.)
Reprinted in Part IV of 1947-*1*.

1911

1. AN INTRODUCTION TO MATHEMATICS. (No. 15 in the *Home University Library of Modern Knowledge*.) London, Williams and Norgate; New York, Henry Holt and Co., 1911. 256 pp.
Reprints: Thornton Butterworth, Ltd., London, 1932. Twelfth impression, Oxford Univ. Press, London and New York, 1942, v, 191 pp.: revised under the direction of J. H. C. Whitehead, the diagrams being redrawn, "a few inaccuracies and typographical errors" corrected, and different books mentioned in the Bibliography.
Translation: German: *Einführung in die Mathematik*. Aus d. Engl. übers. von B. Schenker. Wien, Humboldt Verlag, 1948. (Sammlung "Die Universität," Bd. 3). 222 pp.

2. MATHEMATICS. *Encyclopedia Britannica*, ed. 11, v. 17, pp. 878-883. (Cambridge, Cambridge University Press, 1911.)
Reprints: With one slight omission, in Part IV of 1947-*1*. With slight omissions, under the title, "Mathematics, Nature of," in *Encyclopedia Brittanica*, ed. 14, v. 15, pp. 85-89 (London and New York, 1929.)

773

1912

4. THE PLACE OF MATHEMATICS IN A LIBERAL EDUCATION. *Jour. of the Assn. of Teachers of Mathematics for the Southeastern Part of England,* v. I, no. I, 1912.

Reprinted as "Mathematics and Liberal Education," in Part IV of 1947-1.

1916

1. THE AIMS OF EDUCATION. A Plea for Reform. *Math. Gazette,* v. 8, Jan., 1916, pp. 191-203.

Presidential address to the Mathematical Assn. [England], Jan., 1916.

Reprints: As Chap. I, in *The Organisation of Thought* (1917). With omissions, as Chap. I, in *The Aims of Education and Other Essays* (1929) and as "The Aims of Education" in C. M. Fuess and E. S. Basford, *Unseen Harvests: a Treasury of Teaching* (New York, Macmillan Co., 1947), pp. 92-102.

Partial Reprints: Approximately the first half, with slight omissions, in *New Republic,* v. 58, 1929, pp. 244-246.

1919

2. ADDRESS ON FOUNDER'S DAY. Stanley Technical Trade School, South Norwood, London. Feb. 1, 1919. Coventry and Son, South Norwood, S.E., England. 8 pp.

Reprinted as "Education and Self-Education," in Part III of 1947-1.

1920

2. EINSTEIN'S THEORY; An Alternative Suggestion. *The* (London) *Times Educational Supplement,* Feb. 12, 1920, p. 83.

Reprinted in Part IV of 1947-1.

1921

2. SCIENCE IN GENERAL EDUCATION. *Proc. of Second Congress of Universities of the Empire* (London, G. Bell & Sons, 1921), pp. 31-39.

Reprinted in Part III of 1947-1.

1922

6. UNIFORMITY AND CONTINGENCY. *Proc. Aristotelian Soc.,* n.s., v. 23, 1922-23, pp. 1-18.

Reprinted in Part II of 1947-1 (pp. 132-148).

1923

3. THE FIRST PHYSICAL SYNTHESIS. Chap. VI, pp. 161-178, in: *Science and Civilization*, essays arranged and edited by F. S. Marvin (The Unity Series, v. VI). London, Oxford University Press, 1923.

Reprint of Whitehead's chapter: In Part IV of 1947-*1*.

1925

1. SCIENCE AND THE MODERN WORLD. Lowell Institute Lectures, 1925. New York, The Macmillan Company, 1925. xii, 296 pp.

Reprints: By Macmillan, 1926 and later years, xii, 304 pp. By Cambridge, 1926, xii, 304 pp.; 1927 and later years, xii, 266 pp.; cheap re-issue, 1932, 1947, xii, 266 pp. Penguin Books, London, 1938 ('Pelican Series'), 246 pp.; 1942, 288 pp. New American Library, New York, 1948 ('Pelican Mentor Books'), x, 212 pp. Talking Ed. for the Blind: National Institute for the Blind, London, 1938.

Partial Reprints: Chap. I, with omissions, in Theodore Morrison, *Readings for Citizens at War* (New York, Harper & Brothers, 1943), pp. 262-269. Chap. II, as Chap. III in G. P. Adams and others, comp., *Selected Writings in Philosophy* (New York, D. Appleton-Century Co., 1939), pp. 33-51. Chap. IX, in Saxe Commins and Robert N. Linscott, *The World's Great Thinkers*, v. 4, *Man and the Universe: The Philosophers of Science* (New York, Random House, 1947), pp. 339-358. For reprints of Chap. XII, see entry under 1925-*3*.

Translations: Italian: *La Scienza e il Mondo Moderno*. Con una introd. di Antonio Banfi. Milano, Bompiani, 1945 (Idee nuove, v. 19). 237 pp. German: *Wissenschaft und Moderne Welt*. Mit einer Einl. von Leopold Deuel und einen Nachw. des Herausgebers (Walter Robert Corti. (Aus dem Amerikan. übers. von Gertrud Tschiedel und Francois Bondy.) Zürich, Morgarten Verlag, Conzett & Huber, 1949. 283 pp.

3. RELIGION AND SCIENCE. *Atlantic Monthly*, v. 136, August, 1925, pp. 200-207.

Reprints: As Chap. XII, in *Science and the Modern World* (1925-*1*). W. Lippman and A. Nevins, *A Modern Reader*, 2nd ed., pp. 375-384 (Boston, Heath & Co., 1946); Atlantic Monthly's *Atlantic Harvest*, pp. 560-571 (Boston, Little, Brown & Co., 1947); S. W. Schneider and J. A. Sanford, *A College Book of Prose*, 2nd ed., pp. 382-392 (Boston, Ginn & Co., 1947); F. E. Ward, *English for Communication*, pp. 461-472 (New York, Macmillan Co., 1949).

1926

1. RELIGION IN THE MAKING. Lowell Institute Lectures, 1926. New York, The Macmillan Co., 1926. 160 pp.

Reprinted in Part I of 1947-*1*.

1927

2. ENGLAND AND THE NARROW SEAS. *Atlantic Monthly*, v. 139, June, 1927, pp. 791-798.

Reprinted in Part I of 1947-*1*.

1929

1. PROCESS AND REALITY. An essay in cosmology. Gifford Lectures delivered in the University of Edinburgh during the session 1927-28. New York, The Macmillan Co., 1929. xii, 547 pp.

American ed. reprinted, 1949, by Social Science Publishers (now The Humanities Press), New York, and distributed through the Social Science Bookstore.

Partial Reprint: Part I, Chap. I, "Speculative Philosophy," with minor omissions, in: *Classic American Philosophers*, pp. 437-451 (New York, Appleton-Century-Crofts, Inc., 1951), Max H. Fisch, Editor.

3. THE AIMS OF EDUCATION AND OTHER ESSAYS. New York, The Macmillan Co., 1929. vi, 247 pp.

Reprints: with an Introductory Note by Felix Frankfurter (first published as a letter in the *N. Y. Times*, Jan. 8, 1948. New York, New American Library, 1949 ('Mentor Books'). 166 pp.

1930

1. AN ADDRESS. Delivered at the Celebration of the Fiftieth Anniversary of the Founding of Radcliffe College. *Radcliffe Quarterly*, v. 14, no. 1, Jan., 1930, pp. 1-5.

Reprinted as "Historical Changes," in Part III of 1947-*1*.

1932

2. SYMPOSIUM IN HONOR OF THE SEVENTIETH BIRTHDAY OF ALFRED NORTH WHITEHEAD. Cambridge, Mass., Harvard University Press, 1932. 29 pp.

Consists of comments on Whitehead's work by C. J. Ducasse, M. R. Cohen, W. P. Montague, W. H. Sheldon, and A. O. Lovejoy, and a reply (pp. 22-29) by Whitehead. The occasion was a dinner at the Harvard Club in Boston, February 14, 1931.

Printed for private circulation only.

Partial Reprint: Whitehead's reply, with the last paragraph and references to other speakers omitted, as "Process and Reality," in Part II of 1947-*1*.

1933

1. ADVENTURES OF IDEAS. New York, The Macmillan Co., 1933. xii, 392 pp.

Reprints: Penguin Books, Ltd., Harmondsworth, Middlesex, England, 1942 ('Pelican Series'). 288 pp.

Partial Reprints: Chap. IV, with slight omissions, in: Ruth Nanda Anshen, ed., *Freedom, its Meaning* (New York, Harcourt, Brace & Co., 1940), pp. 42-67. Chap. V, Sects. VI and VII, under title, "From Force to Persuasion," in: R. E. Hoople and others, *Preface to Philosophy: Book of Readings* (New York, Macmillan Co., 1946), pp. 287-289. Approximately one-fifth of Chap. II, half of Chap. XIX, and with slight omissions, Chap. XX, in: *Classic American Philosophers*, pp. 454-470 (New York, Appleton-Century-Crofts, Inc., 1951), Max H. Fisch, Editor.

Translation: Spanish: *Aventuras de las Ideas.* Trad. Carlos Botet. Barcelona, Imp. Miguza, 1947. 374 pp.

Reprints: *Educational Record*, v. 14, Oct., 1933, pp. 454-467. Also in Part III of 1947-*1*.

1934

1. NATURE AND LIFE. Chicago, The University of Chicago Press, 1934. 46 pp.

Reprint: In *Modes of Thought* (1938): Lecture I as Chap. VII, with title, "Nature Lifeless"; Lecture II as Chap. VIII, with title, "Nature Alive."

Partial Reprints: Lecture II, with slight alterations and omissions, as "Philosophy of Life," in *Twentieth Century Philosophy: Living Schools of Thought*, ed. Dagobert D. Runes (New York, Philosophical Library, 1943), pp. 129-144. About three-fifths of Lecture I and five-sixths of Lecture II, in *Classic American Philosophers*, pp. 418-437 (Appleton-Century-Crofts, Inc., 1951), Max H. Fisch, Editor.

Translation: Spanish: Naturaleza y Vida; Estudio Preliminar. Trad. y notas de Risieri Frondizi. Buenos Aires, Imprenta Lopez, 1941 (Filosofía contemporánea, III). 88 pp.

Reprinted, *without* the "Corrigenda," in Part IV of 1947-*1*.

1935

2. THE AIM OF PHILOSOPHY. *Harvard Alumni Bull.*, v. 38, Nov. 15, 1935, pp. 234-235.

"This is an address which Professor Whitehead delivered on October 25 at the annual reception to graduate students in the Department of Philosophy."

Reprints, with the omission of the first and the addition of a final paragraph: as the Epilogue, pp. 233-238, to *Modes of Thought* (1938); as "The Aim of Philosophy," in D. J. Bronstein and others, *Basic Problems of Philosophy* (New York, Prentice-Hall, 1947), pp. 705-708.

3. LETTER. In: J. H. Muirhead, ed., *Bernard Bosanquet and His Friends* (London, George Allen & Unwin, Ltd., 1935), p. 316.

A brief tribute to Bernard Bosanquet, under the heading "In Memoriam."

1936

1. MEMORIES. *Atlantic Monthly*, v. 157, June, 1936, pp. 672-679.

Reprinted in Part I of 1947-*1*.

2. HARVARD: THE FUTURE. *Atlantic Monthly*, v. 158, Sept., 1936, pp. 260-270.

Occasioned by the tercentenary celebration of Harvard College.

Reprinted in Part III of 1947-*1*.

1937

1. REMARKS. *Philos. Rev.*, v. 46, March, 1937, pp. 178-186.

Read before the Eastern Division of the Amer. Philos. Assn., as a response to the Symposium on Whitehead's Philosophy, Cambridge, Mass., Dec. 29, 1936.

Reprints: *Proc. & Addresses, Amer. Philos. Assn.*, v. 10, 1936, pp. 178-186; with the first paragraph omitted, as "Analysis of Meaning," in Part II of 1947-*1*.

1938

1. MODES OF THOUGHT. Six lectures delivered in Wellesley College, Massachusetts [1937-38] and two lectures in the University of Chicago [1933]. New York, The Macmillan Co., 1938. viii, 241 pp.

Translation: Spanish: *Modos de Pensamiento*. Trad. de Joaquín Xirau. Buenos Aires, Editorial Losada, s. a., 1944 (Biblioteca filosófica, pub. bajo la dirección de Francisco Romero), 199 pp.

1939

1. AN APPEAL TO SANITY. *Atlantic Monthly*, v. 163, March, 1939, pp. 309-320.

Reprinted in Part I of 1947-*1*.

2. JOHN DEWEY AND HIS INFLUENCE. In: Schilpp, Paul Arthur, ed., *The Philosophy of John Dewey*, Evanston & Chicago, Northwestern University, 1939 (*The Library of Living Philosophers*, v. 1), pp. 477-478.

This volume published in England by the Cambridge University Press, 1943; 2nd Amer. ed., Tudor Publishing Co., N. Y., 1951.

Reprinted in Part II of 1947-*1*.

INDEX

Aaron, R. I., 425
Absolute, 505; theory of space, 121
Absoluteness, in nature of things, 612
Absolutes, intuitions as, 124, 612
Abstraction, 599, 672, 679, 681, 685; of classes, 146; method of extensive, 26, 39, 60, 74, 113, 218; process of constructive, 259; relative, 122n
Achievement, 698; doctrine of, 457
Ackermann, Wilhelm, 143n
Action, world of, 685
Active entities, 695
Active tone, 278, 281, 283; private, 282
Active world, 694
Activity, 439, 685, 689; pattern of, 284
Acts, 312; finite, 687; meaning of, 687
Actual, entity(-ies), 232f, 239, 326, 357f, 362, 446; events, 341; existents, 342f; occasion(s), 98, 316, 357, 390, 396; processes, 344.
Actuality, 93, 360; concept of, 569; final, 358; finite, 691; the nature of, 370; pure, 516; vacuous, 408
Adaptation, 442
Adjectives, 312
Adjustment, 442f, 446, 454
Adler, Alfred, 298
Adventure, 280, 505, 564, 607; unity of, 506
Adventures of Ideas, 47, 115, 117f, 122n, 268, 298, 353, 357, 359, 360n, 366n, 371n, 372, 373n, 378, 440, 442, 455, 456, 491, 504, 563f, 573, 591f, 595, 597, 601, 606f, 625f, 630, 632, 637, 640, 650
Adventures of the universe, 511
Aesthetic beauty, grades of, 692
Aesthetic experience as ultimate category, 618
Aesthetics, 324; reduction of ethics to, 615
Aesthetic, transcendental, of Kant, 76
Affective tone, 278, 280
Aggregation, principle of, 63
Agnasparta, Matthew of, 552
Agnosticism, 373
Aims, ideal, 573

Aims and Achievements of Scientific Method, The, 80
Aims of Education, 21, 55, 122n, 475, 507f, 632f, 635ff, 639
Albertus Magnus, 167
Alexander, Samuel, 89, 120, 169, 325, 347, 362, 364, 407, 410
Algebra, abstract, 127; classical interpretation of, 135; of classes, 134; extended beyond field of number, 677; linear, 128; of logic, invention of, 25; nonnumerical, 128; numerical, 128; propositional interpretation of, 135; universal, 124
Algebraic language, 677
All, 534
All-One, 386
Alteration, 135
America, influence of, 89
American Philosophical Association, 119, 324
American Youth Commission, 634
Amoebae, respectable, 563n
Analysis of Matter, 76, 234n
Analysis of Mind, 235n
Analytic set theory, 159
Anarchic appetition, 339f; element, 340
Anarchy, 340
"Anatomy of Some Scientific Ideas, The," 55, 59, 62
Animal faith, 103, 282
Animism, 248f
Anthropomorphic rendering of nature, 295
Anticipation, 695
Anti-Dühring, 252
Anti-intellectualism, of Whitehead, 56
Any, notion of, 676
Appearance, objects of immediate, 77
Appearance and Reality, 362
Appetition for an end, 447
Appreciation, acts of, 295
Appreciative perceptions, 299
A priori, 347; dogmatism, 54
Aquinas, St. Thomas, 364, 425
Archaeus, 248
Aristotle, 134, 167, 203, 252, 269f, 279,

779

INDEX